REEDS
WESTERN
ALMANAC
2016

ADLARD COLES NAUTICAL

EDITORS **Perrin Towler and Mark Fishwick**

Free updates are available at www.reedsalmanacs.co.uk

IMPORTANT SAFETY NOTE AND LEGAL DISCLAIMER

This Almanac provides basic navigational data for planning and executing passages. The tidal prediction data has been reproduced by permission of national hydrographic offices. Chartlets illustrate items in the text, orientate the user and highlight key features; they should not be relied on for navigational purposes and must always be used in conjunction with a current, corrected navigational chart. Any waypoint or position listed in this Almanac must first be plotted on the appropriate chart to assess its accuracy, safety in the prevailing circumstances and relevance to the Skipper's intentions.

Navigational guidance or suggestions are based on the accumulated experience of editors, agents, harbour masters and users. They are generic and in compiling a passage plan or pilotage notebook all other available publications and information should be consulted. They take no account of the characteristics of individual vessels nor the actual or forecast meteorological conditions, sea or tidal state. These need to be checked with appropriate local authorities for the intended area of operation prior to departure.

While every care has been taken in compiling the Almanac, it is a human endeavour with many contributors. Despite rigorous checking there may be inadvertent errors or inaccuracies, and omissions resulting from the time of notification in relation to the publication date. To the extent that the editors or publishers become aware of these, corrections will be published on the website www.reedsalmanacs.co.uk (requires registration). Readers should therefore regularly check the website between January and June for any such corrections. Data in this Almanac is corrected up to Weekly Edition 25/2015 of Admiralty Notices to Mariners.

The publishers, editors and their agents accept no responsibility for any errors or omissions, or for any accident, loss or damage (including without limitation any indirect, consequential, special or exemplary damages) arising from the use or misuse of, or reliance upon, the information contained in this Almanac.

The use of any data in this Almanac is entirely at the discretion of the Skipper or other individual with responsibility for the command, conduct or navigation of the vessel in which it is relied upon.

ADVERTISEMENT SALES

Enquiries about advertising space should be addressed to:

adlardcoles@bloomsbury.com

Reeds Nautical Almanac
An imprint of Bloomsbury Publishing Plc
50 Bedford Square, London, WC1B 3DP
1385 Broadway, New York, NY 10018, USA

www.bloomsbury.com

Tel: +44 (0)207 631 5600
Fax: +44 (0)207 631 5800
info@reedsalmanacs.co.uk
editor.britishisles@reedsalmanacs.co.uk
editor.continental@reedsalmanacs.co.uk
www.reedsalmanacs.co.uk

Almanac manager Chris Stevens

Reeds Western Almanac 2016 – ISBN 978 1 4729 1941 0

British Library Cataloguing-in-Publication Data
A catalogue record for this book is available from
the British Library.

Library of Congress Cataloguing-in-Publication data
has been applied for.

REEDS, ADLARD COLES NAUTICAL and the Buoy logo are
trademarks of Bloomsbury Publishing Plc

First published 2015

© Nautical Data Ltd 1999-2003
© Adlard Coles Nautical 2004–2015
Cover photo © Getty Images

Bloomsbury Publishing Plc makes every effort to ensure that the papers used in the manufacture of our books are natural, recyclable products made from wood grown in well-managed forests. Our manufacturing processes conform to the environmental regulations of the country of origin.

To find out more about our authors and books visit www.bloomsbury.com. Here you will find extracts, author interviews, details of forthcoming events and the option to sign up for our newsletters.

Printed by Bell & Bain Ltd.

Come what may!

PANTAENIUS
Sail & Motor Yacht Insurance

Germany · Great Britain* · Monaco · Denmark · Austria · Spain · Sweden · USA · Australia
Plymouth · Phone +44 17 52 22 36 56

pantaenius.co.uk

Reference Contents

Navigational Contents

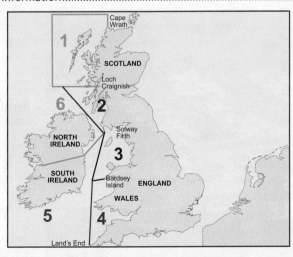

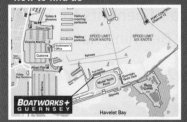

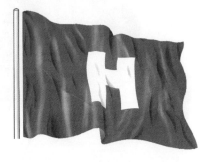
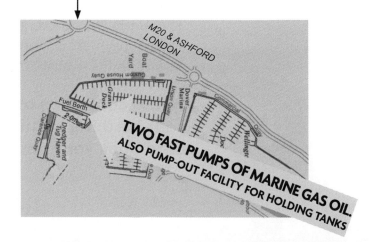

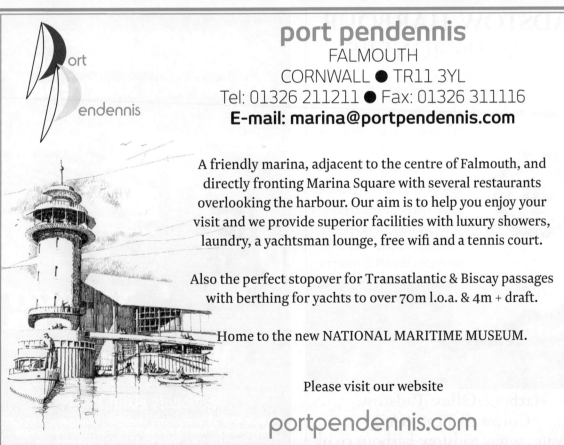

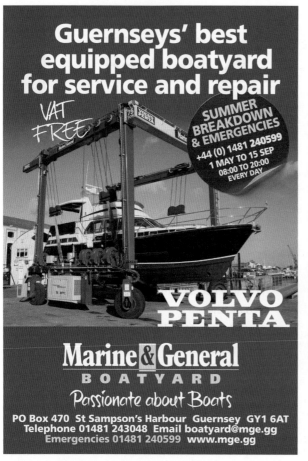

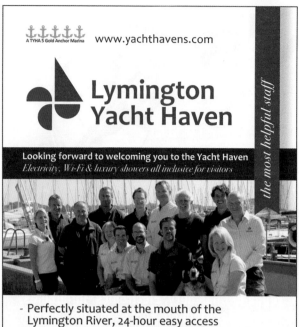

TAKE THE EASY ROUTE
with eSeries powered by LightHouse™ II

LightHouse™ II

e Series

- **Completely redesigned** for clarity and simplicity, eSeries with LightHouse II makes everything easier
- **More Powerful** with smarter touch controls and all new features
- **Point and Steer** with Evolution's 9-axis autopilot control
- **Connect anywhere** onboard with Wi-Fi and Raymarine mobile apps
- **Network** with any LightHouse powered MFD

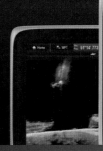

For more information, go to
www.raymarine.com

Raymarine®

xxix

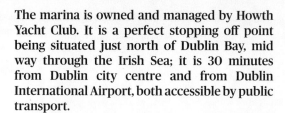

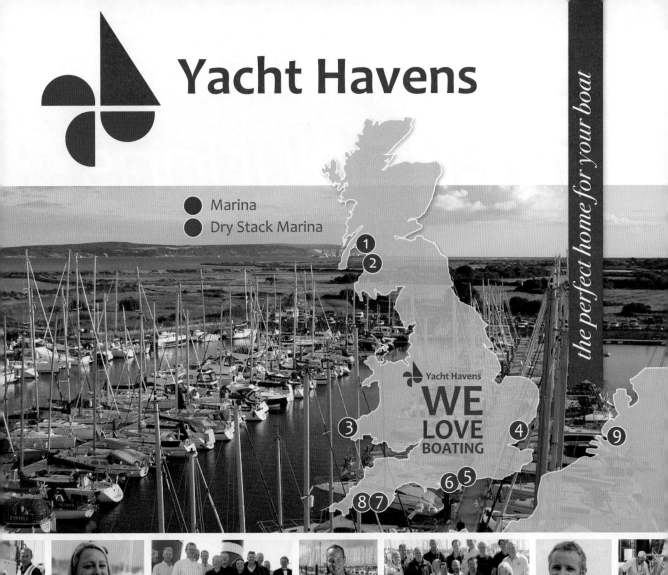

Reference data

0.1 THE ALMANAC

• Acknowledgements

The Editors thank the many official bodies and individuals for information and advice given in the compilation of this Almanac. These include: UKHO, Trinity House, HM Nautical Almanac Office, SHOM, HMSO, HM Revenue & Customs, Meteorological Office, BBC, IBA, MCA, RNLI, ABP, countless Harbourmasters and our many individual Harbour Agents.

• Permissions

Chartlets, tidal stream diagrams and curves are reproduced from Admiralty charts and publications (ALL, ASD, ATT and ALRS) by permission of the UKHO (Licence No GB DQ – 001 – Adlard Coles) and the Controller of HMSO.

UK and foreign tidal predictions are supplied by and with the permission of UKHO.

Extracts from the *International Code of Signals 1969* and *Meteorological Office Weather Services for Shipping* are published by permission of the Controller of HMSO.

Ephemerides are derived from HM Nautical Almanac by permission of HM Nautical Almanac Office and the Council for the Central Laboratory of the Research Councils.

• Disclaimer

No National HO has verified the information in this product and none accepts liability for the accuracy of reproduction or any modifications made thereafter. No National HO warrants that this product satisfies national or international regulations regarding the use of the appropriate products for navigation.

Chartlets in this Almanac are not intended to be used for navigation. Always consult fully corrected official charts. See 0.27, Harbour Information, for more details.

• Improvements

Suggestions, however minor, for improving or correcting this Almanac are always welcome, especially if based on personal experience. All will be carefully considered. Please send your comments by email, if possible, direct to the relevant Editor (see below) or to info@reedsalmanacs.co.uk. Otherwise, a note to Adlard Coles Nautical (see page v) will be forwarded as necessary.

Perrin Towler (editor.britishisles@reedsalmanacs.co.uk) is responsible for all the Areas in this Almanac; Mark Fishwick (editor.continental@reedsalmanacs.co.uk) is responsible for the sections on weather and communications in the Reference Data chapter.

• Notifying errors

Although every care has been taken in compiling this Almanac, errors may still occur. Please let us know if you spot any.

• Harbour Agents

Our harbour agents provide invaluable local information which may not appear in official sources. Vacancies are advertised on our website www.reedsalmanacs.co.uk. If you would like to earn a free copy of Reeds Nautical Almanac please apply to the relevant editor, giving brief details of your experience and the area you could cover.

• Sources of corrections

This Almanac is corrected to Weekly edition No. 25/2014 of Admiralty Notices to Mariners.

Corrections to Admiralty charts and publications can be downloaded from the UKHO website or obtained from Admiralty Chart Agents (ACA) and certain Port Authorities.

• Updates

Free monthly updates, from January to June, can be downloaded at www.reedsalmanacs.co.uk. Please register online.

0.2 SYMBOLS AND ABBREVIATIONS

The following more common Symbols and Abbreviations feature in Reeds Almanacs and in some Admiralty charts and publications. Those symbols in the tinted box immediately below are frequently used within the text describing each port.

	Alongside berth
Ⓒ	Automatic telling machine (ATM), cashpoint
Ⓑ	Bank
	Bottled gas available, Calor Gas, Camping Gaz,or Kosangas
	Boatyard
	Boat hoist (+tons)
	Crane (+ tons)
	Chandlery
	Customs
	Diesel (supply by hose)
	Diesel (in cans)
	Electrical repairs
Ⓔ	Electronic repairs
	Fresh water supply
	Food shop/supermarket
Ⓗ	Hospital
≠	In transit with, ie ldg marks/lts
@	Internet café/access
	Landing place/steps/ladder
LB, ♦	Lifeboat, inshore lifeboat
	Light float, minor
	Lt float, major; Light vessel or Lanby
	Licensed bar, Public house, Inn
©	National Coastwatch Institution (NCI)
	Marine engineering repairs
	Mooring buoy
	Petrol (supply by hose)
	Petrol (in cans)
✉	Post Office
	Pump out facility
✕	Restaurant/cafe
	Rigger
	Sailmaker
	Shipwright (esp wooden hulls)
	Shower
	Shore power (electrical)
	Slipway
Ⓥ	Visitors' berths
	Visitors' mooring
	Wind turbine
	Weather forecast available
	Yacht Club/(YC), Sailing Club(SC)

abm	Abeam
ABP	Associated British Ports
ACA	Admiralty Chart, AC Agent
ACN	Adlard Coles Nautical (Publisher)
Aff Mar	Affaires Maritimes
AIS	Automatic Identification System
aka	Also known as
ALL	Admiralty List of Lights
ALRS	Admiralty List of Radio Signals
Al	Alternating light
ANWB	Association of road & waterway users (Dutch)
ATT	Admiralty Tide Tables

Reference data

ATT	Atterisage (landfall/SWM) buoy
Auto	Météo Répondeur Automatique
B.	Bay, Black
BE	Belgian chart
Bk	Broken (nature of seabed)
Bkwtr	Breakwater
BMS	Bulletin Météorologique Spécial (Strong wind/Gale warning)
Bn, bcn(s)	Beacon, beacon(s)
BSH	German Hydrographic Office/chart(s)
BST	British Summer Time (= DST)
Bu	Blue
By(s)	Buoy, buoys
C.	Cape, Cabo, Cap
c	Coarse (sand; nature of seabed)
ca	Cable (approx 185m long)
Cas	Castle
CD	Chart datum (tidal)
CEVNI	Code Européen de Voies de la Navigation Intérieure (inland waterway signs etc)
cf	Compare, cross-refer to
CG	Coast Guard, HM Coastguard (in the UK)
CGOC	Coast Guard Operations Centre (UK)
chan	Channel (navigational)
Ch	Channel (VHF)
Ch, ✠	Church
Chy	Chimney
Co	Coral (nature of seabed)
Col	Column, pillar, obelisk
CPA	Closest Point of Approach
CROSS	Centre Régional Opérationnel de Surveillance et Sauvetage (= MRCC)
CRS	Coast Radio Station
CRT	Canal and River Trust
C/S	COSPAS/SARSAT (satellite)
Cy	Clay (nature of seabed)
Dec	Declination (of the Sun) abbr: December
Defib	Automated External Defibrillator
dest	Destroyed
DF, D/F	Radio Direction Finding
DG	De-gaussing (range)
DGPS	Differential GPS
Dia	Diaphone (fog signal)
Dir Lt	Directional light
discont	Discontinued
DLR	Dockland Light Railway
Dn(s)	Dolphin(s)
DR	Dead Reckoning or Dries (secondary tides)
DSC	Digital Selective Calling
DST	Daylight Saving Time
DW	Deep Water (route)
DYC	Dutch Yacht Chart(s)
DZ	Danger Zone (buoy)
E	East
ECM	East cardinal mark (buoy/beacon)
ED	Existence doubtful. European Datum
EEA	European Economic Area
Elev	Elevation
Ent	Entrance, entry, enter
EP, △	Estimated position
ETA	Estimated Time of Arrival
ETD	Estimated Time of Departure
F	Fixed light
f	Fine (eg sand; nature of seabed)
F&A	Fore and aft (berth/mooring)
FFL	Fixed and Flashing light
Fl	Flashing light
FM	Frequency Modulation
Foc	Free of charge
Fog Det lt	Fog Detector light
Freq, Fx	Frequency
FS	Flagstaff, Flagpole
ft	Foot, feet
Ft,	Fort
FV	Fishing vessel
G	Gravel (nature of seabed), Green
GC	Great Circle
GDOP	Geometric Dilution of Precision (GPS)
GHA	Greenwich Hour Angle
GLA	General Lighthouse Authority
GMDSS	Global Maritime Distress & Safety System
grt	Gross Registered Tonnage
Gy	Grey
H, h, Hrs	Hour(s)
H–, H+	Minutes before, after the whole hour
H24	Continuous
HAT	Highest Astronomical Tide
HF	High Frequency
HFP	High Focal Plane (buoy)
HIE	Highlands & Islands Enterprise
HJ	Day service only, sunrise to sunset
HM	Harbour Master
HMRC	HM Revenue & Customs
HMSO	Her Majesty's Stationery Office
HN	Night service only, sunset to sunrise
HO	Office hours, Hydrographic Office
(hor)	Horizontally disposed (lights)
hPa	Hectopascal (= 1millibar)
HT	High Tension (overhead electricity line)
HW	High Water
HX	No fixed hours
IALA	International Association of Marine Aids to Navigation and Lighthouse Authorities
iaw	In accordance with
IDM	Isolated Danger Mark (buoy/beacon)
IHO	International Hydrographic Organisation
IMO	International Maritime Organisation
INMARSAT	International Maritime Satellite Organisation
intens	Intensified (light sector)
IPTS	International Port Traffic Signals
IQ	Interrupted quick flashing light
IRPCS	International Regulations for the Prevention of Collisions at Sea
Is, I	Island, Islet
ISAF	International Sailing Federation
Iso	Isophase light
ITU	International Telecommunications Union
ITZ	Inshore Traffic Zone (TSS)
IUQ	Interrupted ultra quick flashing light
IVQ	Interrupted very quick flashing light
kn	Knot(s)
kW	Kilowatts
L	Lake, Loch, Lough
Lat	Latitude
LAT	Lowest Astronomical Tide
Lanby,	Large automatic navigational buoy
Ldg	Leading (light)
LF	Low frequency
L Fl	Long flash
LH	Left hand
LNG	Liquefied Natural Gas
LNTM	Local Notice To Mariners

LOA	Length overall
Long, lng	Longitude
LPG	Liquefied Petroleum Gas
LT	Local time
Lt(s), ☆ ☆	Light(s)
M	Moorings. Nautical (sea) mile(s). Mud
m	Metre(s)
Mag	Magnetic. Magnitude (of star)
Mb, mb	Millibar (= 1 hectopascal, hPa)
MCA	Maritime and Coastguard Agency
Met/Météo	Meteorology/Météorologie (weather)
MHWN	Mean High Water Neaps
MHWS	Mean High Water Springs
MHz	Megahertz
ML	Mean Level (tidal)
MLWN	Mean Low Water Neaps
MLWS	Mean Low Water Springs
MMSI	Maritime Mobile Service Identity
Mo	Morse
Mon	Monument. Abbrev: Monday
MRCC	Maritime Rescue Co-ordination Centre
MRSC	Maritime Rescue Sub-Centre (not in the UK)
MSI	Maritime Safety Information
N	North
Navi	Navicarte (French charts)
NB	Nota Bene. Notice Board
NCM	North Cardinal Mark (buoy/beacon)
ND	No Data (secondary tides)
NGS	Naval Gunfire Support (buoy)
NM	Notice(s) to Mariners
NMOC	National Maritime Operations Centre (HMCG)
np	Neap tides
NP	Naval Publication (plus number)
NRT	Net registered tonnage
NT	National Trust (land/property)
Obscd	Obscured
Obstn	Obstruction
Oc	Occulting light
ODAS	Ocean Data Acquisition System (buoy)
Or	Orange (see also Y)
OT	Other times
P	Pebbles
(P)	Preliminary (NM)
PA	Position approximate
Pax	Passenger(s)
PC	Portuguese chart
PD	Position doubtful
PHM	Port-hand Mark (buoy/beacon)
PLA	Port of London Authority
Pos	Position
Prog	Prognosis (weather charts)
prom	Prominent
PSSA	Particularly Sensitive Sea Area
Pt(e).	Point(e)
Pta	Punta (point)
Q	Quick flashing light
QHM	Queen's Harbour Master
qv	Refer to (quod vide)
R	Red. River.
Racon	Radar transponder beacon
Ramark	Radar beacon
RCD	Recreational Craft Directive
RG	Emergency RDF station
RH	Right hand
Rk, Rky	Rock, Rocky (nature of seabed)
RNLI	Royal National Lifeboat Institution
ROI	Republic of Ireland
R/T	Radiotelephony
Ru	Ruins
RYA	Royal Yachting Association
S	South, Sand (nature of seabed)
S, St, Ste	Saint(s)
SAMU	Service d'Aide Médicale Urgente (ambulance)
SAR	Search and Rescue
SBM	Single buoy mooring
SC	Sailing Club. Spanish chart
SCM	South Cardinal Mark (buoy/beacon)
SD	Sailing Directions,Semi-diameter (of sun) Sounding of doubtful depth
sf	Stiff (nature of seabed)
Sh	Shells (nature of seabed). Shoal
SHM	Starboard-hand Mark (buoy/beacon); Simplified Harmonic Method (tides)
SHOM	Service Hydrographique et Océanographique de la Marine (FrenchHO/Chart)
Si	Silt (nature of seabed)
SIGNI	Signalisation de la Navigation Intérieure
SMS	Short Message Service (mobile texting)
so	Soft (eg mud; nature of seabed)
SOLAS	Safety of Life at Sea (IMO Convention)
Sp	Spire
sp	Spring tides
SPM	Special Mark (buoy/beacon)
SR	Sunrise
SRR	Search and Rescue Region
SS	Sunset. Signal Station
SSB	Single Sideband (radio)
St	Stones (nature of seabed)
Stbd	Starboard
subm	Submerged
SWM	Safe Water Mark (buoy/beacon)
sy	Sticky (eg mud; nature of seabed)
(T), (Temp)	Temporary
tbc	To be confirmed
tbn	To be notified
TD	Temporarily Discontinued (fog signal)
TE	Temporarily Extinguished (light)
tfn	Till further notice
Tr, twr	Tower
T/R	Traffic Report (route notification)
TSS	Traffic Separation Scheme
uncov	Uncovers
UQ	Ultra Quick flashing light
UT	Universal Time (= approx GMT)
Var	Variation (magnetic)
(vert)	Vertically disposed (lights)
Vi	Violet
vis	Visibility, visible
VLCC	Very large crude carrier (Oil tanker)
VNF	Voie Navigable de France (canals)
VQ	Very Quick flashing light
VTS	Vessel Traffic Service
W	West. White
WCM	West Cardinal Mark (buoy/beacon)
Wd	Weed (nature of seabed)
wef	With effect from
WGS	World Geodetic System (GPS datum)
wi-fi	Wireless Fidelity (internet access)
WIG	Wing in ground effect (craft)
WIP	Work in progress
Wk, ⌐ ⊕	Wreck (see also Fig 1(1))
WMO	World Meteorological Organisation
WPT, ⊕	Waypoint
WZ	Code for UK coastal navigation warning
Y	Yellow, Amber, Orange

0.3   PASSAGE PLANNING FORM

DATE:........................   FROM: ....   TO: ....   DIST: ....nm

ALTERNATIVE DESTINATION(S): ....

WEATHER FORECAST: ....
....

FORECASTS AVAILABLE DURING PASSAGE: ....
....

TIDES

DATE:................................	DATE:................................	DATE:................................
PLACE:..............................	PLACE:..............................	PLACE:..............................
HW	HW	HW ....
LW	LW	LW ....
HW	HW	HW ....
LW	LW	LW ....

COEFFICIENT: ....

HEIGHT OF TIDE AT: ....
.....................hrs ....m   ....hrs ....m   ....hrs ....m

DEPTH CONSTRAINTS: ....

TIDAL STREAMS AT: ....

TURNS .... AT ....   TOTAL SET (FM .... TO ....): ....° ....M

TURNS .... AT ....   TOTAL SET (FM .... TO ....): ....° ....M

NET TIDAL STREAM FOR PASSAGE: ....° ....M

ESTIMATED TIME: ....hrs ETD: ....   ETA: ....

SUN/MOON	SUNRISE:	SUNSET:	
	MOONRISE:	MOONSET:	PHASE: ....

WAYPOINTS	NO	NAME	TRACK/DISTANCE (TO NEXT WAYPOINT)
	....	....	.... / ....
	....	....	.... / ....
	....	....	.... / ....
	....	....	.... / ....
	....	....	.... / ....

DANGERS   CLEARING BEARINGS/RANGES/DEPTHS
....
....

LIGHTS/MARKS EXPECTED ....
....
....

COMMUNICATIONS   PORT/MARINA ....   VHF ....   ☎ ....

PORT/MARINA ....   VHF ....   ☎ ....

NOTES (CHARTS PREPARED & PAGE NUMBERS OF RELEVANT PILOTS / ALMANACS / ETC): ....
....
....

0.4 PASSAGE PLANNING

All passages by any vessel that goes to sea *must* be planned. 'Going to sea' is defined as proceeding beyond sheltered waters. Full passage planning requirements may be found in Chapter V of the International Convention for Safety of Life at Sea (SOLAS), but more digestible guidance for small craft is in the MCA's Pleasure Craft Information Pack at: **www.dft. gov.uk/mca/pleasure_craft_information_packdec07-2.pdf.**

Although the passage plan does not have to be recorded on paper, in the event of legal action a written plan is clear proof that the required planning has been completed. A suggested passage planning form is on the previous page. When completed this would constitute a reasonable passage plan. The blank form may be photocopied and/or modified.

Although spot checks on small craft are unlikely, the MCA could, following an accident or incident, take action under the Merchant Shipping Act if it could be proved that the skipper did not have a reasonable passage plan.

All passage plans should at least consider the following:

- **Weather.** Check the weather forecast and know how to get regular updates during the passage.
- **Tides.** Check tidal predictions and determine if there are any limiting depths at your port of departure, during the passage and at the port of arrival (and at alternative ports, if applicable). Tidal streams will almost certainly affect the plan.
- **Vessel.** Confirm she is suitable for the intended trip, is properly equipped, and has sufficient fuel, water and food on board.
- **Crew.** Take into account your crew's experience, expertise and stamina. Cold, tiredness and seasickness can be debilitating – and skippers are not immune.
- **Navigation.** Make sure you are aware of all navigational dangers by consulting up to date charts, pilot books and this Almanac. Never *rely* on GPS for fixing your position.
- **Contingency plan.** Consider bolt holes which can be entered *safely* in an emergency.
- **Information ashore.** Make sure someone ashore knows your plans, when they should become concerned and what action to take if necessary. Be sure to join the Coastguard Voluntary Identification Scheme.

0.5 POSITIONS FROM GPS

GPS uses the World Geodetic System 84 datum (WGS84). With the exception of much of the coast of Ireland and the west coast of Scotland, Admiralty charts of UK waters have now been converted to WGS84. Harbour chartlets in this Almanac are referenced to WGS84.

If the chart in use is not referenced to WGS84, positions read from the GPS receiver must be converted to the datum of the chart in use. This is printed on the chart and gives the Lat/Long corrections to be applied. They can be significant. There are two options:

- Set the receiver to WGS84. Before plotting positions, manually apply the corrections given on the chart. This option is advised by UKHO.
- Set the receiver to the datum of the chart in use; the datum corrections will be applied by the receiver's software. This method is not the most accurate due to the random nature of the differences.

0.6 VHF COMMUNICATIONS

Radio Telephony (R/T)

VHF radio (Marine band 156·00–174·00 MHz) is used by most vessels. Range is slightly better than the line of sight between aerials, typically about 20M between yachts and up to 65M to a shore station depending on aerial heights. It always pays to fit a good aerial, as high as possible.

VHF sets may be **Simplex**, ie transmit and receive on the same frequency, so only one person can talk at a time. **Semi-Duplex** (most modern sets), transmit and receive on different frequencies, or **full Duplex**, ie simultaneous Semi-Duplex, so conversation is normal, but two aerials are needed.

Marine VHF frequencies are known by their international channel number (Ch), as shown below.

Channels are grouped according to three main purposes, but some have more than one purpose.

> *Public correspondence:* **(via Coast radio stations)**
> Ch 26, 27, 25, 24, 23, 28, 04, 01, 03, 02, 07, 05, 84, 87, 86, 83, 85, 88, 61, 64, 65, 62, 66, 63, 60, 82, 78, 81.
> All channels can be used for Duplex.
>
> *Inter-ship:*
> Ch 06*, 08*, 10, 13, 09, 72*, 73, 69, 77*, 15, 17.
> These are all Simplex channels. * for use in UK.
>
> *Port Operations:*
> Simplex: Ch 12, 14, 11, 13, 09, 68, 71, 74, 69, 73, 17, 15.
> Duplex: Ch 20, 22, 18, 19, 21, 05, 07, 02, 03, 01, 04, 78, 82, 79, 81, 80, 60, 63, 66, 62, 65, 64, 61, 84.

The following channels have one specific purpose:

Ch 0 (156·00 MHz): SAR ops, not available to yachts.

Ch 10 (156·50 MHz), **23** (161·750 MHz), **84** (161·825 MHz) and **86** (161·925 MHz): MSI broadcasts. The optimum channel number is stated on Ch 16 in the announcement prior to the broadcast itself.

Ch 13 (156·650 MHz): Inter-ship communications relating to safety of navigation; a possible channel for calling a merchant ship if no contact on Ch 16.

Ch 16 (156·80 MHz): Distress, Safety and calling. Ch 16, in parallel with DSC Ch 70, will be monitored by ships, CG rescue centres (and, in some areas, any remaining Coast Radio Stations) for Distress and Safety until further notice. Yachts should monitor Ch 16. After an initial call, stations concerned **must** switch to a working channel, except for Distress and Safety matters.

Ch 67 (156·375 MHz): Small craft safety channel used by all UK CG centres, accessed via Ch 16.

Ch 70 (156·525 MHz): Digital Selective Calling for Distress and Safety purposes under GMDSS.

Ch 80 (157·025 MHz): Primary working channel between yachts and UK marinas.

Ch M (157·85 MHz): Secondary working channel, formerly known as Ch 37, but no longer.

Ch M2 (161·425 MHz): for race control, with Ch M as stand-by. YCs may apply to use Ch M2.

Your position should be given as Lat/Long or the vessel's bearing and distance *from* a charted object, eg 'My position 225° Fastnet Rock 4M' means you are 4M SW of the Fastnet Rock (*not* 4M NE). Use the 360° True bearing notation and the 24-hour clock (0001–2359), specifying UT or LT.

0.7   DISTRESS CALLS

Distress signal - MAYDAY

Distress only applies to a situation where a *vessel or person is in grave and imminent danger and requires immediate assistance*. A MAYDAY call should usually be sent on VHF Ch 16 or MF 2182 kHz, but any frequency may be used if help would thus be obtained more quickly.

Distress, Urgency and Safety messages from vessels at sea are free of charge. A Distress call has priority over all other transmissions. If heard, cease all transmissions that may interfere with the Distress call or messages, and listen on the frequency concerned.

Brief your crew so they are all able to send a Distress message. The MAYDAY message format (below) should be displayed near the radio. Before making the call:

- Switch on radio (check main battery switch is ON)
- Select HIGH power (25 watts)
- Select VHF Ch 16 (or 2182 kHz for MF)
- Press and hold down the transmit button, and say slowly and distinctly:

- **MAYDAY MAYDAY MAYDAY**
- **THIS IS** ....
  (name of boat, spoken three times)
- **MAYDAY** ....
  (name of boat spoken once)
- **CALLSIGN / MMSI Number** ....
  (Following a DSC alert)
- **MY POSITION IS** ....
  (latitude and longitude, true bearing and distance *from* a known point, or general location)
- **Nature of distress** ....
  (sinking, on fire etc)
- **Help required** ....
  (immediate assistance)
- **Number of persons on board** ....
- **Any other important, helpful information** ....
  (you are taking to the liferaft; distress rockets are being fired etc)
- **OVER**

On completion of the Distress message, release the transmit button and listen. The boat's position is of vital importance and should be repeated if time allows. If an acknowledgement is not received, check the set and repeat the Distress call.

Vessels with GMDSS equipment should make a MAYDAY call on Ch 16, including their MMSI and callsign, *after* sending a DSC Distress alert on VHF Ch 70 or MF 2187·5 kHz.

0.7.1   MAYDAY acknowledgement

In coastal waters an immediate acknowledgement should be expected, as follows:

MAYDAY ....
(name of station sending the Distress message, spoken three times)

THIS IS ....
(name of station acknowledging, spoken three times)

RECEIVED MAYDAY

If you hear a Distress message, write down the details and, if you can help, acknowledge accordingly - but only after giving an opportunity for the nearest Coastguard station or some larger vessel to do so.

0.7.2   MAYDAY relay

If you hear a Distress message from a vessel, and it is not acknowledged, you should pass on the message as follows:

MAYDAY RELAY ....
(spoken three times)

THIS IS ....
(name of vessel re-transmitting the Distress message, spoken three times), followed by the intercepted message.

0.7.3   Control of MAYDAY traffic

A MAYDAY call imposes general radio silence until the vessel concerned or some other authority (eg the nearest Coastguard) cancels the Distress. If necessary the station controlling Distress traffic may impose radio silence as follows:

SEELONCE MAYDAY, followed by its name or other identification, on the Distress frequency.

If some other station nearby believes it necessary to do likewise, it may transmit:

SEELONCE DISTRESS, followed by its name or other identification.

0.7.4   Relaxing radio silence

When complete radio silence is no longer necessary, the controlling station may relax radio silence as follows, indicating that restricted working may be resumed:

MAYDAY

ALL STATIONS, ALL STATIONS, ALL STATIONS

THIS IS ....
(name or callsign)

The time ....

The name of the vessel in distress ....

PRUDONCE

Normal working on the Distress frequency may then be resumed, having listened carefully before transmitting. Subsequent calls from the casualty should be prefixed by the Urgency signal (0.8).

If Distress working continues on other frequencies these will be identified. For example, PRUDONCE on 2182 kHz, but SEELONCE on VHF Ch 16.

0.7.5   Cancelling radio silence

When the problem is resolved, the Distress call must be cancelled by the co-ordinating station using the prowords SEELONCE FEENEE as follows:

MAYDAY

ALL STATIONS, ALL STATIONS, ALL STATIONS

THIS IS ....(name or callsign)

The time ....

The name of the vessel in distress ....

SEELONCE FEENEE

0.8 URGENCY AND SAFETY CALLS

Urgency signal - PAN PAN

The radio Urgency prefix, consisting of the words PAN PAN spoken three times, indicates that a vessel, or station, has *a very urgent message concerning the safety of a ship or person*. It may be used when urgent medical advice is needed.

This is an example of an Urgency call:

> PAN PAN, PAN PAN, PAN PAN
>
> ALL STATIONS, ALL STATIONS, ALL STATIONS
>
> THIS IS YACHT SEABIRD, SEABIRD, SEABIRD
>
> Zero eight five degrees Ballagan Point one point five miles
>
> Dismasted and propeller fouled
>
> Drifting north west towards Limestone Rocks
>
> Require urgent tow
>
> OVER

PAN PAN messages take priority over all traffic except Distress, and are sent on Ch 16 or 2182 kHz. They should be cancelled when the urgency is over.

If the message is long (eg a medical call) or communications traffic is heavy, it may be passed on a working frequency after an initial call on Ch 16 or 2182 kHz. At the end of the initial call you should indicate that you are switching to a working frequency.

If you hear an Urgency call react in the same way as for a Distress call.

0.8.1 Safety signal - SÉCURITÉ

The word SÉCURITÉ (pronounced SAY-CURE-E-TAY) spoken three times, indicates that the station is about to transmit an important navigational or meteorological warning. Such messages usually originate from a CG Centre or a Coast Radio Station, and are transmitted on a working channel after an announcement on the distress/calling channel (Ch 16 or 2182 kHz).

Safety messages are usually addressed to 'All stations', and are often transmitted at the end of the first available silence period. An example of a Sécurité message is:

> SÉCURITÉ, SÉCURITÉ, SÉCURITÉ ....
>
> THIS IS ....
> (CG Centre or Coast Radio Station callsign, spoken three times)
>
> ALL STATIONS ....
> (spoken three times) followed by instructions to change channel, then the message.

0.9 GMDSS

The Global Maritime Distress and Safety System (GMDSS) came into force in 1999. Most seagoing vessels over 300 tons are required by SOLAS to comply with GMDSS, but it is not compulsory for yachts. However, it is important that the principles of the system are understood, and you should at least consider fitting compliant equipment depending on your cruising area. Full details may be found in ALRS Vol 5 (NP 285).

0.9.1 Purpose

GMDSS enables a coordinated SAR operation to be mounted rapidly and reliably anywhere at sea. To this end, terrestrial and satellite communications and navigation equipment is used to alert SAR authorities ashore and ships in the vicinity to a Distress incident or Urgency situation. GMDSS also promulgates MSI (Maritime Safety Information).

0.9.2 Sea areas

The type of equipment carried by a vessel depends of her operating area. The four GMDSS Areas are:

A1	An area within R/T coverage of at least one VHF Coastguard or Coast radio station in which continuous VHF alerting is available via DSC. Range: 20–50M from the CG/CRS.
A2	An area, excluding sea area A1, within R/T coverage of at least one MF CG/CRS in which continuous DSC alerting is available. Range: approx 50–250M from the CG/CRS.
A3	An area between 76°N and 76°S, excluding sea areas A1 and A2, within coverage of HF or an Inmarsat satellite in which continuous alerting is available.
A4	An area outside sea areas A1, A2 and A3, ie the polar regions, within coverage of HF.

In each Area, in addition to a Navtex receiver, certain types of radio equipment must be carried by GMDSS vessels: In A1, VHF DSC; A2, VHF and MF DSC; A3, VHF, MF and HF or SatCom; A4, VHF, MF and HF.

0.9.3 Digital Selective Calling (DSC)

GMDSS comprises 'sub-systems' which are coordinated through Maritime Rescue Coordination Centres (MRCC) to ensure safety at sea. DSC is one of the 'sub-systems' of GMDSS. It uses terrestial communications for making initial contact and, in a distress situation, provides the vessel's identity, nature of distress and position (entered manually or automatically if linked with the GPS). In all DSC messages every vessel and relevant shore station has a 9-digit Maritime Mobile Service Identity (MMSI) which is in effect an automatic electronic callsign. Dedicated frequencies are: VHF Ch 70, MF 2187·5 kHz. A thorough working knowledge of the following procedure is needed.

A typical VHF/DSC Distress alert might be sent as follows:

- Briefly press the (red, guarded) Distress button. The set automatically switches to Ch 70 (DSC Distress channel). Press again for 5 seconds to transmit a basic Distress alert with position and time. The radio then reverts to Ch 16.

- If time permits, select the nature of the distress from the menu, eg Collision, then press the Distress button for 5 seconds to send a full Distress alert.

A CG/CRS should automatically send an acknowledgement on Ch 70 before replying on Ch 16. Ships in range should reply directly on Ch 16. When a DSC Distress acknowledgement has been received, or after about 15 seconds, the vessel in distress should transmit a MAYDAY message by voice on Ch 16, including its MMSI.

0.10 HM COASTGUARD - CONTACT DETAILS OF CG CENTRES

†MILFORD HAVEN COASTGUARD
51°42'N 05°03'W. MMSI 002320017
Gorsewood Drive, Hakin, Milford Haven, SA73 2HD.
☎ 01646 690909. 🖷 01646 692176.
Area: Friog to Marsland Mouth (near Bude).

†HOLYHEAD COASTGUARD
53°19'N 04°38'W. MMSI 002320018
Prince of Wales Rd, Holyhead, Anglesey LL65 1ET.
☎ 01407 762051. 🖷 01407 764373.
Area: Mull of Galloway to Friog (1·6M S of Barmouth).

†*BELFAST COASTGUARD
54°40'N 05°40'W. MMSI 002320021
Bregenz House, Quay St, Bangor, Co Down BT20 5ED.
☎ 02891 463933. 🖷 02891 469886.
Area: L Foyle to Carlingford inc Firth of Clyde and islands.

†*STORNOWAY COASTGUARD
58°12'N 06°22'W. MMSI 002320024
Battery Point, Stornoway, Isle of Lewis H51 2RT.
☎ 01851 702013. 🖷 01851 704387.
Area: Cape Wrath to Mull, Western Isles and St Kilda.

†Monitors DSC MF 2187.5 kHz. *Broadcasts Gunfacts/Subfacts.

0.11 NATIONAL COASTWATCH INSTITUTION

The National Coastwatch Institution (NCI) - www.nci.org. uk is manned by over 2000 volunteers keeping a visual watch during daylight hours along the English and Welsh coast throughout the year assisting in the protection of life at sea. There are 50 operational stations (2015) All NCI stations monitor VHF Ch 16 and provide actual weather, sea state, hazards and local information on request on their dedicated channel **VHF Ch 65**. Many are equipped with AIS, DSC and radar.

0.12 REPUBLIC OF IRELAND (COAST GUARD)

The Irish Coast Guard co-ordinates SAR operations around the coast of Eire via Dublin MRCC, Malin Head and Valentia MRSCs and remote sites.

It may liaise with the UK and France during any rescue operation within 100M of the Irish coast. It is part of the Dept of Marine, Leeson Lane, Dublin 2. ☎ (01) 6783454; 🖷 (01) 6783459. The Irish EPIRB Registry is at the same address; ☎ (01) 6199280; 🖷 (01) 6621571.

The MRCC/MRSCs are co-located with the Coast radio stations of the same name and manned by the same staff.

All stations keep watch H24 on VHF Ch 16 and DSC Ch 70. If ashore dial 999 or 112 in an emergency and ask for Marine Rescue. Details of the MRCC/MRSCs are as follows:

DUBLIN (MRCC)
53°20'N 06°15W. DSC MMSI 002500300 (+2187·5 kHz).
☎ +353 1 662 0922/3; 🖷 +353 1 662 0795.
Area: Carlingford Lough to Youghal.

VALENTIA (MRSC)
51°56'N 10°21'W.DSC MMSI 002500200 (+2187·5 kHz).
☎ +353 669 476 109; 🖷 +353 669 476 289.
Area: Youghal to Slyne Head.

MALIN HEAD (MRSC)
55°22'N 07°20W. DSC MMSI 002500100 (+2187·5 kHz).
☎ +353 74 9370103; 🖷 +353 74 9370221.
Area: Slyne Head to Lough Foyle.

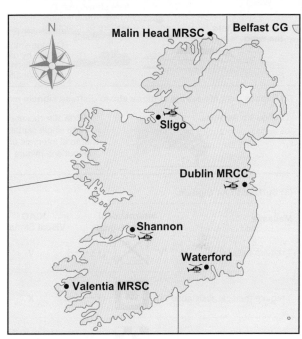

Fig 0(1) Irish CG centres and boundaries

0.12.1 SAR resources

The Irish Coast Guard provides some 50 units around the coast and is on call H24. The RNLI maintains four stations around the coast and operates 42 lifeboats. Additionally, six community-run inshore rescue boats are available.

Sikorsky S-61 helicopters, based at Dublin, Waterford, Shannon and Sligo, can respond within 15 to 45 minutes and operate to a radius of 200M. They are equipped with infrared search equipment and can uplift 30 survivors.

Military and civilian aircraft and vessels, together with the Garda (police) and lighthouse service, can also be called upon.

Some stations provide specialist cliff climbing services. They are manned by volunteers, who are trained in first aid and equipped with inflatables, breeches buoys, cliff ladders etc. Their ☎ numbers (the Leader's residence) are given, where appropriate, under each port.

Fig 0(2)   Distress and life saving signals

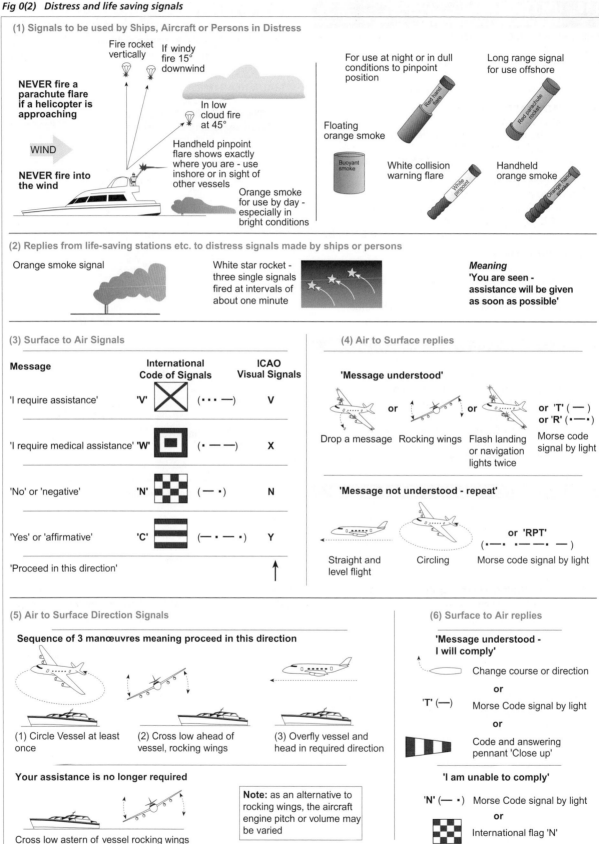

(1) Signals to be used by Ships, Aircraft or Persons in Distress

Fire rocket vertically

If windy fire 15° downwind

NEVER fire a parachute flare if a helicopter is approaching

In low cloud fire at 45°

WIND

Handheld pinpoint flare shows exactly where you are - use inshore or in sight of other vessels

NEVER fire into the wind

Orange smoke for use by day - especially in bright conditions

For use at night or in dull conditions to pinpoint position

Long range signal for use offshore

Red hand flare

Red parachute rocket

Floating orange smoke

Buoyant smoke

White collision warning flare

White pinpoint

Handheld orange smoke

Orange hand smoke

(2) Replies from life-saving stations etc. to distress signals made by ships or persons

Orange smoke signal

White star rocket - three single signals fired at intervals of about one minute

Meaning
'You are seen - assistance will be given as soon as possible'

(3) Surface to Air Signals

Message	International Code of Signals		ICAO Visual Signals
'I require assistance'	'V'	(· · · —)	V
'I require medical assistance'	'W'	(· — —)	X
'No' or 'negative'	'N'	(— ·)	N
'Yes' or 'affirmative'	'C'	(— · — ·)	Y
'Proceed in this direction'			↑

(4) Air to Surface replies

'Message understood'

or   or   or 'T' (—)
or 'R' (· — ·)

Drop a message   Rocking wings   Flash landing or navigation lights twice   Morse code signal by light

'Message not understood - repeat'

or 'RPT'
(· — · · — · —)

Straight and level flight   Circling   Morse code signal by light

(5) Air to Surface Direction Signals

Sequence of 3 manœuvres meaning proceed in this direction

(1) Circle Vessel at least once

(2) Cross low ahead of vessel, rocking wings

(3) Overfly vessel and head in required direction

Your assistance is no longer required

Cross low astern of vessel rocking wings

Note: as an alternative to rocking wings, the aircraft engine pitch or volume may be varied

(6) Surface to Air replies

'Message understood - I will comply'

Change course or direction

or

'T' (—)   Morse Code signal by light

or

Code and answering pennant 'Close up'

'I am unable to comply'

'N' (— ·)   Morse Code signal by light

or

International flag 'N'

0.13 NAVTEX

NAVTEX is the prime method of disseminating MSI to at least 200 miles offshore. A dedicated aerial and receiver with an LCD screen (or integrated printer) are required. The user selects which stations and message categories are recorded for automatic display or printing.

Two frequencies are used. On the international frequency, 518kHz, messages are always available in English with excellent coverage of Europe. Interference between stations is minimised by scheduling time slots and and by limiting transmission power. NAVTEX information applies only to the geographical area for which each station is responsible.

On the national frequency 490kHz (for clarity shown in red throughout this section) the UK/ROI issues inshore waters forecasts and coastal station actuals. Elsewhere it is used mainly for transmissions in the national language. 490khz stations have different identification letters from 518kHz. NAVTEX is particularly useful when preoccupied handling your vessel as you will not miss potentially important information.

0.13.1 Message numbering
Each message is prefixed by a four-character group:

The first character is the code letter of the transmitting station (eg **E** for Niton).

The 2nd character is the message category, see 0.12.2.

The third and fourth are message serial numbers, running from 01 to 99 and then re-starting at 01.

The serial number 00 denotes urgent messages which are always printed.

Messages which are corrupt or have already been printed are rejected. Weather messages are dated and timed. All NAVTEX messages end with NNNN.

0.13.2 Message categories

A*	Navigational warnings
B*	Meteorological warnings
C	Ice reports
D*	SAR info and Piracy attack warnings
E	Weather forecasts
F	Pilot service
G	AIS
H	LORAN
I	Spare
J	SATNAV
K	Other electronic Navaids
L	Navwarnings additional to **A**
M-U	Spare
V-Y	Special services – as allocated
Z	No messages on hand

* These categories cannot be rejected by the receiver.

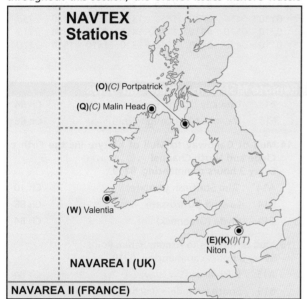

NAVTEX Stations

(O)(C) Portpatrick
(Q)(C) Malin Head
(W) Valentia
(E)(K)(I)(T) Niton

NAVAREA I (UK)
NAVAREA II (FRANCE)

Fig 0(3) NAVTEX stations/areas – UK & Ireland

0.13.3 UK/ROI 518 kHz stations
Weather message times (UT) are in bold. Extended outlook times (2-3 days beyond the shipping forecast period) are in italics.

O –	**Portpatrick** Lundy clockwise to SE Iceland.	**0220**	**0620**	**1020**	**1420**	**1820**	**2220**
Q –	**Malin Head** sea areas Shannon, Rockall, Malin & Bailey,		**0640**			**1840**	
E –	**Niton** Thames clockwise to Fastnet, excluding Trafalgar.	*0040*	**0440**	**0840**	1240	**1640**	2040

0.13.4 UK/ROI 490 kHz stations
These provide forecasts for UK inshore waters (to 12M offshore), a national 3 day outlook for inshore waters and, at times in bold, reports of actual weather at the places listed below. To receive these reports select message category 'V' (0.12.2) on your NAVTEX receiver. Times (UT) of transmissions are listed in chronological order.

Actual Met data includes: Sea level pressure (mb), wind direction and speed (kn), weather, visibility (M), air and sea temperatures (°C), dewpoint temperature (°C) and mean wave height (m).

C –	**Portpatrick** Land's End to Shetland	0020	0420	0820	**1220**	**1620**	2020

North Rona, Stornoway, South Uist, Lusa (Skye bridge), Tiree, Macrihanish, Belfast, Malin Head, Belmullet, St Bees Head, Ronaldsway, Crosby (Liverpool), Valley, Aberporth, Roches Point, Valentia, St Mawgan.

0.13.5 NAVTEX broadcast times in Ireland
Times of weather messages are shown in **bold**. Gale warnings are usually transmitted 4 hourly.

METAREA I (Co-ordinator – UK)		Transmission times (UT)					
Q –	**Malin Head**, Ireland	0240	**0640**	1040	1440	**1840**	2240
W –	**Valentia**, Ireland	0340	**0740**	1140	1540	**1940**	2340

0.14 MSI BROADCASTS BY HM COASTGUARD

MSI (Maritime Safety Information) is routinely broadcast every 3 hours at the times below. VHF working channels are announced on Ch 16.

Each broadcast contains one of 3 different Groups of MSI:
Group A, the full broadcast, contains the Shipping forecast, a new Inshore waters forecast and 24 hrs outlook, Gale warnings, a Fisherman's 3 day forecast* (1 Oct-31 Mar), Navigational (WZ) warnings and Subfacts & Gunfacts

‡ where appropriate. Times of 'A' broadcasts are in bold.

Group B contains a new Inshore waters forecast, plus the previous outlook, and Gale warnings. 'B' broadcast times are in plain type.

Group C is a repeat of the Inshore forecast and Gale warnings (as per the previous Group A or B) plus new Strong wind warnings. 'C' broadcast times are italicised. HM Coastguard modernisation is due to end December 2015 and might affect information on this page.

Broadcasts of shipping and inshore waters forecasts by HM Coastguard

Coastguard	Shipping forecast areas	Inshore areas	Broadcast times UT							
			B	C	A	C	B	C	A	C
Milford Haven	Lundy, Fastnet, Irish Sea	9, 10	0150	*0450*	**0750**	*1050*	1350	*1650*	**1950**	*2250*
Holyhead	Irish Sea	10-12	0130	*0450*	**0730**	*1050*	1330	*1650*	**1930**	*2250*
Belfast‡	Irish Sea, Malin	13, 14	0210	*0510*	**0810**	*1110*	1410	*1710*	**2010**	*2310*
Stornoway‡*	Rockall, Malin, Hebrides, Bailey, Fair Is, Faeroes, SE Iceland	15-17	0110	*0410*	**0710**	*1010*	1310	*1610*	**1910**	*2210*

Inshore waters forecast areas - Remote MSI transmitters and times

9 Land's End to St David's Head, inc the Bristol Channel
Every 3 hours commencing 0150

A9	Trevose Head	Ch 84
B9	Hartland Point	Ch 86
C9	Combe Martin (N Devon)	Ch 23
D9	Severn Bridges	Ch 86
E9	St Hilary (Barry)	Ch 23
F9	Monkstone (Tenby)	Ch 84
G9	St Ann's (Milford Haven)	Ch 84

10 St David's Head to Great Orme Head inc St George's Channel
Every 3 hours commencing 0150

A10	Dinas Head (Fishguard)	Ch 86
B10	Blaenplwyf (Aberystwyth)	Ch 84
C10	South Stack (Holyhead)	Ch 23
D10	Great Orme	Ch 86

11 Great Orme Head to the Mull of Galloway
Every 3 hours commencing, 0130

A11	Moel-y-Parc(N Wales)	Ch 23
B11	Langthwaite (Lancaster)	Ch 84
C11	Caldbeck (Carlisle)	Ch 23

12 Isle of Man
Every 3 hours commencing, 0130

A12	Snaefell (Isle of Man)	Ch 86

13) Lough Foyle to Carlingford Lough
Every 3 hours commencing, 0210

A13	Slievemartin (Rostrevor)	Ch 86
B13	Orlock Head (Bangor)	Ch 84
C13	Black Mountain (Belfast)	Ch 23
D13	West Torr (Fair Head)	Ch 86

E13	Limvady (Lough Foyle)	Ch 84
F13	Navar (Lower Lough Erne)	Ch 86

14 Mull of Galloway to Mull of Kintyre inc the Firth of Clyde and North Channel
Every 3 hours commencing, 0210

A14	Rhu Staffnish (Kintyre)	Ch 10
B14	Lawhill (Ardrossan)	Ch 86
C14	Clyde (Greenock)	Ch 84

15 Mull of Kintyre to Arnamurchan Point
Every 3 hours commencing, 0210

A15	Kilchiaran (SW Islay)	Ch 84
B15	South Knapdale (Loch Fyne)	Ch 23
C15	Torosay (E Mull)	Ch 10
D15	Glengorm (N Mull)	Ch 84
E15	Tiree	Ch 23, MF1883kHz

16 The Minch
Every 3 hours commencing 0110

A16	Arisaig (S of Mallaig)	Ch 86
B16	Drumfearn (SE Skye)	Ch 23
C16	Skriag (Portree, Skye)	Ch 10
D16	Rodel (S Harris)	Ch 84
E16	Melvaig (Loch Ewe)	Ch 86
F16	Portnaguran (E Lewis)	Ch 23

17 Arnamurchan Point to Cape Wrath
Every 3 hours commencing 0110

A17	Barra	Ch 10
B17	Clettreval (N Uist)	Ch 23
C17	Forsnaval (W Lewis)	Ch 84
D17	Butt of Lewis	Ch 10, MF1743 kHz

0.15 OTHER UK WEATHER BROADCASTS

BBC Radio 4 Shipping forecast

BBC Radio 4 broadcasts shipping forecasts at:

0048, 0520 LT[1]	LW, MW, FM
1201 LT	LW only
1754 LT	LW, FM (Sat/Sun)

[1] Includes weather reports from coastal stations

Frequencies

LW		198 kHz
MW	**London and N Ireland:**	720 kHz
	Redruth:	756 kHz
	Plymouth & Enniskillen:	774 kHz
	Carlisle:	1485 kHz
FM	**England:**	92·4–94·6 MHz
	Scotland:	91·3–96·1 MHz 103·5–104·9 MHz
	Wales:	92·8–96·1 MHz & 103·5–104·9 MHz
	N Ireland	93·2–96·0 MHz 103·5–104·6 MHz

The Shipping Forecast contains:

Time of issue; summary of gale warnings in force at that time; a general synopsis of weather systems and their expected development and movement over the next 24 hours; sea area forecasts for the same 24 hours, including wind direction/ force, weather and visibility in each; and an outlook for the following 24 hours.

Gale warnings for all affected areas are broadcast at the earliest break in Radio 4 programmes after receipt, as well as after the next news bulletin.

Weather reports from coastal stations follow the 0048 and 0520 shipping forecasts. They include wind direction and force, present weather, visibility, and sealevel pressure and tendency, if available. The stations are shown in Fig 0(5).

0.15.1 BBC Radio 4 Inshore waters forecast

A forecast for UK inshore waters (up to 12M offshore), valid for 24 hrs, is broadcast after the 0048 and 0520 coastal station reports. It includes forecasts of wind direction and force, weather, visibility and sea state.

Reports of actual weather are broadcast from all the stations below after the 0048 inshore waters forecast and also after the 0520 forecast, except those in italics: Scilly*, Valentia, *Milford Haven, Aberporth, Valley, Liverpool(Crosby),* Ronaldsway, Malin Head; *Machrihanish*;* Stornoway. An asterix* denotes an automatic station.

0.15.2 Terms used in weather bulletins

Speed of movement of pressure systems	
Slowly	< 15 knots
Steadily	15–25 knots
Rather quickly	25–35 knots
Rapidly	35–45 knots
Very rapidly	> 45 knots

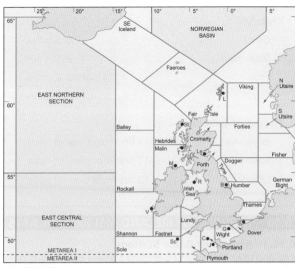

Fig 0(4) UK – Forecast areas

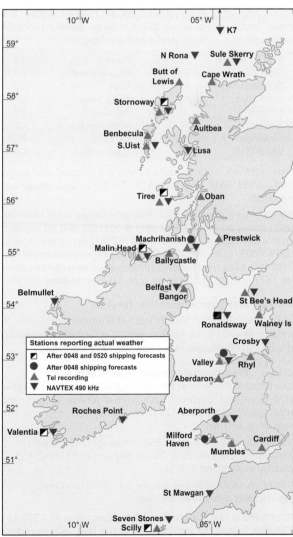

Fig 0(5) Stations reporting actual weather via BBC Radio 4, telephone recordings or NAVTEX

Visibility

Good	> 5 miles
Moderate	2–5 miles
Poor	1000 metres–2 miles
Fog	< 1000 metres

Timing of gale warnings

Imminent:	Within 6 hrs from time of issue
Soon:	6–12 hrs from time of issue
Later:	> 12 hrs from time of issue

Barometric pressure changes (tendency)

Rising or falling slowly: Pressure change of 0·1 to 1·5 hPa/mb in the preceding 3 hours.

Rising or falling: Pressure change of 1·6 to 3·5 hPa/mb in the preceding 3 hours.

Rising or falling quickly: Pressure change of 3·6 to 6 hPa/mb in the preceding 3 hours.

Rising or falling very rapidly: Pressure change of more than 6 hPa/mb in the preceding 3 hours.

Now rising (or falling): Pressure has been falling (rising) or steady in the preceding 3 hours, but at the observation time was definitely rising (falling).

0.16 REPUBLIC OF IRELAND MSI BROADCASTS

0.16.1 Irish Coast Radio Stations

CRS and their VHF channels are listed below and shown in Fig 0(7). See also: www.malinheadcoastguardradio.com/index.htm. Weather bulletins for 30M offshore and the Irish Sea are broadcast on VHF at 0103, 0403, 0703, 1003, 1303, 1603, 1903 and 2203UT after an announcement on Ch 16. Broadcasts are made 1 hour earlier when DST is in force. Bulletins include gale warnings, synopsis and a 24-hour forecast.

MALIN HEAD	23	Bantry	23
Glen Head	24	Mizen Head	04
Donegal Bay	02	Cork	26
Belmullet	83	Mine Head	83
Clifden	26	Rosslare	23
Galway	04	Wicklow Head	02
Shannon	28	DUBLIN	83
VALENTIA	24	Carlingford	04

Gale warnings are broadcast on these VHF channels on receipt and at 0033, 0633, 1233 and 1833 UT, after an announcement on Ch 16.

MF Valentia Radio broadcasts forecasts for sea areas Shannon and Fastnet on 1752 kHz at 0833 & 2033 UT, and on request. Gale warnings are broadcast on 1752 kHz on receipt and at 0303, 0903, 1503 and 2103 (UT) after an announcement on 2182 kHz. Malin Head does not broadcast weather information on 1677 kHz. At Dublin there is no MF transmitter.

0.16.2 Met Éireann weather services

Met Éireann (the Irish Met Office) is at Glasnevin Hill, Dublin 9, Ireland. ☎ +353 1 806 4200 www.met.ie. General forecasting division (H24, charges may apply) ☎ +353 1 806 4255.

0.16.3 Weatherdial telephone forecasts

The latest sea area forecasts and gale warnings are available H24 from Met Éireann's Weatherdial service as recorded messages. Dial ☎ 1550 123 (from within ROI only) plus the following suffixes:

850 Munster; 851 Leinster; 852 Connaught; 853 Ulster; 854 Dublin (plus winds in Dublin Bay and HW times); 855 Coastal waters and Irish Sea.

1550 calls cost €0.95 per min inc VAT from landlines, significantly more from mobiles.

Weatherdial Fax provides similar forecasts: dial 🖷 1570 131 838 and follow the instructions on the line, using product code 0010 for the Marine help page. Calls cost €1.75 per min incl. VAT.

0.16.4 Radio Telefís Éireann (RTE) Radio 1

RTE Radio 1 broadcasts weather bulletins daily at 0602, 1255, 1657 & 2355LT (1hr earlier when DST is in force) on 567kHz (Tullamore), 729kHz (Cork) and FM (88·2–95·2MHz).

Bulletins contain a situation, forecast and coastal reports for Irish Sea and coastal waters. The forecast includes: wind, weather, vis, swell (if higher than 4m) and a 24 hrs outlook.

Gale warnings are included in hourly news bulletins on FM & MF.

Coastal reports include wind, weather, visibility, pressure, with pressure change over the last 3 hrs described as:

Steady	=	0–0·4 hPa change
Rising/falling slowly	=	0·5–1·9
Rising/falling	=	2·0–3·4
Rising/falling rapidly	=	3·5–5·9
Rising/falling very rapidly	=	> 6·0

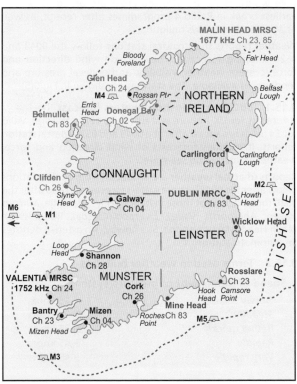

Fig 0(6) shows CRS, Met buoys M1–M6, PROVINCES and headlands named in forecasts

0.17 AUTOMATIC IDENTIFICATION SYSTEM (AIS)

Automatic Identification System (AIS) allows information to be provided to other ships and shore authorities; it is required by SOLAS to be fitted to most vessels over 300 GRT. AIS is widely used to automatically and continuously identify, track and display other vessels and their movements.

Each ship's course and speed vector is shown by a symbol on an AIS screen or overlaid on radar, chart plotter or PC. This data may also appear in a text box as heading, COG & SOG, range, CPA, position, ship's name, and her status – under power or sail, anchored, constrained by draught, restricted in her ability to manoeuvre, not under command, fishing etc.

Many lights, buoys and other aids to navigation (AtoN) are now fitted with AIS, and the number is growing rapidly. On Admiralty charts, these are shown by a magenta circle and the notation 'AIS'. Not all transmitted information is available to all users; it depends on the display system fitted.

AIS Class B transmitters/transceivers for non-SOLAS vessels are available, but are not mandatory. Later sets can receive aids to navigation (A2N) data, showing virtual marks and MMSI numbers from buoys and lighthouses.

Caveats: Many vessels are not fitted with AIS, and some may not have it switched on; some only display 3 lines of text, not a plot; in busy areas only the strongest signals may be shown; AIS may distract a bridge watchkeeper from his visual and radar watch; unlike eyes and radar, AIS does not yet feature in the Colregs; GPS/electronic failures invalidate AIS.

In areas of traffic concentration Class B transmitters may be excluded from the network if no time slots are available.

It is not a radar despite what some advertisements may imply.

0.18 CALCULATING CLEARANCES BELOW OVERHEAD OBJECTS

A diagram often helps when calculating vertical clearance below bridges, power cables etc. Fig 0(7) shows the relationship to CD. The height of such objects as shown on the chart is usually measured above HAT, so the actual clearance will almost always be more. The height of HAT above CD is given at the foot of each page of the tide tables. Most Admiralty charts now show clearances above HAT, but check the **Heights** block below the chart title.

To calculate clearances, insert the dimensions into the following formula, carefully observing the conventions for brackets:

Masthead clearance = (Height of object above HAT + height of HAT above CD) minus (height of tide at the time + height of the masthead above waterline)

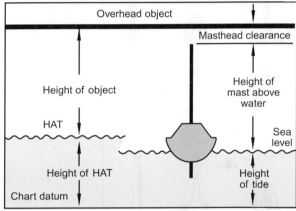

Fig 0(7) Calculating masthead clearance

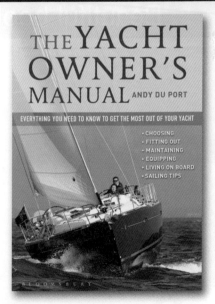

0.19 IALA BUOYAGE

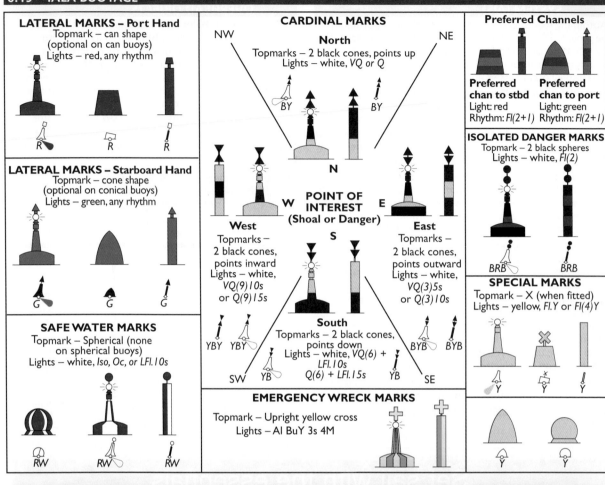

LATERAL MARKS – Port Hand
Topmark – can shape
(optional on can buoys)
Lights – red, any rhythm

R   R   R

LATERAL MARKS – Starboard Hand
Topmark – cone shape
(optional on conical buoys)
Lights – green, any rhythm

G   G   G

SAFE WATER MARKS
Topmark – Spherical (none
on spherical buoys)
Lights – white, Iso, Oc, or LFl.10s

RW   RW   RW

CARDINAL MARKS

NW   NE

North
Topmarks – 2 black cones, points up
Lights – white, VQ or Q

BY   BY

N

W   **POINT OF**   E
            INTEREST
          (Shoal or Danger)

West   **S**   **East**
Topmarks –   Topmarks –
2 black cones,   2 black cones,
points inward   points outward
Lights – white,   Lights – white,
VQ(9)10s   VQ(3)5s
or Q(9)15s   or Q(3)10s

YBY YBY   BYB   BYB

South
Topmarks – 2 black cones,
points down
Lights – white, VQ(6) +
LFl.10s
Q(6) + LFl.15s

SW   YB   YB   SE

EMERGENCY WRECK MARKS
Topmark – Upright yellow cross
Lights – Al BuY 3s 4M

Preferred Channels

Preferred   **Preferred**
chan to stbd   **chan to port**
Light: red   Light: green
Rhythm: Fl(2+1)   Rhythm: Fl(2+1)

ISOLATED DANGER MARKS
Topmark – 2 black spheres
Lights – white, Fl(2)

BRB   BRB

SPECIAL MARKS
Topmark – X (when fitted)
Lights – yellow, Fl.Y or Fl(4)Y

Y   Y   Y

Y   Y

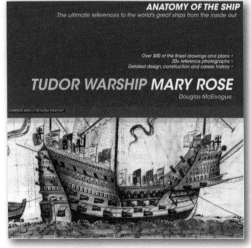

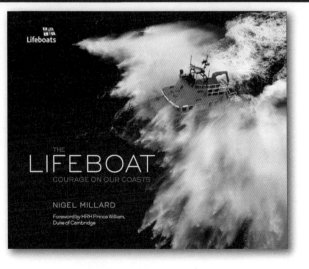

Beautiful books from Conway

0.20 FLAGS AND ENSIGNS

UK WHITE ENSIGN

UK BLUE ENSIGN

UK RED ENSIGN

AUSTRALIA

AUSTRIA

BASQUE FLAG

BELGIUM

CANADA

CYPRUS

DENMARK

FINLAND

FRANCE

GERMANY

GREECE

GUERNSEY

JERSEY

IRELAND

ISRAEL

ITALY

LIBERIA

MALTA

MONACO

MOROCCO

NETHERLANDS

NEW ZEALAND

NORWAY

PANAMA

POLAND

PORTUGAL

SOUTH AFRICA

SPAIN

SWEDEN

SWITZERLAND

TUNISIA

TURKEY

USA

0.21 LIGHTS AND SHAPES

Rule 24

Vessels being towed and towing

Vessel towed shows sidelights (forward) and sternlight

Tug shows two masthead lights, sidelights, sternlight, yellow towing light

Rule 24

Towing by day — Length of tow more than 200m

Towing vessel and tow display diamond shapes. By night, the towing vessel shows three masthead lights instead of two as for shorter tows

Rule 25

Motor sailing

Cone point down, forward. At night the lights of a power-driven vessel underway

Rule 26

Vessel fishing

All-round red light over all-round white, plus sidelights and sternlight when making way

Rule 26

Fishing/Trawling

A shape consisting of two cones point to point in a vertical line one above the other

Rule 26

Vessel trawling

All-round green light over all-round white, plus sidelights and sternlight when making way

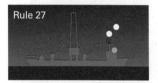

Rule 27

Vessel restricted in her ability to manoeuvre

All-round red, white, red lights vertically, plus normal steaming lights when making way

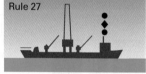

Rule 27

Three shapes in a vertical line: ball, diamond, ball

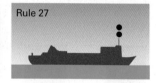

Rule 27

Not under command

Two all-round red lights, plus sidelights and sternlight when making way

Two balls vertically

Rule 27

Dredger

All round red, white, red lights vertically, plus two all-round red lights (or two balls) on foul side, and two all-round green (or two diamonds) on clear side

Rule 27

Divers down

Letter 'A' International Code

Rule 28

Constrained by draught

Three all-round red lights in a vertical line, plus normal steaming lights. By day — a cylinder

Rule 29

Pilot boat

All-round white light over all-round red, plus sidelights and sternlight when underway, or anchor light

Rule 30

Vessel at anchor

All-round white light; if over 50m, a second light aft and lower

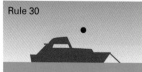

Rule 30

Ball forward

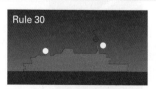

Rule 30

Vessel aground

Anchor light(s), plus two all-round red lights in a vertical line

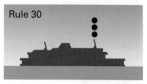

Rule 30

Three balls in a vertical line

0.22 NAVIGATION LIGHTS

LIGHTS FOR TYPICAL YACHT WITH 3 OPTIONAL VARIANTS

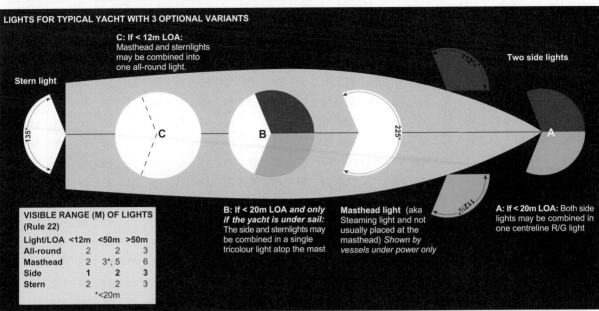

C: If < 12m LOA: Masthead and sternlights may be combined into one all-round light.

Two side lights

Stern light

135°

225°

112½°

112½°

B: If < 20m LOA and only if the yacht is under sail: The side and sternlights may be combined in a single tricolour light atop the mast

Masthead light (aka Steaming light and not usually placed at the masthead) *Shown by vessels under power only*

A: If < 20m LOA: Both side lights may be combined in one centreline R/G light

VISIBLE RANGE (M) OF LIGHTS (Rule 22)			
Light/LOA	<12m	<50m	>50m
All-round	2	2	3
Masthead	2	3*, 5	6
Side	1	2	3
Stern	2	2	3
		*<20m	

PLAN VIEWS OF LIGHTS FOR SAILING VESSELS UNDERWAY AND UNDER SAIL ONLY

Note: If motor-sailing, the lights appropriate for a power-driven vessel must be shown, as below

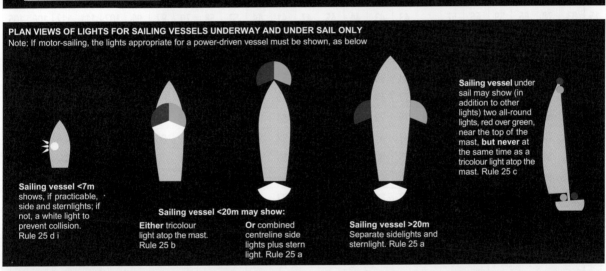

Sailing vessel <7m shows, if practicable, side and sternlights; if not, a white light to prevent collision. Rule 25 d i

Sailing vessel <20m may show:

Either tricolour light atop the mast. Rule 25 b

Or combined centreline side lights plus stern light. Rule 25 a

Sailing vessel >20m Separate sidelights and sternlight. Rule 25 a

Sailing vessel under sail may show (in addition to other lights) two all-round lights, red over green, near the top of the mast, **but never** at the same time as a tricolour light atop the mast. Rule 25 c

PLAN VIEWS OF LIGHTS FOR POWER-DRIVEN VESSELS UNDERWAY AND SAILING CRAFT UNDER POWER

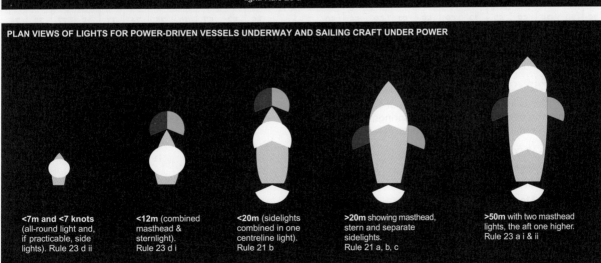

<7m and <7 knots (all-round light and, if practicable, side lights). Rule 23 d ii

<12m (combined masthead & sternlight). Rule 23 d i

<20m (sidelights combined in one centreline light). Rule 21 b

>20m showing masthead, stern and separate sidelights. Rule 21 a, b, c

>50m with two masthead lights, the aft one higher. Rule 23 a i & ii

0.23 TIDAL COEFFICIENTS 2016

Date	Jan am	Jan pm	Feb am	Feb pm	Mar am	Mar pm	Apr am	Apr pm	May am	May pm	June am	June pm	July am	July pm	Aug am	Aug pm	Sept am	Sept pm	Oct am	Oct pm	Nov am	Nov pm	Dec am	Dec pm
1	52	47	41	37	47	42	36		43	46	63	69	68	73	78	82	90	92	90	90	84	82	80	79
2	43	40	35	34	37	34	37	40	50	56	75	81	77	82	86	90	93	93	90	89	81	78	78	76
3	37	37		36	33		46	53	63	71	87	92	86	90	92	93	92	90	87	85	76	72	74	71
4		38	39	44	35	40	61	70	78	86	96	100	93	95	94	93	88	85	82	78	69	64	68	64
5	40	43	50	57	46	53	79	88	93	100	102	103	96	96	92	90	82	77	75	70	60	55	61	57
6	48	53	64	71	61	70	96	103	105	109	103	102	96	94	87	83	73	68	65	60	51	46	54	51
7	58	63	78	84	78	87	109	114	112	113	100	97	92	88	79	75	62	57	55	49	42	39	49	48
8	68	74	90	96	94	101	117	118	112	110	92	87	84	80	70	64	51	45	44	39	38	40	49	52
9	78	83	100	104	107	112	117	115	106	101	82	76	75	70	59	53	40	35	35	32	43			55
10	87	90	107	108	115	116	111	105	95	88	70	64	65	59	48	43	32			32	48	55	61	67
11	93	95	108	106	116	114	99	91	81	74	59	54	54	49	39	35	31	32	35	40	63	71	73	80
12	95	96	103	99	111	105	82	73	66	59	49	46	45	42		34	36	41	47	55	79	86	86	92
13	95	93	94	88	99	91	65	57	53	48		44		39	34	36	48	56	64	72	94	100	97	101
14	91	87	81	73	83	74	50	45		45	43	43	38	39	40	46	64	72	81	88	105	109	104	106
15	83	78	66	59	66	57		43	43	44	45	47	41	44	52	58	79	87	96	102	111	112	106	105
16	74	68	53	50	50	46	43	45	46	48	50	53	48	52	64	71	93	99	108	111	111	109	103	99
17	64	60		49		44	49	54	52	56	57	61	57	62	77	83	104	108	114	114	105	100	95	90
18	57		50	53	45	48	59	64	60	63	64	68	67	71	88	93	110	111	113	111	94	87	84	78
19	56	56	58	64	53	58	68	72	67	70	71	74	75	79	97	100	111	108	106	101	79	72	71	65
20	59	62	69	74	64	69	76	79	73	75	77	79	83	86	102	103	105	100	94	86	64	58	59	53
21	67	72	79	83	75	79	81	83	77	79	80	82	88	90	102	101	93	86	77	69	52	48	49	45
22	76	81	87	89	82	85	84	85	80	81	82	83	91	91	98	94	78	70	61	54	46	45	43	
23	85	88	91	92	87	89	85	85	81	81	82	81	91	90	89	83	61	54	48			46	42	43
24	90	92	92	91	89	89	84	82	80	79	80	78	87	85	77	70	49		45	45	49	52	45	47
25	92	92	90	87	89	87	80	78	77	75	75	73	81	77	63	58	46	46	47	51	56	60	51	55
26	91	89	85	81	86	83	75	71	72	69	70	67	73	68		53	49	54	55	60	63	67	58	62
27	87	84	78	73	80	77	67	63	65	62	64	62	64	60	50	50	59	65	65	70	70	73	66	69
28	80	76	68	63	73	68	58	53	58	56	60			58	53	57	70	76	74	77	75	77	72	75
29	71	67	58	53	63	58	49	46	54	53	60	60	57	57	62	68	80	84	80	82	78	79	77	79
30	61	56			52	47	44			53	62	65	60	63	73	79	86	88	84	84	80	80	81	82
31	51	46			42	39			55	59			68	73	83	87			85	85			82	82

Tidal coefficients indicate the magnitude of the tide on any particular day without having to look up and calculate the range, and thus determine whether it is springs, neaps or somewhere in between. This table is valid for all areas covered by this Almanac and is based on Brest. Typical values are:

120	Very big spring tide
95	**Mean spring tide**
70	Average tide
45	**Mean neap tide**
20	Very small neap tide

0.24 CALCULATING TIDAL STREAM RATES

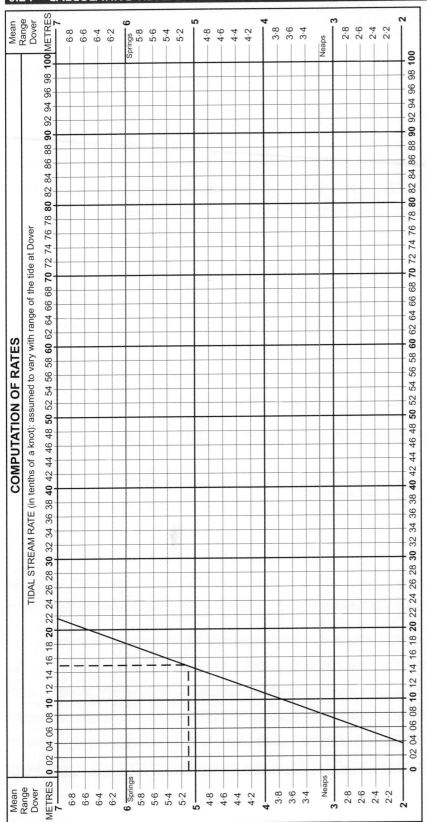

The tidal stream rate at any time may be calculated, assuming that it varies with the range of the tide at Dover. In tidal stream atlases, and on the tidal stream chartlets in this Almanac, the rates are shown in tenths of a knot. Thus '05,27' translates as 0·5k at Neaps and 2·7kn at Springs.

Example: Calculate the tidal stream rate off the north tip of Skye at 0420 UT on a day when the tide at Dover is:

UT	Ht (m)
0328	1·4
0819	6·3
1602	1·1
2054	6·4

The tidal stream chartlet for HW Dover –4 shows '08,18': a mean Neap rate of 0·8kn and a Spring rate of 1·8kn.

On the figure to the right, from the horizontal Rates axis mark 08 on the horizontal blue Neaps line; likewise 18 on the Springs line. Join these two marks with a diagonal. From the range 5·1 on the vertical axis go horizontally to cut the diagonal just drawn. From this point go vertically to the Rates axis, top or bottom, and read off the predicted rate of 15 (1·5kn).

Times are in UT - add 1 hour in non-shaded areas to convert to BST

0.25 SUNRISE/SET TIMES 2016

The table shows times of Sunrise (SR) and Sunset (SS) for every 3rd day as the times of Sunrise and Sunset never change by more than 8 minutes (and often by only 1–3 minutes) between the given dates.

The table is based on Longitude 0°, so longitude corrections are required. To calculate this add 4 minutes of time for every degree West of Greenwich; subtract if East.

LATITUDE 56°N

	Rise	Set	Rise	Set	Rise	Set	Rise	Set	Rise	Set	Rise	Set
	JANUARY		FEBRUARY		MARCH		APRIL		MAY		JUNE	
1	08 31	15 36	07 56	16 32	06 51	17 35	05 30	18 39	04 15	19 40	03 22	20 35
4	08 30	15 39	07 50	16 38	06 43	17 41	05 22	18 45	04 09	19 46	03 19	20 39
7	08 29	15 44	07 44	16 45	06 35	17 48	05 14	18 51	04 02	19 52	03 16	20 42
10	08 27	15 48	07 38	16 52	06 28	17 54	05 06	18 57	03 56	19 58	03 15	20 45
13	08 24	15 53	07 31	16 58	06 20	18 00	04 59	19 04	03 50	20 04	03 14	20 47
16	08 21	15 59	07 24	17 05	06 12	18 06	04 51	19 10	03 45	20 09	03 13	20 49
19	08 17	16 05	07 17	17 11	06 04	18 13	04 44	19 16	03 40	20 15	03 13	20 50
22	08 13	16 11	07 10	17 18	05 56	18 19	04 36	19 22	03 35	20 20	03 13	20 51
25	08 08	16 17	07 03	17 24	05 48	18 25	04 29	19 28	03 30	20 25	03 15	20 51
28	08 03	16 23	06 56	17 31	05 40	18 31	04 22	19 34	03 26	20 29	03 16	20 50
31	07 58	16 30			05 32	18 37			03 23	20 34		

	Rise	Set	Rise	Set	Rise	Set	Rise	Set	Rise	Set	Rise	Set
	JULY		AUGUST		SEPTEMBER		OCTOBER		NOVEMBER		DECEMBER	
1	03 19	20 49	04 05	20 07	05 05	18 53	06 04	17 34	07 08	16 19	08 07	15 31
4	03 21	20 47	04 10	20 01	05 11	18 46	06 10	17 26	07 14	16 12	08 12	15 28
7	03 25	20 45	04 16	19 54	05 17	18 38	06 16	17 19	07 20	16 06	08 16	15 27
10	03 28	20 42	04 22	19 47	05 22	18 30	06 22	17 11	07 27	16 00	08 20	15 25
13	03 32	20 38	04 28	19 41	05 28	18 22	06 28	17 03	07 33	15 55	08 24	15 25
16	03 37	20 34	04 34	19 33	05 34	18 14	06 34	16 56	07 39	15 50	08 26	15 25
19	03 42	20 30	04 39	19 26	05 40	18 06	06 40	16 49	07 45	15 45	08 29	15 26
22	03 47	20 25	04 45	19 19	05 46	17 58	06 47	16 41	07 51	15 41	08 30	15 27
25	03 52	20 20	04 51	19 11	05 52	17 50	06 53	16 34	07 57	15 37	08 31	15 29
28	03 57	20 15	04 57	19 04	05 58	17 42	06 59	16 27	08 02	15 33	08 32	15 32
31	04 03	20 09	05 03	18 56			07 06	16 21			08 31	15 35

LATITUDE 50°N

	Rise	Set	Rise	Set	Rise	Set	Rise	Set	Rise	Set	Rise	Set
	JANUARY		FEBRUARY		MARCH		APRIL		MAY		JUNE	
1	07 59	16 08	07 34	16 53	06 43	17 43	05 36	18 32	04 36	19 19	03 56	20 01
4	07 58	16 11	07 30	16 58	06 36	17 48	05 30	18 37	04 31	19 24	03 54	20 04
7	07 57	16 15	07 25	17 04	06 30	17 53	05 23	18 42	04 26	19 28	03 52	20 06
10	07 56	16 19	07 20	17 09	06 24	17 57	05 17	18 47	04 21	19 33	03 51	20 08
13	07 54	16 23	07 15	17 14	06 17	18 02	05 11	18 51	04 16	19 37	03 50	20 10
16	07 52	16 27	07 10	17 19	06 11	18 07	05 04	18 56	04 12	19 41	03 50	20 12
19	07 50	16 32	07 04	17 24	06 04	18 12	04 58	19 01	04 08	19 45	03 50	20 13
22	07 47	16 37	06 59	17 29	05 58	18 17	04 53	19 05	04 05	19 49	03 51	20 13
25	07 43	16 41	06 53	17 34	05 51	18 21	04 47	19 10	04 02	19 53	03 52	20 13
28	07 40	16 46	06 47	17 39	05 45	18 26	04 41	19 15	03 59	19 56	03 53	20 13
31	07 36	16 51			05 38	18 31			03 56	20 00		

	Rise	Set	Rise	Set	Rise	Set	Rise	Set	Rise	Set	Rise	Set
	JULY		AUGUST		SEPTEMBER		OCTOBER		NOVEMBER		DECEMBER	
1	03 55	20 12	04 30	19 42	05 15	18 43	06 00	17 38	06 50	16 36	07 37	16 01
4	03 57	20 11	04 34	19 37	05 20	18 37	06 05	17 31	06 55	16 31	07 41	15 59
7	04 00	20 10	04 38	19 32	05 24	18 30	06 10	17 25	07 00	16 27	07 44	15 59
10	04 03	20 08	04 43	19 27	05 29	18 24	06 14	17 18	07 05	16 22	07 48	15 58
13	04 06	20 05	04 47	19 21	05 33	18 17	06 19	17 12	07 10	16 18	07 51	15 58
16	04 09	20 02	04 52	19 16	05 38	18 11	06 24	17 06	07 15	16 14	07 53	15 59
19	04 13	19 59	04 56	19 10	05 42	18 04	06 29	17 00	07 20	16 11	07 55	16 00
22	04 16	19 56	05 01	19 04	05 47	17 57	06 34	16 54	07 24	16 08	07 57	16 01
25	04 20	19 52	05 05	18 58	05 51	17 51	06 39	16 49	07 29	16 05	07 58	16 03
28	04 24	19 48	05 09	18 52	05 56	17 44	06 44	16 43	07 33	16 03	07 58	16 05
31	04 28	19 43	05 14	18 45			06 49	16 38			07 59	16 08

0.26 MOONRISE/SET TIMES 2016

The table gives the times of Moonrise (MR) and Moonset (MS) for every 3rd day; interpolation is necessary for other days. The aim is simply to indicate whether the night in question will be brightly moonlit, partially moonlit or pitch black – depending, of course, on the level of cloud cover. The table is based on Longitude 0°. To correct for longitude, add 4 minutes of time for every degree West; subtract if East. ** Indicates that the phenomenon does not occur.

LATITUDE 56°N

	Rise JAN	Set JAN	Rise FEB	Set FEB	Rise MAR	Set MAR	Rise APR	Set APR	Rise MAY	Set MAY	Rise JUN	Set JUN
1	** **	11 25	01 04	10 55	00 58	09 55	02 26	11 01	02 12	12 19	01 57	15 24
4	02 15	12 27	04 13	12 39	03 47	12 14	04 11	14 43	03 30	16 26	03 29	19 30
7	05 30	14 02	06 42	15 43	05 45	15 52	05 31	19 00	04 58	20 40	06 07	22 27
10	08 09	16 53	08 16	19 46	07 07	20 07	07 07	23 06	07 24	23 50	09 37	23 59
13	09 48	20 45	09 32	23 53	08 35	** **	09 40	01 09	10 45	01 04	13 03	00 40
16	11 01	** **	11 13	02 24	10 50	02 22	12 58	03 00	14 09	02 14	16 20	01 40
19	12 31	03 22	13 55	05 14	13 59	04 28	16 19	04 07	17 27	03 13	19 28	03 06
22	15 01	06 32	17 17	06 51	17 21	05 41	19 36	05 07	20 37	04 31	21 48	05 36
25	18 23	08 23	20 39	07 55	20 40	06 40	22 42	06 30	23 08	06 44	23 16	09 09
28	21 47	09 30	23 55	08 58	23 50	07 56	00 25	08 51	00 17	10 04	00 03	13 06
31	** **	10 31			01 40	10 02			01 33	14 00		

	Rise JUL	Set JUL	Rise AUG	Set AUG	Rise SEP	Set SEP	Rise OCT	Set OCT	Rise NOV	Set NOV	Rise DEC	Set DEC
1	01 26	17 07	02 37	18 55	05 02	18 54	06 17	18 00	08 31	17 38	09 21	17 32
4	03 48	20 18	06 07	20 29	08 30	19 55	09 36	19 07	11 23	19 36	11 25	20 29
7	07 16	22 02	09 38	21 31	11 47	21 06	12 35	20 53	13 21	22 41	12 45	** **
10	10 47	23 06	12 56	22 37	14 43	23 01	14 47	23 48	14 40	01 11	13 55	02 51
13	14 06	** **	16 00	** **	16 51	01 00	16 15	02 19	15 57	05 23	15 42	07 02
16	17 16	01 05	18 21	02 13	18 16	04 49	17 32	06 32	17 59	09 31	18 52	10 07
19	19 47	03 25	19 50	05 55	19 34	09 02	19 22	10 42	21 16	12 12	22 34	11 40
22	21 22	06 56	21 05	10 00	21 30	12 57	22 21	13 35	** **	13 34	00 53	12 40
25	22 34	10 53	22 45	13 56	** **	15 33	00 41	15 05	03 05	14 33	04 12	13 45
28	** **	14 52	00 28	16 52	02 50	16 59	04 08	16 06	06 23	15 40	07 15	15 28
31	01 37	18 09	03 51	18 31			07 27	17 10			09 29	18 19

LATITUDE 50°N

	Rise JAN	Set JAN	Rise FEB	Set FEB	Rise MAR	Set MAR	Rise APR	Set APR	Rise MAY	Set MAY	Rise JUN	Set JUN
1	** **	11 25	00 50	11 11	00 37	10 17	02 02	11 25	01 57	12 32	02 01	15 16
4	02 03	12 41	03 49	13 04	03 22	12 39	03 59	14 53	03 31	16 21	03 49	19 06
7	05 06	14 27	06 20	16 04	05 30	16 05	05 35	18 52	05 16	20 19	06 32	22 04
10	07 45	17 16	08 09	19 50	07 09	20 02	07 27	22 43	07 50	23 26	09 50	23 49
13	09 38	20 53	09 42	23 40	08 53	23 51	10 04	00 44	11 01	00 47	13 01	00 39
16	11 07	** **	11 36	02 02	11 15	01 57	13 12	02 45	14 10	02 10	16 05	01 53
19	12 52	03 02	14 18	04 50	14 16	04 09	16 19	04 05	17 14	03 23	19 02	03 30
22	15 26	06 07	17 28	06 39	17 24	05 36	19 22	05 18	20 13	04 53	21 26	06 01
25	18 37	08 08	20 29	07 56	20 29	06 49	22 18	06 53	22 44	07 10	23 08	09 21
28	21 46	09 29	23 38	09 12	23 27	08 16	** **	09 15	00 00	10 19	00 05	13 00
31	** **	10 43			01 14	10 27			01 32	13 59		

	Rise JUL	Set JUL	Rise AUG	Set AUG	Rise SEP	Set SEP	Rise OCT	Set OCT	Rise NOV	Set NOV	Rise DEC	Set DEC
1	01 44	16 46	03 02	18 32	05 13	18 47	06 15	18 05	08 12	17 58	08 54	17 58
4	04 14	19 53	06 21	20 18	08 25	20 02	09 19	19 25	10 56	20 02	11 04	20 49
7	07 32	21 49	09 36	21 34	11 29	21 25	12 09	21 19	13 02	22 59	12 38	** **
10	10 48	23 07	12 41	22 53	14 17	23 27	14 26	** **	14 35	01 19	14 04	02 44
13	13 53	** **	15 35	00 03	16 31	01 22	16 08	02 29	16 09	05 12	16 07	06 38
16	16 52	01 28	17 59	02 37	18 12	04 57	17 42	06 24	18 25	09 06	19 14	09 43
19	19 24	03 51	19 43	06 05	19 47	08 52	19 47	10 18	21 36	11 51	22 42	11 30
22	21 12	07 09	21 14	09 53	21 54	12 32	22 44	13 11	** **	13 27	00 51	12 44
25	22 40	10 50	23 08	13 34	** **	15 11	00 55	14 55	03 01	14 39	03 56	14 02
28	** **	14 32	00 54	16 28	03 02	16 50	04 07	16 09	06 05	16 00	06 49	15 55
31	02 02	17 44	04 06	18 19			07 12	17 27			09 07	18 41

Reference data

0.27 INTERNATIONAL CODE OF SIGNALS

Code flags, phonetic alphabet (NATO/ITU), Morse code, single-letter signals. INTERNATIONAL PORT TRAFFIC SIGNALS.

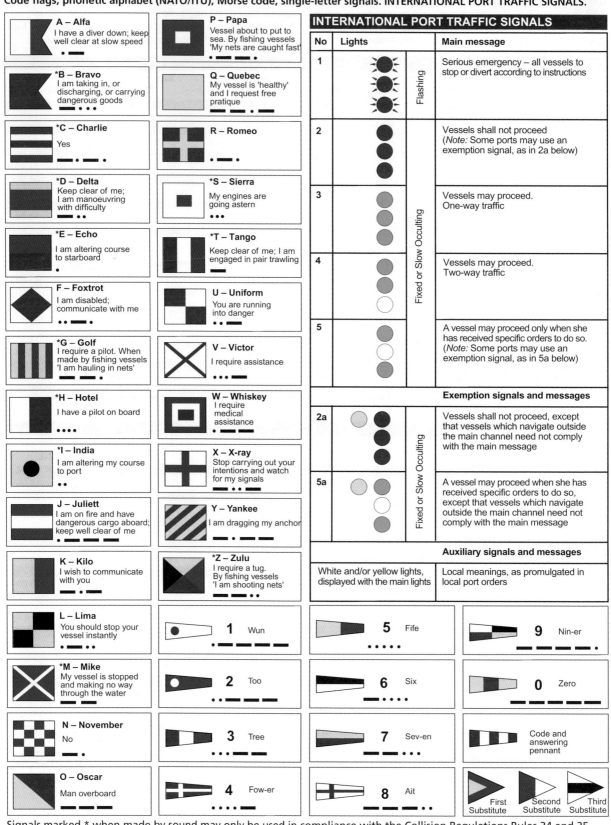

A – Alfa
I have a diver down; keep well clear at slow speed
· ▬

*B – Bravo
I am taking in, or discharging, or carrying dangerous goods
▬ · · ·

*C – Charlie
Yes
▬ · ▬ · ▬

*D – Delta
Keep clear of me; I am manoeuvring with difficulty
▬ · ·

*E – Echo
I am altering course to starboard
· ▬

F – Foxtrot
I am disabled; communicate with me
· · ▬ ·

*G – Golf
I require a pilot. When made by fishing vessels 'I am hauling in nets'
▬ ▬ ·

*H – Hotel
I have a pilot on board
· · · ·

*I – India
I am altering my course to port
· ·

J – Juliett
I am on fire and have dangerous cargo aboard; keep well clear of me
· ▬ ▬ ▬

K – Kilo
I wish to communicate with you
▬ · ▬

L – Lima
You should stop your vessel instantly
· ▬ · ·

*M – Mike
My vessel is stopped and making no way through the water
▬ ▬

N – November
No
▬ ·

O – Oscar
Man overboard
▬ ▬ ▬

P – Papa
Vessel about to put to sea. By fishing vessels 'My nets are caught fast'
· ▬ ▬ ·

Q – Quebec
My vessel is 'healthy' and I request free pratique
▬ ▬ · ▬

R – Romeo
· ▬ ·

*S – Sierra
My engines are going astern
· · ·

*T – Tango
Keep clear of me; I am engaged in pair trawling
▬

U – Uniform
You are running into danger
· · ▬

V – Victor
I require assistance
· · · ▬

W – Whiskey
I require medical assistance
· ▬ ▬

X – X-ray
Stop carrying out your intentions and watch for my signals
▬ · · ▬

Y – Yankee
I am dragging my anchor
▬ · ▬ ▬

*Z – Zulu
I require a tug. By fishing vessels 'I am shooting nets'
▬ ▬ · ·

1 Wun
· ▬ ▬ ▬ ▬

2 Too
· · ▬ ▬ ▬

3 Tree
· · · ▬ ▬

4 Fow-er
· · · · ▬

INTERNATIONAL PORT TRAFFIC SIGNALS

No	Lights		Main message
1		Flashing	Serious emergency – all vessels to stop or divert according to instructions
2		Fixed or Slow Occulting	Vessels shall not proceed (*Note:* Some ports may use an exemption signal, as in 2a below)
3		Fixed or Slow Occulting	Vessels may proceed. One-way traffic
4		Fixed or Slow Occulting	Vessels may proceed. Two-way traffic
5		Fixed or Slow Occulting	A vessel may proceed only when she has received specific orders to do so. (*Note:* Some ports may use an exemption signal, as in 5a below)

Exemption signals and messages

No	Lights		Main message
2a		Fixed or Slow Occulting	Vessels shall not proceed, except that vessels which navigate outside the main channel need not comply with the main message
5a		Fixed or Slow Occulting	A vessel may proceed when she has received specific orders to do so, except that vessels which navigate outside the main channel need not comply with the main message

Auxiliary signals and messages

White and/or yellow lights, displayed with the main lights	Local meanings, as promulgated in local port orders

5 Fife
· · · · ·

6 Six
▬ · · · ·

7 Sev-en
▬ ▬ · · ·

8 Ait
▬ ▬ ▬ · ·

9 Nin-er
▬ ▬ ▬ ▬ ·

0 Zero
▬ ▬ ▬ ▬ ▬

Code and answering pennant

First Substitute   Second Substitute   Third Substitute

Signals marked * when made by sound may only be used in compliance with the Collision Regulations Rules 34 and 35.

0.28   AREA INFORMATION

The 6 geographic Areas are arranged as follows:

An Area map which includes harbours, principal lights, TSS, MRCCs, NCI stations, airports, main ferry routes, magnetic variation and a distance table. Wind farms and other offshore energy installations are not routinely shown.

Tidal stream chartlets showing hourly rates and set.

Lights, buoys and waypoints (LBW) listing positions and characteristics of selected lights and other marks, their daytime appearance, fog signals and Racons. Arcs of visibility and alignment of sector/leading lights are true bearings as seen from seaward. Lights are white unless otherwise stated; any colours are shown between the bearings of the relevant arcs. AIS is widely fitted to navigational marks, but not normally shown in LBW. See the relevant official charts/publications for details.

Passage Information (PI) is at Section 4 in each Area. Further information is geographically arranged between the harbour entries.

Special notes giving data specific to a country or area.

Harbour information (see below).

0.29   HARBOUR INFORMATION

Each harbour entry is arranged as follows:

HARBOUR NAME followed by the County or Unitary Council (or foreign equivalent) and the lat/long of the harbour entrance, or equivalent, for use as the final waypoint.

Harbour ratings (❀ ◊ ✿), inevitably subjective, which grade a port based on the following criteria:

Ease of access:

❀❀❀   *Can be entered in almost any weather from most directions and at all states of tide, by day or night.*

❀❀   *Accessible in strong winds from most directions; possible tidal or pilotage constraints.*

❀   *Only accessible in calm, settled conditions by day with little or no swell; possible bar and difficult pilotage.*

Facilities available:

◊◊◊   *Good facilities for vessel and crew.*

◊◊   *Most domestic needs catered for, but limited boatyard facilities.*

◊   *Possibly some domestic facilities, but little else.*

Ambience:

✿✿✿   *An attractive place; well worth visiting.*

✿✿   *Average for this part of the coast.*

✿   *Holds no particular attraction.*

CHARTS show Admiralty (AC), Imray, and foreign charts, all smallest scale first. Admiralty Leisure Folios (56XX), which cover most of the UK, Channel Islands and Ireland, and Imray 2000 series folios (2X00) are also shown.

TIDES include a time difference (usually on Dover in the UK), ML, Duration and the harbour's Standard Port. Time and height differences for nearby Secondary Ports are also shown. Tidal coefficients are tabled at 0.22.

SHELTER assesses how protected a harbour is from wind, sea, surge and swell. It warns of any access difficulties and advises on safe berths and anchorages.

NAVIGATION gives guidance on the approach and entry, and shows the position of the approach waypoint with its bearing and distance to the harbour entrance or next significant feature. Some waypoints may not be shown on the chartlet. Access times are only stated where a lock, gate, sill or other obstruction restricts entry. Otherwise the minimum charted depth of water in the approaches, where it is less than 2m, is usually shown, but always consult up to date official charts.

Chartlets are based on official charts augmented with local information. Due to their scale, they may not cover the whole area referred to in the text nor do they show every depth, mark, light or feature.

The chartlets are not intended to be used for navigation; positions taken from them should not be used as waypoints in chart plotters. The publisher and editors disclaim any responsibility for resultant accidents or damage if they are so used. The largest scale official chart, properly corrected, should always be used.

Drying areas and an indicative 5m depth contour are shown as: Dries ▓▓ <5m ▓▓ >5m ▓▓

Wrecks around the UK which are of archaeological or historic interest are protected by law. Sites are listed under harbour entries or in Passage Information. Unauthorised interference, including anchoring and diving on these sites, may lead to a substantial fine.

LIGHTS AND MARKS describes, in more detail than is shown on the chartlets, any unusual characteristics of marks, their appearance by day and features not listed elsewhere.

COMMUNICATIONS shows the telephone area code followed by local telephone and VHF contact details for: MRCC/CG, weather, police, doctor/medical, harbourmaster/office, other. Marina contact details are not usually duplicated if they are shown under the marina entry. International telephone calls from/to the UK are described in Special Notes, as are national numbers for emergency services: normally 112 in the EU; 999 in the UK. Radio callsigns, if not obvious, are in *italics*.

FACILITIES describes berthing options and facilities in harbours, marinas and yacht clubs (see the free **Reeds Marina Guide** for detailed marina plans in the UK, Channel Islands and Ireland). Water, electricity, showers and toilets are available in marinas unless otherwise stated. Most yacht clubs welcome visiting crews who belong to a recognised club and arrive by sea. Any rail and air links are also shown.

The overnight cost of a visitor's alongside berth (AB), *correct with regard to information supplied at the time of going to press (Summer 2015)*, is the average charge per metre LOA (unless otherwise stated) during high season, usually June to Sept. It includes VAT, harbour dues and, where possible, any tourist taxes (per head). The cost of pile moorings, ▣s or ⌁s, where these are the norm, may also be given. Shore electricity is usually free abroad but extra in the UK.

The number of ◐ berths is a marina's estimate of how many visitors may be accommodated at any one time. It is always advisable to call the marina beforehand.

TransEurope Marinas (www.transeuropemarinas.com) is an expanding grouping of independent marinas in the UK and abroad. Many hold Blue Flags and 4 or 5 Gold Anchor Awards; it is a condition of membership that they are well-equipped and maintain high standards. They operate a discounted reciprocal berthing scheme and are shown by the symbol ⊕.

Rover Tickets, offering good discounts, are available for many berthing facilities in Scotland and the offlying islands.

0.30 ENVIRONMENTAL GUIDANCE

- Comply with regulations for navigation and conduct within Marine Nature Reserves, Particularly Sensitive Sea Areas (PSSA) and National Water Parks.
- In principle never ditch rubbish at sea, keep it on board and dispose of it in harbour refuse bins.
- Readily degradable foodstuffs may be ditched at sea when >3M offshore (>12M in the English Channel).
- Foodstuffs and other materials which are not readily degradable should never be ditched at sea.
- Sewage. If you do not have a holding tank, only use the onboard heads when well offshore. A holding tank should be fitted as soon as possible as many countries require them. Pump-out facilities (♺) are shown in the text. Do not pump out holding tanks until more than 3M offshore.
- Do not discharge foul water into a marina, anchorage or moorings area and minimise on washing-up water.
- Deposit used engine oil and oily waste ashore at a recognised facility. Do not allow an automatic bilge pump to discharge oily bilge water overboard.
- Dispose of toxic waste, (eg some antifoulings, cleaning chemicals, old batteries) at an approved disposal facility.
- Row ashore whenever possible – to minimise noise, wash and disturbance. Land at recognised places.
- Respect wild birds, plants, fish and marine animals. Avoid protected nesting sites and breeding colonies.
- Do not anchor or dry out on vulnerable seabed species, eg soft corals, eel grass.

0.31 DISTANCES (M) ACROSS THE IRISH SEA

Approximate distances in nautical miles are by the most direct route, avoiding dangers and allowing for TSS.

Scotland England Wales / Ireland	Port Ellen (Islay)	Campbeltown	Troon	Portpatrick	Mull of Galloway	Kirkcudbright	Maryport	Fleetwood	Pt of Ayre (IOM)	Port St Mary (IOM)	Liverpool	Holyhead	Pwllheli	Fishguard	Milford Haven	Swansea	Avonmouth	Ilfracombe	Padstow	Longships
Tory Island	75	107	132	119	134	170	185	215	156	167	238	207	260	279	307	360	406	372	372	399
Malin Head	45	76	101	88	103	139	154	184	125	136	207	176	229	248	276	329	375	341	341	368
Lough Foyle	33	61	86	73	88	124	139	169	110	121	192	161	214	233	261	314	360	320	326	353
Portrush	31	50	76	64	80	116	131	161	102	113	184	153	206	225	253	306	352	308	318	345
Carnlough	42	35	57	32	45	81	96	126	67	78	149	115	168	187	215	268	314	265	280	307
Larne	51	39	58	24	37	72	88	118	58	70	141	106	159	178	206	259	305	254	271	298
Carrickfergus	64	48	65	26	34	69	85	115	55	66	138	101	154	173	201	254	300	249	266	293
Bangor	63	48	64	22	30	65	81	111	51	62	134	97	150	169	197	250	296	245	262	289
Strangford L.	89	72	84	36	30	63	76	97	41	37	107	69	121	141	167	219	265	214	231	258
Carlingford L.	117	100	112	64	60	90	103	112	70	51	118	67	111	124	149	202	248	197	214	241
Dun Laoghaire	153	136	148	100	93	119	126	120	93	69	119	56	82	94	109	162	208	157	174	201
Wicklow	170	153	165	117	108	133	140	127	108	83	123	56	67	71	90	143	189	138	155	182
Arklow	182	165	177	129	120	144	149	133	117	93	131	64	71	65	79	132	179	128	144	167
Rosslare	215	202	208	161	154	179	180	164	152	125	156	90	83	55	58	109	157	110	119	137
Tuskar Rock	216	203	209	162	155	179	182	165	152	126	152	91	82	48	51	105	150	103	112	130
Dunmore East	250	237	243	196	189	213	216	199	186	160	189	127	116	79	76	130	177	124	127	136
Youghal	281	268	274	227	220	244	247	230	217	191	220	158	147	110	103	156	200	148	139	138
Crosshaven	300	287	293	246	239	263	266	249	236	210	239	177	166	131	118	170	216	163	151	144
Baltimore	346	333	339	292	285	309	312	295	282	256	285	223	212	172	160	209	254	198	178	161
Fastnet Rock	354	341	347	300	293	317	320	303	290	264	293	231	220	181	169	216	260	207	185	170

Yacht Havens

the perfect home for your boat

Marina
Dry Stack Marina

Yacht Havens
WE LOVE BOATING

9 Prime Marina Locations... *with the most helpful staff*

Whether you're looking for an annual berth, a safe winter haven or a visitor berth in a new cruising area, you'll find first-rate facilities and a warm welcome from our friendly, experienced team at whichever Yacht Havens location you choose.

Attractive berthing rates and flexible contracts to save you money, superb modern facilities for your enjoyment, free Wi-Fi at every berth for your convenience, and the freedom to exchange berths with other Yacht Havens.

We can provide you with the best boating experience across the UK, and now the Netherlands. Just ask us what we can do for you.

1 Largs Yacht Haven
Largs, Ayrshire
Tel: 01475 675333

2 Troon Yacht Haven
Troon, Ayrshire
Tel: 01292 315553

3 Neyland Yacht Haven
Neyland, Pembrokeshire
Tel: 01646 601601

4 Fambridge Yacht Haven
River Crouch, Essex
Tel: 01621 740370

5 Lymington Yacht Haven
Lymington, Hampshire
Tel: 01590 677071

6 Haven Quay
Lymington, Hampshire
Tel: 01590 677072

7 Plymouth Yacht Haven
Plymouth, Devon
Tel: 01752 404231

8 Yacht Haven Quay
Plymouth, Devon
Tel: 01752 481190

NEW!
9 Jachthaven Biesbosch
Drimmelen, Netherland
Tel: +31(0)162 68 22 49

CALL US TODAY OR VISIT **www.yachthavens.com**

West Scotland

Cape Wrath to Solway Firth

W Scotland

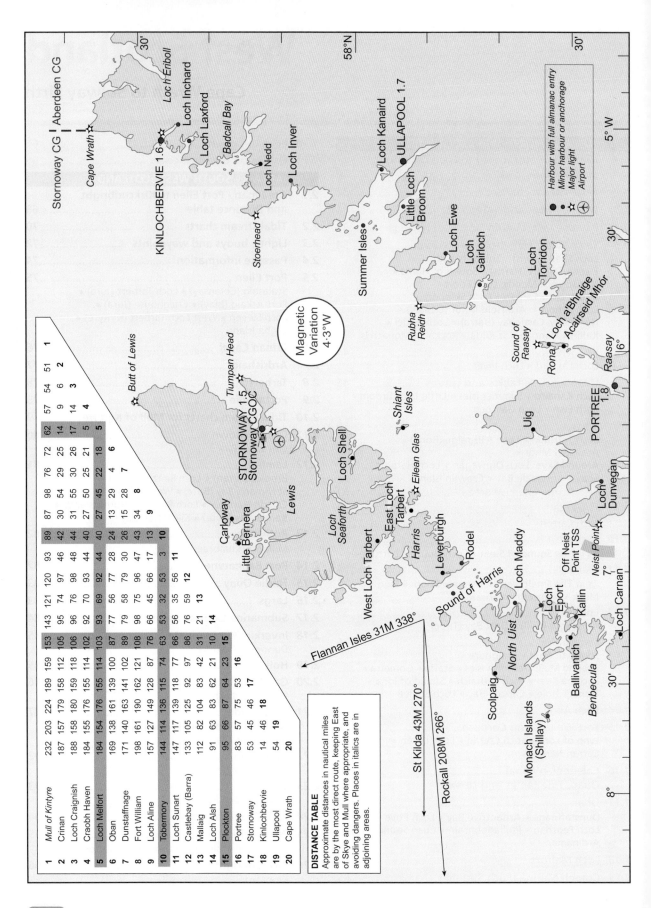

Magnetic Variation 4·3°W

Flannan Isles 31M 338°

St Kilda 43M 270°

Rockall 208M 266°

Harbour with full almanac entry
Minor harbour or anchorage
Major light
Airport

Mull of Kintyre	232	203	224	189	159	153	143	121	120	93	89	87	98	76	72	62	57	54	51	**1**
Crinan	187	157	179	158	112	105	95	74	97	46	42	30	54	29	25	14	9	6	**2**	
Loch Craignish	188	158	180	159	118	106	96	76	98	48	44	31	55	30	26	17	14	**3**		
Craobh Haven	184	155	176	155	114	102	92	70	93	44	40	27	50	25	21	5	**4**			
Loch Melfort	184	154	176	155	114	103	93	69	92	44	40	27	45	22	18	**5**				
Oban	169	138	161	139	100	87	77	56	77	28	24	13	29	4	**6**					
Dunstaffnage	171	140	163	141	102	89	79	58	79	30	26	15	28	**7**						
Fort William	198	161	190	162	121	108	98	75	96	47	43	34	**8**							
Loch Aline	157	127	149	128	87	76	66	45	66	17	13	**9**								
Tobermory	144	114	136	115	74	63	53	32	53	3	**10**									
Loch Sunart	147	117	139	118	66	56	35	56	**11**											
Castlebay (Barra)	133	105	125	92	97	86	76	59	**12**											
Mallaig	112	82	104	83	42	31	21	**13**												
Loch Alsh	91	63	83	62	21	10	**14**													
Plockton	95	66	87	64	23	**15**														
Portree	83	57	75	53	**16**															
Stornoway	53	45	46	**17**																
Kinlochbervie	14	46	**18**																	
Ullapool	54	**19**																		
Cape Wrath	**20**																			

DISTANCE TABLE
Approximate distances in nautical miles are by the most direct route, keeping East of Skye and Mull where appropriate, and avoiding dangers. Places in italics are in adjoining areas.

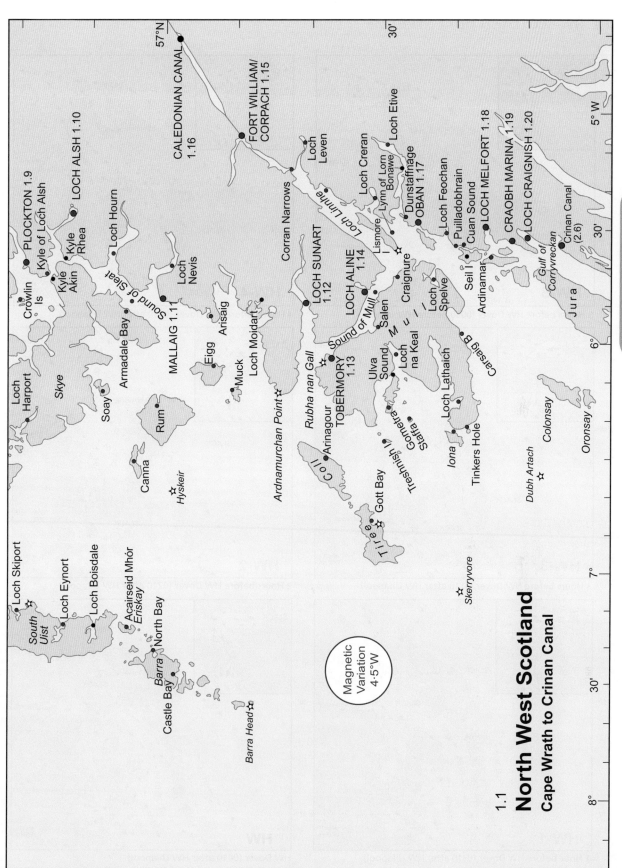

1.1

North West Scotland
Cape Wrath to Crinan Canal

Magnetic Variation 4·5°W

CALEDONIAN CANAL 1.16
FORT WILLIAM/ CORPACH 1.15
PLOCKTON 1.9
LOCH ALSH 1.10
MALLAIG 1.11
LOCH SUNART 1.12
LOCH ALINE 1.14
TOBERMORY 1.13
Loch Leven
Loch Creran
Loch Etive
Lynn of Lorn
Dunstaffnage
OBAN 1.17
Loch Feochan
Puilladobhrain
Cuan Sound
LOCH MELFORT 1.18
CRAOBH MARINA 1.19
LOCH CRAIGNISH 1.20
Crinan Canal (2.6)
Corran Narrows
Loch Linnhe
Salen
Craignure
Sound of Mull
Mull
Loch Spelve
Seil I
Ardinamar
Ardnamurchan Point
Rubha nan Gall
Arinagour
Coll
Ulva Sound
Loch na Keal
Gometra
Staffa
Treshnish I
Loch Lathaich
Iona
Tinkers Hole
Gott Bay
Tiree
Carsaig B
Jura
Gulf of Corryvreckan
Skerryvore
Dubh Artach
Colonsay
Oronsay
Lismore I
Loch Harport
Skye
Soay
Canna
Rum
Hyskeir
Eigg
Muck
Arisaig
Loch Moidart
Loch Nevis
Loch Hourn
Sound of Sleat
Armadale Bay
Kyle Rhea
Kyle Akin
Crowlin Is
Kyle of Loch Alsh
Loch Skiport
Loch Eynort
Loch Boisdale
Acairseid Mhór
Eriskay
North Bay
South Uist
Barra
Castle Bay
Barra Head

57°N
30'
5°W
30'
6°W
30'
7°W
8°W

1.2 NW SCOTLAND TIDAL STREAMS

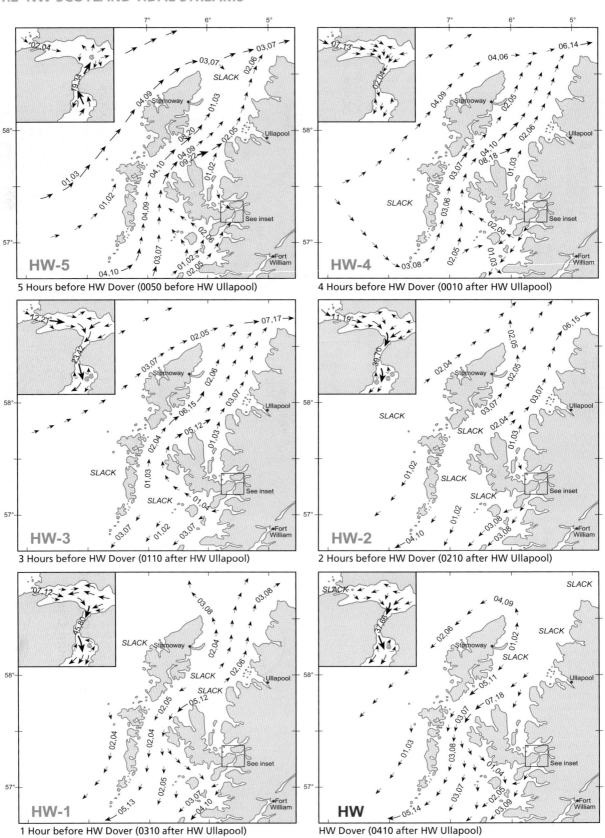

5 Hours before HW Dover (0050 before HW Ullapool)

4 Hours before HW Dover (0010 after HW Ullapool)

3 Hours before HW Dover (0110 after HW Ullapool)

2 Hours before HW Dover (0210 after HW Ullapool)

1 Hour before HW Dover (0310 after HW Ullapool)

HW Dover (0410 after HW Ullapool)

Southward 2.2   Mull of Kintyre 2.10

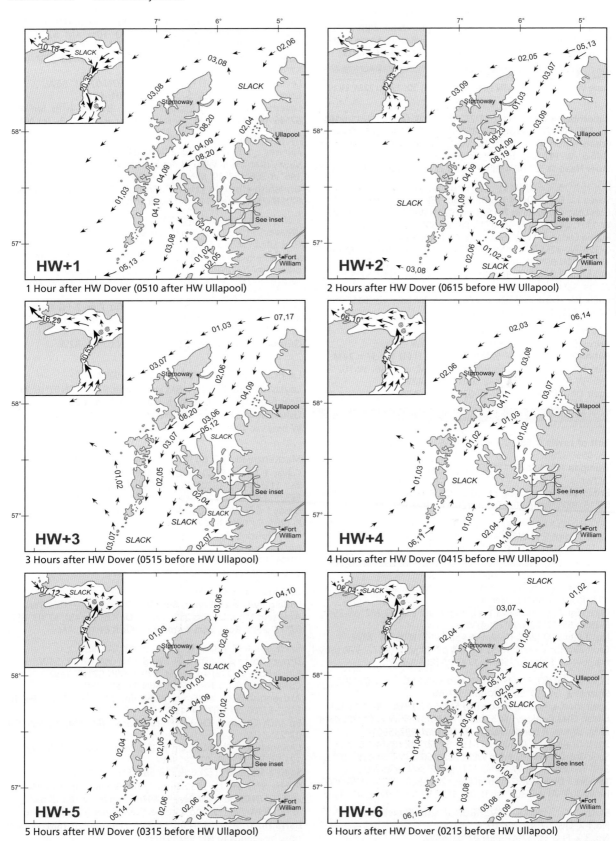

HW+1
1 Hour after HW Dover (0510 after HW Ullapool)

HW+2
2 Hours after HW Dover (0615 before HW Ullapool)

HW+3
3 Hours after HW Dover (0515 before HW Ullapool)

HW+4
4 Hours after HW Dover (0415 before HW Ullapool)

HW+5
5 Hours after HW Dover (0315 before HW Ullapool)

HW+6
6 Hours after HW Dover (0215 before HW Ullapool)

NW Scotland

1.3 LIGHTS, BUOYS AND WAYPOINTS

Bold print = light with a nominal range of 15M or more. CAPITALS = place or feature. *CAPITAL ITALICS* = light-vessel, light float or Lanby. *Italics* = Fog signal. ***Bold italics*** = Racon. Some marks/buoys are fitted with AIS (MMSI No); see relevant charts.

CAPE WRATH TO LOCH TORRIDON

Cape Wrath ☆ 58°37'·54N 04°59'·99W Fl (4) 30s 122m **22M**; W twr.

LOCH INCHARD and LOCH LAXFORD

Kinlochbervie Dir lt 327° ☆ 58°27'·49N 05°03'·08W WRG 15m **16M** vis: 326°-FG-326·5°-AlGW-326·8°-FW-327·3°-AlRW-327·5°-FR-328°.
Creag Mhòr Dir lt 147°; Iso WRG 2s 16m 4M; vis: 136·5°-R -146·5°-W-147·5°-G-157·5°; 58°26'·99N 05°02'·45W.
Stoer Head ☆ 58°14'·43N 05°24'·07W Fl 15s 59m **24M**; W twr.

LOCH INVER, SUMMER ISLES and ULLAPOOL

Soyea I ≰ Fl (2) 10s 34m 6M; 58°08'·56N 05°19'·67W.
Glas Leac ≰ Fl WRG 3s 7m 5M; vis: 071°- W-078°-R-090°-G-103°-W-111°, 243°-W-247°-G-071°; 58°08'·68N 05°16'·36W.
Rubha Cadail ≰ Fl WRG 6s 11m W9M, R6M, G6M; W twr; vis: 311°-G-320°-W-325°-R-103°-W-111°-G-118°-W-127°-R-157°-W-199°; 57°55'·51N 05°13'·40W.
Ullapool Pt ≰ Iso R 4s 8m 6M; W twr; vis: 258°-108°; 57°53'·59N 05°09'·93W.
Cailleach Head ≰ Fl (2) 12s 60m 9M; W twr; vis: 015°-236°; 57°55'·81N 05°24'·23W.

LOCH EWE and LOCH GAIRLOCH

Fairway ◿ L Fl 10s; 57°51'·98N 05°40'·09W.
Rubha Reidh ☆ 57°51'·52N 05°48'·72W Fl (4) 15s 37m **24M**.
Glas Eilean ≰ Fl WRG 6s 9m W6M, R4M; vis: 080°-W-102°-R-296°-W-333°-G-080°; 57°42'·79N 05°42'·42W.
Sgeir Dhubh Mhór ⌁; 57°42'·02N 05°42'·72W

OUTER HEBRIDES – EAST SIDE

LEWIS

Butt of Lewis ☆ 58°30'·89N 06°15'·84W Fl 5s 52m **25M**; R twr; vis: 056°-320°.
Tiumpan Head ☆ 58°15'·66N 06°08'·29W Fl (2) 15s 55m **25M**; W twr.
Broad Bay Tong ⌁ Ldg Lts 320°, Oc R 8s 8m 4M; 58°14'·48N 06°19'·98W. Rear, 70m from front, Oc R 8s 9m 4M.

STORNOWAY

Arnish Point ≰ Fl WR 10s 17m W9M, R7M; W ○ twr; vis: 088°-W-198°-R-302°-W-013°; 58°11'·50N 06°22'·16W.
Sandwick Bay, NW side ≰ Oc WRG 6s 10m 9M; vis: 334°-G-341°-W-347°-R-354°; 58°12'·20N 06°22'·11W.
No. 1 Pier SW corner ≰ Q WRG 5m 11M; vis: shore-G-335°-W-352°-R-shore; 58°12'·36N 06°23'·43W.
Creed Estuary ≰ Iso WRG 10s 24m 5M; vis: 277°-G-282°-W-290°-R-295°; 58°12'·03N 06°23'·47W.
No. 3 Pier ≰ Q (2) G 10s 7m 2M 58°12'·31N 06°23'·28W.
Glumaig Hbr ≰ Iso WRG 3s 8m 3M; 58°11'·27N 06°22'·9W; grey framework twr; vis: 150°-G-174°-W-180°-R-205°.

LOCH ERISORT, LOCH SHELL and EAST LOCH TARBERT

Shiants ◣ QG; 57°54'·57N 06°25'·70W.
Sgeir Inoe ◣ Fl G 6s; W twr; 57°50'·93N 06°33'·93W.
Eilean Glas (Scalpay) ☆ 57°51'·41N 06°38'·55W Fl (3) 20s 43m **23M**; W twr, R bands; ***Racon (T) 16-18M***; 992356014.
Sgeir Graidach ⌁ Q (6) + L Fl 15s; 57°50'·36N 06°41'·37W.
Sgeir Ghlas ≰ Iso WRG 4s 9m W9M, R6M, G6M; W ○ twr; vis: 282°-G-319°-W-329°-R-153°-W-164°-G-171°; 57°52'·36N 06°45'·24W.
Tarbert ≰ Dir Iso WRG 4s 9m 4M; vis : 290°-Iso G-297°-Al WG-300°-Iso W-303°-Al WR-306°-Iso R306°-313°; 57°53'·82N 06°47'·93W.

SOUND OF HARRIS, LEVERBURGH and BERNERAY

No.1 ◣ QG; 57°41'·20N 07°02'·67W.
No. 3 ◣ Fl G 5s; 57°41'·86N 07°03'·44W.

No. 4 ◿ Fl R 5s; 57°41'·76N 07°03'·63W.
Suilven ◿ Fl (3)R 10s; 57°41'·68N 07°04'·36W.
Cabbage ◿ Fl (2) R 6s; ***Racon (T) 5M (3cm)***; 57°42'·13N 07°03'·96W.
Leverburgh Ldg Lts 014·7°. Front, Q 10m 4M 57°46'·23N 07°02'·04W. Rear, Oc 3s 12m 4M.
Jane's Tower ⌁ Q (2) G 5s 6m 4M; vis: obscured 273°-318°; 57°45'·76N 07°02'·12W.
Leverburgh Reef ⌁ Fl R 2s 4m 57°45'·97N 07°01'·86W.
Laimhrig Mhor ≰ Q G; 57°45'·92N 07°01'·65W.
Leverburgh Pier Ldg Lts 063°. Front, Iso Bu 4s 8s 6m 4M; 57°46'·00N 07°01'·61W, metal col. Rear, Iso Bu 4s 8s 7m 4M.

NORTH UIST

Fairway ◿ L Fl 10s; 57°40'·23N 07°01'·39W.
Vallay Island ≰ Fl WRG 3s 4m 8M; vis: 206°-W-085°-G-140°-W-145°-R-206°; 57°39'·69N 07°26'·42W.
Griminish Hbr Ldg Lts 183°. Front, QG 6m 4M; 57°39'·38N 07°26'·75W. Rear, 110m from front, QG 7m 4M.

LOCH MADDY and GRIMSAY

Weaver's Pt ≰ 57°36'·49N 07°06'·00W Fl 3s 24m 7M; W hut.
Glas Eilean Mòr ≰ 57°35'·95N 07°06'·70W Fl (2) G 4s 8m 5M.
Vallaquie Is Dir lt 207·5°/ 255·5° ≰ 57°35'·50N 07°09'·40W; W pillar; vis:Fl (3) WRG 8s 11m W5M, R5M, G5M; shore - G -205°-W-210°-R-240°; Fl (3) WRG 8s 11m W8M, R8M, G8M; 249°-G-254°-W-257°-R-262°.
Lochmaddy Ldg Lts 298°. Front, Ro-Ro Pier 2 FG (vert) 8m 4M. Rear, 110m from front, Oc G 8s 10m 4M; vis: 284°-304°; 57°35'·76N 07°09'·36W.
Grimsay No. 1 ◿ Fl (2) R 8s; 57°28'·26N 07°11'·82W.

SOUTH UIST and LOCH CARNAN

Landfall ⌁ L Fl 10s; 57°22'·27N 07°11'·52W.
Ldg Lts 222°. Front Fl R 2s 7m 5M; W ◇ on post; 57°22'·00N 07°16'·34W. Rear, 58m from front, Iso R 10s 11m 5M; W ◇ on post.
Ushenish ☆ (S Uist) 57°17'·90N 07°11'·57W Fl W 20s 54m **W19M**; W twr; vis: 193°- 018°.

LOCH BOISDALE

MacKenzie Rk ◿ Fl (3) R 15s 3m 4M; 57°08'·24N 07°13'·71W.
Calvay E End ≰ Fl (2) WRG 10s 16m W7M, R7M, G7M; W twr; vis: 111°-W-190°-G-202°-W-286°-R-111°; 57°08'·53N 07°15'·38W; 992351139.
Gasay I ≰ Fl WR 5s 10m W7M, R7M; W twr; vis: 120°-W-284°-R-120°; 57°08'·93N 07°17'·39W.
Loch Boisdale Dir lt ≰, 292·5°; WRG 4s 4m 5M; vis: 287·5°-IsoG-290·5°-AlWG-292°-IsoW-293°-AlW-294·5°-IsoR-298·5°; 57°09'·19N 07°18'·24W.
2 FG 8m 3M on dn; 57°09'·13N 07°18'·18W.

LUDAIG and ERISKAY

Ludaig Bwtr ≰ 2 FR (vert) 6m 3M; 57°06'·17N 07°19'·49W.
Acairseid Mhor Ldg Lts 285°. Front, Oc R 6s 9m 4M; 57°03'·89N 07°17'·25W. Rear, 24m from front, Oc R 6s 10m 4M.

BARRA, CASTLEBAY and VATERSAY SOUND

Drover Rocks ⌁ Q (6) + L Fl 15s; 57°04'·08N 07°23'·54W.
Binch Rock ⌁ Q (6) + L Fl 15s; 57°01'·60N 07°17'·12W.
Curachan ⌁ Q (3) 10s; 56°58'·56N 07°20'·51W.
Ardveenish ≰ Oc WRG 6m 9/6M; vis: 300°-G-304°-W-306°-R-310°; 57°00'·21N 07°24'·43W.
Bo Vich Chuan ⌁ Q(6)+L Fl 15s; ***Racon (M) 5M***; 56°56'·15N 07°23'·31W.
Channel Rk ≰ Fl WR 6s 4m W6M, R4M; vis: 121·5°-W-277°-R-121·5°; 56°56'·24N 07°28'·94W.
Sgeir a Scape ◣ Fl (2) G 8s; 56°56'·25N 07°27'·21W.
Rubha Glas. Ldg Lts 295°. Front ⌁ FBu 9m 6M; Or △ on W twr; 56°56'·77N 07°30'·64W. Rear ⌁, 457m from front, FBu 15m 6M; Or ▽ on W twr; vis: 15° and 8° respectively either side of ldg line.
Barra Hd ☆ 56°47'·12N 07°39'·21W Fl 15s 208m **18M**; W twr; obsc by islands to NE; 992351095.

OUTER HEBRIDES – WEST SIDE

Flannan I ☆, Eilean Mór Fl (2) 30s 101m **20M**; W twr; 58°17'·29N 07°35'·29W, obsc in places by Is to W of Eilean Mór.
Rockall ⚡ Fl 15s 19m 8M (unreliable); 57°35'·76N 13°41'·27W.
Gasker Lt ⚡ Fl (3) 10s 38m 10M; 57°59'·05N 07°17'·20W.
Whale Rock ⚡ Q (3) 10s 5m 5M; *Racon (T)*; 57°54'·40N 07°59·91W.
Haskeir I ☆ 57°41'·96N 07°41·31W Fl 20s 44m **24M**; W twr; *Racon (M) 17–15M*; 992351140.
Monach Isles ☆ Fl (2) 15s 47m **18M**; R brick twr; 57°31'·55N 07°41'·68W.

EAST LOCH ROAG

Aird Laimishader Carloway ⚡ Fl 6s 63m 8M; W hut; obsc on some brgs; 58°17'·06N 06°49'·50W.
Ardvanich Pt ⚡ Fl G 3s 4m 2M; 58°13'·48N 06°47'·68W.
Tidal Rk ⚡ Fl R 3s 2m 2M (sync with Ardvanich Pt above); 58°13'·45N 06°47'·57W.
Grèinam ⚡ Fl WR 6s 8m W8M, R7M; W bn; vis: R143°-169°, W169°-143°; 58°13'·30N 06°46'·16W.

LOCH ROAG

Rubha Domhain ⚡ Fl G 5s 9m 1M; post; 58°12'·96N 06°45'·40W.
Bogha na Muilne ⚡ Fl (2) 10s; 58°12'·70N 06°54'·23W.
Mia Vaig Bay ⚡ Fl G 2s 2m 1M; bn; 58°11'·83N 06°56'·60W.

NORTH UIST and SOUTH UIST

Vallay I ⚡ Fl WRG 3s 8M; vis: 206°-W-085°-G-140°-W-145°-R-206°; 57°39'·70N 07°26'·34W.
Falconet twr ⚡ FR 25m 8M (3M by day); shown 1hr before firing, changes to Iso R 2s 15 min before firing until completion; 57°22'·04N 07°23'·58W.

ST KILDA

Ldg Lts 270°. Front, Oc 5s 26m 3M; 57°48'·32N 08°34'·31W. Rear, 100m from front, Oc 5s 38m 3M; sync.

LOCH TORRIDON TO MALLAIG

LITTLE MINCH and W SKYE

Eugenie Rock ⚡ Q 6 + LF 15s; 57°46'·47N 06°27'·28W.
Eilean Trodday ⚡ Fl (2) WRG 10s 52m W12M, R9M, G9M; W Bn; vis: W062°-R088°-130°-W-322°-G-062°; 57°43'·63N 06°17'·93W; 992351084.
Uig, Edward Pier Hd ⚡ 57°35'·09N 06°22'·29W Iso WRG 4s 9m W7M, R4M, G4M; vis: 180-W-006°-G-050°-W-073°-R-180°.
Waternish Pt ⚡ Fl 20s 21m 8M; W twr; 57°36'·48N 06°37'·99W.
Loch Dunvegan, Uiginish Pt ⚡ Fl WRG 3s 16m W7M,R5M,G5M; W lattice twr; vis: 041°-G-132°-W-145°-R-148°-W-253°-R-263°-W-273°-G-306°, (>148° obsc by Fiadhairt Pt); 57°26'·84N 06°36'·53W.
Neist Point ☆ 57°25'·41N 06°47'·30W Fl 5s 43m **16M**; W twr.
Loch Harport, Ardtreck Pt ⚡ 57°20'·38N 06°25'·80W Fl 6s 18m 9M; small W twr.

RONA, LOCH A'BHRAIGE and INNER SOUND

Na Gamhnachain ⚡ Q; 57°35'·89N 05°57'·71W.
Rona NE Point ☆ 57°34'·69N 05°57'·54W Fl 12s 69m **19M**; W twr; vis: 050°-358°; 992351045.
Loch A'Bhraige, Sgeir Shuas ⚡ Fl R 2s 6m 3M; vis: 070°-199°; 57°35'·02N 05°58'·61W.
Ldg Lts 136·5°. Front, ⚡ Q WRG 3m W4M, R3M; vis: 135°-W-138°-R-318°-G-135°; 57°34'·41N 05°58'·09W. Rear, ⚡ Iso 6s 28m 5M.
Ru Na Lachan ⚡ Oc WR 8s 21m 10M; twr; vis: 337°-W-022°-R-117°-W-162°; 57°29'·02N 05°52'·15W.

SOUND OF RAASAY, PORTREE and CROWLIN ISLANDS

Sgeir Mhór ⚡ Fl G 5s; 57°24'·57N 06°10'·53W.
Eilean Beag ⚡ Fl 6s 32m 6M; W Bn; 57°21'·21N 05°51'·42W.
Eyre Pt ⚡ Fl WR 3s 6m W9M R6M; W clad framework twr; vis: 215°-W-267°-R-288°-W-063°; 57°20'·01N 06°01'·28W.
Sgeir Thraid ⚡ Q 12m 3M; metal twr; 57°19'·82N 05°56'·51W.
Sgeir Ghobhlach ⚡ Fl(3)10s 10m 3M; metal twr; 57°15'·69N 05°52'·25W.

LOCH CARRON

Sgeir Golach ⚡ Fl 10s 5m 3M; 57°21'·20N 05°39'·01W.
Eilean a Chait Lt ho (dis) 13M; 57°20'·96N 05°38'·87W.
Bogha Dubh Sgeir ⚡ Fl (2)R 6s 4m 2M; 57°20'·92N 05°37'·85W.

RAASAY and LOCH SLIGACHAN

Suisnish ⚡ 2 FG (vert) 8m 2M; 57°19'·87N 06°03'·91W.
Eyre Point ⚡ Fl WR 3s 6m W9M, R6M; W twr; vis: 215°-W-266°-R- 288°-W-063°; 57°20'·01N 06°01'·29W.

KYLEAKIN and KYLE OF LOCH ALSH

Carragh Rk ⚡ Fl (2) G 12s; *Racon (T) 5M*; 57°17'·18N 05°45'·36W.
Bow Rk ⚡ Fl (2) R 12s; 57°16'·71N 05°45'·85W.
Fork Rks ⚡ Fl G 6s; 57°16'·85N 05°44'·93W.
Black Eye Rk ⚡ Fl R 6s; 57°16'·72N 05°45'·31W.
Eileanan Dubha East ⚡ Fl (2) 10s 9m 8M; vis: obscured 104°-146°; 57°16'·56N 05°42'·32W.
8 Metre Rock ⚡ Fl G 6s 5m 4M; 57°16'·60N 05°42'·69W.
String Rock ⚡ Fl R 6s; 57°16'·50N 05°42'·89W.
Sgeir-na-Caillich ⚡ Fl (2) R 6s 3m 4M; 57°15'·59N 05°38'·90W.

SOUND OF SLEAT

Kyle Rhea ⚡ Fl WRG 3s 7m W8M, R5M, G5M; W Bn; vis: shore-R-219°-W-228°-G-338°-W-346°-R-shore; 57°14'·22N 05°39'·93W.
Sandaig I, NW point ⚡ Fl 6s 13m 8M; W twr; 57°10'·05N 05°42'·29W.
Ornsay, SE end ⚡ Oc 8s 18m 12M; W twr; vis: 157°-030°; 57°08'·60N 05°46'·85W.
Pt. of Sleat ⚡ Fl 3s 20m9M; W twr; 57°01'·08N 06°01'·08W.

MALLAIG and LOCH NEVIS ENTRANCE

Sgeir Dhearg ⚡ QG; 57°00'·74N 05°49'·50W.
Northern Pier E end ⚡ Iso WRG 4s 6m W9M, R6M, G6M; Gy twr; vis: 181°-G-185°-W-197°-R-201°. Fl G 3s 14m 6M; same structure; 57°00'·47N 05°49'·50W.
Sgeir Dhearg ⚡ 57°00'·63N 05°49'·61W Fl (2) WG 8s 6m 5M; Gy Bn; vis: 190°-G-055°-W-190°.

SMALL ISLES AND WEST OF MULL

CANNA and RUM

Canna, E end Sanday Is ⚡ Fl 10s 32m 9M; W twr; vis: 152°-061°; 57°02'·82N 06°28'·02W.
Loch Scresort ⚡ Q; 57°00'·79N 06°14'·61W.

HYSKEIR, EIGG, MUCK and ARISAIG

Humla ⚡ Fl G 6s 3m 4M 57°00'·46N 06°37'·39W.
Hyskeir ☆ 56°58'·16N 06°40'·83W Fl (3) 30s 41m **24M**; W twr. *Racon (T) 14-17M*; 992351094.
SE point Eigg (Eilean Chathastail) ⚡ Fl 6s 24m 8M; W twr; vis: 181°-shore; 56°52'·25N 06°07'·28W.
Eigg, Sgeir nam Bagh (Ferry Terminal) ⚡ Dir 245°; Fl WRG 3s 9m W14, R11, G11; H24; steel pole; vis: 242·5°-G-244°-W-246°-R-247·5°. 2FR(vert) on same structure; 56°52'·79N 06°07'·56W.
Isle of Muck (Port Mor) ⚡ Dir Fl WRG 3s 7m W14, R11, G11, by day W1, R1, G1; steel twr; vis: 319·5°-G-321°-W-323°-R-324·5°; 56°49'·96N 06°13'·64W.
Bogha Ruadh⚡ Fl G 5s 4m 3M; 56°49'·56N 06°13'·05W.
Bo Faskadale ⚡ Fl (3) G 18s; 56°48'·18N 06°06'·37W.
Ardnamurchan ☆ 56°43'·63N 06°13'·58W Fl (2) 20s 55m **22M**; Gy twr; vis: 002°-217°.
Cairns of Coll, Suil Ghorm ⚡ Fl 12s 23m 10M; W twr; 56°42'·26N 06°26'·75W.

TIREE, COLL and ARINAGOUR

Loch Eatharna, Pier Head ⚡ Dir 325°; Oc WRG 7s 6m 2M; vis: 316°-G-322°-W-328°-R-334°; 56°36'·86N 06°31'·29W.
Loch Eatharna, Bogha Mór ⚡ Fl G 6s; 56°36'·65N 06°30'·90W.
Roan Bogha ⚡ Q (6) + L Fl 15s 3m 5M; 56°32'·23N 06°40'·18W.
Placaid Bogha ⚡ Fl G 4s; 56°33'·22N 06°44'·06W.
Scarinish ⚡ Fl 3s 11m 12M; W □ twr; vis: 210°-030°; S side of ent, 56°30'·02N 06°48'·26W.
Cairn na Burgh More (Treshnish Is), Fl (3) 15s 36m 8M; solar panels on framework tr; 56°31'·05N 06°22'·95W.

Gott Bay Ldg Lts 286·5°. Front FR 8m; 56°30'·61N 06°47'·82W. Rear 30m from front FR 11m.
Skerryvore ☆ Fl 10s 46m **23M**; Gy twr; *Racon (M) 18M*. 56°19'·36N 07°06'·88W; 992351091.

LOCH NA KEAL and LOCH NA LÀTHAICH
Sgeir a Charraigein ⚓ Q(6) + LFl 15s; 56°28'·29N 06°07'·71W.
Eileanan na Liathanaich, SE end ⚓ Fl WR 6s 12m W8M, R6M; vis: R088°- W108°-088°; 56°20'·56N 06°16'·38W.

DUBH ARTACH
Dubh Artach ☆ 56°07'·94N 06°38'·08W Fl (2) 30s 44m **20M**; Gy twr, R band; 992351088.

SOUND OF MULL

LOCH SUNART, TOBERMORY and LOCH ALINE
Ardmore Pt ⚓ Fl (2) 10s 18m 13M; 56°39'·37N 06°07'·70W.
New Rks ⚓ Fl G 6s 56°39'·05N 06°03'·30W.
Rubha nan Gall ☆ 56°38'·33N 06°04'·00W Fl 3s 17m **15M**; W twr.
Tobermory Slip ⚓ Iso WRG 3s 5m 4M; vis: 220°-G-232°-W-244°-R-256°; metal column; 56°37'·41N 06°03'·77W.
Eileanan Glasa (Dearg Sgeir) ⚓ 56°32'·25N 05°54'·80W Fl 6s 7m 8M; W ○ twr.
Fiunary Spit ⚓ Fl G 6s; 56°32'·66N 05°53'·17W.
Fishnish Ferry Slip ⚓ Iso WRG 3s 5m 4M; vis: 158°-G-170°-W-195°-R-230°; metal column; 56°30'·89N 05°48'·61W.
Loch Aline, ⚓ Dir 357°; Oc WRG 6s 2m 4M; vis: 353°-G-356°-W-358°-R-002°; Or concrete plinth; 56°32'·38N 05°46'·47W.
Ardtornish Pt ⚓ Fl (2) WRG 10s 8m W8M, R6M, G6M; W twr; vis: G shore- 301°-W-308°-R-342°-W-057°-R-095°-W-108°-G-shore; 56°31'·09N 05°45'·21W.
Craignure Ldg Lts 240·9°. Front, FR 10m; 56°28'·26N 05°42'·28W. Rear, 150m from front, FR 12m; vis: 225·8°-255·8°.

MULL TO CALEDONIAN CANAL AND OBAN
Lismore ☆, SW end 56°27'·34N 05°36'·45W Fl 10s 31m **17M**; W twr; vis: 237°-208°.
Lady's Rk ⚓ Fl 6s 12m 5M; Red clad lattice tower on W base 56°26'·92N 05°37'·05W; 992351093.
Duart Pt ⚓ Fl (3) WR 18s 14m W5M, R3M; vis: 162°-W-261°-R-275°-W-353°-R-shore; 56°26'·84N 05°38'·77W.

LOCH LINNHE
Corran Shoal ⚓ QR 56°43'·69N 05°14'·39W.
Corran Pt ⚓ Iso WRG 4s 12m W10M, R7M, G7M; W twr; vis: shore-R-195°-W-215°-G-020°-W-030°-R-shore; 56°43'·25N 05°14'·54W.
Corran Narrows NE ⚓ Fl 5s 4m 4M; W twr; vis: S shore-214°; 56°43'·62N 05°13'·90W.
Clovullin Spit ⚓ Fl (2) R 15s; 56°42'·29N 05°15'·56W.
Cuil-cheanna Spit ⚓ Fl G 6s; 56°41'·17N 05°15'·72W.
Mc Lean Rk ⚓ QR 56°49'·80N 05°07'·04W.
Eilean na Creiche ⚓ Fl (2) 5s; 56°50'·25N 05°07'·02W.
Eilean na Craobh ⚓ Fl (2) R 6s 4m 2M; 56°50'·43N 05°07'·95W.

FORT WILLIAM and CALEDONIAN CANAL
Corpach, Caledonian Canal Lock ent ⚓ Iso WRG 4s 6m 5M; W twr; vis: G287°- W310°- R335°-030°; 56°50'·52N 05°07'·44W.

LYNN OF LORN
Sgeir Bhuidhe Appin ⚓ Fl (2) WR 7s 8m W9M R6M; W Bn; vis: W013·5°- R184°-220°; 56°33'·63N 05°24'·65W.
Appin Point ⚓ Fl G 6s; 56°32'·69N 05°25'·97W.
Dearg Sgeir, off Aird's Point ⚓ Fl WRG 2s 2m W3M, R1M, G1M; vis: 196°-R-246°-W-258°-G-041°-W-058°-R-093°-W-139°; 56°32'·20N 05°25'·22W.
Rubha nam Faoileann (Eriska) ⚓ QG 2m 2M; G col; vis 128°-329°; 56°32'·20N 05°24'·11W.
Branra Rk ⚓ Fl(2) 10s 4m 5M; metal frame on W twr; 56°32'·02N 05°26'·60W.

OBAN
N spit of Kerrera ⚓ Fl R 3m 4M; W post; 56°25'·32N 05°29'·29W.
Dunollie ⚓ Fl (2) WRG 6s 6m W8M, R6M, G6M; vis: 351°-G- 020°-W-047°-R-120°-W-138°-G-143°; 56°25'·37N 05°29'·05W.
Rubh'a'Chruidh ⚓ Q R 3m 2M; W col, R bands; 56°25'·49N 05°29'·56W.
Kerrera ⚓ QR; 56°24'·15N 05°30'·81W.
Corran Ledge ⚓ VQ (9) 10s; 56°25'·19N 05°29'·11W.
Oban Bay ⚓ Q; 56°24'·92N 05°29'·23W.
Sgeir Rathaid ⚓ Q(6)+L Fl 15s; 56°24'·75N 05°29'·37W.
North Pier ⚓ 2 F G (vert); metal post; 56°24'·89N 05°28'·49W.
Ro-Ro Jetty ⚓ 2 F G (vert); post on dn; 56°24'·69N 05°28'·65W.
Northern Lt Pier ⚓ 2 F G (vert); metal post; 56°24'·71N 05°28'·91W.

OBAN TO LOCH CRAIGNISH
Heather Is ⚓ Fl R 2·5s 11m 2M; 56°24'·41N 05°30'·24W.
Ferry Rks SE ⚓ Q (3) 10s; 56°23'·99N 05°30'·53W.
Sgeirean Dubha ⚓ Fl (2) 12s 7m 5M; W ○ twr; 56°22'·81N 05°32'·27W.
Sgeir an Fheuran ⚓ Fl G 3s; 56°22'·80N 05°31'·94W.
Bogha Nuadh ⚓ Q (6) + LFl 15s; 56°21'·69N 05°37'·87W; 992351090.
Bogha Ghair ⚓ Q (3) 10s; 56°16'·50N 05°40'·44W.
Bono Rock ⚓ Q (9) 15s; 56°16'·21N 05°41'·22W.
Fladda ⚓ Fl (2) WRG 9s 13m W11M, R9M, G9M; W twr; vis: 169°-R-186°-W-337°-G-344°-W-356°-R-026°; 56°14'·89N 05°40'·83W.
Dubh Sgeir (Luing) ⚓ Fl WRG 6s 9m W6M, R4M. G4M; W twr; vis: W000°- R010°- W025°- G199°-000°; *Racon (M) 5M*; 56°14'·76N 05°40'·20W.
The Garvellachs, Eileach an Naoimh, SW end ⚓ Fl 6s 21m 9M; W Bn; vis: 240°-215°; 56°13'·04N 05°49'·06W.

LOCH MELFORT and CRAOBH HAVEN
Melfort Pier ⚓ Dir FR 6m 3M; (Apr -Nov); 56°16'·14N 05°30'·19W.
⚓ 56°12'·88N 05°33'·59W.
Craobh Marina Bkwtr Hd ⚓ Iso WRG 5s 10m, W5M, R3M, G3M; vis:114°-G-162°-W-183°-R-200°; 56°12'·78N 05°33'·52W.

1.4 PASSAGE INFORMATION

More passage information is threaded between the harbours in this area. It is essential to carry large scale charts and current pilot books for this area which is only partially covered between Ardnamurchan Point and the Shiant Isles by Admiralty Leisure Folio 5616. **Bibliography:** *Clyde Cruising Club Sailing Directions-Kintyre to Arnamurchan, CCC Sailing Directions-Ardnamurchan to Cape Wrath, CCC Sailing Directions-Outer Hebrides*(all Imray/Clyde Cruising Club, Lawrence). *The Yachtsman's Pilot to Skye and Northwest Scotland* (Imray/Lawrence). The *North West Coast of Scotland Pilot* (Admiralty NP66B) covers the whole area.

Scotland's west coast provides splendid, if boisterous, sailing and matchless scenery. In summer the long daylight hours and warmth of the Gulf Stream compensate for the lower air temperatures and higher wind speeds experienced when depressions run typically north of Scotland. Inshore winds are often unpredictable, due to geographical effects of lochs, mountains and islands offshore; calms and squalls can alternate rapidly.

Good anchors, especially on kelp/weed, are essential. ⚓s are listed but it should not be assumed that these will always be available. Particularly in N of area, facilities are very dispersed. A 'Rover Ticket' from Highland Council allows berthing for 15 days; the scheme includes: Kinlochbervie, Lochinver, Gairloch, Kyle of Lochalsh, Kyleakin, Portree and Uig. VHF communications with shore stations may be limited by high ground. Beware ever more fish farms in many inlets. Local magnetic anomalies occur in Kilbrannan Sound, Passage of Tiree, Sound of Mull, Canna, and East Loch Roag. Submarines exercise throughout these waters.

OUTER HEBRIDES

(AC 1785, 1794, 1795) The E sides of these Is have many good, sheltered ⚓s, but W coasts give little shelter. The CCC's *Outer Hebrides SDs* or *The Western Isles* (Imray) are advised.

▶ *The Minches and Sea of the Hebrides can be very rough, particularly in the Little Minch between Skye and Harris, and around Shiant Is where tide runs locally 4kn at sp, and heavy overfalls can occur. The NE going stream on both shores begins at HW Ullapool -0340 (HW Dover +0430), with the strongest flow from mid channel to the Skye coast. There is a W going counter tide E of Vaternish Pt.*

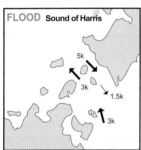

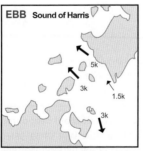

The SW going stream on both shores begins at HW Ullapool +0240 (HW Dover –0130), with the strongest flow from mid channel to the Skye coast, sp rates 2·5kn. The E going stream in Sound of Scalpay runs at up to 2k.The E going flood and W going ebb in Sound of Scalpay run at up to 2k.◀

▶ **Sound of Harris.** *The behaviour of tidal streams is complicated and varies from day to night, springs to neaps, and winter to summer. In the NE part of the Sound, at springs, the stream sets SE from Ullapool +0535 to –0035. At neaps, in the summer, the stream sets SE during the day and NW during the night. To the SW of the Sound, the NW stream starts at Ullapool –0545; the SE stream starts at Ullapool +0025. The approximate maximum rates are as shown. For more detailed information refer to the Admiralty West Coast of Scotland Pilot.*◀

From N to S, the better harbours in the Outer Hebrides include:

Lewis. Stornoway; Loch Grimshader (beware Sgeir a'Chaolais, dries in entrance); Loch Erisort; Loch Odhairn; Loch Shell. Proceeding S from here, or to E Loch Tarbert beware Sgeir Inoe (dries 2·3m) 3M ESE of Eilean Glas lt ho at SE end of Scalpay.

Harris. E Loch Tarbert; Loch Scadaby; Loch Stockinish; Loch Finsby; W Loch Tarbert; Loch Rodel (⚓). A well marked ferry channel connects Leverburgh (South Harris) to Berneray.

N Uist. Loch Maddy (⚓); Loch Eport, Kallin Hbr (⚓).

S Uist. Loch Carnan (⚓); Loch Skiport; Loch Eynort; Loch Boisdale (⚓).

Barra. Castlebay (⚓), and Berneray, on N side, E of Shelter Rk.

There are numerous ⚓s. Bratanish Mor in L Roag is very sheltered and provides respite on W coast

Activity at the Hebrides Range, S. Uist ☎(01870) 604441, is broadcast daily at 0950LT and Mon-Fri 1100-1700LT on VHF Ch 12 (Ch 73 in emergency) and on MF 2660 kHz.

CAPE WRATH TO ULLAPOOL

(AC 1785, 1794) C Wrath (lt fog sig) is a steep headland (110m).

▶ *To N of it the E-going stream begins at HW Ullapool – 0350, and W-going at HW Ullapool + 0235, sp rates 3kn. Eddies close inshore cause almost continuous W-going stream E of Cape, and N-going stream SW of it. Where they meet is turbulence, with dangerous seas in bad weather.* ◀

Duslic Rk, 7ca NE of lt ho, dries 3·4m. 6M SW of C Wrath, islet of Am Balg (45m)is foul for 2ca around.

There are ⚓ in Loch Inchard (AC 2503), the best shelter being in Kinlochbervie on N shore; also good ⚓s among Is along S shore of Loch Laxford, entered between Ardmore Pt and Rubha Ruadh. Handa Is to WSW is a bird sanctuary. Handa Sound is navigable with care, but beware Bogha Morair in mid-chan and associated overfalls.

▶ *Tide turns 2hrs earlier in the Sound than offshore. Strong winds against tide raise a bad sea off Pt of Stoer.*◀

The best shelter is 8M S at Loch Inver (AC 2504), with good ⚓ off hotel near head of loch. ⚓s to the N of Loch Inver may be found at Kylesku, Culkein Drumbeg, Drumbeg, Loch Nedd and Loch Roe. To the S lies Enard Bay.

ULLAPOOL TO LOCH TORRIDON

(AC 1794, 2210, 5616) The Summer Isles (AC 2501), 12M NW of the major fishing port of Ullapool, offer some sheltered ⚓s and tight approaches. The best include the bay on E side of Tanera Mor; off NE of Tanera Beg (W of Eilean Fada Mor); and in Caolas Eilean Ristol, between the island and mainland.

Loch Ewe (AC 3146) provides good shelter and easy access. Best ⚓s are in Poolewe Bay (beware Boor Rks off W shore) and in SW corner of Loch Thuirnaig (entering, keep close to S shore to avoid rocks extending from N side). Off Rubha Reidh (lt) seas can be dangerous.

▶ *The NE-going stream begins at HW Ullapool –0335; the SW-going at HW Ullapool +0305. Sp rates 3kn, but slacker to SW of point.* ◀

Longa Is lies N of ent to Loch Gairloch (AC 2528). The channel N of it is navigable but narrow at E end. Outer loch is free of dangers, but exposed to swell. Best ⚓ is on S side of loch in Caolas Bad a' Chrotha, W of Eilean Horrisdale.

Entering L Torridon (AC 2210) from S or W beware Murchadh Breac (dries 1·5m) 3ca NNW of Rubha na Fearna. Best ⚓s are SW of Eilean Mor (to W of Ardheslaig); in Loch a 'Chracaich, 7ca further SE; E of Shieldaig Is; and near head of Upper L Torridon.

▶ *Streams are weak except where they run 2-3kn in narrows between L Shieldaig and Upper L Torridon.*◀

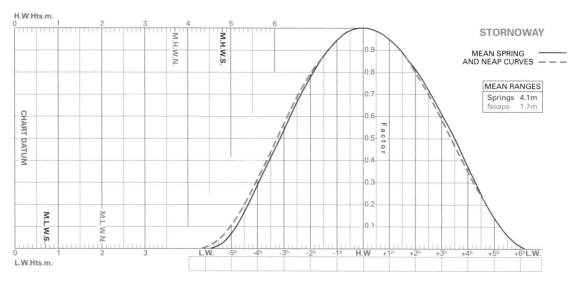

1.5 STORNOWAY

Lewis (Western Isles) **58°11'·58N 06°21'·82W** ✿✿✿✿☁☁✿✿

CHARTS AC 1785, 1794, 2529; Imray C67

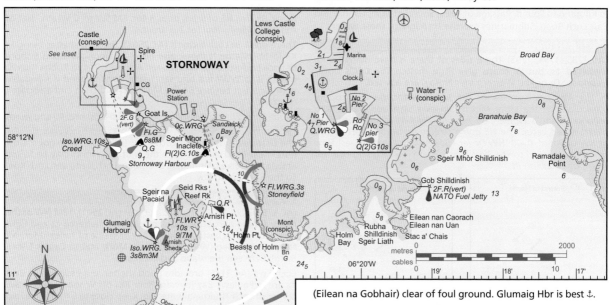

TIDES

Standard Port STORNOWAY (→)

Times				Height (metres)			
High Water		Low Water		MHWS	MHWN	MLWN	MLWS
0100	0700	0300	0900	4·8	3·7	2·0	0·7
1300	1900	1500	2100				
Differences CARLOWAY (W Lewis)							
−0040	+0020	−0035	−0015	−0·7	−0·5	−0·3	0·0
LITTLE BERNERA (W Lewis)							
−0021	−0011	−0017	−0027	−0·5	−0·6	−0·4	−0·2
WEST LOCH TARBERT (W Harris)							
−0015	−0015	−0046	−0046	−1·1	−0·9	−0·5	0·0

SHELTER Good. New marina (2014), max LOA 24m, in Inner Hbr, has depths to 3m. Visitors should report to Stornoway Port Authority; large boats may request berth on 80m pontoon on Esplanade Quay. Ferries use W side No 3 pier, and commercial vessels on Nos 1 and 2 Piers. South'ly swells can make anchoring uncomfortable. ⚓ on chartlet at: Poll nam Portan to W of inner chan in bay NW of Goat Is (Eilean na Gobhair) clear of foul ground. Glumaig Hbr is best ⚓.

NAVIGATION WPT 58°09'·98N 06°20'·87W, 343°/2·3M to Oc WRG lt. Access to the harbour is straightforward at all states of the tide. Reef Rk, N of Arnish Pt to W of entrance, indicated by PHM, QR. To E side of entrance an unlit G bn marks the Beasts of Holm, a rky patch. This lies off Holm Pt, on which is a conspic memorial. A local magnetic anomaly exists over a small area in mid-hbr, 1·75ca N of Seid Rks PHM bn.

LIGHTS AND MARKS Arnish sheds are conspic 3ca SW of Arnish Pt lt, W sector 302°-013° covers ent. Then in turn follow W sectors of: Sandwick Bay lt (close E of water tr, 3 power stn chys; all conspic), then Creed Estuary, Iso WRG 10s, across the harbour, and No 1 Pier, Q WRG. Lit bns in inner hbr mark appr chan to marina.

COMMUNICATIONS (Code 01851) CGOC 702013; Police 101; Dr 703145; ⊖ 703626. HM 702688.
HM VHF Ch 12 16 (H24).

FACILITIES **Marina** 80⌒ inc 8🅥, £2/m/day, £10/m/wk; ⚓ ♠ wi-fi. **Piers 1 & 2** ⚓ ⌑(10t) ⌐. **Pier 3** ⚓ ⌑(mob) ♠(road tanker). **Services** ✕ ♦ ⌸ ⌸ ACA. **Town** ⌸ ⌸ ⌸ ⌸ ⌧ Ⓑ ⌸ ⌸ ✕ ⌸ ⇌ (Ferry to Ullapool, bus to Garve), ✈.

STANDARD TIME (UT)
For Summer Time add ONE hour in **non-shaded areas**

STORNOWAY LAT 58°12′N LONG 6°23′W
TIMES AND HEIGHTS OF HIGH AND LOW WATERS

Dates in red are **SPRINGS**
Dates in blue are NEAPS

YEAR 2016

JANUARY

Day	Time	m	Time	m	Time	m	Time	m
1 F	0506	1.9	1113	4.1	1754	1.8		
2 SA	0010	3.7	0556	2.1	1223	3.9	1850	2.0
3 SU	0123	3.7	0658	2.3	1342	3.8	2000	2.1
4 M	0233	3.7	0816	2.3	1453	3.8	2113	2.1
5 TU	0334	3.8	0931	2.2	1553	3.9	2213	1.9
6 W	0425	4.0	1031	2.0	1642	4.0	2300	1.7
7 TH	0506	4.3	1118	1.8	1723	4.2	2341	1.5
8 F	0543	4.5	1200	1.5	1800	4.4		
9 SA	0020	1.3	0617	4.7	1240	1.3	1835	4.5
10 SU ●	0058	1.1	0652	4.9	1319	1.0	1912	4.7
11 M	0135	1.0	0728	5.1	1358	0.9	1951	4.8
12 TU	0213	0.9	0807	5.1	1439	0.8	2033	4.7
13 W	0253	0.9	0849	5.1	1520	0.8	2117	4.6
14 TH	0334	1.0	0935	5.0	1604	0.9	2206	4.4
15 F	0419	1.2	1027	4.8	1652	1.1	2304	4.2
16 SA ◐	0510	1.4	1128	4.5	1746	1.3		
17 SU	0013	4.0	0610	1.7	1239	4.3	1849	1.6
18 M	0131	3.9	0725	1.9	1355	4.2	2005	1.7
19 TU	0248	4.0	0849	1.9	1510	4.2	2125	1.7
20 W	0358	4.1	1008	1.7	1617	4.3	2234	1.6
21 TH	0455	4.4	1111	1.5	1714	4.4	2329	1.4
22 F	0541	4.6	1203	1.2	1801	4.6		
23 SA	0015	1.2	0621	4.8	1249	1.0	1841	4.7
24 SU ○	0057	1.0	0658	4.9	1330	0.9	1919	4.7
25 M	0135	1.0	0732	5.0	1408	0.8	1954	4.7
26 TU	0211	1.0	0805	4.9	1443	0.9	2027	4.6
27 W	0245	1.0	0836	4.8	1518	1.0	2101	4.5
28 TH	0319	1.1	0908	4.7	1552	1.1	2135	4.3
29 F	0354	1.3	0941	4.4	1628	1.4	2213	4.1
30 SA	0430	1.6	1018	4.2	1706	1.6	2300	3.9
31 SU	0509	1.8	1105	4.0	1749	1.9		

FEBRUARY

Day	Time	m	Time	m	Time	m	Time	m
1 M ◑	0004	3.7	0556	2.1	1214	3.7	1844	2.1
2 TU	0126	3.6	0700	2.3	1347	3.6	2000	2.2
3 W	0241	3.7	0828	2.3	1507	3.6	2126	2.1
4 TH	0346	3.8	0952	2.2	1612	3.8	2229	1.9
5 F	0437	4.1	1052	1.9	1701	4.0	2317	1.6
6 SA	0519	4.4	1139	1.5	1742	4.3	2359	1.3
7 SU	0557	4.7	1221	1.1	1820	4.5		
8 M ●	0039	1.0	0633	5.0	1302	0.8	1856	4.8
9 TU	0119	0.8	0710	5.2	1342	0.5	1935	4.9
10 W	0158	0.6	0750	5.3	1423	0.4	2015	4.9
11 TH	0238	0.5	0831	5.3	1503	0.4	2057	4.8
12 F	0318	0.6	0915	5.2	1545	0.5	2142	4.6
13 SA	0402	0.8	1005	4.9	1630	0.9	2235	4.4
14 SU	0449	1.2	1103	4.6	1719	1.2	2340	4.1
15 M ◐	0545	1.5	1215	4.2	1817	1.6		
16 TU	0102	3.9	0656	1.8	1337	4.0	1932	1.9
17 W	0227	3.8	0829	1.9	1459	3.9	2105	1.9
18 TH	0345	4.0	1001	1.8	1612	4.0	2224	1.8
19 F	0445	4.2	1105	1.5	1708	4.2	2319	1.5
20 SA	0532	4.4	1154	1.2	1751	4.4		
21 SU	0003	1.3	0609	4.6	1237	1.0	1827	4.5
22 M ○	0042	1.1	0642	4.8	1313	0.8	1900	4.6
23 TU	0118	0.9	0712	4.9	1347	0.8	1930	4.7
24 W	0151	0.9	0741	4.9	1419	0.8	2000	4.6
25 TH	0222	0.9	0809	4.8	1450	0.8	2029	4.5
26 F	0253	1.0	0837	4.6	1521	1.0	2100	4.4
27 SA	0325	1.1	0907	4.5	1552	1.2	2133	4.2
28 SU	0357	1.3	0940	4.2	1625	1.4	2211	4.0
29 M	0433	1.6	1019	4.0	1702	1.7	2302	3.8

MARCH

Day	Time	m	Time	m	Time	m	Time	m
1 TU ◑	0514	1.8	1113	3.7	1746	1.9		
2 W	0016	3.6	0606	2.1	1241	3.5	1849	2.2
3 TH	0145	3.6	0725	2.2	1420	3.5	2028	2.2
4 F	0300	3.7	0908	2.1	1537	3.6	2155	2.0
5 SA	0401	3.9	1022	1.8	1635	3.9	2251	1.7
6 SU	0450	4.2	1114	1.4	1720	4.2	2336	1.3
7 M	0531	4.6	1158	1.0	1759	4.5		
8 TU	0018	0.9	0609	5.0	1241	0.6	1836	4.8
9 W ●	0058	0.6	0648	5.2	1321	0.3	1914	5.0
10 TH	0138	0.4	0728	5.4	1402	0.1	1953	5.1
11 F	0219	0.3	0810	5.4	1442	0.1	2035	5.0
12 SA	0300	0.4	0855	5.2	1524	0.3	2119	4.7
13 SU	0344	0.6	0945	4.8	1607	0.7	2210	4.4
14 M	0431	1.0	1045	4.4	1653	1.1	2314	4.1
15 TU ◐	0525	1.4	1200	4.1	1749	1.6		
16 W ◑	0038	3.8	0636	1.7	1324	3.8	1902	1.9
17 TH	0206	3.8	0814	1.9	1447	3.7	2043	2.0
18 F	0326	3.9	0948	1.7	1600	3.8	2207	1.9
19 SA	0428	4.0	1050	1.5	1654	4.0	2301	1.6
20 SU	0513	4.3	1136	1.2	1734	4.2	2344	1.4
21 M	0549	4.4	1215	1.0	1808	4.4		
22 TU	0021	1.1	0620	4.6	1250	0.8	1837	4.5
23 W ○	0056	1.0	0648	4.7	1322	0.7	1905	4.6
24 TH	0127	0.9	0715	4.7	1352	0.7	1933	4.6
25 F	0158	0.8	0742	4.6	1421	0.8	2001	4.6
26 SA	0228	0.9	0809	4.5	1450	0.9	2030	4.5
27 SU	0258	1.0	0838	4.4	1520	1.0	2101	4.3
28 M	0330	1.2	0911	4.2	1551	1.3	2137	4.1
29 TU	0405	1.4	0951	3.9	1625	1.5	2223	3.9
30 W	0444	1.6	1042	3.7	1706	1.8	2327	3.7
31 TH ◑	0533	1.9	1202	3.5	1802	2.0		

APRIL

Day	Time	m	Time	m	Time	m	Time	m
1 F	0054	3.6	0644	2.0	1341	3.4	1933	2.2
2 SA	0215	3.7	0824	2.0	1501	3.6	2114	2.0
3 SU	0321	3.9	0946	1.7	1604	3.8	2219	1.7
4 M	0415	4.2	1044	1.3	1652	4.2	2308	1.3
5 TU	0501	4.6	1131	0.8	1734	4.5	2352	0.8
6 W	0544	4.9	1215	0.4	1813	4.8		
7 TH ●	0035	0.5	0624	5.2	1257	0.2	1852	5.1
8 F	0117	0.3	0707	5.3	1339	0.0	1932	5.1
9 SA	0159	0.2	0751	5.3	1420	0.1	2014	5.0
10 SU	0243	0.3	0838	5.1	1502	0.3	2059	4.8
11 M	0327	0.5	0930	4.7	1545	0.7	2150	4.5
12 TU	0416	0.9	1033	4.3	1632	1.2	2254	4.2
13 W	0511	1.3	1147	3.9	1725	1.6		
14 TH ◐	0015	3.9	0620	1.6	1306	3.7	1835	2.0
15 F	0138	3.8	0750	1.8	1424	3.6	2008	2.1
16 SA	0255	3.8	0919	1.7	1535	3.7	2134	2.0
17 SU	0358	3.9	1021	1.5	1629	3.8	2232	1.7
18 M	0446	4.1	1107	1.3	1709	4.0	2316	1.5
19 TU	0522	4.2	1146	1.1	1742	4.2	2355	1.3
20 W	0554	4.2	1220	0.9	1812	4.4		
21 TH	0029	1.1	0622	4.4	1253	0.8	1840	4.5
22 F ○	0102	1.0	0650	4.5	1323	0.8	1908	4.6
23 SA	0133	0.9	0717	4.5	1353	0.8	1936	4.6
24 SU	0204	0.9	0746	4.4	1422	0.9	2005	4.5
25 M	0235	1.0	0817	4.3	1452	1.0	2037	4.4
26 TU	0308	1.1	0853	4.1	1524	1.2	2115	4.2
27 W	0344	1.2	0935	3.9	1559	1.4	2200	4.0
28 TH	0424	1.4	1029	3.7	1641	1.7	2300	3.9
29 F	0514	1.6	1143	3.6	1735	1.9		
30 SA ◑	0016	3.8	0619	1.8	1309	3.5	1856	2.0

Chart Datum: 2·71 metres below Ordnance Datum (Newlyn). HAT is 5·5 metres above Chart Datum.

NW Scotland

》FREE monthly updates. Register at 《
www.reedsnauticalalmanac.co.uk

39

STANDARD TIME (UT)
For Summer Time add ONE hour in **non-shaded areas**

STORNOWAY LAT 58°12′N LONG 6°23′W
TIMES AND HEIGHTS OF HIGH AND LOW WATERS

Dates in red are **SPRINGS**
Dates in blue are **NEAPS**

YEAR **2016**

MAY

Day	Time m		Day	Time m	
1 SU	0134 3.8 / 0746 1.8 / 1425 3.6 / 2030 1.9		**16** M	0317 3.8 / 0938 1.6 / 1552 3.7 / 2150 1.9	
2 M	0242 3.9 / 0907 1.5 / 1530 3.9 / 2142 1.6		**17** TU	0409 3.9 / 1029 1.5 / 1636 3.9 / 2241 1.7	
3 TU	0341 4.2 / 1009 1.2 / 1623 4.2 / 2237 1.3		**18** W	0450 4.0 / 1111 1.3 / 1713 4.1 / 2323 1.5	
4 W	0432 4.5 / 1101 0.8 / 1708 4.5 / 2326 0.9		**19** TH	0526 4.1 / 1149 1.1 / 1746 4.3	
5 TH	0519 4.8 / 1148 0.5 / 1750 4.8		**20** F	0001 1.3 / 0557 4.2 / 1223 1.0 / 1816 4.4	
6 F	0012 0.6 / 0603 5.1 / 1234 0.3 / ●1831 5.0		**21** SA	0036 1.1 / 0628 4.3 / 1256 1.0 / ○1845 4.5	
7 SA	0057 0.4 / 0648 5.1 / 1317 0.2 / 1913 5.1		**22** SU	0110 1.0 / 0658 4.3 / 1327 0.9 / 1915 4.5	
8 SU	0142 0.3 / 0735 5.1 / 1400 0.3 / 1956 5.0		**23** M	0143 1.0 / 0729 4.3 / 1358 1.0 / 1946 4.5	
9 M	0228 0.3 / 0824 4.9 / 1443 0.5 / 2043 4.8		**24** TU	0216 1.0 / 0803 4.2 / 1431 1.0 / 2021 4.5	
10 TU	0314 0.5 / 0918 4.6 / 1527 0.8 / 2134 4.5		**25** W	0251 1.0 / 0841 4.1 / 1505 1.2 / 2100 4.4	
11 W	0403 0.8 / 1019 4.2 / 1613 1.2 / 2234 4.3		**26** TH	0329 1.1 / 0926 4.0 / 1542 1.3 / 2146 4.2	
12 TH	0457 1.2 / 1126 3.9 / 1704 1.6 / 2345 4.1		**27** F	0411 1.3 / 1019 3.9 / 1626 1.5 / 2242 4.1	
13 F	0559 1.5 / 1236 3.7 / 1806 1.9 ◑		**28** SA	0500 1.4 / 1124 3.7 / 1719 1.7 / 2348 4.0	
14 SA	0100 3.8 / 0712 1.7 / 1347 3.6 / 1921 2.0		**29** SU	0601 1.5 / 1238 3.7 / 1828 1.8 ◐	
15 SU	0212 3.8 / 0831 1.7 / 1455 3.6 / 2043 2.0		**30** M	0058 4.0 / 0713 1.5 / 1350 3.7 / 1950 1.8	
			31 TU	0207 4.0 / 0828 1.4 / 1457 3.9 / 2104 1.6	

JUNE

Day	Time m		Day	Time m	
1 W	0309 4.2 / 0935 1.2 / 1555 4.1 / 2207 1.4		**16** TH	0414 3.8 / 1033 1.6 / 1641 4.0 / 2249 1.7	
2 TH	0406 4.4 / 1033 0.9 / 1646 4.4 / 2302 1.1		**17** F	0457 3.9 / 1116 1.4 / 1719 4.1 / 2332 1.5	
3 F	0459 4.7 / 1125 0.7 / 1732 4.7 / 2353 0.8		**18** SA	0535 4.0 / 1154 1.3 / 1753 4.3	
4 SA	0548 4.8 / 1213 0.6 / 1816 4.9		**19** SU	0011 1.3 / 0609 4.2 / 1230 1.2 / 1825 4.5	
5 SU	0042 0.6 / 0636 4.9 / 1259 0.5 / ●1859 5.0		**20** M	0048 1.5 / 0642 4.2 / 1305 1.1 / ○1857 4.6	
6 M	0130 0.5 / 0724 4.9 / 1344 0.5 / 1943 4.9		**21** TU	0124 1.1 / 0716 4.3 / 1339 1.0 / 1930 4.6	
7 TU	0216 0.5 / 0813 4.7 / 1427 0.7 / 2028 4.8		**22** W	0200 1.0 / 0752 4.3 / 1414 1.0 / 2007 4.6	
8 W	0303 0.6 / 0904 4.5 / 1511 0.9 / 2116 4.6		**23** TH	0238 0.9 / 0831 4.3 / 1451 1.1 / 2046 4.6	
9 TH	0350 0.8 / 0956 4.2 / 1555 1.2 / 2207 4.4		**24** F	0317 0.9 / 0914 4.2 / 1530 1.1 / 2131 4.5	
10 F	0438 1.1 / 1052 4.0 / 1641 1.5 / 2304 4.1		**25** SA	0359 1.0 / 1004 4.1 / 1613 1.3 / 2222 4.4	
11 SA	0529 1.3 / 1153 3.7 / 1732 1.7		**26** SU	0446 1.1 / 1101 4.0 / 1703 1.5 / 2321 4.3	
12 SU	0009 3.9 / 0626 1.6 / 1257 3.6 / ◑1831 1.9		**27** M	0540 1.3 / 1207 3.9 / 1803 1.6 ◐	
13 M	0118 3.8 / 0730 1.7 / 1402 3.6 / 1941 2.1		**28** TU	0027 4.2 / 0642 1.4 / 1319 3.8 / 1914 1.7	
14 TU	0224 3.7 / 0839 1.8 / 1504 3.6 / 2055 2.0		**29** W	0137 4.1 / 0753 1.4 / 1428 3.9 / 2031 1.7	
15 W	0324 3.7 / 0942 1.7 / 1557 3.8 / 2158 1.9		**30** TH	0245 4.2 / 0904 1.3 / 1533 4.1 / 2142 1.5	

JULY

Day	Time m		Day	Time m	
1 F	0349 4.3 / 1011 1.2 / 1630 4.3 / 2246 1.3		**16** SA	0429 3.8 / 1044 1.7 / 1652 4.0 / 2305 1.7	
2 SA	0448 4.4 / 1108 1.0 / 1720 4.5 / 2342 1.0		**17** SU	0513 3.9 / 1128 1.5 / 1730 4.2 / 2349 1.5	
3 SU	0541 4.6 / 1200 0.9 / 1806 4.7		**18** M	0551 4.1 / 1207 1.3 / 1805 4.5	
4 M	0033 0.8 / 0629 4.7 / 1247 0.8 / ●1849 4.9		**19** TU	0028 1.3 / 0626 4.2 / 1245 1.1 / ○1838 4.6	
5 TU	0121 0.6 / 0715 4.7 / 1331 0.8 / 1931 4.9		**20** W	0107 1.0 / 0700 4.4 / 1322 1.0 / 1913 4.8	
6 W	0206 0.6 / 0759 4.7 / 1413 0.8 / 2012 4.9		**21** TH	0145 0.8 / 0736 4.5 / 1358 0.9 / 1950 4.9	
7 TH	0249 0.6 / 0842 4.5 / 1453 0.9 / 2052 4.7		**22** F	0223 0.7 / 0815 4.5 / 1436 0.9 / 2029 4.9	
8 F	0330 0.8 / 0925 4.3 / 1533 1.1 / 2133 4.5		**23** SA	0302 0.7 / 0856 4.5 / 1515 0.9 / 2112 4.8	
9 SA	0412 1.0 / 1009 4.1 / 1614 1.3 / 2216 4.3		**24** SU	0343 0.7 / 0942 4.4 / 1557 1.0 / 2159 4.7	
10 SU	0454 1.2 / 1058 3.9 / 1656 1.6 / 2305 4.0		**25** M	0427 0.9 / 1034 4.2 / 1644 1.2 / 2255 4.5	
11 M	0539 1.5 / 1155 3.7 / 1743 1.8		**26** TU	0516 1.1 / 1136 4.0 / 1738 1.5 ◐	
12 TU	0006 3.8 / 0630 1.7 / 1301 3.6 / ◑1839 2.0		**27** W	0001 4.3 / 0612 1.3 / 1250 3.9 / 1844 1.7	
13 W	0121 3.7 / 0731 1.9 / 1409 3.6 / 1949 2.1		**28** TH	0115 4.1 / 0720 1.5 / 1406 3.9 / 2005 1.8	
14 TH	0232 3.6 / 0843 1.9 / 1512 3.7 / 2107 2.1		**29** F	0230 4.0 / 0839 1.6 / 1518 4.0 / 2128 1.7	
15 F	0335 3.7 / 0951 1.8 / 1606 3.8 / 2214 2.0		**30** SA	0342 4.1 / 0956 1.5 / 1622 4.2 / 2240 1.4	
			31 SU	0445 4.2 / 1059 1.3 / 1714 4.5 / 2337 1.2	

AUGUST

Day	Time m		Day	Time m	
1 M	0537 4.4 / 1151 1.2 / 1758 4.7		**16** TU	0531 4.1 / 1144 1.4 / 1742 4.5	
2 TU	0026 0.9 / 0622 4.6 / 1236 1.0 / ●1838 4.9		**17** W	0007 1.2 / 0606 4.3 / 1224 1.1 / 1816 4.8	
3 W	0111 0.7 / 0702 4.6 / 1317 0.9 / 1915 4.9		**18** TH	0046 0.9 / 0641 4.6 / 1302 0.9 / ○1851 5.0	
4 TH	0151 0.6 / 0739 4.7 / 1356 0.8 / 1950 4.9		**19** F	0125 0.6 / 0716 4.7 / 1339 0.7 / 1928 5.1	
5 F	0229 0.6 / 0815 4.6 / 1432 0.9 / 2024 4.8		**20** SA	0203 0.5 / 0754 4.8 / 1418 0.6 / 2007 5.2	
6 SA	0305 0.7 / 0850 4.4 / 1508 1.0 / 2057 4.6		**21** SU	0242 0.4 / 0834 4.8 / 1457 0.6 / 2050 5.1	
7 SU	0340 0.9 / 0926 4.3 / 1544 1.2 / 2131 4.4		**22** M	0322 0.5 / 0917 4.6 / 1539 0.8 / 2136 4.9	
8 M	0416 1.2 / 1004 4.1 / 1620 1.4 / 2208 4.1		**23** TU	0405 0.7 / 1006 4.4 / 1624 1.1 / 2231 4.6	
9 TU	0454 1.4 / 1050 3.8 / 1700 1.7 / 2254 3.9		**24** W	0451 1.0 / 1107 4.2 / 1716 1.4 / 2340 4.3	
10 W	0535 1.7 / 1152 3.7 / 1746 2.0 ◐		**25** TH	0545 1.4 / 1226 4.0 / 1822 1.7	
11 TH	0002 3.7 / 0626 1.9 / 1311 3.6 / 1845 2.2		**26** F	0102 4.0 / 0653 1.7 / 1350 3.9 / 1948 1.9	
12 F	0136 3.5 / 0736 2.1 / 1424 3.6 / 2009 2.3		**27** SA	0224 3.9 / 0821 1.9 / 1508 4.0 / 2124 1.8	
13 SA	0255 3.5 / 0903 2.1 / 1529 3.8 / 2137 2.1		**28** SU	0340 4.0 / 0949 1.8 / 1615 4.2 / 2237 1.5	
14 SU	0400 3.6 / 1012 1.9 / 1622 4.0 / 2239 1.9		**29** M	0442 4.1 / 1052 1.6 / 1706 4.4 / 2331 1.2	
15 M	0451 3.8 / 1102 1.7 / 1704 4.2 / 2326 1.6		**30** TU	0530 4.3 / 1140 1.3 / 1747 4.6	
			31 W	0015 1.0 / 0609 4.5 / 1222 1.1 / 1822 4.8	

Chart Datum: 2·71 metres below Ordnance Datum (Newlyn). HAT is 5·5 metres above Chart Datum.

》》 **FREE** monthly updates. Register at 《
www.reedsnauticalalmanac.co.uk

STANDARD TIME (UT)	STORNOWAY LAT 58°12′N LONG 6°23′W	Dates in red are SPRINGS
For Summer Time add ONE hour in **non-shaded areas**	TIMES AND HEIGHTS OF HIGH AND LOW WATERS	Dates in blue are NEAPS

YEAR 2016

SEPTEMBER

Day	Time m	Time m		Day	Time m	Time m
1 TH ●	0055 0.8 / 0643 4.6	1300 1.0 / 1854 4.9		**16** F ○	0021 0.8 / 0617 4.7	1238 0.8 / 1827 5.2
2 F	0131 0.7 / 0715 4.7	1335 0.9 / 1925 4.9		**17** SA	0100 0.5 / 0653 5.0	1317 0.6 / 1905 5.4
3 SA	0204 0.7 / 0746 4.8	1408 0.9 / 1954 4.8		**18** SU	0139 0.3 / 0730 5.1	1357 0.5 / 1945 5.4
4 SU	0236 0.8 / 0816 4.6	1441 1.0 / 2023 4.7		**19** M	0219 0.2 / 0810 5.0	1437 0.5 / 2028 5.3
5 M	0308 0.9 / 0847 4.4	1513 1.1 / 2053 4.5		**20** TU	0259 0.4 / 0853 4.9	1520 0.7 / 2116 5.0
6 TU	0339 1.1 / 0920 4.3	1547 1.6 / 2126 4.2		**21** W	0342 0.7 / 0941 4.6	1606 1.0 / 2213 4.6
7 W	0413 1.4 / 0958 4.0	1622 1.6 / 2205 4.0		**22** TH	0428 1.1 / 1043 4.3	1659 1.4 / 2328 4.2
8 TH	0449 1.7 / 1049 3.8	1703 1.9 / 2300 3.7		**23** F ◐	0520 1.5 / 1207 4.0	1806 1.7
9 F ◐	0532 1.9 / 1206 3.7	1755 2.1		**24** SA	0054 3.9 / 0629 1.9	1335 3.9 / 1938 1.9
10 SA	0037 3.5 / 0631 2.2	1334 3.6 / 1912 2.3		**25** SU	0217 3.8 / 0805 2.1	1455 4.0 / 2118 1.8
11 SU	0214 3.5 / 0807 2.3	1447 3.9 / 2055 2.2		**26** M	0333 3.9 / 0937 2.0	1601 4.2 / 2226 1.5
12 M	0328 3.6 / 0938 2.1	1547 3.9 / 2209 1.9		**27** TU	0432 4.1 / 1037 1.7	1651 4.4 / 2315 1.3
13 TU	0423 3.8 / 1035 1.8	1634 4.2 / 2259 1.6		**28** W	0516 4.3 / 1123 1.5	1729 4.6 / 2355 1.1
14 W	0506 4.1 / 1119 1.5	1714 4.5 / 2341 1.2		**29** TH	0551 4.5 / 1202 1.2	1802 4.7
15 TH	0542 4.4 / 1159 1.1	1750 4.9		**30** F	0031 0.9 / 0621 4.6	1238 1.1 / 1831 4.8

OCTOBER

Day	Time m	Time m		Day	Time m	Time m
1 SA ●	0105 0.8 / 0650 4.7	1311 1.0 / 1859 4.8		**16** SU ○	0034 0.4 / 0629 5.1	1254 0.6 / 1842 5.4
2 SU	0136 0.8 / 0718 4.7	1343 1.0 / 1926 4.8		**17** M	0115 0.3 / 0708 5.2	1336 0.4 / 1925 5.4
3 M	0206 0.8 / 0746 4.7	1414 1.0 / 1954 4.7		**18** TU	0156 0.3 / 0749 5.2	1418 0.5 / 2010 5.3
4 TU	0236 1.0 / 0815 4.6	1445 1.1 / 2023 4.5		**19** W	0238 0.4 / 0832 5.0	1503 0.6 / 2101 5.0
5 W	0306 1.2 / 0846 4.4	1517 1.3 / 2055 4.3		**20** TH	0321 0.8 / 0922 4.7	1551 0.9 / 2201 4.6
6 TH	0337 1.4 / 0921 4.3	1552 1.5 / 2133 4.0		**21** F	0407 1.2 / 1023 4.4	1645 1.3 / 2316 4.2
7 F	0412 1.7 / 1006 4.0	1631 1.8 / 2224 3.8		**22** SA ◐	0500 1.6 / 1146 4.2	1753 1.7
8 SA	0451 1.9 / 1110 3.8	1720 2.0 / 2349 3.6		**23** SU	0039 3.9 / 0607 2.0	1312 4.0 / 1920 1.9
9 SU ◐	0544 2.2 / 1241 3.7	1828 2.2		**24** M	0158 3.8 / 0737 2.2	1430 4.0 / 2052 1.8
10 M	0130 3.5 / 0710 2.4	1401 3.8 / 2006 2.2		**25** TU	0312 3.9 / 0907 2.1	1537 4.2 / 2200 1.6
11 TU	0249 3.6 / 0854 2.2	1506 4.0 / 2130 1.9		**26** W	0411 4.0 / 1010 1.9	1628 4.3 / 2248 1.4
12 W	0349 3.9 / 1000 1.9	1558 4.3 / 2225 1.5		**27** TH	0454 4.2 / 1057 1.7	1707 4.5 / 2328 1.2
13 TH	0436 4.2 / 1048 1.5	1642 4.6 / 2311 1.1		**28** F	0528 4.4 / 1137 1.4	1739 4.6
14 F	0515 4.6 / 1131 1.2	1723 4.9 / 2353 0.7		**29** SA	0004 1.1 / 0558 4.6	1213 1.3 / 1808 4.7
15 SA	0552 4.8 / 1212 0.8	1802 5.2		**30** SU ●	0037 1.0 / 0626 4.7	1247 1.2 / 1836 4.7
				31 M	0108 1.0 / 0654 4.8	1319 1.1 / 1904 4.7

NOVEMBER

Day	Time m	Time m		Day	Time m	Time m
1 TU	0138 1.0 / 0722 4.8	1350 1.1 / 1932 4.6		**16** W ○	0136 0.4 / 0732 5.3	1403 0.5 / 1958 5.2
2 W	0208 1.1 / 0751 4.7	1421 1.2 / 2002 4.5		**17** TH	0220 0.6 / 0818 5.1	1450 0.7 / 2050 4.9
3 TH	0238 1.2 / 0822 4.6	1454 1.3 / 2036 4.3		**18** F	0304 0.9 / 0907 4.9	1540 0.9 / 2149 4.6
4 F	0310 1.4 / 0857 4.4	1529 1.5 / 2115 4.1		**19** SA	0351 1.2 / 1005 4.6	1633 1.2 / 2256 4.2
5 SA	0344 1.6 / 0940 4.3	1609 1.7 / 2206 3.9		**20** SU	0442 1.6 / 1116 4.3	1734 1.6
6 SU	0423 1.9 / 1036 4.1	1654 2.0 / 2316 3.7		**21** M ◐	0009 4.0 / 0541 2.0	1235 4.1 / 1845 1.8
7 M ●	0513 2.1 / 1152 3.9	1757 2.0		**22** TU	0123 3.8 / 0654 2.2	1351 4.1 / 2005 1.9
8 TU	0045 3.6 / 0626 2.3	1313 4.0 / 1919 2.1		**23** W	0234 3.8 / 0816 2.2	1459 4.1 / 2117 1.8
9 W	0204 3.7 / 0801 2.2	1421 4.0 / 2042 1.9		**24** TH	0336 3.9 / 0929 2.1	1555 4.1 / 2212 1.7
10 TH	0310 3.9 / 0917 2.0	1520 4.3 / 2146 1.5		**25** F	0424 4.1 / 1024 1.9	1639 4.2 / 2257 1.5
11 F	0403 4.2 / 1014 1.6	1610 4.6 / 2238 1.2		**26** SA	0502 4.3 / 1108 1.7	1715 4.4 / 2335 1.4
12 SA	0448 4.6 / 1102 1.3	1656 4.9 / 2325 0.8		**27** SU	0535 4.5 / 1147 1.5	1748 4.5
13 SU	0529 4.9 / 1148 0.9	1740 5.2		**28** M	0010 1.3 / 0605 4.6	1224 1.4 / 1818 4.5
14 M ○	0009 0.6 / 0609 5.1	1233 0.7 / 1824 5.3		**29** TU ●	0043 1.2 / 0635 4.7	1257 1.3 / 1847 4.6
15 TU	0053 0.4 / 0653 5.3	1318 0.5 / 1910 5.3		**30** W	0115 1.2 / 0704 4.8	1330 1.2 / 1917 4.5

DECEMBER

Day	Time m	Time m		Day	Time m	Time m
1 TH	0146 1.2 / 0734 4.8	1403 1.2 / 1949 4.5		**16** F	0206 0.7 / 0806 5.2	1440 0.7 / 2039 4.9
2 F	0217 1.3 / 0806 4.7	1437 1.3 / 2024 4.4		**17** SA	0250 0.9 / 0853 5.0	1528 0.8 / 2130 4.6
3 SA	0250 1.4 / 0842 4.6	1513 1.4 / 2104 4.2		**18** SU	0334 1.2 / 0942 4.8	1616 1.1 / 2224 4.3
4 SU	0325 1.5 / 0923 4.5	1553 1.5 / 2151 4.1		**19** M	0420 1.5 / 1037 4.5	1707 1.4 / 2323 4.0
5 M	0405 1.7 / 1013 4.3	1638 1.6 / 2249 3.9		**20** TU	0510 1.8 / 1141 4.2	1802 1.7
6 TU	0452 1.9 / 1114 4.2	1732 1.8		**21** W ◐	0029 3.8 / 0606 2.0	1253 4.0 / 1905 1.9
7 W ◐	0001 3.8 / 0552 2.1	1226 4.1 / 1839 1.8		**22** TH	0139 3.7 / 0713 2.2	1405 3.9 / 2015 2.0
8 TH	0118 3.8 / 0711 2.1	1337 4.2 / 1954 1.8		**23** F	0247 3.8 / 0829 2.3	1510 3.9 / 2124 1.8
9 F	0228 4.0 / 0830 2.0	1442 4.3 / 2105 1.6		**24** SA	0345 3.9 / 0941 2.1	1605 4.0 / 2220 1.8
10 SA	0330 4.2 / 0938 1.8	1541 4.5 / 2207 1.3		**25** SU	0433 4.1 / 1037 2.0	1651 4.1 / 2306 1.7
11 SU	0423 4.5 / 1036 1.4	1634 4.8 / 2300 1.0		**26** M	0512 4.3 / 1123 1.8	1729 4.2 / 2345 1.5
12 M	0510 4.8 / 1128 1.1	1725 5.0 / 2349 0.8		**27** TU	0547 4.5 / 1202 1.6	1803 4.3
13 TU	0554 5.0 / 1217 0.9	1813 5.1		**28** W	0021 1.4 / 0618 4.6	1239 1.4 / 1835 4.4
14 W ○	0036 0.7 / 0637 5.2	1306 0.7 / 1901 5.2		**29** TH ●	0055 1.3 / 0649 4.7	1314 1.3 / 1906 4.5
15 TH	0122 0.7 / 0721 5.3	1353 0.6 / 1949 5.1		**30** F	0128 1.2 / 0720 4.8	1349 1.2 / 1939 4.5
				31 SA	0201 1.2 / 0753 4.8	1424 1.1 / 2013 4.5

Chart Datum: 2·71 metres below Ordnance Datum (Newlyn). HAT is 5·5 metres above Chart Datum.

NW Scotland

》》 **FREE** monthly updates. Register at 《 www.reedsnauticalalmanac.co.uk

41

Visitor moorings mentioned in this section are inspected annually, have pick up buoys, can take yachts <15tons, and there is no charge <7days. Refer to www.w-isles.gov.uk/harbour master.

TIDES

Standard Port STORNOWAY (←—)

Times				Height (metres)			
High Water		Low Water		MHWS	MHWN	MLWN	MLWS
0100	0700	0300	0900	4·8	3·7	2·0	0·7
1300	1900	1500	2100				
Differences East side of Outer Hebrides, N to S							
LOCH SHELL (Harris)							
−0013	0000	0000	−0017	0·0	−0·1	−0·1	0·0
EAST LOCH TARBERT (Harris)							
−0025	−0010	−0010	−0020	+0·2	0·0	+0·1	+0·1
LOCH MADDY (N Uist)							
−0044	−0014	−0016	−0030	0·0	−0·1	−0·1	0·0
LOCH CARNAN (S Uist)							
−0050	−0010	−0020	−0040	−0·3	−0·5	−0·1	−0·1
LOCH SKIPORT (S Uist)							
−0100	−0025	−0024	−0024	−0·2	−0·4	−0·3	−0·2
LOCH BOISDALE (S Uist)							
−0055	−0030	−0020	−0040	−0·7	−0·7	−0·3	−0·2
BARRA (North Bay)							
−0103	−0031	−0034	−0048	−0·6	−0·5	−0·2	−0·1
CASTLE BAY (Barra)							
−0115	−0040	−0045	−0100	−0·5	−0·6	−0·3	−0·1
BARRA HEAD (Berneray)							
−0115	−0040	−0045	−0055	−0·8	−0·7	−0·2	+0·1

SHELTER

LOCH SHELL, Lewis, **57°59'·00N 06°25'·50W**. AC 1794. HW −0437 on Dover; ML 2·7m. See 1.5. Pass S of Eilean Iuvard; beware rks to W of Is. ‡ in Tob Eishken, 2½M up loch on N shore (beware rk awash on E side of ent), or at head of loch (exposed to E winds; dries some distance). **Facilities:** ⊠/Stores at Lemreway.

SHIANT ISLANDS, Lewis, **57°53'·68N 06°21'·37W**. AC 1794, 1795. Tides as Loch Shell 1.5. Beware strong tidal streams and overfalls in Sound of Shiant. Strictly a fair weather ‡; in W winds ‡ E of Mol Mor, isthmus between Garbh Eileen (159m) and Eileen an Tighe. In E winds ‡ W of Mol Mor. No lights or facilities.

EAST LOCH TARBERT, Harris, **57°49'·98N 06°41'·07W**. AC 2905. HW −0446 on Dover; ML 3·0m; Duration 0605. See 1.5. Appr via Sound of Scalpay; beware Elliot Rk (2m) 2½ca SSW of Rubha Crago. A bridge (57°52'·80N 06°41'·73W) joins Scalpay to Harris (20m ht). Bridge lts: Centre Oc 6s; N side Iso G 4s 35m; S side Iso R 4s 35m. Eileen Glas lt ho at E end of Scalpay, Fl (3) 20s 43m 23M; W tr, R bands. In Sound of Scalpay, stream sets W from HW +3, and E from HW −3. ‡ off Tarbert WSW of Steamer pier in 2·5m. ☎(01589) 502444. **Facilities:** ⚓ 🛢 🛢 Dr, ⊠ 🛒 ✕ 🍴 ferry to Uig. Alternatively Scalpay N Hbr gives good shelter. Beware rk 5ca off Aird an Aiseig, E side of ent. SHM buoy marks wk off Coddem; 5ca E of the is a rk, depth 1·1m. Ldg Lt Dir Iso WRG 4s 9m 4M. Both piers have 2FG (vert) lts; ‡ 7ca N, in 3m. **Facilities:** ⚓ ⊠ 🛒 Ferry to Harris.

LOCH STOCKINISH, Harris. AC 1757. Entr via Loch Chlual marked by metal Bn Fl R 2s at 57°48'·49N 06°48'·79W and SCM Q(6)+L Fl 15s atop B/Y perch at 57°48'·56N 06°48'·81W; pier landing and fish farms in loch.

LOCH RODEL, Harris. AC 2802. 3⚓s at **57°44'·2N 06°57'·4W** in Poll an Tigh-mhàil; enter from SW past jetties. No lts.

SOUND OF HARRIS, **57°43'N 06°58'W**. Passages through this difficult Sound are detailed in the *W Coast of Scotland Pilot*. The Stanton and Outer Stromay Chans off the Harris shore are the most feasible for yachts. AC 2802 shows the ferry routes from Leverburgh to Berneray.

LOCH MADDY, North Uist, **57°35'·98N 07°06'·07W**. AC 2825. HW −0500 on Dover. See 1.5. With strong wind against tide there can be bad seas off ent. Appr clear, but from S beware submerged rk ½ca N of Leacnam Madadh. Lts: Weaver's Pt Fl 3s 21m 7M; Glas Eilean Mor Fl (2) G 4s 8m 5M; Rubna Nam Pleac Fl R 4s 7m 5M. Inside loch: Ruigh Liath QG 6m 5M; Vallaquie Is Dir Fl (3) WRG 8s. Ferry pier ldg lts 298°: front 2FG(vert) 4M; rear Oc G 8s 10m 4M, vis 284°-304°. Pontoon lit Fl R 3s. 2⚓s Bagh Aird nam Madadh;

2 ⚓s W of and 4 ⚓s SW of ferry pier ☎(01870) 602425; 2⚓s E of Oronsay. ‡s: clear S of ferry pier; NE of Vallaquie Is; Charles Hbr; Oronsay (‡ not advised due to moorings), tidal berth on private pier; Sponish Hbr; Loch Portain. VHF Ch **12** 16. Port Manager ☎(01876) 5003337(day), 5003226(night). **Facilities:** Lochmaddy, 26🛏 2♥ on lit pontoon (Fl R 3s 2M) £2/night inc ⚡, ⚓ 🛢 🛢 🍴 ⊠ Ⓑ 🛒; Loch Portain ⊠ Shop, Bus to Benbecula.

LOCH EPORT, North Uist, **57°33'·45N 07°08'·12W**. AC 2825, but not the head of loch. Tides, approx as L Maddy; 3kn sp stream. On the S side of ent are rks, some drying. The ent proper is clean but very narrow (about 100m) for 5ca, then widens. Follow the charted clearing line 082°. Best ‡s are: Bàgh a' Bhiorain (S of chan; line up cairn and Bu boulder on 129°); and Acairseid Lee (N bank) E or W of Deer Is. ⊠ 🛒 ✕ 🍴 at Clachan, head of loch.

KALLIN, Grimsay. **57°28'·9N 07°12'·2W**. AC 2904. 1⚓ in NE of hbr. 3 chan lt buoys and 2 FR (vert) on hbr bkwtr. ☎(01870) 602425.

LOCH CARNAN, South Uist, **57°22'·03N 07°16'·39W**. AC 2825. Tides, see 1.5. SWM buoy, L Fl 10s, at 57°22'·30N 07°11'·57W is almost 2M E of app chan proper, marked by Nos 1 and 2 buoys, Fl G 2·5s and Fl R 2s, at 57°22'·45N 07°14'·90W. Round No 3 PHM buoy, Fl R 5s, between Gasay and Taigh Iamain, then pick up ldg lts 222° to Sandwick Quay; front Fl R 2s, rear Iso R 10s, both 5M, W ◇s on posts. Power stn and 2 chys are conspic close to SE of quay. ☎(01870) 602425 for permission to berth on the quay (MoD property). ‡ or 2⚓s about 2ca WNW of the quay in deep water. ☎(01870) 610238. The passage S of Gasay is unmarked and needs careful pilotage.

LOCH SKIPPORT, South Uist, **57°19'·98N 07°13'·67W**. AC 2904, 2825. HW −0602 on Dover; see 1.5. Easy ent 3M NNE of Hecla (604m). No lights, but 2¼M SSE is Usinish lt ho Fl WR 20s 54m 19/15M. ‡s at: Wizard Pool in 7m; beware Float Rk, dries 1·2m; on N side of Caolas Mor in 7m; Bagh Charmaig in 5m. Linne Arm has narrow ent, many fish farms and poor holding. No facilities.

LOCH EYNORT, South Uist, **57°13'·13N 07°16'·87W**. AC 2825. Tides: interpolate between Lochs Skipport and Boisdale, see 1.5. ‡s in the outer loch at Cearcdal Bay and on the N side just before the narrows are exposed to the E. The passage to Upper L Eynort is very narrow and streams reach 5-7kn; best not attempted unless local fishermen offer guidance. Good ‡ inside at Bàgh Lathach.

LOCH BOISDALE, South Uist, **57°08'·78N 07°16'·07W**. AC 2770. HW −0455 on Dover; ML 2·4m; Duration 0600. See 1.5. Good shelter except in SE gales when swell runs right up the 2M loch. From N, approach between Rubha na Cruibe and Calvay Is leading line 245°: Holisgeir (0·3m) on with pier (ru). From S beware Clan Ewan Rk, which dries 1·2m, and McKenzie Rk (2·4m), marked by PHM lt buoy Fl (3) R 15s. A new harbour with marina is formed by a causeway from Rubha Bhuailt to Gasay, with two b'waters (G 6s & Fl R 6s with traffic sigs) and an entrance to the N with access from the channel to Boisdale Hbr which lies N of Gasay Is. Off E end beware rock and further development. ‡ off pier in approx 4m, or SW of Gasay Is in approx 9m. 4⚓s NE of pier; ☎(01870) 602425. There are fish cages W of Rubha Bhuailt. Lts: Dir Lt 292·5° WRG 4s 4m 5M, Ro-Ro jetty hd Iso RG 4s 8m 2M; close SE, Eilean Dubh Fl (2) R 5s. E Calvay Is Fl (2) WRG 10s 16m 7M. Gasay Is Fl WR 5s 10m 7M, opposite shore, Fl G 6s 3m 3M; See 1.3. ☎(0187) 700288. **Facilities:** ⚓ (on pier), 🛢 ⊠ ✕ 🍴. Ferry to mainland.

ACAIRSEID MHÓR, Eriskay, ⊕ **57°03'·78N 07°16'·35W**. AC 2770. Tides approx as for North Bay (Barra), see 1.5. Ben Scrien (183m) is a conspicous, pointed peak N of the harbour. Leading lts 285°, both Oc R 6s 9/10m 4M, W △ ▽ on orange posts, lead for 0·5M from the waypoint between two drying rocks into the outer loch. A SHM buoy, Fl G 6s, marks a rock drying 3m. Possible 🛏 on pontoon; 2⚓s (perhaps submerged at HW) are at 57°03'·95N 07°17'·40W on S side of inner loch, opp pier, 2 FG (vert). ☎(01870) 602425. ⊠ 🛒 ✕ 🍴 at Haun, 1·5M at N end of island.

NORTH BAY, Barra, **57°00'·11N 07°24'·67W**. AC 2770. Tides see 1.5. Well marked approach to inlet sheltered from both S and W winds. There are ⚓s in N part of Bay Hirivagh, ‡ 1ca WNW of Black Island or temporarily 🛏 on the quay in 4·5m. WPT 56°58'·68N 07°20'·31W is about 200m NE of Curachan ECM buoy, Q (3) 10s, and in the white sector (304°-306°) of Ardveenish Dir ☆ 305°, Oc WRG 3s, 2·5M to the WNW. ⚓ 🛒 🍴 bus to Castlebay.

CASTLE BAY, Barra, **56°56´·78N 07°29´·67W**. AC 2769. HW –0525 on Dover; ML 2·3m; Duration 0600. See 1.5. Very good shelter & holding. Best ⚓ is in approx 8m NW of Kiessimul Castle; NE of castle are rocks. About 20🅰s lie to W of the pier; they may be encroaching on the recommended ⚓ ☎(01870) 602425. Alternatively ⚓ in Vatersay Bay in approx 9m. W end of Vatersay Sound is closed by a causeway. Beware rocks NNW of Sgeir Dubh a conspic W/G tower, Q(3)G 6s 6m 5M, which leads 283° in transit with Sgeir Liath bn. Channel Rock, 2ca to the South, is marked by Fl WR 6s 4m 6/4M. Close-in leading lts 295°, both FBu 6M on W framework towers: front 9m Or △ on Rubha Glas; rear 457m from front, 15m Or ▽, vis: 15° and 8° respectively either side of ldg line. ☎(01871) 810306.
Facilities: 🔱 ⛴ 🔥 ✉ 🛒 ✕ 🏪. Ferry to mainland.

ISLANDS WEST OF THE OUTER HEBRIDES (N TO S)

TIDES
Standard Port STORNOWAY (←—)

Times				Height (metres)			
High Water		Low Water		MHWS	MHWN	MLWN	MLWS
0100	0700	0300	0900	4·8	3·7	2·0	0·7
1300	1900	1500	2100				
Differences West side of Outer Hebrides, N to S							
SCOLPAIG (W North Uist)							
–0033	–0033	–0040	–0040	–1·0	–0·9	–0·5	0·0
BALIVANICH (W Benbecula)							
–0103	–0017	–0031	–0045	–0·7	–0·6	–0·5	–0·2
FLANNAN ISLES							
–0026	–0016	–0016	–0026	–0·9	–0·7	–0·6	–0·2
VILLAGE BAY (St Kilda)							
–0040	–0040	–0045	–0045	–1·4	–1·1	–0·8	–0·3
ROCKALL							
–0055	–0055	–0105	–0105	–1·8	–1·5	–0·9	–0·2
SHILLAY (Monach Islands)							
–0103	–0043	–0047	–0107	–0·6	–0·7	–0·7	–0·3

SHELTER
FLANNAN ISLES, Western Isles, centred on **58°17´·28N 07°35´·27W** (Eilean Mór). AC 2524, 2721. Tides, as above. Uninhabited group of several rky islets, 18M WNW of Gallan Head (Lewis). The main islet is Eilean Mór where landing can be made on SW side in suitable conditions. Lt ho, Fl (2) 30s 101m 20M, is a 23m high W tr on NE tip of Eilean Mór; the lt is obscured by islets to the W which are up to 57m high. No recommended ⚓s and the few charted depths are by lead-line surveys.

ST KILDA, Western Isles, **57°48´·28N 08°33´·07W**. AC 2721, 2524. Tides at Village Bay, Hirta: HW –0510 on Dover; ML 1·9m; Duration 0615; see above. A group of four isles and three stacks, the main island is Hirta. The facility is now manned by a civilian company, Qinetiq ☎(01870) 604443, based at South Uist. Hirta is owned by National Trust for Scotland, who employ a Seasonal Warden, ☎01870 604628. ⚓ in Village Bay, SE-facing, in approx 5m about 1·5ca off the pier. Ldg lts 270°, both Oc 5s 26/38m 3M. If wind is between NE and SSW big swells enter the bay; good holding, but untenable if winds strong. Levenish Is (55m) is 1·5M E of Hirta with offlying rks. Courtesy call to *Kilda Radio* VHF Ch 16 **12** 73 (HJ) before landing; or Qinetic ☎(01870) 604406 (HO), 604612 (OT). Alternative ⚓ at Glen Bay on N side is only safe in S & E winds. Facilities: 🔱 from wells near landings.

ROCKALL, 57°35´·7N 13°41´·2W. AC 1128, 2524. Tides, as above. A 19m high granite rock, 200M W of N Uist. Best access by helicopter. Lt, Fl 15s 13M, is often extinguished for long periods due to weather damage. Helen's Reef, 1·4m, on which the sea breaks is 2M ENE.

MONACH ISLANDS (Heisker Is), centred on **57°31´·28N 07°38´·07W**. AC 2721, 2722. Tides, see 1.5 Shillay. The group lies 5M SW of N Uist and 8M WNW of Benbecula. The 5 main islands (W-E) are Shillay, Ceann Iar, Shivinish, Ceann Ear and Stockay; all uninhabited. Many rky offliers from NW through N to SE of the group. On Shillay there is a conspic red brick lt ho, Fl (2) 15s. ⚓s at: E of lt ho; Croic Hbr, bay N of Shivinish; and S Hbr on W side of Shivinish.

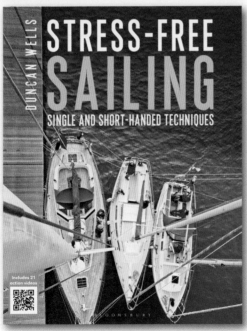
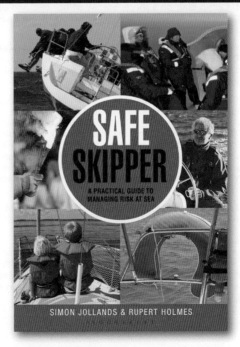

1.6 KINLOCHBERVIE

Highland 58°27'·26N 05°02'·78W ✴✴✴❋⚓⚓⚓⭐⭐

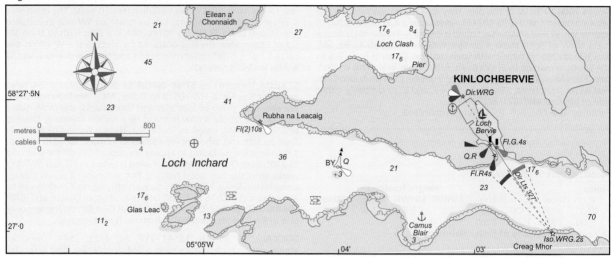

CHARTS AC 1954, 1785, 2503; Imray C67

TIDES –0400 Dover; ML 2·7; Duration 0610

Standard Port ULLAPOOL (→)

Times				Height (metres)			
High Water		Low Water		MHWS	MHWN	MLWN	MLWS
0000	0600	0300	0900	5·2	3·9	2·1	0·7
1200	1800	1500	2100				
Differences LOCH BERVIE							
+0017	+0020	+0015	+0015	–0·4	–0·2	–0·1	+0·1

SHELTER Very good in Kinlochbervie Hbr off the N shore of Loch Inchard. A useful passage port, only 14.5 track miles S of Cape Wrath. It is an active FV port, but yachts ⌒ on pontoon (contact HM for details); NE side ⚓ is shoal/foul. If full, ⚓ at Loch Clash, open to W, but sheltered in winds n through SE; landing jetty in 2·7m. Other ⚓s at: Camus Blair on S shore, 5ca SW of hbr ent, and up the loch at L Sheigra, Achriesgill Bay and 5ca short of the head of the loch.

NAVIGATION WPT 58°27'·34N 05°05'·08W (at mouth of Loch Inchard), 100°/1·3M to hbr ent. The sides of the loch are clean, but keep to N side of Loch Inchard to clear Bodha Ceann na Saile NCM and rk (3m depth) almost in mid-chan.

LIGHTS AND MARKS From offshore in good vis Ceann Garbh, a conspic mountain 900m (6M inland), leads 110° toward ent of Loch Inchard. Rubha na Leacaig, Fl (2) 10s 30m 8M, marks N side of loch ent. Dir ☆ WRG (H24) 15m 16M, Y framework tr (floodlit) leads 327° into hbr; see 1.3 for vis sectors. The 25m wide ent chan (and hbr) is dredged 4m and marked by 2 PHM poles, Fl R 4s and QR, and by a SHM pole, Fl G 4s. On S shore of loch Creag Mhòr, Dir Oc lt WRG 2.8s 16m 9M, is aligned 147°/327° with hbr ent chan; see 1.3.

COMMUNICATIONS (Code 01971) CGOC (01851) 702013; ☎ (0141) 887 9369 (H24); Police 101; Dr 502002. HM 521235, mob 07901 514350.

VHF Ch **14** 16 HX. Ch 06 is used by FVs in the Minches.

FACILITIES harbours@highland.gov.uk ⌒ (pontoon) £1.50<10m for 48hrs to E side of hbr; 8 Ⓥ in new development with ⛽ and ⚓ to W side. ⚓ ⛽ at FV quay, 🏪🛒⛽🔧✉️🛏️🍴✕🅿 (Mission & Hbr Office), 🗑. In summer, bus to Inverness.

ANCHORAGES & HBRS BETWEEN KINLOCHBERVIE & ULLAPOOL

LOCH LAXFORD Highland, **58°24'·78N 05°07'·18W**. AC 2503. HW –0410 on Dover. ML 2·7m. See 1.6. Ent between Rubha Ruadh and Ardmore Pt, 1M ENE, clearly identified by 3 isolated mountains (N-S) Ceann Garbh, Ben Arkle and Ben Stack. The many ⚓s in the loch include: Loch a'Chadh-fi, on N/NE sides of islet (John Ridgeway's Adventure School on Pt on W side of narrows has moorings); Bagh nah-Airde Beag, next bay to E, (beware rk 5ca off SE shore which covers at MHWS); Weaver's Bay on SW shore, 3M from ent (beware drying rk off NW Pt of ent); Bagh na Fionndalach Mor on SW shore (4-6m); Fanagmore Bay on SW shore (beware head of bay foul with old moorings). Beware many fish farming cages. Facilities: none, nearest stores at Scourie (5M).

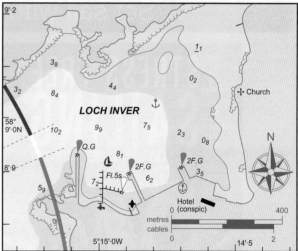

LOCH INVER Highland, **58°08'·98N 05°15'·08W**. AC 2504. HW –0433 on Dover; ML 3·0m. See 1.6. Good shelter in all weathers at head of loch in busy fishing hbr on S side. Appr N or S of Soyea Is, Fl (2) 10s 34m 6M; beware rock drying 1·7m about 50m off Kirkaig Point (S side of ent). Glas Leac, a small islet 7ca WSW of hbr, may be passed on either side. ⚡, Fl WRG 3s, has 3 different approaches (see 1.3) covering the chans N and S of Soyea Is and into the hbr. The church, hotel (S side) and white ho (N side) are all conspic. A 22-berth marina is between the breakwater (QG) and the first FV pier. Or, in W'ly gales, ⚓ in the lee of bkwtr in about 8m; or where HM directs. Other ⚓s on S shore of Loch Inver. VHF Ch 12 16. HM ☎(01571) 844247; mob 07958 734610. Health Centre 01571 844452. Facilities: ⚓ 🏪🛏️🖥️🅿 (Leisure Centre), 🛒🍴✉️⛽.

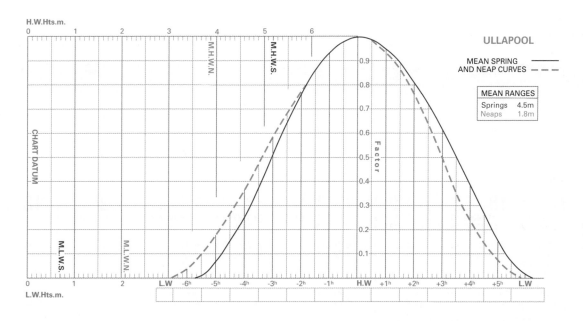

ULLAPOOL

| | MEAN SPRING | —— |
| | AND NEAP CURVES | --- |

MEAN RANGES	
Springs	4·5m
Neaps	1·8m

1.7 ULLAPOOL

Highland **57°53′·70N 05°09′·38W** ✿✿✿✿♤♤♧♧

CHARTS AC 1794, 2500, 2501, 2509; Imray C67

TIDES –0415 Dover; ML 3·0; Duration 0610

Standard Port ULLAPOOL (→)

Times				Height (metres)			
High Water		Low Water		MHWS	MHWN	MLWN	MLWS
0000	0600	0300	0900	5·2	3·9	2·1	0·7
1200	1800	1500	2100				
Differences LOCH LAXFORD							
+0015	+0015	+0005	+0005	–0·3	–0·4	–0·2	0·0
BADCALL BAY							
+0005	+0005	+0005	+0005	–0·7	–0·5	–0·5	+0·2
LOCH NEDD							
0000	0000	0000	0000	–0·3	–0·2	–0·2	0·0
LOCH INVER							
–0005	–0005	–0005	–0005	–0·2	0·0	0·0	+0·1
SUMMER ISLES (Tanera Mor)							
–0005	–0005	–0010	–0010	–0·1	+0·1	0·0	+0·1
LOCH EWE (Mellon Charles, 57°51′N 05°38′W)							
–0005	–0010	–0005	–0005	–0·1	–0·1	–0·1	+0·1
LOCH GAIRLOCH							
–0012	–0011	–0011	–0011	–0·2	+0·1	–0·2	+0·2

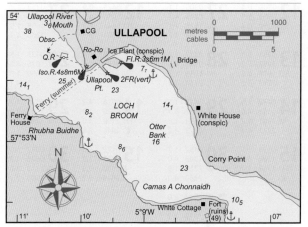

SHELTER A commercial port but yachts welcome. Good ⚓ E of pier, 8⚓ or possible ⌴ on pier (consult HM). Convenient landing inside pier, which may be busy with tourist vessels. Loch Kanaird (N of ent to Loch Broom) has good ⚓ E of Isle Martin. Possible ⚓s 6ca S of Ullapool Pt, and beyond the narrows 3ca ESE of W cottage. The upper loch is squally in strong winds.

NAVIGATION WPT L Broom ent 57°55′·78N 05°15′·08W, 129°/3.5M to Ullapool Pt lt. N of Ullapool Pt extensive drying flats off the mouth of Ullapool R are marked by QR buoy. Beware fish pens and unlit buoys SE of narrows off W shore.

LIGHTS AND MARKS Rhubha Cadail, N of L. Broom ent, Fl WRG 6s 11m 9/6M. Cailleach Hd, W of ent, Fl (2) 12s 60m 9M. Ullapool Pt Iso R 4s 8m 6M; grey mast, vis 258°-108°.

COMMUNICATIONS (Code 01854) CG (non-emergency) 613076; Police 101; Dr Dr 08454 242424; Dentist 613289 or 612660; ⊖ (0141) 887 9369. HM 612724, mob 07734 004843.

Ullapool Harbour Ch 14 16 (H24).

FACILITIES Pier ⚓ ♠ ♨; **Loch Broom SC Services:** ♠ ✎ & GRP repairs Mobile Marine Services ☎633719, mob 07866 516067, ☏ Ⓔ ✕ A.Morgan ☎666383; **Town** ☏ ☏ (0700-2100), @ at Captains Cabin, Library and Ceilidh Place Hotel, all domestic facilities, ☔ at swimming pool, ☕ ✕ ⌂ ⇌ (bus to Garve). Daily buses to Inverness (✈)(no Sunday bus service. **Ferries:** Stornoway; 2-3/day; 2¾ Hrs; Calmac (www.calmac.co.uk).

ADJACENT ANCHORAGES

LOCH KANAIRD, 57°56′·60N 05°12′·20W. AC 2500. HW –0425 Dover; See 1.7; streams are weak and irreg. Situated E of the entrance to Loch Broom, S of the Summer Is and protected by Isle Martin. Good ⚓ (tripping line recommended) ENE of Sgeir Mhor or E of Isle Martin, N of Rubha Beag (also ⌴ on pontoon). Beware cables and marine farms. Ent from S (1ca wide) between two rocky spits, leading line E extremity of Isle Martin in transit with dark streak on cliff behind brg 000°. Ent from N, deep and clear of dangers. Facilities: Ardmair Boat Centre P. Fraser ☎(01854) 612054, ♠ ⚓ ☔ some repairs. Isle Martin, Landing permitted (voluntary donation to Trust ☎(01854) 612531).

STANDARD TIME (UT)
For Summer Time add ONE hour in **non-shaded** areas

ULLAPOOL LAT 57°54'N LONG 5°09'W
TIMES AND HEIGHTS OF HIGH AND LOW WATERS

Dates in red are SPRINGS
Dates in blue are NEAPS

YEAR **2016**

JANUARY

Day	Time m	Time m	Time m	Time m
1 F	0516 2.0	1119 4.3	1759 2.0	
2 SA	0014 4.1	0606 2.2	1227 4.1	1855 2.2
3 SU	0125 4.0	0709 2.4	1346 4.0	2005 2.3
4 M	0236 4.0	0826 2.5	1459 4.0	2118 2.2
5 TU	0339 4.1	0940 2.4	1600 4.2	2218 2.1
6 W	0430 4.4	1037 2.1	1649 4.3	2306 1.8
7 TH	0511 4.6	1124 1.9	1730 4.5	2347 1.6
8 F	0548 4.8	1206 1.6	1807 4.7	
9 SA	0026 1.4	0623 5.1	1246 1.3	1842 4.9
10 SU ●	0105 1.2	0658 5.3	1325 1.1	1919 5.1
11 M	0143 1.0	0734 5.4	1405 0.9	1958 5.1
12 TU	0221 1.0	0813 5.5	1445 0.8	2039 5.1
13 W	0301 1.0	0855 5.4	1526 0.8	2123 5.0
14 TH	0342 1.1	0941 5.3	1610 1.0	2213 4.8
15 F	0428 1.3	1033 5.1	1658 1.2	2310 4.6
16 SA ◐	0519 1.5	1134 4.8	1752 1.4	
17 SU	0018 4.4	0619 1.8	1246 4.6	1855 1.7
18 M	0133 4.3	0733 2.0	1400 4.5	2010 1.8
19 TU	0250 4.3	0856 2.0	1516 4.5	2130 1.8
20 W	0402 4.5	1014 1.8	1625 4.6	2240 1.7
21 TH	0500 4.7	1117 1.6	1721 4.8	2335 1.5
22 F	0547 5.0	1209 1.3	1808 4.9	
23 SA	0022 1.3	0627 5.2	1255 1.1	1849 5.1
24 SU ○	0105 1.1	0704 5.3	1336 0.9	1926 5.1
25 M	0143 1.0	0738 5.3	1413 0.9	2001 5.1
26 TU	0219 1.0	0811 5.3	1449 1.0	2035 5.0
27 W	0254 1.1	0842 5.1	1523 1.0	2108 4.8
28 TH	0328 1.2	0914 5.0	1558 1.2	2143 4.7
29 F	0402 1.4	0947 4.7	1633 1.5	2220 4.4
30 SA	0438 1.7	1024 4.5	1711 1.7	2306 4.2
31 SU	0518 2.0	1110 4.2	1754 2.0	

FEBRUARY

Day	Time m	Time m	Time m	Time m
1 M ◐	0009 4.0	0605 2.2	1220 4.0	1848 2.2
2 TU	0128 3.9	0710 2.4	1350 3.9	2005 2.3
3 W	0243 3.9	0837 2.5	1511 3.9	2131 2.3
4 TH	0350 4.1	0958 2.3	1618 4.1	2235 2.0
5 F	0442 4.4	1057 2.0	1707 4.3	2324 1.7
6 SA	0525 4.7	1144 1.6	1748 4.6	
7 SU	0006 1.4	0602 5.0	1227 1.2	1826 4.9
8 M ●	0047 1.1	0639 5.3	1308 0.9	1903 5.2
9 TU	0126 0.8	0717 5.5	1349 0.6	1941 5.3
10 W	0206 0.6	0756 5.7	1429 0.4	2021 5.4
11 TH	0245 0.6	0837 5.7	1509 0.4	2103 5.3
12 F	0326 0.7	0922 5.5	1551 0.6	2149 5.0
13 SA	0410 0.9	1011 5.2	1636 0.9	2241 4.7
14 SU	0457 1.2	1110 4.9	1725 1.3	2346 4.4
15 M ◐	0553 1.6	1221 4.5	1824 1.7	
16 TU	0104 4.2	0704 1.9	1341 4.3	1939 2.0
17 W	0229 4.2	0836 2.1	1505 4.2	2111 2.0
18 TH	0350 4.3	1005 1.9	1619 4.3	2230 1.9
19 F	0451 4.5	1110 1.6	1715 4.5	2326 1.6
20 SA	0538 4.7	1200 1.3	1759 4.7	
21 SU	0011 1.4	0615 5.0	1242 1.1	1835 4.9
22 M ○	0050 1.1	0648 5.1	1319 0.9	1907 5.0
23 TU	0126 1.0	0718 5.2	1353 0.8	1938 5.0
24 W	0159 0.9	0747 5.2	1425 0.9	2007 5.0
25 TH	0230 0.9	0815 5.1	1456 0.9	2037 4.9
26 F	0301 1.0	0843 5.0	1526 1.0	2107 4.8
27 SA	0332 1.2	0913 4.8	1557 1.2	2140 4.6
28 SU	0405 1.4	0947 4.6	1631 1.5	2218 4.3
29 M	0441 1.7	1026 4.3	1708 1.8	2307 4.1

MARCH

Day	Time m	Time m	Time m	Time m
1 TU ◐	0522 2.0	1118 4.0	1753 2.1	
2 W	0019 3.9	0615 2.2	1246 3.8	1857 2.3
3 TH	0147 3.8	0734 2.4	1423 3.8	2035 2.4
4 F	0304 3.9	0914 2.3	1542 3.9	2201 2.1
5 SA	0407 4.2	1027 1.9	1641 4.2	2258 1.8
6 SU	0456 4.5	1119 1.5	1725 4.6	2343 1.4
7 M	0537 4.9	1204 1.0	1804 4.9	
8 TU	0025 1.0	0616 5.3	1247 0.6	1842 5.2
9 W ●	0106 0.6	0655 5.6	1327 0.3	1920 5.4
10 TH	0146 0.4	0735 5.8	1408 0.1	2000 5.5
11 F	0226 0.3	0817 5.7	1449 0.2	2041 5.4
12 SA	0308 0.4	0902 5.5	1530 0.4	2126 5.1
13 SU	0351 0.7	0952 5.2	1614 0.8	2217 4.8
14 M	0438 1.0	1052 4.8	1701 1.2	2321 4.4
15 TU ◐	0533 1.5	1206 4.4	1757 1.7	
16 W	0041 4.2	0643 1.8	1327 4.1	1912 2.1
17 TH	0209 4.0	0819 2.0	1453 4.0	2051 2.2
18 F	0333 4.1	0952 1.9	1607 4.1	2214 2.0
19 SA	0435 4.3	1055 1.6	1700 4.3	2309 1.7
20 SU	0520 4.5	1141 1.3	1741 4.6	2352 1.4
21 M	0556 4.7	1221 1.1	1815 4.7	
22 TU	0029 1.2	0627 4.9	1256 0.9	1844 4.9
23 W ○	0104 1.0	0655 5.0	1328 0.8	1913 5.0
24 TH	0135 0.9	0722 5.0	1358 0.8	1940 5.0
25 F	0205 0.9	0749 5.0	1427 0.8	2008 4.9
26 SA	0235 0.9	0816 4.9	1456 0.9	2037 4.8
27 SU	0305 1.1	0846 4.7	1526 1.1	2108 4.7
28 M	0337 1.2	0919 4.5	1558 1.3	2144 4.4
29 TU	0412 1.5	0958 4.3	1631 1.6	2228 4.2
30 W	0452 1.7	1048 4.0	1715 1.9	2330 4.0
31 TH ◐	0542 2.0	1206 3.8	1812 2.2	

APRIL

Day	Time m	Time m	Time m	Time m
1 F	0058 3.9	0652 2.2	1344 3.7	1943 2.3
2 SA	0219 3.9	0830 2.1	1504 3.9	2122 2.1
3 SU	0327 4.1	0952 1.8	1608 4.2	2227 1.7
4 M	0422 4.5	1049 1.4	1657 4.5	2316 1.3
5 TU	0508 4.9	1137 0.9	1739 4.9	
6 W	0000 0.9	0550 5.3	1221 0.5	1818 5.2
7 TH ●	0043 0.5	0631 5.6	1304 0.2	1858 5.5
8 F	0125 0.3	0714 5.7	1345 0.1	1938 5.5
9 SA	0207 0.2	0758 5.6	1427 0.1	2020 5.4
10 SU	0250 0.3	0845 5.4	1509 0.4	2106 5.2
11 M	0335 0.6	0938 5.1	1553 0.8	2157 4.8
12 TU	0423 0.9	1040 4.6	1641 1.2	2301 4.5
13 W	0518 1.4	1152 4.3	1735 1.7	
14 TH ◐	0018 4.2	0626 1.7	1309 4.0	1846 2.0
15 F	0142 4.0	0754 1.9	1430 3.9	2019 2.2
16 SA	0304 4.0	0922 1.8	1542 4.0	2143 2.0
17 SU	0407 4.2	1025 1.6	1635 4.2	2240 1.8
18 M	0453 4.3	1112 1.4	1715 4.4	2325 1.5
19 TU	0530 4.5	1152 1.2	1749 4.6	
20 W	0003 1.3	0601 4.7	1227 1.0	1819 4.7
21 TH	0037 1.1	0630 4.8	1259 0.9	1847 4.9
22 F ○	0109 1.0	0658 4.8	1330 0.9	1915 4.9
23 SA	0140 0.9	0725 4.8	1359 1.0	1943 4.9
24 SU	0211 1.0	0754 4.7	1429 1.0	2012 4.8
25 M	0242 1.0	0825 4.6	1459 1.1	2044 4.7
26 TU	0315 1.1	0900 4.5	1532 1.3	2121 4.5
27 W	0350 1.3	0942 4.3	1608 1.5	2206 4.3
28 TH	0431 1.5	1035 4.0	1650 1.8	2305 4.1
29 F	0521 1.7	1147 3.9	1746 2.0	
30 SA ◐	0022 4.0	0626 1.9	1312 3.8	1906 2.1

Chart Datum: 2·75 metres below Ordnance Datum (Newlyn). HAT is 5·9 metres above Chart Datum.

》》 FREE monthly updates. Register at 《《
www.reedsnauticalalmanac.co.uk

STANDARD TIME (UT)
For Summer Time add ONE hour in **non-shaded areas**

ULLAPOOL LAT 57°54'N LONG 5°09'W
TIMES AND HEIGHTS OF HIGH AND LOW WATERS

Dates in red are **SPRINGS**
Dates in blue are NEAPS

YEAR 2016

NW Scotland

MAY

Day	Time	m	Day	Time	m
1 SU	0140	4.0	**16** M	0326	4.0
	0751	1.9		0942	1.7
	1428	3.9		1558	4.0
	2040	2.0		2159	1.9
2 M	0248	4.2	**17** TU	0417	4.1
	0913	1.6		1034	1.6
	1534	4.2		1642	4.2
	2150	1.7		2249	1.7
3 TU	0348	4.5	**18** W	0458	4.3
	1015	1.3		1117	1.4
	1627	4.5		1719	4.4
	2245	1.3		2331	1.5
4 W	0439	4.8	**19** TH	0534	4.4
	1107	0.9		1155	1.2
	1713	4.9		1752	4.6
	2334	0.9			
5 TH	0526	5.1	**20** F	0008	1.3
	1155	0.5		0605	4.5
	1756	5.2		1230	1.1
				1822	4.7
6 F ●	0019	0.6	**21** SA ○	0043	1.2
	0610	5.4		0635	4.6
	1240	0.3		1302	1.0
	1837	5.4		1852	4.8
7 SA	0105	0.4	**22** SU	0116	1.1
	0656	5.5		0706	4.6
	1324	0.2		1334	1.0
	1919	5.4		1922	4.9
8 SU	0150	0.3	**23** M	0149	1.0
	0742	5.4		0737	4.6
	1407	0.3		1406	1.1
	2003	5.3		1953	4.8
9 M	0235	0.4	**24** TU	0223	1.0
	0832	5.2		0811	4.6
	1451	0.5		1438	1.1
	2050	5.1		2027	4.8
10 TU	0321	0.6	**25** W	0258	1.1
	0926	4.9		0849	4.5
	1536	0.9		1513	1.2
	2141	4.8		2106	4.7
11 W	0410	0.9	**26** TH	0335	1.2
	1026	4.6		0933	4.3
	1623	1.2		1551	1.4
	2241	4.5		2152	4.5
12 TH	0504	1.2	**27** F	0418	1.3
	1131	4.2		1025	4.2
	1715	1.6		1635	1.6
	2350	4.2		2247	4.4
13 F ◐	0605	1.6	**28** SA	0507	1.5
	1239	4.0		1129	4.1
	1818	2.0		1729	1.8
				2354	4.2
14 SA	0104	4.0	**29** SU ○	0606	1.6
	0717	1.8		1242	4.0
	1352	3.9		1839	1.9
	1934	2.1			
15 SU	0220	4.0	**30** M	0106	4.2
	0835	1.8		0718	1.6
	1501	3.9		1354	4.0
	2055	2.1		1959	1.9
			31 TU	0214	4.3
				0834	1.5
				1500	4.2
				2113	1.7

JUNE

Day	Time	m	Day	Time	m
1 W	0316	4.5	**16** TH	0423	4.1
	0941	1.3		1038	1.7
	1559	4.5		1646	4.3
	2215	1.4		2256	1.8
2 TH	0413	4.7	**17** F	0505	4.2
	1039	1.0		1122	1.5
	1650	4.7		1724	4.4
	2310	1.1		2339	1.6
3 F	0506	5.0	**18** SA	0542	4.3
	1132	0.8		1201	1.4
	1737	5.0		1759	4.6
4 SA	0000	0.8	**19** SU	0017	1.4
	0555	5.2		0616	4.5
	1221	0.6		1237	1.2
	1821	5.2		1831	4.8
5 SU ●	0049	0.6	**20** M ○	0055	1.2
	0644	5.2		0649	4.6
	1307	0.5		1312	1.1
	1905	5.3		1903	4.9
6 M	0136	0.5	**21** TU	0131	1.1
	0732	5.2		0723	4.6
	1352	0.6		1347	1.1
	1950	5.3		1937	4.9
7 TU	0223	0.5	**22** W	0207	1.0
	0821	5.1		0759	4.7
	1436	0.7		1422	1.1
	2035	5.1		2013	4.9
8 W	0309	0.6	**23** TH	0244	1.0
	0911	4.9		0838	4.6
	1520	0.9		1459	1.1
	2123	4.9		2053	4.9
9 TH	0356	0.9	**24** F	0323	1.0
	1003	4.6		0921	4.6
	1605	1.2		1538	1.2
	2214	4.6		2137	4.8
10 F	0444	1.1	**25** SA	0405	1.1
	1058	4.3		1010	4.4
	1652	1.5		1622	1.4
	2310	4.4		2228	4.7
11 SA	0535	1.4	**26** SU	0452	1.2
	1157	4.1		1107	4.3
	1743	1.8		1712	1.5
				2328	4.5
12 SU ◐	0013	4.1	**27** M ◐	0545	1.3
	0631	1.7		1212	4.2
	1300	3.9		1812	1.7
	1843	2.0			
13 M	0122	4.0	**28** TU	0035	4.4
	0736	1.8		0647	1.5
	1406	3.9		1322	4.2
	1953	2.1		1923	1.8
14 TU	0231	3.9	**29** W	0144	4.4
	0844	1.9		0758	1.5
	1509	3.9		1430	4.2
	2105	2.1		2039	1.7
15 W	0333	4.0	**30** TH	0251	4.4
	0947	1.8		0910	1.5
	1602	4.1		1535	4.4
	2206	2.0		2150	1.6

JULY

Day	Time	m	Day	Time	m
1 F	0356	4.6	**16** SA	0436	4.0
	1017	1.3		1049	1.8
	1634	4.6		1656	4.3
	2253	1.3		2310	1.8
2 SA	0455	4.7	**17** SU	0520	4.2
	1115	1.1		1134	1.6
	1725	4.9		1735	4.5
	2348	1.0		2354	1.5
3 SU	0548	4.9	**18** M	0558	4.4
	1207	1.0		1214	1.4
	1812	5.1		1811	4.7
4 M ●	0039	0.8	**19** TU ○	0034	1.3
	0637	5.0		0633	4.6
	1255	0.8		1252	1.2
	1855	5.2		1845	4.9
5 TU	0127	0.6	**20** W	0113	1.1
	0723	5.1		0708	4.7
	1339	0.8		1329	1.0
	1937	5.2		1920	5.1
6 W	0212	0.6	**21** TH	0151	0.9
	0807	5.0		0744	4.9
	1422	0.8		1407	0.9
	2018	5.2		1956	5.2
7 TH	0255	0.7	**22** F	0229	0.7
	0850	4.9		0822	4.9
	1502	0.9		1444	0.9
	2059	5.0		2035	5.2
8 F	0336	0.8	**23** SA	0308	0.7
	0933	4.7		0903	4.9
	1543	1.1		1524	0.9
	2140	4.8		2118	5.1
9 SA	0417	1.0	**24** SU	0349	0.8
	1016	4.4		0948	4.7
	1623	1.4		1606	1.1
	2223	4.5		2206	5.0
10 SU	0459	1.3	**25** M	0433	0.9
	1104	4.2		1040	4.6
	1706	1.6		1653	1.3
	2311	4.3		2302	4.7
11 M	0544	1.6	**26** TU ◐	0522	1.1
	1200	4.0		1142	4.4
	1753	1.9		1747	1.5
12 TU ◐	0012	4.0	**27** W	0008	4.5
	0635	1.8		0618	1.4
	1304	3.9		1254	4.2
	1849	2.1		1853	1.7
13 W	0124	3.9	**28** TH	0121	4.4
	0737	2.0		0726	1.6
	1411	3.9		1407	4.2
	2000	2.2		2012	1.8
14 TH	0237	3.8	**29** F	0236	4.3
	0849	2.1		0845	1.7
	1516	3.9		1521	4.3
	2116	2.2		2134	1.7
15 F	0343	3.9	**30** SA	0349	4.4
	0956	2.0		1002	1.6
	1611	4.1		1626	4.5
	2220	2.0		2245	1.5
			31 SU	0452	4.6
				1106	1.4
				1720	4.7
				2343	1.2

AUGUST

Day	Time	m	Day	Time	m
1 M	0545	4.8	**16** TU	0537	4.4
	1158	1.2		1151	1.5
	1805	5.0		1747	4.8
2 TU ●	0032	1.0	**17** W	0012	1.3
	0629	4.9		0612	4.7
	1244	1.0		1231	1.2
	1844	5.1		1822	5.1
3 W	0117	0.8	**18** TH ○	0052	0.9
	0709	5.0		0647	4.9
	1326	0.9		1309	0.9
	1921	5.2		1858	5.3
4 TH	0157	0.7	**19** F	0130	0.7
	0747	5.0		0723	5.1
	1404	0.9		1347	0.7
	1956	5.2		1935	5.5
5 F	0235	0.7	**20** SA	0209	0.5
	0823	5.0		0800	5.2
	1441	0.9		1425	0.6
	2030	5.1		2014	5.5
6 SA	0311	0.8	**21** SU	0248	0.4
	0858	4.8		0840	5.2
	1517	1.0		1505	0.7
	2103	4.9		2056	5.4
7 SU	0346	1.0	**22** M	0328	0.5
	0933	4.6		0923	5.0
	1552	1.2		1546	0.8
	2137	4.7		2143	5.2
8 M	0422	1.2	**23** TU	0411	0.7
	1011	4.4		1012	4.8
	1629	1.5		1632	1.1
	2215	4.4		2238	4.9
9 TU	0459	1.5	**24** W	0457	1.1
	1056	4.2		1113	4.5
	1708	1.8		1724	1.4
	2301	4.1		2348	4.6
10 W ◐	0541	1.8	**25** TH ◐	0552	1.5
	1156	4.0		1229	4.3
	1755	2.1		1830	1.8
11 TH	0009	3.9	**26** F	0107	4.3
	0631	2.1		0700	1.8
	1311	3.9		1351	4.2
	1854	2.3		1955	2.0
12 F	0138	3.8	**27** SA	0229	4.2
	0742	2.2		0828	2.0
	1425	3.9		1513	4.2
	2017	2.4		2128	1.9
13 SA	0259	3.8	**28** SU	0347	4.3
	0908	2.2		0955	1.9
	1532	4.0		1621	4.4
	2141	2.2		2241	1.6
14 SU	0406	3.9	**29** M	0449	4.5
	1018	2.1		1059	1.6
	1627	4.2		1712	4.7
	2243	2.2		2336	1.3
15 M	0457	4.1	**30** TU	0537	4.7
	1109	1.8		1148	1.4
	1710	4.5		1753	4.9
	2330	1.6			
			31 W	0020	1.0
				0616	4.9
				1230	1.1
				1829	5.1

Chart Datum: 2·75 metres below Ordnance Datum (Newlyn). HAT is 5·9 metres above Chart Datum.

》》 **FREE** monthly updates. Register at 《
www.reedsnauticalalmanac.co.uk 《

47

STANDARD TIME (UT)
For Summer Time add ONE hour in **non-shaded areas**

ULLAPOOL LAT 57°54'N LONG 5°09'W
TIMES AND HEIGHTS OF HIGH AND LOW WATERS

Dates in red are **SPRINGS**
Dates in blue are **NEAPS**

YEAR 2016

SEPTEMBER

Time	m		Time	m
1 0100	0.8	**16** 0026	0.8
0650	5.0	0623	5.1
TH 1308	1.0	F 1246	0.8
● 1901	5.2	○ 1833	5.5
2 0136	0.7	**17** 0106	0.5
0723	5.1	0659	5.4
F 1343	0.9	SA 1324	0.6
1931	5.2	1911	5.7
3 0210	0.7	**18** 0145	0.3
0753	5.0	0736	5.5
SA 1416	0.9	SU 1404	0.5
2000	5.1	1951	5.7
4 0242	0.8	**19** 0225	0.3
0823	4.9	0816	5.4
SU 1448	1.0	M 1444	0.5
2030	5.0	2035	5.6
5 0313	1.0	**20** 0306	0.4
0854	4.8	0859	5.2
M 1521	1.2	TU 1527	0.7
2100	4.8	2123	5.3
6 0345	1.2	**21** 0348	0.7
0927	4.6	0948	4.9
TU 1554	1.4	W 1613	1.0
2133	4.5	2220	4.9
7 0418	1.5	**22** 0435	1.1
1004	4.4	1049	4.6
W 1630	1.7	TH 1706	1.4
2212	4.3	2334	4.5
8 0455	1.8	**23** 0529	1.6
1053	4.1	1210	4.3
TH 1711	2.0	F 1813	1.8
2306	4.0	◑	
9 0539	2.1	**24** 0057	4.2
1208	3.9	0638	2.0
F 1803	2.2	SA 1337	4.2
◐		1943	2.0
10 0039	3.8	**25** 0222	4.1
0639	2.3	0813	2.2
SA 1335	3.9	SU 1501	4.2
1918	2.4	2120	1.9
11 0214	3.7	**26** 0340	4.2
0815	2.4	0944	2.1
SU 1450	4.0	M 1608	4.4
2059	2.3	2229	1.7
12 0332	3.9	**27** 0438	4.4
0944	2.2	1045	1.8
M 1552	4.2	TU 1658	4.7
2212	2.0	2319	1.4
13 0428	4.1	**28** 0522	4.7
1041	1.9	1131	1.5
TU 1640	4.5	W 1736	4.9
2303	1.6		
14 0511	4.5	**29** 0001	1.1
1126	1.5	0557	4.9
W 1720	4.8	TH 1210	1.3
2346	1.2	1809	5.0
15 0548	4.8	**30** 0038	1.0
1206	1.2	0628	5.0
TH 1757	5.2	F 1246	1.1
		1838	5.1

OCTOBER

Time	m		Time	m
1 0111	0.9	**16** 0040	0.5
0657	5.1	0635	5.5
SA 1319	1.0	SU 1301	0.6
● 1906	5.2	○ 1849	5.8
2 0142	0.8	**17** 0121	0.3
0725	5.1	0713	5.6
SU 1350	1.0	M 1343	0.4
1933	5.1	1931	5.8
3 0212	0.9	**18** 0203	0.3
0753	5.1	0754	5.6
M 1421	1.1	TU 1425	0.5
2001	5.0	2017	5.6
4 0242	1.0	**19** 0245	0.5
0822	4.9	0839	5.4
TU 1452	1.2	W 1510	0.7
2030	4.8	2108	5.3
5 0312	1.2	**20** 0328	0.8
0852	4.8	0928	5.1
W 1524	1.4	TH 1558	1.0
2103	4.6	2208	4.9
6 0344	1.5	**21** 0416	1.3
0928	4.6	1030	4.7
TH 1559	1.6	F 1652	1.4
2141	4.3	2321	4.5
7 0419	1.7	**22** 0510	1.7
1011	4.3	1149	4.4
F 1638	1.9	SA 1759	1.8
2230	4.1	◐	
8 0500	2.0	**23** 0041	4.2
1112	4.1	0618	2.1
SA 1727	2.1	SU 1315	4.3
2350	3.9	1924	2.0
9 0554	2.3	**24** 0203	4.1
1243	4.0	0747	2.3
SU 1834	2.3	M 1438	4.3
◐		2055	2.0
10 0130	3.8	**25** 0319	4.2
0720	2.5	0916	2.2
M 1404	4.0	TU 1545	4.4
2011	2.3	2203	1.8
11 0251	3.9	**26** 0416	4.4
0902	2.3	1018	2.0
TU 1511	4.2	W 1635	4.6
2134	2.0	2253	1.5
12 0353	4.2	**27** 0459	4.6
1007	2.0	1105	1.7
W 1605	4.5	TH 1714	4.7
2230	1.6	2334	1.3
13 0440	4.5	**28** 0534	4.8
1056	1.6	1145	1.5
TH 1649	4.9	F 1746	4.9
2316	1.2		
14 0520	4.9	**29** 0010	1.2
1138	1.2	0604	4.9
F 1729	5.3	SA 1221	1.3
2358	0.8	1815	5.0
15 0557	5.3	**30** 0044	1.1
1220	0.8	0633	5.1
SA 1809	5.6	SU 1254	1.2
		● 1843	5.0
		31 0115	1.0
		0701	5.1
		M 1326	1.2
		1911	5.0

NOVEMBER

Time	m		Time	m
1 0145	1.1	**16** 0143	0.5
0729	5.1	0738	5.6
TU 1356	1.2	W 1410	0.5
1939	4.9	2005	5.6
2 0215	1.1	**17** 0227	0.6
0757	5.0	0824	5.5
W 1428	1.2	TH 1457	0.7
2009	4.8	2057	5.3
3 0245	1.3	**18** 0312	0.9
0828	4.9	0914	5.2
TH 1500	1.4	F 1546	1.0
2043	4.7	2155	4.9
4 0317	1.5	**19** 0359	1.3
0903	4.7	1011	4.9
F 1535	1.6	SA 1639	1.3
2122	4.4	2301	4.6
5 0352	1.7	**20** 0451	1.7
0945	4.5	1120	4.6
SA 1615	1.8	SU 1740	1.7
2210	4.2		
6 0432	2.0	**21** 0011	4.3
1039	4.3	0551	2.1
SU 1702	2.0	M 1238	4.4
2318	4.0	◑ 1850	1.9
7 0523	2.2	**22** 0126	4.2
1155	4.2	0706	2.3
M 1802	2.2	TU 1357	4.3
●		2008	2.0
8 0047	3.9	**23** 0241	4.2
0636	2.4	0827	2.3
TU 1317	4.2	W 1508	4.3
1923	2.2	2121	1.9
9 0206	4.0	**24** 0342	4.3
0810	2.4	0938	2.2
W 1427	4.3	TH 1603	4.4
2047	2.0	2217	1.8
10 0312	4.2	**25** 0429	4.4
0926	2.1	1032	2.0
TH 1526	4.6	F 1646	4.5
2152	1.6	2302	1.6
11 0407	4.6	**26** 0508	4.6
1021	1.7	1116	1.8
F 1617	4.9	SA 1723	4.7
2244	1.3	2341	1.5
12 0452	4.9	**27** 0541	4.8
1110	1.3	1155	1.6
SA 1703	5.2	SU 1755	4.8
2331	0.9		
13 0533	5.3	**28** 0016	1.4
1155	1.0	0611	5.0
SU 1747	5.5	M 1230	1.5
		1825	4.9
14 0015	0.6	**29** 0050	1.3
0614	5.5	0641	5.1
M 1240	0.7	TU 1304	1.3
○ 1831	5.7	● 1855	4.9
15 0100	0.5	**30** 0121	1.2
0655	5.7	0710	5.1
TU 1325	0.5	W 1337	1.3
1917	5.7	1925	4.9

DECEMBER

Time	m		Time	m
1 0153	1.3	**16** 0214	0.8
0740	5.1	0813	5.5
TH 1409	1.3	F 1447	0.7
1957	4.8	2045	5.3
2 0225	1.3	**17** 0258	0.6
0812	5.0	0859	5.4
F 1443	1.3	SA 1534	0.9
2031	4.7	2136	5.0
3 0258	1.5	**18** 0343	1.2
0848	4.8	0949	5.1
SA 1519	1.4	SU 1622	1.2
2110	4.6	2230	4.7
4 0333	1.6	**19** 0430	1.5
0928	4.8	1043	4.8
SU 1558	1.6	M 1712	1.5
2156	4.4	2328	4.4
5 0413	1.8	**20** 0520	1.9
1017	4.6	1145	4.5
M 1643	1.7	TU 1808	1.8
2252	4.3		
6 0501	2.0	**21** 0032	4.2
1117	4.5	0617	2.2
TU 1737	1.9	W 1256	4.3
		◑ 1910	2.0
7 0004	4.2	**22** 0143	4.1
0601	2.2	0725	2.3
W 1231	4.4	TH 1411	4.2
◑ 1843	1.9	2020	2.1
8 0121	4.2	**23** 0253	4.1
0719	2.2	0840	2.4
TH 1343	4.4	F 1519	4.2
1959	1.9	2129	2.1
9 0230	4.3	**24** 0351	4.2
0839	2.1	0949	2.3
F 1448	4.6	SA 1613	4.3
2110	1.7	2225	2.0
10 0332	4.5	**25** 0438	4.4
0946	1.8	1044	2.1
SA 1547	4.8	SU 1658	4.4
2212	1.4	2311	1.8
11 0426	4.8	**26** 0518	4.6
1043	1.5	1129	1.9
SU 1641	5.1	M 1736	4.5
2306	1.1	2351	1.6
12 0514	5.1	**27** 0553	4.8
1135	1.2	1208	1.7
M 1731	5.3	TU 1811	4.7
2355	0.9		
13 0559	5.4	**28** 0027	1.5
1224	0.9	0624	5.0
TU 1820	5.5	W 1245	1.5
		1842	4.8
14 0043	0.7	**29** 0102	1.4
0643	5.6	0656	5.1
W 1312	0.7	TH 1320	1.4
○ 1908	5.5	● 1914	4.8
15 0129	0.7	**30** 0136	1.3
0727	5.6	0727	5.1
TH 1400	0.6	F 1355	1.3
1956	5.5	1946	4.9
		31 0209	1.3
		0759	5.2
		SA 1430	1.2
		2020	4.9

Chart Datum: 2·75 metres below Ordnance Datum (Newlyn). HAT is 5·9 metres above Chart Datum.

》》**FREE** monthly updates. Register at 《
www.reedsnauticalalmanac.co.uk

ADJACENT ISLANDS

SUMMER ISLES, 58°01'N 05°25'W. AC 2509, 2501. HW –0425 Dover; See 1.7; streams are weak and irregular. In the N apps to Loch Broom some 30 islands and rks, the main ones being Eilean Mullagrach, Isle Ristol, Glas-leac Mor, Tanera Beg, Eilean a' Char, Eilean Fada Mor. Beware rocks at S end of Horse Sound. ⚓s:

Isle Ristol, ⚓ to S of drying causeway and clear of moorings; beware landings frequented by local FVs. Close to slip is lt Fl G 3s. Facilities: 🛒 (at Polbain 2M).

Tanera Beg, ⚓ in the chan to the E inside Eilean Fada Mor.

Tanera Mor, on E side, ⚓ in bay to N off pier or in W corner off stone jetty; beware many moorings and fish pens. Also poss ⚓ close NW of Is and close E of Eilean na Saille, but N of drying rock. Facilities: ☎(01854) 622272 B Wilder for ⚓ ⚓ 🏴 Tea room.

Badentarbat Bay, Temp'y ⚓ NW part of bay ESE of pier which is busy with marina farm activity. Beware N part of bay is shoal. Suitable for Achiltibuie or Polbain on mainland. Facilities: ⚓ ⚓ ⚓ (emerg) ☎(01854) 622261 🛒 ✕.

LITTLE LOCH BROOM, 57°54'·98N 05°24'·68W. AC 2500. HW –0415 Dover as per Ullapool, see 1.7; streams are weak (approx 1kn). Between Loch Broom and Gruinard Bay, entered S of Cailleach Hd it is deep (115m in centre) and shoreline steep to. In approaches beware of Ardross Rk (depth 0.6m) 0.38M ENE of Stattic Pt.

Camusnagaul, on S side of loch 1.6M from head and Dundonnel Hotel, ⚓ to E of hamlet.

Scoraig, inside narrows on N shore in N'lies. ⚓ off jetty clear of submarine cables and marine farm. ✕ C.Dawson ☎01845 613380.

ANCHORAGES BETWEEN LITTLE LOCH BROOM & LOCH GAIRLOCH

LOCH EWE, 57°52'·0N 05°40'·0W (SWM buoy, L Fl 10s). AC 2509, 3146. Tides: See 1.7; HW –0415 on Dover; ML 2·6m; Duration 0610. Shelter in all winds. Easy ent with no dangers in loch. Rhubha Reidh lt, Fl (4) 15s 37m 24M, W tr, is 4·5M W of ent. No 1 buoy Fl (3) G 10s. Loch approx 7M long with Isle Ewe and 2 small islets about 2M from ent in centre; can be passed on either side. Temp ⚓ in bay of Isle of Ewe. Beware unlit buoy A2 between E side Isle Ewe & Aultbea Pier, 2 FG (vert). NATO fuelling jetty and dolphins, all Fl G 4s.

Loch Thurnaig, 1.7M SSE of Isle of Ewe, sheltered ⚓ off Ob na Bà Rùaidhe, SE of pier to W of drying reef. Beware of numerous marine farms in approaches.

Aultbea, ⚓ off Aultbea Hotel on E shore or in NW'lies close E of pier. N part of bay is shoal. Facilities: Dr, 🏴 ✉ 🛒 ✕ 🅿.

Poolewe Bay, ⚓ in SW part of bay in 3·5m, at head of loch: Boor Rks(3m) with drying rocks extending 1ca NW lie off W shore about 9ca NW of Poolewe. Head of Loch dries for a considerable distance. Facilities: ✕ ⚓ ⚓ on pier, 🏴 (at garage) ⚓ ✉ 🛒 ✕ 🅿.

Inverewe Gdns on NE side of bay, ⚓ to SW of Jetty at Port na Cloiche Gile.

LOCH GAIRLOCH, 57°43'N 05°45'W. AC 228, 2528. HW –0440 on Dover. See 1.7. A wide loch facing W. Ent clear of dangers but Submarine Exercise Area (see page 51) to S of Longa Is. Quite heavy seas enter in bad weather. Lts: Glas Eilean Fl WRG 6s 9m 6/4M, Gairloch Pier Hd, QR 9m. HM ☎(01445) 712140.

Badachro, good shelter SW of Eilean Horrisdale on SW side of loch but busy with FVs and local craft. Unlit PHM/SHM mark rock ledges in approach. Passage to S of of Eilean Horrisdale is possible with caution. ⚓ on E side NNW of Sgeir Dhubh Bhea. ✕ 🅿(Bad Inn). HM ☎(01445) 741255 for M availability.

Loch Shieldaig, 6 Blue ⚓ (with payment instructions) at SE end of the loch with many moorings for local craft. If congested ⚓ to SSW of Eilean an t-Sabhail. Beware marine farms.

Flowerdale Bay, ⚓ in approx 6m near Gairloch pier or berth on pontoons (2m depth N side, 3m S side) at pier. HM ☎(01445) 712140. VHF Ch 16 (occas). Gairloch Pier: 🛒 fees charged. ⚓ 🏴 ⚓ 🏴 ⚓ 🔒 ✉ 🛒 🅿 SC, Hotel.

SKYE AND THE INNER SOUND

(AC 1795, 2210, 2209, 2208, 2207, 5616) Skye and the islands around it provide many good and attractive anchorages, of which the most secure are: Acairseid Mhor on the W side of Rona; Portree (1.8); Oronsay, Portnalong, near the entrance to Loch Harport, and Carbost at the head; Loch Dunvegan; and Uig Bay in Loch Snizort. ⚓s at Stein (Loch Dunvegan), Portree, Acairseid Mhor (Rona), Churchton Bay (Raasay) and Armadale Bay (S tip).

▶ *Tides are strong off Rubha Hunish at N end of Skye, and heavy overfalls occur with tide against fresh or strong winds.* ◀

⚓ behind Fladday Is near the N end of Raasay can be squally and uncomfortable; and Loch Scavaig (S. Skye, beneath the Cuillins) more so, though the latter is so spectacular as to warrant a visit in fair weather. Soay Is has a small, safe harbour on its N side, but the bar at entrance almost dries at LW springs.

Between N Skye and the mainland there is the choice of Sound of Raasay or Inner Sound. **The direction of buoyage in both Sounds is Northward.** In the former, coming S from Portree, beware Sgeir Chnapach (3m) and Ebbing Rk (dries 2·9m), both NNW of Oskaig Pt. Beware McMillan's Rk (0·4m depth) in mid-channel, marked by SHM lt buoy.

▶ *At the Narrows (chart 2534) the SE-going stream begins at HW Ullapool –0605, and the NW-going at HW Ullapool +0040; sp rate 1·4kn in mid-chan, but more near shoals each side.* ◀

The channel between Scalpay and Skye narrows to 2.5ca with drying reefs each side and least depth 0·1m. ▶ *Here the E-going stream begins at HW Ullapool +0550, and W-going at HW Ullapool –0010, sp rate 1kn.* ◀

Inner Sound, which is a Submarine exercise area, is wider and easier than Sound of Raasay; the two are connected by Caol Rona and Caol Mor, respectively N and S of Raasay. Dangers extend about 1M N of Rona, and Cow Is lies off the mainland 8M to S; otherwise approach from N is clear to Crowlin Is, which should be passed to W. There is a good ⚓ between Eilean Mor and Eilean Meadhonach.

A military torpedo range in the Inner Sound does not normally restrict passage, but vessels may be requested to keep to the E side of the Sound if it is active. Range activity is broadcast at 0800 and 1800LT first on VHF Ch 16 and then on Ch 8, and is indicated by Red Flags flown on the range building at Applecross, by range vessels and at the naval pier at Kyle of Lochalsh, ☎(01599) 534262.

1.8 PORTREE

Skye (Highland) 57°24'·73N 06°11'·07W ❀❀❀❀⚓⚓❁❁❁

CHARTS AC 2209, 2534, 5616; Imray C66

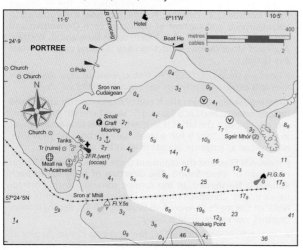

TIDES –0445 Dover; ML no data; Duration 0610

Standard Port ULLAPOOL (→)

Times				Height (metres)			
High Water		Low Water		MHWS	MHWN	MLWN	MLWS
0000	0600	0300	0900	5·2	3·9	2·1	0·7
1200	1800	1500	2100				
Differences PORTREE (Skye)							
–0025	–0025	–0025	–0025	+0·1	–0·2	–0·2	0·0
SHIELDAIG (Loch Torridon)							
–0020	–0020	–0015	–0015	+0·4	+0·3	+0·1	0·0
LOCH A'BHRAIGE (Rona)							
–0020	0000	–0010	0000	–0·1	–0·1	–0·1	–0·2
LOCH SNIZORT (Uig Bay, Skye)							
–0045	–0020	–0005	–0025	+0·1	–0·4	–0·2	0·0
LOCH DUNVEGAN (Skye)							
–0105	–0030	–0020	–0040	0·0	–0·1	0·0	0·0
LOCH HARPORT (Skye)							
–0115	–0035	–0020	–0100	–0·1	–0·1	0·0	+0·1
SOAY (Camus nan Gall)							
–0055	–0025	–0025	–0045	–0·4	–0·2	ND	ND

SHELTER Secure in all but strong S to SW'lies, when Camas Bàn is more sheltered. In the NW of the bay there are 8 ⚓s for <15 tons. Short stay pontoon on pier.

NAVIGATION WPT 57°24'·58N 06°10'·07W, 275°/0·72M to pier. From the S, avoid rks off An Tom Pt (1·5M to E, off chartlet).

LIGHTS AND MARKS Only lts are a SHM buoy Fl G 5s marking Sgeir Mhór, 2 FR (vert) 6m 4M (occas) on the pier and a SPM buoy Fl Y 5s.

COMMUNICATIONS (Code 01478) CGOC (01851) 702013; ⊖ (0141) 887 9369; Police 101; Dr 612013; Ⓗ 612704. HM 612926; Moorings 612341.

VHF Ch 16 12 (occas).

FACILITIES Pier ⚓ ⚓£14 ⚓ ⚓(Mon-Fri).
Town 🅿 🛢 ✉ Ⓑ 🛒 🔧 ✕ 🗄 bus to Kyle of Lochalsh, ⇌.

LOCH TORRIDON Highland, 57°36'N 05°49'W. AC 2210. Tides, see 1.8. Three large lochs: ent to outer loch (Torridon) is 3M wide, with isolated Sgeir na Trian (2m) almost in mid-chan; ⚓s on SW side behind Eilean Mór and in L Beag. L Sheildaig is middle loch with good ⚓ and 2 ⚓s (up to 10 tons) between the Is and village. 1M to the N, a 2ca wide chan leads into Upper L Torridon; many fish cages and prone to squalls. Few facilities, except Shieldaig: ⚓ ✉ 🔧 🗄 Garage; Diabeg: ✕.

LOCH A'BHRAIGE Rona (Highland), 57°34'·6N 05°57'·9W. AC 2479, 2534. HW –0438 on Dover; ML 2·8m; Duration 0605. See 1.8. A good ⚓ in NW of the island, safe except in NNW winds. Beware rks on NE side up to 1ca off shore. Hbr in NE corner of loch head. Ldg lts 137°, see 1.3. Facilities: jetty, ⚓ and a helipad, all owned by MOD (DRA). Before ent, call *Rona* Range Control VHF Ch 13.

Acarseid Mhór is ⚓ on W of Rona. One ⚓ £12, ☎07831 293963. App S of Eilean Garbh marked by W arrow. SD sketch of rks at ent is necessary. ⚓ 🗄 ▷. At **Churchton Bay**, SW tip of Raasay, there are 4 HIE ⚓s; ☎(01478) 612341; ⚓ 🗄 ▷ ✕.

LOCH DUNVEGAN 4 ⚓s off Stein, 57°30'·9N 06°34'·5W. 2 ⚓s off Dunvegan, 57°26'·3N 06°35'·2W. Fuel, ⚓ ✕. ☎(01478) 612341.

LOCH HARPORT Skye (Highland), 57°20'·6N 06°25'·8W. AC 1795. HW –0447 (sp), –0527 (np) on Dover. See 1.8. On E side of Loch Bracadale, entered between Oronsay Is and Ardtreck Pt (W lt ho, Fl 6s 18m 9M). SW end of Oronsay has conspic rk pillar, called The Castle; keep ¼M off-shore here and off E coast of Oronsay which is joined to Ullinish Pt by drying reef. ⚓ Oronsay Is, N side of drying reef (4m), or on E side, but beware rk (dries) 0·5ca off N shore of Oronsay. Fiskavaig Bay 1M S of Ardtreck (7m); Loch Beag on N side of loch, exposed to W winds; Port na Long E of Ardtreck, sheltered except from E winds (beware fish farm); 1 ⚓ off the distillery and 2 ⚓ off *The Old Inn* at Carbost on SW shore. Facilities: Carbost ⚓ ✉ 🛒 ✕ 🗄 🅿(garage). Port na Long ⚓ 🔧 🗄.

LOCH SLIGACHAN Skye (Highland), 57°19'·0N 06°06'·0W. AC 2534. Tides see 1.8. Differences as for Portree. Steep sided sheltered Loch S of Narrows of Raasay. In sheltered weather ⚓ outside in Balmeanach Bay. Entr marked by ECM and SHM. Sconser harbour with ◣ pier and pontoon (lit Fl R 3s 2m 3M) inside narrows used to service fish farms and shellfish beds, which should be avoided.

SOAY HARBOUR Skye (Highland), 57°09'·5N 06°13'·4W. AC 2208. Tides see 1.8. Narrow inlet on NW side of Soay; enter from Soay Sound above half flood to clear bar, dries 1·0m. Appr on 135° from 5ca out to avoid reefs close each side of ent. Cross bar slightly E of mid-chan, altering 20° stbd for best water; ent is 15m wide between boulder spits marked by W poles with Or tops. ⚓ in 3m mid-pool or shoal draught boats can enter inner pool. Good shelter and holding. Camas nan Gall (poor holding); no other facilities.

ARMADALE BAY Skye (Highland), 4M NW of Mallaig. AC 2208. 6 ⚓s £12 at 57°04'·0N 05°53'·6W, ☎(01471) 844216. Bay is sheltered from SE to N winds but subject to swell in winds from N to SE. From S, beware the Eilean Maol & Sgorach rocks. Ferry pier, Oc R 6s 6m 6M, with conspic W shed. Facilities, Skye Yachts ☎01471 844216, M (£12·50), ⚓ at pontoon ◣ 🔧 (not Sat pm or Sun), Free pontoon for tenders, ferry to Mallaig for ⇌. Ardvasar ¾ mile; ◣ HW±3 at ⛟(launching/parking £5), 🅿(not Sun) 🛢 🚻 ▷ ✕ 🗄.

CROWLIN ISLANDS Highland, 57°21'·1N 05°50'·6W. AC 2209, 2498. HW –0435 on Dover, –0020 on Ullapool; HW +0·3m on Ullapool. See 1.7. ⚓ between Eilean Meadhonach and Eilean Mor, appr from N, keep E of Eilean Beg. Excellent shelter except in strong N winds. There is an inner ⚓ with 3½m but ent chan dries. Eilean Beg lt ho Fl 6s 32m 6M, W tr. No facilities.

SUBMARINE EXERCISE INFORMATION

Details of submarine activity in the Exercise Areas north of Mull are broadcast at 0710 and 1910 UT by Stornoway CG on a specified VHF Ch after an initial announcement on Ch 16. Areas are referred to by the names given below, rather than by the numbers indicated on the chartlet. For Areas 22–81 (South of Mull), see page 84.

SUBFACTS

General information on SUBFACTS is also broadcast twice daily at 0620 & 1820 UT on Navtex. Stornoway CGOC will provide SUBFACTS on request; call on Ch 16.

A 'Fisherman's hotline' (☎(01436) 677201) is available on a 24 hour basis and may be used for any queries relating to SUBFACTS from any mariner.

Submarines on the surface and at periscope depth always listen on Ch 16.

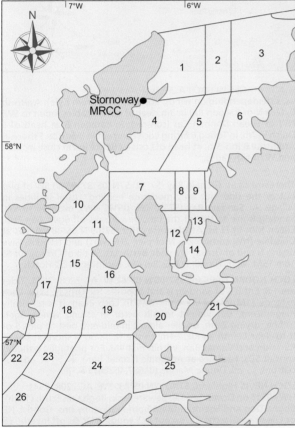

1	Tiumpan	14	Raasay
2	Minch North	15	Neist
3	Stoer	16	Bracadale
4	Shiant	17	Ushenish
5	Minch South	18	Hebrides North
6	Ewe	19	Canna
7	Troddday	20	Rhum
8	Rona West	21	Sleat
9	Rona North	22	Barra
10	Lochmaddy	23	Hebrides Central
11	Dunvegan	24	Hawes
12	Portree	25	Eigg
13	Rona South	26	Hebrides South

1.9 PLOCKTON

Highland 57°20´·52N 05°38´·47W ❀❀👐👐♻♻♻

CHARTS AC 2209, 2528, 5616; Imray C66

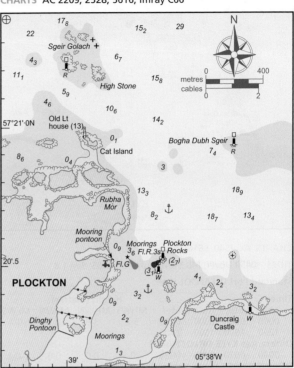

TIDES –0435 Dover; ML 3·5m; Duration 0600; See 1.8

Standard Port ULLAPOOL (→)

Times				Height (metres)			
High Water		Low Water		MHWS	MHWN	MLWN	MLWS
0000	0600	0300	0900	5·2	3·9	2·1	0·7
1200	1800	1500	2100				
Differences PLOCKTON							
+0005	–0025	–0005	–0010	+0·5	+0·5	+0·5	+0·2

SHELTER Good, exposed only to N/NE'lies. 9 Y ⬡s or ⚓ in centre of bay in approx 3·5m. Inner part of bay shoals and dries to the SW.

NAVIGATION WPT 57°21´·16N 05°39´·44W; thence towards Bogha Dubh Sgeir Bn, between Eilean a Chait disused Lt ho and Sgeir Golach Bn / High Stone (1m) to the North. Hawk Rock (0.1m) will be cleared when Duncraig Castle bears 158°. Alter S to the ⚓. Beware Plockton Rks (3·1m) on E side of bay.

LIGHTS AND MARKS See 1.3 and chartlet. Old lt ho (13m) on Eilean a Chait is conspic, as is Duncraig Castle. Sgeir Golach Bn a twr with W panels Fl W 10s, Dubh Sgeir Bn a tower with R panels Fl(2) R 6s and Plockton Rks a PHM Bn Fl R 3s.

COMMUNICATIONS HM (01599) 534589, 📠 534167, Mobile 07802 367253 (at Kyle of Lochalsh); CGOC (01851) 702013; ⊖ (0141) 887 9369; Police101; Dr via HM.

FACILITIES Village ⚓£5, ⛽ ⚓ at 50m dinghy pontoon (H24 except MLWS), Ⓔ 🛢 🗑 ✕ 🗄 ⇌ airstrip, (bus to Kyle of Lochalsh).

ADJACENT MOORINGS

LOCH CARRON Strome Narrows a re not buoyed or lit. Appr on 328° between Sgeir Chreagach and Sgeir Fhada. Fish farms on W shore of Loch Kishorn.

1.10 LOCH ALSH

Highland 57°16'·68N 05°42'·87W ✺✺✺◑◡◡❀❀❀

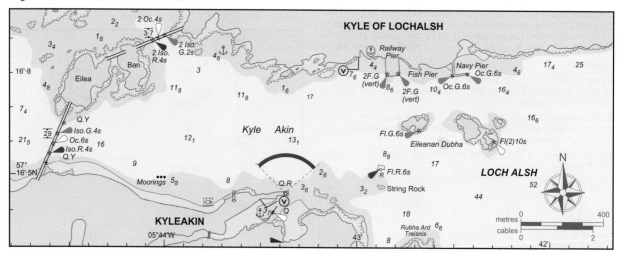

CHARTS AC 2540, 5616; Imray C66

TIDES –0450 Dover; ML 3·0m; Duration 0555; See 1.8

Standard Port ULLAPOOL (→)

Times				Height (metres)			
High Water		Low Water		MHWS	MHWN	MLWN	MLWS
0000	0600	0300	0900	5·2	3·9	2·1	0·7
1200	1800	1500	2100				
Differences KYLE OF LOCHALSH							
–0040	–0020	–0005	–0025	+0·1	0·0	0·0	–0·1
DORNIE BRIDGE (Loch Alsh)							
–0040	–0010	–0005	–0020	+0·1	–0·1	0·0	0·0
GLENELG BAY (Kyle Rhea)							
–0105	–0035	–0035	–0055	–0·4	–0·4	–0·9	–0·1
LOCH HOURN							
–0125	–0050	–0040	–0110	–0·2	–0·1	–0·1	+0·1

SHELTER Kyle of Lochalsh: ⌒ on Railway Pier, with FVs, or on 40m L-shaped pontoon (seasonal), close W of Railway Pier; or ⚓ off the hotel in 11m. **Kyle Akin:** 3 free ⚓s are subject to tidal stream. Lit ❶ pontoon on NW side of hbr for yachts, shoal on N side.

NAVIGATION WPT (from Inner Sound) 57°16'·98N 05°45'·77W, 123°/0·75M to bridge. Chan to bridge is marked by 2 PHM and 2 SHM lt buoys. Bridge to Skye, 29m clearance, is lit Oc 6s in centre of main span, Iso R 4s on S pier and Iso G4s on N pier. The secondary NE span is lit, but has only 3.7m clearance.

LIGHTS AND MARKS See chartlet. Direction of buoyage is N in Kyle Rhea, thence E up Loch Alsh; but W through Kyle Akin and the bridge, ie SHMs are on N side of channel.

COMMUNICATIONS (Code 01599) CGOC (01851) 702013; ☎ (0141) 887 9369; Police 101; Dr, Ⓗ: via HM. Skye bridge 534844. HM 534306, Mobile 07990 971161, Deputy 07771 816900. VHF Ch 11 16.

FACILITIES Kyle of Lochalsh: www.kyleandlochalsh.org.uk/index.asp ⌒pontoon, £15 1st night then £10, ⛽🪝 (Fish pier via HM, Mon-Fri) 🔧🔩🔦Ⓔ🔋✉Ⓑ🛒✕🍴🌐 £2 (honesty box). ⚞ (useful railhead), Bus to Glasgow & Inverness; buses every ½hr to/from Kyleakin.

Kyleakin: ☎534167 or VHF Ch 11, 120m ⌒ (£14/craft) depth varies from 3m to drying. ⚓⛽🛒✕🍴.

ANCHORAGES IN LOCH ALSH (see also 1.8)

⚓s, safe depending on winds, are (clockwise from Kyle): Avernish B, (2ca N of Racoon Rk) in 3m clear of power cables, open to SW; NW of Eilean Donnan Cas (conspic); in Ratagan B at head of L Duich in 7m; in Totaig B facing Loch Long ent in 3·5m; on S shore in Ardintoul B in 5·5m; at head of Loch na Béiste in 7m close inshore and W of fish cages.

SOUND OF SLEAT

There are ⚓s at: **Glenelg Bay (57°12'·57N 05°37'·95W)** SW of pier out of the tide, but only moderate holding. Usual facilities in village. At **Sandaig Bay (57°10'·0N 05°41'·4W)**, exposed to SW. Sandaig Is are to NW of the bay; beware rks off Sgeir nan Eun. Eilean Mór lit Fl 6s. At **Isleornsay Hbr (57°09'N 05°48'W)** 5 ⚓s at Duisdale (NW corner) 2ca N of pier, 2FR (vert) and floodlit. Give drying N end of Ornsay Is a wide berth. Lts: SE tip of Ornsay, Oc 8s 18m 15M, W tr; N end, Fl R 6s 8m 4M. Facilities: ⛽ ✉ Hotels.

LOCH HOURN Highland, **57°08'N 05°42'W**. AC 2208, 2541. Tides see 1.8. Ent is S of Sandaig Is and opposite Isle Ornsay, Skye. Loch extends 11M inland via 4 narrows to Loch Beag; it is scenically magnificent, but violent squalls occur in strong winds. Sgeir Ulibhe, drying 2·1m, bn, lies almost in mid-ent; best to pass S of it to clear Clansman Rk, 2·1m, to the N. ⚓s on N shore at Eilean Ràrsaidh and Camas Bàn, within first 4M. For pilotage further E, consult SDs. Facilities at Arnisdale (Camas Bàn): ⛽🛒✕ 2 ⚓s for patrons, 🍴✉. Doune Marine (01687 462667) ⛽🍴.

LOCH NEVIS Highland, **57°02'·2N 05°43'·3W**. AC 2208, 2541. HW –0515 on Dover. See 1.8. Beware rocks Bogha cas Sruth (1·8m), Bogha Don and Sgeirean Glasa both marked by bns. Good ⚓ NE of Eilean na Glaschoille, except in S winds; 9 Or ⚓s off Inverie, £5 (free if dining), 10m max LOA. Call *Old Forge* VHF Ch 16, M; ✕ 🍴🌐🍴. In strong winds expect violent unpredictable squalls. Enter the inner loch with caution, and ⚓ N or SE of Eilean Maol.

ARISAIG, (Loch nan Ceall), Highland, **56°53'·64N 05°55'·77W** (ent). AC 2207. HW –0515 on Dover; +0030 and +0·9m on Oban. Exposed to strong winds, especially from SE to NW. SDs essential. W mark on Rubh' Arisaig on S side of ent. S Chan is winding, marked by 8 perches. Appr HW+4 to avoid strongest streams LW±1½. Caution: many unmarked rks; no lts. Sheltered ⚓ at head of loch, clear of moorings. Call **Arisaig Marine** ☎(01687) 450224, VHF Ch 16, M; few ⚓s, pontoon (loading, ⛽ & fuel) ⚓ 🔧✕🔦📷🏗(10t) 🔩. **Village** ⛽ at hotel, 🔋✉🛒✕🍴⚞.

KYLE AKIN TO MALLAIG

Approaching Kyle Akin (AC 2540) from W, beware dangerous rks to N, off Bleat Is (at S side of entrance to Loch Carron); on S side of chan, Bogha Beag (dries 1·2m) and Black Eye Rk (depth 3·2m), respectively 6ca and 4ca W of bridge. Pass at least 100m N or S of Eileanan Dubha in Kyle Akin. On S side of chan String Rk (dries) is marked by PHM lt buoy. Kyle Rhea connects Loch Alsh with NE end of Sound of Sleat.

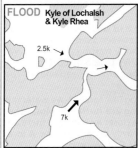 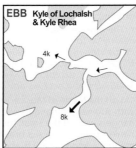

▶ The tidal streams are very strong: N-going stream begins HW Ullapool + 0600, sp rate 6-7kn; S-going stream begins at HW Ullapool, sp rate 8kn. N-going stream in Kyle Rhea begins HW Dover +0140 (HW Ullapool +0555) and runs for 6 hours. The E-going stream in Kyle Akin begins (Sp) HW Dover +0350 (HW Ullapool –0415). (Nps) HW Dover –0415 (HW Ullapool).
S-going stream in Kyle Rhea begins HW Dover –0415 (HW Ullapool) and runs for 6 hours. The W-going stream in Kyle Akin begins (Sp) HW Dover –0015 (HW Ullapool +0400). (Nps) HW Dover +0140 (HW Ullapool +0555). Eddies form both sides of the Kyle with dangerous overfalls off S end in fresh S'ly winds on S-going stream. ◀
Temp ⚓ in Sandaig Bay, 3M to SW.

The Sound of Sleat widens to 4M off Point of Sleat and is exposed to SW winds unless Eigg and Muck give a lee. Mallaig is a busy fishing and ferry harbour, convenient for supplies. Further S the lochs require intricate pilotage. 6M NE of Ardnamurchan Pt (lt, fog sig) are Bo Faskadale rks, drying 0·5m and marked by SHM lt buoy, and Elizabeth Rock with depth of 0·7m.

▶ Ardnamurchan Pt is an exposed headland onto which the ebb sets. With onshore winds, very heavy seas extend 2M offshore and it should be given a wide berth. Here the N-going stream begins at HW Oban – 0525, and the S-going at HW Oban + 0100, sp rates 1·5kn. ◀

ARDNAMURCHAN TO CRINAN

(AC 2171, 2169, 5616) S of Ardnamurchan the route lies either W of Mull via Passage of Tiree (where headlands need to be treated with respect in bad weather); or via the more sheltered Sound of Mull and Firth of Lorne. The former permits a visit to Coll and Tiree, where best ⚓s are at Arinagour (⚓s) and Gott Bay respectively. Beware Cairns of Coll, off the N tip.

The W coast of Mull is rewarding in settled weather, but careful pilotage is needed. Beware tide rip off Caliach Pt (NW corner) and Torran Rks off SW end of Mull (large scale AC 2617 required). Apart from the attractions of Iona and of Staffa (Fingal's Cave), the remote Treshnish Is are worth visiting. The best ⚓s in this area are at Ulva, Gometra, Bull Hole and Tinker's Hole in Iona Sound. The usual passage through Iona Sound avoids overfalls W of Iona, but heed shoal patches. Loch Lathaich on the N side of Ross of Mull is 5M to the E; a good base with ⚓ at Bunessan.

The Sound of Mull gives access to Tobermory, Dunstaffnage Bay, Oban, and up Loch Linnhe through Corran Narrows (where tide runs strongly) to Fort William and to Corpach for the Caledonian Canal. Apart from these places, there are dozens of ⚓s in the sheltered lochs inside Mull, as for example in Loch Sunart with ⚓s at Kilchoan.

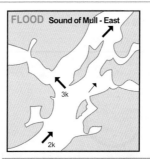 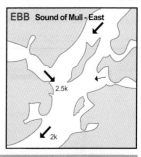

FIRTH OF LORNE AND SOUND OF LUING

▶ Firth of Lorne: the N-going stream begins at HW Oban +0430 (HW Dover –0100). The W-going stream in the Sound of Mull begins at HW Oban –0550 (HW Dover +0105). The ingoing tides at Lochs Feochan, Etive and Creran begin at HW Oban –0350, +0430 and +0600. The S-going stream in the Firth of Lorne begins at HW Oban –0155 (HW Dover +0500). The E-going stream in the Sound of Mull begins at HW Oban –0025 (HW Dover +0555). ◀

On the mainland shore Puilladobhrain is a sheltered ⚓. Cuan Sound is a useful short cut to Loch Melfort, and Craobh Marina. Good shelter, draught permitting, in Ardinamar B, SW of Torsa.

Sound of Luing (AC 2326) between Fladda (lt), Lunga and Scarba on the W side, and Luing and Dubh Sgeir (lt) on the E side, is the normal chan to or from Sound of Jura, despite dangers at the N end and strong tidal streams.

▶ The N- and W-going flood begins at HW Oban + 0430; the S- and E-going ebb at HW Oban –0155. Sp rates are 2·5kn at S end of Sound, increasing to 6kn or more in Islands off N entrance, where there are eddies, races and overfalls. The N- or W-going stream begins in the following sequence: ◀

Dorus Mor:	HW Oban +0330. Sp: 8kn.
Corryvreckan:	HW Oban +0410. Sp: 8.5kn.
Cuan Sound:	HW Oban +0420. Sp: 6kn.
Sound of Jura:	HW Oban +0400. Sp: 4kn.
Sound of Luing:	HW Oban +0430. Sp: 7kn.

The S- or E-going stream begins as follows:

Dorus Mor:	HW Oban –0215. Sp: 8kn.
Corryvreckan:	HW Oban –0210. Sp: 8.5kn.
Cuan Sound:	HW Oban –0200. Sp: 6kn.
Sound of Jura:	HW Oban –0205. Sp: 4kn.
Sound of Luing:	HW Oban –0155. Sp: 7kn.

▶ From the N, beware very strong streams, eddies and whirlpools in Dorus Mór, off Craignish Pt. Streams begin to set W and N away from Dorus Mór at HW Oban +0345, and E and S towards Dorus Mór at HW Oban –0215, sp rates 7kn. ◀

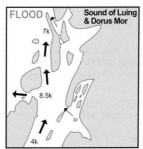 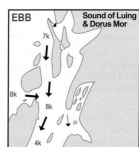

At N end of Sound of Jura (AC 2326) is Loch Craignish. For Gulf of Corryvreckan, Colonsay, Islay, Loch Crinan and passage south through the Sound of Jura, see 2.4.

1.11 MALLAIG

Highland 57°00´·47N 05°49´·47W ✲✲✲⬧⬧⬧⬧✿✿

CHARTS AC 2208, 2541, 5616; Imray C65, C66

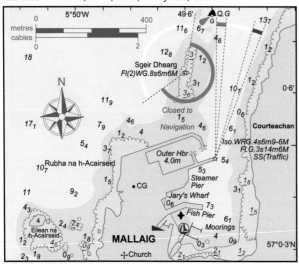

TIDES –0515 Dover; ML 2·9; Duration 0605

Standard Port OBAN (→)

Times				Height (metres)			
High Water		Low Water		MHWS	MHWN	MLWN	MLWS
0000	0600	0100	0700	4·0	2·9	1·8	0·7
1200	1800	1300	1900				
Differences MALLAIG							
+0017	+0017	+0030	+0024	+1·0	+0·7	+0·3	+0·1
INVERIE BAY (Loch Nevis)							
+0030	+0020	+0035	+0020	+1·0	+0·9	+0·2	0·0
BAY OF LAIG (Eigg)							
+0015	+0030	+0040	+0005	+0·7	+0·6	–0·2	–0·2
LOCH MOIDART							
+0015	+0015	+0040	+0020	+0·8	+0·6	–0·2	–0·2
LOCH EATHARNA (Coll)							
+0025	+0010	+0015	+0025	+0·4	+0·3	ND	ND
GOTT BAY (Tiree)							
0000	+0010	+0005	+0010	0·0	+0·1	0·0	0·0

SHELTER Good in SW'lies but open to N. Access H24. Small marina or poss berth on Fish Pier. 12 ⚓s or ⚓ in SE part of hbr clear of moorings. Despite downturn in fishing, Mallaig is a reasonably busy FV harbour, also Skye and Small Isles ferries.

NAVIGATION WPT 57°00´·75N 05°49´·40W, 191°/0·3m to Steamer Pier lt, passing E of Sgeir Dhearg lt bn. The former W chan is permanently closed to navigation.

LIGHTS AND MARKS As chartlet & 1.3. Town lts may obscure Sgeir Dhearg lt. Outer Hbr Pier Hds floodlit. IPTS (3 FR vert at pier hd) when ferries manoeuvring, no other traffic allowed except with HM's permission.

COMMUNICATIONS (Code 01687) CGOC (01851) 702013; ⊖ (0141) 887 9369; Police 101. HM 462154, outside office hrs 462411; Dr 462202.
Mallaig Hbr Radio VHF Ch 09 16 (HO).

FACILITIES ⬭ in marina, £2.40/m/night, short stay <4hrs £12. ⫶◁▷ £3.60 /night. If marina full berth on Fish Pier, £6 for ⚓/fuel/stores. M £15/night ⚓ free but limited space; seek HM permission. ⚓⬛ ⬛⚓⬛/▷ⓘ◁ ✕ ⬟ (Ⅲ) Ⓔ ⬛(mob 10t) ⬮ ACA, wi-fi.
Town ⬚⬛⬛✕⬛⬛Ⓑ⇌.

(AC 2207, 2208, 5616) These consist of Canna, Rum, Eigg and Muck. The hbrs at Eigg (SE end), Rhum (Loch Scresort) and Canna (between Canna and Sanday) are all exposed to E'lies; Canna has best shelter and is useful for the Outer Hebrides. Dangers extend SSW from Canna: at 1M Jemina Rk (depth 1·5m) and Belle Rk (depth 3·6m); at 2M Humla Rk (5m high), marked by buoy and with offlying shoals close W of it; at 5M Hyskeir (lt, fog sig), the largest of a group of small islands; and at 7M Mill Rks (with depths of 1·8m).

▶ *The tide runs hard here, and in bad weather the sea breaks heavily up to 15M SW of Canna. Between Skerryvore and Neist Pt the stream runs generally N and S, starting N-going at HW Ullapool + 0550, and S-going at HW Ullapool –0010. It rarely exceeds 1kn, except near Skerryvore, around headlands of The Small Isles, and over rks and shoals.* ◀

1M off the N side of Muck are Godag Rks, some above water but with submerged dangers extending 2ca further N. Most other dangers around the Small Isles are closer inshore, but there are banks on which the sea breaks heavily in bad weather. A local magnetic anomaly exists about 2M E of Muck.

ANCHORAGES IN THE SMALL ISLES

CANNA The Small Isles, **57°03´·3N 06°29´·4W**. AC 1796, 2208. HW –0457 (Sp), –0550 (Np) on Dover; HW –0035 and –0·4m on Ullapool; Duration 0605. Good shelter, except in strong E'lies, in hbr between Canna and Sanday Is. 10⚓s (£10) around edge of the bay and middle is clear to ⚓ but holding is poor due to kelp. Appr along Sanday shore, keeping N of Sgeir a' Phuirt, dries 4·6m. Ldg marks as in SDs. ⚓ in 3–4m W of Canna pier, off which beware drying rky patch. ⚓ Lt advised due to FVs. Conspic bn, Fl W10s 32m 9M, vis 152°-061°, at E end of Sanday Is. Magnetic anomaly off NE Canna. Facilities: ⚓ ✕ (☎01687 460164), shower at farm (01687 462963) with limited ⬛ ⬛ Note: NTS manage island.

RUM The Small Isles, **57°00´·1N 06°15´·7W**. AC 2207, 2208. HW –0500 on Dover; –0035 and –0·3m on Ullapool; ML 2·4m; Duration 0600. SNH owns Is. The mountains (809m) are unmistakable. Landing is only allowed at L Scresort on E side; no dogs beyond village limit. Beware drying rks 1ca off N point of ent and almost 3ca off S point. ⚓ off slip on S side or further in, to NE of jetty. Hbr is open to E winds/swell. Facilities: ⚓⬛ (eco) by landing pier, ⬛⬛(limited) ✕ ⬟ ferry to Mallaig.

EIGG HARBOUR The Small Isles, **56°52´·6N 06°07´·6W**. AC 2207. HW –0523 on Dover. See 1.11. Entering from N or E use Sgeir nam Bagh (Ferry Terminal) Dir lt 245° Fl WRG 3s, leads between Garbh Sgeir Bn Fl (2) G 10s & Flod Sgeir Bn Fl R 5s. An Sgùrr is a conspic 391m high peak/ridge brg 281°/1·3M from Sgeir nam Bagh. Most of hbr dries, but good ⚓ 1ca NE of Galmisdale Pt pier, except in NE winds when yachts should go through the narrows and ⚓ in South Bay in 6–8m; tide runs hard in the narrows. Also ⚓ in 2·5m at Poll nam Partan, about 2ca N of Flod Sgeir. SE point of Eilean Chathastail Fl 6s 24m 8M, vis 181°-shore, W tr. VHF Ch 08 *Eigg Hbr*. HM ☎ via (01687) 482428. ⚓ repairs. **Pierhead** ▷◁ ⬛⬛⬛ ✕. **Cleadale village** (2M to N) ⬛.

MUCK The Small Isles, **56°49´·8N 06°13´·3W**. AC 2207. Tides approx as Eigg, 1.11. Port Mór at SE end is the main hbr, with a deep pool inside offlying rks, but open to S'lies. Approach: Dir lt Fl WRG 3s 7m 11M (vis 1M by day) leads between Dubh Sgeir (Fl(2) R 10s) and Bogha Ruadh (Fl(2) G 10s) rks; see 1.3. ⚓ towards the NW side of inlet; NE side has drying rks. To N of Is, Bagh a' Ghallanaich is ⚓ protected from S. Few facilities.

1.12 LOCH SUNART
Highland 56°39'·49N 06°00'·07W ✿✿◊◊◊◊✿✿

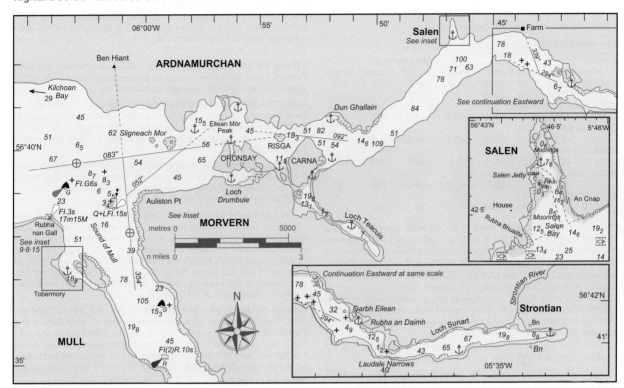

CHARTS AC 5611, 2171, 2392, 2394; Imray C65, 2800

TIDES Salen –0500 Dover; ML 2·0

Standard Port OBAN (→)

Times				Height (metres)			
High Water		Low Water		MHWS	MHWN	MLWN	MLWS
0100	0700	0100	0800	4·0	2·9	1·8	0·7
1300	1900	1300	2000				
Differences SALEN (Loch Sunart)							
–0015	+0015	+0010	+0005	+0·6	+0·5	–0·1	–0·1

SHELTER ✿s at Kilchoan Bay (2M N of Ardmore Pt). ⚓s in Loch Drumbuie (S of Oronsay) sheltered in all winds; in Sailean Mór (N of Oronsay) convenient and easy ent; between Oronsay and Carna; in Loch Teacuis (very tricky ent); E of Carna; Salen Bay, with ✿s and pontoon, open only to SSE (see facilities); Garbh Eilean (NW of Rubha an Daimh), and E of sand spit by Strontian R.

NAVIGATION West WPT, 56°39'·69N 06°03'·07W, 083°/3·7M to Creag nan Sgarbh (NW tip of Orinsay). **South WPT**, 56°38'·00N 06°00'·65W, 1M S of Auliston Pt; there are extensive rky reefs, The Stirks W of this pt. AC 2394 and detailed directions are needed to navigate the 17M long loch, particularly in its upper reaches. Beware Ross Rk, S of Risga; Broad Rk, E of Risga; Dun Ghallain Rk; shoals extending 3ca NNW from Eilean mo Shlinneag off S shore; drying rock 1ca W of Garbh Eilean and strong streams at sp in Laudale Narrows. Fish farms on both sides of the loch.

LIGHTS AND MARKS Unlit. Transits as on the chart: from W WPT, Risga on with N tip of Oronsay at 083°; N pt of Carna on with top of Risga 092°. From S WPT, Ben Hiant bearing 354°, thence Eilean Mor Peak at 052°. Further up the loch, 339° and 294°, as on chartlet, are useful. Other transits are shown on AC 2394.

COMMUNICATIONS (Code 01967) CGOC (01851) 702013; ⊜ (0141) 887 9369; Dr 431231. No VHF, except at Salen Bay (below).

FACILITIES
Kilchoan Bay (56°41'·5N 06°07'·3W); ☎(01972) 510305; 4 ✿s £13/night, ⛴ ⛟ 🏠 🏠 🍺 hotel (1M).

Salen Bay (56°42'·39N 05°46'·17W); www.salenjetty.co.uk ☎(01967) 431510, mob 07909944494. VHF Ch 80 (occas). Keep on E side of entrance to avoid a drying reef on W side. Pontoon 8 🅥, O/night £10< 6m <£2·40 /m, £5 <4hrs; 4 R ✿s(15t) (other moorings private); buoy advised, as bottom is generally foul. ⚓ ⛽ 🅟 🔲 🍺 ✕ 🏠.
Acharacle (2½M), ⊠ 🍺 ≈ (bus to L. Ailort/Ft William), ✈ Oban.
Strontian ⛽ 🏠 ⊠ 🍺 🅑 🏠 hotel, bus to Ft William.

ANCHORAGES IN COLL AND TIREE (Argyll and Bute)
ARINAGOUR, Loch Eatharna, Coll, **56°37'·0N 06°31'·2W**. AC 5611, 2171, 2474. HW –0530 on Dover; ML 1·4m; Duration 0600; see 1.11. Good shelter except with SE swell or strong winds from ENE to SSW. Enter at SHM buoy, Fl G 6s, marking Bogha Mòr. Thence NW to Arinagour ferry pier, 2 FR(vert) 10m and Dir Oc WRG 7s. Beware McQuarrie's Rk (dries 2·9m) 1ca E of pier hd and unmarked drying rks further N on E side of fairway. ✠ and hotel are conspic ahead. Continue N towards old stone pier; ⚓ S of it or use 12✿s S of Dgeir Dubh for boats <10T at £10/night, pay at ferry terminal. Also ⚓ E of Eilean Eatharna. Piermaster ☎(01879) 230347; VHF Ch 31. Facilities: HIE Trading Post ☎230349, ⚓ ⛽ 🅑 🏠 🅟 🍺 ✕. **Village** 🔲 ⛽ 🏠 ⊠ Ferry to Oban (≈).

GOTT BAY, Tiree, **56°30'·74N 06°48'·07W**. AC 5611, 2474. Tides as 1.11; HW –0540 on Dover. HM ☎(01879) 230337, VHF Ch 31. Adequate shelter in calm weather, but exposed in winds ENE to S. (in which case use Wilson hbr in Balephetrish Bay IM W, Ldg lts F.G/Oc.G). The bay, at NE end of island, can be identified by conspic latticed tr at Scarinish about 8ca SW of ent, with lt Fl 3s 11m 16M close by (obscd over hbr). Appr on NW track, keeping to SW side of bay which is obstructed on NE side by Soa Is and drying rks. The ferry pier at S side of ent has FR ldg lts 286½°. ⚓ 1ca NW of pier head in 3m on sand; ⚓ at pier. Facilities: 🏠 🏠 🅑 🍺 ✕ 🏠 ⊠ at Scarinish (½M), Ferry to Oban (≈).

1.13 TOBERMORY

Mull (Argyll and Bute) 56°37'·19N 06°03'·87W ✵✵✵✵☆☆☆☆☆☆

CHARTS AC 5611, 2171, 2390, 2474; Imray C65, 2800

TIDES –0519 Dover; ML 2·4; Duration 0610

Standard Port OBAN (→)

Times				Height (metres)			
High Water		Low Water		MHWS	MHWN	MLWN	MLWS
0100	0700	0100	0800	4·0	2·9	1·8	0·7
1300	1900	1300	2000				
Differences TOBERMORY (Mull)							
+0025	+0010	+0015	+0025	+0·5	+0·6	+0·1	+0·2
CARSAIG BAY (S Mull)							
–0015	–0005	–0030	+0020	+0·1	+0·2	0·0	–0·1
IONA (SW Mull)							
–0010	–0005	–0020	+0015	0·0	+0·1	–0·3	–0·2
BUNESSAN (Loch Lathaich, SW Mull)							
–0015	–0015	–0010	–0015	+0·3	+0·1	0·0	–0·1
ULVA SOUND (W Mull)							
–0010	–0015	0000	–0005	+0·4	+0·3	0·0	–0·1

SHELTER Good, but some swell in strong N/NE winds. 26 🛟s are marked by a blue ⊙ with a Y pick-up. ⚓ clear of fairway, where marked; at SE end of The Doirlinn. Tobermory Harbour Association (THA) manages local and visitors moorings and ⌂ on pontoon.

NAVIGATION WPT 56°37'·59N 06°03'·17W, 224°/0·5M to moorings. N ent is wide and clear of dangers. S ent via The Doirlinn is only 80m wide at HW, and dries at LW; at HW±2 least depth is 2m. The clear channel is N of the central rock and is marked with 2 metal perches. No ⚓ in harbour fairway (buoyed). Keep wash to a minimum.

LIGHTS AND MARKS Rhubha nan Gall, Fl 3s 17m 15M, W tr is 1M N of ent. Ch spire and hotel turret are both conspic.

COMMUNICATIONS (Code 01688) CGOC (01851) 702013; Local CG 302200; Police 101; Dr 302013. Cal-Mac Piermaster 302017; THA Moorings Officer ☎302876, mob 07917 832497.

VHF Ch 16 12 (HO), M.

FACILITIES 25🛟s £15/night 🔧<25'; 50⌂ on pontoon £2.25 inc ⚡; ♦ ⚓; Taigh Solais (THA Harbour Building) 🚻 ▣ 🖥 wi-fi.
Western Isles YC ☎302371. **Town** 🏦 🅿 🔧 🐴 ⓛ ⚓ ACA ✉ Ⓑ 🛒 ✕ 🗒 Divers, ⛴ (ferry to Oban), ✈ (seaplane to Glasgow; helipad on golf course).

SOUND OF MULL Dearg Sgeir Fl 6s 7m 8M marks Eileann Glasa, 2·3M to SE Rubha na Leitrach, 2 F R (vert), marks N ent to Fishnish Bay.

SALEN BAY (Mull, 56°31'·44N 05°56'·82W). Beware Bogha, drying rks 6ca E of the bay; 🛟s £10; 🔧 at Salen Jetty, fee £1/person. **Facilities:** ♦ ♦. **Village:** Dr, 🔧 Ⓔ ✉ 🛒 ✕.

CRAIGNURE, (Mull, 56°28'·37N 05°42'·25W) ldg lts 241°, both FR 10/12m. **Facilities:** 🅿 ✉ 🛒 🗒 Ferry to Oban. Tides, see 1.14.

ANCHORAGES on WEST and SOUTH COASTS OF MULL
(Anti-clockwise from the north. SDs essential) (See AC 5611)
TRESHNISH ISLES 56°29'N 06°31'W. AC 2652. The main Is (N to S) are: Cairn na Burgh, Fladda, Lunga, Bac Mòr and Bac Beag. Tides run hard and isles are exposed to swell, but merit a visit in calm weather. Appr with caution on ldg lines as in CCC SDs; temp ⚓ off Lunga's N tip in 4m.

STAFFA 56°25'·96N 06°20'·34W. AC 2652. Spectacular isle with Fingal's Cave, but same caveats as above. Very temp ⚓ off SE tip where there is landing; beware unmarked rks.

GOMETRA 56°28'·85N 06°23'W. AC 2652. Tides as 1.13. The narrow inlet between Gometra and Ulva Is offers sheltered ⚓, except in S'lies. Appr on 020° between Staffa and Little Colonsay, or N of the former. Beware rks drying 3·2m, to stbd and 5ca S of ent. Inside, E side is cleaner.

LOCH NA KEAL 56°26'N 06°18'W (ent). AC 2652. Tides in 1.13. Appr S of Geasgill Is and N of drying rks off **Inch Kenneth**; E of this Is and in **Sound of Ulva** are sheltered ⚓s, except in S'lies. Beware MacQuarrie's Rk, dries 0·8m.

LOCH LATHAICH Mull, 56°19'·29N 06°15'·47W. AC 2617. HW –0545 on Dover; ML 2·4. See 1.13. Excellent shelter with easy access; good base for cruising W Mull. Eilean na Liathanaich (a group of islets) lie off the ent, marked by a W bn at the E end, Fl WR 6s 12m 8/6M, R088°-108°, W108°-088°. Keep to W side of loch and ⚓ off Bendoran BY in SW, or SE of Eilean Ban off the pier in approx 5m keeping clear of creeler moorings to the E side. Facilities: (Bunessan) ♦ ✉ 🛒 ✕ 🗒.

SOUND OF IONA 56°19'·45N 06°23'·12W. AC 2617. Tides see 1.13. From N, enter in mid-chan; from S keep clear of Torran Rks. Cathedral brg 012° closes the Iona shore past 2 SHM buoys and SCM buoy. Beware a bank 0·1m in mid-sound, between cathedral and Fionnphort; also tel cables and ferries. ⚓ S of ferry close in to Iona, or in Bull Hole. Consult SDs. Crowded in season; limited facilities.

TINKER'S HOLE Ross of Mull, 56°17'·49N 06°23'·07W. AC 2617. Beware Torran Rks, reefs extending 5M S and SW of Erraid. Usual app from S, avoiding Rankin's Rks, drying 0·8m, and rk, dries 2·3m, between Eilean nam Muc and Erraid. Popular ⚓ in mid-pool between Eilean Dubh and Erraid.

CARSAIG BAY Ross of Mull, 56°19'·19N 05°59'·07W. Tides see 1.13. AC 2386. Temp, fair weather ⚓s to N of Gamhnach Mhòr, reef 2m high, or close into NW corner of bay. Landing at stone quay on NE side. No facilities.

LOCH SPELVE Mull, 56°23'N 05°41'W. AC 2387. Tides as Oban. Landlocked water, prone to squalls off surrounding hills. Ent narrows to ½ca due to shoal S side and drying rk N side marked by G pole, Fl G 5s 3m 2M, 56°23'·24N 05°42'·04W. CCC SDs give local ldg lines. ⚓s in SW and NW arms, clear of fish farms. Pier at Croggan; no facilities.

ANCHORAGES ALONG LOCH LINNHE
(AC 5611, 2378, 2379, 2380)
LYNN OF LORN 56°33'N 05°25'·2W. At NE end are ⚓s off **Port Appin**, clear of ferry and cables (beware Appin Rks); and in Airds Bay, open to SW. At NW tip of Lismore, Port Ramsey offers good ⚓s between the 3 main islets.
Linnhe Marina ☎(01631) 730401 offers pontoon and moorings.

LOCH CRERAN 56°32'·14N 05°25'·22W. Tides 1.15. Enter at Airds Pt, Dir lt 050°, Fl WRG 2s, W vis 041-058°. Chan turns 90° stbd with streams of 4kn. Sgeir Callich, rky ridge extends NE to SHM By, Fl G 3s; ⚓ W of it. 🛟s (max LOA 7m) off Barcaldine; also 3🛟s (max LOA 9m) off Creagan Inn, ☎(01631) 573250. Bridge has 12m clearance. Beware of extensive marine farms in loch.

LOCH LEVEN 56°42'N 05°12'W. Tides 1.15. Ballachulish Bay ⚓s: N shore Onich and off St Brides, S shore Kentallen Bay (deep). Approach Ballachulish Bridge (16m clnce) on 114°. Moorings are 4ca to ENE with sheltered ⚓ at Poll an Dùnan, ent W of perch. Loch is navigable 7M to Kinlochleven.
Ballachulish: Hotels, ✉ Ⓑ 🛒 ✕.

CORRAN NARROWS 56°43'·27N 05°14'·34W. AC 2372. Sp rate 6kn. Well buoyed; Corran Pt lt ho, Iso WRG 4s, and lt bn 5ca NE. ⚓ 5ca NW of Pt, off Camas Aiseig pier/slip.

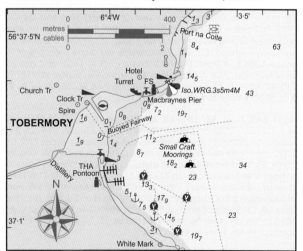

1.14 LOCH ALINE

Highland 56°32'·09N 05°46'·47W ✿✿✿🌢✿✿✿

CHARTS AC 5611, 2390; Imray C65, 2800

TIDES −0523 Dover; Duration 0610

Standard Port OBAN (→)

Times				Height (metres)			
High Water		Low Water		MHWS	MHWN	MLWN	MLWS
0100	0700	0100	0800	4·0	2·9	1·8	0·7
1300	1900	1300	2000				
Differences LOCH ALINE							
+0012	+0012	ND	ND	+0·5	+0·3	ND	ND
SALEN (Sound of Mull)							
+0045	+0015	+0020	+0030	+0·2	+0·2	−0·1	0·0
CRAIGNURE (Sound of Mull)							
+0030	+0005	+0010	+0015	0·0	+0·1	−0·1	−0·1

SHELTER Very good. ⚓s in SE end of loch and in N and E part of loch. Temp berth on old stone slip on W side of ent, depth and ferries permitting. Walk ashore pontoons N of sand mine pier.

NAVIGATION WPT 56°31'·49N 05°46'·37W, 176°/0·9M toldg bn. Bn (bright orange) leads 357°, 100m W of Bogha Lurcain, drying rk off Bolorkle Pt on E side of ent. Buoyed ent is easy, but narrow with a bar (min depth 2·1m); stream runs 2½kn at springs. Beware coasters (which completely fill the ent) from the sand mine going to/from the jetty and ferries to/from Mull. Last 5ca of loch dries.

LIGHTS AND MARKS Ardtornish Pt lt ho, 1M SSE of ent, Fl (2) WRG 10s 7m 8/5M. Lts and buoys as chartlet. War memorial, 9m high, stands on W side of ent. Dir Ldg lt, Oc WRG 6s, 357°, co-located with front ldg bn (Or). 1M up the loch on E side a Y bn with Y ● topmark marks a reef, and ½M further up similar bn marks a larger reef on W side. Clock tr is very conspic at head of loch.

COMMUNICATIONS (Code 01967) CGOC (01851) 702013; ⊖ (0141) 887 9369; Ⓗ (01631) 563727; Dr 421252. No VHF.

FACILITIES Pontoons, www.lochalineharbour.co.uk ☎ 07583 800500, 26⚓ inc ♥ £2·10, 🚾 📷 ⛽. **Village:** ⚓ at pier, ♦ 🏠🍴📮✉🛒 ✕ (Ⓑ ⇌ ✈ at Oban), Ferry to Fishnish Bay (Mull).

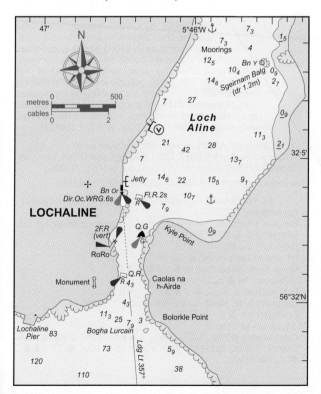

1.15 FORT WILLIAM/CORPACH

Highland 56°48'·99N 05°07'·07W (off Fort William)

CHARTS AC 5611, 2372, 2380, 5617; Imray C65, C63, 2800

TIDES −0535 Dover; ML 2·3; Duration 0610

Standard Port OBAN (→)

Times				Height (metres)			
High Water		Low Water		MHWS	MHWN	MLWN	MLWS
0100	0700	0100	0800	4·0	2·9	1·8	0·7
1300	1900	1300	2000				
Differences CORPACH							
0000	+0020	+0040	0000	0·0	0·0	−0·2	−0·2
LOCH EIL (Head)							
+0025	+0045	+0105	+0025	ND	ND	ND	ND
CORRAN NARROWS							
+0007	+0007	+0004	+0004	+0·4	+0·4	−0·1	0·0
LOCH LEVEN (Head)							
+0045	+0045	+0045	+0045	ND	ND	ND	ND
LOCH LINNHE (Port Appin)							
−0005	−0005	−0030	0000	+0·2	+0·2	+0·1	+0·1
LOCH CRERAN (Barcaldine Pier)							
+0010	+0020	+0040	+0015	+0·1	+0·1	0·0	+0·1
LOCH CRERAN (Head)							
+0015	+0025	+0120	+0020	−0·3	−0·3	−0·4	−0·3

SHELTER Exposed to winds SW thro' N to NE. ⚓s off Fort William pier; in Camus na Gall; SSW of Eilean A Bhealaidh; and off Corpach Basin, where there is also a waiting pontoon. The sea lock is normally available HW±4 during canal hrs. For Caledonian Canal see 1.16.

NAVIGATION Corpach WPT 56°50'·29N 05°07'·07W, 315°/0·32M to lock ent.

Beware McLean Rk, dries 0·3m, buoyed, 8ca N of Fort William. Lochy Flats dry 3ca off the E bank. In Annat Narrows at ent to Loch Eil streams reach 5kn.

LIGHTS AND MARKS Iso WRG 4s lt is at N jetty of sea-lock ent, W310°-335°. A long pier/viaduct off Ft William is unlit.

COMMUNICATIONS (Code 01397) CGOC (01851) 702013; ⊖ 702948; Police 101; Dr 703136. HM 772249.

Corpach Lock VHF Ch **74** 16 (during canal hours).

FACILITIES Fort William: Pier ☎703881 ⬛ ⚓ ⚓. **Town:** 🅿 ✕ ⚒ 🏧 🅛 ACA ✉ Ⓑ 🛒 ✕ 🗑 YC Ⓗ ⇌.
Corpach: Corpach Basin ☎772249 ⚓ ⚓ ⚓ ♦.
Lochaber YC ☎703576 ⚓ ⚓ ⬛ ⚓. **Services** ✕ ✎ 🏧 🅛 Divers.
Village: 🅿 🅿 ✉ Ⓑ 🛒 ✕ 🗑 ⇌.

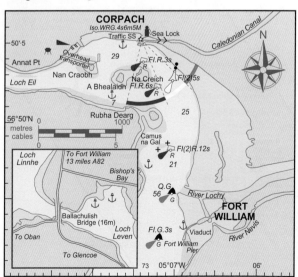

1.16 CALEDONIAN CANAL
Highland ⚓⚓💧💧💧🌼🌼🌼

CHARTS AC 1791, 5617; Imray C63; *Scottish Canals Skippers Guide*

TIDES Tidal differences: Corpach –0455 on Dover; See 1.15. Clachnaharry: +0116 on Dover.

SHELTER Corpach is at the SW ent of the Caledonian Canal, see 1.15; the sea locks at both ends do not open LW±2 at springs. For best shelter transit the sea lock and lie above the double lock. Numerous pontoons along the canal; cost is included in the canal dues.

NAVIGATION The 60M canal consists of 38M through 3 lochs, (Lochs Lochy, Oich and Ness), connected by 22M of canal. Loch Oich is part of a hydro-electric scheme which may vary the water level. The passage normally takes two full days, possibly longer in the summer; absolute minimum is 14 hrs. Speed limit is 5kn in the canal sections. There are 10 swing bridges; road traffic has priority at peak hrs. Do not pass bridges without the keeper's instructions.

LOCKS There are 29 locks: 14 between Loch Linnhe (Corpach), via Lochs Lochy and Oich up to the summit (106ft above sea level); and 15 locks from the summit down via Loch Ness to Inverness.

2012 information

Hours: Winter Mon-Fri 0900-1600
Spring Mon-Sun 0830-1730
Summer Mon-Sun 0800-1730
Autumn Mon-Sun 0830-1730

Dues payable at Corpach: transit/lock fee outward £16/m for 8 day passage or less; return £12/m. £20 per metre is charged for a 2 week sojourn. For regulations and useful booklet *Scottish Canals Skipper's Guide* apply: Canal Manager, Canal Office, Seaport Marina, Muirtown Wharf, Inverness IV3 5LE, ☎(01463) 233140, or download from: www. waterscape.com

LIGHTS AND MARKS See 1.15 for ent lts. Channel is marked by posts, cairns and unlit buoys, PHM on the NW side of the chan and SHM on the SE side.

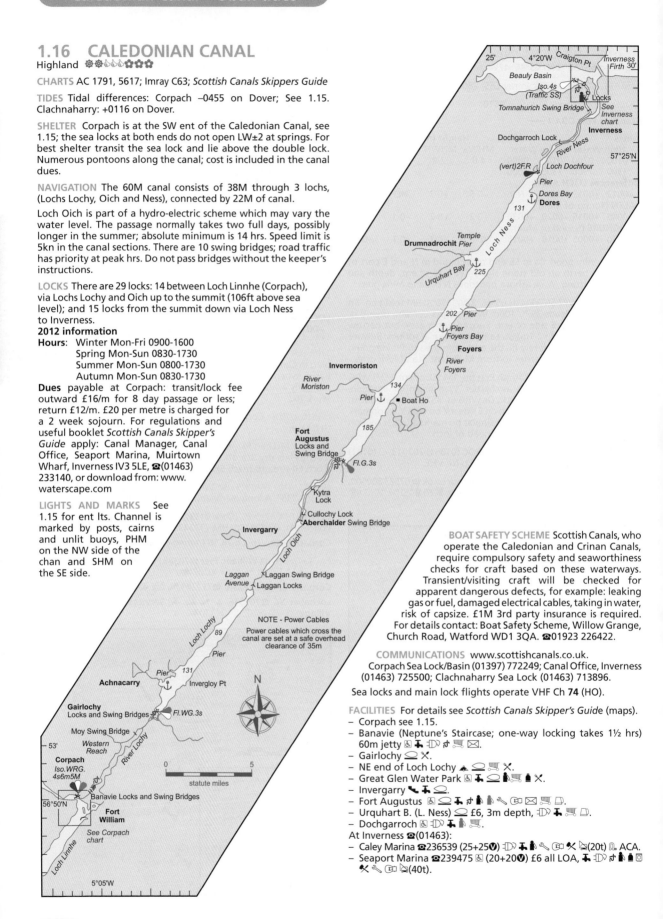

BOAT SAFETY SCHEME Scottish Canals, who operate the Caledonian and Crinan Canals, require compulsory safety and seaworthiness checks for craft based on these waterways. Transient/visiting craft will be checked for apparent dangerous defects, for example: leaking gas or fuel, damaged electrical cables, taking in water, risk of capsize. £1M 3rd party insurance is required. For details contact: Boat Safety Scheme, Willow Grange, Church Road, Watford WD1 3QA. ☎01923 226422.

COMMUNICATIONS www.scottishcanals.co.uk. Corpach Sea Lock/Basin (01397) 772249; Canal Office, Inverness (01463) 725500; Clachnaharry Sea Lock (01463) 713896.

Sea locks and main lock flights operate VHF Ch **74** (HO).

FACILITIES For details see *Scottish Canals Skipper's Guide* (maps).
– Corpach see 1.15.
– Banavie (Neptune's Staircase; one-way locking takes 1½ hrs) 60m jetty 🅿️⚓🛢️⛽🚰📮.
– Gairlochy ⚓✕.
– NE end of Loch Lochy ⚓⚓🛒✕.
– Great Glen Water Park 🅿️⚓⚓🛒🛢️🚰✕.
– Invergarry ⚓⚓⚓.
– Fort Augustus 🅿️⚓⚓🛢️⛽🚰🛒📮🛒🚰.
– Urquhart B. (L. Ness) ⚓ £6, 3m depth, ⛽⚓🚰🚰.
– Dochgarroch 🅿️⛽⚓🚰🛒.
At Inverness ☎(01463):
– Caley Marina ☎236539 (25+25Ⓥ) ⛽⚓🛢️🛒🚰✕⛴️(20t) ⚓ ACA.
– Seaport Marina ☎239475 🅿️ (20+20Ⓥ) £6 all LOA, ⚓⛽🛢️⚓🛒🚰✕🛒⛴️(40t).

STANDARD TIME (UT)
For Summer Time add ONE hour in **non-shaded areas**

OBAN LAT 56°25'N LONG 5°29'W
TIMES AND HEIGHTS OF HIGH AND LOW WATERS

Dates in red are **SPRINGS**
Dates in blue are NEAPS

YEAR 2016

NW Scotland

JANUARY				FEBRUARY				MARCH				APRIL			
Time	m	Time	m	Time	m	Time	m	Time	m	Time	m	Time	m	Time	m
1 0401 1.5 0943 3.4 F 1647 1.9 2215 3.2		**16** 0358 1.1 1000 3.6 SA 1636 1.3 ☾ 2214 3.2		**1** 0452 1.8 1024 3.2 M 1742 2.0 ☽ 2311 3.0		**16** 0546 1.4 1211 3.0 TU 1819 1.5		**1** 0403 1.7 0937 3.2 TU 1640 1.9 ☽ 2217 3.0		**16** 0527 1.3 1145 2.8 W 1750 1.4 2356 2.8		**1** 0538 1.9 1108 2.8 F 1823 1.9		**16** 0123 2.8 0821 1.6 SA 1449 2.8 1956 1.5	
2 0449 1.7 1032 3.2 SA 1743 2.0 ☽ 2317 3.0		**17** 0459 1.3 1107 3.3 SU 1741 1.5 2324 3.1		**2** 0549 1.9 1126 3.0 TU 1849 2.1		**17** 0025 2.9 0706 1.5 W 1405 3.0 1935 1.6		**2** 0459 1.9 1026 3.0 W 1752 2.0 2326 2.9		**17** 0650 1.6 1352 2.8 TH 1907 1.5		**2** 0058 2.9 0705 1.8 SA 1408 2.8 1943 1.7		**17** 0245 3.0 0928 1.5 SU 1535 3.0 2105 1.4	
3 0543 1.8 1139 3.1 SU 1848 2.1		**18** 0610 1.4 1246 3.2 M 1852 1.5		**3** 0101 2.9 0654 2.0 W 1342 3.0 2003 2.0		**18** 0215 3.0 0846 1.5 TH 1527 3.1 2053 1.5		**3** 0613 2.0 1151 2.8 TH 1910 2.0		**18** 0156 2.9 0843 1.5 F 1522 2.9 2031 1.5		**3** 0237 3.1 0827 1.6 SU 1511 3.1 2054 1.4		**18** 0326 3.2 1012 1.3 M 1601 3.2 2156 1.2	
4 0051 3.0 0641 1.9 M 1313 3.1 1959 2.0		**19** 0100 3.0 0729 1.5 TU 1419 3.3 2004 1.5		**4** 0238 3.0 0805 1.9 TH 1505 3.1 2113 1.8		**19** 0332 3.2 1002 1.4 F 1620 3.3 2156 1.3		**4** 0200 2.9 0732 1.9 F 1444 2.9 2028 1.8		**19** 0327 3.1 0953 1.4 SA 1609 3.1 2137 1.3		**4** 0329 3.4 0931 1.2 M 1553 3.3 2150 1.0		**19** 0400 3.4 1048 1.2 TU 1630 3.4 2237 1.0	
5 0214 3.1 0744 1.9 TU 1431 3.2 2104 1.9		**20** 0232 3.2 0851 1.4 W 1527 3.4 2112 1.4		**5** 0334 3.2 0917 1.7 F 1555 3.3 2204 1.5		**20** 0415 3.4 1052 1.2 SA 1654 3.5 2244 1.1		**5** 0311 3.1 0853 1.6 SA 1538 3.1 2132 1.5		**20** 0358 3.3 1038 1.2 SU 1634 3.3 2225 1.1		**5** 0412 3.8 1022 0.8 TU 1630 3.6 2237 0.7		**20** 0435 3.6 1119 1.1 W 1702 3.6 2313 0.9	
6 0309 3.2 0849 1.8 W 1525 3.4 2152 1.7		**21** 0336 3.4 1001 1.3 TH 1619 3.6 2209 1.2		**6** 0419 3.5 1017 1.4 SA 1637 3.5 2246 1.2		**21** 0451 3.7 1133 1.1 SU 1724 3.7 2325 0.9		**6** 0358 3.4 0957 1.3 SU 1614 3.4 2220 1.1		**21** 0430 3.5 1115 1.1 M 1701 3.5 2305 0.9		**6** 0453 4.0 1106 0.5 W 1706 3.9 2322 0.4		**21** 0509 3.7 1148 1.0 TH 1734 3.8 2347 0.9	
7 0355 3.4 0947 1.6 TH 1610 3.5 2231 1.4		**22** 0422 3.6 1056 1.1 F 1700 3.7 2257 1.0		**7** 0459 3.7 1105 1.1 SU 1715 3.7 2324 0.9		**22** 0526 3.8 1209 1.0 M 1755 3.8 ○		**7** 0439 3.7 1046 0.9 M 1656 3.7 2303 0.7		**22** 0503 3.7 1147 1.0 TU 1731 3.7 2341 0.8		**7** 0532 4.2 1147 0.3 TH 1742 4.0 ●		**22** 0542 3.8 1217 0.9 F 1805 3.9 ○	
8 0436 3.6 1036 1.4 F 1651 3.7 2307 1.2		**23** 0503 3.8 1141 1.0 SA 1737 3.8 2340 0.9		**8** 0538 4.0 1148 0.8 M 1750 3.9 ●		**23** 0003 0.8 0600 4.0 TU 1243 0.9 1826 3.9		**8** 0517 4.0 1129 0.6 TU 1730 3.9 2343 0.4		**23** 0537 3.9 1218 0.9 W 1802 3.9 ○		**8** 0005 0.2 0610 4.3 F 1228 0.2 1819 4.1		**23** 0020 0.9 0614 3.9 SA 1247 1.0 1834 3.9	
9 0515 3.8 1120 1.2 SA 1729 3.8 2343 1.0		**24** 0541 4.0 1223 1.0 SU 1811 3.9 ○		**9** 0002 0.6 0614 4.1 TU 1229 0.6 1823 4.0		**24** 0040 0.7 0633 4.0 W 1316 1.0 1856 4.0		**9** 0555 4.2 1210 0.4 W 1804 4.0 ●		**24** 0015 0.7 0608 4.0 TH 1248 0.9 1831 3.9		**9** 0050 0.1 0650 4.2 SA 1310 0.2 1858 4.0		**24** 0052 0.9 0644 3.8 SU 1317 1.0 1904 3.8	
10 0552 4.0 1202 1.0 SU 1804 3.9 ●		**25** 0020 0.8 0617 4.1 M 1302 1.0 1844 3.9		**10** 0042 0.4 0650 4.2 W 1309 0.5 1858 4.0		**25** 0114 0.7 0704 4.0 TH 1347 1.0 1925 3.9		**10** 0024 0.2 0632 4.3 TH 1250 0.3 1839 4.1		**25** 0048 0.8 0639 4.0 F 1317 1.0 1859 3.9		**10** 0135 0.2 0730 4.0 SU 1352 0.3 1939 3.9		**25** 0124 1.0 0713 3.7 M 1344 1.1 1934 3.7	
11 0019 0.9 0628 4.0 M 1243 0.9 1837 3.9		**26** 0059 0.8 0653 4.1 TU 1339 1.1 1917 3.9		**11** 0123 0.4 0727 4.2 TH 1350 0.6 1935 3.9		**26** 0147 0.9 0734 3.9 F 1417 1.2 1954 3.8		**11** 0107 0.1 0709 4.1 F 1330 0.3 1917 4.0		**26** 0120 0.9 0708 3.9 SA 1346 1.1 1927 3.8		**11** 0221 0.4 0812 3.8 M 1437 0.6 2021 3.7		**26** 0153 1.2 0741 3.6 TU 1408 1.3 2005 3.6	
12 0058 0.8 0703 4.1 TU 1324 0.8 1912 3.9		**27** 0136 0.8 0727 4.0 W 1414 1.2 1949 3.8		**12** 0205 0.4 0806 4.0 F 1432 0.6 2015 3.8		**27** 0218 1.0 0803 3.8 SA 1446 1.4 2024 3.7		**12** 0150 0.2 0748 4.1 SA 1412 0.4 1956 3.8		**27** 0150 1.0 0736 3.8 SU 1413 1.2 1956 3.7		**12** 0311 0.7 0857 3.4 TU 1526 0.8 2107 3.4		**27** 0223 1.3 0811 3.4 W 1438 1.4 2041 3.4	
13 0137 0.7 0741 4.0 W 1406 0.9 1951 3.8		**28** 0212 1.0 0800 3.9 TH 1448 1.4 2021 3.7		**13** 0251 0.6 0849 3.8 SA 1518 0.8 2058 3.5		**28** 0249 1.2 0831 3.6 SU 1515 1.5 2055 3.5		**13** 0236 0.4 0829 3.8 SU 1457 0.6 2038 3.6		**28** 0218 1.2 0802 3.6 M 1435 1.4 2027 3.5		**13** 0406 1.1 0951 3.0 W 1620 1.1 2203 3.1		**28** 0301 1.5 0849 3.2 TH 1520 1.6 2125 3.2	
14 0220 0.8 0822 3.9 TH 1451 1.0 2033 3.6		**29** 0248 1.1 0832 3.7 F 1522 1.6 2054 3.5		**14** 0340 0.8 0936 3.5 SU 1610 1.1 2147 3.3		**29** 0323 1.5 0901 3.4 M 1549 1.7 2132 3.3		**14** 0325 0.7 0915 3.5 M 1547 0.9 2125 3.3		**29** 0246 1.4 0831 3.4 TU 1502 1.6 2101 3.3		**14** 0510 1.4 1119 2.8 TH 1722 1.4 ☽ 2325 2.9		**29** 0355 1.6 0939 3.0 F 1621 1.7 2225 3.1	
15 0306 0.9 0908 3.8 F 1540 1.1 2120 3.4		**30** 0325 1.4 0905 3.6 SA 1600 1.7 2131 3.4		**15** 0438 1.1 1035 3.2 M 1710 1.3 ☽ 2249 3.0						**15** 0421 1.2 1010 3.1 TU 1644 1.2 ☽ 2223 3.0		**30** 0322 1.6 0906 3.2 W 1544 1.7 2144 3.1		**15** 0633 1.6 1325 2.7 F 1834 1.5		**30** 0512 1.7 1051 2.8 SA 1740 1.7 ☽ 2356 3.0	
		31 0405 1.6 0941 3.4 SU 1645 1.9 2213 3.2								**31** 0415 1.8 0953 3.0 TH 1656 1.9 ☽ 2246 2.9					

Chart Datum: 2·10 metres below Ordnance Datum (Newlyn). HAT is 4·5 metres above Chart Datum.

》》 **FREE** monthly updates. Register at 《
www.reedsnauticalalmanac.co.uk 《

59

STANDARD TIME (UT)
For Summer Time add ONE hour in **non-shaded areas**

OBAN LAT 56°25'N LONG 5°29'W
TIMES AND HEIGHTS OF HIGH AND LOW WATERS

Dates in red are SPRINGS
Dates in blue are NEAPS

YEAR 2016

MAY

Day	Time m	Time m	Time m	Time m
1 SU	0637 1.7	1247 2.8	1900 1.6	
2 M	0150 3.2	0755 1.5	1429 3.0	2014 1.4
3 TU	0254 3.5	0900 1.2	1520 3.3	2117 1.0
4 W	0343 3.7	0953 0.9	1601 3.6	2211 0.7
5 TH	0427 4.0	1040 0.6	1640 3.8	2301 0.5
6 F	0509 4.1	1124 0.4	1720 4.0	●2348 0.3
7 SA	0551 4.2	1207 0.3	1801 4.1	
8 SU	0034 0.3	0632 4.1	1250 0.3	1842 4.0
9 M	0121 0.3	0714 4.0	1334 0.4	1924 3.9
10 TU	0209 0.5	0757 3.7	1418 0.6	2007 3.7
11 W	0258 0.8	0843 3.4	1506 1.0	2052 3.5
12 TH	0351 1.1	0934 3.1	1557 1.1	2143 3.2
13 F	0451 1.4	1043 2.8	1653 1.3	☽2247 3.0
14 SA	0604 1.6	1237 2.7	1755 1.5	
15 SU	0021 2.9	0735 1.7	1353 2.8	1905 1.5
16 M	0150 2.9	0848 1.6	1444 2.9	2016 1.5
17 TU	0244 3.1	0937 1.5	1522 3.1	2115 1.4
18 W	0325 3.2	1015 1.4	1556 3.3	2201 1.3
19 TH	0403 3.4	1048 1.2	1631 3.5	2239 1.2
20 F	0440 3.6	1117 1.1	1706 3.7	2315 1.1
21 SA	0516 3.7	1147 1.1	1740 3.8	○2351 1.0
22 SU	0551 3.7	1218 1.0	1813 3.8	
23 M	0026 1.0	0624 3.7	1251 1.0	1844 3.8
24 TU	0102 1.1	0655 3.7	1321 1.1	1917 3.7
25 W	0137 1.1	0727 3.6	1351 1.2	1951 3.6
26 TH	0212 1.2	0801 3.4	1425 1.3	2029 3.5
27 F	0253 1.4	0842 3.3	1508 1.4	2114 3.4
28 SA	0345 1.5	0932 3.1	1601 1.4	2210 3.3
29 SU	0451 1.5	1035 3.0	1708 1.5	☽2322 3.2
30 M	0607 1.5	1156 2.9	1823 1.5	
31 TU	0056 3.3	0721 1.4	1332 3.0	1937 1.3

JUNE

Day	Time m	Time m	Time m	Time m
1 W	0217 3.4	0827 1.2	1442 3.2	2047 1.1
2 TH	0316 3.6	0925 1.0	1534 3.5	2148 0.9
3 F	0406 3.8	1016 0.8	1620 3.7	2243 0.7
4 SA	0452 4.0	1104 0.6	1703 3.9	2333 0.5
5 SU	0536 4.0	1149 0.5	●1747 4.0	
6 M	0022 0.5	0619 4.0	1234 0.5	1829 4.0
7 TU	0110 0.6	0702 3.9	1317 0.5	1911 4.0
8 W	0157 0.7	0745 3.7	1401 0.7	1953 3.8
9 TH	0244 0.9	0828 3.5	1446 0.8	2036 3.6
10 F	0333 1.2	0912 3.2	1532 1.1	2120 3.4
11 SA	0424 1.4	1007 3.1	1620 1.3	2209 3.2
12 SU	0521 1.6	1108 2.9	1713 1.5	☽2308 3.0
13 M	0627 1.7	1239 2.8	1809 1.6	
14 TU	0024 2.9	0743 1.8	1348 2.9	1910 1.6
15 W	0144 3.0	0848 1.7	1439 3.0	2013 1.6
16 TH	0243 3.1	0936 1.6	1522 3.2	2111 1.5
17 F	0330 3.3	1014 1.4	1602 3.4	2200 1.4
18 SA	0413 3.4	1048 1.3	1641 3.5	2243 1.3
19 SU	0454 3.6	1121 1.2	1719 3.7	2325 1.2
20 M	0533 3.7	1154 1.1	○1756 3.8	
21 TU	0005 1.1	0609 3.7	1229 1.0	1830 3.8
22 W	0045 1.0	0643 3.7	1303 1.0	1905 3.8
23 TH	0124 1.0	0716 3.6	1337 1.0	1940 3.8
24 F	0203 1.0	0751 3.5	1414 1.0	2019 3.7
25 SA	0245 1.1	0832 3.4	1456 1.1	2102 3.6
26 SU	0333 1.2	0919 3.3	1545 1.2	2153 3.5
27 M	0429 1.3	1013 3.1	1643 1.3	☽2255 3.3
28 TU	0536 1.4	1121 3.0	1752 1.4	
29 W	0015 3.3	0647 1.4	1247 3.0	1907 1.4
30 TH	0147 3.3	0757 1.3	1413 3.2	2022 1.3

JULY

Day	Time m	Time m	Time m	Time m
1 F	0258 3.5	0901 1.1	1517 3.4	2131 1.1
2 SA	0355 3.6	0957 1.0	1608 3.6	2231 0.9
3 SU	0445 3.8	1048 0.8	1654 3.8	2324 0.8
4 M	0530 3.8	1135 0.7	●1737 3.9	
5 TU	0013 0.7	0612 3.9	1220 0.6	1818 4.0
6 W	0059 0.7	0652 3.8	1302 0.6	1858 4.0
7 TH	0144 0.8	0730 3.7	1344 0.7	1937 3.9
8 F	0226 1.0	0808 3.6	1424 0.8	2015 3.8
9 SA	0308 1.2	0845 3.4	1505 1.0	2052 3.6
10 SU	0350 1.4	0923 3.3	1546 1.2	2131 3.4
11 M	0434 1.6	1007 3.1	1631 1.4	2215 3.2
12 TU	0524 1.8	1102 3.0	1720 1.6	☽2308 3.0
13 W	0623 1.9	1222 2.9	1815 1.7	
14 TH	0024 2.9	0733 1.9	1349 2.9	1915 1.8
15 F	0153 3.0	0845 1.8	1450 3.1	2019 1.7
16 SA	0301 3.1	0941 1.6	1538 3.2	2122 1.6
17 SU	0352 3.3	1023 1.4	1622 3.4	2217 1.4
18 M	0437 3.5	1100 1.2	1703 3.6	2304 1.2
19 TU	0519 3.6	1135 1.0	1741 3.8	○2348 1.1
20 W	0557 3.7	1209 0.9	1818 3.9	
21 TH	0029 0.9	0630 3.8	1245 0.8	1852 4.0
22 F	0109 0.8	0702 3.8	1321 0.7	1927 4.0
23 SA	0149 0.8	0737 3.7	1400 0.7	2004 3.9
24 SU	0230 0.8	0815 3.6	1442 0.8	2046 3.8
25 M	0315 0.9	0859 3.4	1529 0.9	2133 3.6
26 TU	0407 1.1	0949 3.3	1623 1.1	☽2229 3.4
27 W	0508 1.3	1050 3.1	1730 1.3	2344 3.2
28 TH	0617 1.4	1215 3.0	1845 1.4	
29 F	0129 3.1	0730 1.4	1359 3.1	2005 1.4
30 SA	0252 3.2	0842 1.3	1515 3.3	2125 1.3
31 SU	0356 3.4	0944 1.1	1608 3.5	2229 1.1

AUGUST

Day	Time m	Time m	Time m	Time m
1 M	0445 3.6	1037 0.9	1650 3.7	2320 0.9
2 TU	0526 3.7	1123 0.8	●1728 3.9	
3 W	0004 0.9	0602 3.8	1206 0.7	1805 4.0
4 TH	0045 0.8	0637 3.9	1246 0.6	1841 4.0
5 F	0124 0.8	0710 3.8	1324 0.7	1916 4.0
6 SA	0202 1.0	0743 3.8	1400 0.8	1949 3.9
7 SU	0237 1.1	0814 3.6	1435 1.0	2021 3.7
8 M	0313 1.3	0846 3.5	1512 1.2	2054 3.5
9 TU	0350 1.5	0922 3.3	1552 1.4	2129 3.3
10 W	0434 1.7	1004 3.1	1637 1.7	☽2209 3.1
11 TH	0528 1.9	1102 3.0	1731 1.8	2303 3.0
12 F	0634 2.0	1249 2.9	1833 1.9	
13 SA	0102 2.9	0750 1.9	1426 3.0	1942 1.9
14 SU	0242 3.0	0906 1.7	1522 3.2	2055 1.7
15 M	0339 3.2	0959 1.5	1606 3.4	2159 1.5
16 TU	0423 3.4	1039 1.2	1646 3.7	2248 1.2
17 W	0503 3.6	1115 1.0	1724 3.9	2331 0.9
18 TH	0539 3.8	1149 0.7	1801 4.0	○
19 F	0011 0.7	0612 3.9	1225 0.5	1835 4.1
20 SA	0051 0.6	0643 3.9	1303 0.4	1909 4.1
21 SU	0130 0.5	0717 3.9	1343 0.4	1946 4.1
22 M	0211 0.6	0755 3.8	1426 0.6	2026 3.9
23 TU	0255 0.7	0836 3.6	1513 0.8	2110 3.6
24 W	0344 0.9	0924 3.3	1607 1.0	2204 3.3
25 TH	0442 1.2	1023 3.1	1713 1.3	☽2320 3.1
26 F	0551 1.4	1152 2.9	1829 1.5	
27 SA	0123 3.0	0707 1.5	1358 3.0	2000 1.5
28 SU	0253 3.1	0826 1.4	1519 3.2	2132 1.4
29 M	0356 3.3	0933 1.2	1606 3.4	2229 1.2
30 TU	0439 3.5	1024 1.0	1639 3.7	2312 1.1
31 W	0511 3.6	1108 0.8	1712 3.9	2349 0.8

Chart Datum: 2·10 metres below Ordnance Datum (Newlyn). HAT is 4·5 metres above Chart Datum.

STANDARD TIME (UT)	OBAN LAT 56°25'N LONG 5°29'W	Dates in red are SPRINGS
For Summer Time add ONE hour in **non-shaded areas**	TIMES AND HEIGHTS OF HIGH AND LOW WATERS	Dates in blue are NEAPS

YEAR **2016**

NW Scotland

SEPTEMBER

Time m	Time m
1 0543 3.8 / 1148 0.7 / TH 1746 4.0 ●	**16** 0516 3.8 / 1126 0.6 / F 1737 4.2 / ○ 2349 0.6
2 0025 0.9 / 0614 3.9 / F 1225 0.7 / 1818 4.1	**17** 0548 4.0 / 1204 0.4 / SA 1812 4.3
3 0059 0.9 / 0645 3.9 / SA 1300 0.7 / 1849 4.1	**18** 0028 0.4 / 0620 4.0 / SU 1244 0.3 / 1847 4.3
4 0132 1.0 / 0714 3.9 / SU 1333 0.8 / 1920 4.0	**19** 0107 0.3 / 0655 4.0 / M 1325 0.3 / 1924 4.2
5 0204 1.1 / 0743 3.8 / M 1406 1.0 / 1950 3.9	**20** 0149 0.4 / 0733 3.9 / TU 1410 0.5 / 2004 4.0
6 0236 1.3 / 0812 3.7 / TU 1439 1.2 / 2019 3.7	**21** 0233 0.6 / 0815 3.7 / W 1458 0.7 / 2049 3.6
7 0310 1.5 / 0845 3.5 / W 1514 1.5 / 2049 3.5	**22** 0322 0.9 / 0902 3.5 / TH 1553 1.1 / 2141 3.3
8 0348 1.7 / 0922 3.3 / TH 1557 1.7 / 2123 3.2	**23** 0419 1.2 / 1000 3.2 / F 1659 1.4 / ☽ 2259 3.0
9 0439 1.9 / 1010 3.1 / F 1651 1.9 / ☽ 2207 3.0	**24** 0526 1.4 / 1134 3.0 / SA 1818 1.6
10 0546 2.0 / 1131 2.9 / SA 1759 2.1 / 2324 2.8	**25** 0117 2.9 / 0642 1.5 / SU 1354 3.0 / 2005 1.6
11 0704 2.0 / 1405 3.0 / SU 1916 2.0	**26** 0250 3.0 / 0806 1.5 / M 1518 3.2 / 2128 1.5
12 0228 2.9 / 0825 1.8 / M 1504 3.2 / 2035 1.8	**27** 0348 3.2 / 0915 1.3 / TU 1553 3.4 / 2217 1.3
13 0324 3.1 / 0927 1.6 / TU 1547 3.5 / 2140 1.5	**28** 0421 3.4 / 1005 1.1 / W 1618 3.7 / 2255 1.1
14 0405 3.4 / 1011 1.2 / W 1625 3.7 / 2228 1.1	**29** 0447 3.6 / 1047 0.9 / TH 1648 3.8 / 2328 1.0
15 0442 3.6 / 1049 0.9 / TH 1701 4.0 / 2310 0.8	**30** 0516 3.8 / 1125 0.8 / F 1720 4.0 / 2359 1.0

OCTOBER

Time m	Time m
1 0547 3.9 / 1200 0.8 / SA 1751 4.1 ●	**16** 0521 4.1 / 1142 0.4 / SU 1747 4.4 / ○
2 0029 0.9 / 0616 4.0 / SU 1234 0.8 / 1821 4.1	**17** 0003 0.4 / 0557 4.2 / M 1225 0.3 / 1825 4.4
3 0100 1.0 / 0645 4.0 / M 1306 0.9 / 1851 4.0	**18** 0045 0.3 / 0634 4.2 / TU 1309 0.4 / 1904 4.2
4 0132 1.1 / 0714 4.0 / TU 1337 1.1 / 1921 3.9	**19** 0127 0.4 / 0715 4.0 / W 1355 0.5 / 1945 4.0
5 0203 1.3 / 0743 3.8 / W 1408 1.3 / 1949 3.7	**20** 0212 0.6 / 0757 3.8 / TH 1445 0.8 / 2030 3.6
6 0233 1.5 / 0815 3.6 / TH 1441 1.6 / 2017 3.5	**21** 0301 0.9 / 0845 3.6 / F 1540 1.1 / 2122 3.3
7 0304 1.7 / 0851 3.4 / F 1519 1.8 / 2049 3.3	**22** 0356 1.1 / 0941 3.3 / SA 1644 1.5 / ☽ 2236 3.0
8 0346 1.9 / 0934 3.2 / SA 1613 2.0 / 2131 3.1	**23** 0459 1.4 / 1106 3.1 / SU 1803 1.7
9 0454 2.0 / 1038 3.0 / SU 1728 2.1 / ☽ 2239 2.9	**24** 0055 2.8 / 0611 1.6 / M 1328 3.1 / 1950 1.7
10 0615 2.0 / 1327 3.0 / M 1850 2.1	**25** 0226 2.9 / 0733 1.6 / TU 1454 3.2 / 2106 1.6
11 0159 2.9 / 0735 1.9 / TU 1434 3.2 / 2010 1.8	**26** 0322 3.1 / 0845 1.4 / W 1526 3.4 / 2153 1.4
12 0258 3.1 / 0844 1.6 / W 1519 3.5 / 2113 1.5	**27** 0351 3.3 / 0938 1.3 / TH 1550 3.6 / 2229 1.3
13 0339 3.4 / 0936 1.3 / TH 1557 3.8 / 2201 1.1	**28** 0416 3.5 / 1021 1.1 / F 1620 3.8 / 2301 1.2
14 0414 3.6 / 1020 0.9 / F 1634 4.1 / 2244 0.8	**29** 0446 3.7 / 1058 1.0 / SA 1652 3.9 / 2330 1.1
15 0448 3.9 / 1101 0.6 / SA 1710 4.3 / 2324 0.5	**30** 0518 3.9 / 1133 1.0 / SU 1724 4.0 / ● 2359 1.1
	31 0549 4.0 / 1206 1.0 / M 1755 4.1

NOVEMBER

Time m	Time m
1 0030 1.1 / 0619 4.1 / TU 1239 1.1 / 1826 4.0	**16** 0024 0.4 / 0618 4.2 / W 1256 0.5 / 1847 4.2
2 0102 1.1 / 0650 4.0 / W 1312 1.2 / 1857 3.9	**17** 0108 0.5 / 0700 4.1 / TH 1343 0.7 / 1930 4.0
3 0134 1.3 / 0721 3.9 / TH 1344 1.4 / 1926 3.8	**18** 0154 0.6 / 0744 4.0 / F 1433 0.9 / 2015 3.7
4 0203 1.4 / 0753 3.8 / F 1416 1.6 / 1955 3.6	**19** 0242 0.9 / 0831 3.7 / SA 1526 1.2 / 2104 3.4
5 0232 1.6 / 0828 3.6 / SA 1452 1.8 / 2029 3.4	**20** 0334 1.1 / 0923 3.5 / SU 1625 1.5 / 2205 3.1
6 0308 1.8 / 0910 3.4 / SU 1542 1.9 / 2113 3.2	**21** 0430 1.4 / 1028 3.2 / M 1736 1.7 / ☽ 2355 2.9
7 0402 1.9 / 1007 3.2 / M 1654 2.0 / ☽ 2216 3.0	**22** 0534 1.5 / 1215 3.1 / TU 1904 1.8
8 0519 2.0 / 1137 3.2 / TU 1816 2.0 / 2359 2.9	**23** 0130 2.9 / 0645 1.6 / W 1353 3.2 / 2025 1.6
9 0638 1.9 / 1346 3.3 / W 1933 1.8	**24** 0231 3.0 / 0758 1.6 / TH 1444 3.3 / 2118 1.7
10 0214 3.1 / 0752 1.7 / TH 1442 3.6 / 2037 1.5	**25** 0310 3.2 / 0900 1.5 / F 1518 3.4 / 2158 1.5
11 0303 3.3 / 0856 1.4 / F 1526 3.8 / 2129 1.2	**26** 0343 3.4 / 0949 1.4 / SA 1551 3.6 / 2232 1.4
12 0342 3.6 / 0948 1.1 / SA 1606 4.1 / 2215 0.9	**27** 0416 3.6 / 1029 1.3 / SU 1624 3.8 / 2302 1.2
13 0419 3.9 / 1036 0.8 / SU 1646 4.3 / 2259 0.6	**28** 0451 3.8 / 1105 1.3 / M 1659 3.9 / 2332 1.2
14 0457 4.1 / 1123 0.6 / M 1726 4.4 / ○ 2341 0.5	**29** 0525 3.9 / 1140 1.2 / TU 1734 4.0 / ●
15 0537 4.2 / 1209 0.5 / TU 1806 4.4	**30** 0004 1.2 / 0558 4.0 / W 1215 1.2 / 1808 4.0

DECEMBER

Time m	Time m
1 0038 1.2 / 0632 4.0 / TH 1251 1.3 / 1840 3.9	**16** 0054 0.6 / 0649 4.2 / F 1334 0.8 / 1919 4.0
2 0111 1.2 / 0704 3.9 / F 1326 1.4 / 1912 3.8	**17** 0139 0.6 / 0733 4.1 / SA 1421 1.0 / 2002 3.8
3 0142 1.3 / 0738 3.8 / SA 1400 1.5 / 1943 3.7	**18** 0224 0.8 / 0816 3.9 / SU 1509 1.2 / 2045 3.5
4 0212 1.4 / 0813 3.7 / SU 1436 1.6 / 2019 3.5	**19** 0311 1.0 / 0901 3.6 / M 1600 1.5 / 2132 3.3
5 0247 1.6 / 0853 3.6 / M 1521 1.7 / 2101 3.3	**20** 0400 1.3 / 0949 3.4 / TU 1655 1.7 / 2228 3.1
6 0333 1.7 / 0943 3.4 / TU 1619 1.8 / 2155 3.2	**21** 0452 1.5 / 1047 3.2 / W 1758 1.9 / ☽ 2351 3.0
7 0433 1.7 / 1048 3.3 / W 1732 1.9 / ☽ 2305 3.1	**22** 0549 1.6 / 1206 3.1 / TH 1912 1.9
8 0546 1.8 / 1218 3.3 / TH 1847 1.8	**23** 0121 3.0 / 0652 1.7 / F 1340 3.1 / 2026 1.9
9 0037 3.1 / 0702 1.7 / F 1354 3.5 / 1955 1.6	**24** 0221 3.1 / 0801 1.8 / SA 1439 3.2 / 2121 1.8
10 0210 3.2 / 0815 1.5 / SA 1454 3.7 / 2056 1.3	**25** 0308 3.2 / 0906 1.7 / SU 1522 3.4 / 2202 1.6
11 0308 3.5 / 0920 1.2 / SU 1543 3.9 / 2148 1.1	**26** 0349 3.4 / 0957 1.6 / M 1601 3.5 / 2237 1.5
12 0355 3.8 / 1017 1.0 / M 1628 4.1 / 2237 0.8	**27** 0428 3.6 / 1039 1.5 / TU 1640 3.7 / 2310 1.3
13 0440 4.0 / 1109 0.8 / TU 1711 4.2 / 2323 0.7	**28** 0506 3.8 / 1118 1.4 / W 1719 3.8 / 2344 1.2
14 0523 4.1 / 1158 0.7 / W 1754 4.2 / ○	**29** 0543 3.9 / 1156 1.3 / TH 1756 3.9 / ●
15 0008 0.6 / 0606 4.2 / TH 1246 0.7 / 1836 4.1	**30** 0018 1.2 / 0619 4.0 / F 1234 1.2 / 1829 3.9
	31 0052 1.1 / 0652 4.0 / SA 1311 1.2 / 1900 3.8

Chart Datum: 2·10 metres below Ordnance Datum (Newlyn). HAT is 4·5 metres above Chart Datum.

》》 FREE monthly updates. Register at 《
www.reedsnauticalalmanac.co.uk

61

1.17 OBAN

Argyll and Bute **56°24'·99N 05°29'·07W** ❀❀❀◊◊◊◊✿✿

CHARTS AC 2171, 2387, 2388, 1790; Imray C65, 2800

TIDES −0530 Dover; ML 2·4; Duration 0610

Standard Port OBAN (←)

Times				Height (metres)			
High Water		Low Water		MHWS	MHWN	MLWN	MLWS
0100	0700	0100	0800	4·0	2·9	1·8	0·7
1300	1900	1300	2000				
Differences DUNSTAFFNAGE BAY							
+0005	0000	0000	+0005	+0·1	+0·1	+0·1	+0·1
CONNEL							
+0020	+0005	+0010	+0015	−0·3	−0·2	−0·1	+0·1
BONAWE							
+0150	+0205	+0240	+0210	−2·0	−1·7	−1·3	−0·5

SHELTER Good shelter in bay except in strong SW/NW winds, but Oban Marina in Ardantrive Bay (Kerrera) is well sheltered from all directions, but as yet has no water on pontoons. The only ⚓s convenient for town are in deep water off the Esplanade and NW of Sailing Club, beware of moorings. Alternatively ⚓ at N end of Kerrera to S of Rubh'a Chruidh Is or Horseshoe Bay and Little Horseshoe Bay, Kerrera Sound. Beware fish farms S of Ardantrive Bay.

NAVIGATION WPT (N) 56°25'·85N 05°30'·0W, 132°/0·7M to Dunollie lt; WPT (S) 56°22'N 05°33'W, 035°/1M to 1·5ca E of Sgeirean Dubha, thence through Kerrera Sound to Oban Bay. Ferry Rks can be passed on either side. Direction of the buoyage is **NE**, thus pass to the E'ward of PHM unlit buoy or to W'ward of the SHM QG buoy. The N'ly SHM buoy must be passed to the W'ward. In Oban Bay beware Sgeir Rathaid, buoyed, in middle of the bay and ferries running to/from Railway Pier.

LIGHTS AND MARKS See 1.3 and chartlet.

COMMUNICATIONS (Code 01631) CGOC (01851) 702013; ⊖ 08457 231110; Police 101; Dr 563175; N Pier ☎562892.

North Pier Ch 12 16 (0900–1700); Railway Pier, *CalMac* Ch 06 12 16; *Oban Marina* Ch 80.

FACILITIES **North Pier** ⬱ ⬱ ⚓ ⏍(15t mob) via Piermaster.
Railway Pier ⬱ ⚓ ⛽(H24, ☎562849) ⬛ ⚓ ACA ⚒ ⏍ divers.
Oban Sailing Club 16 ⛟s £15/night, pay at Y honesty box £5 until 1600; short stay ⬱ (with ⚓), £2/half hour; free for 30 mins.
Oban Marina (Ardantrive Bay) www.obanmarina.com ☎565333; 30 ⛟s £18/nt (20t), £30/nt (50t); 100⬱ £2.35+⏍ ⬛▲⬛⬛ Ⓔ⏍× ⬛⚓(limited) ⍟ ▶(50t). Water taxi to/from Oban (hrly, 0830-2100 Apr, 0730-2300, Oct-Apr 2hrly), free for boat crews.
Town ☎(½M), all facilities, Ⓗ, ⇌ Connel (airstrip) 3M, Glasgow (✈) 3hrs, ferries to Inner & Outer Hebrides.
Heather Is ⛟s 3Y 15t, 1 Gy 20t, 1 Or 50t; £10/nt (pay Ardantrive Fm).

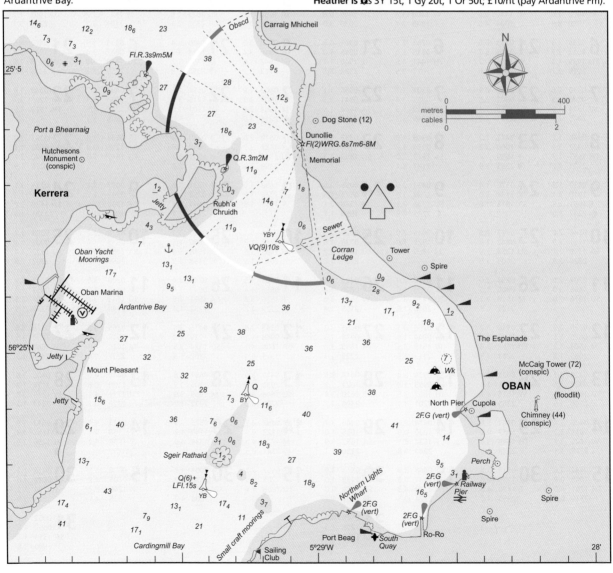

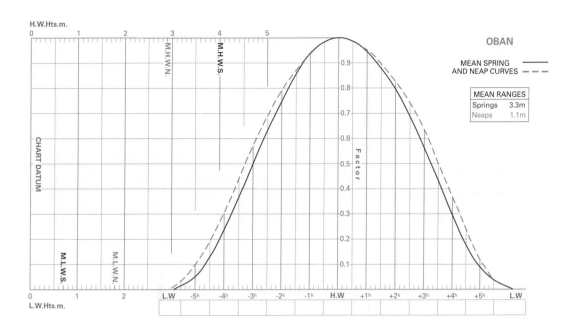

OBAN

MEAN SPRING
AND NEAP CURVES

MEAN RANGES	
Springs	3.3m
Neaps	1.1m

ADJACENT HARBOUR ON MAINLAND TO N OF OBAN

DUNSTAFFNAGE Marina, Argyll and Bute, **56°27'·04N 05°25'·97W**. AC 2388, 5611. Within the bay the tidal stream is rotary setting mainly E through the marina and running strongly through the moorings. Enter between Rubha Garbh and Eilean Mór. No navigational hazards, W and SW sides of bay dry. Use buoyed fairway, keeping clear of moorings, spd limit 4kn.

☎(01631) 566555, VHF Ch37/M1 ◣ (launch H24 except LWS ±2hrs) 200⌂ inc 🅥 £2·45+£3 ⛽ 🅟 ♫(0830-2000 summer) 🅿 ⚒ △ ⛽ 🅡 🖩(40t) ⬟(masting) ✕ 🛒 (½M) 🅟 (¾M), bus, ⇌ Oban (3M).

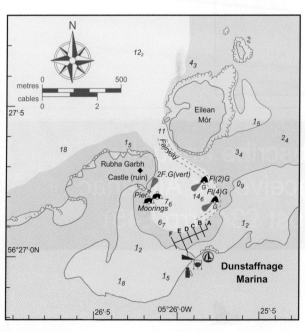

ANCHORAGES ON MAINLAND SHORE OF FIRTH OF LORN

LOCH FEOCHAN, Argyll and Bute, **56°21'·39N 05°29'·77W**. AC 5611, 2387. HW = HW Oban; flood runs 4 hrs, ebb for 8 hrs. Caution: strong streams off Ardentallan Pt. Good shelter, 5M S of Oban and 1·5M SE of Kerrera. Best appr at local slack LW = LW Oban +0200. Narrow buoyed channel, ⚓ off pier, or moor off.

Ardoran Marine ☎(01631) 566123, 🖷 566611; 4 🅐s £10·00 <11m, ◣ ⚓ 🅿 ⚒ 🅡 🖩.

PUILLADOBHRAIN, Argyll and Bute, **56°19'·47N 05°35'·22W**. AC 5611, 2386/2387. Tides as Oban. Popular ⚓ on the SE shore of the Firth of Lorne, approx 7M S of Oban, sheltered by the islets to the W of it. At N end of Ardencaple Bay identify Eilean Dùin (18m) and steer SE keeping 1½ca off to clear a rk awash at its NE tip. Continue for 4ca between Eilean nam Beathach, with Orange drum on N tip, and Dun Horses rks drying 2·7m. Two W cairns on E side of Eilean nam Freumha lead approx 215° into the inner ⚓ in about 4m. Landing at head of inlet. Nearest facilities: 🖂 ☎ at Clachan Br (½M); ☎ ✉ at Clachan Seil.

CUAN SOUND, Argyll and Bute, **56°15'·84N 05°37'·47W**. AC 2386, 2326. Tides see 1.17 SEIL SOUND. Streams reach 6kn at sp; N-going makes at HW Oban +0420, S-going at HW Oban −2. The Sound is a useful doglegged short cut from Firth of Lorne to Lochs Melfort and Shuna, but needs care due to rks fish farms and tides. There are ⚓s at either end to await the tide. At the 90° dogleg, pass close N of Cleit Rk onto which the tide sets; it is marked by a Y △ perch. The chan is only ¾ca wide here due to rks off Seil. Overhead cables (35m) cross from Seil to Luing. There are ⚓s out of the tide to the S of Cleit Rk. No lts/facilities. See CCC SDs.

ARDINAMAR, Luing/Torsa, **56°14'·92N 05°37'·04W**. AC 2326. HW −0555 on Dover; ML 1·7m; see 1.17 SEIL SOUND. A small cove and popular ⚓ between Luing and Torsa, close W of ent to L. Melfort. Appr on brg 290°. Narrow, shallow (about 1m CD) ent has drying rks either side, those to N marked by 2 SHM perches. Keep about 15m S of perches to ⚓ in 2m in centre of cove; S part dries. Few facilities: ✉ 🛒 ☎ at Cullipool 1·5M WNW. 🅿 at Cuan Sound ferry 2M NNW.

1.18 LOCH MELFORT

Argyll and Bute **56°14'·59N 05°34'·07W** ✲✲✲♦♦♦❀❀❀

CHARTS AC 5611, 2169, 2326; Imray C65, 2800

TIDES Loch Shuna –0615 Dover; ML Loch Melfort 1·7; Duration Seil Sound 0615

Standard Port OBAN (←)

Times				Height (metres)			
High Water		Low Water		MHWS	MHWN	MLWN	MLWS
0100	0700	0100	0800	4·0	2·9	1·8	0·7
1300	1900	1300	2000				
Differences LOCH MELFORT							
–0055	–0025	–0040	–0035	–1·2	–0·8	–0·5	–0·1
SEIL SOUND							
–0035	–0015	–0040	–0015	–1·3	–0·9	–0·7	–0·3

SHELTER Good at Kilmelford Yacht Haven in Loch na Cille; access at all tides for 3m draught, W lts at end of pier and along its length. Or lt at Melfort Pier (Fearnach Bay at N end of loch): pier/pontoon in 2m, but chan to inner hbr dries; good ⚓ in N winds. ⚓'ge sheltered from S to W at Kames Bay clear of moorings and rocks. Beware extensive marine farm activity inshore NE of Arduaine Point.

NAVIGATION WPT 56°13'·90N 05°34'·80W, 000°/3·5ca to Eilean Gamhna. Pass either side of Eilean Gamhna. 8ca NE lies Campbell Rk (1·8m). A rk drying 1m lies 1½ca ESE of the FS on Eilean Coltair. The S side of L Melfort is mostly steep-to, except in Kames Bay. At Loch na Cille, beware drying reef ¾ca off NE shore (PHM perch), and rk near S shore (SHM perch); boats may obscure perches.

LIGHTS AND MARKS A Dir FR ☆ 6m 3M on Melfort pier (also depth gauge) and a Dir FG ☆ close NE on the shore are not ldg lts, nor do they form a safe transit. Approach on a N'ly track keeping them an equal angle off each bow.

COMMUNICATIONS (Code 01852) Police 101; Ⓗ (01631) 567500; CGOC (01851) 702013; ⊜ (0141) 887 9369.

Kilmelford VHF Ch **80** M (HO).

FACILITIES

Melfort Pier melharbour@aol.com ☎200333, ⌣ < 6m or ⚙ £12/day, ⚓ ◻ @ wi-fi, hotel accommodation.

Kilmelford Yacht Haven ☎ 200248, ▦ 200343, ⚓ HW±4; ⌣£16/craft (any LOA) ⛟(Mon-Sat 0800-2000) ⛽ ◻ 🏪(20t) ✕ ✎ 🅿.

Kilmelford Village (1¼M): ✉ 🏪 ✕ 🍺.

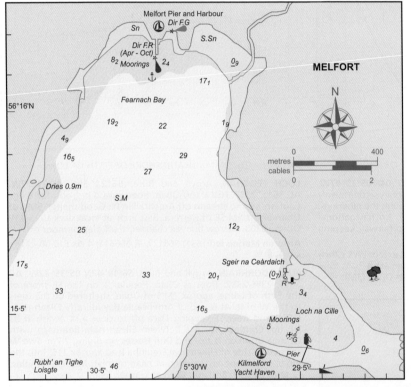

MELFORT

Subscribe annually
and receive the Almanac
for just £34 (rrp £45)

REEDS 2016 NAUTICAL ALMANAC

1.19 CRAOBH MARINA (L SHUNA)

Argyll & Bute **56°12'·80N 05°33'·54W** ❀❀❀❀✿✿✿ ✿✿✿

CHARTS AC 5611, 2169, 2326; Imray C65, 2800

TIDES HW Loch Shuna −0100 Oban; −0615 Dover; Seil Sound Duration 0615, ML 1·4. For tidal figures see 1.18.

SHELTER Very good. Craobh (pronounced Croove) Marina (access H24) on SE shore of Loch Shuna is enclosed by N and S causeways between islets. The ent is between 2 bkwtrs on the N side. In the marina, a shoal area S of the E bkwtr is marked by 9 PHM and 2 SHM buoys. A Y perch in W corner of hbr marks a spit; elsewhere ample depth. There are ⚓s in Asknish Bay 1M to the N, and in the bays E of Eilean Arsa and at Bàgh an Tigh-Stòir, S of Craobh.

NAVIGATION WPT 56°13'·01N 05°33'·57W, 173°/2ca to ent. Tidal streams in Loch Shuna are weak. Beware fish farm 2ca N of Shuna, lobster pots in appr's and unmarked rks (dr 1·5m) 4ca NNE of ent. An unlit SHM buoy marks a rk (1m) 150m NNW of the W bkwtr. 1M N of marina, Eich Donna, an unmarked reef (1·5m), lies between Eilean Creagach and Arduaine Pt.

LIGHTS AND MARKS The W sector, 162°-183°, of Dir Lt, Iso WRG 5s 10m 5/3M, on E bkwtr hd leads 172° between the close-in rks above. Multi coloured marina buildings are conspic.

COMMUNICATIONS (Code 01852) CGOC (01851) 702013; ✆ (0141) 887 9369; Police 101; Ⓗ (01546) 602323.

VHF Ch M 80 (summer 0830-2000; winter 0830-1800).

FACILITIES **Craobh Marina** ☎500222 mob 07917 805386; ◣ (launch/recovery £3.70/m); (200+50 Ⓥ) £2·30; ▮ ▲ △ ⌂ ⊠ ☡(30t)

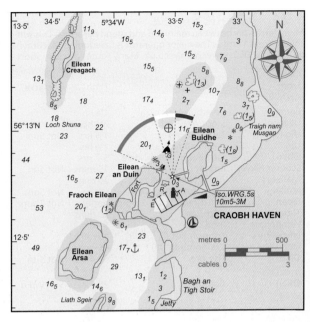

⌂(12t) ⚒ ⚓ ⛽ Ⓔ ⊡ ✗ SC, Divers.

Village: ⊠(Kilmelford) Ⓑ(Fri) 🍴 ⛟ ⇌ (Oban by bus) ✈ (Glasgow).

1.20 LOCH CRAIGNISH

Argyll and Bute **56°07'·99N 05°35'·07W** ❀❀❀❀✿✿✿ ✿✿✿

CHARTS AC 5611, 2169, 2326; Imray C65, C63, 2800

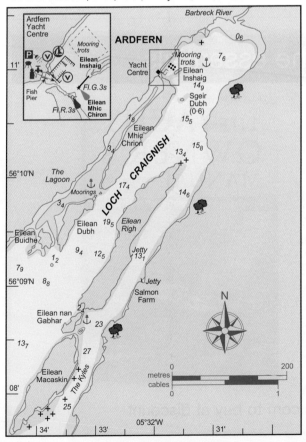

TIDES +0600 Dover; ML (Loch Beag)1·2; Duration (Seil Sound) 0615

Standard Port OBAN (←)

Times				Height (metres)			
High Water		Low Water		MHWS	MHWN	MLWN	MLWS
0100	0700	0100	0800	4·0	2·9	1·8	0·7
1300	1900	1300	2000				
Differences LOCH BEAG (3M SSW of Ardfern)							
−0110	−0045	−0035	−0045	−1·6	−1·2	−0·8	−0·4

NOTE: HW Ardfern is approx HW Oban −0045; times/heights much affected by local winds and barometric pressure

SHELTER Beware squalls in E'lies, especially on E side of loch. Good at Ardfern, 56°11'·0N 05°31'·8W, access H24 appr chan unlit; ⚓s at:
- Eilean nan Gabhar; appr from E chan and ⚓ E of island.
- Eilean Righ; midway up the E side of the island.
- Eilean Dubh in the 'lagoon' between the island and mainland bounded by moorings to the NE and SW of the entrance.

NAVIGATION WPT 56°07'·59N 05°35'·37W (off chartlet) between Dorus Mór and Liath-sgier Mhòr.

Beware: strong tidal streams (up to 8kn) in Dorus Mór; a reef extending 1ca SSW of Eilean Macaskin; rk 1½ca SSW of Eilean Dubh; fish cages especially on E side of loch; a drying rock at N end of Ardfern ⚓ with a rock awash ¼ca E of it. (These 2 rks are ½ca S of the more S'ly of little islets close to mainland.) The main fairway is free from hazards, except for Sgeir Dhubh (0·6m), an unmarked rk 3½ca SSE of Ardfern, with a reef extending about ½ca all round. Ardfern is 1ca W of Eilean Inshaig.

LIGHTS AND MARKS Ent to Ardfern Yacht Centre marked by PHM buoy, Fl R 3s, and end of floating breakwater, Fl G 3s, which extends 90m SW from Eilean Inshaig.

COMMUNICATIONS CGOC (01851) 702013; ✆ (0141) 887 9369; Dr (01546) 602921; Ⓗ (01546) 602449.

Ardfern Yacht Centre VHF Ch 80 M (office hrs).

FACILITIES **Ardfern Yacht Centre** www.ardfernyacht.co.uk ☎ 01852 500247; 12 ⚓ £1·40) 87+20 Ⓥ ⌂£2·20; ◣ (HW±3, £1·75/m) ⚓ ▶(HO) ⚒ ⚓ ⛽ △ ⌂(40t) ⌂(25t) ⚓ ACA.
Village ⊠ 🍴 ✗ ⛟ Ⓑ(Fri) ⇌(Oban) ✈(Glasgow).

1.21 FERRIES

Many ferries ply between mainland and island harbours. This summary may prove useful when plans or crews change in remote places. It covers Areas 1 and 2. The major operator is Caledonian MacBrayne: Head Office, The Ferry Terminal, Gourock PA19 1QP. For reservations: ☎08000 665000; www.calmac.co.uk. Many routes are very short and may not be pre-bookable; seasonal routes are marked *.

CalMac

From	To	Time	Remarks
Areas 8			
Berneray	Leverburgh	1¼	
Ullapool	Stornoway	2¾ hrs	
Uig (Skye)	Tarbert (Harris)	1¾ hrs	Not Sun
Uig	Lochmaddy (N Uist)	1¾ hrs	
Oban	Castlebay/Lochboisdale	5-7 hrs	
Sconser (Skye)	Raasay	15 mins	Not Sun
Mallaig*	Armadale (Skye)	20 mins	
Mallaig	Eigg-Muck-Rum-Canna	Varies	Not Sun
Oban	Coll-Tiree	Varies	Not Thurs
Tobermory	Kilchoan	35 mins	
Fionnphort	Iona	5 mins	
Lochaline	Fishnish (Mull)	15 mins	
Oban	Craignure (Mull)	45 mins	
Oban	Lismore	50 mins	Not Sun
Areas 8/9			
Oban	Colonsay	2¼ hrs	Sun/W/Fri
Area 9			
Kennacraig	Port Askaig/Colonsay	Varies	Wed
Kennacraig	Port Ellen	2h 10m	
Kennacraig	Port Askaig	2 hrs	
Tayinloan	Gigha	20 mins	
Ardrossan	Brodick	55 mins	
Claonaig	Lochranza (Arran)	30 mins	
Largs	Cumbrae Slip	10 mins	
Tarbert (L Fyne)	Portavadie*	25 mins	
Colintraive	Rhubodach (Bute)	5 mins	
Wemyss Bay	Rothesay (Bute)	35 mins	
Gourock	Dunoon	20 mins	

Other Island Ferry Operators

From	To	Operator	Telephone
Areas 8			
Corran - V	Ardgour	Highland Council	01855 841243
Easdale - P	Seil	Area Manager	01631 562125
Firth of Lorn - P	Colonsay	K & ✉ Byrne	01951 200320
	Uisken (Ross of Mull)		
	Scalasaig (Colonsay)		
	Tarbert (Jura)		
	Port Askaig (Islay)		
Jura - V	Port Askaig (Islay)	Serco Denholm	01496 840681
Kerrara - P	Oban	Oban Yachts	01631 565333
Kilgregan - P	Gourock	Clyde Marine Motoring	01475 721281
Lismore - P	Port Appin	Area Manager	01631 562125
Loch Nevis - P	Mallaig	Bruce Watt	01687 462233
Luing - P/V	Seil	Area Manager	01631 562125
Morvern	Sunart	Pre-book via	01688 302851
Mull	Drimnin	Sound of Mull	or mobile
Ardnamurchan	Tobermoray Kilchoan	Transport	07799 608199
Skye - V	Glenelg	IOSFCIC	01599 522236
Staffa - P	Iona	D Kirkpatrick	01681 700373
Staffa - P	Mull	Gordon Grant	01681 700338
Staffa - P	Mull	Turus Mara	01688 400242

P = Passenger only   V = Cars and Passengers

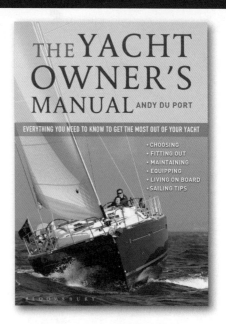

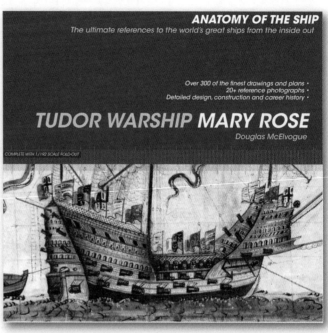
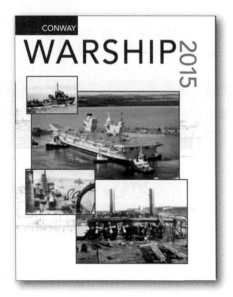
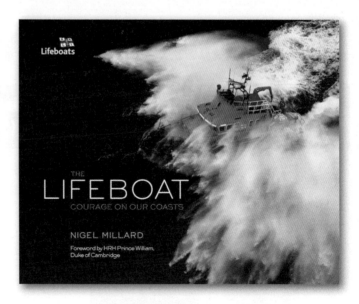

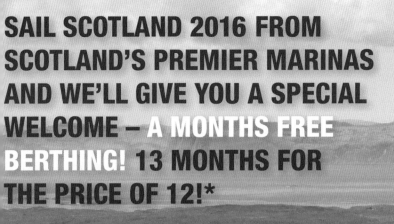

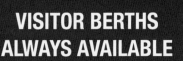

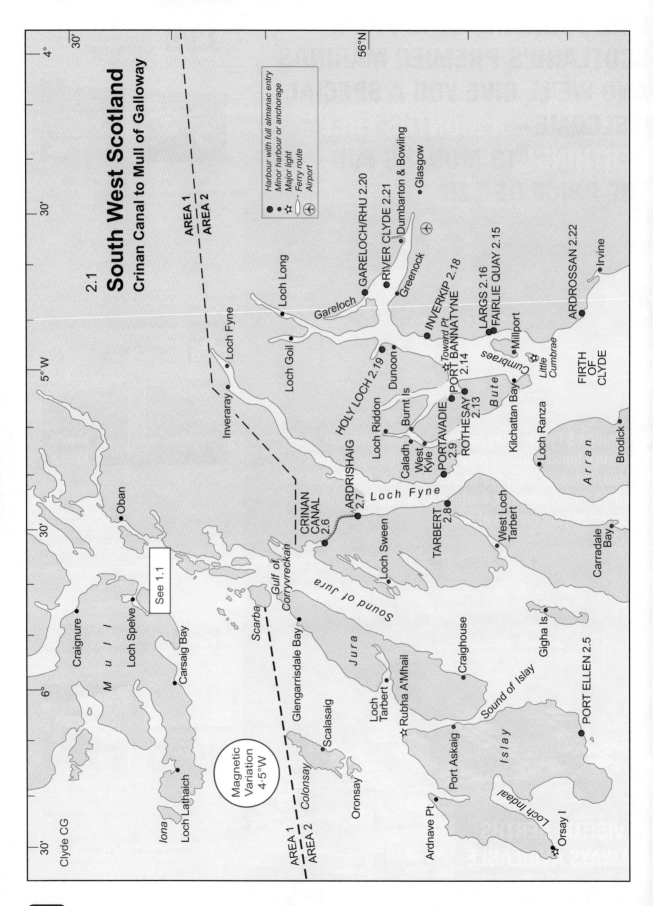

2.1
South West Scotland
Crinan Canal to Mull of Galloway

Magnetic Variation 4·5°W

See 1.1

Harbour with full almanac entry
Minor harbour or anchorage
Major light
Ferry route
Airport

AREA 1
AREA 2

AREA 1
AREA 2

GARELOCH/RHU 2.20
RIVER CLYDE 2.21
Dumbarton & Bowling
Glasgow
Greenock
INVERKIP 2.18
Toward Pt
PORT BANNATYNE 2.14
LARGS 2.16
FAIRLIE QUAY 2.15
ARDROSSAN 2.22
Irvine
Millport
Little Cumbrae
FIRTH OF CLYDE
Cumbraes
Kilchattan Bay
Loch Ranza
Brodick

Loch Long
Loch Fyne
Loch Goil
Dunoon
HOLY LOCH 2.19
Burnt Is
Loch Riddon
Caladh
West Kyle
PORTAVADIE 2.9
ROTHESAY 2.13
Bute
Arran
Carradale Bay

Inveraray

ARDRISHAIG 2.7
CRINAN CANAL 2.6
Loch Sween
Loch Fyne
TARBERT 2.8
West Loch Tarbert

Gulf of Corryvreckan
Scarba
Glengarrisdale Bay
Jura
Sound of Jura
Craighouse
Loch Tarbert
Rubha A'Mhail
Port Askaig
Sound of Islay
Islay
Ardnave Pt
Loch Indaal
Orsay I
PORT ELLEN 2.5
Gigha Is

Clyde CG
Iona
Loch Lathaich
Craignure
Loch Spelve
Carsaig Bay
Oban
Mull
Colonsay
Scalasaig
Oronsay

Gareloch

56°N

30'
4°
30'
5°W
30'
6°
30'

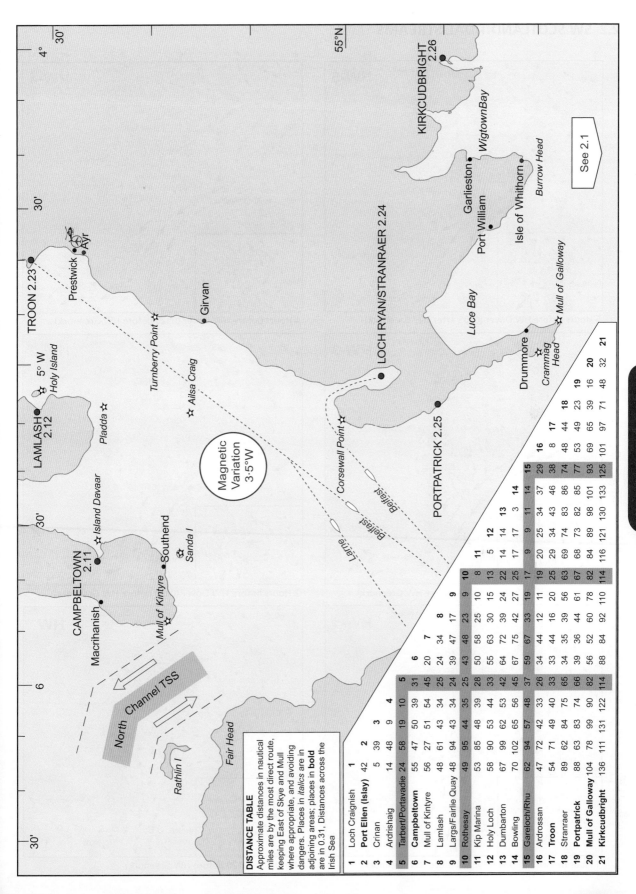

KIRKCUDBRIGHT 2.26

Wigtown Bay

Garlieston

Port William

Isle of Whithorn

Burrow Head

See 2.1

TROON 2.23

5° W

Holy Island

Prestwick

Ayr

Girvan

Turnberry Point

Ailsa Craig

LOCH RYAN/STRANRAER 2.24

Luce Bay

Magnetic Variation 3·5W

Corsewall Point

Belfast

PORTPATRICK 2.25

Drummore

Crammag Head

Mull of Galloway

LAMLASH 2.12

Pladda

Island Davaar

CAMPBELTOWN 2.11

Macrihanish

Mull of Kintyre

Southend

Sanda I

Larne

Belfast

North Channel TSS

Fair Head

Rathlin I

SW Scotland

DISTANCE TABLE

Approximate distances in nautical miles are by the most direct route, keeping East of Skye and Mull where appropriate, and avoiding dangers. Places in *italics* are in adjoining areas; places in **bold** are in 0.31, Distances across the Irish Sea

		1	2	3	4	5	6	7	8	9	10	11	12	13	14	15	16	17	18	19	20	21
1	Loch Craignish	**1**																				
2	**Port Ellen (Islay)**	42	**2**																			
3	Crinan	5	39	**3**																		
4	Ardrishaig	14	48	9	**4**																	
5	Tarbert/Portavadie	24	58	19	10	**5**																
6	**Campbeltown**	55	47	50	39	31	**6**															
7	Mull of Kintyre	56	27	51	54	45	20	**7**														
8	Lamlash	48	61	43	34	25	24	34	**8**													
9	Largs/Fairlie Quay	48	94	43	34	24	39	47	17	**9**												
10	Rothesay	49	95	44	35	25	43	48	23	9	**10**											
11	Kip Marina	53	85	48	39	28	50	58	25	10	8	**11**										
12	Holy Loch	58	90	53	44	33	55	63	30	15	13	5	**12**									
13	Dumbarton	67	99	62	53	42	64	72	39	24	22	14	14	**13**								
14	Bowling	70	102	65	56	45	67	75	42	27	25	17	17	3	**14**							
15	Gareloch/Rhu	62	94	57	48	37	59	67	33	19	17	9	9	11	14	**15**						
16	Ardrossan	47	72	42	33	26	34	44	12	11	19	20	25	34	37	29	**16**					
17	**Troon**	54	71	49	40	33	33	44	16	20	25	29	34	43	46	38	8	**17**				
18	Stranraer	89	84	75	74	65	35	35	39	56	67	69	74	83	86	74	48	44	**18**			
19	Portpatrick	88	63	83	83	66	39	36	44	61	67	68	73	82	85	77	53	49	23	**19**		
20	**Mull of Galloway**	104	78	99	90	82	56	52	60	78	82	84	89	98	101	93	69	65	39	16	**20**	
21	Kirkcudbright	136	111	131	122	114	88	84	92	110	114	116	121	130	133	125	101	97	71	48	32	**21**

2.2 SW SCOTLAND TIDAL STREAMS

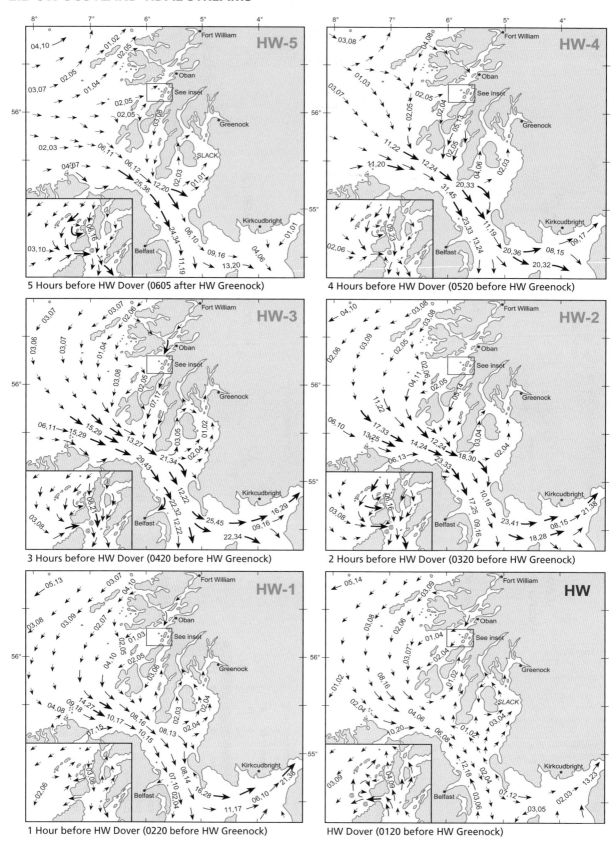

5 Hours before HW Dover (0605 after HW Greenock)

4 Hours before HW Dover (0520 before HW Greenock)

3 Hours before HW Dover (0420 before HW Greenock)

2 Hours before HW Dover (0320 before HW Greenock)

1 Hour before HW Dover (0220 before HW Greenock)

HW Dover (0120 before HW Greenock)

Northward 1.2   Mull of Kintyre 2.10   Irish Sea 3.2, 4.2   North Ireland 6.2

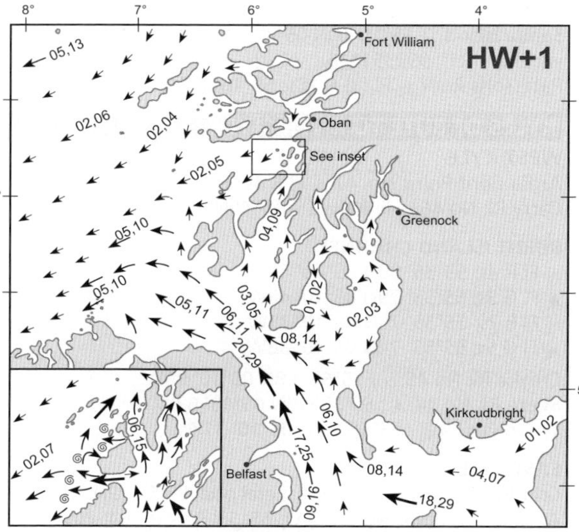

HW+1

1 Hour after HW Dover (0020 before HW Greenock)

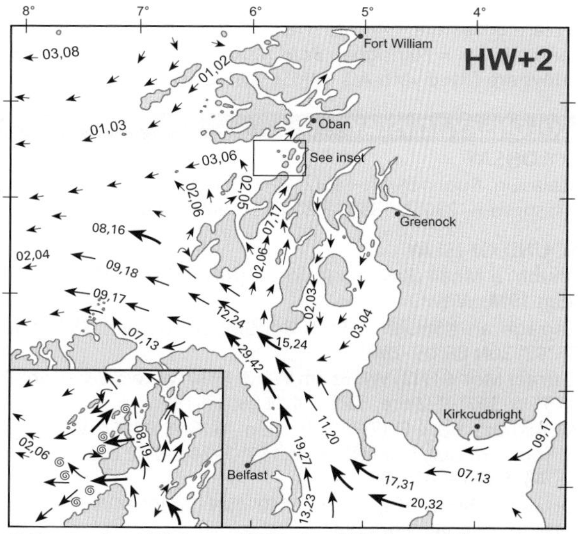

HW+2

2 Hours after HW Dover (0040 after HW Greenock)

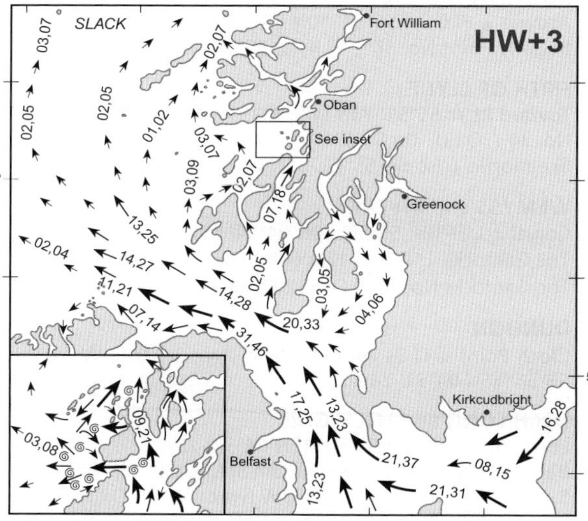

HW+3

3 Hours after HW Dover (0140 after HW Greenock)

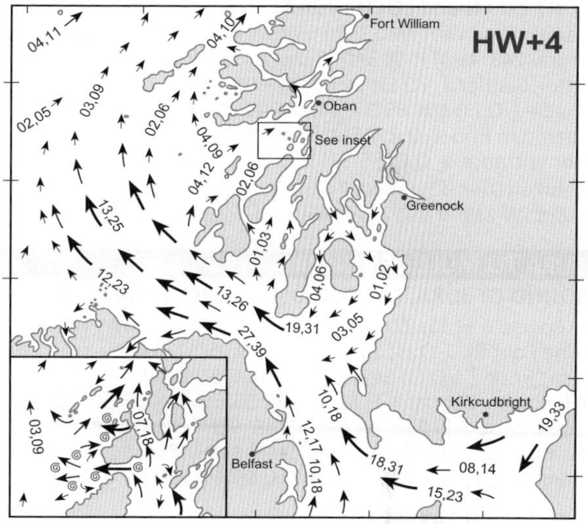

HW+4

4 Hours after HW Dover (0240 after HW Greenock)

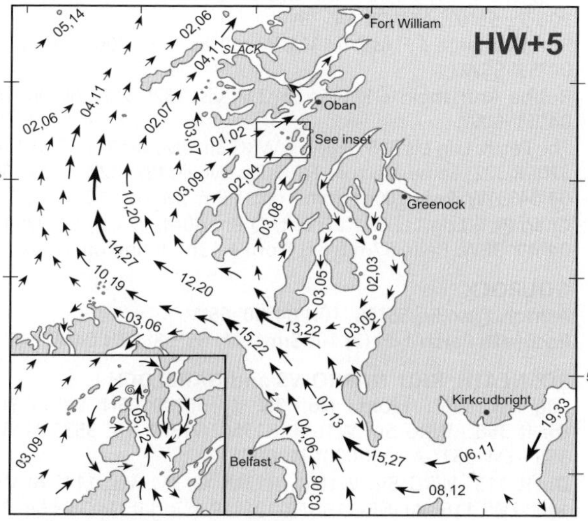

HW+5

5 Hours after HW Dover (0340 after HW Greenock)

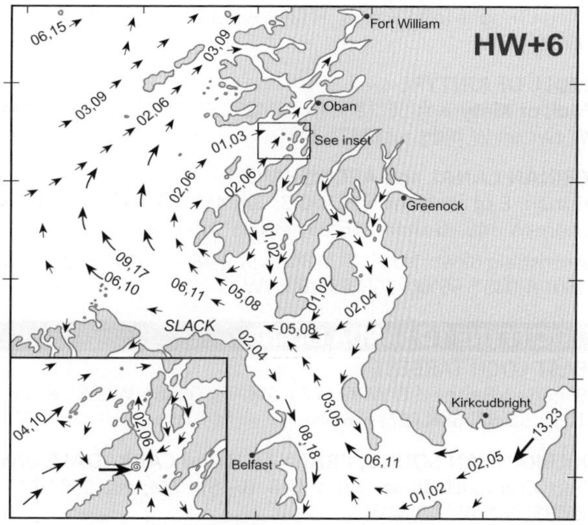

HW+6

6 Hours after HW Dover (0440 after HW Greenock)

SW Scotland

71

2.3 LIGHTS, BUOYS AND WAYPOINTS

Bold print = light with a nominal range of 15M or more. CAPITALS = place or feature. *CAPITAL ITALICS* = light-vessel, light float or Lanby. *Italics* = Fog signal. ***Bold italics*** = Racon. Some marks/buoys are fitted with AIS (<u>MMSI No</u>); see relevant charts.

COLONSAY TO ISLAY

COLONSAY
Scalasaig, Rubha Dubh ⚓ Fl (2) WR 10s 8m W8M, R6M; W bldg; vis: shore-R- 230°-W-337°-R-354°; 56°04'·01N 06°10'·90W.

SOUND OF ISLAY
Rhubh' a Mháil (Ruvaal) ☆ 55°56'·18N 06°07'·46W Fl (3) 15s 45m **19M**; W twr.
Carragh an t'Struith ⚓ Fl 3s 8m 9M; W twr; vis: 354°-180°; 55°52'·30N 06°05'·78W.
Carraig Mòr ⚓ Fl (2) WR 6s 7m W8M, R6M; W twr; vis: shore-R-175°-W-347°-R-shore; 55°50'·42N 06°06'·13W.
McArthur's Hd ⚓ Fl (2) WR 10s 39m W13M, R10M; W twr; W in Sound of Islay from NE coast,159°-R-244°-W-E coast of Islay; 55°45'·84N 06°02'·90W.
Orsay Is, **Rhinns of Islay** ☆ 55°40'·40N 06°30'·84W Fl 5s 46m **24M**; W twr; vis: 256°-184°.

PORT ELLEN and LOCH INDAAL
Carraig Fhada ⚓ Fl WRG 3s 20m W8M, R6M, G6M; W☐twr; vis: W shore- 248°-G-311°-W-340°-R-shore; 55°37'·22N 06°12'·71W.
Otter Gander ⚓ VQ (3) 5s; 55°36'·60N 06°12'·34W.
Fhada ⚓ Q (3) 10s; 55°37'·21N 06°12'·41W.
Sgeir nan Ron ⚓ Q R; 55°45'·53N 06°17'·32W.
Hbr entrance ▲ Q G; 55°37'·55N 06°11'·45W.
Rubh'an Dùin ⚓ Fl (2) WR 7s 15m W11M, R8M; W twr; vis: shore-R-218°-W-249°-R-350°-W-shore; 55°44'·70N 06°22'·28 W.

JURA TO MULL OF KINTYRE

SOUND OF JURA, CRAIGHOUSE, L SWEEN and GIGHA
Skervuile ⚓ Fl 15s 22m 9M; 55°36'·60N 06°12'·34W; W twr.
Nine Foot Rk ⚓ Q (3) 10s; 55°52'·44N 05°52'·91W.
Goat Rock ⚓ VQ (3) 5s; 55°50'·12N 05°55'·67W.
Eilean nan Gabhar ⚓ Fl 5s 9m 8M; 55°50'·01N 05°56'·25W.
Craighouse ⚓ Fl R 6s 3m 5M; 55°49'·98N 05°56'·43W.
Na Cùiltean ⚓ Fl 10s 9m 9M; 55°48'·64N 05°54'·90W.
Gamhna Gigha ⚓ Fl (2) 6s 7m 5M; 55°43'·78N 05°41'·08W.

WEST LOCH TARBERT
Dunskeig Bay ⚓ Q (2) 10s 11m 8M; 55°45'·22N 05°35'·00W.
Eileen Tráighe (off S side) ⚓ Fl (2) R 5s 5m 3M; R post; 55°45'·37N 05°35'·75W.

MULL OF KINTYRE
Mull of Kintyre ☆ 55°18'·64N 05°48'·25W Fl (2) 20s 91m **24M**; W twr on W bldg; vis: 347°-178°.

CRINAN CANAL and ARDRISHAIG
Crinan, E of lock ent ⚓ Fl WG 3s 8m 4M; W twr, R band; vis: shore-W-146°-G-shore; 56°05'·48N 05°33'·37W.
Ardrishaig Bkwtr Hd ⚓ L Fl WRG 6s 9m 4M; vis: 287°-G-339°-W-350°-R-035°; 56°00'·76N 05°26'·59W.

LOCH FYNE TO SANDA ISLAND

EAST LOCH TARBERT
Eilean na Beithe ⚓ Fl WRG 3s 7m 5M; vis: G036°- W065°- R078°-106°; 55°52'·68N 05°19'·62W.

KILBRANNAN SOUND, CRANNAICH and CARRADALE BAY
Port Crannaich Bkwtr Hd ⚓ Fl R 10s 5m 6M; vis: 099°-279°; 55°35'·60N 05°27'·84W.

CAMPBELTOWN LOCH to SANDA ISLAND
Davaar N Pt ☆ 55°25'·69N 05°32'·42W Fl (2) 10s 37m **23M**; W twr; vis: 073°-330°.
Sanda Island ☆ 55°16'·50N 05°35'·01W Fl 10s 50m **15M**; W twr; vis: 242°-121°; <u>992351116</u>.
Patersons Rock ⚓ Fl (3) R 18s; 55°16'·90N 05°32'·48W.

KYLES OF BUTE TO RIVER CLYDE

WEST KYLE
Ardlamont Point No. 47 ⚓ Fl R 4s; 55°49'·59N 05°11'·76.
Carry Rk No 46 ⚓ Fl R 4s; 55°51'·40N 05°12'·14W.

BURNT ISLAND CHANNEL
⚓ Fl R 4s; 55°55'·80N 05°10'·46W.
▲ Fl G 3s; 55°55'·79N 05°10'·48W.
⚓ Fl R 2s; 55°55'·76N 05°10'·39W.
▲ Fl G 5s; 55°55'·74N 05°10'·38W.
Creyke Rk No 45 ⚓ ; 55°55'·68N 05°10'·89W.
Beere Rk No 44 ▲ ; 55°55'·10N 05°10'·63W.
Wood Fm Rk ⚓ ; 55°55'·42N 05°10'·31W.

EAST KYLE
Colintrave Pt ⚓ Fl R 3s 7m 2M; metal post; 55°55'·39N 05°09'·22W.
Ardmaleish Point No. 41 ⚓ Q; 55°53'·02N 05°04'·70W.

ROTHESAY SOUND
Ardyne ▲ Fl G 3s; 55°52'·10N 05°03'·20W.
Bogany Point No. 36 ⚓ Fl R 4s; 55°50'·78N 05°01'·41W.

FIRTH OF CLYDE
Toward Pt ☆ 55°51'·73N 04°58'·79W Fl 10s 21m **22M**; W twr.
No. 34 ⚓ Q (3) 10s; 55°51'·44N 04°59'·11W.
Skelmorlie ⚓ Iso 5s; 55°51'·65N 04°56'·34W.

WEMYSS and INVERKIP
Cowal ⚓ L Fl 10s; 55°56'·00N 04°54'·83W.
The Gantocks ⚓ Fl R 6s 12m 6M; ○ twr; 55°56'·45N 04°55'·08W.
The Gantocks No. 31 ⚓ Q; 55°56'·56N 04°55'·13W.

DUNOON
Cloch Point ⚓ Fl 3s 24m 8M; W ○ twr, B band, W dwellings; 55°56'·55N 04°52'·74W.

LOCH LONG and LOCH GOIL
Loch Long ⚓ Oc 6s; 55°59'·15N 04°52'·42W.
Baron's Pt No. 3 ⚓ Oc (2) Y 10s 5m 3M; 55°59'·18N 04°51'·12W.
Ravenrock Pt ⚓ Fl 4s 12m 10M; W twr on W col. Dir lt 204°, WRG 9m (same twr); vis: 201·5°-F R-203°-Al WR(W phase incr with brg)-203·5°-FW-204·5°-Al WG(G phase incr with brg)-205°-FG-206·5°; 56°02'·14N 04°54'·39W.
Port Dornaige ⚓ Fl 6s 8m 11M; W col; vis: 026°-206°; 56°03·75N 04°53'·65W.
Rubha Ardnahein ⚓ Fl R 5s 3m 3M; vis: 132°-312°; 56°06'·15N 04°53'·60W.
The Perch, Ldg Lts 318° Front, F WRG 3m 5M; vis: 311°-G-317°-W-320°-R-322°. Same structure, Fl R 3s 3m 3M; vis: 187°-322'; 56°06'·90N 04°54'·31W. Rear, 700m from front, F 7m 5M; vis: 312°-322·5°.
Cnap Pt ⚓ Ldg Lts 031°. Front, Q 8m 10M; W col; 56°07'·40N 04°49'·96W. Rear, 87m from front F 13m; R line on W twr.

GOUROCK
Ashton ⚓ Iso 5s; 55°58'·10N 04°50'·65W.
Rosneath Patch ⚓ Fl (2) 10s 5m 10M; 55°58'·52N 04°47'·45W.

ROSNEATH, RHU NARROWS and GARELOCH
Ldg Lts 356°. **Front, No. 7N** ⚓ 56°00'·05N 04°45'·36W Dir lt 356°. WRG 5m **W16M**, R13M, G13M; vis: 353°-Al WG-355°- FW-357°-Al WR-000°-FR-002°.
Dir lt 115° WRG 5m **W16M**, R13M, G13M; vis: 111°-Al WG-114°-FW- 116°-Al WR-119°-FR-121°. Passing lt Oc G 6s 6m 3M;

G △ on G pile . Rear, Ardencaple Castle Centre ⚓ 56°00'·54N 04°45'·43W 2 FG (vert) 26m 12M; twr on Castle NW corner; vis: 335°-020°.

No. 8N Lt Bn ⚓ 55°59'·09N 04°44'·21W Dir lt 080° WRG 4m; **W16M**, R13M,G13M;vis: 075°-FG-077·5°-Al WG-079·5°-FW-080·5°-AltWR-082·5°-FR-085°. **Dir lt 138°** WRG 4m **W16M**, R13M, G13M; vis: 132°-FG-134°-Al WG- FW137°-139°-Al WR-142°. Passing lt Fl Y 3s 6m 3M.

Gareloch No. 1 Lt Bn ⚓ VQ (4) Y 5s 9m; Y 'X' on Y structure; 55°59'·12N 04°43'·89W.

No. 3N Lt Bn ⚓ 56°00'·07N 04°46'·72W Dir lt 149° WRG 9m **W16M**, R13M, G13M F & Al; vis: 144°-FG-145°-Al WG-148°-FW-150°-Al WR-153°-FR-154°. Passing lt Oc R 8s 9m 3M.

Rosneath DG Jetty ⚓ 2 FR (vert) 5M; W col; vis: 150°-330°; 56°00'·39N 04°47'·51W.

Rhu Pt ⚓ Dir lt 318° WRG **W16M**, R13M, G13M; vis: 315°-Al WG-317°-F-319°-Al WR-321°-FR-325°; Dir W; vis: 325°-QW-340°-FW-345°-OcW-350°; 56°00'·95N 04°47'·20W.

Limekiln No. 2N Lt Bn ⚓ 56°00'·67N 04°47'·64W Dir lt 295° WRG 5m **W16M**, R13M, G13M F & Al; R □ on R Bn; vis: 291°-Al WG- 294°-FW- 296°-Al WR-299°-FR-301°.

Mambeg Dir lt 331°, Q (4) WRG 8s 10m 14M; vis: 328·5°-G-330°-W- 332°-R-333°; H24; 56°03'·74N 04°50'·47W.

GREENOCK and PORT GLASGOW
Anchorage Lts in line 196°. Front, FG 7m 12M; Y col; 55°57'·62N 04°46'·58W. Rear, 32m from front, FG 9m 12M. Y col.

Lts in line 194·5°. Front, FG 18m; 55°57'·45N 04°45'·91W. Rear, 360m from front, FG 33m.

Steamboat Quay, W end ⚓ FG 12m 12M; B&W chequered col; vis 210°-290°; 55°56'·25N 04°41'·44W. From here to Glasgow Lts on S bank are Fl G and Lts on N bank are Fl R.

CLYDE TO MULL OF GALLOWAY

HUNTERSTON CHANNEL
'C' ⚓ Fl G 5s; 55°48'·10N 05°55'·30W.
Hun 1 ⚓ (Y) Fl (4) Y 15s; 55°48'·10N 04°54'·21W.
Hun 3 ⚓ Fl R 2s; 55°47'·60N 04°53'·52W.

LARGS and FAIRLIE
Approach ⚓ L Fl 10s; 55°46'·40N 04°51'·85W.
Fairlie Patch ⚓ Fl G 1·5s; 55°45'·38N 04°52'·34W.

MILLPORT and GREAT CUMBRAE
Tomont End Daymark 55°47'·56N 04°54'·10W.
Tattie Pier ⚓ WRG 3s 5m 4M; vis: 222°-G-234°-W-246°-R-258°; metal column; 55°47'·20N 04°53'·89W.
Ldg Lts 333°. Pier Head front, 55°45'·04N 04°55'·85W FR 7m 5M. Rear, 137m from front, FR 9m 5M.
Mountstuart ⚓ L Fl 10s; 55°48'·00N 04°57'·57W.
Runnaneun Pt (Rubha'n Eun) ⚓ Fl R 6s 8m 12M; W twr; 55°43'·79N 05°00'·23W.
Little Cumbrae Is, Cumbrae Elbow ⚓ Fl 6s 28m 14M; W twr; vis: 334°-193°; 55°43'·22N 04°58'·06W.

ARDROSSAN
Approach Dir lt 055°, WRG 15m W14M, R11M, G11M; vis: 050°-F G-051·2°-Alt WG(W phase inc with Brg)- 053·8°-FW-056·2°-Alt WR(R phase inc with brg)-058·8°-FR-060°; 55°38'·66N 04°49'·22W. Same structure FR 13m 6M; vis: 325°-145°.
Lt ho Pier Hd ⚓ Iso WG 4s 11m 9M; W twr; vis: 035°-W-317°-G-035°; 55°38'·47N 04°49'·57W.

IRVINE
Ldg Lts 051°. Front, FG 10m 5M; 55°36'·40N 04°41'·57W. Rear, 101m from front, FR 15m 5M; G masts, both vis: 019°-120°.

TROON
Troon Approach ⚓ Fl G 4s; 55°33'·06N 04°41'·34W.
W Pier Hd ⚓ Fl (2) WG 5s 11m 9M; W twr; vis: 036°-G-090°-W-036°; 55°33'·07N 04°41'·02W.
Lady I ⚓ Fl 2s 19m 11M; W Tr R vert stripes; *Racon (T) 13-11M;* 55°31'·63N 04°44'·05W.

ARRAN, RANZA, LAMLASH and BRODICK
Pillar Rk Pt ☆ (Holy Island), 55°31'·04N 05°03'·65W Fl (2) 20s 38m **18M**; W □ twr.
Holy Is SW end ⚓ Fl G 3s 14m 6M; W twr; vis: 282°-147°; 55°30'·73N 05°04'·21W.

Pladda ☆ 55°25'·50N 05°07'·12W Fl (3) 30s 40m **17M**; W twr.

AYR and AILSA CRAIG
S Pier Hd ⚓ Q 7m 7M; R twr; vis: 012°-161°. Also FG 5m 5M; vis: 012°-082°; 55°28'·17N 04°38'·74W.
Ldg Lts 098°. Front, FR 10m 5M; Tfc sigs; 55°28'·15N 04°38'·38W. Rear, 130m from front Oc R 10s 18m 9M.
Maidens Hbr, E side ⚓ Fl G 5s 4m 3M; 55°20'·24N 04°49'·20W.
Maidens Hbr, W side ⚓ Fl R 3s 4m 2M; 55°20'·23N 04°49'·19W.
Turnberry Point ⚓, near castle ruins 55°19'·57N 04°50'·69W Fl 15s 29m 12M; W twr.

Ailsa Craig ☆ 55°15'·12N 05°06'·52W Fl 4s 18m **17M**; W twr; vis: 145°-028°.

GIRVAN
S Pier Hd ⚓ 2 FG (vert) 8m 4M; W twr; 55°14'·72N 04°51'·90W.

LOCH RYAN and STRANRAER
Milleur Point ⚓ Q; 55°01'·28N 05°05'·66W.
Fairway ⚓ Iso 4s; 54°59'·77N 05°03'·82W.
Forbes Shoal ⚓ QR; 54°59'·47N 05°02'·96W.
Loch Ryan W ⚓ QG; 54°59'·23N 05°03'·24W .
Cairn Pt ⚓ Fl (2) R 10s 14m 12M; W twr; 54°58'·46N 05°01'·85W.
Cairnryan ⚓ Fl R 5s 5m 5M; 54°57'·77N 05°00'·99W.
Stranraer No.1 ⚓ Oc G 6s; 54°56'·67N 05°01'·32W.
No. 3 ⚓ QG; 54°55'·87N 05°01'·60W.
No. 5 ⚓ Fl G 3s; 54°55'·08N 05°01'·86W.
E Pier Hd ⚓ 2 FR (vert) 9m; 54°54'·61N 05°01'·60W.

Corsewall Point ☆ 55°00'·41N 05°09'·58W Fl (5) 30s 34m **22M**; W twr; vis: 027°-257°.
Black Head Old Lighthouse (disused); W tower, 22m; 54°51'·70N 05°08'·80W.

PORTPATRICK
Ldg Lts 050·5°. Front, FG (occas); 54°50'·50N 05°07'·02W. Rear, 68m from front, FG 8m (occas).

Crammag Hd ☆ 54°39'·90N 04°57'·92W Fl 10s 35m **18M**; W twr.
Mull of Galloway ☆, SE end 54°38'·08N 04°51'·45W Fl 20s 99m **28M**; W twr; vis: 182°-105°.

MULL OF GALLOWAY and WIGTOWN BAY
Port William Ldg Lts 105°. Front, Pier Hd Fl G 3s 7m 3M; 54°45'·66N 04°35'·28W. Rear, 130m from front, FG 10m 2M.
Isle of Whithorn ⚓ Fl WR 3s 20m 6/4M; vis: 310°-W-005°- R-040°; 54°41'·79N 04°21'·54W.
Whithorn Ldg Lts 335°. Front, Oc R 8s 7m 7M; Or ♦; 54°42'·01N 04°22'·05W. Rear, 35m from front, Oc R 8s 9m 7M; Or ♦, synch.

Little Ross ⚓ Fl 5s 50m 12M; W twr; obsc in Wigtown B when brg more than 103°; 54°45'·93N 04°05'·10W.

KIRKCUDBRIGHT BAY and KIPPFORD
Little Ross NNE end of Is ⚓ Fl (2) 5s 21m 5M; Stone bcn; 54°46'·06N 04°05'·02W.
Hestan I, E end ⚓ Fl (2) 10s 42m 9M; 54°49'·95N 03°48'·53W.

2.4 PASSAGE INFORMATION

More passage information is threaded between the harbours in this area. Conditions in the SW of Scotland are generally less rugged south of Mull but good charts and up to date Pilots are still essential. Admiralty Leisure Folios 5611 covers the Mull of Kintyre to Point of Ardnamurchan, 5610, the Firth of Clyde. 5613, Irish Sea eastern part including Isle of Man, covers the Scottish coast south of the Clyde to Kirkcudbright. **Bibliography:** *The Yachtsman's Pilot, Clyde to Colonsay* (Imray/Lawrence). *Clyde Cruising Club Sailing Directions-Firth of Clyde including Solway Firth and North Channel* (Imray/Clyde Cruising Club, Lawrence). The *South West Coast of Scotland Pilot* (Admiralty NP66A) covers the whole area.

Submarines regularly exercise in this area, see **2.17, SUBMARINE EXERCISE AREAS** and SUBFACTS for information on this activity.

Some of the following more common *Gaelic* terms may help with navigation: *Acairseid*: anchorage. *Ailean*: meadow. *Aird, ard*: promontory. *Aisir, aisridh*: passage between rocks. *Beag*: little. *Beinn*: mountain. *Bo, boghar, bodha*: rock. *Cala*: harbour. *Camas*: channel, bay. *Caol*: strait. *Cladach*: shore, beach. *Creag*: cliff. *Cumhamn*: narrows. *Dubh, dhubh*: black. *Dun*: castle. *Eilean, eileanan*: island. *Garbh*: rough. *Geal, gheal*: white. *Glas, ghlas*: grey, green. *Inis*: island. *Kyle*: narrow strait. *Linn, Linne*: pool. *Mor, mhor*: large. *Mull*: promontory. *Rinn, roinn*: point. *Ruadh*: red, brown. *Rubha, rhu*: cape. *Sgeir*: rock. *Sruth*: current. *Strath*: river valley. *Tarbert*: isthmus. *Traigh*: beach. *Uig*: bay.

CORRYVRECKAN TO CRINAN

(AC 2326, 2343) Between Scarba and Jura is the Gulf of Corryvreckan (AC 2343) which is best avoided, and should never be attempted by small craft except at slack water and in calm conditions. (In any event the Sound of Luing is always a safer and not much longer alternative.) The Gulf has a least width of 6ca and is free of dangers apart from its very strong tides which, in conjunction with a very uneven bottom, cause extreme turbulence. This is particularly dangerous with strong W winds over a W-going (flood) tide which spews out several miles to seaward of the gulf, with overfalls extending 5M from the W of ent (The Great Race). Keep to the S side of the gulf to avoid the worst turbulence and the whirlpool known as The Hag, in depths of only 29m, as opposed to more than 100m in the fairway.

▶ *The W-going stream in the gulf begins at HW Oban + 0410, and the E-going at HW Oban − 0210. Sp rate W-going is 8·5kn, and E-going about 6kn. The range of tide at sp can vary nearly 2m between the E end of the gulf (1·5m) and the W end (3·4m), with HW 30mins earlier at the E end. Slack water occurs at HW Oban +0400 and −0230 and lasts almost 1 hr at Nps, but only 15 mins at sps. On the W-going (flood) stream eddies form both sides of the gulf, but the one on the N (Scarba) shore is more important. Where this eddy meets the main stream off Camas nam Bairneach there is violent turbulence, with heavy overfalls extending W at the division of the eddy and the main stream.* ◀

There are temp ⚓s with the wind in the right quarter in Bàgh Gleann a' Mhaoil in the SE corner of Scarba, and in Bàgh Gleann nam Muc at N end of Jura but the latter has rks in approaches E and SW of Eilean Beag.

SE of Corryvreckan is Loch Crinan, which leads to the Crinan Canal. Beware Black Rk, 2m high and 2ca N of the canal sea lock, and dangers extending 100m from the rock.

WEST OF JURA TO ISLAY

(AC 2481, 2168) The W coasts of Colonsay and Oronsay (AC 2169) are fringed with dangers up to 2M offshore. A narrow drying channel crossed by an overhead cable (10m) separates them.

The Sound of Islay presents no difficulty; hold to the Islay shore, where all dangers are close in. There are ⚓s in the Sound, but holding is mostly poor. The best places are alongside at Port Askaig, or at ⚓ off the distillery in Bunnahabhain B, 2·5M to the N.

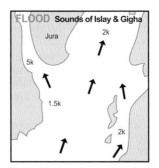
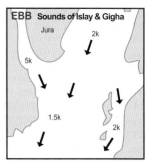

▶ *The N-going stream begins at HW Oban + 0440, and the S-going at HW Oban − 0140. Main flood begins HW Oban +0545. Streams turn approx 1 hr earlier in Gigha Sd and at Kintyre and Jura shores. S going stream for 9hrs close inshore between Gigha and Machrihanish starting HW Oban −0530.*

Main ebb begins HW Oban −0015. Streams turn 1 hr earlier in Gigha Sd, Kintyre and Jura shores. Overfalls off McArthur's Hd. The Sp rates are 2·5kn at N entrance and 1·5kn at S entrance, but reaching 5kn in the narrows off Port Askaig. There are overfalls off McArthur's Hd (Islay side of S entrance) during the S-going stream. ◀

The N coast of Islay and Rhinns of Islay are very exposed. In the N there is an ⚓ SE of Nave Island at entrance to Loch Gruinart; beware Balach Rks which dry, just to N.

▶ *To the SW off Orsay (lt), Frenchman's Rks and W Bank there is a race and overfalls which should be cleared by 3M. Here the NW-going stream begins at HW Oban + 0530, and the SE-going at HW Oban − 0040; Sp rates are 6-8kn inshore, but decrease to 3kn 5M offshore.* ◀

Loch Indaal gives some shelter; beware rks extending from Laggan Pt on E side of ent. Off the Mull of Oa there are further overfalls. Port Ellen, the main hbr on Islay, has HIE ⚓s; there are some dangers in approach, and it is exposed to S; see AC 2474.

SOUND OF JURA TO GIGHA

(AC 2397, 2396, 2168) From Crinan to Gigha the Sound of Jura is safe if a mid-chan course is held. Ruadh Sgeir (lt) are rocky ledges in mid-fairway, about 3M W of Crinan. Loch Sween (AC 2397) can be approached N or SE of MacCormaig Islands, where there is an attractive ⚓ on NE side of Eilean Mor, but exposed to NE. Coming from N beware Keills Rk and Danna Rk. Sgeirean a Mhain is a rk in fairway 1·5M NE of Castle Sween (conspic on SE shore). ⚓ at Tayvallich, near head of loch on W side.

W Loch Tarbert (AC 2477) is long and narrow, with good ⚓s and lts near ent, but unmarked shoals. On entry give a berth of at least 2½ca to Eilean Traighe off N shore, E of Ardpatrick Pt. Dun Skeig, an isolated hill, is conspic on S shore. Good ⚓ near head of loch, 1M by road from E Loch Tarbert, Loch Fyne.

On W side of Sound, near S end of Jura, are The Small Is (AC 2396) across the mouth of Loch na Mile. Beware Goat Rk (dries 0·3m) 1.5ca off S'most Is, Eilean nan Gabhar, behind which is good ⚓. Also possible to go alongside Craighouse Pier (HIE ⚓). Another ⚓ is in Lowlandman's B, about 3M to N, but exposed to S winds; Ninefoot Rks with depth of 2·4m and ECM lt buoy lie off ent. Skervuile (lt) is a reef to the E, in middle of the Sound.

S of W Loch Tarbert, and about 2M off the Kintyre shore, is Gigha Is (AC 2475). Good ⚓s on E side in Druimyeon B and Ardminish B (HIE ⚓s), respectively N and S of Ardminish Pt. Outer and Inner Red Rks (least depth 2m) lie 2M SW of N end of Gigha Is. Dangers extend 1M W off S end of Gigha Is. Gigalum Is and Cara Is are off the S end. Gigha Sound needs very careful pilotage, since there are several dangerous rks, some buoyed/lit, others not.

▶ *The N-going stream begins at HW Oban + 0430, and S-going at HW Oban − 0155, sp rates 1·3kn.* ◀

HARBOURS AND ANCHORAGES IN COLONSAY, JURA, ISLAY AND THE SOUND OF JURA

SCALASAIG, Colonsay, **56°04′·14N 06°10′·86W**. AC 2169. HW +0542 on Dover; ML 2·2m. See 2.5. Conspic monument ½M SW of hbr. Beware group of rks N of pier hd marked by bn. 2❂ berths run by CMAL on N side of pier, inner end approx 2·5m. Inner hbr to SW of pier is safe, but dries. Ldg lts 262°, both FR 8/10m on pier. Also ⚓ clear of cable in **Loch Staosnaig**; SW of Rubha Dubh lt, Fl (2) WR 10s 8m 8/6M; shore-R-230°-W-337°-R-354°. Facilities: 🏪 🅿 🛒 (all at ✉), 🔧 Hotel ☎(01951) 200316, Dr (0951) 200328.

LOCH TARBERT, W Jura, **55°57′·69N 06°00′·06W**. AC 2169, 2481. Tides as Rubha A'Mhàil (N tip of Islay). See 2.5. HW −0540 on Dover; ML 2·1m; Duration 0600. Excellent shelter inside the loch, but subject to squalls in strong winds; ⚓ outside in Glenbatrick Bay in approx 6m in S winds, or at Bagh Gleann Righ Mor in approx 2m in N winds. To enter inner loch via Cumhann Beag, there are four pairs of ldg marks (W stones) at approx 120°, 150°, 077°, and 188°, the latter astern, to be used in sequence; pilot book required. There are no facilities.

PORT ASKAIG, Islay, **55°50′·87N 06°06′·26W**. AC 2168, 2481. HW +0610 on Dover; ML 1·2m. See 2.5. Hbr on W side of Sound of Islay. ⚓ close inshore in 4m or secure to ferry pier. Beware strong tide/eddies. ✫ FR at LB. Facilities: 🔧(on pier) 🏪 🅿 ✉ 🛒 ✕ Hotel ferries to Jura and Kintyre. Other ⚓s in the Sound at: Bunnahabhain (2M N); Whitefarland Bay, Jura, opp Caol Ila distillery; NW of Am Fraoch Eilean (S tip of Jura); Aros Bay, N of Ardmore Pt.

CRAIGHOUSE, SE Jura, **55°49′·99N 05°56′·31W**. AC 2168, 2481, 2396. HW +0600 on Dover; ML 0·5m; Duration 0640 np, 0530 sp. See 2.5. Good shelter, but squally in W winds. Enter between lit bn on SW end of Eilean nan Gabhar, Fl 5s 7m 8M vis 225°-010°, and unlit bn close SW. There are 16 Jura Dev Trust ⚓s (£10/night) N of pier (☎(01496) 810332), where yachts may berth alongside; or ⚓ in 5m at the N end of Loch na Mile (poor holding in heavy weed). Facilities: very limited, short stay pontoon 🔧 🏪 🅿 ✉ 🛒 ✕ 🍴. **Lowlandman's Bay** is 1M further N, with ECM buoy, Q (3) 10s, marking Nine Foot Rk (2·4m) off the ent. ⚓ to SW of conspic houses, off stone jetty.

LOCH SWEEN, Argyll and Bute, **55°55′·69N 05°41′·26W**. AC 2397. HW +0550 on Dover; ML 1·5m; Duration = 0610. See 2.6 Carsaig Bay. Off the ent to loch, **Eilean Mòr** (most SW'ly of MacCormaig Isles) has tiny ⚓ on N side in 3m; local transit marks keep clear of two rks, 0·6m and 0·9m. Inside the loch, beware Sgeirean a'Mhain, a rk in mid-chan to S of Taynish Is, 3M from ent. Good shelter in Loch a Bhealaich (⚓ outside **Tayvallich** in approx 7m on boulders) or enter inner hbr to ⚓ W of central reef. There are no lights. Facilities: 🅿 🛒 ✉ with 🔧 ✕. Close to NE are ⚓s at **Caol Scotnish** and **Fairy Is**, the former obstructed by rks 3ca from ent.

WEST LOCH TARBERT, Argyll and Bute, (Kintyre), **55°45′N 05°36′W**. AC 2476. Tides as Gigha Sound, 2.5. Good shelter. En S of Eilean Traighe, Fl (2) R 5s, and NW of Dun Skeig, Q (2) 10s, where there is conspic conical hill (142m). Avoid shallows inshore to each side. Loch is lit for 5M by 3 bns, QG, QR and QG in sequence, up to Kennacraig ferry pier, 2FG (vert). PHM buoy, QR, is 2½ca NW of pier. Caution: many drying rks and fish farms outside the fairway and near head of loch. ⚓s are NE of Eilean Traighe (beware weed and ferry wash); near Rhu Pt, possible ⚓s; NE of Eilean dà Gallagain, and at loch hd by pier (ru). Tarbert (2.8) is 1·5M walk/bus.

GIGHA ISLAND, Argyll and Bute, **55°40′·6N 05°44′·0W**. AC 2168, 2475. HW +0600 on Dover; ML 0·9m; Duration 0530. See 2.5. **Ardminish Bay**: 23 Gigha Heritage Trust ⚓s in the centre (£10) 17 rated at 15t and 6 at 25t or ⚓ NE of Ferry Jetty. Refurbished pontoon and walkway for landing. Reefs extend off both points, the S'ly reef marked by an unlit PHM buoy. Kiln Rk (dries 1·5m) is close NE of the old ferry jetty. **Druimyeon Bay** is more sheltered in E'lies, but care needed entering from S. ⚓s sheltered from winds in Kilnaughton Bay, Port Mór (S-W), Bàgh na Dòirlinne (SE-S), W Tarbert Bay (NE). Caolas Gigalum (⚓ 50m SE of pier) is safe in all but NE-E winds. Beware many rks in Gigha Sound. Lts: Fl (2) 6s, on Gamhna Gigha (off NE tip); WCM buoy Fl (9) 15s marks Gigalum Rks, at S end of Gigha. **Ardminish** ☎(01583) 505254: 🔧 🏪 🅿 🅿 🅿 ✉ 🛒 ✕ 🍴.

2.5 PORT ELLEN

Islay (Argyll and Bute) **55°37′·29N 06°12′·26W** ❄❄⚓⚓⚓✿✿

CHARTS AC 2168, 2476; Imray C64

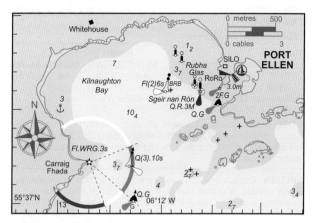

TIDES HW +0620 np, +0130 sp on Dover; ML 0·6. Sea level is much affected by the weather, rising by 1m in S/E gales; at nps the tide is sometimes diurnal and range negligible.

Standard Port OBAN (←—)

Times				Height (metres)			
High Water		Low Water		MHWS	MHWN	MLWN	MLWS
0100	0700	0100	0800	4·0	2·9	1·8	0·7
1300	1900	1300	2000				
Differences PORT ELLEN (S Islay)							
−0530	−0050	−0045	−0530	−3·1	−2·1	−1·3	−0·4
SCALASAIG (E Colonsay)							
−0020	−0005	−0015	+0005	−0·3	−0·2	−0·3	0·0
GLENGARRISDALE BAY (N Jura)							
−0020	0000	−0010	0000	−0·4	−0·2	0·0	−0·2
CRAIGHOUSE (SE Jura)							
−0230	−0250	−0150	−0230	−3·0	−2·4	−1·3	−0·6
RUBHA A'MHÀIL (N Islay)							
−0020	0000	+0005	−0015	−0·3	−0·1	−0·3	−0·1
ARDNAVE POINT (NW Islay)							
−0035	+0010	0000	−0025	−0·4	−0·2	−0·3	−0·1
ORSAY ISLAND (SW Islay)							
−0110	−0110	−0040	−0040	−1·4	−0·6	−0·5	−0·2
BRUICHLADDICH (Islay, Loch Indaal)							
−0105	−0035	−0110	−0110	−1·8	−1·3	−0·4	+0·3
PORT ASKAIG (Sound of Islay)							
−0030	−0035	−0015	−0025	−1·8	−1·3	−0·7	−0·2
GIGHA SOUND (Sound of Jura)							
−0450	−0210	−0130	−0410	−2·5	−1·6	−1·0	−0·1
MACHRIHANISH							
−0520	−0350	−0340	−0540	Mean range 0·5 metres.			

SHELTER Good shelter on pontoons (3m at MLWS), but in S winds swell sets into the bay. W of Rubha Glas rocks marked by 3 bns with reflective topmarks. In W'lies ⚓ in Kilnaughton Bay, N of Carraig Fhada lt ho; or 4M ENE at Loch-an-t-Sàilein.

NAVIGATION WPT 55°36′·69N 06°12′·06W, 326°/0·63M to Carraig Fhada lt ho. Beware Otter Rk 4M SE of hbr marked by ECM, rks on both sides of ent and in NE corner of bay. Keep close to pier.

LIGHTS AND MARKS On W side 10 radio masts (103m) and Carraig Fhada lt ho (conspic), Fl WRG 3s 20m 8/6M; keep in W sector until past the SHM lt buoy. Sgeir nan Ròn Bn Q R, dolphin off Ro-Ro Pier 2 FG (vert) and marina pontoon Fl G 4s. Limit of dredged area around pier and pontoons area marked by buoys.

COMMUNICATIONS CGOC (02891) 463933. Moorings are run by local community.

FACILITIES Marina (30⛵ inc ❂, ⚓ in bay), portellenmarina.co.uk ☎300301 for fuel/assistance, dredged to 3m, ⚓ £12<10m>£14, 🚻/🚿 🅿 🍴. **Village:** 🔧 🅿 ✉ 🛒 ✕ 🅿 @.

2.6 CRINAN CANAL

Argyll and Bute **56°05'·50N 05°33'·38W** Crinan ✿❀⚓⚓✿✿✿

CHARTS AC 2326, 2476; Imray C65, C63.

TIDES –0608 Dover; ML 2·1; Duration 0605; HW Crinan is at HW Oban –0045

Standard Port OBAN (←)

Times				Height (metres)			
High Water		Low Water		MHWS	MHWN	MLWN	MLWS
0100	0700	0100	0800	4·0	2·9	1·8	0·7
1300	1900	1300	2000				
Differences CARSAIG BAY (56°02'N 05°38'W)							
–0105	–0040	–0050	–0050	–2·1	–1·6	–1·0	–0·4

NOTE: In the Sound of Jura, S of Loch Crinan, the rise of tide occurs mainly during the 3½ hrs after LW; the fall during the 3½ hrs after HW. At other times the changes in level are usually small and irregular.

SHELTER Complete shelter in canal basin; yachts are welcome. Good shelter in Crinan Hbr (E of Eilean da Mheinn) but full of moorings, contact Crinan Boatyard. Except in strong W/N winds, ⚓ E of the canal ent, clear of fairway or SW of Eilean da Mheinn. Good holding in Gallanach Bay on N side of L Crinan in about 3m.

NAVIGATION WPT 56°05'·70N 05°33'·64W, 146°/0·27M to Fl WG 3s lt. Beware Black Rock (2m high) in appr NE of ldg line 146° to dir Fl WG 3s lt. Off NW corner of chartlet, no ⚓ in a nearly rectangular shellfish bed, 6ca by 6ca. SPM lt buoys mark each corner: Fl (4) Y 12s at the NE and NW corners, Fl Y 6s at the SW and SE corners; the latter being about 100m NE of Black Rock.

CANAL Canal is 9M (14.5km) long with 15 locks and 7 opening bridges. Transit time is at least 6 hrs, observing the 4kn speed limit. Entry at all tides. Max LOA: 26·82m, 6.09m beam, 2·7m draught (add 0.10m to salt water draught. If >2.2m contact Canal Office or Sea Locks 24 hrs in advance to confirm canal level will allow passage – there may be some delay to raise water levels) mast 28.95m. The canal operates Mon-Fri in winter months increasing to 6/7 days in peak season. Contact Crinan Canal Office for timings or consult www.scottishcanals.co.uk. Periods of closure may be expected during winter months. It is closed between Christmas and New Year. Long warps and fenders are essential; sea locks can be turbulent at low tide and care is to be taken handling warps – always take a turn round a suitable cleat. Do not pump out bilges or heads in the canal. Water points are supplied but not hoses. Bellanoch pontoons / moorings are reserved for long term berth holders and should not be used by those in transit.

BOAT SAFETY SCHEME Transit craft may be subject to random safety checks on gas systems. £1M 3rd party insurance is required. See also 1.16.

LIGHTS AND MARKS Crinan Hotel is conspic W bldg. A conspic chy, 3ca SW of hotel, leads 187° into Crinan Hbr. E of sea-lock: Dir Fl WG 3s 8m 4M, vis 114°-W-146°-G-280°. Ent: 2 FG (vert) and 2FR (vert).

COMMUNICATIONS (Code 01546) CGOC (02891) 463933; Police 101; Dr 462001. Canal Office 603210 (HO). Sea lock 830285 (for advice at w/e and if no response to VHF – staff carry phone). VHF Ch **74** 16 only at sea locks.

FACILITIES Canal Office (Mon-Fri), www.scottishcanals.co.uk. All fees are under review; contact office for details. ⚓⛴🛶 *Skippers Guide* is essential reading; **Sea Basin** ⌣ (overnight rate available). Use shore toilets, not yacht heads, whilst in canal.

Services: Crinan Boatyard www.crinanboatyard.co.uk ☎830232; ⬛🛢⚓🛠⚒ 🅿🏧🅿🗐🗙 C(5t), ✕.

Village ✉ Ⓑ 🍴 🛒 🗙 (Ardrishaig), ⇌ (Oban), ✈ (Glasgow).

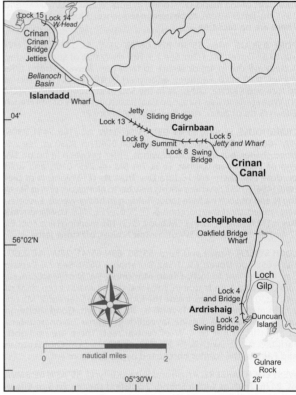

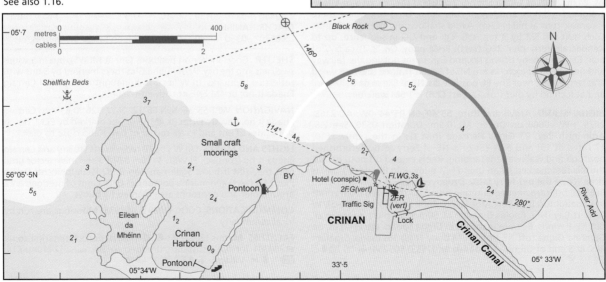

MULL OF KINTYRE

(AC 2126, 2199, 2798) From Crinan to Mull of Kintyre is about 50M. Passage round the Mull of Kintyre within 2 or 3 miles of the coast requires great care. Races exist S and SW of the Mull, and fresh to strong S winds cause dangerous breaking seas especially during E-going (flood) tidal streams. Best to keep at least 3 miles offshore and S of Sanda Island.

▶*In Sanda Sound the W-going stream starts HW Dover –0110, and the E-going stream starts HW Dover +0500. Sp rates 5kn. Close W of the Mull the N-going stream starts at HW Dover –0130, and the S-going stream at HW Dover +0430. Sp rates 5kn. Careful timing is needed, especially W-bound.*◀

The Traffic Separation Scheme in the North Channel, is only 2M W of the Mull and limits sea-room in the ITZ.

Sanda Sound separates Sanda Island and its rocks and islets from Kintyre. On the mainland shore beware Macosh Rks (dry, PHM lt buoy), forming part of Barley Ridges, 2ca offshore; and Arranman's Barrels, drying and submerged, marked by PHM lt buoy. A tidal turbine is sited 4ca SE off Rat Stane just outside a line joining the 2 buoys, with a lattice twr SPM, X topmark, Fl Y 5s. Sanda Is provides useful stopping point while waiting for the tide. Beware Paterson's Rk (9ca E, dries). There is good ⚓ on N side in Sanda Roads. Approach with Boat Ho bearing 155°; beware strong tidal stream across entrance, and drying rocks in middle of bay. See Plan on AC 2126.

▶ *Once E of Mull of Kintyre, tidal conditions and pilotage much improve.*◀

MULL OF KINTYRE TO UPPER LOCH FYNE

(AC 2126, 2383, 2381, 2382). Campbeltown is entered N of Island Davaar (lt). 1·5M N off lt ho is Otterard Rk (depth 3·8m), with Long Rk (dries 1·1m) 5ca W of it; only Otterard Rock is buoyed.

▶*E of Island Davaar tide runs 3kn at Sp, and there are overfalls.*◀

Kilbrannan Sound runs 21M from Island Davaar to Skipness Pt, where it joins Inchmarnock Water, Lower Loch Fyne and Bute Sound.

▶*There are few dangers apart from overfalls off Carradale Pt and on Erins Bank, 10M S of Skipness, on S-going stream.*◀

Good ⚓ in Carradale Bay, off Torrisdale Castle.

Lower L Fyne (AC 2381) is mainly clear of dangers to East L Tarbert. On E shore beware rks off Ardlamont Pt; 4M to NW is Skate Is which is best passed to W. 3M S of Ardrishaig beware Big Rk (depth 2·1m). Further N, at entrance to Loch Gilp (mostly dries), note shoals (least depth 1·5m) round Gulnare Rk, PHM lt buoy; also Duncuan Is with dangers extending SW to Sgeir Sgalag (depth 0·6m), buoyed.

Where Upper L Fyne turns NE (The Narrows) it is partly obstructed by Otter Spit (dries 0·9m), extending 8ca WNW from E shore and marked by lt bn. The stream runs up to 2kn here. A buoyed/lit rk, depth less than 2m, lies about 7ca SW of Otter Spit bn. In Upper L Fyne (AC 2382) off Minard Pt, the chan between rks and islands in the fairway is buoyed/lit.

2.7 ARDRISHAIG

Argyll and Bute 56°00'·78N 05°26'·62W ✿✿⚓⚓✿✿

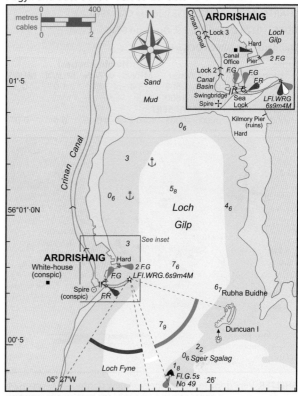

CHARTS AC 5610, 2131, 2381; Imray C63, 2900

TIDES +0120 Dover; ML 1·9; Duration 0640

Standard Port GREENOCK (→)

Times				Height (metres)			
High Water		Low Water		MHWS	MHWN	MLWN	MLWS
0000	0600	0000	0600	3·4	2·8	1·0	0·3
1200	1800	1200	1800				
Differences ARDRISHAIG							
+0006	+0006	-0015	+0020	0·0	0·0	+0·1	–0·1
INVERARAY							
+0011	+0011	+0034	+0034	–0·1	+0·1	–0·5	–0·2

SHELTER Hbr is sheltered except from strong E'lies; do not berth on pier or ⚓ due to commercial vessels H24. Sea lock into the Crinan Canal is usually left open, however, a waiting pontoon has been installed outside the lock, with restricted depth, for use in fair weather only. Access at all tides. Complete shelter in the canal basin, or beyond lock No 2. Also ⚓ 2ca N of hbr, off the W shore of L Gilp. Head of Loch Fyne dries for nearly 1M.

NAVIGATION WPT No 48 PHM buoy, Fl R 4s, 56°00'·18N 05°26'·31W, 345°/0·6M to bkwtr lt. Dangerous drying rocks to E of appr chan are marked by No 49 Fl.G.5s SHM buoy.

LIGHTS AND MARKS Conspic W Ho on with block of flats leads 315°between Nos 48 and 49 buoys. Bkwtr lt, L Fl WRG 6s, W339°-350°. Pier is floodlit. Other lights as plan.

COMMUNICATIONS (Code 01546) CGOC (02891) 463933; Police 101; Dr 462001. Canal Office 603210 (Mon-Fri); Sea lock 602458. VHF Ch **74** 16.

FACILITIES Pier/Hbr ☎603210, ⬤ (fees under review) ⚓ ⚓.

Crinan Canal www.scottishcanals.co.uk **Sea Lock** ☎602458, ⬤ ⚓⚓⚓✕⬤; dues, see 2.6. **Services:** ⬤⚓⚓⬤⬤⬤.
Village: ✉ ⑧ ⬤ ✕ ⬤ ⇌ (Oban), ✈ (Glasgow or Campbeltown).

2.8 TARBERT

Tarbert (entrance) 55°52′·05N 05°24′·22W ✿✿✿✿✿✿✿✿✿

CHARTS AC 5610, 2131, 2381; Imray C63, 2900

TIDES +0120 Dover; ML 1·9; Duration 0640

Standard Port GREENOCK (⟶)

Times				Height (metres)			
High Water		Low Water		MHWS	MHWN	MLWN	MLWS
0000	0600	0000	0600	3·4	2·8	1·0	0·3
1200	1800	1200	1800				
Differences EAST LOCH TARBERT							
–0005	–0005	0000	–0005	+0·2	+0·1	0·0	0·0

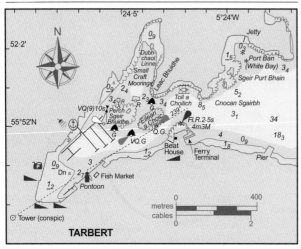

TARBERT

SHELTER Very good in all weathers on new pontoons. Access H24. 100 🅥 ⌣ on pontoons (call on VHF Ch 14 for berth); only use Fish Quay if directed by HM.

NAVIGATION WPT 55°52′·02N 05°23′·03W, 270°/0·7M to Fl R 2·5s lt. Ent is 60m wide and well marked. Cock Isle divides the ent in half: Main hbr to the S, Buteman's Hole to the N, where ⌕s are fouled by heavy moorings and lost chains. Speed limit 3kn.

LIGHTS AND MARKS Outer ldg lts 252° to S ent: Fl R 2·5s on with Cock Is lt QG. Inner ldg line 239°: same QG, G column, on with conspic ✠ tr. Note: The W sector, 065°-078°, of Eilean na Beithe ⚡, Fl WRG 3s 7m 5M (on E shore of Lower Loch Fyne), could be used to position for the initial appr to Tarbert.

COMMUNICATIONS (Code 01880) CGOC (02891) 463933; Police 101; Ⓗ (01546) 602323. HM 820344, www.tarbertharbour.co.uk. VHF Ch **14** (0900-1700LT).

FACILITIES Yacht Berthing Facility, www.tarbertharbour.co.uk, ⌣ £2.54, 🕂 ⬚⑂.

Fish Quay 🕂 🅐(Mon-Fri 0800-1800); **Tarbert YC** ⚓.

Town ⌂ 🕿(0800-1800) 🔋🔌✕🔧☎⌂🏧🍴🏦 ACA, 🚂 ✉ Ⓑ ✕ ⬚ ⇌ (bus to Glasgow), ✈ (Glasgow/Campbeltown).

ANCHORAGES IN LOCH FYNE
• *Beware discarded wires on seabed throughout the area.*

In Lower L Fyne there is a ⚓ at Kilfinan Bay, 🕿(01700) 821201. In Upper Loch Fyne: 10 ⚓ for patrons of the Oyster Bar at Cairndow 6M N of Inverary; ⚓ SSW of pier in 4m or dry out NW of the pier; 🕂 (on pier), 🔋✉🚂✕⬚ bus to Glasgow. On NW bank at Port Ann, Loch Gair and Minard Bay; and on SE bank at Otter Ferry, Sailors' Bothy run by Otter Ferry Pier Association with dinghy pontoon, 🅿 and toilets (15⚓s at Oyster Catcher Inn), Strachur Bay (pontoon and 5⚓s off Creggans Inn, 🕿(01369) 860279) and St Catherine's.

2.9 PORTAVADIE

Tarbert (entrance) 55°52′·23N 05°18′·98W ✿✿✿✿✿✿✿

CHARTS AC 5610, 2131, 2381; Imray C63, 2900

TIDES +0120 Dover; ML 1·9; Duration 0640

Standard Port GREENOCK (⟶)

Times				Height (metres)			
High Water		Low Water		MHWS	MHWN	MLWN	MLWS
0000	0600	0000	0600	3·4	2·8	1·0	0·3
1200	1800	1200	1800				
Differences PORTAVADIE							
–0005	–0005	0000	–0005	+0·2	+0·1	0·0	0·0

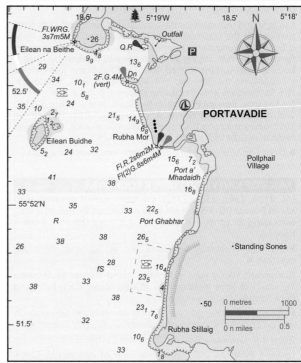

SHELTER Very good in a well protected deep water facility. Access H24. 230 🅥 ⌣ on pontoons with assistance available (call on VHF Ch 80 for berth). If arriving after hours use S, A, B or ⌣ pontoons.

NAVIGATION WPT 55°52′·00N 05°19′·20W, 027°/0·27M to entrance. When approaching from north pass SW of Eilean Buidhe which has fish farm to the NE. Inshore passage may be used with local knowledge. From the S Clear Sgat Mor and round Rubha Stillaig avoiding fish farm inshore. Portavadie has a narrow entrance between lit breakwaters. Speed limit 3kn.

LIGHTS AND MARKS Eilean na Beithe to North Fl WRG 3s 7m 5M 036°-G-065°-W-078°-R-106° marks access to Glenan Bay and inshore passage NE of Eilean Buidhe. Sgat Mor Fl 3s 9m 12M. Entrance marked by beacons PH Fl R 2s 6m 2M; SH Fl (2) G 8s 6m 4M.

COMMUNICATIONS (Code 01880) CGOC (02891) 463933; Police 101. VHF Ch **80** (0900-1700LT).

FACILITIES Marina, www.portavadiemarina.com 🕿811075, 206 ⚓ ⌣ inc 🅥 £2.15, 🔋🔌🔋✕☎⌂🍴🏪(12t) 🏧✕⬚ wi-fi, small shop, ✈ (Glasgow). Other local shops at Kames (2.5M).

ADJACENT ANCHORAGES
Glenan Bay to NW ⚓ in 15m steep to bay open to SW.

Asgog B1.5M to S entered between Sgat Mor and Sgat Beag. ⚓ in 15M to E of Eilean Aoidhe.

2.10 TIDAL STREAMS AROUND THE MULL OF KINTYRE

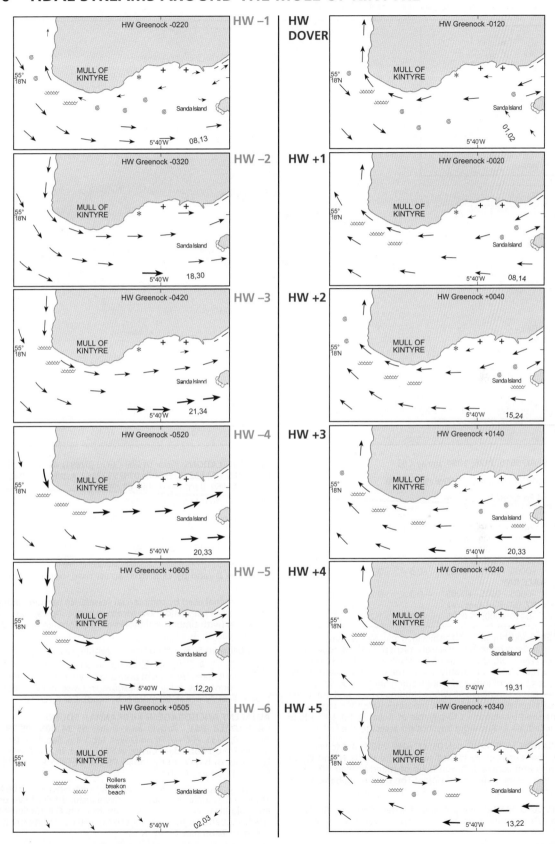

2.11 CAMPBELTOWN
Argyll & Bute 55°25'·90N 05°32'·56W Hbr ent ❁❁❁⬙⬙✿✿✿

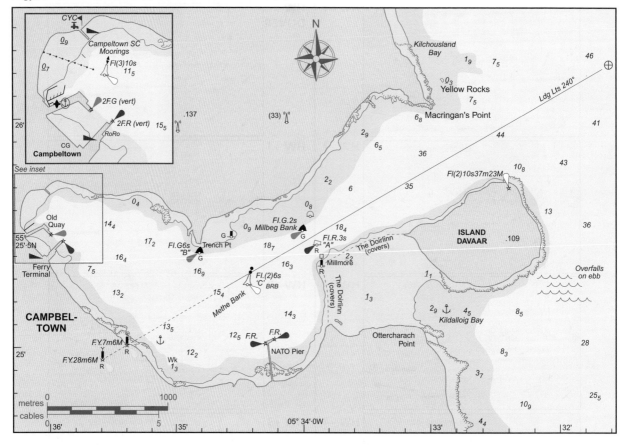

CHARTS AC 5610, 2126, 1864; Imray C63

TIDES +0125 Dover; ML 1·8; Duration 0630

Standard Port GREENOCK (→)

Times				Height (metres)			
High Water		Low Water		MHWS	MHWN	MLWN	MLWS
0000	0600	0000	0600	3·4	2·8	1·0	0·3
1200	1800	1200	1800				
Differences CAMPBELTOWN							
−0025	−0005	−0015	+0005	−0·5	−0·3	+0·1	+0·2
CARRADALE BAY							
−0015	−0005	−0005	+0005	−0·3	−0·2	+0·1	+0·1
SOUTHEND, (Mull of Kintyre)							
−0030	−0010	+0005	+0035	−1·3	−1·2	−0·5	−0·2

SHELTER Good, but gusts off the hills in strong SW'lies. Main harbour dredged to 9m for commercial vessels. Yacht pontoon dredged 3·0m is close NW of Old Quay and gives excellent sheltered berthing. Yachts >12m LOA should notify ETA to the berthing master by ☎. Good ⚓ on S side of loch, E of front leading light. ⚓ possible in N of harbour, but is exposed to SE winds. Holding is poor and great care must be taken not to foul local SC moorings (large Y buoys). Some may be used by visitors - £10 payable at Royal Hotel. S of Island Davaar temp ⚓ in Kildalloig Bay, but no access to the loch.

NAVIGATION WPT 55°26'·24N 05°31'·61W, 240°/1·4M to first chan buoys. The ent is easily identified by radio masts N and NE of Trench Pt and conspic lt ho on N tip of Island Davaar off which streams are strong (4kn sp). Caution: The Doirlinn, a bank drying 2·5m which covers at HW, is close S of the ldg line.

LIGHTS AND MARKS See 2.4 and chartlet. Otterard Rk (3·8m depth, off chartlet, 1·5M NNE of Island Davaar), is marked by ECM lt buoy.

COMMUNICATIONS (Code 01586) CGOC (02891) 463933; Police 101; Dr 552105. HM 552552 mobile 07825 732862, Asst HM 551242 mobile 07876 580950. Berthing mobile 07798 524821.

VHF Ch 13 16 (Mon-Fri 0900-1700).

FACILITIES Yacht pontoon (10+20❂) £1.70, ⚓ ⬗.

Aqualibrium: dedicated facilities for yacht crews, opposite pontoon: @ 🚾/⬙ ▢ ✕ swimming pool, gym, sauna, creche and library.

Royal Hotel – payment of berthing fees: @ 🚾/⬙ ▢ ✕.

Old Quay D (and by cans from across road, opposite pontoon), ⚓ ⬩ LB.

Ferry Terminal used by commercial vessels. No berthing alongside without HM's permission. The attached public slipway has a drying out berth (with timber keel blocks and upright leaning posts) for FVs and yachts, ⚓ ⬗.

Campbeltown SC ⬆ (dinghies), ⬚ regular racing.

Town 🅿 🛈 🏧 ⬩ ⚒ 🔧 Ⓔ ⬚(10t) ⬩ ACA, 🍽(2) ✕ 🛏 ✉ Ⓑ; ♿🚾 about 100m from yacht pontoon (keypad, number displayed on pontoon). Bus 3/day to Glasgow, ✈ twice daily to Glasgow, (nearest ⇌ Arrochar, 90 miles N by road). Car hire/taxi.

ADJACENT ANCHORAGE IN KILBRANNAN SOUND
CARRADALE BAY, Argyll and Bute, **55°34'·40N 05°28'·66W**. AC 5610, 2131, HW+0115 on Dover. ML 1·8m. See 2.11. Good ⚓ 1 M S in 7m off Torrisdale Castle in SW corner. In N & E winds ⚓ in NE corner of bay, W of Carradale Pt. 3ca E of this Pt, a PHM buoy Fl (2) R 12s marks Crubon Rk.

In S & E winds a swell sets into bay, when good shelter can be found 1M N in **Carradale Harbour** (Port Crannaich); if full of FVs, use 4❂ immediately to N or ⚓ 100m N of Hbr. Bkwtr lt, Fl R 10s 5m 6M. Call HM Campbeltown for overnight berth, £10 pay in honesty box. Facilities: ⚓ on pier, ✉ 🛒 ✕ ⬚.

2.12 LAMLASH

Isle of Arran, N Ayrshire **55°32'·00N 05°07'·06W** ⚓⚓⚓⚓⚓⚓⚓⚓⚓

CHARTS AC 5610, 2131, 2220, 1864; Imray C63

TIDES +0115 Dover; ML no data; Duration 0635

Standard Port GREENOCK (→)

Times				Height (metres)			
High Water		Low Water		MHWS	MHWN	MLWN	MLWS
0000	0600	0000	0600	3·4	2·8	1·0	0·3
1200	1800	1200	1800				
Differences LAMLASH							
–0016	–0036	–0024	–0004	–0·2	–0·2	ND	ND
BRODICK BAY							
–0013	–0013	–0008	–0008	–0·2	–0·1	0·0	+0·1
LOCH RANZA							
–0015	–0005	–0010	–0005	–0·4	–0·3	–0·1	0·0

SHELTER Very good in all weathers. Lamlash is a natural hbr with sheltered ⚓s as follows: off Lamlash except in E'lies – depth may be 20m but shoals rapidly to the W; off Kingscross Point, good except in strong N/NW winds; off the NW of Holy Island in E'lies. ⚓ off Lamlash Pier. Dry out against pier if in need of repairs. See also Brodick 5M N, and Loch Ranza 14M N (RH col).

NAVIGATION WPT 55°32'·63N 05°03'·06W, 270°/1M to N Chan buoy (Fl R 6s).

Beware: submarines exercise frequently in this area (see 2.17), and also wreck of landing craft (charted) off farmhouse on Holy Is.

LIGHTS AND MARKS See 2.4 and chartlet.

COMMUNICATIONS (Code 01770) CGOC (02891) 463933; Police 101; ℍ 600777. No VHF.

FACILITIES Lamlash Old Pier ⌐ (£3–£5), ⚓ ⚓ ✕ ⚓; Arran YC ☎01770 600333 25⚓ £10. Village (Lamlash/Brodick) ⚓ ⚓ ✕ ✕ ⚓ ⊠ ⚓ ⇌ (bus to Brodick, Ferry to Ardrossan), ✈ (Glasgow or Prestwick).

OTHER HARBOURS ON ARRAN (AC 2724, 2131, 2126)

BRODICK, Arran, **55°35'·50N 05°08'·66W**. AC 2131, 2220, 1864. HW +0115 on Dover; ML 1·8m; Duration 0635. See 2.12. Shelter good except in E winds. ⚓ W of ferry pier in 3m; on NW side just below Castle in 4·5m, or further N off Merkland Pt in 3-4m. Also 10⚓s. There are no navigational dangers but the bay is in a submarine exercise area; see 2.17. Lts: Ro Ro pier dolphin 2 F R (vert) 9m 4M and 2 F G (vert) 9m 4M on pier hd. Facilities: ⚓ ⚓ ⚓ (at pier hd) ⚓ ⊠ ⓑ ⚓ ✕ ⚓. Ferry to Ardrossan.

LOCH RANZA, Arran, **55°42'·60N 05°17'·96W**. AC 2131, 2383, 2221. HW +0120 on Dover; ML 1·7m; Duration 0635. See 2.12. Good shelter, but swell enters loch in N'lies. The 850m mountain 4M to S causes fierce squalls in the loch in S winds. Beware Screda Reef extending SW off Newton Pt. 12⚓s. ⚓ in 5m off castle (conspic); holding is suspect in soft mud. Dinghy landing and temp ⚓ on pontoon at Lochranza. 2F G lts on RoRo pier at Coillemore. S shore dries. Facilities: ⚓ ⚓ at ferry slip, ⊠ ⚓ ✕. Ferry to Claonaig.

HARBOURS AND ANCHORAGES AROUND BUTE (Clockwise from Garroch Head, S tip of Bute) (AC 2131, 1906/7)

ST NINIAN'S BAY, Bute, **55°48'·15N 05°07'·86W**. AC 2221, 2383. Inchmarnock Is gives some shelter from the W, but Sound is exposed to S'lies. At S end, beware Shearwater Rk, 0·9m, almost in mid-sound. ⚓ in about 7m, 2ca E of St Ninian's Pt; beware drying spit to S of this Pt. Or ⚓ off E side of Inchmarnock, close abeam Midpark Farm.

WEST KYLE, Bute, **55°54'N 05°12'·7W**. AC1906. Tides, see 2.13 (Tighnabruaich). On W bank PHM buoys, each Fl R 4s, mark Ardlamont Pt, Carry Pt and Rubha Ban; N of which are two Fl Y buoys (fish farms). ⚓ close off Kames or Tighnabruaich, where space allows; or in Black Farland Bay (N of Rubha Dubh). Some ⚓s off Kames and Royal Hotels, maintained by them on a 'use at own risk basis': Kames Hotel ☎(01700) 811489; Kyles of Bute Hotel 811350; Royal Hotel 811239; and Tighnabruaich Hotel 811615. Facilities: ⚓ ⚓ ⚓ ⚓.

CALADH HARBOUR, Argyll and Bute, **55°56'·00N, 05°11'·73W**. AC 1906. HW (Tighnabruaich) +0015 on Dover; ML 2·1m. See 2.13. Perfectly sheltered natural hbr on W side of ent to Loch Riddon. Enter Caladh Hbr to N or S of Eilean Dubh; keep to the middle of the S passage. When using the N ent, keep between R and G bns to clear a drying rk marked by perch. ⚓ in the middle of hbr clear of moorings. No facilities/stores; see West Kyle above.

LOCH RIDDON, Argyll and Bute, **55°57'N 05°11'·6W**. AC 1906. Tides, see 2.13. Water is deep for 1·3M N of Caladh and shore is steep-to; upper 1·5M of loch dries. ⚓ on W side close N of Ormidale pier; on E side at Salthouse; off Eilean Dearg (One Tree Is); and at NW corner of Fearnoch Bay.

BURNT ISLANDS, Bute, **55°55'·76N 05°10'·39W**. AC 1906. Tides, see 2.16. The three islands (Eilean Mor, Fraoich and Buidhe) straddle the East Kyle. There are 2 channels: North, between Buidhe and the other 2 islets, is narrow, short and marked by 2 SHM buoys (the NW'ly one is Fl G 3s), and one PHM buoy, Fl R 2s. South chan lies between Bute and Fraoich/Mor; it is unlit, but marked by one PHM and two SHM buoys. Depths may be less than charted. A SHM buoy, Fl G 3s, is off Rubha a' Bhodaich, 4ca ESE. Direction of buoyage is to SE. Sp streams reach 5kn in N Chan and 3kn in S Chan. ⚓ in Wreck Bay, Balnakailly Bay or in the lee of Buidhe and Mor in W'lies; also W of Colintraive Pt, clear of ferry and cables. There are 6⚓s off the hotel, ☎(01700) 841207.

KILCHATTAN BAY, Bute, **55°45'N 05°01'·1W**. AC 1907. Bay is deep, but dries 3ca off the W shore. Temp ⚓s only in offshore winds: off the village on SW side, or on N side near Kerrytonlia Pt. Rubh' an Eun Lt, Fl R 6s, is 1·1M to SSE. Facilities: ⚓ ⊠ ⚓ bus to Rothesay.

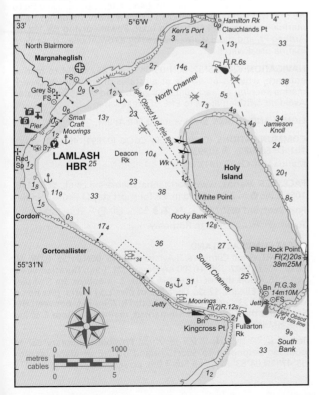

2.13 ROTHESAY

Isle of Bute, Argyll and Bute **55°50′·32N 05°03′·08W**
❀❀❀♢♢❀❀

CHARTS AC 5610, 2131, 1907, 1906, 1867; Imray C63, 2900

TIDES +0100 Dover; ML 1·9; Duration 0640

Standard Port GREENOCK (→)

Times				Height (metres)			
High Water		Low Water		MHWS	MHWN	MLWN	MLWS
0000	0600	0000	0600	3·4	2·8	1·0	0·3
1200	1800	1200	1800				
Differences ROTHESAY BAY							
−0020	−0015	−0010	−0002	+0·2	+0·2	+0·2	+0·2
RUBHA A'BHODAICH (Burnt Is)							
−0020	−0010	−0007	−0007	−0·2	−0·1	+0·2	+0·2
TIGHNABRUAICH							
+0007	−0010	−0002	−0015	0·0	+0·2	+0·4	+0·5

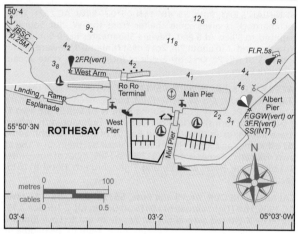

SHELTER Good in Outer and Inner Harbours (max 2m draught and very limited space for LOA > 40ft), and on pontoons S of West Arm, but beware of very strong easterly flow towards the rocks on the E side of the harbour due to wash during ferry manoeuvres (and whilst berthed). No berthing on north and east faces of Main Pier. Good ⚓ off Isle of Bute SC in west side of bay. Exposed to N/NE; **Port Bannatyne Marina** (Kames Bay) offers better shelter.

NAVIGATION WPT 55°51′·00N 05°02′·76W, 194°/0·69M to Outer hbr ent. From E keep 1ca off Bogany Pt PHM buoy, Fl R 4s. Call HM for bridge openings to Inner Harbour. Entry/exit to/from hbr controlled by traffic lights. Extreme care needed; very limited room to manoeuvre.

LIGHTS AND MARKS Lts as chartlet, hard to see against shore lts. Conspicuous church spire leads 190° to outer harbour. Port Sigs:

● (3 vert) = Harbour closed to all traffic movements.

● (2 vert) + ○ = Harbour open.

COMMUNICATIONS (Code 01700) CGOC (02891) 463933; Police 101; Dr 503985; ⊞ 503938. HM 503842; Bute Berthing Co mob 07799 724225. *Bute Berthing* Ⓜ; *Rothesay Harbour* Ch **12** 16.

FACILITIES 68 ⊇ Ⓥ (Bute Berthing Co) call ahead for availability. £16 for 8m LOA, £21 for 11m LOA, short stay £6, ⚒ ▃ ⤙ ⏚ ↦ ⚓ ⚓ ⚓ on Pier; ♦ by arrangement weekdays (min 200 galls).

Town (Wed – early closing) ☎ ☎ (closes 1800) @(0900-1700) ✉ Ⓑ ⛟ ✗ ⌷ ⥥ (ferry to Wemyss Bay) ✈(Glasgow).

2.14 PORT BANNATYNE

Isle of Bute, Argyll and Bute **55°51′·75N 05°05′·17W**
❀❀♢♢❀❀

CHARTS AC 5610, 2131, 1907, 1906, 1867; Imray C63, 2900

TIDES As for Rothesay

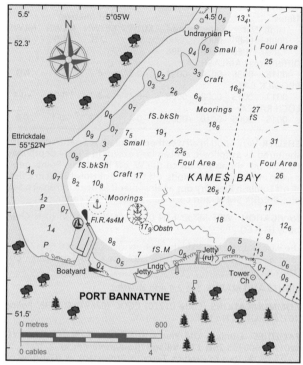

SHELTER Well sheltered from westerly winds and protected by stone breakwater. Marina situated in SW corner of Kames Bay provides secure alongside berth in 2.4m. Alternatively ⚓ in 11m to NE of b'water clear of small craft along N shore. moorings NE of marina – beware sunken fishing boat. Beware drying rks 1ca off Ardbeg Pt, and shoal water, marked by a row of piles, close W of marina breakwater.

NAVIGATION WPT 55°52′·00N 05°04′·00W, 252°/0·7M to marina entrance, which is accessible at all states of the tide. Approach marina keeping at least 20m clear of the end of the breakwater. Avoid no ⚓/fishing areas to ENE of breakwater.

LIGHTS AND MARKS Breakwater lt Fl R 4s 2M.

COMMUNICATIONS (Code 01700) CGOC (02891) 463933; Police 101; Dr 503985; ⊞ 503938.
Marina VHF Ch 37 (M1).

FACILITIES Marina, www.portbannatynemarina.co.uk, ☎503116, 105⊇ inc Ⓥ in 2·5m, £2·00/m, £6 for short stay (4 hrs) ⌁ wi-fi.
Port Boatyard ☎502719 ▃ ⤙ ⏚ ♦ ⚒ ⚒ ⊡ Ⓔ ♠ ⚓ ⚓(15t) ⚓.
Town ⛟ ✉ ⌷ ✗ bus to Rothesay.

GREAT CUMBRAE ISLAND

MILLPORT, Great Cumbrae, N Ayrshire, **55°45′·00N 04°55′·82W**. AC 5610, 1867, 1907. HW +0100 on Dover; ML 1·9m; Duration 0640. See 2.16. Good shelter, except in S'lies. ⚓ in approx 3m S of pier or E of the Eileans. 12 ⚓s 1½ca SSE of pier. Ldg marks: pier hd on with ⊕ twr 333°; or ldg lts 333°, both FR 7/9m 5M, between the Spoig and the Eileans, QG. Unmarked, drying rk is close E of ldg line. HM ☎(01475) 530826.

Town ▃ ☎ ☎ ♦ ⏚ ⚓ ✉ ⛟ ✗ ⌷. Possible temporary ⊇ on pontoon belonging to SportScotland off NE of island (approx 55°47′·1N 04°53′·8W) in 3.5m–4.5m; no services.

2.15 FAIRLIE QUAY

N Ayrshire 55°46'·07N 04°51'·78W ✿⚓✿✿

CHARTS AC 5610, 2131, 1907, 1867; Imray C63, 2900

TIDES +0105 Dover; ML 1·9; Duration 0640

Standard Port GREENOCK (→)

Times				Height (metres)			
High Water		Low Water		MHWS	MHWN	MLWN	MLWS
0000	0600	0000	0600	3·4	2·8	1·0	0·3
1200	1800	1200	1800				
Differences MILLPORT							
–0005	–0025	–0025	–0005	0·0	–0·1	0·0	+0·1

SHELTER Access H24. Poor shelter; pontoon subject to swell in fresh conditions and wash from passing vessels. Craft should not be left unsupervised unless calm settled weather is forecast. Cumbrae Island gives shelter from westerlies; Largs Channel is open to S or N winds.

NAVIGATION WPT 55°46'·08N 04°51'·84W. From S beware Hunterston Sands, Southannan Sands and outfalls from Hunterston Power Stn (conspic).

LIGHTS AND MARKS Lts as on chartlet. Fairlie Quay, 2 FG (vert) N & S ends of Pier.

COMMUNICATIONS (Code 01475) CGOC (02891) 463933; Dr 673380; Ⓗ 733777; Police 101. Fairlie Quay 568267.

Fairlie Quay Marina Ch **80** M (H24).

FACILITIES Fairlie Quay Fuel H24: ⬧⬧⚒⬧ ⬧⬧⬧⬧ (80t) ⬧. **Fairlie YC; Town** ✉Ⓑ🛒✕ ⬧≈ (Fairlie & Largs; 50 mins to Glasgow), ✈.

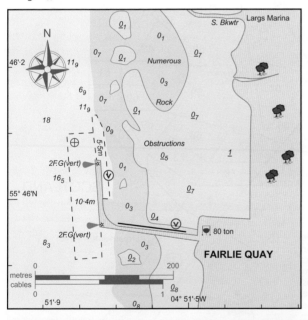

FAIRLIE QUAY

2.16 LARGS

N Ayrshire 55°46'·40N 04°51'·84W ✿✿✿⚓⚓✿✿

CHARTS AC 5610, 2131, 1907, 1867; Imray C63, 2900

TIDES +0105 Dover; ML 1·9; Duration 0640

Standard Port GREENOCK (→)

Times				Heights (metres)			
High Water		Low Water		MHWS	MHWN	MLWN	MLWS
0000	0600	0000	0600	3·4	2·8	1·0	0·3
1200	1800	1200	1800				.
Differences MILLPORT							
–0005	–0025	–0025	–0005	0·0	–0·1	0·0	+0·1

SHELTER Excellent in Largs Yacht Haven, access all tides (2·5m in ent; 3m deep berths). 7 pontoons; ❼ on 'C/D'. Cumbrae Is gives shelter from W'lies; Largs Chan is open to S or N winds.

NAVIGATION WPT 55°46'·40N 04°51'·84W, SWM lt buoy, off ent. From S beware Hunterston Sands, Southannan Sands and outfalls from Hunterston Power Stn (conspic). From the S bkwtr to Fairlie Quay is a restricted, no ⚓ area.

LIGHTS AND MARKS 'Pencil' monument (12m) conspic 4ca N of ent. Lts as on chartlet. Largs Pier, 2 FG (vert) when vessel expected.

COMMUNICATIONS (Code 01475) CGOC (02891) 463933; Dr 673380; Ⓗ 733777; Police 101; Largs SC 670000.

Largs Yacht Haven Ch **80** M (H24).

FACILITIES Largs Yacht Haven www.yachthavens.com ☎ 675333, (730⬚ inc ❼), £2·90; ⬧▬(H24)⬧⬧⬧(H24)⬧⬧⚒⬧⬧Ⓔ⬧⬧ ⬧(70t) ⬧(17t) Divers, ice, ✕⬧. **Town** (1M) ✉Ⓑ🛒✕⬧≈ (50 mins to Glasgow), ✈.

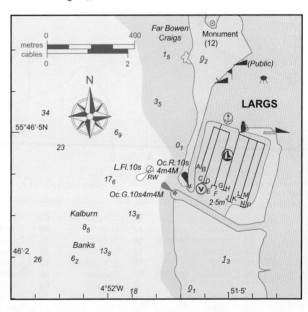

LARGS

ARRAN, BUTE AND FIRTH OF CLYDE

(AC1906, 1907) Arran's mountains tend to cause squalls or calms, but there are good ⚓s at Lamlash, Brodick and Loch Ranza. Sannox Rock (depth 1·5m) is 2½ca off Arran coast 8M N of Lamlash. 1ca off W side of Inchmarnock is Tra na-h-uil, a rock drying 1·5m. In Inchmarnock Sound, Shearwater Rk (depth 0·9m) lies in centre of S entrance.

The Kyles of Bute are attractive channels N of Bute, and straightforward apart from the Burnt Islands where it is best to take the north channel, narrow but well buoyed, passing between Eilean Buidhe and Eilean Fraoich/Eilean Mor. ▶*Spring stream may reach 5kn.*◀ Caladh Hbr is a beautiful ⚓ 7ca NW of Burnt Is.

The N lochs in Firth of Clyde are less attractive. Loch Goil is worth a visit; Loch Long is squally with few ⚓s but no hidden dangers; Gareloch has Rhu Marina, Faslane submarine base and small craft moorings at the northern end. ▶ *Navigation in Firth of Clyde is straightforward since tidal streams are weak, seldom exceeding 1kn. It is however a busy area with many large commercial vessel movements and extensive naval training which takes place involving submarines, ships and aircraft. All users are recommended to read The Clydeport CLYDE LEISURE NAVIGATION GUIDE – www.clydeport.co.uk.* ◀ Channels are well marked; but beware unlit moorings. There are marinas on the mainland at Largs, Holy Loch, Portavadie and Inverkip. Rothesay Hbr on E Bute, and Kilchattan B (⚓ 6M to S) are both sheltered from SSE to WNW.

2.17 SUBMARINE EXERCISE AREAS

Submarines keep a constant listening watch on Ch 16. Submarines on the surface comply strictly with IRPCS; submarines at periscope depth will not close to within 1500 yds of a FV without her express agreement.

A 'Fisherman's hotline' (☎(01436) 677201) is available on a 24 hour basis and may be used for any queries relating to SUBFACTS from any mariner.

SUBFACTS broadcasts detail submarine activity in the exercise areas between Barra and the Isle of Man. They are transmitted by CGOC Belfast at 0710 and 1910 on a specified VHF Ch after an initial announcement on Ch 16.

The areas are referred to by the names given in the table for Areas 1–26 (North of Mull), see page 51.

General information on SUBFACTS is also broadcast twice daily at 0620 & 1820 UT on Navtex.

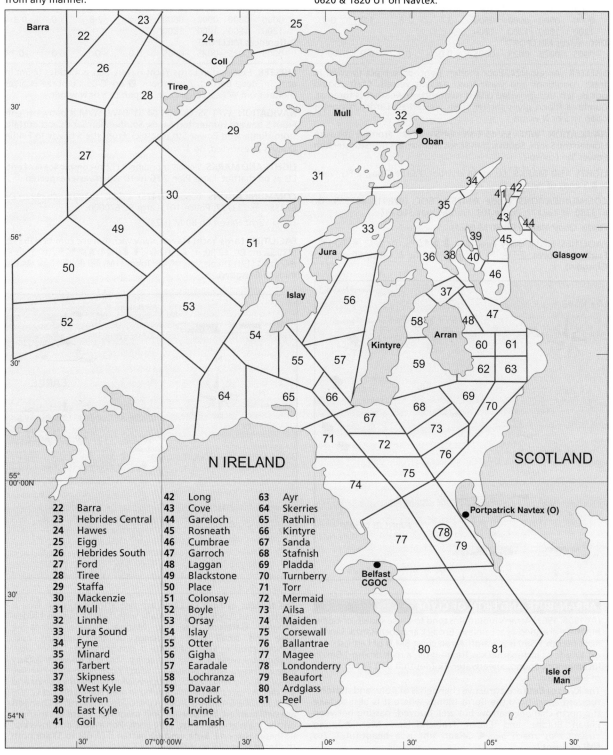

		42	Long	63	Ayr
22	Barra	43	Cove	64	Skerries
23	Hebrides Central	44	Gareloch	65	Rathlin
24	Hawes	45	Rosneath	66	Kintyre
25	Eigg	46	Cumbrae	67	Sanda
26	Hebrides South	47	Garroch	68	Stafnish
27	Ford	48	Laggan	69	Pladda
28	Tiree	49	Blackstone	70	Turnberry
29	Staffa	50	Place	71	Torr
30	Mackenzie	51	Colonsay	72	Mermaid
31	Mull	52	Boyle	73	Ailsa
32	Linnhe	53	Orsay	74	Maiden
33	Jura Sound	54	Islay	75	Corsewall
34	Fyne	55	Otter	76	Ballantrae
35	Minard	56	Gigha	77	Magee
36	Tarbert	57	Earadale	78	Londonderry
37	Skipness	58	Lochranza	79	Beaufort
38	West Kyle	59	Davaar	80	Ardglass
39	Striven	60	Brodick	81	Peel
40	East Kyle	61	Irvine		
41	Goil	62	Lamlash		

2.18 INVERKIP (KIP MARINA)

Inverclyde 55°54'·50N 04°53'·00W ✿✿✿♒♒♒♠♠

CHARTS AC 5610, 2131, 1907; Imray C63, 2900

TIDES +0110 Dover; ML 1·8; Duration 0640

Standard Port GREENOCK (→)

Times				Height (metres)			
High Water		Low Water		MHWS	MHWN	MLWN	MLWS
0000	0600	0000	0600	3·4	2·8	1·0	0·3
1200	1800	1200	1800				
Differences WEMYSS BAY							
–0005	–0005	–0005	–0005	0·0	0·0	+0·1	+0·1

SHELTER Excellent inside marina. Chan and marina are dredged 3·5m; accessible H24. Inverkip Bay is exposed to SW/NW winds.

NAVIGATION WPT 55°54'·49N 04°52'·95W, Kip SHM buoy, Fl G 5s, at ent to buoyed chan; beware shifting bank to the N.

LIGHTS AND MARKS SHM 55°54'·55N 04°54'·47W Fl G 1·06M 093° to entr which is ½M N of conspic chmy (238m). SPM buoy marks sewer outfall off Ardgowan Pt. From Kip SHM buoy, 3 SHM and 3 PHM buoys mark 365m long appr chan.

COMMUNICATIONS (Code 01475) CGOC (02891) 463933; Police 101; Dr 520248; ⊞ 33777.

Kip Marina Ch **80** M (H24). *Clydeport Estuary Radio* VHF Ch **12** 16 (H24). Info on weather and traffic available on request.

FACILITIES Kip Marina www.scottishmarinas.co.uk ☎521485; 625◠ inc 🅥, £2.25, £12 <5hrs, ♠🔔🔲⚓🗝️⚒ ⓔ △ ▣(50t) ◠◖ Diver, 🛒 ✕ 🏠 YC. **Town** ✉ Ⓑ (Gourock), ⇌ ✈ (Glasgow).

ADJACENT ANCHORAGE
DUNOON, Argyll and Bute, **55°56'·70N 04°55'·20W**. AC 5610, 2131, 1907, 1994. Use Greenock tides. Temp ⚓ in West or East Bays (S and N of Dunoon Pt). The former is open to the S; the latter more shoal. The Gantocks, drying rks 3ca SE of Dunoon Pt, have W ○ bn tr, Fl R 6s 12m 6M. 2FR (vert) on ferry pier. Facilities: 🏠🏨🔲♠ ✉🛒 ✕ 🏠 ferry to Gourock. 3⚓s off Innellan, 3·7M S of Dunoon, ☎(01369) 830445.

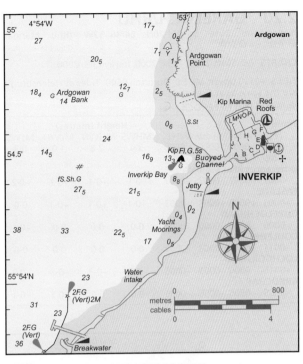

ANCHORAGE IN THE UPPER FIRTH OF CLYDE

GOUROCK, Inverclyde, **55°58'·00N 04°49'·00W**. AC 5610, 2131, 1994, Imray C63, 2900 Series; OS 63. Use Greenock tides. ⚓ in West Bay, beware of moorings. It is exposed in NW/NE'lies. Beware foul ground in Gourock Bay. No navigational dangers, but much shipping and ferries in the Clyde. The S edge of the Firth of Clyde recommended channel lies 2ca N of Kempock Pt. The pier at the S end of Gourock Bay is disused and unsafe. Facilities: Royal Gourock YC ☎632983 ♠⚓⚒🗝️△🛒✕🏠. **Town:** 🏠🏨✉Ⓑ🛒✕ 🏠⇌ Ferry (to Dunoon) ✈ (Glasgow).

2.19 HOLY LOCH

Argyll 55°59'·03N 04°56'·82W ✿✿✿♒♒♒✿✿✿

CHARTS AC 5610, 2131, 1994; Imray C63, 2900

TIDES +0122 Dover; ML 2·0; Duration 0640

Standard Port GREENOCK (→)

SHELTER Good, but exposed to to E/NE.

NAVIGATION WPT 55°59'·03N 04°55'·75W 270° to marina ent 0.60M. No offshore dangers. Holy Loch is controlled by QHM Clyde but navigation is not restricted; keep well clear of ferries when entering or leaving the loch.

LIGHTS AND MARKS No 30 SCM 55°58'·75N 04°53'·82W off Strone Pt. 2FR at SE end of pier. Marina floodlit.

COMMUNICATIONS (Code 01369) CGOC (02891) 463933; Police 101; Dr 703279; ⊞ 704341.

Holy Loch Marina Ch 80 M.

FACILITIES Marina www.holylochmarina.co.uk ☎701800, 270◠+ 🅥 in 3m £2.64, 2nd night ½ price; short stay £5.50. ♠🔔♠🔲🚿▣(25t) ◖◗✕. Possible ◠ on breakwater pontoon for larger yachts in depth >5m, but open to the E. Commercial timber yard operating alongside marina facilities. **Holy Loch SC** ☎702707.

Sandbank (town) PO, 🛒 🏠 ✕ Ferries from Hunter's Quay to McInroy's Pt, Gourock, connecting with trains and coaches to Glasgow Airport. Good local area bus service.

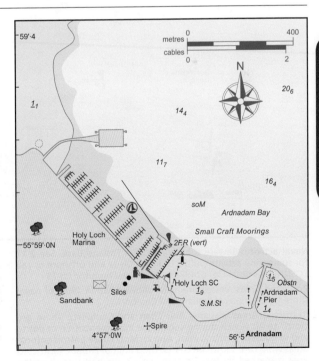

2.20 GARELOCH/RHU

Argyll and Bute **56°00'·70N 04°46'·57W** (Rhu Marina)
✿✿✿⚓⚓⚓✿✿✿

CHARTS AC 5610, 2131, 1994, 2000; Imray C63, 2900

TIDES +0110 Dover; ML 1·9; Duration 0640. Tides at Helensburgh are the same as at Greenock.

Standard Port GREENOCK (→)

Times				Height (metres)			
High Water		Low Water		MHWS	MHWN	MLWN	MLWS
0000	0600	0000	0600	3·4	2·8	1·0	0·3
1200	1800	1200	1800				
Differences RHU MARINA							
–0007	–0007	–0007	–0007	–0·1	–0·1	–0·1	–0·2
FASLANE							
+0003	+0003	+0003	+0003	+0·1	+0·1	+0·1	0·0
GARELOCHHEAD							
0000	0000	0000	0000	0·0	0·0	0·0	–0·1
COULPORT							
–0011	–0011	–0008	–0008	0·0	0·0	0·0	0·0
LOCHGOILHEAD							
+0015	0000	–0005	–0005	–0·2	–0·3	–0·3	–0·3
ARROCHAR							
–0005	–0005	–0005	–0005	0·0	0·0	–0·1	–0·1

BYELAWS Loch Long and Gareloch are Dockyard Ports under the jurisdiction of the Queen's Harbour Master. All submarines and other warships at anchor or underway have an Exclusion Zone around them enforced by MOD Police.

SHELTER Rhu Marina rock bkwtr 1m above MHWS, now extended with submerged section (end marked by SHM Fl G 5s) replacing floating wavebreak, protects the berths from strong winds from E to S. Helensburgh Pier is a temp'y drying berth, rather exposed, used by occas steamers. ⚓ E of marina or in Rosneath Bay. Moorings N of the narrows at Stroul B & Clynder; and at the head of the loch. Clyde Naval Base at Faslane must be avoided by yachts.

NAVIGATION WPT 55°59'·29N 04°45'·26W, 356°/1·3M to bn No 7. Beaches between Cairndhu Pt and Helensburgh Pier are strewn with large boulders above/below MLWS. Gareloch ent is via Rhu Narrows. Marina entrance not easy to find at night between pontoon breakwater and Fl G Bn of marina entrance; beware cross-tides. There are large unlit MoD buoys and barges off W shore of Gareloch; for Garelochhead keep to W shore until well clear of Faslane Naval Base.

LIGHTS AND MARKS Ldg/dir lts into Gareloch 356°, 318°, 295°, 329° and 331°. Conspic ✠ tr at Rhu Point.

COMMUNICATIONS (Code 01436) CGOC (02891) 463933; Police 101; Ⓗ (01389) 754121; Dr 672277. QHM 674321.
MoD Police/QHM Ch 16/73. Rhu Marina Ch 80 M (H24 in season).

FACILITIES Rhu Marina, sbell@quaymarinas.com ☎820238; ⚓ (235) ⬭ £2.40 (short stay £12) pontoons A-J, ⚓ ◣ 🔧 🚻 🗑(35t) ⚒ ⚓ 🏧 🔥 🛢 ⏚ ✕ wi-fi.
Royal Northern and Clyde YC ☎820322; club ⚓s, 🔧 ✕ ⌂; **Helensburgh SC** ☎672778 ◣ (dinghies), 🔧 ⚓. **Town** all services, ⇌ ✈ (Glasgow). **DRB Marine** (Rosneath) ☎831231, use jetty only to load, some ⚓s, 🗑(40t). **Silvers Yard** private moorings.

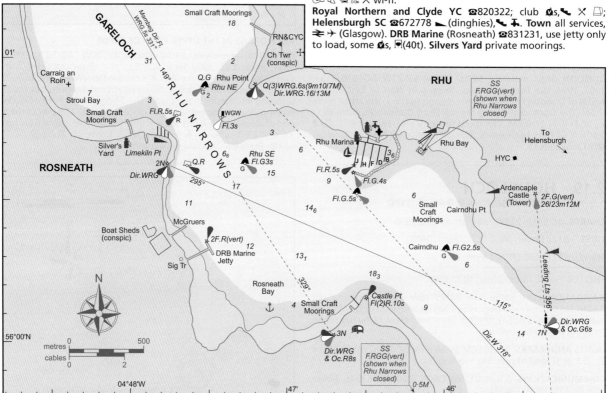

Naval activity: Beware submarines from Faslane Base. See 2.17 for submarine activity (Subfacts) in the Clyde and offshore or call FOSNNI Ops ☎(01436) 674321 Ext 3206 and monitor Ch 73.

Protected Areas: Vessels are never allowed within 150m of naval shore installations at Faslane and Coulport.

Restricted Areas (Faslane, Rhu Chan and Coulport): These are closed to all vessels during submarine movements (see opposite and *W Coast of Scotland Pilot*, App 2). MoD Police patrols enforce areas which are shown on charts. The S limit of Faslane Restricted area is marked by two Or posts with X topmarks on Shandon

foreshore. The W limit is marked by Iso WRG 4s, vis W356°-006°, at Gareloch Oil fuel depot N jetty. The following signals are shown when restrictions are in force:

Entrance to Gareloch

Day & Night: ● ● ● (vert), supplemented by R flag with W diagonal bar.

Faslane and Coulport

Day & Night: ● ● ● (vert), supplemented by International Code pendant over pendant Nine.

LOCH LONG and LOCH GOIL, Argyll and Bute, approx 56°00′N 04°52′·5W to 56°12′·00N 04°45′·00W. AC *5610*, 3746. Tides: See 2.20 for differences. ML 1·7m; Duration 0645.

SHELTER Loch Long is about 15M long. Temp ⚓s (south to north) at: Cove, Blairmore (not in S'lies), Ardentinny, Portincaple, Coilessan (about 1M S of Ardgartan Pt), and near head of loch (Arrochar) on either shore. In Loch Goil ⚓ at Swines Hole and off Carrick Castle (S of the pier, in N'lies a swell builds). Avoid ⚓ near Douglas Pier. The head of the loch is crowded with private/dinghy moorings, and is either too steep-to or too shallow to ⚓. The loch is frequently closed to navigation due to the trial range half way down.

LIGHTS Coulport Jetty, 2FG (vert) each end; Covered Berth L Fl G (SW corner) with 3F G(vert) and F G to NE; Port Dornaige Fl 6s 8m 11M, vis 026°-206°; Dog Rock (Carraig nan Ron) Fl 2s 11M; Finnart Oil Terminal has FG lts and ldg lts 031° QW/FW on Cnap Pt. Upper Loch Long is unlit. Loch Goil ent is marked by 2 PHM buoys (Fl R 3s and QR), a SHM buoy (QG) and ldg lts 318°: front (The Perch) Dir FWRG and Fl R 3s; rear FW. Rubha Ardnahein Fl R5s.

FACILITIES Loch Long (Cove), Cove SC, ⚓ 🛒 ⬚; ⚓(pier); (Portincaple) ✉ 🛒 hotel, ⚓; (Ardentinny) shop, 🛒 ✕ hotel, ⛟; (Blairmore) ━ ⚓ ✉ 🛒; (Arrochar) shops, hotel, ⚓ ⛽ ✉. Loch Goil (Carrick Castle) has 2 blue ☸s (£10/night, max 15t, free wi-fi), 🚾. Lochgoilhead: ⚓ ⛽ ✉ 🛒.

2.21 RIVER CLYDE

Dunbartonshire **55°57′·50N 04°45′·70W** (Tail of the Bank)
❀❀❀❀♻♻♻

CHARTS AC 5610, 2131, 1994, 2007: *BW Skipper's Guide for Forth and Clyde Canal, BW Skipper's Handbook for Lowland Canals;* Imray C63, 2900

TIDES +0122 Dover; ML 2·0; Duration 0640

Standard Port GREENOCK (→)

Times				Height (metres)			
High Water		Low Water		MHWS	MHWN	MLWN	MLWS
0000	0600	0000	0600	3·4	2·8	1·0	0·3
1200	1800	1200	1800				
Differences PORT GLASGOW (55°56′·10N 04°40′·50W)							
+0010	+0005	+0010	+0020	+0·2	+0·1	0·0	0·0
DUMBARTON							
+0015	+0010	+0020	+0040	+0·4	+0·3	+0·1	0·0
BOWLING							
+0020	+0010	+0030	+0055	+0·6	+0·5	+0·3	+0·1
RENFREW							
+0025	+0015	+0035	+0100	+0·9	+0·8	+0·5	+0·2
GLASGOW							
+0025	+0015	+0035	+0105	+1·4	+1·1	+0·8	+0·4

SHELTER Good at Greenock (James Watt Dock Marina), Dumbarton (Sandpoint Marina) and Bowling Harbour.

NAVIGATION WPT 55°57′·50N 04°45′·70W, 1·2M to James Watt Dock (JWD) entrance, which experiences strong tidal streams flowing in the dredged channel across the entrance. Sandpoint Marina and Bowling Harbour are, respectively, about 6M and 9M further up-river. The density of shipping and numerous ferries in the Clyde warrant particular attention. Large vessels manoeuvre at the Greenock Container / Ocean Terminal and masters are to maintain communication with Harbour Control.

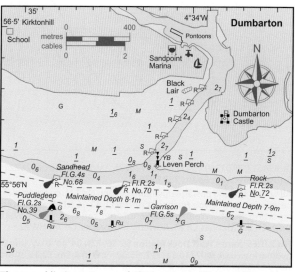

The speed limit upstream of Cloch point is 12kn and 5kn where boards mark Dead Slow. Vessels under sail are not relieved of their obligations under Rules for Narrow Channels and are reminded that E of Bowling vessels may proceed under power alone. All vessels planning an up-river passage are to contact their berth or destination before proceeding. Keep just inboard of chan lateral marks as depths shoal rapidly outboard. For Dumbarton cross the river at 90° at No 39 SHM buoy. Depths in R Leven may be less than charted. For Bowling Hbr cross at No 45 SHM buoy.

LIGHTS AND MARKS The River Clyde is well buoyed/lit.

COMMUNICATIONS (Codes: Greenock 01475; Glasgow 0141, followed by 7 digit Tel No). CGOC (02891) 463933; Police 101;

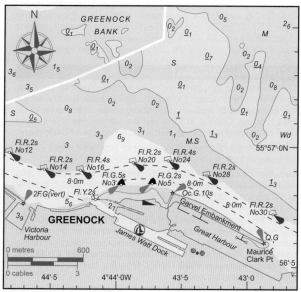

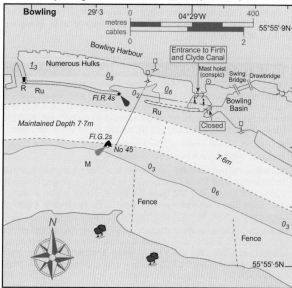

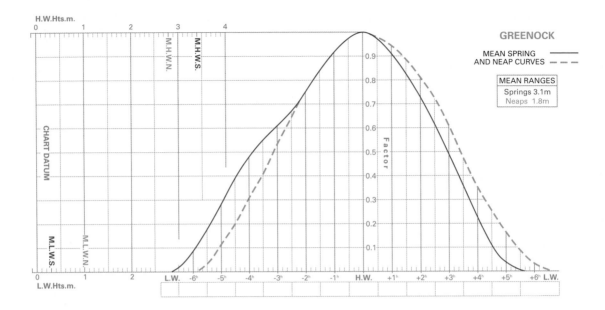

GREENOCK

MEAN SPRING ——————
AND NEAP CURVES – – – –

MEAN RANGES
Springs 3.1m
Neaps 1.8m

Dr 634617; ⊞ 01389 754121. HM 725775; Estuary Control 726221; British Waterways Board 332 6936.

All vessels seeking passage upstream beyond No 1 buoy are to seek permission from *Clyde Harbour Control* Ch **12** 16 (H24) at charted reporting points. Weather/traffic info on request. James Watt Dock Ch 80; Marinas Ch M. Bowling lockkeeper Ch 74, HW±2.

FACILITIES James Watt Dock Marina 55°56'·72N 04°44'·01W. info@jwdmarina.co.uk ☎07710 611117; 65⌒ inc 🅥 in 4.5m, £2.15, short stay £11.50/craft. 🏴 🚾 🔥 🛠 ✕ 🏬 at marina entrance. **Greenock** ✕ ✎ 🏴 ⛽ 🏴 🔩 🏬 ✕ 🏬.

Sandpoint Marina 55°56'·48N 04°34'·07W www.sandpoint-marina. co.uk ☎01389 762396/731500. Limited visitors' berths, £10 per night. VHF Ch **M.** 🔌 📆 🏴 🏴(40t) ⛽ ☎01389 742438. **Town** ✉ Ⓑ 🛒 ✕ 🏬 ⇌ 30 mins to Glasgow.

Bowling Basin 55°55'·8N 04°29'·0W, W end of Forth & Clyde Canal. ☎01389 877969. Basin Lock access dries 0·7m. Call VHF Ch 74 for t lock schedule. *Skipper's Brief* www.scottishcanals.co.uk. **Facilities** ⌒ £3.75, 🔥 🏴/🚾 🏴 by prior notice, 🏴(mast). **Town** 📆 📆 ✉ Ⓑ 🛒 ✕ 🏬 ⇌.

There are no yachting facilities on R Clyde E of Bowling Basin.

GLASGOW 55°55'·94N 04°34'·25W

Clyde Yacht Clubs Association is at 8 St James St, Paisley. ☎8878296. Clyde CC Suite 408, Pentagon Centre, 36 Washington St, Glasgow, G3 8AZ, ☎221 2774.

5kn off and S of Black Hd. Races occur off Copeland Is. Morroch B, Money Hd Mull of Logan and Mull of Galloway.

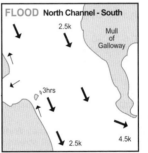

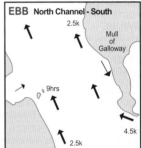

*Irish coast – N-going ebb begins at HW Belfast (HW Dover –0015). Scottish coast – HW Greenock –0250 (HW Dover –0130). Races off Copeland Is and Mull of Galloway. Flood begins 2 hrs early close inshore N of Mull of Galloway. A race SSE of Crammag Hd is bad if wind against tide. Mull of Galloway (lt) is a high (82m), steep-to headland with **a dangerous race extending nearly 3M to S.** On E-going stream it extends NNE into Luce B; on W-going stream it extends SW and W. Give the race a wide berth, or pass close inshore at slack water nps and calm weather. SW wind >F4 against W-going stream, do not attempt inshore route.◄*

FIRTH OF CLYDE TO MULL OF GALLOWAY

(AC 2131, 2126, 2199, 2198) Further S the coast is less inviting, with mostly commercial hbrs until Ardrossan and Troon, NW of which there are various dangers: Troon Rk (depth 5·6m, but sea can break), Lappock Rk (dries 0·6m, marked by bn), and Mill Rk (dries 0·4m, buoyed). Lady Isle (lt, racon) is 2M WSW of Troon.

▶ *There is a severe race off Bennane Hd (8M SSE of Ailsa Craig, conspic) when tide is running strongly.◄*

Loch Ryan offers little for yachtsmen but there is a small marina at Stranraer and ⚓ S of Kirkcolm Pt, inside the drying spit which runs in SE direction 1·5M from the point. There is also a useful ⚓ in Lady Bay, sheltered except from NE. Portpatrick is a useful passage harbour, but not in onshore winds.

▶ **North Channel South:** *Irish coast – the S-going flood begins HW Belfast –0600 (HW Dover +0610). Counter tide off Donaghadee and Island Magee for last 3 hrs of flood. Scottish coast between Corsewall Pt and Mull of Galloway – HW Greenock +0310 (HW Dover +0430). Sp rate off Corsewall Pt is 2–3kn, increasing to*

SCOTLAND – SW COAST

The Scares, two groups of rocks, lie at the mouth of Luce Bay which elsewhere is clear more than 3ca offshore; but the whole bay is occupied by a practice bombing range, marked by 12 DZ SPM lt buoys. Good ⚓ at E Tarbert B awaiting the tide around Mull of Galloway, or good shelter in drying hbr of Drummore.

▶ *Off Burrow Hd there is a bad race in strong W winds with a W-going tide.◄*

Luce Bay Firing Range (D402/403) lies at the NW end. For info on activity ☎(01776) 888792. In Wigtown B the best ⚓ is in Isle of Whithorn B, but exposed to S. It is also possible to dry out in Garlieston.

A tank firing range, between the E side of ent to Kirkcudbright Bay and Abbey Hd, 4M to E, extends 14M offshore. If unable to avoid the area, cross it at N end close inshore. For information contact the Range safety boat 'Gallovidian' on VHF Ch 16, 73. The range operates 0900-1600LT Mon-Fri, but weekend and night firing may also occur.

GREENOCK LAT 55°57'N LONG 4°46'W
TIMES AND HEIGHTS OF HIGH AND LOW WATERS

STANDARD TIME (UT) — For Summer Time add ONE hour in **non-shaded areas**

Dates in red are **SPRINGS** — Dates in blue are **NEAPS**

YEAR 2016

JANUARY

Day	Time m	Time m	Time m	Time m		Day	Time m	Time m	Time m	Time m
1 F	0451 3.1	1016 0.9	1645 3.4	2238 0.8		16 SA	0429 3.4	1008 0.6	1648 3.6	☽ 2248 0.4
2 SA	0538 3.0	1110 1.1	1730 3.3	☾ 2336 1.0		17 SU	0516 3.3	1106 0.7	1742 3.4	2352 0.6
3 SU	0630 2.9	1213 1.2	1822 3.1			18 M	0611 3.2	1213 0.9	1850 3.2	
4 M	0042 1.0	0732 2.9	1324 1.2	1922 3.0		19 TU	0104 0.7	0724 3.0	1331 0.9	2019 3.1
5 TU	0150 1.0	0842 3.0	1432 1.1	2031 3.0		20 W	0216 0.7	0857 3.1	1446 0.8	2144 3.1
6 W	0249 1.0	0948 3.1	1526 1.0	2139 3.1		21 TH	0319 0.6	1009 3.2	1548 0.6	2249 3.3
7 TH	0339 0.9	1041 3.3	1612 0.8	2236 3.2		22 F	0414 0.5	1105 3.4	1640 0.5	2343 3.4
8 F	0421 0.8	1125 3.4	1652 0.6	2324 3.3		23 SA	0502 0.4	1152 3.5	1725 0.3	
9 SA	0500 0.7	1204 3.5	1729 0.5			24 SU	0032 3.4	0546 0.4	1235 3.6	○ 1804 0.3
10 SU	0008 3.4	0536 0.6	1240 3.6	● 1805 0.4		25 M	0116 3.4	0626 0.4	1314 3.7	1841 0.3
11 M	0052 3.4	0614 0.5	1316 3.7	1843 0.3		26 TU	0155 3.3	0704 0.4	1351 3.7	1916 0.3
12 TU	0135 3.5	0656 0.4	1354 3.8	1925 0.3		27 W	0231 3.3	0740 0.4	1426 3.7	1951 0.4
13 W	0218 3.5	0740 0.4	1434 3.8	2010 0.2		28 TH	0304 3.3	0816 0.5	1501 3.7	2028 0.4
14 TH	0301 3.5	0827 0.4	1517 3.8	2058 0.2		29 F	0340 3.3	0854 0.6	1537 3.6	2108 0.5
15 F	0344 3.5	0916 0.5	1601 3.7	2150 0.3		30 SA	0417 3.2	0935 0.7	1614 3.5	2151 0.7
						31 SU	0457 3.1	1019 0.8	1654 3.3	2237 0.8

FEBRUARY

Day	Time m	Time m	Time m	Time m		Day	Time m	Time m	Time m	Time m
1 M	0540 3.0	1111 1.0	1739 3.1	☾ 2332 1.0		16 TU	0539 3.2	1147 0.7	1819 3.1	
2 TU	0631 2.9	1214 1.1	1833 3.0			17 W	0041 0.7	0638 3.0	1311 0.8	1955 2.9
3 W	0040 1.1	0736 2.8	1331 1.2	1937 2.9		18 TH	0159 0.8	0825 2.9	1433 0.8	2140 2.9
4 TH	0156 1.1	0858 2.9	1446 1.0	2053 2.9		19 F	0306 0.7	0954 3.0	1537 0.6	2244 3.1
5 F	0303 1.1	1008 3.0	1543 0.8	2207 3.0		20 SA	0402 0.5	1051 3.2	1628 0.4	2335 3.2
6 SA	0354 0.8	1059 3.2	1628 0.6	2305 3.1		21 SU	0450 0.4	1138 3.4	1711 0.3	
7 SU	0437 0.6	1141 3.4	1707 0.4	2353 3.3		22 M	0020 3.3	0531 0.3	1221 3.5	○ 1749 0.3
8 M	0517 0.5	1220 3.5	● 1746 0.4			23 TU	0100 3.3	0609 0.3	1258 3.6	1822 0.3
9 TU	0037 3.3	0557 0.3	1300 3.6	1825 0.1		24 W	0136 3.3	0643 0.3	1332 3.6	1852 0.3
10 W	0121 3.4	0638 0.2	1340 3.7	1906 0.0		25 TH	0207 3.3	0714 0.3	1404 3.6	1923 0.3
11 TH	0204 3.5	0722 0.2	1422 3.8	1951 0.0		26 F	0237 3.3	0746 0.4	1436 3.6	1957 0.4
12 F	0245 3.5	0808 0.2	1504 3.8	2038 0.0		27 SA	0309 3.3	0820 0.4	1510 3.5	2032 0.4
13 SA	0327 3.5	0855 0.2	1547 3.7	2128 0.1		28 SU	0343 3.3	0918 0.5	1545 3.5	2109 0.5
14 SU	0408 3.5	0946 0.4	1632 3.6	2223 0.3		29 M	0418 3.2	0938 0.6	1623 3.3	2151 0.7
15 M	0451 3.3	1041 0.5	1721 3.4	☾ 2326 0.5						

MARCH

Day	Time m	Time m	Time m	Time m		Day	Time m	Time m	Time m	Time m
1 TU	0456 3.1	1024 0.8	1705 3.1	☾ 2239 0.9		16 W	0513 3.2	1127 0.6	1800 2.9	
2 W	0539 2.9	1121 0.9	1755 2.9	2338 1.0		17 TH	0021 0.8	0607 2.9	1256 0.7	1941 2.7
3 TH	0637 2.7	1231 1.0	1856 2.8			18 F	0140 0.8	0747 2.8	1415 0.7	2130 2.8
4 F	0053 1.1	0756 2.7	1357 1.0	2012 2.8		19 SA	0247 0.8	0932 2.9	1518 0.5	2229 3.0
5 SA	0218 1.0	0927 2.8	1508 0.7	2140 2.9		20 SU	0343 0.6	1030 3.1	1608 0.4	2316 3.1
6 SU	0323 0.8	1028 3.1	1559 0.4	2245 3.1		21 M	0430 0.4	1117 3.3	1650 0.3	2358 3.2
7 M	0412 0.6	1115 3.3	1642 0.2	2334 3.2		22 TU	0512 0.3	1158 3.4	1727 0.2	
8 TU	0455 0.3	1157 3.5	1722 0.0			23 W	0036 3.3	0548 0.3	1236 3.4	○ 1758 0.3
9 W	0019 3.3	0536 0.2	1241 3.6	● 1802 -0.2		24 TH	0109 3.3	0620 0.3	1308 3.4	1826 0.3
10 TH	0103 3.4	0618 0.0	1324 3.7	1845 -0.2		25 F	0139 3.3	0648 0.3	1339 3.4	1855 0.3
11 F	0145 3.5	0702 0.0	1407 3.8	1929 -0.2		26 SA	0208 3.3	0717 0.3	1410 3.4	1926 0.4
12 SA	0226 3.5	0747 0.0	1450 3.8	2016 -0.1		27 SU	0239 3.4	0749 0.3	1443 3.4	1959 0.4
13 SU	0306 3.6	0834 0.0	1533 3.7	2106 0.1		28 M	0310 3.3	0824 0.4	1518 3.4	2037 0.4
14 M	0346 3.5	0924 0.2	1617 3.5	2200 0.4		29 TU	0342 3.3	0905 0.5	1555 3.3	2119 0.6
15 TU	0427 3.4	1019 0.4	1704 3.3	☾ 2303 0.6		30 W	0417 3.1	0951 0.6	1637 3.1	2207 0.7
						31 TH	0456 3.0	1047 0.8	1725 3.0	☾ 2304 0.9

APRIL

Day	Time m	Time m	Time m	Time m		Day	Time m	Time m	Time m	Time m
1 F	0547 2.8	1153 0.8	1824 2.8			16 SA	0111 0.9	0708 2.8	1348 0.6	2102 2.7
2 SA	0012 1.1	0701 2.7	1312 0.8	1938 2.7		17 SU	0218 0.8	0856 2.9	1448 0.5	2201 2.9
3 SU	0133 1.0	0838 2.8	1427 0.6	2108 2.8		18 M	0315 0.7	0958 3.1	1539 0.4	2247 3.1
4 M	0247 0.8	0952 3.0	1525 0.3	2218 3.0		19 TU	0404 0.5	1047 3.2	1622 0.3	2328 3.2
5 TU	0343 0.5	1044 3.2	1612 0.3	2310 3.2		20 W	0446 0.4	1128 3.3	1658 0.3	
6 W	0431 0.3	1131 3.4	1656 -0.2	2356 3.3		21 TH	0005 3.2	0522 0.3	1206 3.3	1730 0.3
7 TH	0515 0.1	1217 3.6	● 1739 -0.3			22 F	0039 3.3	0554 0.3	1239 3.3	○ 1759 0.4
8 F	0040 3.4	0558 -0.1	1304 3.6	1823 -0.1		23 SA	0110 3.3	0622 0.3	1310 3.3	1827 0.4
9 SA	0123 3.5	0642 -0.1	1350 3.7	1908 -0.2		24 SU	0140 3.4	0651 0.3	1342 3.3	1858 0.4
10 SU	0205 3.6	0727 -0.1	1435 3.7	1956 -0.1		25 M	0209 3.4	0722 0.3	1416 3.4	1933 0.4
11 M	0245 3.6	0814 -0.1	1520 3.6	2046 0.1		26 TU	0240 3.4	0759 0.3	1453 3.3	2012 0.5
12 TU	0325 3.6	0904 0.1	1604 3.4	2140 0.3		27 W	0312 3.4	0840 0.4	1532 3.3	2057 0.5
13 W	0406 3.4	1000 0.3	1653 3.2	2242 0.6		28 TH	0346 3.3	0928 0.5	1614 3.2	2146 0.7
14 TH	0451 3.2	1109 0.5	1750 2.9	☾ 2356 0.8		29 F	0425 3.1	1023 0.6	1702 3.0	2243 0.8
15 F	0545 3.0	1233 0.6	1922 2.7			30 SA	0512 3.0	1127 0.6	1758 2.9	☾ 2347 0.9

Chart Datum: 1·62 metres below Ordnance Datum (Newlyn). HAT is 3·9 metres above Chart Datum.

SW Scotland

»» FREE monthly updates. Register at «
www.reedsnauticalalmanac.co.uk

89

GREENOCK LAT 55°57'N LONG 4°46'W

TIMES AND HEIGHTS OF HIGH AND LOW WATERS

STANDARD TIME (UT)
For Summer Time add ONE hour in **non-shaded areas**

Dates in red are **SPRINGS**
Dates in blue are **NEAPS**

YEAR **2016**

MAY

Time	m		Time	m
1 0620	2.8	**16**	0139	0.9
1239	0.6		0758	2.9
SU 1908	2.8	M 1410	0.6
			2116	2.8
2 0058	0.9	**17**	0239	0.8
0752	2.8		0913	3.0
M 1350	0.4	TU 1502	0.5
2031	2.9		2207	3.0
3 0211	0.8	**18**	0331	0.6
0913	3.0		1007	3.1
TU 1451	0.2	W 1546	0.4
2145	3.1		2251	3.1
4 0314	0.5	**19**	0416	0.5
1013	3.2		1052	3.2
W 1543	0.0	TH 1625	0.4
2241	3.2		2330	3.2
5 0406	0.3	**20**	0454	0.4
1105	3.4		1131	3.2
TH 1631	-0.2	F 1700	0.4
2330	3.4		
6 0453	0.1	**21**	0007	3.3
1154	3.5		0528	0.4
F 1717	-0.2	SA 1207	3.2
		○ 1732	0.5
7 0016	3.5	**22**	0041	3.4
0538	-0.1		0559	0.4
SA 1244	3.6	SU 1240	3.2
1802	-0.2		1803	0.5
8 0101	3.6	**23**	0113	3.4
0623	-0.1		0629	0.4
SU 1333	3.6	M 1314	3.3
1849	-0.1		1836	0.5
9 0144	3.6	**24**	0143	3.5
0709	-0.1		0702	0.3
M 1420	3.6	TU 1351	3.3
1938	0.0		1913	0.5
10 0225	3.6	**25**	0214	3.5
0756	-0.1		0739	0.3
TU 1507	3.5	W 1430	3.3
2028	0.2		1954	0.5
11 0306	3.6	**26**	0248	3.5
0846	0.1		0822	0.3
W 1553	3.3	TH 1512	3.3
2121	0.4		2040	0.5
12 0348	3.5	**27**	0325	3.4
0941	0.3		0910	0.4
TH 1642	3.1	F 1555	3.2
2219	0.6		2130	0.6
13 0433	3.3	**28**	0404	3.3
1044	0.4		1004	0.4
F 1738	2.9	SA 1643	3.1
◐ 2323	0.8		2225	0.7
14 0524	3.1	**29**	0451	3.2
1157	0.6		1105	0.5
SA 1847	2.7	SU 1736	3.0
		◑ 2324	0.8
15 0032	0.9	**30**	0551	3.0
0630	2.9		1211	0.4
SU 1309	0.6	M 1839	3.0
2009	2.7		

JUNE

Time	m		Time	m
1 0139	0.7	**16**	0252	0.8
0836	3.1		0912	2.9
W 1420	0.2	TH 1507	0.6
2109	3.1		2206	3.0
2 0245	0.6	**17**	0342	0.7
0944	3.2		1008	2.9
TH 1517	0.1	F 1552	0.6
2212	3.2		2254	3.2
3 0343	0.4	**18**	0425	0.5
1041	3.4		1053	3.1
F 1609	0.0	SA 1631	0.5
2306	3.3		2336	3.3
4 0435	0.2	**19**	0504	0.5
1135	3.4		1133	3.1
SA 1658	-0.1	SU 1708	0.5
2355	3.5		
5 0523	0.0	**20**	0014	3.4
1226	3.5		0539	0.4
SU 1746	0.0	M 1211	3.2
●		○ 1742	0.5
6 0041	3.5	**21**	0048	3.4
0608	0.0		0612	0.4
M 1318	3.5	TU 1249	3.2
1833	0.0		1817	0.5
7 0125	3.6	**22**	0120	3.5
0654	-0.1		0646	0.3
TU 1407	3.4	W 1329	3.2
1921	0.1		1855	0.5
8 0208	3.6	**23**	0153	3.5
0740	0.0		0724	0.3
W 1454	3.3	TH 1411	3.3
2010	0.3		1938	0.5
9 0249	3.6	**24**	0229	3.5
0826	0.1		0806	0.3
TH 1540	3.2	F 1454	3.3
2059	0.4		2024	0.4
10 0330	3.5	**25**	0308	3.5
0916	0.2		0853	0.3
F 1627	3.1	SA 1538	3.3
2150	0.5		2113	0.5
11 0413	3.4	**26**	0349	3.5
1010	0.4		0945	0.3
SA 1715	3.0	SU 1624	3.2
2244	0.7		2205	0.5
12 0459	3.2	**27**	0434	3.4
1110	0.5		1042	0.3
SU 1806	2.9	M 1714	3.2
◑ 2343	0.8	◑ 2301	0.6
13 0551	3.0	**28**	0528	3.2
1216	0.6		1144	0.3
M 1904	2.8	TU 1810	3.1
14 0047	0.9	**29**	0002	0.7
0653	2.9		0637	3.1
TU 1320	0.7	W 1249	0.4
2007	2.8		1915	3.0
15 0153	0.9	**30**	0109	0.7
0804	2.9		0801	3.1
W 1418	0.7	TH 1354	0.3
2111	2.9		2033	3.0

JULY

Time	m		Time	m
1 0220	0.7	**16**	0306	0.8
0919	3.1		0915	2.9
F 1456	0.3	SA 1519	0.7
2146	3.1		2217	3.1
2 0325	0.5	**17**	0357	0.7
1025	3.2		1016	3.0
SA 1553	0.2	SU 1605	0.7
2246	3.3		2307	3.2
3 0421	0.3	**18**	0441	0.5
1122	3.3		1105	3.1
SU 1645	0.1	M 1645	0.6
2339	3.4		2348	3.3
4 0511	0.1	**19**	0519	0.4
1216	3.4		1147	3.1
M 1733	0.1	TU 1722	0.5
●		○	
5 0026	3.5	**20**	0025	3.4
0557	0.1		0554	0.3
TU 1307	3.3	W 1229	3.2
1820	0.2		1758	0.5
6 0111	3.6	**21**	0059	3.5
0640	0.0		0629	0.2
W 1355	3.3	TH 1310	3.2
1905	0.2		1837	0.4
7 0152	3.6	**22**	0135	3.6
0722	0.1		0706	0.2
TH 1440	3.2	F 1353	3.3
1949	0.3		1920	0.4
8 0231	3.6	**23**	0213	3.6
0804	0.1		0748	0.1
F 1522	3.2	SA 1436	3.3
2033	0.4		2005	0.3
9 0310	3.6	**24**	0253	3.6
0846	0.2		0833	0.1
SA 1601	3.1	SU 1520	3.3
2117	0.5		2052	0.3
10 0349	3.5	**25**	0334	3.6
0932	0.4		0922	0.1
SU 1642	3.0	M 1604	3.3
2203	0.6		2142	0.4
11 0429	3.3	**26**	0418	3.5
1022	0.5		1017	0.2
M 1725	3.0	TU 1650	3.3
2253	0.7	◑ 2236	0.5
12 0512	3.2	**27**	0507	3.3
1118	0.7		1117	0.4
TU 1811	2.9	W 1739	3.2
◑ 2348	0.9		2335	0.6
13 0601	3.0	**28**	0606	3.1
1220	0.8		1224	0.5
W 1904	2.8	TH 1838	3.1
14 0053	1.0	**29**	0044	0.7
0657	2.9		0728	3.0
TH 1325	0.8	F 1335	0.5
2006	2.8		1957	3.0
15 0204	1.0	**30**	0202	0.8
0804	2.8		0904	3.0
F 1426	0.8	SA 1443	0.5
2115	2.9		2126	3.0
		31	0314	0.6
			1019	3.1
		SU 1543	0.4
			2234	3.2

AUGUST

Time	m		Time	m
1 0413	0.4	**16**	0416	0.6
1117	3.2		1043	3.0
M 1635	0.3	TU 1622	0.6
2327	3.4		2322	3.3
2 0503	0.2	**17**	0456	0.4
1209	3.3		1129	3.1
TU 1723	0.3	W 1700	0.5
●			
3 0014	3.5	**18**	0001	3.4
0546	0.1		0532	0.2
W 1257	3.3	TH 1211	3.2
1806	0.3	○ 1737	0.4
4 0057	3.6	**19**	0038	3.5
0625	0.1		0608	0.1
TH 1341	3.2	F 1253	3.3
1847	0.3		1816	0.3
5 0135	3.6	**20**	0117	3.6
0702	0.1		0645	0.0
F 1420	3.2	SA 1335	3.3
1925	0.3		1858	0.3
6 0211	3.6	**21**	0157	3.7
0737	0.2		0726	0.0
SA 1454	3.2	SU 1417	3.4
2003	0.4		1943	0.2
7 0246	3.6	**22**	0238	3.7
0814	0.3		0811	0.0
SU 1528	3.1	M 1459	3.4
2041	0.4		2030	0.2
8 0321	3.5	**23**	0319	3.7
0853	0.4		0859	0.1
M 1604	3.1	TU 1541	3.4
2122	0.5		2119	0.3
9 0358	3.4	**24**	0402	3.6
0936	0.5		0951	0.3
TU 1643	3.1	W 1624	3.4
2206	0.7		2212	0.4
10 0436	3.3	**25**	0448	3.4
1023	0.7		1052	0.5
W 1725	3.0	TH 1711	3.3
◐ 2255	0.8	◑ 2312	0.6
11 0519	3.1	**26**	0542	3.1
1118	0.9		1204	0.6
TH 1813	2.9	F 1806	3.1
2355	1.0		
12 0611	2.9	**27**	0026	0.8
1225	1.0		0702	2.9
F 1910	2.8	SA 1323	0.7
			1923	3.0
13 0108	1.1	**28**	0153	0.8
0713	2.8		0904	2.9
SA 1340	1.0	SU 1434	0.7
2021	2.8		2113	3.0
14 0228	1.0	**29**	0306	0.7
0826	2.8		1017	3.0
SU 1446	0.9	M 1533	0.6
2138	3.0		2222	3.2
15 0329	0.8	**30**	0404	0.5
0944	2.9		1111	3.2
M 1539	0.8	TU 1624	0.4
2237	3.1		2314	3.4
		31	0451	0.3
			1158	3.3
		W 1709	0.3
			2358	3.5

Chart Datum: 1·62 metres below Ordnance Datum (Newlyn). HAT is 3·9 metres above Chart Datum.

STANDARD TIME (UT)
For Summer Time add ONE hour in **non-shaded areas**

GREENOCK LAT 55°57'N LONG 4°46'W
TIMES AND HEIGHTS OF HIGH AND LOW WATERS

Dates in red are **SPRINGS**
Dates in blue are **NEAPS**

YEAR 2016

SEPTEMBER

Time	m		Time	m
1 0531	0.2	**16** 0506	0.1	
1240	3.3		1152	3.3
TH 1750	0.3	F 1714	0.3	
●		○		
2 0038	3.6	**17** 0014	3.6	
0607	0.2		0543	0.0
F 1319	3.3	SA 1233	3.4	
1826	0.3		1754	0.2
3 0115	3.6	**18** 0056	3.7	
0638	0.2		0622	-0.1
SA 1352	3.2	SU 1314	3.5	
1859	0.4		1836	0.2
4 0148	3.6	**19** 0139	3.8	
0709	0.3		0704	-0.1
SU 1422	3.2	M 1356	3.5	
1931	0.4		1921	0.1
5 0220	3.6	**20** 0222	3.8	
0741	0.4		0748	0.0
M 1453	3.3	TU 1437	3.6	
2006	0.5		2007	0.2
6 0253	3.6	**21** 0305	3.8	
0816	0.4		0836	0.1
TU 1527	3.3	W 1519	3.6	
2043	0.5		2057	0.3
7 0327	3.5	**22** 0348	3.6	
0853	0.5		0929	0.4
W 1603	3.2	TH 1601	3.5	
2123	0.6		2150	0.5
8 0404	3.4	**23** 0434	3.4	
0934	0.7		1031	0.6
TH 1642	3.1	F 1647	3.4	
2209	0.8		◑ 2254	0.7
9 0445	3.2	**24** 0527	3.1	
1021	0.9		1148	0.8
F 1727	3.0	SA 1741	3.2	
◑ 2303	1.0			
10 0535	3.0	**25** 0017	0.8	
1122	1.1		0653	2.8
SA 1821	2.9	SU 1310	0.9	
			1857	3.0
11 0014	1.1	**26** 0143	0.8	
0635	2.8		0901	2.9
SU 1243	1.2	M 1419	0.9	
1929	2.8		2055	3.0
12 0144	1.1	**27** 0251	0.7	
0749	2.8		1006	3.1
M 1407	1.1	TU 1517	0.7	
2054	2.9		2202	3.2
13 0256	0.9	**28** 0346	0.5	
0916	2.9		1055	3.3
TU 1509	0.9	W 1607	0.5	
2203	3.1		2253	3.4
14 0347	0.6	**29** 0431	0.4	
1022	3.1		1138	3.4
W 1555	0.7	TH 1650	0.4	
2251	3.3		2336	3.5
15 0428	0.3	**30** 0510	0.3	
1110	3.2		1216	3.4
TH 1635	0.5	F 1729	0.4	
2333	3.5			

OCTOBER

Time	m		Time	m
1 0015	3.6	**16** 0518	0.0	
0543	0.3		1210	3.6
SA 1251	3.4	SU 1733	0.2	
● 1803	0.4	○		
2 0050	3.6	**17** 0035	3.8	
0613	0.4		0559	-0.1
SU 1321	3.4	M 1253	3.6	
1833	0.4		1816	0.1
3 0121	3.6	**18** 0121	3.8	
0641	0.4		0643	0.0
M 1349	3.4	TU 1335	3.7	
1902	0.5		1901	0.1
4 0153	3.6	**19** 0206	3.8	
0711	0.4		0729	0.1
TU 1420	3.4	W 1417	3.7	
1934	0.6		1948	0.2
5 0225	3.6	**20** 0251	3.8	
0744	0.5		0817	0.3
W 1453	3.5	TH 1459	3.7	
2009	0.6		2038	0.3
6 0300	3.5	**21** 0336	3.6	
0819	0.6		0911	0.5
TH 1527	3.4	F 1542	3.6	
2048	0.7		2132	0.5
7 0337	3.4	**22** 0424	3.4	
0859	0.8		1012	0.8
F 1604	3.3	SA 1628	3.5	
2133	0.8		◑ 2238	0.7
8 0418	3.3	**23** 0521	3.1	
0944	1.0		1127	1.0
SA 1645	3.2	SU 1721	3.3	
2225	1.0			
9 0505	3.1	**24** 0002	0.8	
1040	1.2		0648	2.9
SU 1736	3.0	M 1246	1.1	
◑ 2331	1.1		1834	3.1
10 0603	2.9	**25** 0121	0.8	
1151	1.3		0837	2.9
M 1843	2.9	TU 1354	1.0	
			2019	3.1
11 0054	1.1	**26** 0226	0.7	
0716	2.8		0940	3.1
TU 1318	1.3	W 1452	0.8	
2005	2.9		2131	3.2
12 0214	0.9	**27** 0320	0.6	
0844	2.9		1028	3.3
W 1431	1.1	TH 1543	0.7	
2122	3.1		2223	3.4
13 0311	0.6	**28** 0405	0.5	
0955	3.1		1110	3.4
TH 1524	0.8	F 1627	0.5	
2217	3.4		2307	3.5
14 0356	0.3	**29** 0444	0.4	
1045	3.3		1147	3.5
F 1609	0.5	SA 1705	0.5	
2304	3.5		2346	3.5
15 0437	0.1	**30** 0518	0.5	
1128	3.4		1220	3.5
SA 1651	0.3	SU 1739	0.5	
2349	3.7	●		
		31 0021	3.5	
			0547	0.5
		M 1251	3.5	
			1809	0.5

NOVEMBER

Time	m		Time	m
1 0054	3.5	**16** 0104	3.8	
0616	0.6		0625	0.1
TU 1321	3.6	W 1317	3.8	
1837	0.6		1844	0.1
2 0126	3.5	**17** 0153	3.8	
0645	0.6		0712	0.2
W 1352	3.6	TH 1400	3.9	
1908	0.6		1932	0.2
3 0200	3.5	**18** 0240	3.7	
0718	0.6		0801	0.4
TH 1424	3.6	F 1443	3.8	
1943	0.6		2021	0.3
4 0236	3.5	**19** 0327	3.5	
0754	0.7		0854	0.6
F 1458	3.6	SA 1526	3.7	
2022	0.7		2115	0.5
5 0314	3.5	**20** 0417	3.4	
0835	0.8		0951	0.8
SA 1533	3.5	SU 1612	3.6	
2107	0.8		2217	0.6
6 0355	3.3	**21** 0512	3.1	
0921	1.0		1057	1.0
SU 1612	3.3	M 1704	3.4	
2159	0.9		◐ 2330	0.8
7 0441	3.1	**22** 0622	3.0	
1015	1.1		1209	1.1
M 1659	3.2	TU 1806	3.2	
◑ 2300	1.0			
8 0535	3.0	**23** 0046	0.9	
1118	1.3		0746	2.9
TU 1800	3.1	W 1318	1.1	
			1926	3.1
9 0011	1.0	**24** 0151	0.8	
0643	3.0		0857	3.0
W 1232	1.3	TH 1420	1.0	
1917	3.1		2044	3.2
10 0127	0.8	**25** 0246	0.7	
0804	3.0		0951	3.2
TH 1347	1.1	F 1513	0.8	
2037	3.2		2145	3.3
11 0230	0.6	**26** 0334	0.7	
0919	3.2		1035	3.3
F 1449	0.9	SA 1559	0.7	
2142	3.4		2233	3.4
12 0323	0.4	**27** 0415	0.6	
1015	3.4		1115	3.5
SA 1541	0.6	SU 1640	0.6	
2236	3.6		2315	3.4
13 0410	0.2	**28** 0451	0.6	
1103	3.5		1151	3.5
SU 1628	0.4	M 1716	0.6	
2326	3.7		2353	3.4
14 0455	0.0	**29** 0524	0.6	
1148	3.7		1225	3.6
M 1714	0.2	TU 1749	0.6	
○		●		
15 0015	3.8	**30** 0027	3.5	
0539	0.0		0555	0.7
TU 1233	3.7	W 1258	3.6	
1758	0.2		1819	0.6

DECEMBER

Time	m		Time	m
1 0102	3.5	**16** 0142	3.7	
0625	0.7		0658	0.3
TH 1329	3.7	F 1346	3.9	
1850	0.6		1918	0.2
2 0138	3.5	**17** 0230	3.6	
0658	0.7		0746	0.4
F 1401	3.7	SA 1429	3.9	
1924	0.6		2005	0.3
3 0215	3.5	**18** 0317	3.5	
0735	0.7		0835	0.5
SA 1435	3.7	SU 1512	3.8	
2003	0.7		2054	0.4
4 0255	3.5	**19** 0404	3.3	
0817	0.8		0926	0.7
SU 1511	3.6	M 1556	3.7	
2047	0.7		2147	0.5
5 0336	3.4	**20** 0452	3.2	
0903	0.9		1020	0.8
M 1550	3.5	TU 1643	3.5	
2137	0.8		2245	0.7
6 0421	3.3	**21** 0543	3.1	
0954	1.0		1121	1.0
TU 1634	3.4	W 1733	3.3	
2233	0.8		◐ 2352	0.8
7 0510	3.2	**22** 0641	3.0	
1051	1.1		1229	1.1
W 1726	3.3	TH 1830	3.2	
◑ 2336	0.8			
8 0608	3.1	**23** 0102	0.9	
1156	1.1		0747	2.9
TH 1833	3.2	F 1337	1.1	
			1936	3.1
9 0044	0.8	**24** 0205	0.9	
0719	3.1		0855	3.0
F 1306	1.1	SA 1438	1.0	
1953	3.2		2048	3.1
10 0151	0.6	**25** 0258	0.9	
0837	3.2		0954	3.2
SA 1415	0.9	SU 1529	0.9	
2108	3.3		2152	3.2
11 0252	0.5	**26** 0345	0.8	
0944	3.3		1042	3.3
SU 1515	0.7	M 1614	0.7	
2211	3.5		2243	3.2
12 0346	0.3	**27** 0426	0.7	
1039	3.5		1124	3.5
M 1609	0.5	TU 1654	0.7	
2307	3.6		2326	3.3
13 0435	0.2	**28** 0503	0.7	
1129	3.6		1203	3.6
TU 1658	0.3	W 1731	0.6	
14 0000	3.7	**29** 0005	3.3	
0523	0.2		0537	0.7
W 1217	3.7	TH 1238	3.6	
○ 1744	0.2	● 1804	0.6	
15 0052	3.7	**30** 0043	3.4	
0610	0.2		0609	0.7
TH 1302	3.8	F 1310	3.7	
1831	0.2		1836	0.6
		31 0120	3.4	
			0642	0.7
		SA 1342	3.7	
			1909	0.6

Chart Datum: 1·62 metres below Ordnance Datum (Newlyn). HAT is 3·9 metres above Chart Datum.

》 FREE monthly updates. Register at 《
www.reedsnauticalalmanac.co.uk

91

SW Scotland

2.22 ARDROSSAN

N Ayrshire **55°38'·50N 04°49'·61W** ⊛⊛♦♦♦♧♧

CHARTS AC 5610, 2126, 2221, 2491, 1866; Imray C63

TIDES +0055 Dover; ML 1·9; Duration 0630

Standard Port GREENOCK (←—)

Times				Height (metres)			
High Water		Low Water		MHWS	MHWN	MLWN	MLWS
0000	0600	0000	0600	3·4	2·8	1·0	0·3
1200	1800	1200	1800				
Differences ARDROSSAN							
–0020	–0010	–0010	–0010	–0·2	–0·2	+0·1	+0·1
IRVINE							
–0020	–0020	–0030	–0010	–0·3	–0·3	–0·1	0·0

SHELTER Good in marina (formerly Eglinton Dock), access at all tides over sill, 5·2m least depth. A storm gate is fitted; max acceptable beam is 8·6m (28ft). Strong SW/NW winds cause heavy seas in the apprs and the hbr may be closed in SW gales. Ferries berth on both sides of Winton Pier.

NAVIGATION WPT 55°38'·13N 04°50'·55W, 055°/0·65M to hbr ent. From the W/NW keep clear of low-lying Horse Isle (conspic W tower on its S end) ringed by drying ledges. The passage between Horse Isle and the mainland is obstructed by unmarked drying rks and should not be attempted. Be aware of following dangers: From the S/SE, Eagle Rk 3ca S of hbr ent, marked by SHM buoy, Fl G 5s. 3ca SE of Eagle Rk lies unmarked Campbell Rk (0·2m). W Crinan Rk (1·1m) is 300m W of hbr ent, marked by PHM buoy, Fl R 4s.

LIGHTS AND MARKS Dir lt WRG 15m W14M, R/G11M (see 2.3); W sector leads 055° to hbr ent between lt ho and detached bkwtr. Lt ho Iso WG 4s 11m 9M, 317°-G-035°, W elsewhere. On S end of detached bkwtr, Fl R 5s 7m 5M.

Traffic Signals, shown H24 from control twr at ent to marina:

3 F ● lts (vert) = hbr and marina closed; no entry/exit for commercial and pleasure vessels.

3 F ● lts (vert) = marina open, hbr closed; pleasure craft may enter/exit the marina, no commercial movements.

2 F ● lts over 1 F ● = hbr open, marina closed; in severe weather marina storm gate is closed. Commercial vessels may enter/exit hbr, subject to approval by Hbr Control on VHF. Pleasure craft must clear the approach channel, ferry turning area (between the detached bkwtr and Winton Pier) and the outer basin. Yachts may not manoeuvre under sail alone until seaward of the outer breakwater.

COMMUNICATIONS (Code 01294) CGOC (02891) 463933; Police 101; Dr 463011. Marina www. clyde marina.com ☎607077.
Clyde Marina VHF Ch 80 M. *Hbr Control* Ch 12 14 16 (H24).

FACILITIES Clyde Marina (252⌒ inc 50Ⓥ) £2·60, short stay £9<4hrs, access H24, office hrs 0900-1800 ▮ ⚓ Ⓑ Ⓔ ▣(50t) ⚓ ✕. **Town** ▮ ⊠ Ⓑ ⛟ ⊗ ✕ ▢. ⇌ ✈ (Prestwick/Glasgow). Ferry to Brodick (Arran).

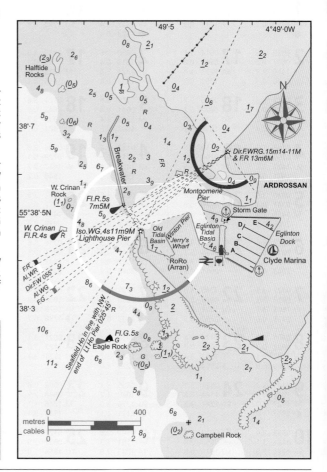

ADJACENT HARBOURS

IRVINE, N Ayrshire, **55°36'·17N 04°42'·07W**. AC 2126, 2220, 1866. HW +0055 on Dover. Tides: see 2.22.

Do not attempt entrance in heavy onshore weather. Goodshelter once across the bar which carries approx 0·5m. The IB-B SPM buoy, Fl Y 3s, is 1·15M from hbr ent, close NW of ldg line. 5 blocks of flats and chimneys are conspic ENE of entrance. Ldg lts 051°: front, FG 10m 5M; rear, FR 15m 5M. The S ent groyne is lit, Fl G 3s; groynes inside the ent have unlit perches. White Pilot tower with mast is conspic 3ca inside entrance.

HM ☎(01294) 487286, ⌨ 487111, VHF Ch 12 (0800-1600 Tues and Thurs; 0800-1300 Wed).

⚓ prohib. Visitors' pontoons on N side or on S side at visitors' quay (2·2m). Berths available above opening footbridge which opens at 5 mins notice ☎08708 403123 or VHF Ch 12 (call *Irvine Bridge*). **Quay** ⌒, 5m<£4<10m<£6<15m £9, ⊾ ⛟ ⏣ ⚠ ⊠(3t).

Town ⏦ ⏦ (1·5km), ▮⛟ ✕⇌✈ (Prestwick).

AYR, S Ayrshire, **55°28'·22N 04°38'·78W**. AC 5610, 2126, 2220, 1866. HW +0050 on Dover; ML 1·8m. Duration 0630. See 2.23.

Good shelter in S dock although berth space limited. After heavy rains large amounts of debris may be washed down the R Ayr. From the W, harbour entrance lies between conspic gasholder to the N and townhall spire to the S. St Nicholas SHM buoy, Fl G 2s, warns of shoals and a separate drying rock (0·8m) 150m S of entrance.

Ldg lts 098°: front, by Pilot Stn, FR 10m 5M R tower, rear (130m from front), Oc R 10s 18m 9M. Traffic signals (near front ldg lt):

2 ● (vert) = hbr closed to incoming traffic.

N Bkwtr Hd, QR 9m 5M. S Pier Hd, Q 7m 7M, vis 012°-161°, and FG 5m 5M, same structure, vis 012°-082°, over St Nicholas Rk. HM ☎(01292) 281687; VHF Ch 14 16.

Ayr Y & CC at S dock, ⚓ limited ⌒ on pontoon on N side of harbour (access key, £10 deposit, from Ship Inn).

Services ✕ ⚓ Ⓑ ⏣.

Town ⏚ ⏦ ⏦ ▮ ⊠ Ⓑ ⛟ ✕ ▢ ⇌.

2.23 TROON

S Ayrshire 55°33′·10N 04°40′·97W ❀❀◊◊❀❀

CHARTS AC 5610, 2126, 2220, 1866; Imray C63

TIDES +0050 Dover; ML 1·9; Duration 0630

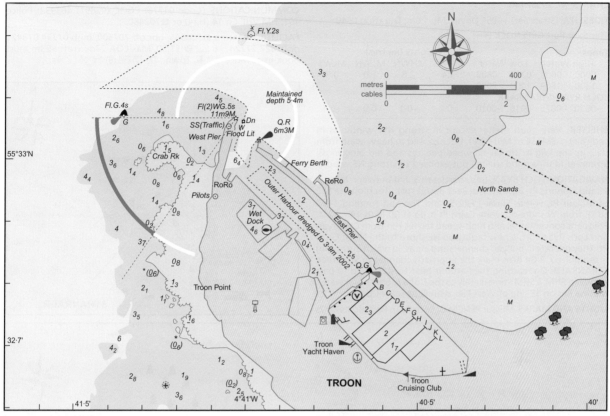

Standard Port GREENOCK (←)

Times				Height (metres)			
High Water		Low Water		MHWS	MHWN	MLWN	MLWS
0000	0600	0000	0600	3·4	2·8	1·0	0·3
1200	1800	1200	1800				
Differences TROON							
−0025	−0025	−0020	−0020	−0·2	−0·2	0·0	0·0
AYR							
−0025	−0025	−0030	−0015	−0·4	−0·3	+0·1	+0·1
GIRVAN							
−0025	−0040	−0035	−0010	−0·3	−0·3	−0·1	0·0

SHELTER Complete in marina (2·4m at ent, 1·6m at SE end); speed limit 5kn. *Strong W winds cause heavy seas in the hbr approach.*

NAVIGATION WPT 55°33′·20N 04°42′·00W, 103°/0·6M to W pier lt. Appr in sector SW to NW. Beware Lady Isle, Fl (4) 30s 19m 8M, W bn, 2·2M SW; Troon Rock (5·6m, occas breaks) 1·1M W; Lappock Rock (0·6m, bn with G barrel topmark) 1·6M NNW; Mill Rock (0·4m) ½M NNE of hbr ent, marked by unlit PHM buoy. Beware wash from high speed ferries in approaches.

LIGHTS AND MARKS No ldg lts. Traffic signals when Fast Ferries arriving/departing. 14m SE of W pier hd lt, Fl (2) WG 5s, there is a floodlit dolphin, W with dayglow patches. A SHM lt buoy, FG, marks the chan in the ent to marina.

COMMUNICATIONS (Code 01292) CGOC (02891) 463933; Police 101; Dr 313593; Ⓗ 610555 (Ayr). HM 281687; Troon CC 311865; Troon YC 316770. HM Ch 14. Marina Ch 80 M (H24).

FACILITIES Troon Yacht Haven ⌂ www.yachthavens.com ☎315553 access all tides 300�+50Ⓥ, £2·70 (short stay £10·20). Ⓥ berth on pontoon **A**, first to stbd. LOA 36m x 3m draught ⌂ at hammerheads. ⚓ ◻ ▮(H24) ▮ ✕ ✎ ⊞ Ⓔ ◻ △(daily pick-up) ▭ (50t) ▭(25t) 🛒 ▭ ✕ ☎311523.

Town ⊠ Ⓑ ⇌ ✈ (Prestwick/Glasgow). Fast RoRo ferry to Larne.

HARBOUR ON THE FIRTH OF CLYDE SOUTH OF TROON

GIRVAN, S Ayrshire, **55°14′·77N 04°51′·87W**. AC 2199, 1866. HW +0043 on Dover; ML 1·8m; Duration 0630. See 2.23.

Good shelter. Brest Rks, 3·5M N of the harbour extend 6ca offshore. Bar carries approx 1·5m. Beware Girvan Patch, 1·7m, 4ca SW of ent. Ch spire (conspic) brg 104° leads between N Bkwtr, Fl R 4s 5m 2M, and S pier, 2 FG (vert) 8m 4M. Inner N groyne, Iso 4s 3m 4M. Traffic sig at root of S pier: 2 B discs (hor)/ 2 ● (hor) = hbr shut.

HM ☎(01465) 713648; VHF Ch 12 16 (HO)

35 � (£2·00) on fingers around perimeter of inner harbour (1·7m). Coasters and FVs berth on adjacent quay: ⚓ ⚓.

Town 🏨 🏪 Ⓑ ⊠ 🛒 ✕ ⇌.

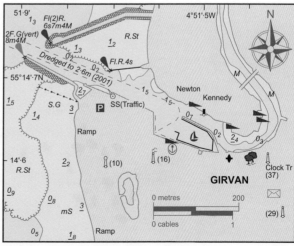

2.24 LOCH RYAN/STRANRAER

Dumfries and Galloway 55°01′N 05°05′W ❄❅🌀🌀❀❀

CHARTS AC 2198, 1403

TIDES HW (Stranraer) +0055 Dover; ML 1.6m; Duration 0640

Standard Port GREENOCK (←)

Times				Heights (metres)			
High Water		Low Water		MHWS	MHWN	MLWN	MLWS
0000	0600	0200	0800	3.4	2.8	1.0	0·3
1200	1800	1400	2000				
LOCH RYAN/STRANRAER							
–0030	–0025	–0010	–0010	–0.2	–0.1	0.0	+0.1

SHELTER Very good shelter except in strong NW winds. ⚓s in Lady Bay, 1·3M SSE of Milleur Pt, but exposed to heavy wash from HSS; in The Wig in 3m (avoid weed patches and old moorings); Stranraer Marina good shelter, but exposed to strong NE winds.

NAVIGATION LOCH RYAN: (see chartlet rhs). Ent between Milleur Pt and Finnarts Pt. Beware The Beef Barrel rock, 1m high 6ca SSE of Milleur Pt, Forbes Shoal ⚓ Fl(2)5s and The Spit running 1·5M to SE from W shore opposite Cairn Pt lt ho Fl (2) R10s 14m 12M. Frequent conventional and high-speed ferries run from Cairnryan and Loch Ryan Port, a new facility on NE shore to the NE of Cairn Pt. They operate in buoyed channels and areas, in which anchoring is prohibited. 3 Gn Bcns mark the approach channel to Stranraer. STRANRAER: On reaching the harbour bear to starboard to pass between PHM & SHM immediately to the E of a rubble breakwater. Marina lies on SE side of West Pier with ⓥ at seaward end.

LIGHTS AND MARKS Milleur Pt NCM Q; Loch Ryan Port ldg lts Iso 2s

9M; Cairn Pt Fl(2) R 10s 14m; Cairnryan ferry terminal Fl R 5s 5m 5M. Stranraer, centre pier hd 2FBu (vert), E pier hd 2FR (vert); PHM Fl R 5s, SHM Fl G 5s.

COMMUNICATIONS (Code 01776) CGOC (02891) 463933; Police 101; HM VHF Ch **14** (H24) or ☎702460.

FACILITIES Marina ☎706565, hbr off 707500; mob 07734 073421 or 07827 277247. 8 🛏 ⓥ £1.50. Max LOA 27m; craft >23m must book in advance ⟨D⟩ ⚓. **Town:** 🅿 🅿 ✉ Ⓑ 🍴 ✕ 🛍 🚉.

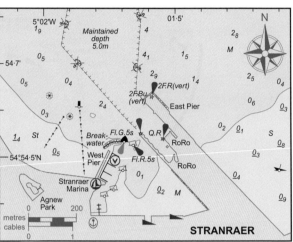

STRANRAER

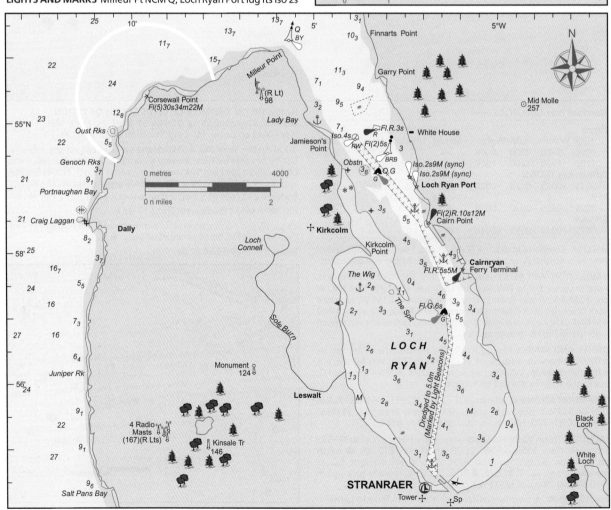

HARBOURS FROM MULL OF GALLOWAY TO WIGTOWN BAY

DRUMMORE, Dumfries and Galloway, **54°41'·57N 04°53'·49W.** AC 2094, 5613. HW +0040m on Dover; ML 3.3m; Duration 0610. Owned by Drummore Hbr Trust the small drying harbour has now silted almost entirely rendering of little interest to passing mariners. Temp'y ⚓ 5.5ca NNE of hbr ent in 4m. Facilities in village: ⌂ ⌂ ▲ ✉ 🛒 ✕ ⌸ ⇌ (bus to Stranraer), ✈ (Carlisle).

PORT WILLIAM, Dumfries and Galloway, **54°45'·70N 04°35'·10W.** AC 1826, 2094, 5613. HW +0035 on Dover; ML 3.7m; Duration 0545. See 2.26. Sheltered harbour dries having approx 1m at HW±2. ⚓ in 3m approx 0.4M off hbr ent. Ldg lts F G 2M on shore Front lt on pier Fl G 3s 3M. HM ☎07734 073419.

ISLE OF WHITHORN, Dumfries and Galloway, **54°41'·91N 04°21'·88W.** AC 1826, 2094, 5613. HW +0035 on Dover; ML 3.7m; Duration 0545. See 2.26. Shelter good but hbr dries, having approx 2.5m at HW±3. On W side of ent beware the Skerries ledge. St Ninian's Tr (Fl WR 3s 20m 6/4M viz: 310°-W-005°-R-040°; W □ tr) is conspic at E side of ent. E pier hd has QG 4m 5M; ldg lts 335°, both Oc R 8s 7/9m 7M, synch, Or masts and ◊. HM ☎07734 073420, www.isleofwhithorn.com; Facilities: ⌂ on quay £4.83/yacht, 2 ⚓ (launching £1.00), ▲ ⌂(by arrangement with HM), ⚓ ✕ ✎ 🛢 ✉ 🛒 ⌸ VHF Ch 08 (occas).

GARLIESTON, Dumfries and Galloway, **54°47'·36N 04°21'·83W.** AC 1826, 2094, 5613. HW +0035 on Dover; ML no data; Duration 0545. See 2.26. Hbr affords complete shelter but dries. Pier hd lt 2FR (vert) 5m 3M. Beware rky outcrops in W side of bay marked by a perch. HM ☎(01988) 600295, Mobile 07734 073422. Facilities: ▲ £3, ⚓ ⌸ on quay, ⚓. **Town:** ⌂ ⌂ 🛒 ✎.

Action and adventure at sea

JERRY GRAYSON AFC
Foreword by HRH The Duke of York, Prince Andrew

RESCUE PILOT
CHEATING THE SEA
BLOOMSBURY

BLOOD RANSOM
STORIES FROM THE FRONT LINE IN THE WAR AGAINST SOMALI PIRACY
JOHN BOYLE
BLOOMSBURY

IN THE FACE OF DANGER; STORIES FROM THE FRONT LINE

Visit www.adlardcoles.com to buy at discount

2.25 PORTPATRICK

Dumfries and Galloway 54°50'·42N 05°07'·18W ✦✦◊◊✿✿

CHARTS AC 2724, 2198; Imray C62

TIDES +0032 Dover; ML 2·1; Duration 0615
Standard Port LIVERPOOL (→)

Times				Heights (metres)			
High Water		Low Water		MHWS	MHWN	MLWN	MLWS
0000	0600	0200	0800	9·4	7·5	3·2	1·1
1200	1800	1400	2000				
Differences PORTPATRICK							
+0038	+0032	0009	–0008	–5·5	–4·4	–2·0	–0·6

SHELTER Good in tiny Inner harbour (on rough stone wall), but entrance is difficult in strong SW/NW winds.

NAVIGATION WPT 54°50'·00N 05°08'·07W, 050°/0·7M to ent. Ent to outer hbr by short narrow chan with hazards either side, including rky shelf covered at HW. Beware cross tides off ent, up to 3kn springs. Barrel buoy (a mooring buoy) marks end of Half Tide Rk; do not cut inside.

LIGHTS AND MARKS Old Lt Ho (W tower, 22m) on Black Head is conspic 1·6M north of entrance. Ldg lts 050·5°, FG (H24) 6/8m: Front on sea wall; rear on bldg; 2 vert orange stripes by day. Conspic features include: TV mast 1M NE, almost on ldg line; large hotel on cliffs about 1½ca NNW of hbr ent; Dunskey Castle (ru) 4ca SE of hbr.

COMMUNICATIONS (Code 01776) CGOC (02891) 463933; Police 101; Ⓗ 702323; RNLI Coxswain (for local advice) 07771 741717. HM 810355.

FACILITIES Hbr ▲ ⚓⚓ (small craft), ⌂£16, ⚓. **Village** ⌂ ▲ (bulk tanker) ▲ ✉ 🛒 ✕ ⌸ ⇌ (bus to Stranraer Ⓑ), ✈ (Prestwick).

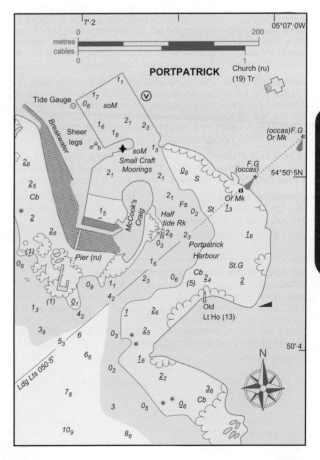

2.26 KIRKCUDBRIGHT

Dumfries and Galloway 54°50'·33N 04°03'·47W ✻❀◊◊✿✿✿

CHARTS AC 1826, 2094, 1346, 1344, 5613; Imray C62

TIDES +0030 Dover; ML 4·1; Duration 0545

Standard Port LIVERPOOL (3.16) (→)

Times				Height (metres)			
High Water		Low Water		MHWS	MHWN	MLWN	MLWS
0000	0600	0200	0800	9·4	7·5	3·2	1·1
1200	1800	1400	2000				
Differences KIRKCUDBRIGHT BAY							
+0020	+0020	+0005	−0005	−1·9	−1·6	−0·8	−0·3
DRUMMORE							
+0035	+0045	+0010	+0015	−3·5	−2·6	−1·2	−0·5
PORT WILLIAM							
+0035	+0035	+0020	−0005	−3·0	−2·3	−1·1	ND
GARLIESTON							
+0030	+0040	+0025	0000	−2·4	−1·8	−0·8	ND
ISLE OF WHITHORN							
+0025	+0030	+0020	0000	−2·5	−2·1	−1·1	−0·4
HESTAN ISLET (Kippford)							
+0030	+0030	+0015	+0020	−1·1	−1·2	−0·8	−0·2
SOUTHERNESS POINT							
+0035	+0035	+0025	+0005	−0·8	−0·8	ND	ND
ANNAN WATERFOOT							
+0055	+0110	+0215	+0305	−2·3	−2·7	−3·0	CD+
TORDUFF POINT							
+0110	+0145	+0515	+0405	−4·2	−5·0	CD+	CD+
REDKIRK							
+0115	+0220	+0710	+0440	−5·6	−6·3	CD+	CD+

NOTES: At Annan Waterfoot, Torduff Pt and Redkirk the LW time differences are for the start of the rise, which at sp is very sudden. CD+ = At LW the tide does not usually fall below CD; ND = No Data.

SHELTER Very good. Depths at LW: 1·0–2·0m at the floating pontoon 300m below quay, visitors should always berth/raft on N side of it. Craft drawing 2·0–3·0m, drying ⚓, and drying out against Town Quay (used H24 by FVs) by advance arrangement with HM. Downriver there are good ⚓s close W, N, and NE of Little Ross and ½ca N of Torrs Pt, except in S'lies which raise heavy swell.

NAVIGATION WPT 54°45'·51N 04°04'·08W, 005°/1·4M to Torrs Pt. The Bar is 1ca N of Torrs Pt; access HW±2½. R Dee has depths of 0·1m to 4·3m. Spring tides run up to 3–4kn. A firing range straddles the ent but no restrictions on transit of firing area; call Range Safety Officer ☎(01557) 500271 (out of hours), 830236 (office hours) or VHF 73 Range Safety Craft, *Gallavidian*, on Ch 16.

LIGHTS AND MARKS Little Ross Lt ho, W of ent, Fl 5s 50m 12M, NNE end of Is, Stone bn Fl (2) 5s 21m 5M. No 1 bn, Fl 3s 7m 3M, on ♦ shed (54°47'·70N). River well lit/marked, 2 Fl G lts at pontoon.

COMMUNICATIONS (Code 01557) CGOC (01407) 762051; Police 101; Dr 330755; HM 331135 Mobile 07709 479663; GM Marine Services (Fuel) 07970 109814.

Ch 12 (0730–1700). *Range Control* Ch 16 73.

KIRKCUDBRIGHT

FACILITIES Pontoon/jetty ⚓ max LOA 60m £1.40 inc ⚑ ⊕ ⚓
Town Quay ⚓ ▲ ▮(by arrangement with HM) ⚒ ⊞ ⚏ ⚓(15t).
KYC ☎330963; **SC** ☎330032 ⚓ ⚓ ⚓.
Town ⊠ Ⓑ ⚸ ✗ ⚎ ⇌ (Dumfries 30M), ✈ (Glasgow 100M).

HARBOUR IN THE SOLWAY FIRTH APPROACHES

KIPPFORD, Dumfries and Galloway, **54°52'·36N 03°48'·93W**. AC 1826, 1346, 5613. HW +0040 on Dover; ML 4·2m (Hestan Is). See 2.26. Good shelter on drying ⚓/pontoons off Kippford, 2·75M up drying Urr Estuary from Hestan Is lt ho Fl (2) 10s 42m 9M. Access via drying, marked, unlit chan. *Clyde Cruising Club* or *Solway Sailing Directions* (from Solway YC) are strongly advised.

Beware Craig Roan on E side of ent. Temp ⚓s NE or W of Hestan Is to await tide. VHF: Ch M call *Kippford Startline* (YC) HW±2 in season. Ch 16 *Kippford Slipway* (Pilotage). Facilities: **Solway YC** www.thesyc.com ☎(01556) 600221; ⚓, ⊕, ⚓ M; **Services**: ⚓ £6, ⚓ ⚓ ⛽ ▲ ⚒ ⚓ ⚓ *Kippford Slipway Ltd* (01556) 620249. **Town** ⚓ ⛽ ⚠ ⊠ ⚸ ⚏.

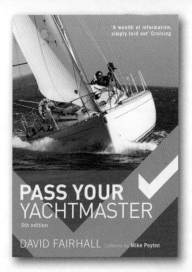
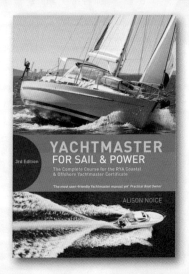
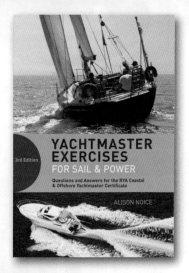
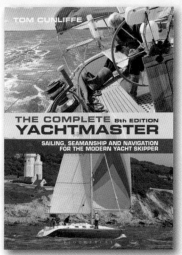
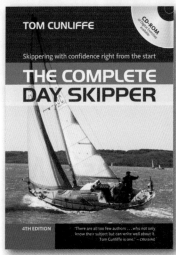

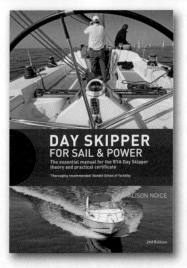
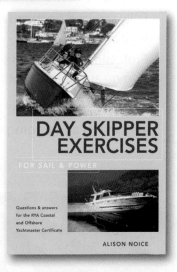

West England, IoM & Wales

Solway Firth to Land's End

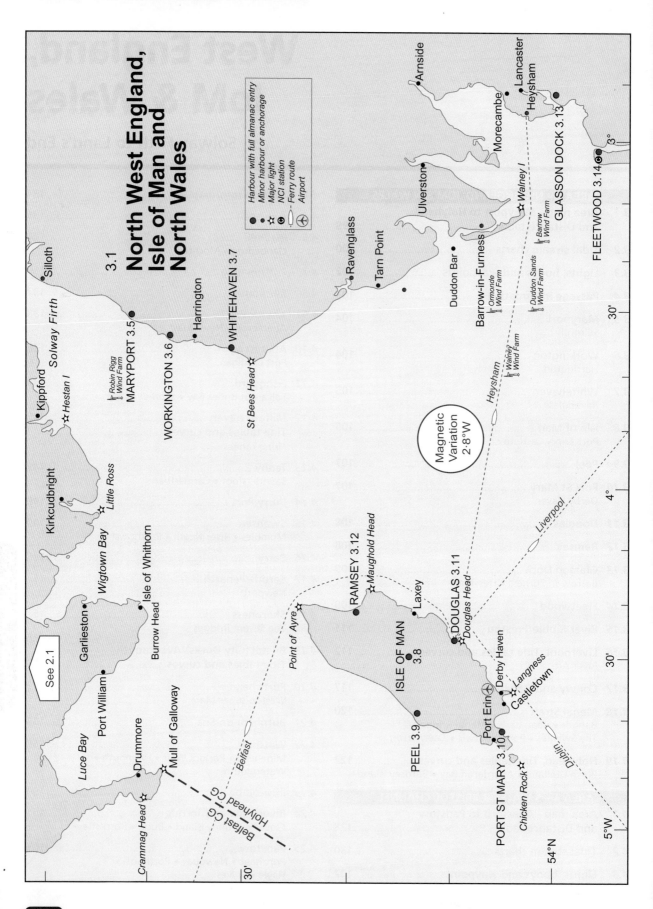

North West England, Isle of Man and North Wales

3.1

Legend:
- ● Harbour with full almanac entry
- • • Minor harbour or anchorage
- ☆ Major light
- ⊙ NCI station
- - - - Ferry route
- ✈ Airport

Magnetic Variation 2·8°W

Silloth
Kippford
Solway Firth
Hestan I
Robin Rigg Wind Farm
MARYPORT 3.5
Harrington
WORKINGTON 3.6
WHITEHAVEN 3.7
St Bees Head
Ravenglass
Tarn Point
Duddon Bar
Barrow-in-Furness
Ormonde Wind Farm
Duddon Sands Wind Farm
Ulverston
Walney I
Barrow Wind Farm
Morecambe
Heysham
Arnside
Lancaster
Heysham
GLASSON DOCK 3.13
FLEETWOOD 3.14
3°

Heysham
Walney Wind Farm

Kirkcudbright
Little Ross
Wigtown Bay
Isle of Whithorn
Garlieston
Burrow Head
Port William
Luce Bay
Drummore
Mull of Galloway
Crammag Head

See 2.1

Liverpool
Belfast
Belfast CG
Holyhead CG
Dublin

Point of Ayre
RAMSEY 3.12
Maughold Head
Laxey
DOUGLAS 3.11
Douglas Head
ISLE OF MAN 3.8
Derby Haven
Langness
Castletown
Port Erin
PEEL 3.9
PORT ST MARY 3.10
Chicken Rock

4°

30'

30'

54°N

5°W

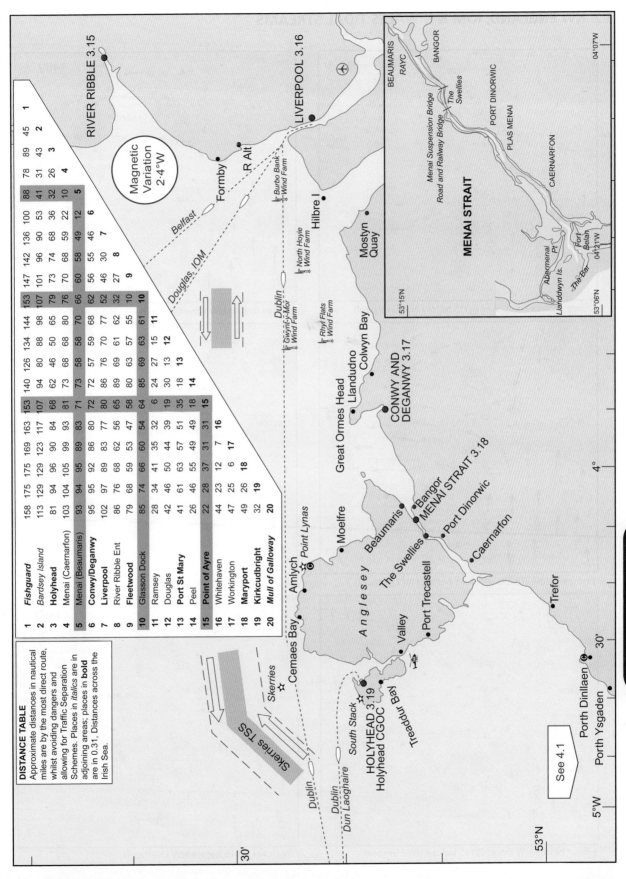

3.2 NW ENGLAND, IOM & N WALES TIDAL STREAMS

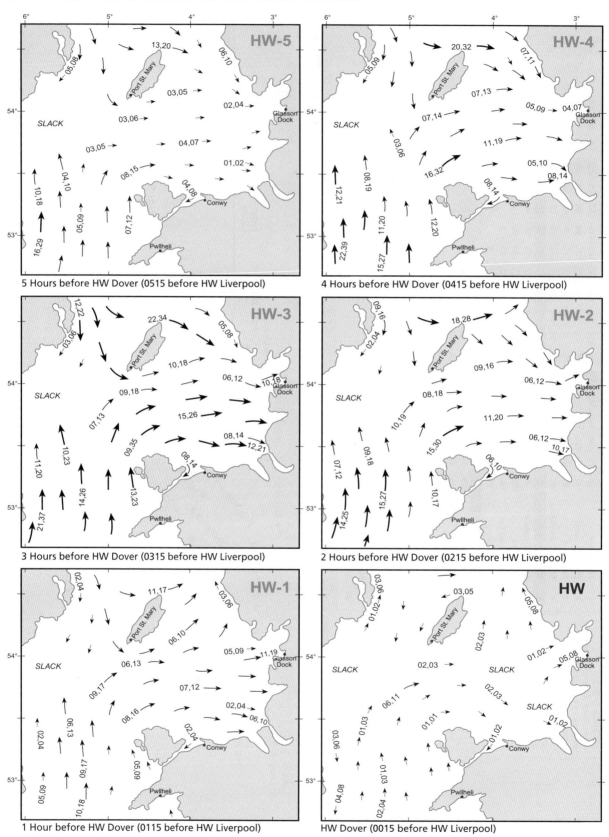

5 Hours before HW Dover (0515 before HW Liverpool)

4 Hours before HW Dover (0415 before HW Liverpool)

3 Hours before HW Dover (0315 before HW Liverpool)

2 Hours before HW Dover (0215 before HW Liverpool)

1 Hour before HW Dover (0115 before HW Liverpool)

HW Dover (0015 before HW Liverpool)

Northward 2.2   Southward 4.2   North Ireland 6.2   Mull of Kintyre 2.10   South Ireland 5.2

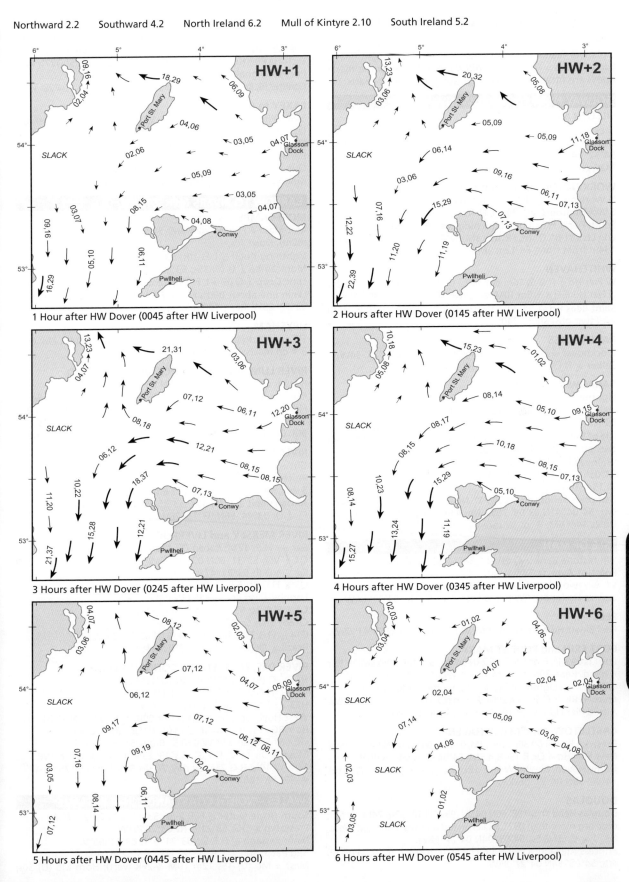

1 Hour after HW Dover (0045 after HW Liverpool)

2 Hours after HW Dover (0145 after HW Liverpool)

3 Hours after HW Dover (0245 after HW Liverpool)

4 Hours after HW Dover (0345 after HW Liverpool)

5 Hours after HW Dover (0445 after HW Liverpool)

6 Hours after HW Dover (0545 after HW Liverpool)

NW England

3.3 LIGHTS, BUOYS AND WAYPOINTS

Bold print = light with a nominal range of 15M or more. CAPITALS = place or feature. *CAPITAL ITALICS* = light-vessel, light float or Lanby. *Italics* = Fog signal. ***Bold italics*** = Racon. Some marks/buoys are fitted with AIS (<u>MMSI No</u>); see relevant charts.

SOLWAY FIRTH TO BARROW-IN-FURNESS

SILLOTH and MARYPORT
Lees Scar ⚓ Fl G 5s 11m 4M; W piles; 54°51'·78N 03°24'·79W.
Groyne Hd ⚓ 2 FG (vert) 4m 4M; Fl Bu tfc signals close by; 54°52'·14N 03°23'·93W.
Maryport S Pier Hd ⚓.Fl 1·5s 10m 6M; 54°43'·07N 03°30'·64W.

WORKINGTON and HARRINGTON
N Workington ⚓ Q; 54°40'·10N 03°38'·18W.
S Workington ⚓ VQ (6) + L Fl 10s; 54°37'·01N 03°38'·58W.
South Pier ⚓ Fl 5s 11m 5M; R bldg; 54°39'·12N 03°34'·67W.
Ldg Lts 131·8°. Front, FR 10m 3M; 54°38'·92N 03°34'·19W. Rear, 134m from front, FR 12m 3M.

WHITEHAVEN
W Pier Hd ⚓ Fl G 5s 16m 8M; W ○ twr; 54°33'·17N 03°35'·92W.
N Pier Hd ⚓ Fl R 5s 8m 10M; W ○ twr; 54°33'·17N 03°35'·75W.
Saint Bees Hd ☆ 54°30'·81N 03°38'·23W Fl (2) 20s 102m **18M**; W○ twr; obsc shore-340°.

RAVENGLASS
Blockhouse ⚓ FG; (Eskdale Range); 54°20'·16N 03°25'·34W.
Selker ⚓ Fl (3) G 10s; *Bell;* 54°16'·14N 03°29'·58W.

BARROW-IN-FURNESS
Lightning Knoll ⚓ L Fl 10s; 53°59'·83N 03°14'·28W.
Halfway Shoal ⚓ QR 19m 10s; R&W chequer Bn; 54°01'·46N 03°11'·88W.
Isle of Walney ☆ 54°02'·92N 03°10'·64W Fl 15s 21m **23M**; stone twr; obsc 122°-127° within 3M of shore.
Walney Chan Ldg Lts 040·7°. No.1 Front ⚓, Q 7m 10M; B Pile; 54°03'·19N 03°09'·22W. No. 2 Rear ⚓, 0·61M from front, Iso 2s 13m 10M; Pile.
Rampside Sands Ldg Lts 005·1°. No. 3 Front ⚓, Q 9m10M; W ○ twr; 54°04'·41N 03°09'·79W. No. 4 Rear ⚓, 0·77M from front, Iso 2s 14m 6M; R col, W face.

ISLE OF MAN
Whitestone Bank ⚓ Q (9) 15s; 54°24'·58N 04°20'·41W.
Point of Ayre ☆ 54°24'·94N 04°22'·13W Fl (4) 20s 32m **19M**; W twr, two R bands, ***Racon (M) 13-15M***.
Low Lt Ho (unlit), RW twr, B base, 54°25'·03N 04°21'·86W.

PEEL
Peel Bkwtr Hd ⚓ Oc 7s 11m 6M; W twr; 54°13'·67N 04°41'·69W.

PORT ERIN and PORT ST MARY
Ldg Lts 099·1°. Front, 54°05'·23N 04°45'·57W FR 10m 5M; W twr, R band. Rear, 39m from front, FR 19m 5M; W col, R band.
Calf of Man Lighthouse (disused), white 8-sided tower.
Chicken Rk ☆ Fl 5s 38m **20M**; ***Racon (C)*** 54°02'·27N 04°50'·32W
Alfred Pier Hd ⚓ Oc R 10s 8m 6M; 54°04'·33N 04°43'·82W.

CASTLETOWN and DERBY HAVEN
Dreswick Pt ⚓ Fl (2) 30s 23m 12M; W twr; 54°03'·29N 04°37'·45W.
New Pier Hd ⚓ Oc R 15s 8m 5M; 54°04'·33N 04°38'·97W.
Derby Haven, Bkwtr SW end ⚓Iso G 2s 5m 5M; W twr, G band; 54°04'·58N 04°37'·06W.

DOUGLAS
Douglas Head ☆ 54°08'·60N 04°27'·95W Fl 10s 32m **24M**; W twr; obsc brg more than 037°. FR Lts on radio masts 1 and 3M West.
No. 1 ⚓ Q (3) G 5s; 54°09'·04N 04°27'·68W.
Princess Alexandra Pier Hd ⚓ Fl R 5s 16m 8M; R mast; *Whis (2) 40s;* 54°08'·84N 04°27'·85W.

Ldg Lts 229·3°, Front ⚓, Oc Bu 10s 9m 5M; W △ R border on mast; 54°08'·72N 04°28'·25W. Rear ⚓, 62m from front, Oc Bu 10s 12m 5M; W ▽ on R border; synch with front.
Victoria Pier Hd ⚓ Iso G 10s 10m 3M; W col; vis: 225°-327°; Intnl Port Tfc Signals; 54°08'·84N 04°28'·08W.
Conister Rk Refuge ⚓ Q 3M; vis: 234°-312°; 54°09'·03N 04°28'·12W.

LAXEY to RAMSEY
Laxey Pier Hd ⚓ Oc R 3s 7m 5M; W twr, R band; obsc when brg less than 318°; 54°13'·50N 04°23'·43W.
Maughold Head ☆ 54°17'·72N 04°18'·58W Fl (3) 30s 65m **21M**.
Bahama ⚓ VQ (6) + L Fl 10s; 54°20'·01N 04°08'·57W.
Queens Pier Dn ⚓ Fl R 5s; 54°19'·28N 04°21'·95W.
King William Bank ⚓ Q (3) 10s; 54°26'·01N 04°00'·08W.

BARROW TO RIVERS MERSEY AND DEE

MORECAMBE
Met Mast ⚓ Fl Y 5s 20m 5M; 54°00'·13N 03°33'·38W; Aero FR (80m), *Horn 30s.*
Lightning Knoll ⚓ L Fl 10s; 53°59'·84N 03°14'·28W.
Morecambe ⚓ Q (9) 15s; 53°52'·00N 03°22'·00W.
Lune Deep ⚓ Q (6) + L Fl 15s; ***Racon (T);*** 53°56'·07N 03°12·90W.
Lts in line about 090°. Front, FR 10m 2M; G mast; 54°04'·41N 02°52'·63W. Rear, 140m from front, FR 14m 2M; G mast.

HEYSHAM
SW Quay Ldg Lts 102·2°. Front ⚓, both F Bu 11/14m 2M; Or & B ♦ on masts; 54°01'·91N 02°55'·22W.

RIVER LUNE, GLASSON DOCK and FLEETWOOD
R Lune ⚓ Q (9) 15s; 53°58'·63N 03°00'·03W.
Fairway No. 1(Fleetwood) ⚓ 53°57'·67N 03°02'·03W Q; *Bell.*
Fleetwood Esplanade Ldg Lts 156°. Front, Iso G 2s 14m 9M; 53°55'·71N 03°00'·56W. Rear, 320m from front, Iso G 4s 28m 9M. Both vis on Ldg line only. (H24) (chan liable to change).

RIVER RIBBLE
Gut ⚓ L Fl 10s; 53°41'·74N 03°08'·98W.
Perches show Fl R on N side, and Fl G on S side of chan.
S side, 14¼M Perch ⚓ Fl G 5s 6m 3M; 53°42'·75N 03°04'·90W.
Jordan's Spit ⚓ Q (9) 15s; 53°35'·76N 03°19'·28W.
FT ⚓ Q; 53°34'·56N 03°13'·20W.

RIVER MERSEY and LIVERPOOL
Bar ⚓ Fl.5s 12M; ***Racon (T) 10M;*** 53°32'·01N 03°20'·98W.
Q1 ⚓ VQ; 53°31'·00N 03°16'·72W.
Q2 ⚓ VQ R; 53°31'·47N 03°14'·95W.
Q3 ⚓ Fl G 3s; 53°30'·95N 03°15'·10W.
Formby ⚓ Iso 4s; 53°31'·13N 03°13'·48W.
C4 ⚓ Fl R 3s; 53°31'·82N 03°08'·51W.
Crosby ⚓ Oc 5s; 53°30'·72N 03°06'·29W.
C14 ⚓ Fl R 3s; R hull; 53°29'·91N 03°05'·34W.
Brazil ⚓ QG; 53°26'·85N 03°02'·23W.

RIVER DEE, MOSTYN and CONNAH'S QUAY
HE1 ⚓ Q (9) 15s; 53°26'·33N 03°18'·08W.
HE2 ⚓ Fl G 2·5s; 53°24'·90N 03°12'·88W.
HE3 ⚓ Q G; 53°24'·55N 03°12'·74W.
West Hoyle Spit (Earwig) Dir lt 090. ⚓ 53°21'·21N 03°24'·07W; Iso WRG 2s W10M, R7M, G7M (day W3M, R2M, G2M).
vis: 087·5°-G-089·5°-W-090·5°-R-092·5°; occasional.
Mostyn Dir Lt ⚓ 177·5°. 53°19'·23N 03°16'·38W Iso WRG 2s 11m W 10M R,G 7M, by day W 3M R,G 2M; vis: 175°-G-177°-W-178°-R-180°; H24.

WALES – NORTH COAST AND INNER PASSAGE
South Hoyle Outer ⚓ Fl R 2·5s; 53°21'·47N 03°24'·70W.
Prestatyn ⚓ QG; 53°21'·51N 03°28'·51W.
Inner Passage ⚓ Fl R 5s; 53°21'·91N 03°31'·95W.
Mid Patch Spit ⚓ QR; 53°22'·25N 03°32'·67W.
Mast ⚓ Mo (U) 15s 12m 10M & 2FR (vert); *Horn Mo (U) 30s;*

Mast (80); 53°28'·84N 03°30'·50W.
W Constable ⚓ Q (9) 15s; *Racon (M) 10M*; 53°23'·14N 03°49'·26W.
N Constable ⚓ VQ; 53°23'·76N 03°41'·42W.

RHYL, LLANDUDNO and CONWY
River Clwyd Outfall ⚓ Q R 7m 2M; 53°19'·45N 03°30'·34W.
Rhyll SWM ⚓ Mo(A) 10s; 53°19'·60N 03°32'·00W.
Llandudno Pier Hd ⚡ 2 FG (vert) 8m 4M; 53°19'·90N 03°49'·51W.
Great Ormes Hd Lt Ho, (unlit); 53°20'·56N 03°52'·17W.
Conwy Fairway ⚓ L Fl 10s; 53°17'·95N 03°55'·58W.
C1 ⚓ Fl G 10s; 53°17'·83N 03°54'·58W.
C2 ⚓ Fl (2) R 10s; 53°17'·94N 03°54'·52W.
River Conwy ent, ⚡ L Fl G 15s 5m 2M; 53°18'·03N 03°50'·86W.

ANGLESEY
Point Lynas ☆ 53°24'·98N 04°17'·35W Oc 10s 39m **18M**; W castellated twr; vis: 109°-315°; H24.

AMLWCH to HOLYHEAD BAY
Main Bkwtr ⚡ Fl G 15s 11m 3M; W mast; vis: 141°-271°; 53°25'·02N 04°19'·91W.
Furlong ⚓ Fl G 2·5s; 53°25'·41N 04°30'·47W.
Archdeacon Rock ⚓ Q; 53°26'·71N 04°30'·87W.
Victoria Bank ⚓ VQ; 53°25'·61N 04°31'·37W.
Coal Rk ⚓ Q (6) + L Fl 15s; 53°25'·91N 04°32'·79W.
Ethel Rk ⚓ VQ; 53°26'·64N 04°33'·67W.
The Skerries ☆ 53°25'·27N 04°36'·50W Fl (2) 15s 36m **20M**; W ○ twr, R band; *Racon (T) 25M*. Iso R 4s 26m 10M; same twr; vis: 233°-252°, sector unreliable > 4M; *Horn (2) 60s*. H24 in periods of reduced visibility; 992351084.
Langdon ⚓ Q (9) 15s; 53°22'·74N 04°38'·74W.
Bolivar ⚓ FL G 2·5s; 53°21'·51N 04°35'·33W.
Wk ⚓ Fl (2) R 10s; 53°20'·43N 04°36'·60W.

HOLYHEAD to SOUTH STACK
Bkwtr Head ⚡ Fl (3) G 10s 21m 14M; W □ twr, B band; Fl Y vis: 174°-226°; *Siren 20s*; 53°19'·86N 04°37'·16W.

Spit ⚓ Fl G 3s; 53°19'·79N 04°37'·15W.
South Stack ☆ 53°18'·41N 04°41'·98W Fl 10s 60m **24M**; (H24); W ○ twr; obsc to N by N Stack and part obsc in Penrhos bay; *Horn 30s*. Fog Det lt vis: 145°-325°.

MENAI STRAIT TO BARDSEY ISLAND
Ten Feet Bank ⚓ QR; 53°19'·47N 04°02'·82W.
Dinmor ⚓ QG; 53°19'·34N 04°03'·32W.
Trwyn-Du ⚡ Fl 5s 19m 12M; W ○ castellated twr, B bands; vis: 101°-023°; *Bell (1) 30s*, sounded continuously; 53°18'·77N 04°02'·44W. FR on radio mast 2M SW.

APPROACHES to BEAUMARIS and BANGOR
(Direction of buoyage ⬗ NE to SW)
Perch Rock ⚓ Fl R 5s; 53°18'·73N 04°02'·09W.

PORT DINORWIC and CAERNARFON
Port Dinorwic Pier Hd ⚡ 53°11'·21N 04°12'·60W F WR 5m 2M; vis: 225°-R- 357°-W-225°.

(Direction of buoyage ⬗ SW to NE)
Caernarfon N Pier Hd ⚡ 2 FG (vert) 5m 2M; 53°08'·72N 04°16'·56W.
Abermenai Point ⚡ Fl WR 3·5s 6m 3M; W mast; vis: 065°-R-245°-W-065°; 53°07'·62N 04°19'·72W.
C1 ⚓ Fl G 5s; 53°06'·85N 04°24'·35W.
C2 ⚓ Fl R 10s; 53°06'·95N 04°24'·46W.
Caernarfon Bar ⚓ L Fl 10s; 53°06'·45N 04°25'·00W.
Llanddwyn I ⚡Fl WR 2·5s 12m W7M, R4M; W twr; vis: 280°-R-015°-W-120°; 53°08'·05N 04°24'·79W.

PORTH DINLLÄEN
CG Stn ⚡ FR when firing 10M N; 52°56'·82N 04°33'·89W.
Careg y Chwislen ⚓ Fl(2) 10s 2M 52°56'·99N 04°33'·51W.

Bardsey I ☆ 52°44'·97N 04°48'·02W Fl (5) 15s 39m **26M**; W□twr, R bands; obsc by Bardsey Is 198°-250° and in Tremadoc B when brg < 260°.

3.4 PASSAGE INFORMATION
More passage information is threaded between the harbours in this area. Admiralty Leisure Folio 5613, Irish Sea eastern part including Isle of Man, covers the Mull of Galloway to Great Ormes Head including the Isle of Man. Folio 5609, North West Wales including Menai Strait, covers Colwyn Bay to Aberystwyth, including Anglesey. **Bibliography:** *Irish Sea Pilot* (Imray/Rainsbury). *Cruising Anglesey and Adjoining Waters* (Imray/Morris).The *West Coasts of England and Wales Pilot* (Admiralty NP37) covers the whole area.

SOLWAY FIRTH
(AC 1346) Between Abbey Hd and St Bees Hd lies the Solway Firth, most of which is encumbered by shifting sandbanks. *Solway SDs* are essential. Off the entrances to the Firth, and in the approaches to Workington, beware shoals over which strong W winds raise a heavy sea. The area N of Silloth is unsurveyed but buoyed channels are navigable as far as Dumfries and Annan on the N shore. Buoys are laid primarily for the aid of pilots.

▶ *Local knowledge is required, particularly in the upper Firth, where streams run very strongly in the channels when the banks are dry, and less strongly over the banks when covered. In Powfoot Channel the flood stream begins at HW L'pool – 0300, and the ebb at HW L'pool + 0100,* **Sp rates up to 6kn.** ◀

The River Nith, approached between Borron Point and Blackshaw Spit, leads to Carsethorn, Glencaple, Kingholm Quay and Dumfries. There are 2 ⚓s at Caresthorn; Kingholm Quay offers drying berths, ⚓ and on pontoons. Local knowledge is essential, but pilotage for visiting yachts is available. Contact

cargo@nith-navigation.co.uk, ☎07801 321457 or 07860 522598, or visit: www.nith-navigation.co.uk.

On the south side of the Solway Firth are Maryport, Workington, Harrington and Whitehaven. South of St Bees Head lies the Nuclear processing plant at Sellafield. The large shallow drying harbour at Ravenglass lies south again with Eskmeals Firing Range. Selker rocks and Black Leg Rk are notable shoals between Ravenglass and the Duddon Estuary. This dries at LW and is only navigable by small shoal draught craft. The Isle of Walney has an airfield and shelters Barrow -in-Furness which is reached by Walney Chan on rounding South East Point.

Morecambe Bay is shallow and mostly dries. Heysham harbour is exclusively for commercial traffic. The R Lune gives access to Port Glasson and the R Wyre to Fleetwood. The Channels which traverse the extensive offshore sandbanks are buoyed and shift frequently. Shell Flat extends 11M off the beach at Blackpool.

WIND FARMS
Robin Rigg wind farm is approximately 7M WNW of Maryport. Be aware of Walney, Ormonde Barrow and West of Duddon Sands wind farms between 6M and 12M off Walney Island. Burbo Bank wind farm is directly S of the approaches to Liverpool with an extension planned to the W. North Hoyle, Gwynt y Mor and Rhyl Flats wind farms WSW lie between 6M and 12M off the coast of N Wales.

An extensive area has been earmarked for development between Anglesey and the Isle of Man. Known collectively as the Celtic Array this will consist of 3 large wind farms. the first of these, Rhiannon, is undergoing public consultation.

NW England

3.5 MARYPORT

Cumbria **54°43'·03N 03°30'·38W** ✿✿❀♦♦♦♧♧♧

CHARTS AC 1826, 1346, 2013, 5613; Imray C62

TIDES +0038 Dover; ML no data; Duration 0550
Standard Port LIVERPOOL (→)

Times				Height (metres)			
High Water		Low Water		MHWS	MHWN	MLWN	MLWS
0000	0600	0200	0800	9·4	7·5	3·2	1·1
1200	1800	1400	2000				
Differences MARYPORT							
+0021	+0036	+0017	+0002	−0·8	−0·9	−0·7	−0·2
SILLOTH							
+0035	+0045	+0040	+0050	−0·2	−0·4	−0·9	−0·3

SHELTER Good in marina, sill 3·1m above CD, 2.5m above sill for entry; at other times Workington is a refuge. Elizabeth Dock gates u/s. Elizabeth Basin dries 2m; commercial, not used by yachts.

NAVIGATION WPT 54°43'·09N 03°32'·47W, 090°/1M to S pier. Overfalls at ent in W/SW winds over ebb. At HW−3 1·8m over bar at ent and in river chan; mud banks cover HW −2. Max speed 4kn.

LIGHTS AND MARKS SHM bn Fl G 5s marks outfall 6ca SW of S pier. SSS displays IPTS signals 2 and 5 (see IPTS 5.20)

COMMUNICATIONS (Code 01900) CGOC (01407) 762051; Police 101; Dr 815544; ⊞ 812634. HM 817440; Hbr Authority 604351.

Port VHF Ch **12** 16. Marina (H24) Ch **12** 16.

FACILITIES Maryport Marina www.maryportmarina.com ☎814431 190⌇ inc ❶ £20.80/craft inc ⚡ ⚓ (±3HW) 🚿 ♿ 🛠 🗼 🔧 (25t) ⚓ **Maryport Yachting Association** www.maryportyachting.co.uk. **Town** 🏧 🏤 ✉ ⑧ ⚒ ✕ 🏬 ⚑ ✈ (Manchester/Newcastle).

3.6 WORKINGTON

Cumbria **54°39'·03N 03°34'·38W** ✿✿♦❀

CHARTS AC 1826, 1346, 2013, 5613; Imray C62

TIDES +0025 Dover; ML 4·5; Duration 0545
Standard Port LIVERPOOL (→)

Times				Height (metres)			
High Water		Low Water		MHWS	MHWN	MLWN	MLWS
0000	0600	0200	0800	9·4	7·5	3·2	1·1
1200	1800	1400	2000				
Differences WORKINGTON							
+0029	+0027	+0014	+0004	−1·1	−1·1	−0·5	−0·1

SHELTER Good. Ent and chan to Prince of Wales Dock are maintained at 1·2m. Berth/moor by prior arrangement with Vanguard SC (☎07707 785328) in drying Tidal Dock; no ⚓ in Turning Basin. Prince of Wales Dock for commercial vessles only. Low (1·8m) fixed railway bridge across ent to inner Tidal Hbr.

NAVIGATION WPT 54°39'·59N 03°35'·38W, 131°/1M to front ldg lt.

- Tide sets strongly across ent. In periods of heavy rain a strong freshet from R Derwent may be encountered in the hbr ent.

LIGHTS AND MARKS Workington Bank, least depth 5·5m, is 2M W of hbr ent; and is marked by NCM and SCM lt buoys (see 3.3). Ldg lts 132°, both FR 10/12m 3M, on W pyramidal trs with R bands. Two sets of F Bu lts in line mark NE and SW edges of chan. There are 16 wind-turbines on shore between ¾M and 2M NE of hbr ent.

COMMUNICATIONS (Code 01900) CGOC (01407) 762051; Police 101; Dr 64866; ⊞ 602244. HM 602301.

VHF Ch 14 16 (HW−2½ to HW+2 approx).

FACILITIES Dock ⚓ 🛠 🔧 ♿.
Vanguard SC www.vanguard-workington.co.uk ☎01228 674238 ⚓ ⚓.
Town 🏧 ✉ ⑧ ⚒ ✕ 🏬 ⚑ ✈ (Carlisle).

MINOR HARBOUR 10M NNE OF MARYPORT

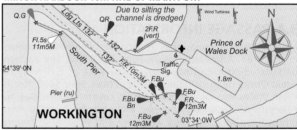

SILLOTH, Cumbria, **54°52'·16N 03°23'·86W**. AC 1826, 1346, 2013, 5613. HW −0050 on Dover; ML no data; Duration 0520. See 3.5. Commercial harbour which welcomes occasional visiting yachts. Appr via English or Middle Chans; requires local knowledge, Beware constantly shifting chans and banks, and unsurveyed areas. East Cote Dir lt 052° FG 15m 12M; vis 046°-058°, intens 052°. Ldg lts, both F, 115°. Groyne 2 FG (vert). Outer hbr dries 2·8m; lock into New Dock (4m) HW−1½ to HW+½. Ent marked by Oc R/G lts. Subtract 1m from height of tide to calculate draught over sill. £24 covers entry/exit and 1 week stay. Traffic sigs on mast at New Dock; must receive permission before proceeding. VHF Ch 16 12. HM ☎(01697) 331358. ⚓ WSW of ent in about 4m off Lees Scar, Fl G 5s 11m 4M; exposed to SW winds. Facilities: ⚓ ✉ ⑧ ✕ 🏬 ⚒.

MINOR HARBOUR 2M S OF WORKINGTON

HARRINGTON, Cumbria, **54°36'·77N 03°34'·29W**. AC 1826, 1346, 2013, 5613. HW +0025 on Dover; Duration 0540; Use Diff's Workington 3.6. Good shelter in small hbr only used by local FVs and yachts; dries 3ca offshore. Ent, marked by PHM perches on N side, difficult in strong W winds. Berth on N wall of inner hbr (free). Call ☎(01946) 823741 Ext 148 for moorings. Limited facilities. **SC** ☎(01946) 830600.

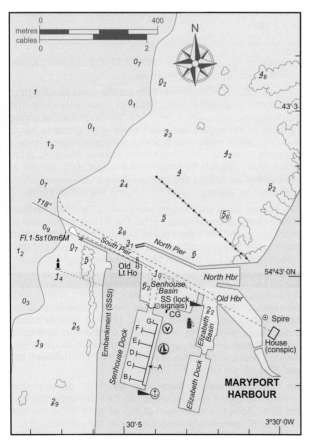

MARYPORT HARBOUR

3.7 WHITEHAVEN

Cumbria **54°33′·18N 03°35′·82W** ❁❁❁♧♧❁❁

CHARTS AC 1826, 1346, 2013, 5613; Imray C62

TIDES +0015 Dover; ML 4·5; Duration 0550

Standard Port LIVERPOOL (→)

Times				Height (metres)			
High Water		Low Water		MHWS	MHWN	MLWN	MLWS
0000	0600	0200	0800	9·4	7·5	3·2	1·1
1200	1800	1400	2000				
Differences WHITEHAVEN							
+0010	+0020	+0005	0000	−1·4	−1·2	−0·8	−0·1
TARN POINT (54°17′N 03°25′W)							
+0010	+0010	+0005	−0005	−1·1	−1·1	−0·7	−0·2
DUDDON BAR (54°09′N 03°20′W)							
+0007	+0007	+0005	−0001	−0·9	−0·9	−0·6	−0·2

SHELTER Very good, entry safe in most weathers. One of the more accessible ports of refuge in NW England, with a marina in the Inner Hbr. Appr chan across the outer hbr is dredged to 1·0m above CD. Sea lock (30m x 13.7m), with sill at CD, maintains 7m within inner hbr. N Hbr is for commercial and FV use.

NAVIGATION WPT 54°33′·34N 03°36′·21W, 133°/4½ca to W pier hd. There are no hazards in the offing. Hold closer to the North Pier, and beware bar at end of W Pier.

LIGHTS AND MARKS Several tall chimneys are charted within 1·5M S of hbr. St Bees Head Lt ho is 2·7M SSW of hbr ent. SHM bn, Fl G 2·5s, 4½ca S of W pierhead marks sewer outfall. IPTS sigs 1-3 shown from N side of lock ent to seaward only at present: priority to inward bound vessels.

COMMUNICATIONS (Code 01946) CGOC (01407) 762051; Police 101; HM 692435; Sealock 694672.

HM VHF Ch 12 16.

FACILITIES Marina ⚓ www.whitehavenmarina.co.uk ☎692435 285 inc ♥ in Inner Harbour (Lowther Marina) and Queen's Dock (Queen's Marina) £2.20, ⚓ ◻ ♦ ♣ ⚒ ⚓ Ⓔ ⚲ ◓(45t) ♨ SC. **Town** Market days Thurs, Sat; ▯ ▯ ✉ Ⓑ ⚒ ✕ ◻ ⇌.

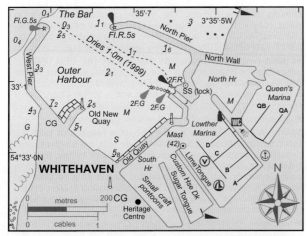

WHITEHAVEN

MINOR HARBOUR BETWEEN ST BEES HD AND MORECAMBE BAY
RAVENGLASS, Cumbria, **54°20′·00N 03°26′·80W** (drying line). AC 1346, 1826, 5613. HW +0020 on Dover; ML no data; Duration 0545. See 3.7 (Tarn Pt). Large drying hbr, into which R's Mite, Irt and Esk flow; approx 2·5m in ent at HW−2. Sellafield power stn with WCM lt buoy and outfall buoys are 5M NNW. FG ☆ (occas) on blockhouse at S side of ent. *Solway Sailing Directions* with pilotage notes by Ravenglass Boating Ass'n, local knowledge advisable. From N beware Drigg Rk and from S Selker Rks, SHM lt buoy, 5M SSW of ent. Firing range D406 close S at Eskmeals; Mon-Thur 0800-1600LT (1500 Fri). When in use R flags flown, R lts at night; *Eskmeals Gun Range* VHF Ch 16 11, ☎(01229) 712245/5. **Village:** ⚓ ⚓ ✉ ◻ ⚒.

3.8 ISLE OF MAN

Charts AC Irish Sea 1826, 1411; 2094 (small scale); 2696 (ports), 5613; Imray C62, Y70

The Isle of Man is one of the British Islands, set in the Irish Sea roughly equidistant from England, Scotland, Wales and Ireland but it is not part of the UK. It has a large degree of self-government. Lights are maintained by the Northern Lighthouse Board. Manx harbours are administered by the IoM Government.

Distances See 3.1 for distances between ports in Area 3 and 0.31 for distances across the Irish Sea, North Channel and St George's Channel.

Harbours and anchorages Most of the harbours are on the E and S sides, but a visit to the W coast with its characteristic cliffs is worth while. The four main harbours are described in an anti-clockwise direction from Peel on the W coast to Ramsey in the NE. There are good ⚓s at: Port Erin in the SW, Castletown and Derby Haven in the SE, and Laxey Bay in the E. All IOM harbours charge the same overnight berthing rate, £1.18/m (multi-hulls £1.76/m).

R/T If contact with local Harbour Offices cannot be established on VHF, vessels should call *Douglas Hbr Control* Ch **12** 16 for urgent messages or other info.

Coastguard Call Holyhead CGOC Ch 16 67 86; the Snaefell (IoM) aerial is linked to the CG network.

Customs The IOM is under the same customs umbrella as the rest of the UK, and there are no formalities on arriving from or returning to the UK.

Weather Forecasts can be obtained direct from the forecaster at Ronaldsway Met Office ☎0900 6243 3200, H24. **Douglas Hbr Control** (3.11) can supply visibility and wind info on request.

MINOR HARBOURS IN THE ISLE OF MAN

PORT ERIN, Isle of Man, **54°05′·31N 04°46′·34W**. AC 2094, 2696, 5613. HW −0020 on Dover; ML 2·9m; Duration 0555. See 3.14. From S and W, Milner's Twr on Bradda Hd is conspic. Ldg lts, both FR 10/19m 5M, lead 099° into the bay. Beware the ruined bkwtr (dries 2·9m) extending N from the SW corner, marked by an unlit SHM buoy. A small hbr on the S side dries 0·8m. Raglan Pier (E arm of hbr), Oc G 5s 8m 5M. 2♂s W of Raglan Pier. Good ⚓ in 3-8m N of Raglan Pier, but exposed to W'lies. Call Port St. Mary Harbour (VHF Ch 12) ☎833205.

CASTLETOWN BAY, Isle of Man, **54°03′·51N 04°38′·57W**. AC 2094, 2696, 5613. HW +0025 on Dover; ML 3·4m; Duration 0555. The bay gives good shelter except in SE to SW winds. From the E, keep inside the race off Dreswick Pt, or give it a wide berth. Beware Lheeah-rio Rks in W of bay, marked by PHM buoy, Fl R 3s, Bell. Hbr dries 3·1m to level sand. Berth in outer hbr or go via swing footbridge (manually opened) into inner hbr below fixed bridge. ⚓ between Lheeah-rio Rks and pier in 3m; or NW of Langness Pt. Lts: Langness lt, on Dreswick Pt, Fl (2) 30s 23m 12M. Hbr S (New) Pier, Oc R 15s 8m 5M; Inner S pier (Irish Quay), Oc R 4s 5m 5M, vis 142°-322°. 150m NW is swing bridge marked by 2 FR (hor). N pier, Oc G 4s 3m (W metal post on concrete column). VHF Ch 12 16 (when vessel due). HM ☎823549; Dr 823597. Facilities: **Outer hbr** ⚓ ⚓ ▭ ◖(mob); **Irish Quay** ⚓ ▭ ◖; **Inner hbr** ⚓ ▭ ◖; **Town** ▯ ▯ ♦ ⚒.

LAXEY, Isle of Man, **54°13′·46N 04°23′·32W**. AC 2094, 5613. HW +0025 on Dover; +0010 and −2·0m on Liverpool; ML 4m; Duration 0550. The bay gives good shelter in SW to N winds. 2 yellow ♂s (seasonal) are close E of hbr ent; 2 more are 1M S in Garwick Bay. ⚓ about 2ca S of pier hds or in Garwick Bay. The hbr dries 3·0m to rk and is only suitable for small yachts. Beware rks on N side of the narrow ent. Keep close to pier after entering to avoid training wall on NE side. ▭ on inside of pier; inner basin is full of local boats. Pier hd lt Oc R 3s 7m 5M, obsc when brg <318°. Bkwtr hd lt Oc G 3s 7m. Harbour Office ☎861663. Facilities: ⚓ ✉ Ⓑ ✕ ◻.

ISLE OF MAN

(Charts 2094, 2696, 5613) For pilotage information and harbours of IoM, see *IOM Sailing Directions, Tidal Streams and Anchorages*, published by Hunter Publications. For notes on crossing the Irish Sea, see 6.4. There are four choices rounding S of IoM:

- In bad weather, or at night, keep S of Chicken Rk.
- In good conditions, pass between Chicken Rk and Calf of Man.
- By day, with winds <F 3 and a reliable engine giving >5kn, Calf Snd between Calf of Man and IoM is navigable. Pass between Kitterland Is and Thousla Rk, marked by bn Fl R 3s 9m 4M.
- Little Sound, a minor unmarked channel, runs E of Kitterland Is.

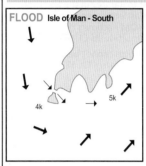
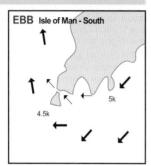

▶ The stream runs strongly through Calf Sound, N-going at HW Liverpool –0145, and S-going at HW Liverpool +0345, Sp rate 3·5kn. W of Calf of Man the stream runs N and S, but changes direction off Chicken Rk running E/W between Calf of Man and Langness Pt. Overfalls extend E from Chicken Rk on E-going stream, beginning at HW L'pool + 0610, and N from the rock on W-going stream, which begins at HW L'pool. The Skerranes (drying) extend 1ca SW Of Langness Pt (lt). Tidal stream run strongly, with eddies and a race. A dangerous sea builds to the E of Langness peninsula in strong winds. Here the NE-going stream begins at HW L'pool +0545, and the SW-going at HW L'pool –0415, sp rates 2·25kn. ◀

⚓ (exposed to the E) in Derby Haven, N of St Michael's Is. From here to Douglas and on to Maughold Hd (lt), there are no dangers more than 4ca offshore.

▶ Inshore the SW-going stream runs for 9 hrs and the NE-going for 3 hrs, since an eddy forms during the second half of the main NE-going stream. Off Maughold Hd the NE-going stream begins at HW L'pool +0500, and the SW-going at HW L'pool –0415. ◀

SE, E and NW of Pt of Ayre are dangerous banks, on which seas break in bad weather. These are Whitestone Bank (least depth 2·0m), Bahama Bank (1·5m), Ballacash Bank (2·7 m), King William Banks (3·3m), and Strunakill Bank (6·7m).

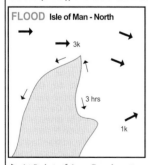
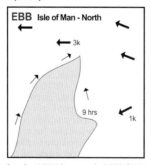

▶ At Point of Ayre E-going stream begins HW Liverpool –0600 (HW Dover –0545). W-going stream at Point of Ayre begins HW L'pool

(HW Dover +0015). A counter tide runs inside the banks to the East. In Ramsey Bay the S-going tide runs for 3 hours from L'pool +0515 (Dover +0530). In Ramsey Bay the N-going tide runs for 9 hours from L'pool –0345 (Dover –0330).◀

The W coast of IOM has few pilotage hazards. A spit with depth of 1·4m runs 2ca offshore from Rue Pt. Jurby Rk (depth 2·7m) lies 3ca off Jurby Hd. Craig Rk (depth 4m) and shoals lie 2·5M NNE of Peel.

BARROW TO CONWY

(AC 2010, 1981, 1978, 5613) Ent to Barrow-in-Furness (AC 3164) is about 1M S of Hilpsford Pt at S end of Walney Island where the lt ho is prominent. W winds cause rough sea in the entrance. Moorings and ⚓ off Piel and Roa Islands, but space is limited.

▶ The stream sets across the narrow channel, which is well marked, but shallow in patches. Stream runs hard on ebb. Coming from the S it is possible with sufficient rise of tide to cross the sands between Fleetwood and Barrow. ◀

Barrow Wind Farm (30 turbines) marked by FR and Fl Y lights and fog signals on some structures is centred approx 7·6M SSW of Barrow-in-Furness. Further W lies the W Duddon Sands Wind Farm (108 turbines). Its W'rn extremity is marked by a tall Met Mast. To the North Walney and Ormonde (30 turbines) wind farms straddle the northern approaches to Barrow and the Lune.

Lune Deep, 2M NW of Rossall Pt, is the entrance to Morecambe Bay (chart 2010), and gives access to the ferry/commercial port of Heysham, Glasson Dock, and Fleetwood; it is well buoyed.

▶ Streams run 3·5kn at sp. ◀

Most of the Bay is encumbered with drying sands, intersected by chans which are subject to change. S of Morecambe B, beware shoals and drying outfall (2·0m) extending 3M W of Rossall Pt. Further S, R. Ribble gives access via a long drying chan to the marina at Preston.

Queen's Channel and Crosby Chan (AC 1951 & 1978) are entered E of the Bar light float. They are well buoyed, dredged and preserved by training banks, and give main access to R Mersey and Liverpool. Keep clear of commercial shipping. From the N the old Formby chan is abandoned, but possible near HW. Towards HW in moderate winds a yacht can cross the training bank (level varies between 2m and 3m above CD) E of Great Burbo Bank, if coming from the W; Rock Chan, which is unmarked and dries in parts, may also be used but beware wrecks. W of Bar Lt Vessel the Douglas oil field, an IMO Area to be Avoided centred on 53°32'·23N 03°34'·70W, effectively separates the traffic flow.

In good weather at neaps, the Dee Estuary (AC 1953, 1978) is accessible for boats able to take the ground. But most of the estuary dries and banks extend 6M seaward. Chans shift, and buoys are moved as required. Main ent is Welsh Chan, but if coming from N, Hilbre Swash runs W of Hilbre Is.

▶ Stream runs hard in chans when banks are dry. ◀

Sailing W from the Dee on the ebb, it is feasible to take the Inner Passage (buoyed) S of West Hoyle Spit, which gives some protection from onshore winds at half tide or below. Rhyl is a tidal hbr marked offshore by a SWM, not accessible in strong onshore winds, but gives shelter for yachts able to take the ground. Abergele Rd, Colwyn B and Llandudno B are possible ⚓s in settled weather and S winds. Conwy and Deganwy harbours offer good shelter in marinas.

▶ Between Point of Ayr and Great Ormes Head the E-going stream begins at HW Liverpool +0600, and the W-going at HW Liverpool –0015, sp rates 3kn. ◀

North Hoyle Wind Farm consists of 30 turbines and is centred on 53°25'·00N 03°27'·00W. Each turbine is 58m high, with 40m diameter blades and clearance of 18m. Many of them are lit. Gwynt-y-Mor Wind Farm centred on 53°28'·20N 03°37'·70W. The area is delineated by cardinal and yellow buoys. Underwater obstructions will exist throughout. Vessels are advised to keep well clear and not enter the area.

3.9 PEEL

Isle of Man 54°13′·61N 04°41′·68W ✿✿⚓⚓✿✿✿

CHARTS AC 2094, 2696, 5613; Imray C62; Y70

TIDES +0005 Dover; ML 2·9; Duration 0545

Standard Port LIVERPOOL (→)

Times				Height (metres)			
High Water		Low Water		MHWS	MHWN	MLWN	MLWS
0000	0600	0200	0700	9·4	7·5	3·2	1·1
1200	1800	1400	1900				
Differences PEEL							
+0010	+0010	-0020	-0030	-4·2	-3·2	-1·7	-0·7

SHELTER Good, except in strong NW to NE winds when ent should not be attempted. 4 Y ⚓s (seasonal) off S groyne in about 2m. Fin keelers may be able to berth on N bkwtr in 5m. The marina is in the Inner Harbour with berthing on pontoons and alongside harbour wall for boats up to 15m LOA. Pass dimensions on Ch 12. Approach dries 1·4m; access approx HW±2 when flapgate lowered and through swing bridge. Maintained depth 2·5m.

NAVIGATION WPT 54°14′·00N 04°41′·78W, 207°/5ca to groyne lt. Beware groyne on S side of harbour ent, submerged at half tide.

LIGHTS AND MARKS Power stn chy (83m, grey with B top) at S end of inner hbr is conspic from W and N; chy brg 203° leads to hbr ent. Groyne lt and Clock Tr (conspic) in transit 200° are almost on same line. Peel Castle and 2 twrs are conspic on St Patrick's Isle to NW of hbr. 207° ldg lts, Fl R 5s. The E and W abutments to the Inner Hbr ent are marked by lts Fl R 3s and Fl G 3s respectively. Traffic signals at marina entrance. Swing bridge has FR lts at centre span. Fl Y lts = flap gate being raised lowered; bridge opening/closing.

COMMUNICATIONS (Code 01624) CGOC (01407) 762051; ☎ 0900 6243 322; Police 697327; Dr 843636. Harbour Office 842338, Mobile 07624 495036.
Peel Hbr VHF Ch 12 16 (HW±2), HO for Swing Bridge – other times call *Douglas Hbr Control* Ch 12 for remote bridge opening.

FACILITIES Outer Hbr, ⌿ see 3.8; **Marina** 120⌿ inc ⓥ, £1.72; access via flapgate; ⚓⚓⚓⚓⚓⚓ ⚓⚓(mob); **Peel Sailing & Cruising Club** ☎842390 ⚑ (key from Harbour Office), ✗ ⚓ ⚓. **Town** ⚓ ⚓⚓⚓ ACA ✉ Ⓑ ⚓ ✗ ⚓ ⚓ (bus to Douglas & ferry), ✈ Ronaldsway.

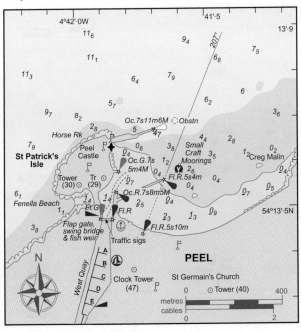

PEEL

3.10 PORT ST MARY

Isle of Man 54°04′·43N 04°43′·73W ✿✿⚓⚓✿✿✿

CHARTS AC 2094, 2696, 5613; Imray C62; Y70

TIDES +0020 Dover; ML 3·2; Duration 0605

Standard Port LIVERPOOL (→)

Times				Height (metres)			
High Water		Low Water		MHWS	MHWN	MLWN	MLWS
0000	0600	0200	0700	9·4	7·5	3·2	1·1
1200	1800	1400	1900				
Differences PORT ST MARY							
+0010	+0020	-0015	-0035	-3·5	-2·7	-1·6	-0·6
CALF SOUND							
+0010	+0010	-0020	-0030	-3·3	-2·7	-1·2	-0·5
PORT ERIN							
+0018	+0010	-0013	-0028	-4·1	-3·3	-1·6	-0·6

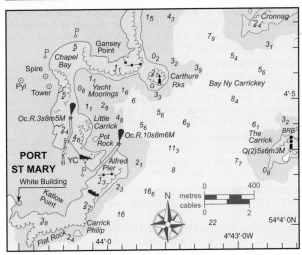

SHELTER Very good except in E or SE winds. ⚓ S of Gansey Pt, but poor holding. 5 yellow ⚓s (seasonal) between Alfred Pier and Little Carrick.

NAVIGATION WPT 54°04′·21N 04°43′·37W, 295°/0·3M to Alfred Pier lt. Rocky outcrops to SE of pier to 2ca offshore. Beware lobster/crab pots, especially between Calf of Man and Langness Pt.

LIGHTS AND MARKS Alfred Pier, Oc R 10s, in transit 295° with Inner Pier, Oc R 3s, W twr + R band, leads clear S of The Carrick Rk, in centre of bay, which is marked by IDM bn, Q (2) 5s 6m 3M. A conspic TV mast (133m), 5ca WNW of hbr, in transit with Alfred Pier lt leads 290° towards the hbr and also clears The Carrick rock.

COMMUNICATIONS (Code 01624) CGOC (01407) 762051; ☎ 0900 6243 322, Police 697327; Dr 832226. HM 833205.
Port St Mary Hbr VHF Ch 12 16 (when vessel due or through Douglas Hbr Control Ch 12).

FACILITIES Alfred Pier ⌿ see 3.8, ⚓⚓⚓⚓ ⚓(mob); **Inner Hbr** dries 2·4m on sand; ⌿⚓⚓⚓⚓ ⚓ ⚓ Ⓐ; **Isle of Man YC** ☎832088, ⚓⚑⚑. **Town** ⚓✉Ⓑ⚓✗⚓⚓ (bus to Douglas, qv for ferries), ✈ Ronaldsway.

MINOR HARBOUR EAST OF CASTLETOWN

DERBY HAVEN, Isle of Man, **54°04′·65N 04°36′·45W.** Tides & charts as above. Rather remote bay exposed only to NE/E winds. ⚓ in centre of bay, NW of St Michael's Island, in 3-5m. A detached bkwtr on NW side of the bay gives shelter to craft able to dry out behind it. Lts: Iso G 2s on S end of bkwtr. Aero FR (occas) at Ronaldsway airport, NW of bay. Facilities: at Castletown (1½M) or Port St Mary.

3.11 DOUGLAS

Isle of Man **54°08'·87N 04°27'·96W** ✹✹✹✹⬡⬡🌸🌸🌸

CHARTS AC 2094, 2696, 5613; Imray C62; Y70

TIDES +0009 Dover; ML 3·8; Duration 0600
Standard Port LIVERPOOL (→)

Times				Height (metres)			
High Water		Low Water		MHWS	MHWN	MLWN	MLWS
0000	0600	0200	0700	9·4	7·5	3·2	1·1
1200	1800	1400	1900				
Differences DOUGLAS							
+0010	+0020	–0020	–0030	–2·5	–2·1	–0·8	–0·3

SHELTER Good except in NE winds. Very heavy seas run in during NE gales. Outer hbr: Victoria and King Edward VIII piers are for commercial vessels/ferries. At inner end of Battery Pier in summer about 18 boats can raft up on pontoon; untenable in NE/E winds. Complete shelter in inner hbr, with possible pontoon berths, flapgate lowers on the flood and rises on the ebb at 4·4m above CD, lifting bridge opens every ½H subject to tide/road traffic conditions (request opening on VHF Ch12).

NAVIGATION WPT 54°09'·01N 04°27'·67W (abeam No 1 SHM buoy, Q (3) G 5s), 229°/0·47M to front ldg lt. Appr from NE of No 1 buoy (to avoid overfalls E of Princess Alexandra Pier) and await port entry sig, or call on VHF Ch 12. There is no bar. Keep clear of large vessels and ferries. Beware concrete step at end of dredged area (◊ mark on King Edward VIII Pier) and cill at ent to inner hbr.

LIGHTS AND MARKS Douglas Head Fl 10s 32m 24M. Ldg lts 229°, both Oc Bu 10s 9/12m 5M, synch; front W △; rear W ▽, both on R border. IPTS Nos 2, 3 and 5 shown from mast on Victoria Pier. Dolphin at N end of Alexandra Pier 2FR (vert).

COMMUNICATIONS (Code 01624) CGOC (01407) 762051; ⚓ 0900 6243 322, Police 697327; ⊞ 650000. Harbour Control 686628 (H24).

Douglas Hbr Control VHF Ch **12** 16 (H24); also broadcasts nav warnings for IoM ports and coastal waters on Ch 12 including weather and tidal info on request.

FACILITIES Outer Hbr ⌓ see 3.8, ⚓ ⌐ ⛴ at pontoon, ⛽ ⌂(mob); **Inner Hbr** (Pontoons, N and S Quays) 110⌓; ♥ according to space, ⌐ ⛴ ⬡ ⌂; **Douglas Bay YC** ☎673965, ⚓ ⌐ ⬡ 0930-2300 ⬚. **Services** ⬡ ⚒ ⚙ ⬚ ⬛ ACA, Divers, Kos. **Town** www.gov.im ⬛ ⊠ Ⓑ ⬚ 🛒 ✗ ⬚ ✈ Ronaldsway. **Ferries** Liverpool; 16/week; 2½ hrs; IoM. Heysham; 16/week; 3½ hrs; Steam Packet (www.steam-packet.com). Also to Dublin and Belfast.

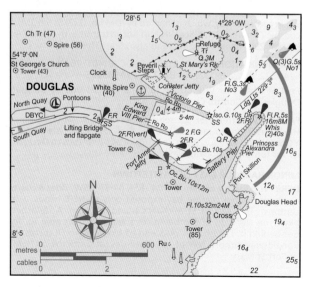

3.12 RAMSEY

Isle of Man **54°19'·44N 04°22'·49W** ✹✹⬡⬡🌸🌸

CHARTS AC 2094, 2696, 5613; Imray C62; Y70

TIDES +0020 Dover; ML 4·2; Duration 0545
Standard Port LIVERPOOL (→)

Times				Height (metres)			
High Water		Low Water		MHWS	MHWN	MLWN	MLWS
0000	0600	0200	0700	9·4	7·5	3·2	1·1
1200	1800	1400	1900				
Differences RAMSEY							
+0010	+0020	–0010	–0020	–2·0	–1·6	–0·9	–0·2

SHELTER Very good in inner harbour but entrance difficult in strong NE-E winds. Hbr dries 1·8m–6m. Access approx HW –2½ to HW +2. Berth on Town quay (S side) or as directed by HM on entry. 5 yellow ⚓s are close to Queen's Pier hd (seasonal). Note: Landing on Queen's Pier is prohibited.

NAVIGATION WPT 54°19'·44N 04°21'·89W, 270°/0·37M to ent. The foreshore dries out 1ca to seaward of the pier hds.

LIGHTS AND MARKS No ldg lts/marks. Relative to hbr ent, Pt of Ayre, Fl (4) 20s 32m 19M, is 5·5M N; Maughold Hd, Fl (3) 30s 65m 21M, is 3M SE; Albert Tr (☐ stone tr 14m, on hill 130m) is conspic 7ca S; and Snaefell (617m) bears 220°/5M. Inside the hbr an Iso G 4s, G SHM post, marks the S tip of Mooragh Bank; it is not visible from seaward. 2FR (hor) on each side mark the centre of swing bridge.

COMMUNICATIONS (Code 01624) CGOC (01407) 762051; ⚓ 0900 6243 322, Police 812234; Dr 813881; ⊞ 811811. Harbour Office 812245, mob 07624 460304.

Ramsey Hbr VHF Ch **12** 16 (0800-1600LT and when a vessel is due); Other times call *Douglas Hbr Control* Ch **12**.

FACILITIES Outer Hbr: E Quay ☎812245, only for commercial vessels (frequent movements H24); **Town Quay** (S side) ⌓ see 3.8, ⛴ ⬡. **Inner Hbr, W Quay** ⌓ ⬡ ⛴ ⌐ (Grid); **N Quay** ⌓ ⛽ ⛴; **Shipyard Quay** ⌐; **Old Hbr** ⚓ ⌐ ⌓; **Manx S&CC** ☎813494, ⌓. **Services** ⬡ ⚒ ⚙ ⬚ Ⓔ. **Town** ⬛ Kos, ⊠ Ⓑ ⬚ 🛒 ✗ ⬚ @ in Library; ⇌ (bus to Douglas for ferries), ✈ Ronaldsway.

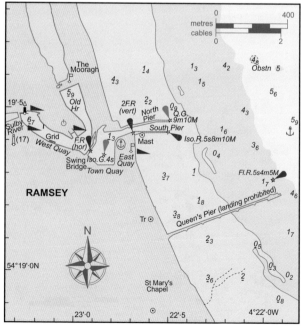

3.13 GLASSON DOCK

Lancashire 53°59'·98N 02°50'·93W ✹✹♨♨♨♨❁❁

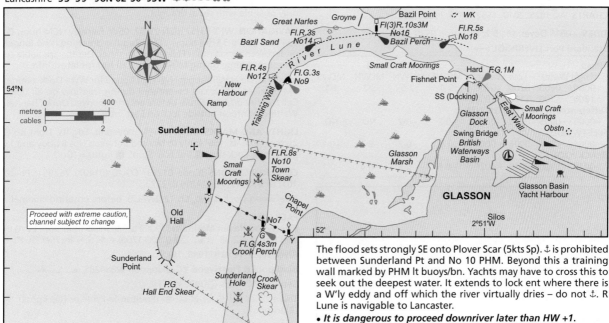

The flood sets strongly SE onto Plover Scar (5kts Sp). ⚓ is prohibited between Sunderland Pt and No 10 PHM. Beyond this a training wall marked by PHM lt buoys/bn. Yachts may have to cross this to seek out the deepest water. It extends to lock ent where there is a W'ly eddy and off which the river virtually dries – do not ⚓. R Lune is navigable to Lancaster.

• **It is dangerous to proceed downriver later than HW +1.**

LIGHTS AND MARKS Plover Scar, Fl 2s, on with Cockersand, FW, leads 084° up to Nos 2/3 buoys; then follow buoyed chan which shifts.

Tfc Sigs at Glasson DockheadW side
- ● = lock manned, but shut – No entry
- ● = lock open, clear to enter
- Fl = gate opening or closing
Tfc Sigs inside lock: ● = gate open ● = gate shut.

COMMUNICATIONS (Code 01524) CGOC (01407) 762051; Police 101 🏥 765944; HM 07910 315606.

VHF Ch 16 **69** (HW–1½ to HW Liverpool).

FACILITIES Glasson Basin Marina www.bwml.co.uk ☎751491; 240 +20🅥 (£12·50/craft); 🛒 ♦ ⚒ 🔧(50t) ⚓.

Glasson SC ☎751089 ♠ ▬ 🗒; **Lune CC** Access only near HW.

Town 🏨 ✉ 🍴 ✕ 🗒 ⇌ (bus to Lancaster 4M), ✈ (Blackpool).

ADJACENT HARBOURS IN MORECAMBE BAY
BARROW-IN-FURNESS, Cumbria, 54°05'·64N 03°13'·44W. AC 1826, 2010, 3164, 5613. HW +0030 on Dover; ML 5·0m; Duration 0530 (⟵). Good shelter but open to SE winds. Drying moorings off Piel and Roa Islands or ⚓ clear of fairway. Marks/lts: Walney Island Lt ho (conspic stone tr), Fl 15s 21m 23M (obsc 122°-127° within 3M of shore). Directions: From Lightning Knoll SWM lt buoy, ldg lts, front Q 7m 14M; rear (6ca from front), Iso 2s 13m 14M (lattice structures) lead 041°/3·7M past Halfway Shoal bn, QR 16m 10M (RY chequers), to Bar lt buoy abeam Walney Is lt ho in dredged chan (call HM for latest depth). Inner Chan ldg lts, front Q 9m 14M, rear Iso 2s 14m 14M, lead 005° past Piel Is. 3M NW at Barrow, commercial docks reached via buoyed/lit Walney Chan, dredged to 2·5m, which must be kept clear. HM ☎(01229) 822911; VHF *Barrow Port Radio* Ch 12 16 (H24).

Piel Is, ruined castle, jetty and moorings on E side. Facilities: Inn.

Roa Is, 5ca N, has jetty at S end and moorings on E & W sides. ▬ (Roa Is Boat Club ☎(01229) 825291). Causeway joins to mainland. Facilities: Hotel at Rampside, 🍴.

HEYSHAM, Lancashire, 54°02'·01N 02°55'·96W. AC 1826, 2010, 1552, 5613. HW +0015 on Dover; ML 5·1m; Duration 0545. See 3.13. Good shelter, but yachts not normally accepted without special reason. Beware high speed ferries and oil rig supply ships. Ldg lts 102°, both F Bu 11/14m 2M, Y+B ◊ on masts. S jetty lt 2 FG (vert); Siren 30s. S pier hd ,Oc G 7·5s 9m 6M. N pier hd, 2FR (vert) 11m, obsc from seaward. Ent sigs: R flag or ● = no entry; no sig = no dep; 2 R flags or 2 ● = no ent or dep. VHF Ch 14 74 16 (H24). HM ☎(01524) 852373. Facilities: ⚓ 🍴 ✕ 🗒 at Morecambe (2M).

CHARTS AC 1826, 1552, 2010, 5613; Imray C62

TIDES +0020 Dover; ML No data; Duration 0535

Standard Port LIVERPOOL (⟶)

Times				Height (metres)			
High Water		Low Water		MHWS	MHWN	MLWN	MLWS
0000	0600	0200	0700	9·4	7·5	3·2	1·1
1200	1800	1400	1900				
Differences BARROW-IN-FURNESS (Ramsden Dock)							
+0020	+0020	+0010	+0010	–0·1	–0·4	0·0	+0·1
ULVERSTON							
+0025	+0045	ND	ND	–0·1	–0·2	ND	ND
ARNSIDE							
+0105	+0140	ND	ND	+0·4	+0·1	ND	ND
MORECAMBE							
+0010	+0015	+0025	+0010	+0·1	–0·1	–0·3	0·0
HEYSHAM							
+0014	+0012	+0002	–0003	+0·2	–0·1	–0·1	+0·1
GLASSON DOCK							
+0025	+0035	+0215	+0235	–2·8	–3·1	ND	ND
LANCASTER							
+0115	+0035	DR	DR	–5·1	–5·0	DR	DR

NOTE: At Glasson Dock LW time differences give the end of a LW stand which lasts up to 2 hrs at sp.

SHELTER Very good in marina, sea lock (9m wide) opens into Glasson Dock HW–¾ to HW (Liverpool) (daylight hrs only Nov-Mar) Inner lock/swing bridge lead into BWML basin. There are no safe LW berths on the outer quay walls.

NAVIGATION WPT 53°58'·63N 03°00'·03W (Lune WCM), 4·2M to Plover Scar. Enter buoyed chan at HW–1½ (-1¼ Nps). It changes frequently. For latest info call Port Commission (☎01524 751724).

3.14 FLEETWOOD

Lancashire 53°55'·49N 03°00'·15W ✧✧✧✧♦♦♦✿✿

CHARTS AC 1826, 2010, 1552, 5613; Imray C62

TIDES +0015 Dover; ML 5.2; Duration 0530

Standard Port LIVERPOOL (→)

Times				Height (metres)			
High Water		Low Water		MHWS	MHWN	MLWN	MLWS
0000	0600	0200	0700	9·4	7·5	3·2	1·1
1200	1800	1400	1900				
Differences WYRE LIGHTHOUSE							
−0005	−0005	0000	−0005	−0·2	−0·2	ND	ND
FLEETWOOD							
−0004	−0004	−0006	−0006	0·0	−0·2	−0·1	+0·1
BLACKPOOL							
−0010	0000	−0010	−0020	−0·5	−0·5	−0·4	−0·1

SHELTER Excellent in Fleetwood Haven Marina. Sheltered ⚓, clear of turning circle, off Knott End pier on E bank to await tide. Passage up-river to Skippool (5M) needs local knowledge and is only possible with shoal draught.

NAVIGATION WPT 53°57'·67N 03°02'·05W, Fairway NCM buoy, Q, 134°/3ca to No 3 SHM buoy, VQ.G. Regular dredging is no longer undertaken to maintain Fleetwood channel. Depths are liable to frequent change owing to siltation. Call HM for latest info.

Ideally arrive at WPT about HW-1½ if bound for Wyre Dock marina, 3M up-river, which can be entered during freeflow on all tides. Call *Fleetwood Dock Radio* before entering buoyed Dock Channel. Waiting pontoon outside lock on East Jetty.

LIGHTS AND MARKS Chan is well buoyed/lit. Ldg lts, front Iso G 2s; rear Iso G 4s, 156° (only to be used between Nos 8 buoy and 11 perch bn). Lock sigs: ● lights = 'Stop'; ● lights = 'Go'.

COMMUNICATIONS (Code 01253) CGOC (01407) 762051; Police 101; Dr 873312. HM (ABP) 872323.
Fleetwood Dock Radio, Ch 12 (HW±2), before entering channel.

FACILITIES
Fleetwood Haven Marina ☎879062 ⚓ 340 inc 🅥 (max 20m LOA) in two basins, £2.35, ♿ ▬ 🖪 🐟(0800-1700) ⛽ ✕ 🛁 🚻 🛒(75t) ✕.

River Wyre YC ☎811948, 1🅥.

Blackpool & Fleetwood YC (Skippool) ☎884205, ▬ ⌷ ⛽ 🛁.

Services ✕ ⚒ 🖭 Ⓔ(☎823535) ⚓ 🛁.

Town 🏧 🏧 ✉ Ⓑ 🚆 ✕ 🛒 ⇌ (Poulton-le-Fylde or Blackpool), ✈ (Blackpool).

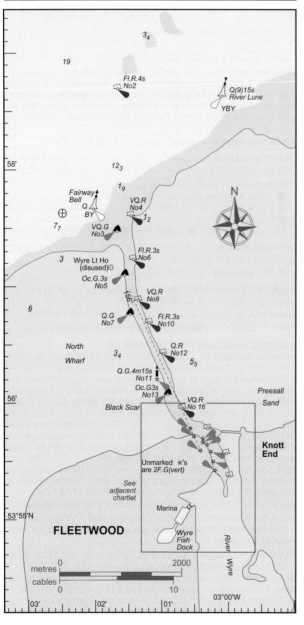

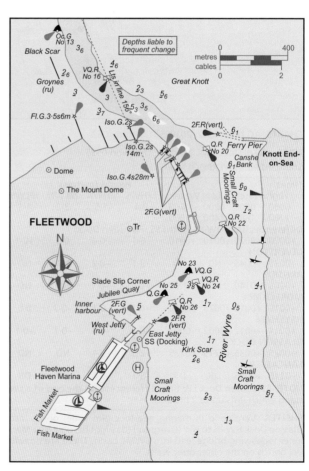

3.15 RIVER RIBBLE/PRESTON

Lancashire 53°43'·51N 03°00'·08W ✿✿⚓♦♦♦✿✿

CHARTS AC 1826, 1981, 5613; Imray C62

TIDES +0013 Dover; ML No data; Duration 0520

Standard Port LIVERPOOL (→)

Times				Height (metres)			
High Water		Low Water		MHWS	MHWN	MLWN	MLWS
0000	0600	0200	0700	9·4	7·5	3·2	1·1
1200	1800	1400	1900				
Differences PRESTON							
+0015	+0015	+0330	+0305	−4·1	−4·2	−3·1	−1·0

LW time differences give the end of a LW stand lasting 3½ hrs.

SOUTHPORT							
−0015	−0005	ND	ND	−0·4	−0·4	ND	ND
FORMBY							
−0010	−0005	−0025	−0025	−0·4	−0·2	−0·3	−0·1

SHELTER Good in Preston Marina (5m depth) 15M upriver. Possible drying berths on the N bank at Lytham or Freckleton, or 2M up R Douglas access only near HW.

NAVIGATION WPT **A** 53°41'·75N 03°08'·90W, Gut SWM lt buoy. The chartlet shows only the outer 6M of the estuary. Due to changes to the Gut Channel and South Gut, best water is now in the Gut Channel which almost dries but not to the extent shown on AC 1981. It is navigable approx HW±2. South Gut is no longer discernible and should not be used without local knowledge.

Leave WPT **A** at HW Liverpool −2 then track 070°/2·6M to WPT **B** (53°42'·90N 03°05'·00W). Continue up Gut Channel leaving the first 3 perches about 100m to starboard. Leave 11½M perch 100m to port. The river trends 080° between training walls (dry 3m), marked by lit perches. The remaining channel is straightforward but night entry is not advised.

LIGHTS AND MARKS 14½M perch is the most seaward channel mark. Up-river of 11½M perch there is a PHM buoy and perch (off chartlet), both Fl R 5s. 4 SHM perches, Fl G 5s, lead to 5M perch, Fl

(2) G 10s, marking mouth of unlit R Douglas. 3M and 2M perches are Fl G 5s; 1M perch is Fl G 10s. Warton airfield beacon, Mo (WQ) G 9s occas, is N abeam 6M perch, Fl G 5s.

COMMUNICATIONS (Code 01772) CGOC (01407) 762051; Police 101; Ⓗ 710408. Preston locks 726871. At Preston, for locks call *Riversway* Ch **16** 14 (HW −1½ to +2); Marina Ch 80 (HO); Douglas BY Ch 16 when vessel due.

FACILITIES Waiting berth (2m draught) outside storm gates (usually open). Traffic lts at marina lock; plan below. Lockmaster on duty HW±2, on daylight tides (0700-2000 Apr-Sep by Lavers Liverpool Tide Tables). This and tidal height should permit locking from −1 HW +2 on demand. Swing bridge opens in unison with locks. From 1 Oct-31 Mar contact marina to book locking 24 hrs in advance.

Preston Marina www.prestonmarina.co.uk ☎733595, mob 07770 505094, £1·60, ♿ ♠ ⛽ ✕ ⚒ ⤮(25t, 45t by arrangement) ⚓ ACA 🛒 ✕.

Douglas BY, ☎812462 mob 07967 184528, ⤥ ⚓£0·70 ⚓ ♠ ✕ ⚒ ⤮(20t) ⚓.

Freckleton BY ☎632439 mob 07957 820881, ⤥ ⚓£5/yacht ⚓ ⚒ ⚓.

Ribble Cruising Club ☎(01253) 739983.

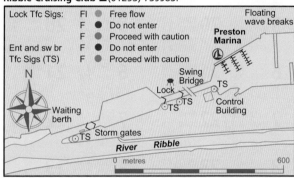

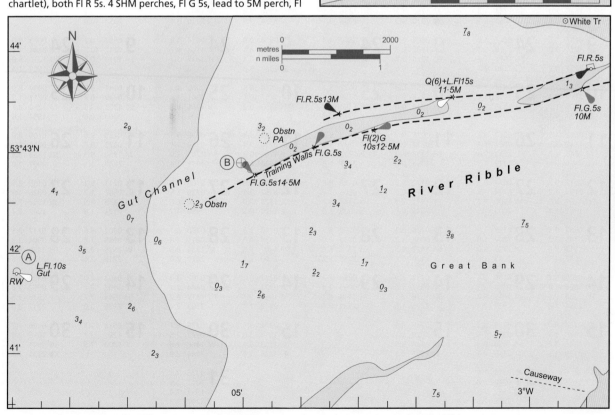

STANDARD TIME (UT)
For Summer Time add ONE hour in **non-shaded areas**

LIVERPOOL (GLADSTONE DOCK) LAT 53°27'N LONG 3°01'W
TIMES AND HEIGHTS OF HIGH AND LOW WATERS

Dates in red are **SPRINGS**
Dates in blue are **NEAPS**

YEAR 2016

JANUARY

Day	Time	m	Day	Time	m
1 F	0314 / 0943 / 1534 / 2226	8.0 / 2.9 / 8.1 / 2.9	**16** SA	0314 / 0956 / 1539 / 2229 ☽	8.7 / 2.1 / 8.9
2 SA	0404 / 1030 / 1629 / 2319 ☽	7.6 / 3.3 / 7.7 / 3.2	**17** SU	0411 / 1052 / 1640 / 2329	8.3 / 2.4 / 8.5 / 2.3
3 SU	0504 / 1131 / 1734	7.3 / 3.5 / 7.4	**18** M	0518 / 1200 / 1751	8.0 / 2.6 / 8.3
4 M	0026 / 0612 / 1245 / 1843	3.3 / 7.3 / 3.6 / 7.4	**19** TU	0042 / 0634 / 1320 / 1906	2.5 / 7.9 / 2.7 / 8.2
5 TU	0135 / 0720 / 1357 / 1948	3.2 / 7.4 / 3.3 / 7.6	**20** W	0200 / 0748 / 1438 / 2018	2.5 / 8.1 / 2.4 / 8.4
6 W	0235 / 0819 / 1457 / 2044	2.9 / 7.8 / 2.9 / 7.9	**21** TH	0310 / 0853 / 1546 / 2120	2.2 / 8.5 / 2.0 / 8.6
7 TH	0327 / 0908 / 1548 / 2131	2.5 / 8.2 / 2.5 / 8.3	**22** F	0410 / 0948 / 1644 / 2213	1.9 / 8.8 / 1.6 / 8.9
8 F	0413 / 0951 / 1636 / 2212	2.1 / 8.6 / 2.0 / 8.6	**23** SA	0502 / 1036 / 1734 / 2259	1.7 / 9.1 / 1.3 / 9.1
9 SA	0457 / 1031 / 1721 / 2252	1.8 / 9.0 / 1.7 / 8.9	**24** SU	0547 / 1118 / 1818 / 2340 ○	1.5 / 9.3 / 1.2
10 SU	0540 / 1110 / 1805 / 2332 ●	1.5 / 9.3 / 1.4 / 9.1	**25** M	0627 / 1156 / 1858	1.4 / 9.4 / 1.1
11 M	0622 / 1149 / 1848	1.3 / 9.5 / 1.2	**26** TU	0017 / 0702 / 1233 / 1933	9.2 / 1.4 / 9.4 / 1.3
12 TU	0012 / 0704 / 1231 / 1931	9.3 / 1.2 / 9.6 / 1.1	**27** W	0052 / 0734 / 1306 / 2005	9.1 / 1.6 / 9.2 / 1.5
13 W	0055 / 0745 / 1314 / 2012	9.3 / 1.3 / 9.6 / 1.1	**28** TH	0125 / 0804 / 1339 / 2035	8.9 / 1.8 / 9.0 / 1.8
14 TH	0138 / 0826 / 1358 / 2054	9.2 / 1.4 / 9.5 / 1.3	**29** F	0159 / 0833 / 1413 / 2103	8.6 / 2.1 / 8.7 / 2.1
15 F	0224 / 0909 / 1446 / 2139	9.0 / 1.7 / 9.2 / 1.6	**30** SA	0235 / 0905 / 1450 / 2135	8.3 / 2.5 / 8.3 / 2.5
			31 SU	0314 / 0942 / 1532 / 2215	7.9 / 2.8 / 7.9 / 2.9

FEBRUARY

Day	Time	m	Day	Time	m
1 M	0402 / 1030 / 1624 / 2310 ☽	7.5 / 3.2 / 7.5 / 3.3	**16** TU	0449 / 1135 / 1726	8.0 / 2.6 / 8.0
2 TU	0503 / 1135 / 1734	7.2 / 3.5 / 7.2	**17** W	0013 / 0608 / 1300 / 1847	2.7 / 7.7 / 2.8 / 7.8
3 W	0026 / 0618 / 1259 / 1854	3.4 / 7.2 / 3.5 / 7.2	**18** TH	0139 / 0730 / 1425 / 2007	2.8 / 7.8 / 2.6 / 7.9
4 TH	0147 / 0732 / 1416 / 2006	3.2 / 7.4 / 3.2 / 7.5	**19** F	0257 / 0841 / 1537 / 2112	2.6 / 8.2 / 2.1 / 8.3
5 F	0252 / 0834 / 1519 / 2103	2.8 / 7.9 / 2.6 / 8.0	**20** SA	0400 / 0937 / 1635 / 2204	2.2 / 8.6 / 1.7 / 8.6
6 SA	0347 / 0924 / 1613 / 2151	2.3 / 8.4 / 2.1 / 8.5	**21** SU	0451 / 1023 / 1722 / 2246	1.8 / 8.9 / 1.4 / 8.9
7 SU	0436 / 1009 / 1703 / 2234	1.8 / 8.9 / 1.5 / 8.9	**22** M	0533 / 1102 / 1801 / 2323 ○	1.6 / 9.2 / 1.2 / 9.1
8 M	0523 / 1051 / 1750 / 2315 ●	1.4 / 9.4 / 1.1 / 9.3	**23** TU	0608 / 1137 / 1836 / 2356	1.4 / 9.3 / 1.1 / 9.1
9 TU	0608 / 1132 / 1835 / 2357	1.0 / 9.7 / 0.7 / 9.6	**24** W	0640 / 1210 / 1907	1.4 / 9.3 / 1.2
10 W	0651 / 1214 / 1918	0.8 / 9.9 / 0.6	**25** TH	0027 / 0709 / 1241 / 1935	9.1 / 1.4 / 9.2 / 1.3
11 TH	0039 / 0733 / 1258 / 1959	9.7 / 0.8 / 10.0 / 0.6	**26** F	0058 / 0737 / 1312 / 2001	9.0 / 1.5 / 9.1 / 1.5
12 F	0122 / 0813 / 1341 / 2039	9.6 / 0.9 / 9.9 / 0.8	**27** SA	0128 / 0805 / 1342 / 2028	8.8 / 1.7 / 8.8 / 1.8
13 SA	0206 / 0854 / 1427 / 2120	9.3 / 1.2 / 9.5 / 1.2	**28** SU	0200 / 0835 / 1413 / 2058	8.6 / 2.0 / 8.5 / 2.2
14 SU	0252 / 0937 / 1516 / 2205	8.9 / 1.6 / 9.1 / 1.8	**29** M	0234 / 0909 / 1448 / 2133	8.2 / 2.4 / 8.1 / 2.6
15 M	0345 / 1029 / 1614 / 2301 ☽	8.5 / 2.1 / 8.5 / 2.3			

MARCH

Day	Time	m	Day	Time	m
1 TU	0313 / 0950 / 1530 / 2218 ☽	7.8 / 2.9 / 7.6 / 3.1	**16** W	0424 / 1117 / 1705 / 2348	8.0 / 2.5 / 7.8 / 2.9
2 W	0404 / 1044 / 1630 / 2324	7.4 / 3.2 / 7.2 / 3.4	**17** TH	0544 / 1243 / 1830	7.6 / 2.8 / 7.5
3 TH	0517 / 1203 / 1756	7.1 / 3.4 / 7.0	**18** F	0118 / 0709 / 1409 / 1952	3.0 / 7.6 / 2.6 / 7.7
4 F	0054 / 0642 / 1334 / 1924	3.4 / 7.2 / 3.2 / 7.3	**19** SA	0240 / 0822 / 1520 / 2057	2.8 / 8.0 / 2.2 / 8.1
5 SA	0215 / 0756 / 1447 / 2032	3.0 / 7.7 / 2.6 / 7.8	**20** SU	0343 / 0918 / 1615 / 2146	2.3 / 8.4 / 1.8 / 8.5
6 SU	0318 / 0854 / 1548 / 2125	2.4 / 8.3 / 2.0 / 8.4	**21** M	0432 / 1002 / 1700 / 2225	2.0 / 8.7 / 1.5 / 8.8
7 M	0413 / 0943 / 1641 / 2211	1.8 / 8.9 / 1.4 / 9.0	**22** TU	0511 / 1040 / 1736 / 2259	1.7 / 9.0 / 1.3 / 9.0
8 TU	0503 / 1028 / 1730 / 2254	1.2 / 9.5 / 0.8 / 9.5	**23** W	0544 / 1113 / 1808 / 2330 ○	1.5 / 9.1 / 1.2 / 9.1
9 W	0550 / 1111 / 1816 / 2337 ●	0.8 / 9.9 / 0.4 / 9.8	**24** TH	0614 / 1144 / 1837	1.4 / 9.2 / 1.2
10 TH	0634 / 1154 / 1859	0.5 / 10.1 / 0.2	**25** F	0000 / 0641 / 1215 / 1903	9.1 / 1.3 / 9.1 / 1.3
11 F	0019 / 0716 / 1238 / 1940	9.9 / 0.4 / 10.2 / 0.2	**26** SA	0030 / 0710 / 1245 / 1931	9.1 / 1.4 / 9.0 / 1.4
12 SA	0102 / 0757 / 1322 / 2020	9.8 / 0.5 / 10.0 / 0.5	**27** SU	0100 / 0739 / 1314 / 1959	8.9 / 1.5 / 8.8 / 1.7
13 SU	0145 / 0838 / 1407 / 2100	9.5 / 0.8 / 9.6 / 1.1	**28** M	0130 / 0811 / 1344 / 2029	8.7 / 1.8 / 8.5 / 2.0
14 M	0231 / 0921 / 1456 / 2143	9.1 / 1.4 / 9.1 / 1.7	**29** TU	0202 / 0844 / 1417 / 2103	8.4 / 2.1 / 8.2 / 2.4
15 TU	0321 / 1011 / 1553 / 2236 ☽	8.5 / 2.0 / 8.4 / 2.4	**30** W	0239 / 0922 / 1458 / 2144	8.1 / 2.5 / 7.8 / 2.9
			31 TH	0326 / 1011 / 1553 / 2242 ☽	7.7 / 2.9 / 7.4 / 3.3

APRIL

Day	Time	m	Day	Time	m
1 F	0433 / 1122 / 1712	7.4 / 3.2 / 7.1	**16** SA	0050 / 0637 / 1341 / 1923	3.1 / 7.6 / 2.6 / 7.6
2 SA	0006 / 0557 / 1252 / 1842	3.4 / 7.3 / 3.0 / 7.3	**17** SU	0209 / 0750 / 1449 / 2029	2.9 / 7.8 / 2.3 / 7.9
3 SU	0135 / 0716 / 1412 / 1957	3.0 / 7.7 / 2.5 / 7.8	**18** M	0312 / 0848 / 1543 / 2117	2.6 / 8.2 / 2.0 / 8.3
4 M	0245 / 0821 / 1517 / 2056	2.4 / 8.3 / 1.9 / 8.5	**19** TU	0401 / 0933 / 1627 / 2156	2.2 / 8.5 / 1.7 / 8.6
5 TU	0345 / 0914 / 1614 / 2145	1.8 / 9.0 / 1.2 / 9.1	**20** W	0440 / 1011 / 1703 / 2230	1.9 / 8.7 / 1.5 / 8.8
6 W	0438 / 1002 / 1706 / 2230	1.2 / 9.5 / 0.7 / 9.5	**21** TH	0513 / 1044 / 1735 / 2301	1.7 / 8.9 / 1.4 / 8.9
7 TH	0527 / 1047 / 1753 / 2314 ●	0.7 / 9.9 / 0.3 / 9.9	**22** F	0544 / 1117 / 1805 / 2332 ○	1.5 / 8.9 / 1.3 / 9.0
8 F	0613 / 1132 / 1837 / 2357	0.4 / 10.2 / 0.1 / 10.0	**23** SA	0614 / 1148 / 1834	1.4 / 9.0 / 1.3
9 SA	0657 / 1217 / 1919	0.2 / 10.2 / 0.2	**24** SU	0003 / 0644 / 1219 / 1903	9.0 / 1.4 / 8.9 / 1.4
10 SU	0041 / 0739 / 1303 / 2000	9.9 / 0.3 / 9.9 / 0.6	**25** M	0034 / 0717 / 1250 / 1934	8.9 / 1.6 / 8.7 / 1.6
11 M	0125 / 0822 / 1350 / 2040	9.6 / 0.7 / 9.5 / 1.1	**26** TU	0105 / 0750 / 1322 / 2007	8.8 / 1.7 / 8.5 / 1.9
12 TU	0211 / 0907 / 1439 / 2124	9.1 / 1.2 / 8.9 / 1.8	**27** W	0139 / 0826 / 1357 / 2042	8.4 / 1.9 / 8.3 / 2.3
13 W	0302 / 0958 / 1535 / 2216	8.6 / 1.8 / 8.3 / 2.4	**28** TH	0217 / 0904 / 1439 / 2123	8.3 / 2.3 / 8.0 / 2.6
14 TH	0403 / 1102 / 1644 / 2325 ☽	8.0 / 2.4 / 7.7 / 3.0	**29** F	0304 / 0952 / 1533 / 2217	8.0 / 2.6 / 7.6 / 3.0
15 F	0518 / 1221 / 1803	7.7 / 2.7 / 7.5	**30** SA	0406 / 1055 / 1644 / 2331 ☽	7.7 / 2.8 / 7.4 / 3.1

Chart Datum: 4·93 metres below Ordnance Datum (Newlyn). HAT is 10·3 metres above Chart Datum.

》》 FREE monthly updates. Register at 《
www.reedsnauticalalmanac.co.uk 《

STANDARD TIME (UT)
For Summer Time add ONE hour in **non-shaded areas**

LIVERPOOL (GLADSTONE DOCK) LAT 53°27′N LONG 3°01′W
TIMES AND HEIGHTS OF HIGH AND LOW WATERS

Dates in red are SPRINGS
Dates in blue are NEAPS

YEAR 2016

MAY

Time	m		Time	m
1 0523	7.7	**16** 0122	3.1
1215	2.7	0705	7.7
SU 1806	7.5	M 1405	2.5
		1945	7.7
2 0054	2.9	**17** 0226	2.9
0639	7.9	0806	7.9
M 1334	2.3	TU 1500	2.3
1921	8.0	2038	8.0
3 0209	2.4	**18** 0318	2.6
0746	8.4	0855	8.1
TU 1443	1.8	W 1546	2.1
2024	8.5	2121	8.3
4 0313	1.8	**19** 0401	2.3
0843	9.0	0937	8.4
W 1544	1.3	TH 1625	1.9
2117	9.0	2158	8.6
5 0410	1.3	**20** 0438	2.0
0935	9.4	1014	8.6
TH 1638	0.8	F 1700	1.7
2205	9.5	2232	8.8
6 0502	0.8	**21** 0513	1.7
1024	9.8	1049	8.7
F 1728	0.5	SA 1733	1.6
● 2251	9.7	○ 2305	8.9
7 0551	0.5	**22** 0548	1.6
1112	10.0	1123	8.8
SA 1814	0.4	SU 1806	1.5
2337	9.9	2338	9.0
8 0638	0.3	**23** 0622	1.5
1159	9.9	1156	8.8
SU 1858	0.4	M 1840	1.5
9 0022	9.8	**24** 0011	9.0
0723	0.4	0658	1.5
M 1247	9.7	TU 1230	8.7
1940	0.7	1914	1.6
10 0108	9.5	**25** 0046	8.9
0808	0.7	0735	1.6
TU 1334	9.3	W 1305	8.6
2023	1.2	1950	1.8
11 0154	9.1	**26** 0122	8.8
0854	1.2	0813	1.7
W 1423	8.8	TH 1344	8.4
2107	1.8	2028	2.1
12 0243	8.7	**27** 0203	8.6
0945	1.7	0853	2.0
TH 1516	8.3	F 1427	8.2
2156	2.4	2110	2.3
13 0340	8.2	**28** 0250	8.3
1042	2.2	0940	2.2
F 1617	7.8	SA 1519	8.0
◔ 2256	2.9	2201	2.6
14 0445	7.8	**29** 0348	8.1
1150	2.6	1036	2.3
SA 1726	7.5	SU 1623	7.8
		◑ 2304	2.7
15 0008	3.1	**30** 0455	8.1
0555	7.6	1144	2.3
SU 1300	2.6	M 1735	7.8
1838	7.5		
		31 0017	2.7
		0606	8.2
		TU 1258	2.2
		1847	8.1

JUNE

Time	m		Time	m
1 0131	2.4	**16** 0227	2.9
0714	8.5	0812	7.8
W 1409	1.8	TH 1459	2.5
1953	8.5	2041	8.0
2 0240	2.0	**17** 0318	2.6
0815	8.9	0901	8.0
TH 1513	1.5	F 1545	2.2
2051	8.9	2124	8.3
3 0342	1.5	**18** 0402	2.3
0912	9.2	0944	8.3
F 1611	1.1	SA 1625	2.0
2143	9.2	2203	8.6
4 0439	1.1	**19** 0444	2.0
1005	9.5	1023	8.5
SA 1704	0.9	SU 1704	1.8
2232	9.5	2240	8.8
5 0532	0.8	**20** 0524	1.7
1055	9.6	1100	8.6
SU 1753	0.7	M 1742	1.6
● 2320	9.6	○ 2315	8.9
6 0622	0.6	**21** 0604	1.5
1144	9.6	1136	8.7
M 1840	0.8	TU 1820	1.5
		2352	9.1
7 0006	9.6	**22** 0643	1.4
0709	0.6	1212	8.8
TU 1232	9.5	W 1859	1.5
1923	1.0		
8 0052	9.5	**23** 0029	9.1
0755	0.8	0723	1.4
W 1319	9.2	TH 1251	8.8
2006	1.4	1937	1.6
9 0137	9.2	**24** 0109	9.0
0841	1.2	0803	1.5
TH 1405	8.8	F 1332	8.7
2048	1.8	2017	1.7
10 0223	8.8	**25** 0151	8.9
0926	1.6	0844	1.6
F 1452	8.4	SA 1416	8.6
2132	2.3	2059	2.0
11 0311	8.4	**26** 0237	8.8
1014	2.1	0928	1.8
SA 1542	8.0	SU 1505	8.4
2220	2.7	2146	2.2
12 0405	8.0	**27** 0329	8.6
1107	2.5	1018	1.9
SU 1639	7.6	M 1601	8.2
◑ 2316	3.1	◔ 2241	2.4
13 0506	7.7	**28** 0429	8.4
1207	2.7	1117	2.1
M 1742	7.4	TU 1706	8.1
		2346	2.5
14 0021	3.2	**29** 0536	8.3
0610	7.6	1225	2.1
TU 1309	2.8	W 1817	8.1
1848	7.4		
15 0127	3.2	**30** 0058	2.4
0714	7.6	0646	8.4
W 1408	2.7	TH 1338	2.0
1949	7.7	1926	8.3

JULY

Time	m		Time	m
1 0212	2.2	**16** 0235	3.0
0753	8.6	0826	7.7
F 1447	1.8	SA 1506	2.6
2030	8.6	2051	8.0
2 0321	1.8	**17** 0329	2.6
0855	8.9	0916	8.0
SA 1550	1.6	SU 1554	2.3
2127	8.9	2136	8.4
3 0423	1.4	**18** 0418	2.2
0952	9.1	0959	8.3
SU 1646	1.3	M 1639	1.9
2219	9.2	2216	8.7
4 0519	1.1	**19** 0503	1.8
1044	9.3	1039	8.6
M 1737	1.2	TU 1722	1.7
● 2307	9.4	○ 2255	9.0
5 0610	0.9	**20** 0547	1.5
1133	9.3	1117	8.8
TU 1824	1.1	W 1804	1.5
2353	9.5	2333	9.2
6 0657	0.8	**21** 0630	1.2
1218	9.3	1156	9.0
W 1908	1.2	TH 1845	1.3
7 0036	9.4	**22** 0012	9.4
0740	0.9	0711	1.1
TH 1301	9.1	F 1236	9.1
1948	1.4	1926	1.3
8 0118	9.2	**23** 0053	9.4
0822	1.2	0752	1.1
F 1342	8.8	SA 1317	9.1
2026	1.7	2006	1.3
9 0157	8.9	**24** 0135	9.4
0901	1.6	0832	1.2
SA 1421	8.5	SU 1400	9.0
2102	2.1	2046	1.5
10 0238	8.6	**25** 0220	9.2
0938	2.0	0913	1.4
SU 1503	8.2	M 1446	8.7
2139	2.5	2130	1.8
11 0322	8.2	**26** 0308	9.0
1017	2.4	0958	1.7
M 1549	7.8	TU 1538	8.5
2220	2.9	◑ 2219	2.1
12 0412	7.8	**27** 0404	8.6
1103	2.8	1051	2.0
TU 1644	7.5	W 1638	8.2
◑ 2312	3.2	2320	2.4
13 0511	7.5	**28** 0510	8.3
1201	3.0	1157	2.3
W 1747	7.3	TH 1751	8.0
14 0019	3.4	**29** 0034	2.5
0618	7.3	0624	8.2
TH 1308	3.1	F 1314	2.4
1855	7.4	1906	8.0
15 0131	3.3	**30** 0155	2.4
0726	7.4	0739	8.2
F 1411	2.9	SA 1429	2.2
1958	7.6	2017	8.3
		31 0309	2.1
		0847	8.5
		SU 1536	2.0
		2118	8.7

AUGUST

Time	m		Time	m
1 0414	1.7	**16** 0353	2.2
0946	8.8	0936	8.2
M 1635	1.7	TU 1615	2.0
2210	9.1	2152	8.8
2 0510	1.3	**17** 0442	1.7
1036	9.0	1017	8.7
TU 1725	1.4	W 1702	1.6
● 2256	9.3	2232	9.2
3 0559	1.0	**18** 0529	1.3
1121	9.2	1057	9.1
W 1810	1.3	TH 1746	1.3
2338	9.4	○ 2312	9.5
4 0642	0.9	**19** 0613	1.0
1201	9.2	1136	9.3
TH 1850	1.3	F 1829	1.0
		2352	9.7
5 0017	9.4	**20** 0656	0.7
0720	1.0	1216	9.5
F 1239	9.1	SA 1911	0.9
1925	1.4		
6 0053	9.3	**21** 0033	9.8
0756	1.2	0736	0.7
SA 1314	8.9	SU 1258	9.5
1958	1.6	1951	1.0
7 0128	9.1	**22** 0116	9.8
0828	1.5	0816	0.8
SU 1348	8.7	M 1340	9.3
2029	1.9	2031	1.2
8 0202	8.8	**23** 0200	9.5
0858	1.9	0855	1.1
M 1423	8.4	TU 1425	9.0
2059	2.3	2113	1.6
9 0239	8.4	**24** 0247	9.2
0928	2.3	0938	1.6
TU 1503	8.1	W 1515	8.6
2133	2.7	2200	2.0
10 0320	8.0	**25** 0342	8.7
1003	2.7	1028	2.1
W 1549	7.7	TH 1614	8.2
◑ 2217	3.1	◑ 2300	2.4
11 0411	7.5	**26** 0449	8.2
1052	3.1	1133	2.6
TH 1646	7.3	F 1730	7.8
2316	3.4		
12 0517	7.2	**27** 0019	2.7
1201	3.4	0609	7.9
F 1758	7.2	SA 1257	2.8
		1852	7.8
13 0034	3.5	**28** 0146	2.6
0635	7.1	0731	7.9
SA 1321	3.3	SU 1419	2.6
1913	7.4	2008	8.2
14 0153	3.2	**29** 0302	2.2
0749	7.3	0842	8.3
SU 1429	3.0	M 1528	2.3
2017	7.8	2109	8.6
15 0258	2.8	**30** 0406	1.7
0848	7.8	0939	8.6
M 1525	2.5	TU 1625	1.9
2108	8.3	2159	9.0
		31 0459	1.4
		1025	8.9
		W 1712	1.6
		2241	9.2

Chart Datum: 4·93 metres below Ordnance Datum (Newlyn). HAT is 10·3 metres above Chart Datum.

NW England

》》 FREE monthly updates. Register at 《
www.reedsnauticalalmanac.co.uk 《

113

STANDARD TIME (UT)
For Summer Time add ONE hour in **non-shaded areas**

LIVERPOOL (GLADSTONE DOCK) LAT 53°27'N LONG 3°01'W
TIMES AND HEIGHTS OF HIGH AND LOW WATERS

Dates in red are **SPRINGS**
Dates in blue are **NEAPS**

YEAR 2016

SEPTEMBER		OCTOBER		NOVEMBER		DECEMBER	
Time m	Time m	Time m	Time m	Time m	Time m	Time m	Time m
1 0543 1.1 1104 9.1 TH 1752 1.4 ● 2319 9.4	**16** 0506 1.1 1033 9.3 F 1725 1.1 ○ 2248 9.8	**1** 0553 1.3 1114 9.2 SA 1800 1.5 ● 2327 9.3	**16** 0527 0.6 1049 9.8 SU 1747 0.8 ○ 2306 10.2	**1** 0619 1.6 1148 9.2 TU 1830 1.7	**16** 0634 0.6 1157 10.0 W 1900 0.7	**1** 0624 1.7 1158 9.1 TH 1842 1.8	**16** 0009 9.8 0702 1.0 F 1231 9.8 1935 0.8
2 0621 1.1 1140 9.2 F 1827 1.4 2353 9.4	**17** 0552 0.7 1113 9.6 SA 1810 0.8 2329 10.0	**2** 0623 1.3 1145 9.2 SU 1829 1.5 2358 9.2	**17** 0612 0.4 1132 10.0 M 1832 0.6 2350 10.2	**2** 0003 9.0 0648 1.7 W 1219 9.1 1901 1.8	**17** 0020 10.0 0717 0.8 TH 1243 9.8 1946 0.9	**2** 0016 8.8 0657 1.8 F 1231 9.0 1918 1.8	**17** 0057 9.5 0747 1.3 SA 1317 9.5 2022 1.1
3 0655 1.1 1212 9.2 SA 1859 1.4	**18** 0635 0.5 1154 9.8 SU 1852 0.7	**3** 0651 1.4 1214 9.2 M 1857 1.6	**18** 0654 0.4 1215 10.0 TU 1915 0.6	**3** 0035 8.9 0718 1.8 TH 1250 8.9 1934 1.9	**18** 0109 9.6 0801 1.3 F 1330 9.5 2033 1.2	**3** 0050 8.7 0732 2.0 SA 1306 8.9 1955 2.0	**18** 0144 9.2 0831 1.7 SU 1404 9.2 2109 1.5
4 0026 9.3 0724 1.3 SU 1244 9.1 1927 1.6	**19** 0011 10.1 0716 0.5 M 1236 9.8 1933 0.7	**4** 0028 9.1 0718 1.6 TU 1245 9.0 1926 1.8	**19** 0035 10.1 0736 0.7 W 1259 9.7 1959 0.9	**4** 0107 8.6 0750 2.1 F 1323 8.7 2009 2.2	**19** 0159 9.1 0846 1.8 SA 1421 9.0 2125 1.7	**4** 0125 8.5 0808 2.3 SU 1343 8.7 2034 2.2	**19** 0232 8.7 0916 2.2 M 1452 8.8 2157 2.0
5 0057 9.1 0752 1.5 M 1315 8.9 1955 1.8	**20** 0055 10.0 0756 0.7 TU 1319 9.6 2014 1.0	**5** 0059 8.9 0745 1.8 W 1316 8.8 1956 2.0	**20** 0123 9.7 0817 1.2 TH 1345 9.4 2044 1.3	**5** 0140 8.3 0824 2.5 SA 1359 8.4 2047 2.6	**20** 0253 8.6 0936 2.4 SU 1517 8.5 2222 2.2	**5** 0205 8.3 0848 2.6 M 1425 8.5 2117 2.5	**20** 0321 8.3 1003 2.7 TU 1544 8.4 2250 2.5
6 0128 8.9 0819 1.8 TU 1347 8.6 2024 2.1	**21** 0140 9.7 0836 1.1 W 1404 9.2 2057 1.4	**6** 0130 8.6 0814 2.2 TH 1348 8.5 2029 2.4	**21** 0212 9.2 0901 1.8 F 1436 8.8 2135 1.9	**6** 0220 8.0 0904 2.9 SU 1443 8.1 2133 2.9	**21** 0353 8.1 1035 2.9 M 1621 8.1 ◗ 2328 2.6	**6** 0251 8.0 0934 2.9 TU 1516 8.2 2209 2.7	**21** 0416 7.8 1057 3.1 W 1643 8.0 ◗ 2348 2.8
7 0201 8.5 0846 2.2 W 1422 8.3 2057 2.5	**22** 0228 9.2 0918 1.7 TH 1454 8.7 2146 2.0	**7** 0203 8.2 0847 2.6 F 1424 8.1 2107 2.8	**22** 0308 8.5 0952 2.4 SA 1537 8.3 ◗ 2238 2.4	**7** 0309 7.7 0954 3.3 M 1540 7.8 ◗ 2232 3.1	**22** 0501 7.7 1146 3.2 TU 1732 7.9	**7** 0348 7.8 1032 3.1 W 1619 8.1 ◗ 2312 2.7	**22** 0519 7.6 1201 3.3 TH 1748 7.7
8 0236 8.1 0919 2.6 TH 1501 7.9 2136 2.9	**23** 0323 8.6 1008 2.3 F 1554 8.2 ◗ 2248 2.5	**8** 0242 7.8 0927 3.0 SA 1509 7.7 2155 3.1	**23** 0416 8.0 1058 3.0 SU 1651 7.9 2355 2.7	**8** 0414 7.4 1102 3.5 TU 1654 7.6 2348 3.1	**23** 0038 2.7 0615 7.6 W 1300 3.2 1843 7.9	**8** 0457 7.7 1142 3.1 TH 1730 8.1	**23** 0051 2.9 0627 7.5 F 1310 3.4 1855 7.7
9 0318 7.6 1002 3.1 F 1550 7.5 ◗ 2228 3.3	**24** 0433 8.0 1116 2.9 SA 1712 7.8	**9** 0334 7.4 1021 3.5 SU 1612 7.4 ◗ 2302 3.4	**24** 0536 7.6 1221 3.2 M 1811 7.8	**9** 0536 7.4 1225 3.3 W 1812 7.8	**24** 0145 2.6 0726 7.8 TH 1407 3.0 1948 8.0	**9** 0024 2.6 0611 7.9 F 1258 2.9 1841 8.3	**24** 0153 2.7 0734 7.6 SA 1413 3.2 1958 7.8
10 0416 7.2 1103 3.5 SA 1701 7.2 2343 3.5	**25** 0010 2.8 0556 7.7 SU 1243 3.1 1836 7.8	**10** 0450 7.1 1141 3.6 M 1736 7.3	**25** 0114 2.6 0657 7.7 TU 1342 3.0 1926 8.0	**10** 0107 2.7 0654 7.8 TH 1341 2.9 1920 8.3	**25** 0243 2.4 0823 8.1 F 1502 2.8 2040 8.3	**10** 0137 2.3 0722 8.3 SA 1409 2.5 1946 8.7	**25** 0248 2.7 0830 7.9 SU 1508 2.9 2051 8.1
11 0540 6.9 1229 3.6 SU 1825 7.2	**26** 0136 2.6 0721 7.8 M 1407 2.9 1953 8.1	**11** 0029 3.3 0621 7.2 TU 1310 3.4 1856 7.7	**26** 0225 2.3 0807 8.0 W 1448 2.7 2027 8.4	**11** 0216 2.2 0759 8.3 F 1445 2.3 2018 8.9	**26** 0332 2.2 0909 8.4 SA 1548 2.5 2124 8.5	**11** 0244 1.9 0823 8.7 SU 1513 2.0 2045 9.1	**26** 0335 2.5 0916 8.3 M 1554 2.6 2136 8.3
12 0111 3.4 0708 7.1 M 1351 3.2 1939 7.6	**27** 0250 2.2 0831 8.2 TU 1515 2.4 2054 8.5	**12** 0149 2.8 0738 7.7 W 1421 2.8 2000 8.2	**27** 0322 2.0 0859 8.4 TH 1541 2.3 2115 8.7	**12** 0316 1.7 0853 8.9 SA 1542 1.7 2110 9.4	**27** 0412 1.9 0946 8.7 SU 1626 2.2 2202 8.7	**12** 0343 1.5 0918 9.2 M 1612 1.5 2139 9.5	**27** 0416 2.2 0955 8.6 TU 1635 2.3 2215 8.5
13 0225 2.8 0817 7.7 TU 1455 2.7 2037 8.2	**28** 0350 1.8 0924 8.6 W 1609 2.1 2141 8.9	**13** 0253 2.2 0836 8.3 TH 1519 2.2 2052 8.9	**28** 0409 1.8 0941 8.7 F 1623 2.1 2154 8.9	**13** 0411 1.2 0941 9.4 SU 1635 1.2 2158 9.8	**28** 0448 1.9 1021 8.9 M 1701 2.0 2237 8.9	**13** 0438 1.1 1008 9.5 TU 1706 1.1 2230 9.7	**28** 0454 2.0 1032 8.8 W 1713 2.1 2251 8.7
14 0325 2.2 0909 8.3 W 1550 2.1 2124 8.8	**29** 0439 1.5 1006 8.9 TH 1652 1.8 2221 9.1	**14** 0349 1.6 0923 9.0 F 1612 1.6 2138 9.4	**29** 0448 1.6 1016 8.9 SA 1659 1.9 2229 9.1	**14** 0501 0.8 1026 9.8 M 1725 0.9 ○ 2245 10.1	**29** 0520 1.8 1053 9.0 TU 1735 1.9 ● 2310 8.9	**14** 0529 0.9 1056 9.8 W 1758 0.8 ○ 2320 9.8	**29** 0530 1.8 1106 9.0 TH 1751 1.8 ● 2326 8.8
15 0418 1.6 0952 8.8 TH 1639 1.6 2207 9.4	**30** 0519 1.3 1042 9.1 F 1728 1.6 2255 9.3	**15** 0439 1.0 1007 9.5 SA 1701 1.1 2222 9.9	**30** 0521 1.6 1047 9.1 SU 1730 1.8 ● 2301 9.1	**15** 0548 0.6 1112 10.0 TU 1813 0.7 2333 10.1	**30** 0552 1.7 1125 9.1 W 1808 1.8 2343 8.9	**15** 0617 0.7 1144 9.9 TH 1847 0.7	**30** 0606 1.7 1141 9.0 F 1828 1.7
			31 0551 1.5 1118 9.2 M 1800 1.7 2332 9.1				**31** 0000 8.9 0642 1.7 SA 1216 9.2 1906 1.6

Chart Datum: 4·93 metres below Ordnance Datum (Newlyn). HAT is 10·3 metres above Chart Datum.

》》 FREE monthly updates. Register at 《
www.reedsnauticalalmanac.co.uk

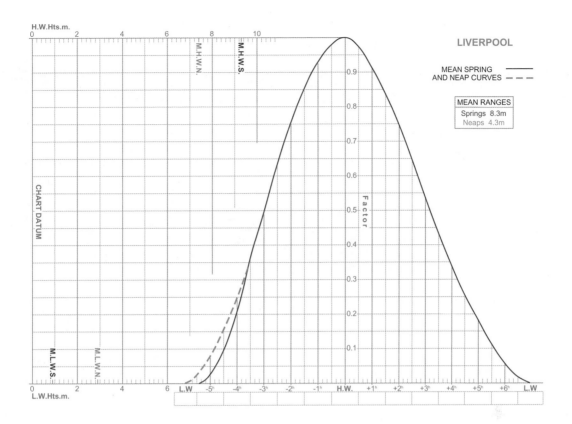

LIVERPOOL

MEAN SPRING
AND NEAP CURVES – – –

MEAN RANGES
Springs 8.3m
Neaps 4.3m

3.16 LIVERPOOL

Merseyside 53°24'·22N 03°00'·28W (Liver Bldg) ❄❄❄❄💧💧💧❀❀

CHARTS AC 1826, 1978, 1951, 3490, 5613; Imray C62, C52

TIDES +0015 Dover; ML 5·2; Duration 0535

Standard Port LIVERPOOL (GLADSTONE DOCK) (←)

Times				Height (metres)			
High Water		Low Water		MHWS	MHWN	MLWN	MLWS
0000	0600	0200	0700	9·4	7·5	3·2	1·1
1200	1800	1400	1900				
Differences EASTHAM (River Mersey)							
+0014	+0014	+0006	+0006	+0·2	0·0	–0·4	–0·5
HALE HEAD (River Mersey)							
+0035	+0030	ND	ND	–2·5	–2·6	ND	ND
WIDNES (River Mersey)							
+0045	+0050	+0355	+0340	–4·3	–4·5	–2·8	–0·6
FIDDLER'S FERRY (River Mersey)							
+0105	+0120	+0535	+0445	–6·0	–6·4	–2·7	–0·6
HILBRE ISLAND (River Dee)							
–0011	–0008	–0013	–0018	–0·4	–0·3	+0·1	+0·2
MOSTYN DOCKS (River Dee)							
–0015	–0010	–0025	–0025	–0·9	–0·8	ND	ND
CONNAH'S QUAY (River Dee)							
+0005	+0020	+0350	+0335	–4·7	–4·5	DR	DR
CHESTER (River Dee)							
+0110	+0110	+0455	+0455	–5·4	–5·5	DR	DR
COLWYN BAY							
–0015	–0015	ND	ND	–1·6	–1·4	ND	ND
LLANDUDNO							
–0009	–0021	–0031	–0038	–1·7	–1·6	–0·9	–0·6

NOTE: LW time differences at Connah's Quay give the end of a LW stand lasting about 3¾hrs at sp and 5hrs at nps. A bore occurs in the R Dee at Chester.

SHELTER Good at marinas in Brunswick/Coburg docks and in Canning/Albert Docks. Fair weather ⚓ on the SW side of river. Strong winds from any direction raise a swell on the bar. Wind against tide causes steep, breaking seas in outer reaches of River Mersey with disturbed waters into the Crosby Channel.

NAVIGATION WPT 53°32'·02N 03°20'·98W, Bar light float, 111°/2·8M to Q1 NCM lt F. From Q1 to marina is 15·5M via Queens and Crosby Channels. Both have training banks which cover and it is unsafe to navigate between these and the floats/buoys. Sp tidal streams exceed 5kn within the river. Elsewhere great caution is needed as the whole area (R Dee, R Mersey to R Alt and N to Morecambe Bay) is littered with sandbanks and damaged training walls. Local knowledge is advisable inshore outside marked passages.

Leeds and Liverpool Canal (BWB) gives access to E Coast, ent at Stanley Dock. Max draught 1·0m, air draught 2·2m, beam 4·3m, LOA 18·3m. Liverpool to Goole 161M, 103 locks.

Manchester Ship Canal, ent at Eastham Locks (outer wall bn Iso YR 4s), leads 31M to Salford Quays or R Weaver for boatyards at Northwich. Obtain licence from MSC Co ☎0151 327 1461.

R Dee: WPT 53°25'·13N 03°13'·17W, Hilbre Swash HE2 ECM buoy, Q (3) 10s, (chan shifts). From the W use Welsh Chan. The Dee estuary mostly dries.

LIGHTS AND MARKS Bar SWM lt float, Fl 5s Racon. Keep 5ca clear of SPM, 5ca W of Bar lt float. Formby SWM buoy, Iso 4s, is at the ent to Queen's Chan which is marked by light floats and buoys, and 3 NCM buoys, numbered Q1-Q12. Crosby Chan is similarly marked, C1-C23. From Crosby SWM buoy, Oc 5s, the track up-river is approx 145°. The Liver Bldg (twin spires) and Port of Liverpool Bldg (dome) are conspic on the E bank opposite Birkenhead Docks.

COMMUNICATIONS (Code 0151) CGOC (01407) 762051; Police 101; Ⓗ 709 0141. Port Ops 949 6134/5; ⚕949 6095.

Contact *Mersey VTS* Ch **12** 16 (H24) before Bar lighted Buoy. Nav /gale warnings are broadcast on receipt on Ch 12. Movements, nav warnings and weather are b/cast on Ch 09 at HW–3 and –2. *Canning Dock/Liverpool Marina* Ch **M**. Eastham Locks Ch 07 (H24). Manchester Ship Canal Ch 14. Liverpool NTM for further detail.

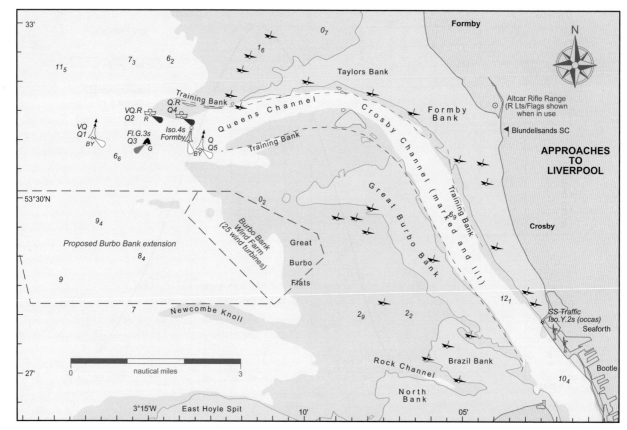

APPROACHES TO LIVERPOOL

FACILITIES Liverpool Marina entrance is 1M S of the Liver Bldg, abeam Pluckington Bank WCM buoy. **IPTS** (sigs 2, 3 & 5) from conspic black control bldg at lock ent. 2m depth over sill at Brunswick Dock lock (width 8m) approx HW ±2¼ sp, ±1½ nps, 0600-2200 Mar-Oct. Pontoons inside, min depth 3·5m; night locking by arrangement. www.liverpoolmarina.co.uk ☎7076777 (0600-2200 Mar–Oct). 350 ⬭, £2·20; ⬛ 🔧◎⬛🚿⬛ (½M) 🔧⬛🔧⬛🔧⬛🔧🔧 (60t), ⬛ @ wi-fi, ⬛ ✕ (☎7076888).

Albert Dock ☎7096558; access HW–2 to HW via Canning Dock, but not on every tide. VHF Ch M when manned, ⬭🔌🔧.

Royal Mersey YC ☎6453204, ⬛⬛⬛⬛⬛🔧✕⬛.

W Kirby SC ☎6255579, M (in Dee Est) ⬛⬭ (at HW), ⬛🔧⬛ (30t) ⬛.

Hoylake SC ☎6322616, ⬛⬛🔧⬛.

City all facilities, ⬛✈.

ADJACENT ANCHORAGE
RIVER ALT, Merseyside, **53°31´·42N 03°03´·80W**. AC 1978, 1951, 5613. HW –0008 on Dover. Good shelter but only for LOA <8·5m x 1·2m draught on a HW of at least 8m. Mersey E training wall can be crossed HW±2. Entrance to channel (shifts frequently) is E of C14 PHM lt float. The channel runs SE of, and parallel to the large fixed marks on the training wall (outer is a R basket; inner a Y cross), then between R and G perches. Inadvisable to ⚓ in R Alt without local knowledge; pick up a free mooring off the SC and contact club. Facilities are very limited. **Blundell Sands SC** ☎(0151) 9292101 (occas), ⬛⬛(at HW) 🔧⬛.

ADJACENT HARBOUR
RHYL, Denbigh, **53°19´·0N 03°30´·4W**. AC 1978, 1951, 5613. Good shelter for vessels able to take the ground on pontoons in outer hbr. Inner hbr dries. Strong tides rip across ent between SWM and Hope's Nose, but training and harbour walls now renovated to make entry achievable with care. Lifting bridge divides hbrs and opens on req Ch 14. Contact HM prior to visit: ☎01745 360625.

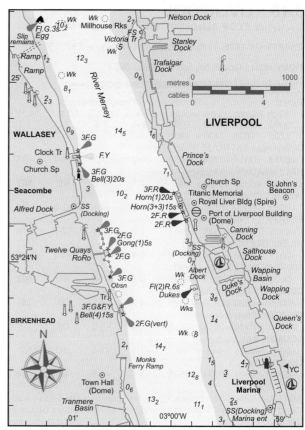

LIVERPOOL

3.17 CONWY AND DEGANWY

Conwy 53°17'·48N 03°50'·23W (marina) ✹❀⌂⌂⌂⌂❀❀❀
Deganwy 53°17'·41N 03°49'·66W (marina) ✹❀⌂⌂⌂❀❀❀

CHARTS AC 5609, 1826, 1977, 1978, 1463; Imray C52

TIDES −0015 Dover; ML 4·3; Duration 0545

Standard Port HOLYHEAD (→)

Times				Height (metres)			
High Water		Low Water		MHWS	MHWN	MLWN	MLWS
0000	0600	0500	1100	5·6	4·4	2·0	0·7
1200	1800	1700	2300				
Differences CONWY							
+0025	+0035	+0120	+0105	+2·3	+1·8	+0·6	+0·4

NOTE: HW Conwy is approx HW Liverpool −0040 sp and −0020 nps.

SHELTER Good in river, except in NW gales. Good in marinas.

NAVIGATION Hbr guide www.conwy.gov.uk/harbourandseaboard WPT 53°17'·95N 03°55'·58W, Fairway buoy LFl 10s; 095°/6·2ca to channel between C1/C2 buoys.

After C1/C2 buoys the channel up to Deganwy is marked by lit lateral marks in sequence: C2A, C4, then paired SHM/PHM: C3/C6, C5/C8, C7/C10, C9/C12, C11/C14. C16 (Fl R 6s) at narrows into R Conwy. A bar, dries 1·0m, forms at The Scabs adjacent to No 6 PHM. Perch Lt bcn Fl G 15s 5M marks turn to river ent. 10kn speed limit above.

Beware unlit moorings throughout the harbour, Beacons Jetty in the narrows and unlit pontoons upstream from Bodlondeb Pt. Spring ebb runs at 5kn and vacant moorings may be submerged.

North Deep, a buoyed inshore passage (close SW of Gt Orme's Hd to Deganwy Point), is only advised with local knowledge.

LIGHTS AND MARKS Penmaenmawr SPM outfall buoy (SW of C1 buoy) is not a channel mark. The 4 towers of Conwy castle and the 2 adjacent bridge towers are conspic once in the river.

COMMUNICATIONS (Code 01492) CGOC (01407) 762051; Police 101; Dr 592424; HM 596253.

HM Ch **14**. Summer 0900-1700LT daily; winter, same times Mon-Fri). Marinas, pre-call Ch 80 (H24) for a berth. N Wales CC launch Ch **M** water taxi.

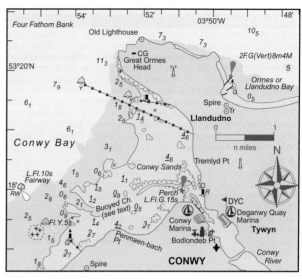

FACILITIES Beacons Jetty ⚓ HW±3.

Conwy Marina ⚓ www.quaymarinas.com ☎593000. Access when height of tide above CD exceeds 3·5m; waiting pontoon outside. Gate times are on an electronic noticeboard. Obey R/G entry lts. 505⌂ inc ♥, £2·60m; (short stay £10·95) ⚓ ⛽ ⚓ ⚓(0700-2200) ⚓ ⚓ ⚓ ⚓ ⚓ Ⓔ ⚓ ⚓ ⚓(30t) ⚓ ✕ ⚓ wi-fi.

Deganwy Quay Marina ⚓ www.quaymarinas.com ☎576888. Access when height of tide above CD exceeds 4m, approx HW ±3¼. Keep close to 3 lit PHM lt marking the appr channel (see below). Min depth in chan is 2·5m when gate open. Obey R/G entry lights. 150⌂ inc ♥, £2·60 (short stay £10·95) ⚓ ⛽ ⚓ ⚓(0700-2200) ⚓ ⚓ ⚓ ✕ ⚓ ⚓ Ⓔ ⚓(20t) ✕ ⚓ wi-fi.

Harbour Above Bodlondeb Pt contact HM for: ⚓'s, pontoon ⌂ £13; **Town Quay** 3 drying ⌂ £11<8m>£12·50<12·3m; ⚓ ⚓ ⚓ ⚓ (Town Quay HW±2, call Ch 14 to confirm).

N Wales Cruising Club (Conwy) ☎593481, ⚓ ⌂ ⚓ ⚓.

Conwy YC (Deganwy) ☎583690, ⚓ ⚓ ⚓ ✕ ⚓.

Town ⚓ ⚓ ✉ Ⓑ ⚓ ✕ ⚓ ⇌ ✈ (Liverpool).

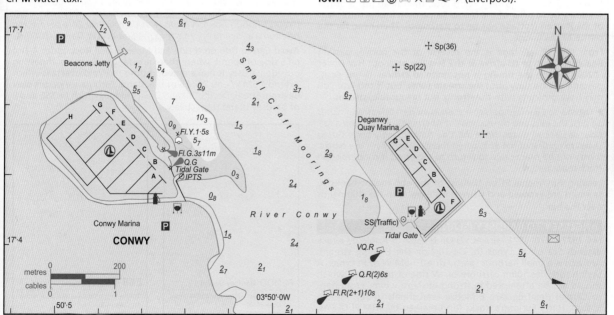

MENAI STRAIT

(AC 1464, Imray C52) From NE to SW the main features of this narrow, 16 mile channel are: Puffin Is, where the Strait begins at its North-East entrance; Beaumaris; Garth Pt at Bangor; Menai Suspension Bridge (29m); The Swellies, a narrow 1M stretch with strong tidal streams and dangers mid-stream; Britannia Bridge, both road and rail (26m), with cables close W at elevation of 21m; Port Dinorwic; Caernarfon; Abermenai Pt and Fort Belan, which mark the SW end of Strait; and Caernarfon Bar. The following brief notes cover only very basic pilotage. For detailed directions see the UKHO *West Coasts of England and Wales Pilot*, or *Cruising Anglesey and Adjoining Waters* by Ralph Morris.

▶*The Swellies should be taken near local HW slack, and an understanding of tidal streams is essential. The tide is about 1 hour later, and sp range about 2·7m more, at the NE end of the Strait than at the SW end. Levels differ most at 1hr after HW at the NE end where sea level is > 1·8m above the level at the SW end and at about 4¾hrs before HW at the NE end where sea level is > 1·8m below the level at the SW end.*

Normally the stream runs as follows (referred to HW Dover).

Interval fm HW	Direction
–0110 to +0340	SW between Garth Pt and Abermenai Pt.
+0340 to +0510	Outwards from The Swellies, (NE towards Garth Pt / SW towards Abermenai Pt)
+0510 to -0110	NE between Abermenai Pt and Garth Pt.

See diagram on adjacent page.

Sp rates are generally about 3kn, **but more in narrows, eg 5kn off Abermenai Pt, 6kn between the bridges, and 8kn through The Swellies.** *Timings and rates of streams may be affected by strong winds in either direction and storm surges in the Irish Sea.*◀

Note: Direction of buoyage becomes NE off Caernarfon.

From SW to NE, aim to arrive at the Swellies early HW Dover –0300 to take the E-going tidal stream to pass Menai bridge between HW Dover –0230 to –0200. Better to arrive too early, and wait, than too late and risk not making it through the narrows before the stream turns to the W. Approach the S arch of Britannia Bridge keeping the white pyramid in line with the centre of the arch. Once through the bridge run parallel to the shore until abeam the pyramid. At this point, look astern and keep the white leading marks (beneath the S arch of the bridge) in line. When Price's Point is abeam, turn to starboard to pass 20-30m S of Swelly Perch rock, then head just S of the Anglesey (ie N) pillar of the Menai Suspension Bridge until clear of the Platters (cottage abeam to starboard). Then head for the centre of the bridge.

From the NE, pilotage is the reverse of the above, passing Beaumaris in time to arrive at the Swellies at about HW Dover –0200, though the timing is not quite so critical. If too early, passage will be slow until the stream turns, but if too late you may have difficulty with the strong, but favourable, stream.

▶ *Caernarfon Bar is impassable even in moderately strong winds against the ebb, and the narrows at Abermenai Pt demand a fair tide, or slackish water, since the tide runs strongly here. Going seaward on first of the ebb, when there is water over the banks, it may not be practicable to return to the Strait if conditions on the bar are bad.*◀

Leaving Abermenai Pt on the last of the ebb means banks to seaward are exposed and there is little water in the channel or over the bar.

ANGLESEY TO BARDSEY ISLAND

(AC 1977, 1970, 1971 Imray C52) On N coast of Anglesey a race extends 5ca off Pt Lynas (lt, Oc 10s) on the E-going stream. Amlwch is a small harbour (partly dries) 1·5M W of Pt Lynas. A drying rock lies 100m offshore on W side of approach, which should not be attempted in strong onshore winds. From here to Carmel Head beware E Mouse (and shoals to SE), Middle Mouse, Harry Furlong's Rocks (dry) marked by SHM Fl G 2½s, Victoria Bank (least depth 1·8m) and W Mouse (with dangers to W & SW). Further offshore are the shoals of Archdeacon Rk, Coal Rk and Ethel Rk which lie in the red sector of Skerries Lt Ho.

Cardinal buoys mark their position. The outermost of these dangers is 2M offshore. Overfalls and races occur at headlands and over the many rocks and shoals along this coast.

In good conditions by day and at slack water, Carmel Hd can be rounded close inshore following a track outside East Mouse, inshore of Middle & West Mouse, staying N of Furlong SHM and passing S of Victoria Bank. Short, steep seas break here in even moderate winds against tide and can be dangerous. The best passage at night or in bad weather, is to pass 1M off Skerries, in the TSS ITZ. Holyhead (port of refuge), is accessible H24 in all weathers. The marina is within New Harbour; beware fast ferries across the entrance and note the TSS.

▶*Between Carmel Hd and The Skerries the NE-going stream begins at HW Dover +0530 (HW Holyhead +0615), and the SW-going at HW Dover –0045 (HW Holyhead +0005),* **Sp rates 5kn.** *1M NW of Skerries the stream turns 0130 later, running less strongly.* **Flood and Ebb tides close to the coast runs at over 5k springs,** *and at about 2.5kn 7 miles offshore. The brief period of slack water offshore is HW Dover –0100 and +0500. There is no significant counter tide in Holyhead Bay, where slack water lasts longer.*◀

▶*Races occur off N Stack and S Stack. There is a severe and dangerous race off South Stack starting at HW -0600 on the flood (**Sp rate 5kn**) extending 8nm to the Skerries and another dangerous race off Carmel Hd (Sp rate 6kn). Races are less extensive on SSW-going stream, which begins at HW Holyhead +0020, (**Sp rate 5kn**).*◀

The W coast of Anglesey is rugged with rks, some drying, up to 1·5M offshore. Races run off Penrhyn Mawr and Rhoscolyn Hd, between which is Maen Piscar a dangerous, drying rock (1·2m).

▶*A W-going eddy occurs E of Penrhyn Mawr during the SE-going stream and eddies form in Abraham's Bosom and Gogarth Bay.*◀

E of Llanddwyn Is, Pilot's Cove is a good ⚓ to await suitable conditions.

On the Lleyn Peninsula Porth Dinllaen is a good ⚓, but exposed to NW through N to SE. Braich y Pwll is the steep, rky point at end of Lleyn Peninsula (AC 1971). About 1M N of it and up to 1M offshore lie The Tripods, a bank on which there are overfalls and steep seas with wind against tide.

▶*Bardsey Sound, 1.5M wide, can be used by day in moderate winds.* **Stream reaches 8kn at Sp, and passage should be made at slack water,** *which occurs about 2¼ hrs after local high and low water: HW Dover –0100 (HW Holyhead –0010) going E, or westbound LW Dover –0100 (LW Holyhead +0030). An eddy ('Young flood') flows W from N of Carreg Ddu 2hrs before the tide turns allowing approach to the Snd at HW Dover +0500.*◀

Avoid Carreg Ddu on N side and Maen Bugail Rock (dries 4·1m) on S side of Sound, where there are dangerous races. If passing outside Bardsey Is make a good offing to avoid overfalls which extend 1·5M W and 2·5M S of the island. Turbulence occurs over Bastram Shoal, Devil's Tail and Devil's Ridge, which lie SSE and E of Bardsey Island respectively.

FLOOD Bardsey Sound

The tide turns to the NW or NE (flood) as follows:
(a): Dover +0300;
(b): Dover +0500;
(c): Dover +0600.
These times are approximate.

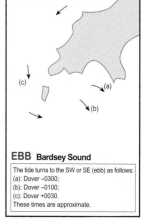

EBB Bardsey Sound

The tide turns to the SW or SE (ebb) as follows:
(a): Dover –0300;
(b): Dover –0100;
(c): Dover +0030.
These times are approximate.

NOTE: There is a strong eddy down tide off Bardsey Island and overfalls throughout the area.

FLOOD

(T): turning → : < 2k ➡ : 2-4k ⫸ : 4k +

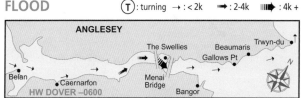

LOCAL LW: Caernarfon HW Dover –0555. Port Dinorwic –0620.
Menai –0540. Beaumaris –0605.

HW DOVER –0500

HW DOVER –0400

HW DOVER –0300

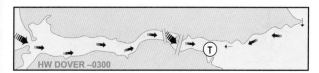

HW DOVER –0200

SLACK WATER IN THE SWELLIES: HW Dover –0200 to –0230.

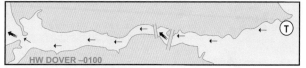

HW DOVER –0100

LOCAL HW: Belan: HW Dover –0115. Caernarfon: –0105.
Port Dinorwic: –0050.

EBB

(T): turning → : < 2k ➡ : 2-4k ⫸ : 4k +

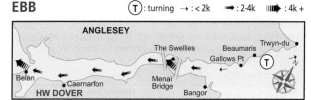

LOCAL HW: Menai –0005. Beaumaris –0010.

HW DOVER +0100

HW DOVER +0200

HW DOVER +0300

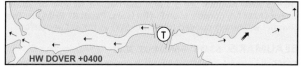

HW DOVER +0400

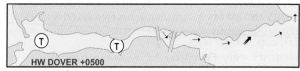

HW DOVER +0500

LOCAL LW: Belan: HW Dover +0520.

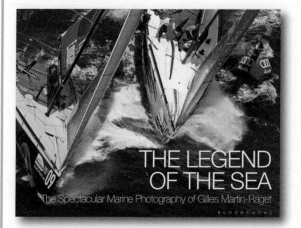

N Wales

3.18 MENAI STRAIT

Gwynedd/Isle of Anglesey ⚓❀❀❀❀❀

CHARTS AC 5609, 1464, Imray C52. NOTE: The definitive Pilot book is *Cruising Anglesey and Adjoining Waters* by Ralph Morris.

TIDES –0035 Dover (Sp), 0020 (Np)
Standard Port HOLYHEAD (⟶)

Times				Height (metres)			
High Water		Low Water		MHWS	MHWN	MLWN	MLWS
0000	0600	0500	1100	5·6	4·4	2·0	0·7
1200	1800	1700	2300				
Differences BEAUMARIS							
+0025	+0010	+0055	+0035	+2·0	+1·6	+0·5	+0·1
MENAI BRIDGE							
+0030	+0010	+0100	+0035	+1·7	+1·4	+0·3	0·0
PORT DINORWIC							
–0015	–0025	+0030	0000	0·0	0·0	0·0	+0·1
CAERNARFON							
–0030	–0030	+0015	–0005	–0·4	–0·4	–0·1	–0·1
FORT BELAN							
–0040	–0015	–0025	–0005	–1·0	–0·9	–0·2	–0·1
LLANDDWYN ISLAND							
–0115	–0055	–0030	–0020	–0·7	–0·5	–0·1	0·0

NORTH EAST ENTRANCE

SHELTER Reasonable ⚓ N of Trwyn Du in Southerly winds or in outer road in settled conditions to await a favourable tide.

NAVIGATION WPT 53°19´·48N 04°03´·28W, 137°/1M to Perch Rk.

- In N'ly gales seas break on Ten Feet Bank and there are high, steep breaking seas in Puffin Sound.
- In N Strait keep to buoyed chan, nearer Anglesey taking care to avoid the SHM marking a wreck W of B1 SHM.

LIGHTS AND MARKS See 3.3 and chartlet. At NE end of Strait, Trwyn-Du Lt ho, Conspic tr on Puffin Is and Perch Rk PHM bn. The channel is laterally buoyed (direction SW) as far as Caernarfon.

BEAUMARIS 53°15´·66N 04°05´·38W

TIDES Beaumaris –0025 Dover; ML Beaumaris 4·2; Duration 0540

SHELTER Reasonable off Beaumaris except from NE winds. ⚓ S of B10 PHM buoy.

LIGHTS AND MARKS Beaumaris pier has light 2Fl (3) G 10s 6M.

COMMUNICATIONS (Code 01248); Dr (emergency) 384001; Police 101; CGOC (01407) 762051.

FACILITIES **Royal Anglesey YC** www.royalangleseyyc.org.uk ☎810295, ⚓ ⚓ ⚓ ✕ 🏠.
North West Venturers' YC, at Gallows Pt www.nwyc.org.uk ⚓.
Power Marine ⚓ ✕ ✎ ⬚ Ⓔ 🏴(20t) ⬚(2t).
Town 🅿 ⬚ ✉ Ⓑ ⇌ (bus to Bangor), ✈ (Anglesey/Liverpool).

BANGOR 53°14´·46N 04°07´·58W

SHELTER Good, but open to winds from N to NE, at Dickies BY or Port Penrhyn dock. Dock and approaches dry approx 3m.

COMMUNICATIONS (Code 01248) Penrhyn HM ☎352525.

FACILITIES Dickies, Port Penrhyn, www.dickies.co.uk ☎363400, 5⬚ £15/night, ⚓ ⬚ ✕ ✎ ⬚ Ⓔ ⚓ ⬚ 🏴(30t) ⬚ 🅿.
Town (1M) 🅿 🅿 ⛽ ✉ Ⓑ ⇌ ✈ (Anglesey/Liverpool).

MENAI BRIDGE 53°13´·20N 04°09´·79W

COMMUNICATIONS (Code 01248) Piermaster Menai Bridge 712312, mobile 07990 531595. At Menai Bridge, all moorings are private. Pier is owned and managed by Bangor University.

FACILITIES St George's Pier (Fl G 10s)⚓ at all tides.

The Marine Club, Porth Daniel, ☎717484, ⚓ ⬚ ⚓ ⚓ ⚓ ⬚ ⬚

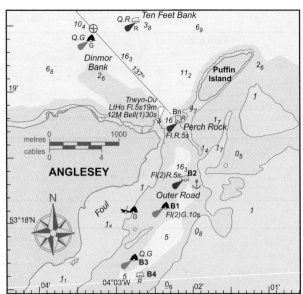

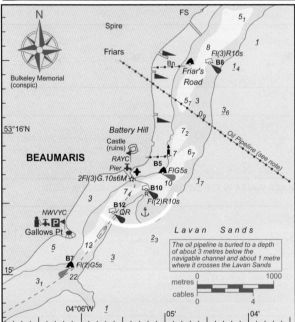

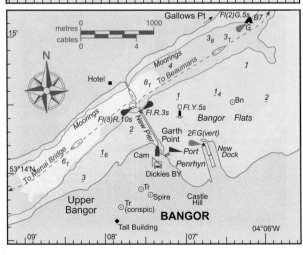

THE SWELLIES

NAVIGATION

- The passage should only be attempted at slack HW, which is –0145 HW Dover.
- The shallow rky narrows between the bridges may be dangerous for yachts at other times, when the stream can reach 8kn.
- At slack HW Sp there is 3m over The Platters and the outcrop off Price Pt, which can be ignored.
- For shoal-draught boats passage is also possible at slack LW Nps, when there are depths of 0·5m close E of Britannia Bridge.
- The bridges and power cables have a least clearance of 21m at MHWS. Night passage is not recommended.

LIGHTS AND MARKS See 3.3. and chartlet.
Britannia Bridge, E side ldg lts 231°, both FW. Br lts, both sides: Centre span Iso 5s 27m 3M; S end, FR 21m 3M; N end, FG 21m 3M.

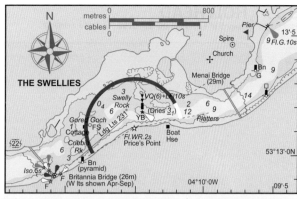

PORT DINORWIC/Y Felinheli 53°11'·20N 04°13'·70W

LIGHTS AND MARKS Pier Hd F WR 5m 2M, vis R225°- W357°-225°.

COMMUNICATIONS(Code 01248); Dr 670423. Marina 671500.
Dinorwic Marina VHF Ch, *Plas Menai Centre Menai Base* Ch **80** M.

FACILITIES Port Dinorwic Marina ⊕ portdinorwic.co.uk ☎ 671500; **Tidal basin** dries at Sp; lock (width 9·7m) opens HW±2. ⬛ 180⬭ 🅱🗚🖉⬛⬛🗚⬛🗚🗚⬛⬛🅔⬛🗚(15t).

Dinas Boatyard ☎671642, ⬛🗚🗚⬛⬛⬛ all 🗚 facilities ⬛.
Town 🅔 ✉ (Bangor or Caernarfon), 🅑 ⇌ (Bangor), ✈ (Liverpool).

Plas Menai (between Port Dinorwic and Caernarfon), Sailing and Sports Centre ☎670964, 🅺, day moorings only.

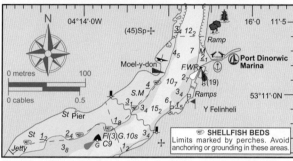

CAERNARFON 53°08'·51N 04°16'·83W ✻✻🖤💧💧💧❀❀❀

SHELTER Good in Victoria Dock Marina, access HW±2 via lifting cill, traffic lts (HO); pontoons at SW end in 2m, **Ⓥ** to starboard of ent. In river hbr (S of conspic castle) berth against wall, dries to mud/gravel, access HW±3 via swing bridge; for opening sound B (—···). ⚓ off Foel Ferry only with local knowledge; temp ⚓ off Abermenai Pt, sheltered from W, but strong streams. **Ⓥ** waiting 1½ca SW of C9.

COMMUNICATIONS (Code 01286) Police 101; 🏥 01248 384384; Dr (emergency) 01248 384001. HM 672118, Mobile 07786 730865.
Victoria Dock Marina Ch **80**. *Caernarfon Hbr* Ch **14** 16 (HJ).

FACILITIES River £9·60<20'<£13·20<30'<£18 /craft, ⬛⬛⬛⬛.
Victoria Dock ☎672346, 46 ⬭ £2·35, ⬛⬛⬛⬛.
Caernarfon SC ☎(01248) 672861,⬛⬛.
Royal Welsh YC ☎(01248) 672599, ⬛.

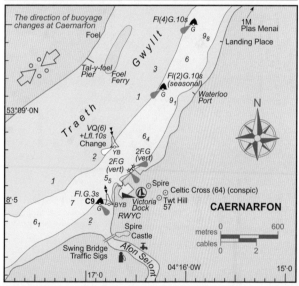

SOUTH WEST ENTRANCE – CAERNARFON BAR

NAVIGATION A dangerous sea can build in even a moderate breeze against tide, especially if a swell is running. Bar Chan should not be used at any time other than local HW-3 to HW+3. Caernarfon Bar shifts often and unpredictably see website at www.caernarfon-hbr.demon.co.uk/buoy_e.htm. **Direction of buoyage changes to NE at Caernarfon.**

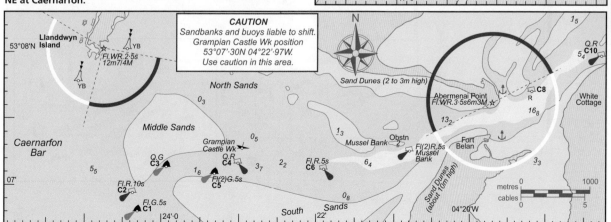

3.19 HOLYHEAD

Isle of Anglesey 53°19'·72N 04°37'·07W ✿✿✿♦♦♦✿✿

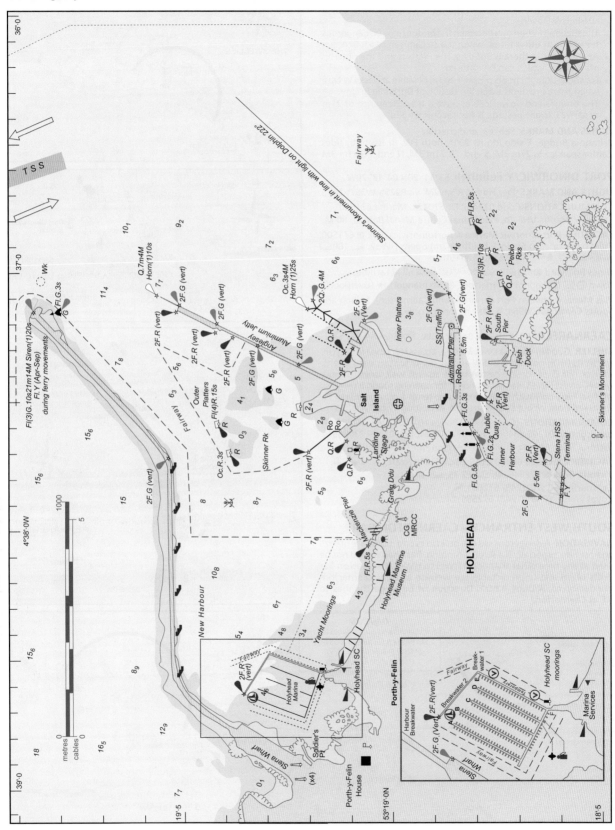

TSS

Fairway

Skinner's Monument in line with light on Dolphin 222°

Fl.R.5s
R 2₂

R 2₂

Peibio
Rks

Fl(3)R.10s
R
Q.R

Fl.G.3s
G

Wk

4·6

5·7

Q.7m4M
Horn(1)10s
7₁

2F.G (vert)

2F.G (vert)

Anglesey Aluminium Jetty

Oc.3s4M
Horn (1)25s

2Q.4M

2F.G (vert)

Inner Platters
3·8

2F.G(vert)

2F.G(vert)

2F.R (vert)

South Pier

11·4

7₈

Fl(3)G.10s21m14M Siren(1)120s
FI.Y (Apr–Sep)
during ferry movements

2F.R (vert)

2F.R (vert)

5₆

*Outer
Platters*

6₃

4₁

5₆
G

5

2F.G (vert)

2F.R (vert)

SS:(Traffic)

RoRo

Admiralty Pier

Fish
Dock

Skinner's Monument

Fairway

Oc.R.3s
R

Fl(4)R.15s
R

Skinner Rk

0₃

2₄

R

2₈

G

Ro
Ro

**Salt
Island**

Q.R

Fl.G.3s

2F.R
(Vert)

Stena HSS
Terminal

15₆

15

8

8₇

9

Q.R

*Landing
Stage*

6₅

Fl.G.2s Public
Quay

Inner
Harbour

5·5m

F.Y

2F.G (vert)

Mackenzie Pier

Graig Ddu

Fl.G.5s

2F.G

HOLYHEAD

15₆

16₅

18

8₉

12₉

10₅

New Harbour

5₄

6₇

4₈

3₄

Yacht Moorings

6₃

4₃

Fl.R.5s

CG
MRCC

*Holyhead Maritime
Museum*

metres 0
cables 0
1000

5

4°38'·0W

7₉

7₇

Fl.R.5s

*Soldier's
Pt*

Siena Wharf

0₁

Porth-y-Felin
House

(x4)

2F.R (vert)

Fairway

Holyhead
Marina

4₆

Holyhead SC

Porth-y-Felin

Harbour
Breakwater

2F.G (Vert)

Siena
Wharf

2F.R(vert)

Fairway

Break-
water 1

Breakwater 2

A
B
C
D
E

Fairway

Holyhead SC
moorings

Marina
Services

19'·5

53°19'·0N

18'·5

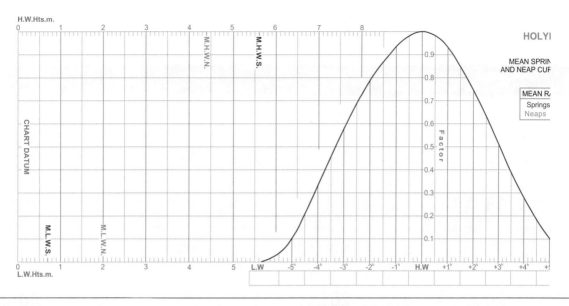

N Wales

CHARTS AC 5609, 1826, 1970, 1977, 1413, 2011; Imray C61, C52

TIDES –0050 Dover; ML 3·2; Duration 0615

Standard Port HOLYHEAD (→)

Times				Height (metres)			
High Water		Low Water		MHWS	MHWN	MLWN	MLWS
0000	0600	0500	1100	5·6	4·4	2·0	0·7
1200	1800	1700	2300				
Differences TRWYN DINMOR (W of Puffin Is)							
+0025	+0015	+0050	+0035	+1·9	+1·5	+0·5	+0·2
MOELFRE (NE Anglesey)							
+0025	+0020	+0050	+0035	+1·9	+1·4	+0·5	+0·2
AMLWCH (N Anglesey)							
+0020	+0010	+0035	+0025	+1·6	+1·3	+0·5	+0·2
CEMAES BAY (N Anglesey)							
+0020	+0025	+0040	+0035	+1·0	+0·7	+0·3	+0·1
TREARDDUR BAY (W Anglesey)							
–0045	–0025	–0015	–0015	–0·4	–0·4	0·0	+0·1
PORTH TRECASTELL (SW Anglesey)							
–0045	–0025	–0005	–0015	–0·6	–0·6	0·0	0·0
TREFOR (Lleyn peninsula)							
–0115	–0100	–0030	–0020	–0·8	–0·9	–0·2	–0·1
PORTH DINLLAEN (Lleyn peninsula)							
–0120	–0105	–0035	–0025	–1·0	–1·0	–0·2	–0·2
PORTH YSGADEN (Lleyn peninsula)							
–0125	–0110	–0040	–0035	–1·1	–1·0	–0·1	–0·1
BARDSEY ISLAND							
–0220	–0240	–0145	–0140	–1·2	–1·2	–0·5	–0·1

SHELTER Accessible at all times. Good in marina, least depth 2m, and on YC moorings which are uncomfortable in strong NE-E winds. Temporary visitors' berths on E side of marina floating breakwater are exposed to the east. ⌕ not recommended – foul ground. Strong NW-NE winds raise an uncomfortable sea.

NAVIGATION WPT 53°20´·12N 04°37´·27W, 165°/0·28M to Bkwtr Lt ho. Small craft should leave Spit SHM buoy to starboard and maintain a safe distance from bkwtr to allow for obstns before heading for marina/moorings. Yachts should keep well clear of commercial shipping and the Outer Platters. Beware numerous fishing markers close to the breakwater. No ⌕ in the fairways.

Frequent HSS and Ro-Ro ferries to and from Ireland use inner hbr south of aluminium jetty and comply with a mini-TSS 100-500m off bkwtr hd.

LIGHTS AND MARKS Ldg marks 165°: bkwtr lt ho on with chy (127m, grey + B top; R lts); chy and Holyhead Mountain (218m) are conspic from afar. Cranes on aluminium jetty conspic closer to.

COMMUNICATIONS (Code 01407) CGOC 762051; Police 101; Dr via CGOC. Marina 764242; Port Control 763071.

Holyhead Marina and *Holyhead SC*: Ch **M**. Monitor *Holyhead* Ch 14 16 (H24) for ferry traffic. Broadcast of local nav info/warnings 1200 (UT) daily on Ch 14.

FACILITIES Marina www.holyheadmarina.co.uk, ☎764242; 500⌂ + Ⓥ, £2.60, short stay £7/craft, ⌁ Ⓞ ⬧ (0800-1800) ⬧ ⚒ ▣ Ⓔ ⌂ ▣(15t) ⌁ ✕ ⌂ wi-fi.

Inner Hbr ☎762304, used by Stena HSS; not advised for yachts.

Holyhead SC (HSC) ☎762526; M £8.00, ⌁ ⚓ ⚓ launch (call Ch M: 0900-2100, Fri/Sat to 2330) ✕ ⌂.

Town ▣ ✉ Ⓑ ⌂ Ⓞ ✕ ⌂ ⇌ ✈ (Anglesey/Liverpool). Ferry/HSS to Dun Laoghaire and Dublin.

MINOR HARBOURS (HW –0240 on Dover, see table (←)). May be useful, in settled conditions only, on passage N, see Pl.

Trearddur Bay (3M south) **53°16´·66N 04°37´·50W**. AC 1970, 5609,Imray C52. ⌕ (private, small craft only) or poss ⌕; open to prevailing SW'lies.

PORTH DINLLAEN, Gwynedd, **52°56´·68N 04°33´·66W**. AC 1971, 1512. Shelter good in S to W winds but strong NNW to NNE winds cause heavy seas in the bay. Beware Carreg-y-Chad (1·8m) 0·75M SW of the point, and Carreg-y-Chwislen (dries, with unlit IDM Bn) 2ca ENE of the point. From N, Garn Fadryn (369m) brg 182° leads into the bay. Best ⌕ 1ca S of LB ho in approx 2m.
HM ☎(01758) 720276. Facilities: ⌂ ⌂ by landing stage.

Morfa Nefyn (1M) ▣ ⌂ ✕ ⌂.

ABERDARON BAY, Gwynedd, **52°47´·75N 04°42´·82W**. AC 5609, 1410, 1411, 1971, 5609. In SE appr to bay are 2 islets Ynys Gwylan-fawr and Ynys Gwylan-bâch with a deep water passage between them, also passage between Ynys Gwylan-fawr and Trwyn Gwningaer (shore). ⌕ 4ca SSW of church in 5-10m, limited protection and subject to swell at times but sheltered in winds from W through N to NE. **Do not leave craft unattended due to poor holding ground**. Dinghy landing with care on shingle beach at Porth Simddy or Meudwy, W side of bay.

Village limited facilities: ⚓ ✉ ✕ ⌂ ⇌ (Pwllheli).

BARDSEY ISLAND – YNYS ENNLI, Gwynedd, **52°45´·00N 04°47´·40W**. AC 5609, 1410, 1411, 1971. Island of historical interest with ruined abbey and religious settlement since 6th century (now a managed farm and nature reserve, see 0.29). ⌕ W of Pen Cristin in appr to Henllwyn Cove in 4m is sheltered in winds from WSW through N to NE but is subject to swell at times. Small craft may ⌕ in the cove with caution, but beware isolated rocks and shoals. Landing at jetty in rocks marked by small boathouse at top of slip.

STANDARD TIME (UT)
For Summer Time add ONE hour in **non-shaded areas**

HOLYHEAD   LAT 53°19'N   LONG 4°37'W
TIMES AND HEIGHTS OF HIGH AND LOW WATERS

Dates in **red** are **SPRINGS**
Dates in blue are NEAPS

YEAR 2016

JANUARY

	Time	m		Time	m
1 F	0235 0835 1450 2117	4.8 1.9 4.9 1.8	**16** SA ◑	0230 0836 1452 2112	5.2 1.3 5.4 1.2
2 SA ◗	0327 0927 1544 2215	4.6 2.2 4.7 2.0	**17** SU	0330 0938 1555 2218	4.9 1.6 5.2 1.4
3 SU	0430 1031 1650 2321	4.4 2.4 4.6 2.1	**18** M	0442 1051 1709 2331	4.8 1.7 5.0 1.6
4 M	0540 1143 1802	4.4 2.4 4.6	**19** TU	0600 1208 1827	4.8 1.7 5.0
5 TU	0026 0647 1250 1908	2.1 4.6 2.2 4.7	**20** W	0043 0712 1319 1937	1.5 4.9 1.6 5.1
6 W	0123 0743 1346 2003	1.9 4.8 2.0 4.8	**21** TH	0149 0813 1422 2037	1.4 5.2 1.3 5.2
7 TH	0211 0828 1433 2048	1.7 5.0 1.7 5.0	**22** F	0245 0903 1515 2127	1.2 5.4 1.1 5.4
8 F	0253 0908 1514 2128	1.5 5.3 1.4 5.2	**23** SA	0332 0948 1601 2211	1.1 5.6 0.9 5.5
9 SA	0332 0946 1554 2207	1.2 5.5 1.1 5.2	**24** SU ○	0414 1029 1643 2252	1.0 5.7 0.8 5.5
10 SU ●	0410 1023 1633 2245	1.0 5.7 0.9 5.5	**25** M	0452 1107 1721 2329	1.0 5.8 0.8 5.5
11 M	0449 1102 1713 2325	0.9 5.8 0.8 5.6	**26** TU	0529 1144 1758	0.9 5.7 0.8
12 TU	0529 1142 1754	0.8 5.9 0.7	**27** W	0005 0603 1220 1833	5.4 1.0 5.6 1.0
13 W	0007 0610 1225 1837	5.6 0.8 5.9 0.7	**28** TH	0040 0638 1254 1908	5.3 1.2 5.5 1.1
14 TH	0052 0654 1310 1924	5.5 0.9 5.8 0.8	**29** F	0115 0714 1328 1945	5.1 1.4 5.3 1.4
15 F	0139 0742 1358 2014	5.4 1.1 5.6 1.0	**30** SA	0151 0752 1406 2025	4.9 1.6 5.1 1.6
			31 SU	0232 0836 1449 2112	4.7 1.9 4.8 1.9

FEBRUARY

	Time	m		Time	m
1 M ◗	0322 0928 1543 2210	4.5 2.1 4.6 2.1	**16** TU	0411 1027 1647 2307	4.8 1.6 4.8 1.7
2 TU	0427 1035 1657 2322	4.4 2.3 4.4 2.2	**17** W	0535 1150 1814	4.6 1.7 4.7
3 W	0546 1154 1819	4.4 2.3 4.4	**18** TH	0027 0657 1309 1933	1.8 5.0 1.6 4.8
4 TH	0036 0659 1306 1930	2.1 4.5 2.1 4.6	**19** F	0140 0803 1416 2034	1.6 5.0 1.4 5.0
5 F	0138 0757 1404 2024	1.9 4.6 1.8 4.8	**20** SA	0237 0855 1508 2120	1.4 5.2 1.1 5.2
6 SA	0228 0844 1452 2109	1.6 5.1 1.4 5.1	**21** SU	0322 0937 1550 2159	1.2 5.4 0.9 5.3
7 SU	0311 0924 1534 2149	1.2 5.4 1.0 5.4	**22** M ○	0401 1014 1627 2234	1.0 5.6 0.8 5.4
8 M ●	0351 1004 1614 2228	0.9 5.7 0.7 5.6	**23** TU	0435 1048 1701 2307	0.9 5.6 0.8 5.4
9 TU	0431 1043 1655 2308	0.7 5.9 0.7 5.7	**24** W	0507 1121 1732 2339	0.9 5.6 0.8 5.4
10 W	0511 1124 1736 2350	0.5 6.1 0.3 5.8	**25** TH	0539 1153 1804	0.9 5.6 0.9
11 TH	0553 1207 1819	0.5 6.1 0.3	**26** F	0010 0610 1225 1835	5.4 1.0 5.5 1.0
12 F	0032 0636 1252 1903	5.7 0.5 6.0 0.5	**27** SA	0042 0643 1256 1908	5.3 1.1 5.3 1.2
13 SA	0118 0722 1338 1952	5.5 0.7 5.8 0.8	**28** SU	0115 0717 1330 1943	5.1 1.3 5.1 1.4
14 SU	0206 0813 1430 2046	5.3 1.0 5.5 1.1	**29** M	0151 0756 1408 2024	4.9 1.6 4.9 1.7
15 M ◗	0302 0914 1530 2150	5.0 1.4 5.1 1.5			

MARCH

	Time	m		Time	m
1 TU ◗	0233 0842 1454 2114	4.7 1.9 4.6 2.0	**16** W ◗	0345 1009 1631 2245	4.8 1.6 4.7 1.9
2 W	0327 0942 1558 2222	4.5 2.1 4.3 2.2	**17** TH	0510 1133 1803	4.6 1.7 4.5
3 TH	0444 1100 1730 2346	4.3 2.2 4.3 2.2	**18** F	0009 0638 1255 1923	1.9 4.6 1.6 4.6
4 F	0611 1224 1855	4.4 2.1 4.4	**19** SA	0124 0747 1400 2021	1.8 4.8 1.4 4.8
5 SA	0102 0721 1332 1957	2.0 4.7 1.7 4.7	**20** SU	0221 0838 1450 2105	1.5 5.1 1.2 5.0
6 SU	0200 0815 1425 2045	1.6 5.0 1.3 5.1	**21** M	0305 0918 1530 2140	1.3 5.3 1.0 5.2
7 M	0247 0859 1509 2127	1.2 5.4 0.8 5.4	**22** TU	0341 0952 1604 2212	1.1 5.4 0.8 5.3
8 TU	0329 0940 1551 2207	0.8 5.7 0.5 5.7	**23** W	0413 1024 1635 2242	0.9 5.5 0.8 5.4
9 W ●	0409 1021 1632 2247	0.5 6.0 0.2 5.8	**24** TH	0443 1055 1705 2311	0.9 5.5 0.8 5.4
10 TH	0450 1103 1714 2329	0.3 6.2 0.1 5.9	**25** F	0513 1126 1734 2341	0.8 5.5 0.8 5.4
11 F	0533 1147 1757	0.2 6.2 0.1	**26** SA	0544 1157 1804	0.9 5.4 1.0
12 SA	0012 0616 1232 1842	5.9 0.3 6.1 0.3	**27** SU	0012 0615 1229 1836	5.3 1.0 5.3 1.1
13 SU	0057 0703 1320 1930	5.7 0.5 5.8 0.7	**28** M	0045 0649 1302 1909	5.2 1.2 5.1 1.3
14 M	0144 0755 1411 2023	5.4 0.8 5.4 1.1	**29** TU	0120 0726 1339 1948	5.0 1.4 4.9 1.6
15 TU ◗	0238 0855 1512 2126	5.1 1.2 5.0 1.5	**30** W	0159 0810 1422 2035	4.8 1.6 4.6 1.9
			31 TH ◗	0249 0906 1521 2139	4.6 1.9 4.4 2.1

APRIL

	Time	m		Time	m
1 F	0356 1019 1647 2302	4.4 2.0 4.3 2.2	**16** SA	0607 1227 1858	4.6 1.6 4.5
2 SA	0524 1144 1818	4.4 1.9 4.4	**17** SU	0055 0717 1332 1956	1.9 4.7 1.5 4.7
3 SU	0023 0641 1256 1926	2.0 4.6 1.6 4.7	**18** M	0154 0809 1422 2039	1.7 4.9 1.3 4.9
4 M	0127 0740 1353 2017	1.6 5.0 1.1 4.9	**19** TU	0238 0850 1502 2114	1.5 5.1 1.1 5.1
5 TU	0218 0829 1441 2101	1.2 5.4 0.7 5.4	**20** W	0315 0925 1536 2145	1.2 5.2 1.0 5.2
6 W	0303 0914 1525 2143	0.7 5.7 0.4 5.7	**21** TH	0347 0957 1606 2215	1.1 5.3 0.9 5.3
7 TH ●	0346 0957 1608 2224	0.4 6.0 0.1 5.9	**22** F ○	0417 1029 1636 2244	1.0 5.4 0.9 5.4
8 F	0429 1041 1652 2307	0.2 6.2 0.2 6.0	**23** SA	0448 1100 1706 2315	0.9 5.4 1.0 5.4
9 SA	0513 1127 1736 2351	0.1 6.2 0.1 5.9	**24** SU	0519 1132 1737 2347	0.9 5.3 1.0 5.4
10 SU	0559 1214 1822	0.2 6.0 0.4	**25** M	0552 1205 1809	1.0 5.2 1.1
11 M	0037 0647 1304 1910	5.7 0.4 5.7 0.7	**26** TU	0020 0627 1240 1844	5.3 1.1 5.1 1.3
12 TU	0126 0740 1357 2003	5.5 0.7 5.3 1.2	**27** W	0057 0705 1318 1923	5.2 1.3 4.9 1.5
13 W	0219 0840 1458 2105	5.1 1.1 4.9 1.6	**28** TH	0137 0749 1403 2010	5.0 1.5 4.7 1.7
14 TH	0323 0951 1614 2219	4.8 1.5 4.6 1.9	**29** F	0225 0843 1459 2110	4.8 1.6 4.5 1.9
15 F ◗	0442 1110 1740 2341	4.6 1.6 4.5 2.0	**30** SA ◗	0327 0950 1615 2226	4.6 1.7 4.4 2.0

Chart Datum: 3·05 metres below Ordnance Datum (Newlyn). HAT is 6·3 metres above Chart Datum.

》》 **FREE** monthly updates. Register at 《
www.reedsnauticalalmanac.co.uk

HOLYHEAD   LAT 53°19′N   LONG 4°37′W
TIMES AND HEIGHTS OF HIGH AND LOW WATERS

YEAR 2016

MAY

Time	m	Time	m
1 0444	4.6	**16** 0012	2.0
1108	1.7	0632	4.6
SU 1741	4.5	M 1251	1.6
2345	1.9	1916	4.6
2 0601	4.8	**17** 0113	1.9
1219	1.4	0729	4.7
M 1851	4.8	TU 1344	1.5
		2003	4.8
3 0052	1.6	**18** 0203	1.7
0704	5.0	0815	4.9
TU 1320	1.1	W 1427	1.3
1946	5.1	2041	5.0
4 0147	1.2	**19** 0243	1.5
0758	5.4	0854	5.0
W 1412	0.7	TH 1504	1.2
2034	5.5	2115	5.1
5 0236	0.8	**20** 0319	1.3
0847	5.7	0929	5.1
TH 1459	0.4	F 1537	1.1
2118	5.7	2147	5.2
6 0323	0.5	**21** 0351	1.2
0934	5.9	1003	5.2
F 1545	0.2	SA 1609	1.0
● 2202	5.8	○ 2219	5.3
7 0409	0.3	**22** 0424	1.1
1022	6.0	1036	5.2
SA 1631	0.2	SU 1640	1.0
2247	5.9	2251	5.4
8 0456	0.2	**23** 0458	1.0
1110	6.0	1110	5.2
SU 1717	0.3	M 1713	1.1
2333	5.9	2325	5.4
9 0544	0.3	**24** 0533	1.0
1159	5.8	1145	5.2
M 1804	0.5	TU 1748	1.1
10 0020	5.8	**25** 0001	5.4
0634	0.5	0609	1.1
TU 1250	5.6	W 1223	5.1
1853	0.8	1825	1.2
11 0109	5.5	**26** 0039	5.3
0726	0.7	0649	1.2
W 1342	5.2	TH 1303	5.0
1944	1.2	1906	1.4
12 0201	5.2	**27** 0121	5.2
0823	1.1	0734	1.3
TH 1440	4.9	F 1349	4.8
2041	1.6	1953	1.6
13 0300	5.0	**28** 0209	5.0
0927	1.4	0826	1.4
F 1547	4.6	SA 1443	4.7
☽ 2147	1.9	2049	1.7
14 0407	4.7	**29** 0305	4.9
1037	1.6	0927	1.5
SA 1701	4.5	SU 1549	4.6
2301	2.0	☽ 2157	1.8
15 0521	4.6	**30** 0412	4.9
1147	1.7	1036	1.4
SU 1815	4.5	M 1704	4.6
		2310	1.7
		31 0524	4.9
		1145	1.3
		TU 1815	4.8

JUNE

Time	m	Time	m
1 0018	1.5	**16** 0119	1.9
0631	5.1	0733	4.7
W 1249	1.1	TH 1347	1.6
1916	5.0	2004	4.8
2 0118	1.2	**17** 0207	1.7
0731	5.3	0821	4.8
TH 1346	0.8	F 1430	1.5
2009	5.3	2045	5.0
3 0213	0.9	**18** 0249	1.5
0825	5.5	0902	4.9
F 1437	0.6	SA 1508	1.3
2058	5.5	2121	5.1
4 0304	0.7	**19** 0327	1.3
0917	5.7	0939	5.1
SA 1527	0.5	SU 1543	1.2
2145	5.7	2155	5.3
5 0353	0.5	**20** 0403	1.2
1007	5.8	1014	5.1
SU 1614	0.5	M 1618	1.1
● 2231	5.8	○ 2230	5.4
6 0443	0.4	**21** 0439	1.0
1056	5.8	1050	5.2
M 1702	0.5	TU 1653	1.1
2318	5.8	2306	5.5
7 0532	0.4	**22** 0516	1.0
1146	5.7	1128	5.2
TU 1749	0.7	W 1730	1.0
		2344	5.5
8 0005	5.7	**23** 0555	0.9
0620	0.5	1207	5.2
W 1235	5.5	TH 1809	1.1
1835	0.9		
9 0052	5.6	**24** 0024	5.5
0710	0.8	0635	0.9
TH 1324	5.2	F 1249	5.1
1923	1.2	1851	1.2
10 0140	5.3	**25** 0106	5.4
0801	1.0	0719	1.0
F 1415	4.9	SA 1334	5.0
2013	1.5	1937	1.3
11 0230	5.1	**26** 0153	5.3
0855	1.3	0808	1.1
SA 1509	4.7	SU 1424	4.9
2107	1.8	2029	1.4
12 0325	4.8	**27** 0244	5.2
0953	1.6	0903	1.2
SU 1610	4.5	M 1522	4.8
☽ 2209	2.0	☽ 2129	1.6
13 0426	4.6	**28** 0344	5.2
1056	1.7	1006	1.3
M 1715	4.4	TU 1631	4.8
2317	2.1	2238	1.6
14 0532	4.5	**29** 0452	5.0
1159	1.8	1115	1.3
TU 1821	4.5	W 1743	4.8
		2348	1.5
15 0021	2.1	**30** 0603	5.1
0637	4.6	1222	1.2
W 1257	1.7	TH 1850	5.0
1917	4.6		

JULY

Time	m	Time	m
1 0055	1.4	**16** 0129	2.0
0710	5.2	0747	4.6
F 1325	1.1	SA 1356	1.7
1950	5.2	2013	4.8
2 0156	1.1	**17** 0220	1.7
0811	5.3	0836	4.8
SA 1422	0.9	SU 1440	1.5
2043	5.4	2055	5.1
3 0252	0.9	**18** 0303	1.4
0906	5.5	0917	5.0
SU 1514	0.8	M 1520	1.3
2132	5.6	2133	5.3
4 0344	0.7	**19** 0342	1.2
0957	5.6	0955	5.1
M 1602	0.7	TU 1557	1.1
● 2219	5.7	○ 2209	5.4
5 0433	0.5	**20** 0420	1.0
1045	5.6	1032	5.3
TU 1648	0.7	W 1634	1.0
2304	5.8	2246	5.6
6 0520	0.5	**21** 0458	0.8
1131	5.5	1110	5.4
W 1732	0.8	TH 1712	0.9
2348	5.7	2325	5.7
7 0605	0.6	**22** 0537	0.7
1216	5.4	1150	5.4
TH 1815	0.9	F 1752	0.8
8 0031	5.6	**23** 0006	5.7
0648	0.8	0617	0.7
F 1300	5.2	SA 1232	5.4
1856	1.1	1833	0.9
9 0114	5.4	**24** 0048	5.7
0731	1.0	0700	0.7
SA 1342	5.0	SU 1315	5.3
1939	1.4	1918	1.0
10 0156	5.2	**25** 0133	5.6
0815	1.3	0747	0.9
SU 1425	4.8	M 1403	5.2
2024	1.6	2007	1.2
11 0240	5.0	**26** 0222	5.4
0903	1.5	0839	1.0
M 1513	4.6	TU 1456	5.2
2113	1.9	☽ 2104	1.4
12 0329	4.7	**27** 0319	5.2
0956	1.8	0939	1.3
TU 1609	4.4	W 1600	4.8
☽ 2212	2.1	2211	1.6
13 0429	4.5	**28** 0427	5.0
1058	1.9	1049	1.4
W 1714	4.4	TH 1715	4.8
2320	2.2	2326	1.6
14 0537	4.4	**29** 0544	4.9
1202	2.0	1202	1.5
TH 1822	4.4	F 1831	4.8
15 0029	2.1	**30** 0040	1.5
0646	4.5	0659	5.0
F 1303	1.9	SA 1312	1.4
1923	4.6	1938	5.0
		31 0149	1.3
		0806	5.1
		SU 1414	1.2
		2035	5.3

AUGUST

Time	m	Time	m
1 0248	1.0	**16** 0238	1.5
0902	5.3	0855	4.9
M 1507	1.1	TU 1456	1.4
2123	5.5	2109	5.3
2 0338	0.8	**17** 0319	1.1
0950	5.4	0934	5.2
TU 1552	0.9	W 1535	1.1
● 2207	5.7	2146	5.5
3 0423	0.7	**18** 0358	0.8
1033	5.5	1011	5.4
W 1634	0.8	TH 1613	0.8
2249	5.7	○ 2224	5.8
4 0504	0.6	**19** 0436	0.6
1113	5.5	1049	5.6
TH 1713	0.8	F 1651	0.7
2328	5.7	2303	5.9
5 0543	0.7	**20** 0515	0.4
1152	5.4	1128	5.7
F 1751	0.9	SA 1731	0.6
		2344	6.0
6 0006	5.6	**21** 0556	0.4
0620	0.8	1210	5.6
SA 1229	5.3	SU 1812	0.6
1827	1.0		
7 0043	5.5	**22** 0027	5.9
0657	1.0	0638	0.5
SU 1305	5.1	M 1253	5.5
1903	1.3	1856	0.8
8 0119	5.3	**23** 0112	5.8
0734	1.2	0724	0.7
M 1342	5.0	TU 1340	5.4
1942	1.5	1945	1.0
9 0156	5.1	**24** 0201	5.5
0814	1.5	0815	1.0
TU 1422	4.8	W 1431	5.1
2025	1.8	2042	1.3
10 0238	4.8	**25** 0258	5.2
0859	1.8	0914	1.3
W 1509	4.6	TH 1535	4.9
☽ 2115	2.0	☽ 2150	1.6
11 0329	4.6	**26** 0408	4.9
0954	2.0	1027	1.6
TH 1609	4.4	F 1654	4.5
2218	2.2	2312	1.7
12 0438	4.4	**27** 0534	4.8
1102	2.2	1148	1.8
F 1724	4.4	SA 1819	4.8
2335	2.3		
13 0558	4.3	**28** 0033	1.6
1216	2.1	0657	4.8
SA 1838	4.5	SU 1304	1.7
		1930	5.0
14 0050	2.1	**29** 0145	1.4
0713	4.5	0805	5.0
SU 1321	2.0	M 1408	1.5
1940	4.7	2027	5.2
15 0150	1.8	**30** 0242	1.1
0810	4.7	0857	5.2
M 1412	1.7	TU 1458	1.2
2028	5.0	2113	5.5
		31 0328	0.9
		0939	5.3
		W 1539	1.1
		2153	5.6

Chart Datum: 3·05 metres below Ordnance Datum (Newlyn). HAT is 6·3 metres above Chart Datum.

N Wales

STANDARD TIME (UT)
For Summer Time add ONE hour in **non-shaded areas**

HOLYHEAD   LAT 53°19'N   LONG 4°37'W
TIMES AND HEIGHTS OF HIGH AND LOW WATERS

Dates in red are **SPRINGS**
Dates in blue are **NEAPS**

YEAR 2016

SEPTEMBER

Time	m		Time	m
1 0407	0.8	**16** 0331	0.7
1016	5.4	0947	5.6
TH 1616	0.9	F 1548	0.7
● 2229	5.7	○ 2159	5.9
2 0443	0.7	**17** 0410	0.4
1051	5.5	1025	5.8
F 1651	0.9	SA 1627	0.5
2304	5.7	2239	6.1
3 0517	0.7	**18** 0450	0.3
1124	5.5	1105	5.9
SA 1724	0.9	SU 1708	0.4
2338	5.6	2321	6.2
4 0550	0.8	**19** 0532	0.3
1157	5.4	1147	5.9
SU 1757	1.0	M 1751	0.4
5 0011	5.5	**20** 0005	6.1
0622	1.0	0615	0.4
M 1230	5.3	TU 1231	5.8
1830	1.2	1836	0.6
6 0044	5.3	**21** 0052	5.9
0655	1.2	0702	0.7
TU 1303	5.1	W 1318	5.5
1905	1.4	1926	0.9
7 0118	5.1	**22** 0143	5.6
0731	1.5	0753	1.1
W 1339	5.0	TH 1410	5.3
1944	1.7	2025	1.3
8 0156	4.9	**23** 0242	5.2
0811	1.8	0854	1.5
TH 1421	4.7	F 1514	5.0
2030	2.0	◖ 2136	1.6
9 0241	4.6	**24** 0357	4.8
0900	2.0	1010	1.9
F 1514	4.5	SA 1636	4.8
◖ 2128	2.2	2300	1.7
10 0343	4.4	**25** 0528	4.7
1005	2.3	1134	2.0
SA 1627	4.4	SU 1804	4.8
2244	2.3		
11 0512	4.3	**26** 0023	1.7
1126	2.3	0652	4.8
SU 1752	4.5	M 1252	1.9
		1917	5.0
12 0008	2.2	**27** 0133	1.5
0638	4.4	0756	5.0
M 1244	2.1	TU 1355	1.6
1903	4.7	2013	5.2
13 0116	1.9	**28** 0227	1.2
0742	4.7	0844	5.2
TU 1342	1.8	W 1442	1.4
1957	5.0	2056	5.4
14 0208	1.5	**29** 0310	1.0
0829	5.0	0922	5.3
W 1428	1.4	TH 1521	1.2
2040	5.4	2133	5.6
15 0252	1.1	**30** 0346	0.9
0909	5.3	0955	5.4
TH 1509	1.1	F 1555	1.1
2120	5.7	2206	5.6

OCTOBER

Time	m		Time	m
1 0419	0.9	**16** 0344	0.4
1026	5.5	1000	5.9
SA 1626	1.0	SU 1604	0.5
● 2238	5.6	○ 2215	6.2
2 0449	0.9	**17** 0426	0.2
1056	5.5	1042	6.0
SU 1657	1.0	M 1647	0.4
2310	5.6	2300	6.3
3 0519	0.9	**18** 0509	0.3
1127	5.5	1125	6.0
M 1728	1.1	TU 1732	0.4
2341	5.5	2346	6.2
4 0550	1.1	**19** 0555	0.5
1158	5.4	1211	5.9
TU 1801	1.2	W 1820	0.6
5 0013	5.4	**20** 0035	5.9
0621	1.3	0642	0.8
W 1231	5.3	TH 1259	5.7
1835	1.4	1912	0.9
6 0047	5.2	**21** 0129	5.5
0655	1.5	0735	1.2
TH 1306	5.1	F 1353	5.4
1912	1.6	2012	1.2
7 0123	5.0	**22** 0229	5.1
0733	1.8	0836	1.6
F 1345	4.9	SA 1456	5.1
1955	1.9	◖ 2122	1.5
8 0206	4.7	**23** 0344	4.8
0818	2.0	0949	2.0
SA 1434	4.7	SU 1614	4.9
2050	2.1	2242	1.7
9 0303	4.4	**24** 0511	4.7
0919	2.3	1111	2.1
SU 1538	4.5	M 1739	4.9
◖ 2201	2.2		
10 0426	4.3	**25** 0000	1.7
1039	2.4	0631	4.7
M 1704	4.5	TU 1228	2.0
2325	2.1	1851	5.0
11 0559	4.4	**26** 0109	1.6
1201	2.2	0734	4.9
TU 1821	4.7	W 1330	1.8
		1948	5.1
12 0037	1.8	**27** 0202	1.4
0707	4.7	0821	5.1
W 1306	1.9	TH 1419	1.6
1920	5.1	2032	5.3
13 0134	1.4	**28** 0245	1.2
0758	5.1	0901	5.3
TH 1357	1.5	F 1458	1.4
2008	5.4	2108	5.4
14 0221	1.0	**29** 0320	1.1
0841	5.4	0930	5.4
F 1441	1.1	SA 1531	1.3
2051	5.8	2141	5.5
15 0303	0.7	**30** 0352	1.0
0921	5.7	1000	5.5
SA 1522	0.7	SU 1602	1.2
2133	6.0	● 2213	5.5
		31 0422	1.0
		1030	5.4
		M 1633	1.1
		2244	5.5

NOVEMBER

Time	m		Time	m
1 0451	1.1	**16** 0451	0.4
1100	5.6	1108	6.1
TU 1704	1.2	W 1717	0.4
2316	5.5	2332	6.1
2 0522	1.2	**17** 0538	0.6
1131	5.5	1155	6.0
W 1737	1.2	TH 1808	0.6
2348	5.4		
3 0554	1.3	**18** 0022	5.8
1205	5.4	0627	0.9
TH 1812	1.4	F 1244	5.8
		1900	0.8
4 0023	5.2	**19** 0116	5.5
0627	1.5	0718	1.2
F 1240	5.3	SA 1337	5.5
1849	1.5	1958	1.1
5 0100	5.0	**20** 0214	5.2
0705	1.7	0815	1.6
SA 1320	5.1	SU 1435	5.3
1931	1.7	2101	1.4
6 0143	4.8	**21** 0321	4.9
0749	2.0	0920	1.9
SU 1406	4.9	M 1543	5.0
2022	1.9	◗ 2212	1.7
7 0236	4.6	**22** 0436	4.7
0845	2.2	1034	2.1
M 1504	4.8	TU 1658	4.9
● 2126	2.0	2324	1.8
8 0347	4.5	**23** 0552	4.7
0957	2.3	1147	2.2
TU 1617	4.7	W 1810	4.9
2242	2.0		
9 0514	4.5	**24** 0030	1.7
1117	2.2	0657	4.8
W 1735	4.8	TH 1253	2.1
2355	1.8	1911	5.0
10 0627	4.8	**25** 0127	1.6
1226	1.9	0748	4.9
TH 1841	5.1	F 1346	1.9
		2000	5.1
11 0056	1.4	**26** 0213	1.5
0724	5.1	0829	5.1
F 1323	1.5	SA 1430	1.7
1935	5.4	2041	5.2
12 0149	1.0	**27** 0251	1.4
0812	5.4	0904	5.3
SA 1412	1.2	SU 1506	1.5
2023	5.7	2117	5.3
13 0235	0.7	**28** 0325	1.3
0855	5.7	0936	5.4
SU 1458	0.8	M 1540	1.4
2109	6.0	2150	5.4
14 0320	0.5	**29** 0357	1.2
0938	5.9	1007	5.5
M 1543	0.5	TU 1612	1.3
○ 2155	6.2	● 2223	5.4
15 0405	0.4	**30** 0428	1.2
1022	6.1	1038	5.6
TU 1629	0.4	W 1645	1.2
2243	6.2	2255	5.4

DECEMBER

Time	m		Time	m
1 0500	1.2	**16** 0525	0.7
1111	5.6	1141	6.0
TH 1719	1.2	F 1757	0.6
2329	5.3		
2 0533	1.3	**17** 0010	5.8
1145	5.5	0612	0.9
F 1754	1.3	SA 1230	5.9
		1846	0.7
3 0005	5.2	**18** 0101	5.5
0608	1.4	0700	1.1
SA 1222	5.5	SU 1318	5.7
1832	1.4	1938	1.0
4 0044	5.1	**19** 0152	5.2
0646	1.6	0750	1.5
SU 1301	5.3	M 1409	5.4
1913	1.5	2032	1.3
5 0126	5.0	**20** 0246	4.8
0729	1.7	0844	1.8
M 1345	5.2	TU 1503	5.1
2001	1.6	2130	1.6
6 0215	4.8	**21** 0346	4.7
0820	1.9	0944	2.0
TU 1437	5.1	W 1604	4.9
2057	1.7	◗ 2234	1.8
7 0315	4.7	**22** 0453	4.6
0922	2.0	1052	2.2
W 1539	5.0	TH 1712	4.7
◗ 2202	1.7	2339	1.9
8 0428	4.7	**23** 0602	4.5
1034	2.0	1201	2.2
TH 1650	5.0	F 1820	4.7
2313	1.6		
9 0544	4.8	**24** 0040	1.9
1145	1.9	0704	4.7
F 1800	5.1	SA 1304	2.1
		1921	4.8
10 0019	1.4	**25** 0135	1.8
0648	5.0	0754	4.9
SA 1250	1.6	SU 1357	2.0
1903	5.3	2011	4.9
11 0119	1.2	**26** 0221	1.7
0744	5.3	0836	5.1
SU 1346	1.3	M 1441	1.7
1959	5.6	2053	5.0
12 0212	0.9	**27** 0300	1.5
0834	5.6	0913	5.2
M 1438	1.0	TU 1519	1.5
2051	5.8	2131	5.2
13 0302	0.7	**28** 0335	1.4
0921	5.8	0947	5.4
TU 1528	0.7	W 1554	1.4
2141	6.0	2205	5.3
14 0350	0.6	**29** 0408	1.3
1007	6.0	1020	5.5
W 1616	0.5	TH 1628	1.2
○ 2231	6.0	● 2239	5.4
15 0437	0.6	**30** 0442	1.2
1054	6.1	1053	5.6
TH 1707	0.5	F 1703	1.1
2321	5.9	2314	5.3
		31 0516	1.2
		1129	5.6
		SA 1739	1.1
		2350	5.3

Chart Datum: 3·05 metres below Ordnance Datum (Newlyn). HAT is 6·3 metres above Chart Datum.

》》**FREE** monthly updates. Register at 《
www.reedsnauticalalmanac.co.uk

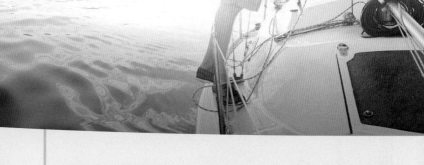

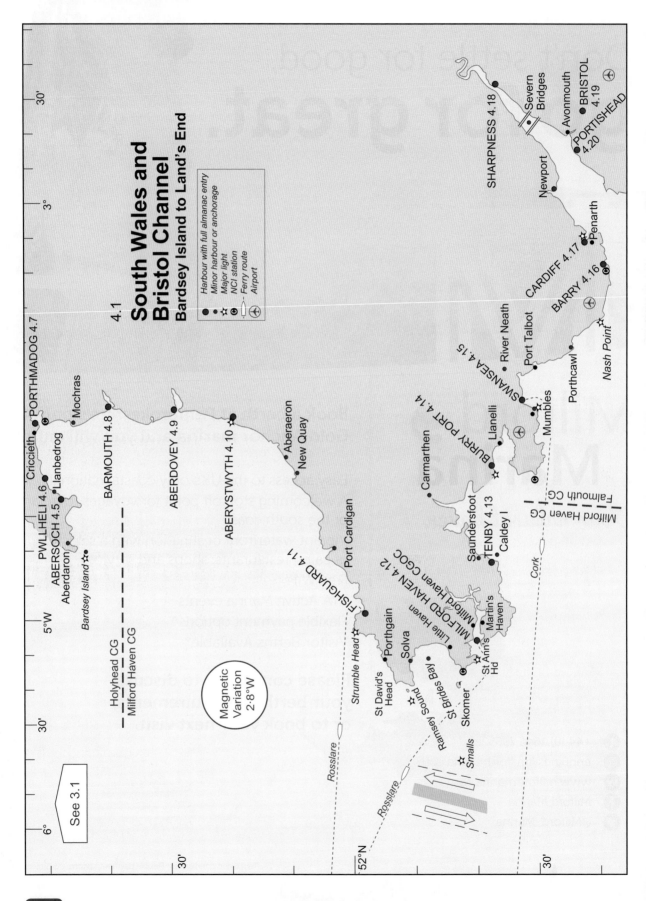

4.1

South Wales and Bristol Channel

Bardsey Island to Land's End

- ● Harbour with full almanac entry
- ● Minor harbour or anchorage
- ☆ Major light
- ☼ NCI station
- ⛴ Ferry route
- ✈ Airport

See 3.1

Magnetic Variation 2·8'W

Holyhead CG
Milford Haven CG

PORTHMADOG 4.7
Criccieth
PWLLHELI 4.6
Llanbedrog
ABERSOCH 4.5
Aberdaron
Bardsey Island ☆
Mochras
BARMOUTH 4.8
ABERDOVEY 4.9
ABERYSTWYTH 4.10
Aberaeron
New Quay
Port Cardigan
FISHGUARD 4.11
Strumble Head ☆
St David's Head
Porthgain
Solva
Little Haven
Ramsey Sound
St Brides Bay
Skomer
Smalls ☆
St Ann's Hd
Martin's Haven
MILFORD HAVEN 4.12
Milford Haven CGOC
Carmarthen
Saundersfoot
TENBY 4.13
Caldey I
BURRY PORT 4.14
Llanelli
Mumbles
SWANSEA 4.15
River Neath
Port Talbot
Porthcawl
Nash Point ☆
BARRY 4.16
CARDIFF 4.17
Penarth
Newport
SHARPNESS 4.18
Severn Bridges
Avonmouth
BRISTOL 4.19
PORTISHEAD 4.20

Milford Haven CG
Falmouth CG

Cork
Rosslare
Rosslare
Rosslare

5°W
6°
30'
30'
30'
3°
30'
52°N
30'

128

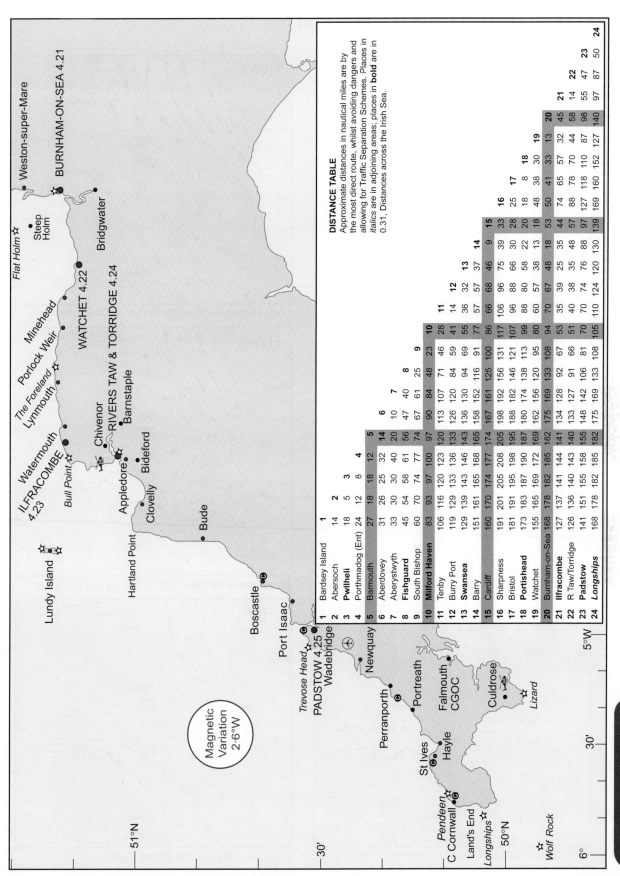

DISTANCE TABLE

Approximate distances in nautical miles are by the most direct route, whilst avoiding dangers and allowing for Traffic Separation Schemes. Places in *italics* are in adjoining areas; places in **bold** are in 0.31, Distances across the Irish Sea.

		1	2	3	4	5	6	7	8	9	10	11	12	13	14	15	16	17	18	19	20	21	22	23	24
1	Bardsey Island	1																							
2	Abersoch	14	**2**																						
3	**Pwllheli**	18	5	**3**																					
4	Porthmadog (Ent)	24	12	8	**4**																				
5	Barmouth	27	18	18	12	**5**	**14**																		
6	Aberdovey	31	26	25	32	18	**6**																		
7	Aberystwyth	33	30	30	40	20	10	**7**																	
8	**Fishguard**	45	54	58	61	56	47	40	**8**																
9	South Bishop	60	70	74	77	74	67	61	25	**9**															
10	**Milford Haven**	83	93	97	100	97	90	84	48	23	**10**														
11	Tenby	106	116	120	123	120	113	107	71	46	28	**11**													
12	Burry Port	119	129	133	136	133	126	120	84	59	41	14	**12**												
13	**Swansea**	129	139	143	146	143	136	130	94	69	55	36	32	**13**											
14	Barry	151	161	165	168	165	158	152	116	91	77	57	57	37	**14**										
15	**Cardiff**	160	170	174	177	174	167	161	125	100	86	66	68	46	9	**15**									
16	Sharpness	191	201	205	208	205	192	156	131	117	106	96	75	39	33	**16**									
17	Bristol	181	191	195	198	195	188	182	146	121	107	96	88	66	30	28	25	**17**							
18	**Portishead**	173	183	187	190	187	180	174	138	113	99	88	80	58	22	20	18	8	**18**						
19	Watchet	155	165	169	172	169	162	156	120	95	80	60	57	38	13	18	48	38	30	**19**					
20	**Burnham-on-Sea**	168	178	182	185	182	175	169	133	108	94	70	67	48	18	53	50	41	33	13	**20**				
21	**Ilfracombe**	127	137	141	144	144	134	128	92	67	53	35	39	25	35	44	74	65	57	32	45	**21**			
22	R Taw/Torridge	126	136	140	143	140	133	127	91	66	51	40	38	35	48	57	88	78	70	44	13	14	**22**		
23	**Padstow**	141	151	155	158	155	148	142	106	81	70	70	74	76	88	97	127	118	110	87	58	55	47	**23**	
24	*Longships*	168	178	182	185	182	175	169	133	108	105	110	124	120	130	139	169	160	152	127	140	97	98	50	**24**

Magnetic Variation 2·6°W

5°W

30'

6°

51°N

30'

50°N

Weston-super-Mare

BURNHAM-ON-SEA 4.21

Steep Holm

Flat Holm

Bridgwater

WATCHET 4.22

Minehead

Porlock Weir

The Foreland

Lynmouth

RIVERS TAW & TORRIDGE 4.24

Watermouth

Chivenor

Barnstaple

ILFRACOMBE 4.23

Bull Point

Appledore

Bideford

Clovelly

Hartland Point

Bude

Lundy Island

Boscastle

Port Isaac

Trevose Head

PADSTOW 4.25

Wadebridge

Newquay

Perranporth

Portreath

Falmouth CGOC

Culdrose

Lizard

St Ives

Hayle

Pendeen

C Cornwall

Land's End

Longships

Wolf Rock

4.2 S WALES & BRISTOL CHANNEL TIDAL STREAMS

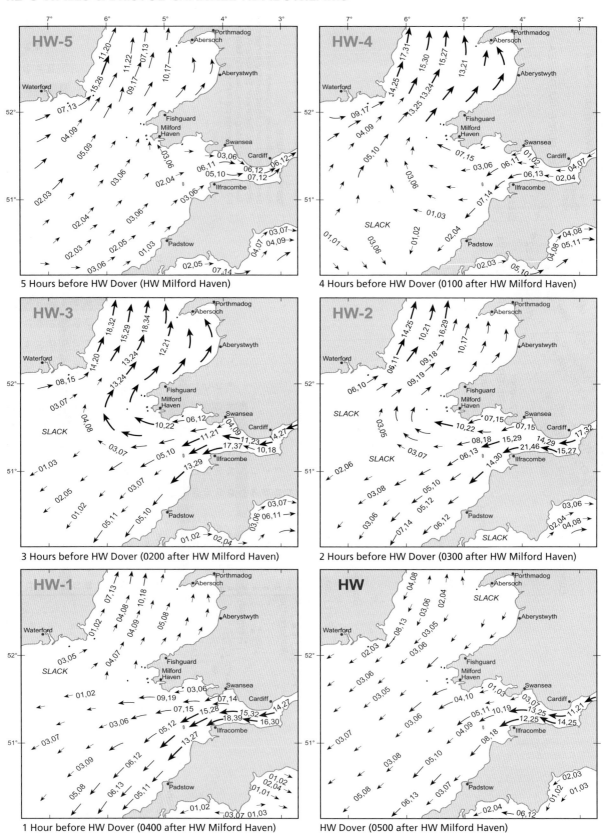

5 Hours before HW Dover (HW Milford Haven)

4 Hours before HW Dover (0100 after HW Milford Haven)

3 Hours before HW Dover (0200 after HW Milford Haven)

2 Hours before HW Dover (0300 after HW Milford Haven)

1 Hour before HW Dover (0400 after HW Milford Haven)

HW Dover (0500 after HW Milford Haven)

Northward 3.2   South Ireland 5.2

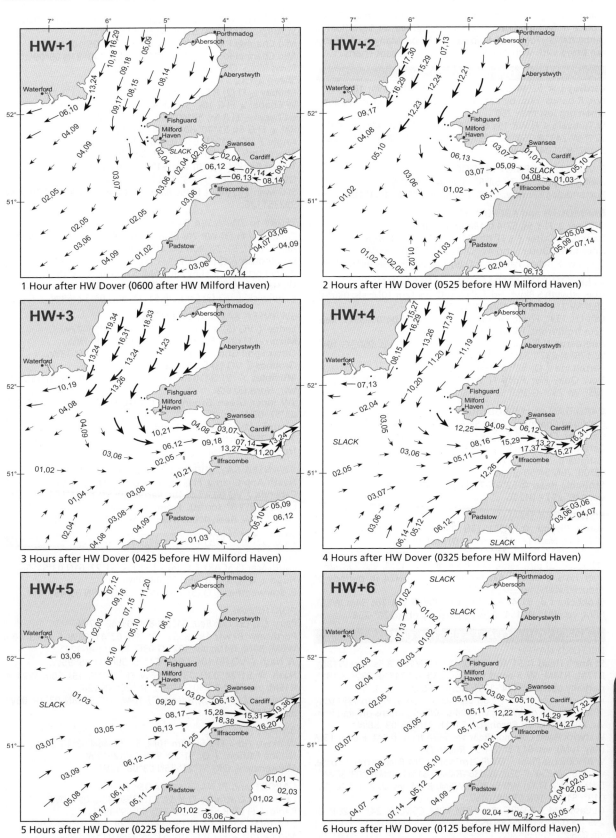

1 Hour after HW Dover (0600 after HW Milford Haven)

2 Hours after HW Dover (0525 before HW Milford Haven)

3 Hours after HW Dover (0425 before HW Milford Haven)

4 Hours after HW Dover (0325 before HW Milford Haven)

5 Hours after HW Dover (0225 before HW Milford Haven)

6 Hours after HW Dover (0125 before HW Milford Haven)

4.3 LIGHTS, BUOYS AND WAYPOINTS

Bold print = light with a nominal range of 15M or more. CAPITALS = place or feature. *CAPITAL ITALICS* = light-vessel, light float or Lanby. *Italics* = Fog signal. ***Bold italics*** = Racon. Many marks/buoys are fitted with with AIS (<u>MMSI No</u>); see relevant charts.

CARDIGAN BAY (SEE ALSO 9.10.4)

Bardsey I ☆ 52°44'·98N 04°48'·01W Fl R 10s 39m **18M**; W □ twr, R bands; obsc by Bardsey I 198°-250° and in Tremadoc B when brg less than 260°.
St Tudwal's ⚓ Fl WR 15s 46m W14, R10M; vis: 349°-W-169°-R-221°-W-243°-R-259°-W-293°-R-349°; obsc by East I 211°-231°; 52°47'·92N 04°28'·30W.

PWLLHELI and PORTHMADOG

Pwllheli App ⚓ Iso 2s; 52°53'·03N 04°22'·90W.
Porthmadog Fairway ⚓ L Fl 10s; 52°53'·01N 04°11'·10W.

BARMOUTH and ABERDOVEY

Diffuser ⚓ Fl Y 5s; 52°43'·19N 04°05'·38W.
Barmouth Outer ⚓ L Fl 10s; 52°42'·62N 04°04'·83W.
Aberdovey Outer ⚓ Iso 4s; 52°32'·00N 04°05'·56W.
Cynfelyn Patches, Patches ⚓ Q (9) 15s; 52°25'·83N 04°16'·41W.

ABERYSTWYTH, ABERAERON and NEW QUAY

Aberystwyth S Bkwtr Hd ⚓ Fl (2) WG 10s 12m 10M; vis: 030°-G-053°-W-210°; 52°24'·40N 04°05'·52W.
Ldg Lts 133°. Front, FR 4m 5M; 52°24'·37N 04°05'·39W. Rear, 52m from front, FR 7m 6M.
Aberaeron N Pier ⚓ Fl (4) WRG 15s 10m 6M; vis: 050°-G-104°-W-178°-R-232°; 52°14'·61N 04°15'·87W.
Carreg Ina ⚓ Q; 52°13'·25N 04°20'·75W.
New Quay Pier Hd ⚓ Fl WG 3s 12m W8M, G5M; G △; vis: 135°-W- 252°-G-295; 52°12'·95N 04°21'·35W.

CARDIGAN and FISHGUARD

Cardigan Channel ⚓ Fl (2) 5s; 52°06'·44N 04°41'·43W.
Cardigan Cliff Base Bn 1 ⚓ Fl R 4s 3M; 52°07'·05N 04°41'·39W.
Cardigan Cliff Base Bn 2 ⚓ Fl R 2s 3M; 52°06'·91N 04°41'·34W.
Fishguard N Bkwtr Hd ⚓ Fl G 4·5s 18m 13M; *Bell (1) 8s;* 52°00'·76N 04°58'·23W.
Strumble Head ☆ 52°01'·79N 05°04'·43W Fl (4) 15s 45m **26M**; vis: 038°-257°; (H24).

BISHOPS and SMALLS

South Bishop ☆ 51°51'·14N 05°24'·74W Fl 5s 44m **16M**; W ○ twr; *Horn (3) 45s;* ***Racon (O)10M***; (H24).
The Smalls ☆ 51°43'·27N 05°40'·19W Fl (3) 15s 36m **18M**; ***Racon (T);*** *Horn (2) 60s.* Same twr, Iso R 4s 33m 13M; vis: 253°-285° over Hats & Barrels Rk; both Lts shown H24 in periods of reduced visibility; <u>992351123</u>.
Skokholm I ⚓, 51°41'·64N 05°17'·22W Fl WR 10s 54m W8M, R8M; vis: 301°-W-154°-R-301°; partially obsc 226°-258°.

WALES – SOUTH COAST – BRISTOL CHANNEL

MILFORD HAVEN

St Ann's Head ☆ 51°40'·87N 05°10'·42W Fl WR 5s 48m **W18M, R17M**; W 8-sided twr; vis: 233°-W-247°-R-332°-W131°, partially obscured 124°-129°; *Horn (2) 60s.*
W Blockhouse Point ⚓ Ldg Lts 022·5°. Front, F 54m 13M (day 10M); B stripe on W twr; vis: 004·5°-040·5°; intens on lead line. vis: 004·5°-040·5°; ***Racon (Q);*** 51°41'·31N 05°09'·56W.
Watwick Point Common Rear ☆, 0·5M from front, F 80m **15M** (day 10M); vis: 013·5°-031·5°; ***Racon (Y).***
W Blockhouse Point ⚓ Q WR 21m W9M, R7M; R lantern on W base: vis: 220°-R-020°-W-036°-R-049°; 51°41'·31N 05°09'·56W.
Dale Fort ⚓ Fl (2) WR 5s 20m W5M, R3M; vis: 222°-R-276°-W-019°; 51°42'·16N 05°09'·01W.
Gt Castle Hd ⚓ F WRG 27m W5M, R3M, G3M; vis: 243°-R-281°-G-299°-W-029°; 51°42'·68N 05°07'·06W. Co-located Dir WRG (040°); vis: 038·25°-G-039°-AlWG-039·5°-W-040·5°-AlWR-041°-R-041·75°

(**not** used in conjunction with the front ldg light below)
Ldg Lts ≠ 039·7° **Front,** Oc 4s 27m **15M**; vis: 031·2°-048·2°. **Rear,** 890m from front. Oc 8s 53m **15M** (day 10M); vis: 031·2°-048·2°.
St Ann's ⚓ Fl R 2·5s; 51°40'·25N 05°10'·51W.
Mid Channel Rks ⚓ Q (9) 15s; 51°40'·18N 05°10'·14W.
Mid Channel Rk ⚓ Fl (3) G 7s 18m 8M; 51°40'·31N 05°09'·83W.
Rows Rks ⚓ Q R; 51°40'·22N 05°09'·02W.
Sheep ⚓ QG; 51°40'·06N 05°08'·31W.
Millbay ⚓ Fl (2) R 5s; 51°41'·05N 05°09'·45W.
W Chapel ⚓ Fl G 10s; 51°40'·98N 05°08'·67W.
E Chapel ⚓ Fl R 5s; 51°40'·87N 05°08'·15W.
Rat ⚓ Fl G 5s; 51°40'·80N 05°07'·86W.
Angle ⚓ VQ; 51°41'·63N 05°08'·27W.
Thorn Rock ⚓ Q (9) 15s; 51°41'·53N 05°07'·76W.
Turbot Bank ⚓ VQ (9) 10s; 51°37'·41N 05°10'·08W.
ODAS Fl(5) Y 20s; 51°36'·70N 05°08'·70W.
St Gowan ⚓ Q (6) + L Fl 15s, ***Racon (T) 10M***; 51°31'·93N 04°59'·77W; <u>992351126</u>.

TENBY to SWANSEA BAY

Caldey I ⚓ Fl (3) WR 20s 65m W13M, R9M; vis: R173°- W212°-R088°-102°; 51°37'·90N 04°41'·08W.
Woolhouse ⚓ Q (6) + L Fl 15s; 51°39'·35N 04°39'·69W.
Burry Port Inlet ⚓ Fl 5s 7m 6½M; 51°40'·62N 04°15'·06W.
W. Helwick ⚓ (9) 15s; ***Racon (T) 10M***; 51°31'·40N 04°23'·65W.
E. Helwick ⚓ VQ (3) 5s; *Bell;* 51°31'·80N 04°12'·68W.

SWANSEA BAY and SWANSEA

Ledge ⚓ VQ (6) + L Fl 10s; 51°29'·93N 03°58'·77W.
Mixon ⚓ Fl (2) R 5s; *Bell;* 51°33'·12N 03°58'·78W.
Outer Spoil Gnd ⚓ Fl Y 2·5s; 51°32'·11N 03°55'·73W.
Grounds ⚓ VQ (3) 5s; 51°32'·81N 03°53'·47W.
Mumbles ☆ 51°34'·01N 03°58'·27W Fl (4) 20s 35m **15M**; W twr; *Horn (3) 60s.*
SW Inner Green Grounds ⚓ Q(6)+L Fl 15s; *Bell;* 51°34'·06N 03°57'·03W.
Swansea Lts in line 020°. Front: E Breakwater head, Oc G 4s 5m 2M & 2FG(vert) 10m 6M; 51°36'·38N 03°55'·62W. Rear, 3·1ca from front: FG 6M.

SWANSEA BAY, RIVER NEATH and PORT TALBOT

Neath App Chan ⚓ Fl G 5s; 51°35'·71N 03°52'·83W.
Cabenda ⚓ VQ (6) + L Fl 10s; ***Racon (Q)***; 51°33'·36N 03°52'·23W.
Ldg Lts 059·8° (occas). Front, Oc R 3s 12m 6M; 51°34'·92N 03°48'·10W. Rear, 400m from front, Oc R 6s 32m 6M.

BRISTOL CHANNEL – NORTH SHORE (EASTERN PART)

W Scar ⚓ Q (9) 15s, *Bell,* ***Racon (T) 10M***; 51°28'·31N 03°55'·57W.
South Scar (S SCAR) ⚓ Q (6) + L Fl 15s; 51°27'·61N 03°51'·58W.
Hugo ⚓ Q R; 51°28'·55N 03°48'·03W.
E. Scarweather ⚓ Q (3) 10s; *Bell;* 51°27'·98N 03°46'·76W.

PORTHCAWL

Fairy ⚓ Q (9) 15s; *Bell;* 51°27'·86N 03°42'·07W.
Porthcawl Bkwtr Hd ⚓ Fl 51°28'·39N 03°41'·98W F WRG 10m W6M, R4M, G4M; vis: 302°-G-036°-W-082°-R-122°.
W Nash ⚓ VQ (9) 10s ; *Bell;* 51°25'·99N 03°45'·95W.
Nash ☆ 51°24'·03N 03°33'·06W Fl (2) WR 15s 56m **W21M, R16M**; vis: 280°-R-290°-W-100°-R-120°-W-128°.
Breaksea ⚓ L Fl 10s; ***Racon (T) 10M***; 51°19'·88N 03°19'·08W; <u>992351124</u>.

BARRY

W Bkwtr Hd ⚓ Fl 2·5s 12m 10M; 51°23'·46N 03°15'·52W.
N. One Fathom ⚓ Q; 51°20'·94N 03°12'·17W.
Mackenzie ⚓ QR; 51°21'·75N 03°08'·24W.

CARDIFF and PENARTH ROADS

Lavernock Outfall ⚓ Fl Y 5s; 51°23'·95N 03°09'·50W.
Ranie ⚓ Fl (2) R 5s; 51°24'·23N 03°09'·39W.
S Cardiff ⚓ Q (6) + L Fl 15s; *Bell;* 51°24'·18N 03°08'·57W.
Mid Cardiff ⚓ Fl (3) G 10s; 51°25'·60N 03°08'·09W.

Cardiff Spit ⍭ QR; 51°24'·57N 03°07'·12W.
N Cardiff ⍭ QG; 51°26'·52N 03°07'·19W.
Wrach Chan Dir lt 348·5°. Oc WRG 10s 5m; W3M, R3M, G3M;
vis: 344·5°-G-347°-W-350°-R-352°; H24; 51°27'·16N 03°09'·75W.
Outer Wrach ⍭ Q (9) 15s; 51°26'·20N 03°09'·46W.

FLATHOLM to THE BRIDGE
Flat Holm ☆, SE Pt 51°22'·54N 03°07'·14W Fl (3) WR 10s 50m **W15M,**
R12M; W ○ twr; vis: 106°-R-140°-W-151°-R-203°-W-106°; (H24).
Monkstone ⍭ Fl 5s 13m 12M; R column on W ○ twr; 51°24'·89N
03°06'·01W.
Tail Patch ⍭ QG; 51°23'·53N 03°03'·65W.
Hope ⍭ Q (3) 10s; 51°24'·84N 03°02'·68W.
NW Elbow ⍭ VQ (9) 10s; *Bell*; 51°26'·28N 02°59'·93W.
EW Grounds ⍭ L Fl 10s 7M; *Whis; Racon (T) 7M*; 51°27'·12N
02°59'·95W.

NEWPORT DEEP, RIVER USK and NEWPORT
Newport Deep ⍭ Fl (3) G 10s; *Bell;*51°29'·36N 02°59'·12W.
East Usk ☆ 51°32'·40N 02°58'·01W; Fl (2) WRG 10s 11m
W11M,R10M, G10M; vis: 284°-W-290° -obscured shore-324°-R-
017°-W-037°-G-115°-W-120°. Also Oc WRG 10s 10m W11M,
R9M, G9M; vis: 013°-G-017°-W- 019°-R-023°.
Julians Pill Ldg Lts 062°. Front, FG 5m 4M; 51°33'·30N
02°57'·94W. Rear, 61m from front, FG 8m 4M.

BRISTOL DEEP
N Elbow ⍭ QG; *Bell;* 51°26'·97N 02°58'·65W.
S Mid Grounds ⍭ VQ (6) + L Fl 10s; 51°27'·62N 02°58'·68W.
E Mid Grounds ⍭ Fl R 5s; 51°27'·75N 02°54'·98W.
Clevedon ⍭ VQ; 51°27'·39N 02°54'·93W.
Welsh Hook ⍭ Q (6) + L Fl 15s; 51°28'·53N 02°51'·86W.
Avon ⍭ Fl G 2·5s; 51°27'·92N 02°51'·73W.
Black Nore Pt Lt Ho; W ○ twr on frame; 51°29'·09N 02°48'·05W.
Newcome ⍭ 51°30'·01N 02°46'·71W Fl (3) R 10s.
Denny Shoal ⍭ VQ (6) + L Fl 10s; 51°30'·15N 02°45'·45W.
Cockburn ⍭ 51°30'·45N 02°44'·10W Fl R 2·5s.
W Dock Middle ⍭ 51°29.95'·01N 02°44'·20W Q G.
W Dock Outer ⍭ 51°30'·00N 02°44'·85W Fl G 5s.
Firefly ⍭ Fl (2) G 5s; 51°29'·96N 02°45'·35W.
Portishead Point ☆ 51°29'·68N 02°46'·42W Q (3) 10s 9m **16M**;
B twr, W base; vis: 060°-262°; *Horn 20s.*

PORTISHEAD
Pier Hd ⍭ Iso G 2s 5m 3M; 51°29'·69N 02°45'·27W.
Seabank. Dir WG 6m 5M; vis: 085·8°-FG-086·7°-AltWG-086·9°-FW-
089·7°. 5M; vis: 070·3°-103·3°; by day 1M, vis: 076·8°-096·8°.
Lts in line 086·8°. Q(8) 5M 10/16m; vis: 070·3°-103·3°; day 1M vis:
076·8°-096·8° Front 51°30'·07N 02°43'·80W; Rear, 500m behind.
Knuckle Lts in line 099·6°, Oc G 5s 6m 6M; 51°29'·94N 02°43'·67W.
Rear, 165m from front, FG 13m 6M; vis: 044°-134°.

AVONMOUTH
Royal Edward Dock N Pier Hd ⍭ Fl 4s 15m 10M; vis: 060°-228·5°;
51°30'·49N 02°43'·09W.
King Road Ldg Lts 072·4°. N Pier Hd ⍭ Front, Oc R 5s 5m 9M; W
obelisk, R bands; vis: 062°-082°; 51°30'·49N 02°43'·09W. Rear
⍭, 546m from front, QR 15m 10M; vis: 066°- 078°.

RIVER AVON, CUMBERLAND BASIN and AVON BRIDGE
S Pier Hd ⍭ Oc RG 30s 9m 10M and FBu 4m 1M; vis: 294°-R-
036°-G-194°; 51°30'·37N 02°43'·10W. *Bell(1) 10s.*
Ldg Lts 127·2°. Front ⍭, Iso R 2s 6m 3M, vis: 010°-160°; 51°30'·10N
02°42'·59W. Rear⍭ , Iso R 2s10m 3M, vis: 048°-138°.

WESTON-SUPER-MARE
Pier Hd ⍭ 2 FG (vert) 6m; 51°20'·88N 02°59'·26W.
E Culver ⍭ Q (3) 10s; 51°18'·00N 03°15'·44W.
W Culver ⍭ VQ (9) 10s; 51°17'·47N 03°19'·00W.
Gore ⍭ Iso 5s; *Bell;* 51°13'·94N 03°09'·79W.

BURNHAM-ON-SEA and RIVER PARRETT
Ent ⍭ Fl 7·5s 7m 12M; vis: 074°-164°; 51°14'·89N 03°00'·36W;
Dir lt 076°. F WRG 4m W12M, R10M, G10M; vis: 071°-G- 075°-
W-077°- R-081°.
DZ No. 1 ⍭ Fl Y 2·5s; 51°15'·28N 03°09'·49W.
DZ No. 2 ⍭ Fl Y 10s; 51°13'·77N 03°19'·86W.
DZ No. 3 ⍭ Fl Y 5s; 51°16'·34N 03°14'·98W.

WATCHET, MINEHEAD and PORLOCK WEIR
Watchet W Bkwtr Hd ⍭ Oc G 3s 9m 9M; 51°11'·03N 03°19'·74W.
Watchet E Pier ⍭ 2 FR (vert) 3M; 51°11'·01N 03°19'·72W.
Minehead Bkwtr Hd ⍭ Fl (2) G 5s 4M; vis: 127°-262°; 51°12'·81N
03°28'·36W.
Lynmouth Foreland ☆ 51°14'·73N 03°47'·21W Fl (4) 15s 67m
18M; W ○ twr; vis: 083°-275°; (H24).

LYNMOUTH and WATERMOUTH
River Training Arm ⍭ 2 FR (vert) 6m 5M; 51°13'·90N 03°49'·83W.
Harbour Arm ⍭ 2 FG (vert) 6m 5M; 51°13'·92N 03°49'·84W.
Sand Ridge ⍭ Q G; 51°15'·01N 03°49'·77W.
Copperas Rock ⍭ Fl G 2·5s; 51°13'·78N 04°00'·60W.
Watermouth ⍭ Oc WRG 5s 1m 3M; W △; vis: 149·5°-G-151·5°-W-
154·5°-R-156·5°; 51°12'·93N 04°04'·60W.

ILFRACOMBE to BAGGY POINT
Ldg Lts 188°. Front, Oc 10s 8m 3M; 51°12'·53N 04°06'·65W.
Rear, Oc 10s 6m 3M.
Horseshoe ⍭ Q; 51°15'·02N 04°12'·96W.
Bull Point ☆ 51°11'·94N 04°12'·09W Fl (3) 10s 54m **20M**; W ○ twr,
obscd shore-056°. Same twr; FR 48m 12M; vis: 058°-096°.
Morte Stone ⍭ Fl G 5s; 51°11'·30N 04°14'·95W.
Baggy Leap ⍭ Fl (2) G 10s; 51°08'·92N 04°16'·97W.

BIDEFORD, RIVERS TAW and TORRIDGE
Bideford Fairway ⍭ L Fl 10s; *Bell;* 51°05'·25N 04°16'·25W.
Bideford Bar ⍭ Q G; 51°04'·89N 04°14'·62W.
Instow ☆ Ldg Lts 118°. **Front,** 51°03'·62N 04°10'·66W Oc 6s
22m **15M**; vis: 103·5°-132°. **Rear,** 427m from front, Oc 10s 38m
15M; vis: 103°-132·5°; (H24).
Crow Pt ⍭ Fl WR 2. 5s 8m W6M R5M; vis: 225°-R-232°-W-237°-
R-358°-W- 015°-R-045°; 51°03'·96N 04°11'·39W.

LUNDY
Near North Point ☆ 51°12'·10N 04°40'·65W Fl 15s 48m **17M**;
vis: 009°-285°.
South East Point ☆ 51°09'·72N 04°39'·37W Fl 5s 53m **15M**;
vis: 170°-073°.
Hartland Point ⍭ 51°01'·3N 04°31'·6W Fl (6) 15s 30m 8M;
adjacent to Hartland Point Light House (disused).

BUDE, PADSTOW and NEWQUAY
Compass Point twr 50°49'·71N 04°33'·42W.
Stepper Point (Padstow) ⍭ L Fl 10s 12m 4M; 50°34'·12N
04°56'·72W.
Trevose Head ☆ 50°32'·94N 05°02'·13W Fl 7·5s 62m **21M**.
North Pier Hd (Newquay) ⍭ 2 FG (vert) 5m 2M; 50°25'·07N
05°05'·19W.

HAYLE and ST IVES
The Stones ⍭ Q; 50°15'·64N 05°25'·51W.
Godrevy I ⍭ Fl WR 10s 28m 8M; metal post; vis: 022°-W-101°-
R-145°-W-272°; 50°14'·56N 05°24'·01W;
adjacent to Godrevy Light House (disused).
Hayle App ⍭ QR; 50°12'·26N 05°26'·30W.
St Ives App ⍭ 50°12'·85N 05°28'·42W.
Bann Shoal ⍭ Fl G 2.5s; *Racon (B) 10M*; 50°20'·03N 05°51'·11W;
992351053.
Pendeen ☆ 50°09'·90N 05°40'·30W Fl (4) 15s 59m **16M**; vis: 042°-
240°; between Gurnard Hd and Pendeen it shows to coast.

4.4 PASSAGE INFORMATION

More passage information is threaded between the harbours in this area. Admiralty Leisure Folio 5620 covers South West Wales, 5608 the Bristol Channel and 5603 the approach to Bristol Channel from Land's End. For additional tidal information east of Ilfracombe/Swansea see *Arrowsmith's Bristol Channel Tide Tables* from J.W. Arrowsmith Ltd ☎(0117) 9667545. **Bibliography:** *Bristol Channel and River Severn Cruising Guide*, Milford Haven to St Ives (Imray/Cumberlidge). The *West Coasts of England and Wales Pilot* (Admiralty NP37) covers the whole area.

It is useful to know some Welsh words with navigational significance.

Aber: estuary.	Afon: river.
Bach, bychan, fach: little.	Borth: cove.
Bryn: hill.	Careg, craig: rock.
Coch, goch: red.	Dinas: fort.
Ddu: black.	Fawr, Mawr: big.
Ffrydiau: tide rip.	Llwyd: grey.
Moel: bare conical hill.	Mor: sea.
Morfa: sandy shore.	Mynydd: mountain.
Penrhyn: headland.	Porth: cove.
Ynys, Ynysoedd: island(s).	

CARDIGAN BAY

(AC 1971, 1972, 1973) Harbours are mostly on a lee shore, and/or have bars which make them dangerous to approach in bad weather. Abersoch and Pwllheli offer best shelter from the prevailing westerlies. There may be overfalls off Trwyn Cilan, SW of St Tudwal's Is (lit). In N part of the bay there are three major dangers to coasting yachts: St Patrick's Causeway (Sarn Badrig) runs 12M SW from Mochras Pt. It is mostly large loose stones, and dries (up to 1·5m) for much of its length. In strong winds the sea breaks heavily at all states of tide. The outer end is marked by a WCM light buoy. At the inner end there is a channel about 5ca offshore, which can be taken with care at half tide.

Sarn-y-Bwch runs 4M WSW from Pen Bwch Pt. It is consists of rocky boulders, drying in places close inshore and with least depth 0·3m over 1M offshore. There is a WCM buoy off the W end. NW of Aberystwyth, Sarn Cynfelyn and Cynfelyn Patches extend 6·5M offshore, with depths of 1·5m in places. A WCM buoy is at the outer end. Almost halfway along the bank is Main Channel, 3ca wide, running roughly N/S but not marked.

Aberporth MOD Range occupies much of Cardigan Bay. It is usually active Mon-Fri 0900-1630LT, and some weekends, but times are subject to change. Active danger areas vary in size and location and may include the area off the Range head to the west of Aberporth. Beware of targets and buoys within the danger area, some unlit. Range activity is broadcast on VHF Ch 16 one hour before live firings. Flags are flown either side of the Range head to signify activity in the inner (yellow flags) or outer (red flags) danger areas. If passing through the area during operational hours contact *Aberporth Marine Control* on Ch 16 or Ch 13. Further information may be obtained from Aberporth Marine Control, ☎ (01239) 813760, or Aberporth Range Control ☎(01239) 813480.

If on passage N/S through St George's Chan (ie not bound for Cardigan B or Milford Haven) the easiest route, and always by night, is W of the Bishops and the Smalls, noting the TSS. If bound to/from Milford Haven or Cardigan Bay, passage inside both the Smalls and Grassholm is possible.

RAMSEY SOUND, THE BISHOPS, THE SMALLS TO MILFORD HAVEN

(AC 1478, 1482) The Bishops and the Clerks are islets and rocks 2·5M W and NW of Ramsey Island, a bird sanctuary SSW of St David's Head. N Bishop is the N'ly of the group, 3ca ENE of which is Bell Rock (depth 1·9m). S Bishop (Lt, fog sig) is 3M to the SSW.

Between S Bishop and Ramsey Is the dangers include Daufraich with offlying dangers to the E and heavy overfalls; Llech Isaf and Llech Uchaf drying rocks are further ENE. Carreg Rhoson and other dangers are between Daufraich and N Bishop. The navigable routes between most of these islets and rocks trend NE/SW. Use only by day, in good visibility and with local knowledge. The N/S route close W of Ramsey Is is considered easier than Ramsey Sound.

▶ *2M W of The Bishops the S-going stream begins at Milford Haven +0400, and the N-going at Milford Haven –0230, sp rates 2kn. Between The Bishops and Ramsey Is the SW-going stream begins at Milford Haven +0330, and the NE-going at Milford Haven –0300, sp rates 5kn. Ramsey Sound should be taken at slack water. S-going stream begins at Milford Haven +0300, and the N-going at Milford Haven –0330, sp rates 6kn at The Bitches, where the channel is narrow (2ca), decreasing N & S.* ◀

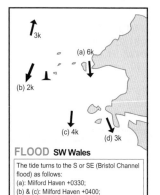

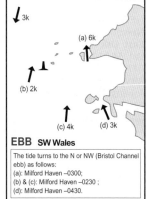

FLOOD SW Wales

The tide turns to the S or SE (Bristol Channel flood) as follows:
(a): Milford Haven +0330;
(b) & (c): Milford Haven +0400;
(d): Milford Haven +0200.

EBB SW Wales

The tide turns to the N or NW (Bristol Channel ebb) as follows:
(a): Milford Haven –0300;
(b) & (c): Milford Haven –0230 ;
(d): Milford Haven –0430.

The Bitches are rocks up to 4m high extending 2ca from E side of Ramsey Island. Other dangers are: Gwahan and Carreg-gafeiliog, both 3m high at N end of Sound, to W and E; Horse Rock (dries 0·9m) almost in mid-channel about 5ca NNE of The Bitches, with associated overfalls; Shoe Rock (dries 3m) at SE end of channel; and rocks extending 5ca SSE from S end of Ramsey Island.

St Brides Bay is a regular anchorage for tankers, but ⊥ only in settled weather/offshore winds as it is a trap in westerlies. Solva is a little hbr with shelter for boats able to take the ground, or ⊥ behind Black Rk (dries 3·6m) in the middle of the entrance.

The Smalls Lt, where there is a Historic Wreck (see 0.29) is 13M W of the Welsh mainland (Wooltack Pt). 2M and 4M E of The Smalls are the Hats and Barrels, rocky patches on which the sea breaks.

▶ *7M E of The Smalls is Grassholm Island with a race either end and strong tidal eddies so that it is advisable to pass about 1M off. The chan between Barrels and Grassholm is 2·5M wide, and here the S-going stream begins at Milford Haven +0440, and the N-going at Milford Haven –0135, sp rates 5kn.* ◀

Five miles of clear water lie between Grassholm and Skomer Is/Skokholm Is to the E. Wildgoose Race, which forms W of Skomer and Skokholm is very dangerous, so keep 2M W of these two Is. To E of Skomer Island Midland Island, and between here and Wooltack Point is Jack Sound, least width about 1ca. Do not attempt it without AC 1482, detailed pilotage directions, and only at slack water neaps.

▶ *Correct timing is important. The S-going stream begins at Milford Haven +0200, and the N-going at Milford Haven –0430, sp rates 6-7kn.* ◀

Rocks which must be identified include, from N to S: On E side of chan off Wooltack Pt, Tusker Rock (2m), steep-to on its W side; and off Anvil Point, The Cable (2·4m), The Anvil and Limpet Rocks (3·7m). On the W side lie the Crabstones (3·7m) and the Blackstones (1·5m).

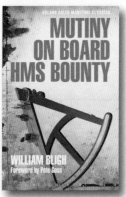
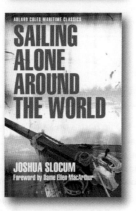
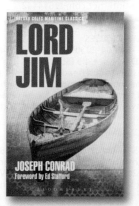

4.5 ABERSOCH

Gwynedd 52°49'·29N 04°29'·20W (⚓) ✵✵♨♨♙♙

CHARTS AC 5609, 1410, 1411, 1971, 1512; Imray C61, C52, C51

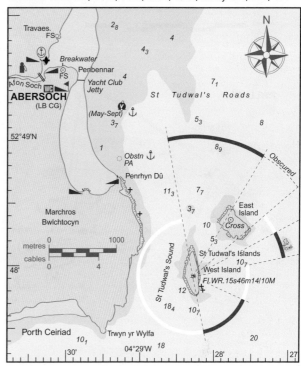

TIDES −0315 Dover; ML 2·5; Duration 0520; Zone 0 (UT)

Standard Port MILFORD HAVEN (→)

Times				Height (metres)			
High Water		Low Water		MHWS	MHWN	MLWN	MLWS
0100	0800	0100	0700	7·0	5·2	2·5	0·7
1300	2000	1300	1900				
Differences ST TUDWAL'S ROADS							
+0155	+0145	+0240	+0310	−2·2	−1·9	−0·7	−0·2
ABERDARON							
+0210	+0200	+0240	+0310	−2·4	−1·9	−0·6	−0·2

SHELTER There are few moorings for visitors. Apply to HM or SC. ⚓ in St Tudwal's Roads clear of moored yachts; sheltered from SSE through S to NE.

NAVIGATION WPT 52°48'·52N 04°26'·13W, 293°/2·4M to YC jetty. There are no navigational dangers, but steer well clear of the drying rks to the E of East Island; Carred y Trai buoy FlR 2·5s is 2ca E of these rks (just off chartlet). St Tudwal's islands themselves are fairly steep-to, except at N ends. St Tudwal's Sound is clear of dangers.

LIGHTS AND MARKS The only lt is on St Tudwal's West Island, Fl WR 15s 46m 14/10M (see chartlet and 4.3).

COMMUNICATIONS (Code 01758) CGOC (01407) 762051; Police 101; Dr 612535. HM 712203.

S Caernarfon YC Ch **80** M.

FACILITIES South Caernarvonshire YC ☎712338, ♦⚓⚓♦⚓✕ ⊡ (May-Sept).

Abersoch Power Boat Club ☎812027.

Services ⚓ ⚓✕✎⊡ R ⊡(12t).

Town ⚓ ACA, ✉ Ⓑ ⚒ ✕ ⊡ ⇌ (Pwllheli), ✈ (Chester).

4.6 PWLLHELI

Gwynedd 52°53′·23N 04°23′·75W ✿✿◊◊◊◊✿✿✿

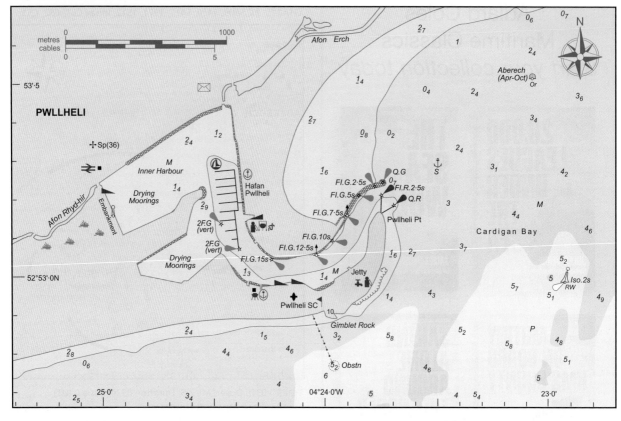

CHARTS AC 1410, 1971, 1512; Imray C61, C52, C51

TIDES –0315 Dover; ML 2·6; Duration 0510

Standard Port MILFORD HAVEN (→)

Times				Height (metres)			
High Water		Low Water		MHWS	MHWN	MLWN	MLWS
0100	0800	0100	0700	7·0	5·2	2·5	0·7
1300	2000	1300	1900				
Differences PWLLHELI							
+0210	+0150	+0245	+0320	–1·9	–1·6	–0·6	–0·1
CRICCIETH							
+0210	+0155	+0255	+0320	–2·0	–1·8	–0·7	–0·3

SHELTER Good in hbr and marina. Drying moorings in inner hbr (SW and NW bights).

NAVIGATION WPT 52°53′·02N 04°23′·07W, SWM lt buoy 299°/0·47M to QG lt at head of Training Arm.

- Ent is safe in most winds, but in strong E to SW winds sea breaks on offshore shoals.
- Ent subject to silting; 3 tide gauges. Average tidal stream 2kn.
- No ⚓ in hbr; 4kn speed limit.

LIGHTS AND MARKS See 4.3 and chartlet. Gimblet Rock (30m) is conspic conical rock 3ca SW of ent.

COMMUNICATIONS (Code 01758) CGOC (01407) 762051; Ⓗ Bangor (A&E) 01248 384384; Police 101; Dr 701457. HM ☎704081. Marina: Ch **80** M H24. HM: VHF Ch **16** (0900-1715).

FACILITIES Marina www.hafanpwllheli.co.uk ☎701219; 420⬲, £2·63+ⅅ £3·22, £13·30 <4hrs. Pontoons are numbered 4–12 from S–N; Pile berths on S side of appr channel.

Services 🅰️🛠️🔧⛽🚿⚓⚓️⛴️Ⓔ🚮◨(50t)⬲(14t)🔧 wi-fi,.
Marina Boat Club ☎612271, ⚓🔧🍴.
Harbour 6 ⚓, £8/craft/day, ⚓🔧🛠️⛽⚓🛠️⛵⚓.
Town ✉️Ⓑ🛒✕🍴⚐✈ (Chester).

YACHT CLUBS South Caernarvonshire YC ☎712338.
Pwllheli SC pwllhelisailingclub@btinternet.com ☎614442.
Marina Boat Club ☎612271, 🔧⚓🍴.

ADJACENT HARBOURS AND ANCHORAGES

LLANBEDROG, Gwynedd, **52°51′·14N 04°28′·09W**. AC 5609, 1410, 1411, 1971, 1512. HW –0245 on Dover, see 4.5 (St Tudwal's Roads). Good ⚓ N of Trwyn Llanbedrog (steep sided headland 131m) 1.0ca ENE of Bcn PHM in 2-3m. Beach has numerous conspicuous bathing huts. Sheltered in winds from N through W to SW. ⚓ well clear of local craft moorings as they have a long scope. Dinghy landing near boathouse.

Village limited facilities: 🔧🏦🏦 (½M) ✕⚐⚞ (Pwllheli).

MOCHRAS, Gwynedd, **52°49′·57N 04°07′·77W**. AC 1971, 1512. HW –0245 on Dover. Small yacht hbr in drying Mochras lagoon on SE side of Shell Is. Bar, about 2ca seaward. Appr advised HW±2, but HW±1 at sp. 3 grey posts, R topmarks, mark NE side of chan. Ebb tide runs strongly in the narrow ent between the sea wall and Shell Is (lt Fl WRG 4s, 079°-G-124°-W-134°-R-179°; Mar-Nov); at sp beware severe eddies inside. Inside ent, buoyed chan runs WSW to Shell Island Yacht Hbr ☎01341 241453.

Facilities: 🔧⚓🔧📷✕⚐. Shifting chan, marked by posts and buoys, runs NE to Pensarn, where permanent moorings limit space. Drying ⬲⚞.

4.7 PORTHMADOG

Gwynedd 52°55'·32N 04°07'·77W ✵⟡⟡⟡❀❀❀

CHARTS AC 1410, 1971, 1512; Imray C61, C51, C52

TIDES −0247 Dover; ML no data; Duration 0455

Standard Port MILFORD HAVEN (→)

Times				Height (metres)			
High Water		Low Water		MHWS	MHWN	MLWN	MLWS
0100	0800	0100	0700	7·0	5·2	2·5	0·7
1300	2000	1300	1900				
Differences PORTHMADOG							
+0235	+0210	ND	ND	−1·9	−1·8	ND	ND

SHELTER Inner hbr (N of Cei Ballast): Good all year round; visitors' drying ⌐ adjacent Madoc YC or afloat rafted on moored yachts. Outer hbr: Summer only, exposed to S winds. Speed limit 6kn in hbr upstream of No 8 buoy.

NAVIGATION WPT, 52°53'·01N 04°11'·10W, (SWM) Head ESE to enter laterally buoyed chan, which turns N at No 4 buoy to the E of N bank before turning NE off Ynys Gyngar (W Ho conspic).

- Channel shifts frequently and may divide but is well marked.
- Channel varies from that charted.
- In SW'lies, short steep-sided seas, especially on the ebb.
- Latest info from HM on request. Advise entering HW±1½.

LIGHTS AND MARKS Fairway buoy RW, L Fl 10s. SPM Fl Y 5s marks outfall 6 Ca to NW. Chan marker buoys Nos 1–9, 12,14, 15, 17 lit (May-Oct), have R/G reflective top marks and reflective numbers. Moel-y-Gest is conspic hill (259m) approx 1M WNW of harbour. Harlech Castle (ru) is about 3M SE of approach channel.

COMMUNICATIONS (Code 01766) CGOC (01407) 762051; Police 101; Dr 512284. HM 512927, mobile (07879) 433147; Pilot 530684. HM Ch 16 **12** (HO and when vessel due). Madoc YC Ch M.

FACILITIES Harbour £8·00 all craft, pilot, ⌐ access HW±4 (£10), ⬧(quay), ⬚ ⬚ ⬚(8t) ⬚ ACA.
Porthmadog SC ☎513546, ⬧⬧⬧.
Madoc YC ☎512976, ⬚ ⬧ ⌐ ⬚ ⬧ ⬚.
Town ⬚⬧⬧⬚⬚⬚⬚ ⇌ ✈ (Chester).

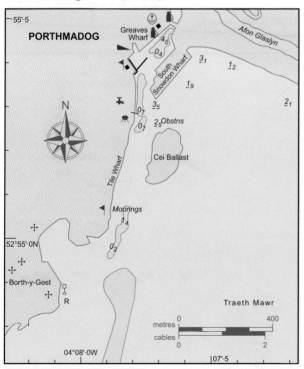

4.8 BARMOUTH

Gwynedd 52°42'·97N 04°03'·07W ✵✵⟡⟡❀❀❀

CHARTS AC 5609, 1410, 1971, 1484; Imray C61, C51

TIDES −0305 Dover; ML 2·6; Duration 0515

Standard Port MILFORD HAVEN (→)

Times				Height (metres)			
High Water		Low Water		MHWS	MHWN	MLWN	MLWS
0100	0800	0100	0700	7·0	5·2	2·5	0·7
1300	2000	1300	1900				
Differences BARMOUTH							
+0207	+0200	+0300	+0233	−2·0	−1·5	−0·6	0·0

SHELTER Good. Entry safe HW±2½, but impossible in strong SW'lies. Exposed ⌁ W of Barmouth Outer buoy in 6 to 10m. In hbr there are 5 ⬧s, a pontoon for up to 10 boats <10m able to take the ground to the N of the quay, at the W end of which is a ♥ berth that dries at half-tide. Secure as directed by HM because of submarine cables and strong tidal streams. Drying ⌁ inside Penrhyn Pt.

NAVIGATION WPT, Barmouth Outer SWM buoy, 52°42'·72N 04°05'·02W, 082°/0·8M to Y Perch lt, QR. Appr from SW between St Patrick's Causeway (Sarn Badrig) and Sarn-y-Bwch. Barmouth can be identified by Cader Idris, a mountain 890m high, 5M ESE. Fegla Fawr, a rounded hill, lies on S side of hbr.

- The Bar, 0·75M W of Penrhyn Pt, min depth 0·3m, is constantly changing. Chan is marked by buoys fitted with radar reflectors and reflective tape and moved as required.
- Spring ebb runs 3–5kn.
- The estuary and river (Afon Mawddach) are tidal and can be navigated for about 7M above railway br (clearance approx 5·5m); but chan is not buoyed, and sandbanks move constantly – local knowledge essential.

LIGHTS AND MARKS Outer SWM L Fl 10s; Bar SHM Fl G; No2 PHM Fl R. Y Perch Sth Cardinal bn Q6 +LFl 15s marks S end of stony ledge extending 3ca SW from Ynys y Brawd across N Bank, 50m to SE PHM, Q R, marks channel. Ynys y Brawd groyne, with bn, Fl R 5s 5M at SE end. NW end of railway bridge is lit, 2 FR (hor).

COMMUNICATIONS (Code 01341) CGOC (01407) 762051; Police 101; Dr 280521. HM 280671 mob 07795 012747; Local information www.barmouthwebcam.co.uk

Call *Barmouth Hbr* VHF Ch **12** 16 (Apr-Sep 0900-1700 later for HW; Oct-Mar 0900-1600); wind and sea state are available.

FACILITIES 3 drying ⬧ M (call HM in advance for deep water ⬧), 8 ⌐ inc 6♥ on pontoon/quay £10/£6 yacht (inc ⬚), ⬚ ⬧ ⬧ 2 ⌐ (HW±3, £10/day). ⬧ ⬧ ⬚ ⬚ at ⬚. **Merioneth YC** ☎280000.
Town ⬚⬚⬚⬚⬚⬚⬚ ✕ ⬧ ⇌ ✈ (Manchester/ L'pool); Ferry to Penrhyn Pt for **Fairbourne** ⬚⬚ ⇌.

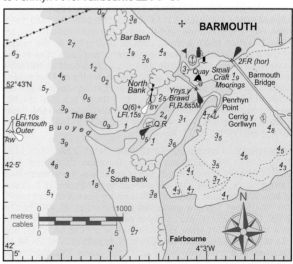

4.9 ABERDOVEY

Gwynedd 52°32'·57N 04°02'·72W (Jetty) ❀❀◊◊◊❀❀❀

CHARTS AC 5609, 1410, 1972, 1484; Imray C61, C51

TIDES –0320 Dover; ML 2·6; Duration 0535. For differences see 4.10.

SHELTER Good except in strong W/SW winds. Berth on jetty in 3m; to the E there is heavy silting.

NAVIGATION WPT Aberdovey Outer SWM buoy, 52°32'·00N 04°05'·56W, 093°/0.43M to Bar buoy.

- Bar and channel constantly shift and are hazardous below half-tide; buoys moved accordingly.
- Enter channel at gateway between Bar SHM and PHM Fl R 5s. Visitors should call HM on VHF before entering.

LIGHTS AND MARKS See 4.3 and chartlet. No daymarks. Lts may be unreliable. Submarine cables (prohib ⚓s) marked by bns with R ◊ topmarks.

COMMUNICATIONS (Code 01654) CGOC (01646) 690909; Police 101; Dr 710414; ℍ 710411. HM 767626, mob 07879 433148.
Call *Aberdovey Hbr* VHF Ch **12** 16.

FACILITIES Jetty/Wharf ⚓ ⤸ ⤳ 5◻ £8·00, ⚡ 🔧 ⬧.
Dovey YC ☎767607, ⤳ (£4.50 if engine <10hp) ⤸ 🔧 ⬜.
Ynyslas BY (S shore) 🚩(16t) 🔧.
Town 🏪 🍴 🏦 ⊠ Ⓑ 🛒 ✕ ⬜ ⇌ ✈ (Birmingham).

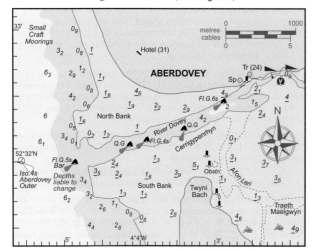

OTHER HARBOURS IN SOUTH PART OF CARDIGAN BAY

ABERAERON, Ceredigion, **52°14'·62N 04°15'·94W**. AC 1410, 1972, 1484. HW –0325 on Dover; +0140 and –1·9m on Milford Haven; ML 2·7m; Duration 0540. A small, popular drying hbr at the mouth of the R Aeron. Short drying piers extend each side of river ent. In strong NW'lies there is little shelter. ◻£8·50/craft on NW wall, only in calm conditions. Foul ground with depths of 1·5m extend 3ca offshore to SW of Aberaeron. Beware Carreg Gloyn (0·3m) 4ca WSW of hbr, and Sarn Cadwgan (1·8m) shoals 5ca N of the hbr ent. Lts (see 4.3 for sectors): N pier Fl (4) WRG 15s 10m 6M. S pier Fl (3) G 10s 11m 6M. VHF **14** 16. HM ☎(01545) 571645 🔧 🐟(from fishermen). YC ☎570077. Town 🏪.

NEW QUAY, Ceredigion, **52°12'·92N 04°21'·22W**. AC 1410, 1972, 1484. HW –0335 on Dover; Duration 0540; see 4.10. Good shelter in offshore winds, but untenable in North Westerlies. Carreg Ina, rks drying 1·3m, are marked by NCM buoy, Q, on E side of bay. 2 Y bns mark sewer outfall running 7ca NNW from Ina Pt. The hbr (dries 1·6m) is protected by a pier; Lt, Fl WG 3s 12m 8/5M; 135°-W-252°-G-295°. Groyne extends 80m SSE of pier head to a starboard bn; close ENE of which is a ECM bn, Q (3) 10s. HM ☎(01545) 560368; Dr ☎560203; YC ☎560516. VHF Ch **14** 16. Facilities: 🔧 🐟(from fishermen) ⤳ (£8·50). Town 🏪(3M) ⊠ ✕ ⬜.

4.10 ABERYSTWYTH

Ceredigion 52°24'·42N 04°05'·47W ❀❀◊◊◊❀❀❀

CHARTS AC 5609, 5620, 1410, 1972, 1484; Imray C61, C51

TIDES – 0330 Dover; ML 2·7; Duration 0540
Standard Port MILFORD HAVEN (→)

Times				Height (metres)			
High Water		Low Water		MHWS	MHWN	MLWN	MLWS
0100	0800	0100	0700	7·0	5·2	2·5	0·7
1300	2000	1300	1900				
Differences ABERDOVEY							
+0215	+0200	+0230	+0305	–2·0	–1·7	–0·5	0·0
ABERYSTWYTH							
+0145	+0130	+0210	+0245	–2·0	–1·7	–0·7	0·0
NEW QUAY							
+0150	+0125	+0155	+0230	–2·1	–1·8	–0·6	–0·1
ABERPORTH							
+0135	+0120	+0150	+0220	–2·1	–1·8	–0·6	–0·1

SHELTER Good, in marina (1·7m) on E side of chan; or dry against Town Quay.

NAVIGATION WPT 52°24'·83N 04°06'·22W,133°/0·6M° to ent. Appr dangerous in strong on-shore winds. The Bar, close off S pier hd, has 0·7m least depth. From N, beware Castle Rks, in R sector of N bkwtr lt; also rks drying 0·5m W of N bkwtr and boulders below S pier hd. Turn 90° port inside narrow ent. E edge of inner hbr chan 0·3m is defined by WCM bn which in line with Y daymark gives a daytime lead into the harbour.

LIGHTS AND MARKS N Bkwtr Hd ≠ 140° Wellington Mon't (on top Pendinas, conspic hill 120m high) clears to S of Castle Rks. Ldg lts 133°, both FR on Ystwyth Bridge, white daymarks. WCM bn on with Y daymark leads 100° across bar into harbour entrance.

COMMUNICATIONS (Code 01970) CGOC (01646) 690909; Police 101; Dr 624855. HM 611433, Mobile 07974 023965; Marina 611422.
HM Ch **14** 16. Marina Ch 80.

FACILITIES Marina (Y Lanfa), ☎611422 ⤳ (launch £10), ◻88+15◐
£2·80+£3⚡ ⛽ 🛁 🔧 🚩(10t) 🛥(15t by arrangement).
Town Quay ⚓ ◻ £8·50/craft, 🔧 🛒 ⚒ ⚙ 📞 Ⓔ 🛥(25t).
YC ☎612907, ⚓ ⤳ ⬜.
Town 🏪 🍴 🏦 ⊠ Ⓑ 🛒 ✕ ⬜ ⇌ ✈ (Swansea).

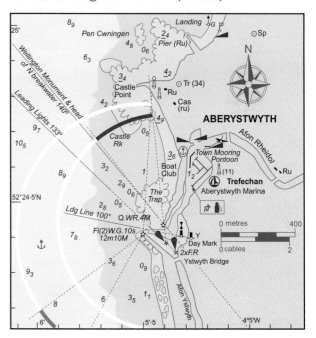

MINOR HARBOUR, 12M NE of Fishguard

PORT CARDIGAN, Ceredigion, **52°07′·02N 04°42′·07W**. AC 1973, 1484. HW –0405 on Dover; ML 2·4m; Duration 0550. Good shelter, but ent dangerous in strong N/NW winds. **Large scale charts are essential;** contact Afon Teifi Fairways Ltd, www.afonteififairways.com or Mooring Master (see below) in advance. The bar has 0·5m or less. ⚓ near Hotel (conspic) on E side of ent (2 bns Fl.R.4s, Fl.R.2s). Chan is usually close to E side marked by W posts; IDM (Fl (2) 5s) should be left to stbd when clear of the bar. ⚓ off Pen-yr-Ergyd. Inside spit pontoon or ⚓s off Teifi Boating Club, Mooring Master ☎(01239) 613966, mob 07799 284206. Upstream to Bryn-Du chan is marked by SWM but shifts constantly. St Dogmaels chan lies between ⚓s and pontoon, Mooring Master ☎07909 830752. Above the Ferry Inn chan runs up to the old bridge (3m clearance)through Netpool with deeper water moorings, Mooring Master ☎07814 035438.
Teifi Boating Club ☎613846, ⚓ ▱; Services: ⚒ ✗.
Town Ⓑ 🛒 🅟 🏧 🏨 ⚓ ⚒ ✗ ▱.

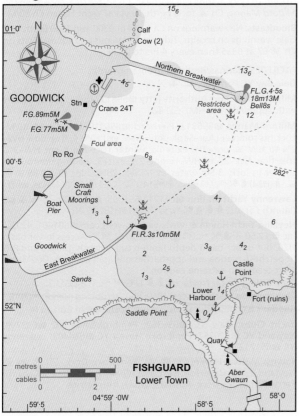

4.11 FISHGUARD

Pembrokeshire **52°00′·12N 04°58′·40W**
Commercial Hbr ✿✿✿✿✿; Lower Hbr ✿✿✿✿✿

CHARTS AC 5620, 1178, 1410, 1973, 1484; Imray C61, C51, C60

TIDES –0400 Dover; ML 2·6; Duration 0550

Standard Port MILFORD HAVEN (→)

Times				Height (metres)			
High Water		Low Water		MHWS	MHWN	MLWN	MLWS
0100	0800	0100	0700	7·0	5·2	2·5	0·7
1300	2000	1300	1900				
Differences FISHGUARD							
+0115	+0100	+0110	+0135	–2·2	–1·8	–0·5	+0·1
PORT CARDIGAN							
+0140	+0120	+0220	+0130	–2·3	–1·8	–0·5	0·0
CARDIGAN (Town)							
+0220	+0150	ND	ND	–2·2	–1·6	ND	ND
PORTHGAIN							
+0055	+0045	+0045	+0100	–2·5	–1·8	–0·6	0·0
RAMSEY SOUND							
+0030	+0030	+0030	+0030	–1·9	–1·3	–0·3	0·0
SOLVA							
+0015	+0010	+0035	+0015	–1·5	–1·0	–0·2	0·0
LITTLE HAVEN							
+0010	+0010	+0025	+0015	–1·1	–0·8	–0·2	0·0
MARTIN'S HAVEN							
+0010	+0010	+0015	+0015	–0·8	–0·5	+0·1	+0·1
SKOMER IS							
–0005	–0005	+0005	+0005	–0·4	–0·1	0·0	0·0

SHELTER Good, except in strong NW/NE winds. Beware large swell, especially in N winds. No ⚓, except SW of ferry quay. Good holding in most of the bay. At Lower town ⚓ off Saddle or Castle Points in 1·4m. Strong S'lies funnel down the hbr.

NAVIGATION WPT 52°01′·02N 04°57′·57W, 237°/0·48M to N bkwtr lt. *Keep at least 1ca clear of N bkwtr head; beware of ferries and High-Speed SeaCats manoeuvring.*

LIGHTS AND MARKS See 4.3 and chartlet. Strumble Hd Lt ho, Fl (4) 15s 45m 26M, is approx 4M WNW of hbr. The SHM (bn) at Aber Gwaun is very small.

COMMUNICATIONS (Code 01348) CGOC (01646) 690909; Police 101; Dr 872802. Commercial Hbr Supervisor 404425.

HM Ch **14** 16. Goodwick Marine Ch M (occas).

FACILITIES Fishguard (Lower town) dries 3·2m; limited 🅿, £5/night, 15⚓ (drying, max 5 tons), ⚓ ⚓ ⛽ 🅿 (from Goodwick Marine) ✗ ⚒ 🅿 🛒 ACA.
Fishguard Bay YC ⚓ ⚓ ▱.
Town 🅿 🅿 🏧 ✉ Ⓑ Ⓑ 🛒 ✗ ▱@ ⇌ ✈ (Cardiff), Ferry to Rosslare; 2/day; 1¾hrs; Stena Line (www.stenaline.ie).

HARBOURS IN ST BRIDES BAY (See AC 5620)

SOLVA, Pembrokeshire, **51°52′·02N 05°11′·67W**. AC 1478. HW –0450 on Dover; ML 3·2m; Duration 0555. See 4.11. Good shelter for small boats that can take the ground. Avoid in strong S winds. Black Scar, Green Scar and The Mare are rks 5ca S. Ent via SSE side; best water near Black Rk in centre of ent. Beware stone spit at Trwyn Caws on W just inside entrance. There are 9 Or ⚓s drying on hard sand (£6.00), drying/rafting ABs for <9·5m LOA; or ⚓ behind the rk in approx 3m. Yachts can go up to the quay (£7.50) Facilities: 🅿 🛒 ✗ ▱ in village. ⚓ on quay, ⚓ (launching £5). HM (01437) 721703 mob 07974 020139, VHF Ch 16 8, ⚓ 🅿. **Solva Boat Owners Assn** ☎721489 mob 07974 020139.

ST BRIDES BAY, Pembrokeshire, **51°49′·02N 05°10′·07W**. AC 1478. HW (Little Haven) –0450 on Dover; ML 3·2m; Duration 0555. See 4.11. A SPM buoy, Fl (5) Y 20s, is midway between Ramsey and Skomer islands at 51°48′·2N 05°20′·0W. Keep at least 100m offshore 1/9-28/2 to avoid disturbing seals, and ditto nesting sea

birds 1/3-31/7. Many good ⚓s, especially between Little Haven and Borough Head in S or E winds or between Solva and Dinas Fawr in N or E winds. In W'lies boats should shelter in Solva (above), Skomer (below) or Pendinas Bach. Tankers ⚓ in mouth of bay. For apprs from the N or S see 4.4. Facilities: (Little Haven) ⚓ (cans) 🅿 🛒 ✗ ▱.

SKOMER, Pembrokeshire, **51°44′·42N 05°16′·77W**. AC 1478, 2878. HW –0455 Dover. See 4.11. The island is a National Nature Reserve (fee payable to Warden on landing) and also a Marine Nature Reserve, extending to Marloes Peninsula. Keep at least 100m offshore 1/9-28/2 to avoid disturbing seals and ditto nesting sea birds 1/3-31/7. There is a 5kn speed limit within 100m of the island. ⚓ in S Haven (N Haven ⚓ due to eel grass). Enter N Haven close to W shore, and land on W side of bay on beach or at steps. In N Haven pick up ⚓s provided. No access to the island from S Haven. For Jack Sound see 4.4. There are no lts, marks or facilities. For info, Marine Conservation Officer ☎(01646) 636736.

4.12 MILFORD HAVEN

Pembrokeshire 51°40'·13N 05°08'·16W ✿✿✿✿♦♦♦✿✿

CHARTS AC 5620, 1410, 1178, 1478, 2878, 3273/4/5; Imray C60, C13, 2600

TIDES −0500 Dover; ML 3·8; Duration 0605

Standard Port MILFORD HAVEN (→)

Times				Height (metres)			
High Water		Low Water		MHWS	MHWN	MLWN	MLWS
0100	0800	0100	0700	7·0	5·2	2·5	0·7
1300	2000	1300	1900				
Differences DALE ROADS							
−0005	−0005	−0008	−0008	0·0	0·0	0·0	−0·1
NEYLAND							
+0002	+0010	0000	0000	0·0	0·0	0·0	0·0
HAVERFORDWEST							
+0010	+0025	DR	DR	−4·8	−4·9	DR	DR
LLANGWM (Black Tar)							
+0010	+0020	+0005	0000	+0·1	+0·1	0·0	−0·1

SHELTER Very good in various places round the hbr, especially in Milford Marina and Neyland Yacht Haven. ⚓s in Dale Bay; off Chapel Bay and Angle Pt on S shore; off Scotch Bay, E of Milford marina; and others beyond Pembroke Dock. Free pontoons (May-Oct) include: Dale Bay, Gelliswick Bay; waiting pontoons off Milford Dock and Hobbs Pt (for Pembroke Dock); and drying pontoons at Dale Beach, Hazelbeach, Neyland and Burton; mainly intended for tenders. It is possible to dry out safely at inshore areas of Dale, Sandy Haven and Angle Bay, depending on weather.

NAVIGATION WPT (W) 51°40'·25N 05°10'·65W. WPT (E) 51°40'·05N 05°08'·06W.

- The tide sets strongly across the ent to the Haven particularly at sp. In bad weather avoid passing over Mid Chan Rks and St Ann's Hd shoal, where a confused sea and swell will be found. Give St Ann's Head a wide berth especially on the ebb, when East Chan by Sheep Island is better.

- Beware large tankers entering/departing the Haven and ferries moving at high speed in the lower Haven. **Keep outside the main shipping channels if possible.**

- Milford Haven Port Authority has a jetty, Port Control and offices near Hubberston Pt. Their launches have G hulls and W upperworks with 'PILOT' in black letters and fly a Pilot flag while on patrol; Fl Bu lt at night. Their instructions must be obeyed. No vessel may pass within 100m of any terminal or any tanker, whether at ⚓ or under way.

River Cleddau is navigable 6M to Picton Pt, at junction of West and East arms, at all tides for boats of moderate draught. Clearance under Cleddau Bridge above Neyland is 36m; and 25m under power cable 1M upstream. Chan to Haverfordwest has 2m at HW and clearances of only 6m below cables and bridge; only feasible for shoal draught/lifting keel and unmasted craft.

Firing Ranges to the S and SE, see 4.13 and AC 1076.

LIGHTS AND MARKS See 4.3 and chartlets. Y SPM have been established in W Angle, Gelliswick, Dale Bays and off Jenkins Pt to prohibit high speed craft and water skiing.

Milford Haven leading lights are specifically for VLCCs entering/leaving hbr and proceeding to/from the oil refineries. The Haven is very well buoyed and lit as far as Cleddau bridge.

Milford Dock ldg lts 348°, both F.Bu, with W ○ daymarks. Dock entry sigs on E side of lock: 2 FG (vert) = gates open, vessels may enter. VHF Ch 18 is normally used for ent/exit by day and night.

COMMUNICATIONS (Code 01646) Lock 696310; CGOC 690909; Police 101; Ⓗ Haverfordwest (01437) 764545; Dr 690674. Port Control 696136/7.

Monitor *Milford Haven Port Control* Ch 12 (H24) while underway in the Haven. *Milford Haven Patrol* launches Ch11/12 (H24). To lock in to Milford Dock marina call *Pierhead*, Ch 14, for clearance, then call *Milford Marina*, Ch ⚓ for a berth. Neyland Yacht Haven Ch 80/M.

Broadcasts: Nav warnings on Ch 12 14 at 0300 and 1500 (both UT). Gale warnings on receipt. Tide hts and winds on request. Bcsts on Ch 16 67 at 0335 then every 4 hrs to 2335.

FACILITIES Marinas/Berthing (from seaward):
Dale Bay YC Pontoon ⚓ ⚓ ✕ ⛟.

Milford Haven Port Authority jetty ☎696133 (occas use by visitors with approval from HM), ⚓ ⚓.

Milford Marina ☎696312, Pierhead ☎696310. VHF Ch 14, 80/M. Lock hrs summer (Apr–Sep): ent HW−5, exit HW−4, free flow HW−2¼ to HW−¼, ent+3½, exit+4½; winter (Oct–Mar): ent HW−3¼, free flow HW−2¼ to HW−¼, ent+2½, exit+3; waiting pontoon or shelter in lock, 3·5m water at MLWS. 280⚓ inc Ⓥ, £2·85 ⚓ ⚓. ⚓ ⚓(H24) ⚓ ✕ ⚓ Ⓔ ⚓ ⚓ ⚓(14t) ⚓ ⚓ ⚓ Ⓑ ⛟ ✕ ⚓ ice, wi-fi.

Lawrenny Yacht Station ☎651212/651065, ⚓ £5, 100⚓; ⚓ ⚓ ⚓ (launch £5) ⚓ ⚓ ⚓ ⚓ ⚓ ✕ ⚓ ⚓ ⚓(15t) ⚓ ⛟ ✕.

Neyland Yacht Haven ⚓, www.yachthavens.com ☎601601, 420⚓ inc Ⓥ £2·50, ⚓ ⚓ ✕ ⚓ ⚓ Ⓔ ⚓ ⚓(20t) ⚓ ⛟✕; Access lower basin H24, but upper basin depth limited (sill + depth gauges and R/G lit perches); marina and approaches dredged annually Oct/March – proceed with extreme caution.

Dale Sailing Co (at Neyland) ⚓ ⚓ LPG ✕ ⚓ ⚓ ⚓(35t) ⚓.

East Llannion Marine: access HW±3, ⚓ scrubbing piles ⚓ ⚓(30t).

Rudder's BY, small but useful, is just upstream of Burton Pt.

Yacht Clubs: Dale YC ☎636362; Pembrokeshire YC ☎692799; Neyland YC ☎600267; Pembroke Haven YC ☎684403; Lawrenny YC ☎651212.

Towns: Milford Haven, ⚓ Ⓑ ⚓. Pembroke Dock; ⚓ Ⓑ ⚓ Ⓗ. Neyland, ⚓ Ⓑ. Haverfordwest, Ⓗ ⚓ Ⓑ ⚓ ✈ (Swansea or Cardiff). Ferry: Pembroke Dock–Rosslare; 2/day; Irish Ferries.

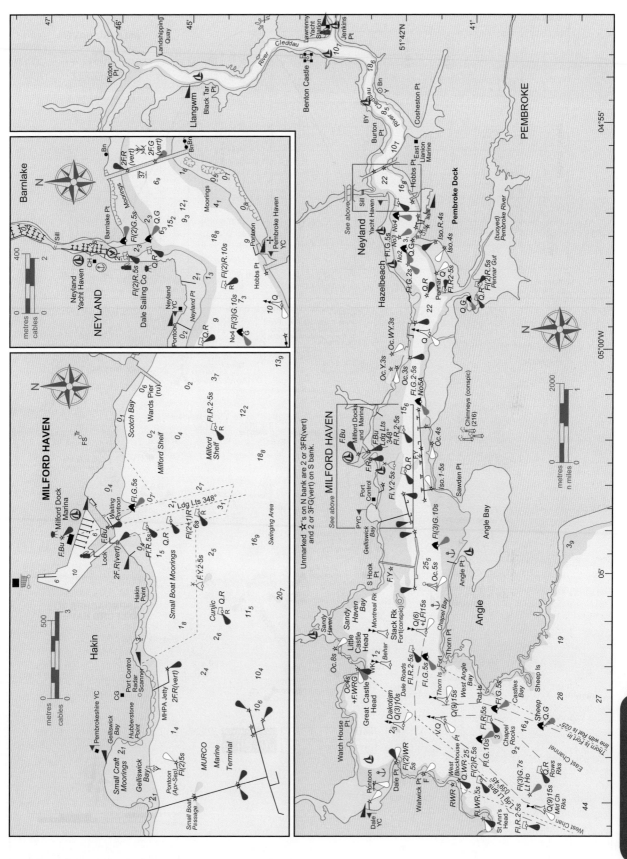

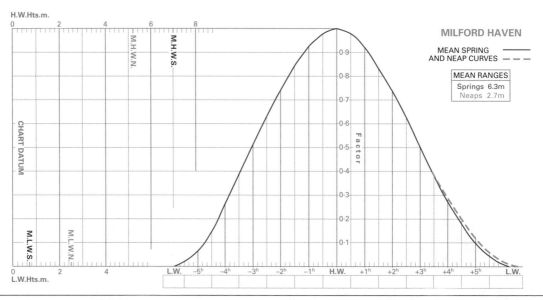

MILFORD HAVEN

MEAN SPRING ——————
AND NEAP CURVES — — —

MEAN RANGES
Springs 6.3m
Neaps 2.7m

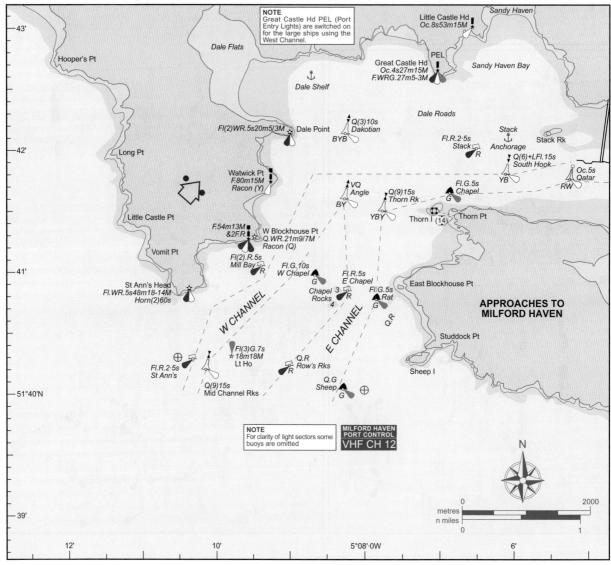

NOTE
Great Castle Hd PEL (Port Entry Lights) are switched on for the large ships using the West Channel.

Little Castle Hd
Oc.8s53m15M

Sandy Haven

Dale Flats

Great Castle Hd
Oc.4s27m15M
F.WRG.27m5-3M

PEL

Sandy Haven Bay

Hooper's Pt

Dale Shelf

Dale Roads

Fl(2)WR.5s20m5/3M   Dale Point

Q(3)10s
Dakotian
BYB

Stack
Anchorage

Stack Rk

Long Pt

Fl.R.2·5s
Stack
R

Q(6)+LFl.15s
South Hook
YB

Oc.5s
Qatar
RW

Little Castle Pt

Watwick Pt
F.80m15M
Racon (Y)

VQ
Angle
BY

Q(9)15s
Thorn Rk
G

Fl.G.5s
Chapel

Vomit Pt

YBY

Thorn I (14)

Thorn Pt

F.54m13M
&2F.R

W Blockhouse Pt
Q.WR.21m9/7M
Racon (Q)

Fl(2).R.5s
Mill Bay
R

Fl.G.10s
W Chapel
G

Fl.R.5s
E Chapel

St Ann's Head
Fl.WR.5s48m18-14M
Horn(2)60s

Chapel
Rocks
3
4
R

Fl.G.5s
Rat
G

East Blockhouse Pt

**APPROACHES TO
MILFORD HAVEN**

W CHANNEL

E CHANNEL

Q.R

Studdock Pt

Fl.R.2·5s
St Ann's

Fl(3)G.7s
18m18M
Lt Ho

Q.R
Row's Rks
R

Sheep I

Q(9)15s
Mid Channel Rks

Q.G
Sheep
G

NOTE
For clarity of light sectors some buoys are omitted

MILFORD HAVEN
PORT CONTROL
VHF CH 12

N

metres 0   2000
n miles 0   1

STANDARD TIME (UT)
For Summer Time add ONE hour in **non-shaded areas**

MILFORD HAVEN   LAT 51°42'N   LONG 5°03'W
TIMES AND HEIGHTS OF HIGH AND LOW WATERS

Dates in red are **SPRINGS**
Dates in blue are NEAPS

YEAR 2016

JANUARY

Time	m	Time	m
1 0419	2.1	**16** 0426	1.4
1030	5.9	1039	6.5
F 1650	2.2	SA 1658	1.5
2256	5.5	◑ 2305	6.1
2 0506	2.4	**17** 0522	1.8
1117	5.6	1136	6.2
SA 1742	2.5	SU 1759	1.8
◑ 2350	5.3		
3 0606	2.6	**18** 0008	5.8
1217	5.4	0630	2.0
SU 1850	2.6	M 1245	5.9
		1912	2.0
4 0100	5.2	**19** 0122	5.7
0719	2.7	0753	2.1
M 1332	5.4	TU 1400	5.8
2003	2.6	2031	1.8
5 0215	5.3	**20** 0239	5.8
0833	2.6	0911	1.9
TU 1442	5.4	W 1514	6.0
2110	2.4	2142	1.8
6 0317	5.6	**21** 0349	6.1
0935	2.3	1018	1.6
W 1540	5.7	TH 1620	6.2
2204	2.1	2241	1.5
7 0408	5.9	**22** 0449	6.4
1026	1.9	1113	1.3
TH 1628	6.0	F 1715	6.5
2249	1.7	2331	1.2
8 0452	6.3	**23** 0538	6.8
1111	1.6	1201	1.1
F 1712	6.4	SA 1802	6.8
2331	1.4		
9 0534	6.7	**24** 0016	1.0
1152	1.3	0621	7.0
SA 1753	6.6	SU 1244	0.9
		○ 1843	6.9
10 0011	1.2	**25** 0056	0.9
0614	6.9	0700	7.0
SU 1234	1.0	M 1322	0.9
● 1834	6.9	1921	6.9
11 0052	1.0	**26** 0133	0.9
0654	7.1	0737	7.0
M 1315	0.8	TU 1357	0.9
1915	7.0	1956	6.8
12 0132	0.8	**27** 0207	1.0
0736	7.2	0811	6.9
TU 1357	0.7	W 1430	1.1
1957	7.0	2029	6.6
13 0214	0.8	**28** 0240	1.2
0818	7.2	0844	6.7
W 1439	0.8	TH 1502	1.3
2039	6.9	2102	6.4
14 0255	0.9	**29** 0311	1.4
0902	7.1	0916	6.5
TH 1521	1.0	F 1532	1.6
2124	6.7	2135	6.1
15 0339	1.1	**30** 0343	1.7
0948	6.8	0950	6.1
F 1607	1.2	SA 1605	1.9
2211	6.4	2210	5.8
		31 0418	2.0
		1028	5.8
		SU 1643	2.2
		2252	5.5

FEBRUARY

Time	m	Time	m
1 0502	2.3	**16** 0601	2.0
1113	5.5	1216	5.7
M 1733	2.5	TU 1840	2.1
◑ 2346	5.2		
2 0604	2.6	**17** 0052	5.5
1214	5.2	0728	2.2
TU 1847	2.7	W 1336	5.5
		2008	2.2
3 0100	5.1	**18** 0219	5.5
0729	2.7	0857	2.1
W 1337	5.1	TH 1500	5.6
2014	2.6	2128	2.0
4 0226	5.2	**19** 0338	5.8
0850	2.5	1008	1.8
TH 1457	5.3	F 1610	5.9
2126	2.3	2230	1.7
5 0333	5.6	**20** 0438	6.2
0954	2.1	1103	1.5
F 1558	5.7	SA 1704	6.3
2221	1.9	2319	1.3
6 0425	6.1	**21** 0525	6.6
1046	1.6	1148	1.1
SA 1649	6.1	SU 1747	6.6
2309	1.4		
7 0512	6.6	**22** 0001	1.1
1132	1.2	0605	6.8
SU 1734	6.6	M 1227	0.9
2353	1.0	○ 1825	6.8
8 0556	7.0	**23** 0038	0.9
1216	0.8	0641	6.9
M 1818	7.0	TU 1301	0.8
●		1859	6.8
9 0035	0.7	**24** 0111	0.8
0638	7.3	0715	7.0
TU 1300	0.5	W 1333	0.8
1900	7.2	1931	6.8
10 0118	0.5	**25** 0143	0.9
0721	7.5	0746	6.9
W 1342	0.3	TH 1403	0.9
1942	7.3	2002	6.7
11 0200	0.4	**26** 0213	1.0
0803	7.5	0815	6.8
TH 1424	0.4	F 1431	1.1
2024	7.3	2031	6.6
12 0241	0.5	**27** 0242	1.1
0846	7.4	0845	6.6
F 1506	0.5	SA 1459	1.3
2107	7.0	2101	6.4
13 0323	0.7	**28** 0311	1.4
0930	7.1	0915	6.3
SA 1548	0.8	SU 1528	1.6
2151	6.7	2132	6.1
14 0407	1.1	**29** 0342	1.7
1017	6.7	0947	6.0
SU 1634	1.3	M 1600	1.9
2240	6.3	2207	5.7
15 0457	1.5		
1110	6.2		
M 1728	1.8		
◑ 2338	5.8		

MARCH

Time	m	Time	m
1 0419	2.1	**16** 0538	2.0
1026	5.6	1151	5.6
TU 1640	2.3	W 1812	2.2
◑ 2252	5.4		
2 0508	2.4	**17** 0027	5.4
1118	5.2	0706	2.3
W 1737	2.6	TH 1314	5.3
2357	5.1	1945	2.4
3 0624	2.7	**18** 0157	5.4
1234	5.0	0839	2.2
TH 1913	2.7	F 1442	5.4
		2109	2.2
4 0127	5.1	**19** 0319	5.7
0804	2.6	0951	1.9
F 1410	5.1	SA 1553	5.8
2045	2.5	2211	1.8
5 0253	5.4	**20** 0418	6.1
0920	2.2	1044	1.5
SA 1526	5.6	SU 1644	6.1
2151	2.0	2259	1.4
6 0355	6.0	**21** 0504	6.4
1019	1.6	1126	1.2
SU 1623	6.1	M 1725	6.5
2243	1.4	2338	1.2
7 0446	6.5	**22** 0543	6.7
1108	1.1	1202	1.0
M 1711	6.6	TU 1801	6.7
2330	0.9		
8 0533	7.0	**23** 0013	1.0
1155	0.6	0616	6.8
TU 1756	7.1	W 1235	0.9
		○ 1833	6.8
9 0015	0.5	**24** 0046	0.9
0617	7.4	0648	6.9
W 1239	0.2	TH 1305	0.9
● 1839	7.4	1904	6.8
10 0059	0.1	**25** 0116	0.9
0701	7.7	0718	6.8
TH 1323	0.1	F 1334	0.9
1922	7.5	1933	6.8
11 0142	0.1	**26** 0146	0.9
0744	7.7	0748	6.8
F 1405	0.1	SA 1402	1.0
2004	7.5	2002	6.7
12 0224	0.2	**27** 0214	1.1
0827	7.6	0815	6.6
SA 1446	0.3	SU 1430	1.2
2047	7.2	2031	6.5
13 0306	0.5	**28** 0244	1.3
0911	7.2	0845	6.4
SU 1528	0.7	M 1458	1.5
2130	6.9	2101	6.2
14 0349	0.9	**29** 0315	1.6
0956	6.7	0916	6.1
M 1612	1.2	TU 1530	1.8
2217	6.4	2135	5.9
15 0437	1.5	**30** 0351	1.9
1048	6.1	0953	5.7
TU 1703	1.8	W 1607	2.1
◑ 2313	5.8	2217	5.6
		31 0436	2.2
		1042	5.4
		TH 1658	2.4
		◑ 2316	5.3

APRIL

Time	m	Time	m
1 0541	2.5	**16** 0126	5.4
1153	5.1	0810	2.3
F 1819	2.6	SA 1411	5.3
		2038	2.3
2 0041	5.2	**17** 0245	5.6
0719	2.5	0920	2.0
SA 1326	5.1	SU 1521	5.6
2002	2.5	2140	2.0
3 0211	5.4	**18** 0346	5.9
0843	2.1	1013	1.7
SU 1450	5.5	M 1613	6.0
2116	2.0	2228	1.6
4 0321	6.0	**19** 0433	6.2
0947	1.5	1055	1.4
M 1552	6.1	TU 1655	6.3
2214	1.4	2308	1.4
5 0417	6.5	**20** 0512	6.5
1040	1.0	1131	1.2
TU 1644	6.7	W 1732	6.5
2304	0.9	2344	1.2
6 0506	7.1	**21** 0547	6.6
1129	0.5	1204	1.1
W 1731	7.1	TH 1805	6.7
2351	0.4		
7 0553	7.5	**22** 0017	1.1
1215	0.2	0619	6.7
TH 1816	7.5	F 1236	1.0
●		○ 1835	6.7
8 0037	0.2	**23** 0049	1.0
0638	7.7	0650	6.7
F 1301	0.0	SA 1306	1.0
1900	7.6	1905	6.8
9 0122	0.1	**24** 0119	1.0
0723	7.7	0720	6.7
SA 1344	0.1	SU 1335	1.1
1944	7.6	1935	6.7
10 0205	0.2	**25** 0150	1.1
0807	7.5	0749	6.6
SU 1426	0.3	M 1405	1.2
2027	7.3	2006	6.6
11 0248	0.5	**26** 0222	1.2
0852	7.1	0821	6.4
M 1508	0.7	TU 1436	1.5
2111	6.9	2038	6.4
12 0333	0.9	**27** 0255	1.5
0938	6.6	0854	6.2
TU 1552	1.3	W 1509	1.7
2158	6.4	2113	6.1
13 0421	1.5	**28** 0333	1.7
1028	6.1	0933	5.9
W 1642	1.8	TH 1548	2.0
2252	5.9	2157	5.8
14 0520	2.0	**29** 0419	2.0
1129	5.5	1022	5.6
TH 1747	2.3	F 1639	2.2
◑		2254	5.6
15 0001	5.5	**30** 0520	2.2
0641	2.3	1129	5.3
F 1247	5.2	SA 1749	2.4
1914	2.4	◑	

Chart Datum: 3·71 metres below Ordnance Datum (Newlyn). HAT is 7·9 metres above Chart Datum.

S Wales

<table>
<tr><td>

STANDARD TIME (UT)
For Summer Time add ONE
hour in **non-shaded areas**

</td><td>

MILFORD HAVEN   LAT 51°42'N   LONG 5°03'W
TIMES AND HEIGHTS OF HIGH AND LOW WATERS

</td><td>

Dates in red are **SPRINGS**
Dates in blue are NEAPS

YEAR 2016

</td></tr>
</table>

MAY

#	Time	m	#	Time	m
1 SU	0010 0642 1252 1921	5.5 2.2 5.3 2.3	**16** M	0158 0833 1436 2056	5.5 2.2 5.5 2.2
2 M	0133 0805 1413 2039	5.6 2.0 5.6 1.9	**17** TU	0302 0930 1532 2149	5.7 1.9 5.7 1.9
3 TU	0245 0913 1519 2142	6.0 1.5 6.1 1.5	**18** W	0353 1016 1618 2233	6.0 1.7 6.0 1.7
4 W	0345 1010 1614 2236	6.5 1.0 6.6 1.0	**19** TH	0437 1056 1658 2312	6.2 1.5 6.3 1.4
5 TH	0439 1102 1705 2327	7.0 0.6 7.1 0.6	**20** F	0515 1132 1734 2348	6.4 1.3 6.5 1.3
6 F	0529 1151 1753	7.3 0.3 7.4	**21** SA	0550 1206 1808	6.5 1.2 6.6
7 SA	0015 0616 1238 1839	0.3 7.5 0.2 7.5	**22** SU	0022 0623 1239 1840	1.2 6.6 1.2 6.7
8 SU	0102 0703 1323 1924	0.2 7.5 0.3 7.5	**23** M	0056 0656 1312 1913	1.1 6.6 1.2 6.7
9 M	0148 0749 1407 2009	0.3 7.3 0.5 7.3	**24** TU	0130 0729 1345 1946	1.1 6.5 1.3 6.6
10 TU	0233 0835 1451 2054	0.6 7.0 0.9 6.9	**25** W	0205 0803 1419 2022	1.2 6.4 1.4 6.5
11 W	0318 0921 1535 2141	1.0 6.6 1.3 6.5	**26** TH	0242 0840 1456 2101	1.4 6.3 1.5 6.3
12 TH	0406 1010 1623 2232	1.4 6.1 1.8 6.0	**27** F	0322 0922 1538 2146	1.5 6.1 1.7 6.1
13 F	0500 1105 1720 2332	1.9 5.6 2.2 5.7	**28** SA	0408 1011 1627 2241	1.7 5.8 2.0 5.9
14 SA	0607 1211 1832	2.2 5.3 2.4	**29** SU	0504 1111 1729 2347	1.9 5.6 2.1 5.8
15 SU	0044 0723 1327 1949	5.5 2.3 5.3 2.4	**30** M	0613 1223 1846	1.9 5.6 2.1
			31 TU	0059 0729 1338 2003	5.9 1.8 5.8 1.9

JUNE

#	Time	m	#	Time	m
1 W	0211 0839 1446 2110	6.1 1.5 6.1 1.5	**16** TH	0307 0932 1537 2153	5.6 1.7 5.7 2.0
2 TH	0315 0941 1546 2210	6.4 1.2 6.5 1.2	**17** F	0358 1019 1623 2238	5.8 1.8 6.0 1.7
3 F	0413 1037 1641 2305	6.8 0.9 6.8 0.8	**18** SA	0442 1100 1704 2319	6.1 1.6 6.3 1.5
4 SA	0507 1129 1733 2356	7.0 0.7 7.1 0.6	**19** SU	0522 1139 1742 2357	6.3 1.4 6.5 1.3
5 SU	0559 1218 1822	7.2 0.5 7.3	**20** M	0559 1215 1818	6.4 1.3 6.6
6 M	0045 0647 1306 1908	0.5 7.2 0.7 7.3	**21** TU	0035 0635 1252 1854	1.2 6.5 1.2 6.7
7 TU	0133 0734 1351 1954	0.5 7.1 0.7 6.9	**22** W	0113 0712 1328 1931	1.1 6.6 1.1 6.8
8 W	0218 0819 1434 2038	0.7 6.9 0.9 6.9	**23** TH	0151 0750 1406 2010	1.1 6.6 1.2 6.7
9 TH	0303 0904 1517 2123	1.0 6.5 1.3 6.6	**24** F	0230 0830 1446 2051	1.1 6.5 1.3 6.6
10 F	0347 0948 1601 2208	1.4 6.2 1.6 6.2	**25** SA	0312 0912 1528 2136	1.2 6.4 1.4 6.5
11 SA	0433 1035 1648 2257	1.7 5.8 2.0 5.9	**26** SU	0357 0959 1615 2226	1.4 6.2 1.6 6.3
12 SU	0525 1128 1743 2354	2.1 5.5 2.3 5.6	**27** M	0447 1053 1709 2324	1.5 6.0 1.8 6.1
13 M	0625 1231 1848	2.4 5.3 2.4	**28** TU	0546 1155 1815	1.7 5.8 1.9
14 TU	0100 0731 1340 1957	5.4 2.3 5.3 2.4	**29** W	0030 0655 1306 1930	6.0 1.7 5.8 1.9
15 W	0208 0836 1443 2100	5.5 2.2 5.5 2.2	**30** TH	0141 0808 1417 2044	6.0 1.7 5.9 1.7

JULY

#	Time	m	#	Time	m
1 F	0250 0917 1523 2150	6.2 1.5 6.2 1.4	**16** SA	0318 0941 1548 2206	5.5 2.1 5.7 2.0
2 SA	0354 1018 1624 2250	6.4 1.2 6.5 1.1	**17** SU	0411 1030 1636 2253	5.8 1.8 6.1 1.7
3 SU	0453 1113 1719 2343	6.7 1.0 6.8 0.9	**18** M	0456 1113 1718 2335	6.1 1.5 6.4 1.4
4 M	0546 1203 1809	6.9 0.8 7.0	**19** TU	0537 1153 1758	6.4 1.3 6.7
5 TU	0033 0635 1251 1855	0.7 7.0 0.7 7.1	**20** W	0016 0617 1233 1836	1.2 6.6 1.1 6.9
6 W	0119 0720 1334 1939	0.7 7.0 0.8 7.1	**21** TH	0056 0656 1313 1916	1.0 6.8 0.9 7.0
7 TH	0202 0802 1416 2020	0.8 6.8 1.0 6.9	**22** F	0136 0736 1353 1957	0.8 6.8 0.9 7.1
8 F	0243 0842 1455 2100	1.0 6.6 1.2 6.7	**23** SA	0217 0817 1433 2038	0.8 6.8 0.9 7.0
9 SA	0322 0921 1533 2138	1.3 6.3 1.5 6.4	**24** SU	0258 0859 1515 2122	0.9 6.7 1.0 6.8
10 SU	0400 1001 1611 2218	1.6 6.0 1.8 6.1	**25** M	0341 0943 1559 2209	1.0 6.5 1.3 6.6
11 M	0439 1043 1653 2303	1.9 5.7 2.1 5.7	**26** TU	0427 1032 1648 2301	1.3 6.2 1.6 6.3
12 TU	0525 1132 1748 2356	2.2 5.4 2.4 5.4	**27** W	0521 1129 1748	1.6 5.9 1.8
13 W	0622 1233 1851	2.4 5.2 2.5	**28** TH	0003 0626 1238 1903	6.0 1.9 5.7 2.0
14 TH	0102 0731 1346 2003	5.3 2.3 5.2 2.5	**29** F	0116 0744 1354 2026	5.8 1.9 5.7 2.0
15 F	0215 0841 1453 2110	5.3 2.4 5.4 2.3	**30** SA	0232 0901 1509 2140	5.9 1.8 5.9 1.7
			31 SU	0343 1007 1615 2242	6.1 1.6 6.3 1.4

AUGUST

#	Time	m	#	Time	m
1 M	0445 1103 1711 2335	6.4 1.3 6.6 1.1	**16** TU	0431 1049 1654 2313	6.0 1.6 6.4 1.4
2 TU	0537 1152 1758	6.7 1.0 6.9	**17** W	0515 1132 1736 2355	6.4 1.2 6.8 1.0
3 W	0021 0622 1236 1841	0.9 6.8 0.9 7.1	**18** TH	0557 1213 1817	6.7 0.9 7.1
4 TH	0104 0703 1316 1920	0.8 6.9 0.8 7.1	**19** F	0036 0637 1254 1857	0.7 7.0 0.7 7.3
5 F	0142 0741 1353 1957	0.8 6.8 0.9 7.0	**20** SA	0118 0718 1335 1939	0.7 7.2 0.6 7.4
6 SA	0218 0816 1428 2032	0.9 6.7 1.1 6.8	**21** SU	0159 0759 1416 2020	0.5 7.2 0.6 7.4
7 SU	0251 0850 1501 2105	1.2 6.5 1.3 6.6	**22** M	0241 0841 1458 2103	0.6 7.0 0.8 7.1
8 M	0323 0924 1533 2139	1.4 6.2 1.6 6.2	**23** TU	0322 0924 1540 2149	0.8 6.8 1.1 6.8
9 TU	0355 0959 1607 2215	1.7 5.9 1.9 5.9	**24** W	0406 1010 1628 2239	1.2 6.4 1.5 6.3
10 W	0430 1039 1648 2259	2.1 5.6 2.3 5.5	**25** TH	0457 1105 1726 2340	1.6 6.0 1.9 5.9
11 TH	0516 1129 1745 2355	2.4 5.3 2.6 5.2	**26** F	0601 1214 1846	2.0 5.7 2.2
12 F	0623 1237 1905	2.6 5.1 2.7	**27** SA	0056 0726 1338 2017	5.6 2.2 5.6 2.2
13 SA	0112 0748 1404 2027	5.1 2.7 5.2 2.6	**28** SU	0221 0851 1501 2135	5.6 2.1 5.8 1.9
14 SU	0237 0903 1514 2134	5.2 2.5 5.4 2.2	**29** M	0338 0959 1608 2235	5.9 1.8 6.1 1.5
15 M	0341 1001 1608 2227	5.6 2.0 5.9 1.8	**30** TU	0437 1053 1700 2324	6.3 1.4 6.6 1.2
			31 W	0524 1138 1744	6.6 1.1 6.9

Chart Datum: 3·71 metres below Ordnance Datum (Newlyn). HAT is 7·9 metres above Chart Datum.

STANDARD TIME (UT)	MILFORD HAVEN LAT 51°42'N LONG 5°03'W	Dates in red are SPRINGS
For Summer Time add ONE hour in **non-shaded areas**	TIMES AND HEIGHTS OF HIGH AND LOW WATERS	Dates in blue are NEAPS

YEAR **2016**

SEPTEMBER

Time	m	Time	m
1 0006 / 0605 / TH 1218 / ● 1822	1.0 / 6.8 / 0.9 / 7.0	**16** 0533 / 1150 / F 1753 / ○	7.0 / 0.8 / 7.3
2 0043 / 0642 / F 1254 / 1858	0.9 / 6.9 / 0.9 / 7.1	**17** 0014 / 0615 / SA 1233 / 1835	0.5 / 7.3 / 0.5 / 7.6
3 0117 / 0716 / SA 1327 / 1930	0.9 / 6.9 / 0.9 / 7.0	**18** 0057 / 0657 / SU 1315 / 1918	0.3 / 7.5 / 0.4 / 7.7
4 0149 / 0747 / SU 1359 / 2001	0.9 / 6.8 / 1.0 / 6.9	**19** 0139 / 0738 / M 1357 / 2000	0.3 / 7.5 / 0.4 / 7.6
5 0218 / 0818 / M 1429 / 2031	1.1 / 6.6 / 1.2 / 6.6	**20** 0221 / 0820 / TU 1439 / 2044	0.4 / 7.3 / 0.6 / 7.3
6 0247 / 0848 / TU 1458 / 2102	1.4 / 6.4 / 1.5 / 6.4	**21** 0302 / 0904 / W 1523 / 2129	0.8 / 7.0 / 1.0 / 6.9
7 0315 / 0919 / W 1529 / 2134	1.7 / 6.1 / 1.8 / 6.0	**22** 0346 / 0950 / TH 1611 / 2220	1.2 / 6.5 / 1.5 / 6.3
8 0347 / 0954 / TH 1605 / 2212	2.0 / 5.8 / 2.2 / 5.6	**23** 0436 / 1045 / F 1710 / ◑ 2321	1.8 / 6.0 / 2.0 / 5.8
9 0425 / 1037 / F 1652 / ◑ 2301	2.4 / 5.4 / 2.5 / 5.3	**24** 0541 / 1155 / SA 1834	2.2 / 5.6 / 2.3
10 0519 / 1139 / SA 1805	2.7 / 5.1 / 2.8	**25** 0040 / 0712 / SU 1324 / 2009	5.4 / 2.4 / 5.5 / 2.3
11 0013 / 0650 / SU 1307 / 1945	5.0 / 2.9 / 5.1 / 2.8	**26** 0210 / 0840 / M 1449 / 2125	5.5 / 2.3 / 5.8 / 2.0
12 0150 / 0825 / M 1436 / 2102	5.0 / 2.6 / 5.4 / 2.4	**27** 0326 / 0946 / TU 1554 / 2222	5.8 / 1.9 / 6.2 / 1.6
13 0309 / 0931 / TU 1538 / 2159	5.5 / 2.2 / 5.9 / 1.9	**28** 0421 / 1037 / W 1642 / 2306	6.2 / 1.5 / 6.6 / 1.3
14 0404 / 1022 / W 1627 / 2247	6.0 / 1.7 / 6.2 / 1.3	**29** 0505 / 1119 / TH 1723 / 2344	6.6 / 1.3 / 6.8 / 1.1
15 0450 / 1107 / TH 1711 / 2331	6.5 / 1.2 / 6.9 / 0.9	**30** 0543 / 1155 / F 1759	6.8 / 1.1 / 7.0

OCTOBER

Time	m	Time	m
1 0017 / 0617 / SA 1229 / ● 1832	1.0 / 6.9 / 1.0 / 7.0	**16** 0551 / 1210 / SU 1813 / ○	7.4 / 0.5 / 7.7
2 0049 / 0648 / SU 1300 / 1902	1.0 / 6.9 / 1.0 / 7.0	**17** 0034 / 0634 / M 1255 / 1856	0.3 / 7.6 / 0.3 / 7.8
3 0119 / 0718 / M 1330 / 1932	1.0 / 6.9 / 1.1 / 6.9	**18** 0118 / 0717 / TU 1339 / 1941	0.3 / 7.6 / 0.4 / 7.7
4 0147 / 0747 / TU 1359 / 2001	1.2 / 6.8 / 1.2 / 6.7	**19** 0201 / 0801 / W 1423 / 2026	0.4 / 7.5 / 0.6 / 7.3
5 0215 / 0816 / W 1428 / 2030	1.4 / 6.6 / 1.5 / 6.5	**20** 0244 / 0846 / TH 1508 / 2113	0.8 / 7.1 / 1.0 / 6.9
6 0243 / 0847 / TH 1459 / 2101	1.6 / 6.3 / 1.8 / 6.1	**21** 0329 / 0934 / F 1557 / 2204	1.3 / 6.6 / 1.5 / 6.3
7 0314 / 0920 / F 1535 / 2136	1.9 / 6.0 / 2.1 / 5.8	**22** 0419 / 1029 / SA 1657 / ◑ 2304	1.8 / 6.2 / 2.0 / 5.8
8 0350 / 1000 / SA 1619 / 2222	2.3 / 5.7 / 2.5 / 5.4	**23** 0523 / 1136 / SU 1817	2.3 / 5.7 / 2.4
9 0438 / 1056 / SU 1721 / ◑ 2329	2.6 / 5.3 / 2.7 / 5.1	**24** 0020 / 0649 / M 1300 / 1947	5.4 / 2.5 / 5.6 / 2.4
10 0555 / 1217 / M 1900	2.9 / 5.2 / 2.8	**25** 0145 / 0815 / TU 1421 / 2100	5.4 / 2.4 / 5.7 / 2.1
11 0102 / 0742 / TU 1351 / 2024	5.1 / 2.7 / 5.4 / 2.4	**26** 0259 / 0921 / W 1526 / 2155	5.7 / 2.1 / 6.1 / 1.8
12 0230 / 0856 / W 1501 / 2127	5.4 / 2.3 / 5.9 / 1.9	**27** 0355 / 1011 / TH 1615 / 2239	6.1 / 1.8 / 6.4 / 1.5
13 0331 / 0952 / TH 1555 / 2218	6.0 / 1.7 / 6.5 / 1.3	**28** 0439 / 1052 / F 1656 / 2316	6.4 / 1.5 / 6.6 / 1.3
14 0421 / 1040 / F 1643 / 2305	6.6 / 1.2 / 6.8 / 0.8	**29** 0516 / 1128 / SA 1732 / 2349	6.7 / 1.3 / 6.8 / 1.2
15 0507 / 1126 / SA 1728 / 2350	7.1 / 0.8 / 7.4 / 0.5	**30** 0550 / 1202 / SU 1805 / ●	6.8 / 1.2 / 6.9
		31 0021 / 0621 / M 1234 / 1835	1.2 / 6.9 / 1.2 / 6.9

NOVEMBER

Time	m	Time	m
1 0051 / 0651 / TU 1304 / 1905	1.2 / 6.9 / 1.2 / 6.8	**16** 0059 / 0700 / W 1323 / 1925	0.4 / 7.6 / 0.5 / 7.6
2 0120 / 0721 / W 1335 / 1935	1.2 / 6.8 / 1.3 / 6.7	**17** 0144 / 0746 / TH 1410 / 2012	0.6 / 7.5 / 0.6 / 7.3
3 0149 / 0751 / TH 1406 / 2006	1.4 / 6.7 / 1.5 / 6.5	**18** 0229 / 0832 / F 1456 / 2059	0.9 / 7.2 / 1.0 / 6.8
4 0220 / 0823 / F 1439 / 2038	1.6 / 6.4 / 1.7 / 6.3	**19** 0315 / 0920 / SA 1546 / 2149	1.3 / 6.8 / 1.4 / 6.4
5 0252 / 0857 / SA 1515 / 2114	1.9 / 6.2 / 2.0 / 6.0	**20** 0404 / 1012 / SU 1641 / 2244	1.8 / 6.3 / 1.9 / 5.9
6 0329 / 0937 / SU 1559 / 2159	2.2 / 5.9 / 2.3 / 5.6	**21** 0501 / 1111 / M 1747 / ◑ 2348	2.2 / 5.9 / 2.2 / 5.5
7 0415 / 1030 / M 1655 / ◑ 2301	2.5 / 5.6 / 2.5 / 5.4	**22** 0612 / 1221 / TU 1905	2.5 / 5.7 / 2.4
8 0520 / 1141 / TU 1815	2.7 / 5.5 / 2.6	**23** 0103 / 0730 / W 1337 / 2017	5.4 / 2.5 / 5.7 / 2.3
9 0021 / 0653 / W 1305 / 1941	5.3 / 2.7 / 5.6 / 2.3	**24** 0216 / 0840 / TH 1444 / 2117	5.5 / 2.3 / 5.8 / 2.1
10 0146 / 0815 / TH 1420 / 2049	5.5 / 2.3 / 5.9 / 1.9	**25** 0317 / 0935 / F 1539 / 2204	5.8 / 2.1 / 6.1 / 1.8
11 0254 / 0917 / F 1521 / 2146	6.0 / 1.8 / 6.5 / 1.4	**26** 0405 / 1021 / SA 1624 / 2245	6.1 / 1.8 / 6.3 / 1.6
12 0350 / 1012 / SA 1614 / 2238	6.5 / 1.3 / 6.9 / 1.0	**27** 0446 / 1100 / SU 1703 / 2321	6.4 / 1.6 / 6.5 / 1.5
13 0440 / 1101 / SU 1703 / 2326	6.9 / 0.9 / 7.3 / 0.6	**28** 0523 / 1136 / M 1739 / 2355	6.6 / 1.5 / 6.6 / 1.4
14 0528 / 1149 / M 1751 / ○	7.4 / 0.6 / 7.6	**29** 0557 / 1210 / TU 1812 / ●	6.7 / 1.4 / 6.7
15 0013 / 0614 / TU 1237 / 1838	0.4 / 7.6 / 0.4 / 7.7	**30** 0027 / 0629 / W 1244 / 1844	1.3 / 6.8 / 1.3 / 6.7

DECEMBER

Time	m	Time	m
1 0059 / 0701 / TH 1316 / 1916	1.3 / 6.8 / 1.3 / 6.6	**16** 0130 / 0734 / F 1359 / 2000	0.6 / 7.4 / 0.7 / 7.2
2 0131 / 0733 / F 1350 / 1949	1.4 / 6.8 / 1.4 / 6.5	**17** 0215 / 0820 / SA 1445 / 2045	0.8 / 7.2 / 0.9 / 6.9
3 0203 / 0807 / SA 1425 / 2024	1.5 / 6.6 / 1.5 / 6.4	**18** 0300 / 0905 / SU 1530 / 2131	1.1 / 6.9 / 1.2 / 6.5
4 0238 / 0843 / SU 1503 / 2102	1.7 / 6.5 / 1.7 / 6.2	**19** 0344 / 0951 / M 1617 / 2217	1.5 / 6.5 / 1.6 / 6.1
5 0317 / 0924 / M 1546 / 2146	1.9 / 6.2 / 1.9 / 5.9	**20** 0431 / 1039 / TU 1707 / 2309	1.9 / 6.2 / 2.0 / 5.7
6 0401 / 1013 / TU 1636 / 2240	2.1 / 6.0 / 2.1 / 5.7	**21** 0524 / 1134 / W 1806 / ◑	2.3 / 5.8 / 2.3
7 0457 / 1114 / W 1739 / 2347	2.3 / 5.8 / 2.2 / 5.6	**22** 0009 / 0627 / TH 1239 / 1913	5.4 / 2.5 / 5.6 / 2.5
8 0608 / 1224 / TH 1856	2.4 / 5.8 / 2.2	**23** 0119 / 0739 / F 1349 / 2023	5.3 / 2.5 / 5.5 / 2.4
9 0102 / 0729 / F 1339 / 2009	5.6 / 2.3 / 6.0 / 1.9	**24** 0227 / 0847 / SA 1453 / 2122	5.5 / 2.4 / 5.6 / 2.2
10 0215 / 0841 / SA 1446 / 2114	5.9 / 1.9 / 6.3 / 1.6	**25** 0326 / 0944 / SU 1548 / 2211	5.7 / 2.2 / 5.8 / 2.0
11 0319 / 0944 / SU 1546 / 2213	6.3 / 1.5 / 6.7 / 1.2	**26** 0415 / 1031 / M 1634 / 2254	6.0 / 1.9 / 6.1 / 1.8
12 0416 / 1040 / M 1642 / 2306	6.8 / 1.1 / 7.0 / 0.9	**27** 0457 / 1112 / TU 1715 / 2332	6.3 / 1.7 / 6.3 / 1.5
13 0508 / 1133 / TU 1735 / 2356	7.1 / 0.8 / 7.3 / 0.7	**28** 0535 / 1150 / W 1752	6.5 / 1.5 / 6.5
14 0559 / 1223 / W 1825 / ○	7.4 / 0.6 / 7.4	**29** 0007 / 0610 / TH 1226 / ● 1827	1.4 / 6.7 / 1.3 / 6.6
15 0044 / 0647 / TH 1312 / 1913	0.6 / 7.5 / 0.5 / 7.4	**30** 0042 / 0645 / F 1302 / 1901	1.3 / 6.8 / 1.2 / 6.6
		31 0116 / 0719 / SA 1337 / 1936	1.2 / 6.8 / 1.2 / 6.6

Chart Datum: 3·71 metres below Ordnance Datum (Newlyn). HAT is 7·9 metres above Chart Datum.

S Wales

》》 FREE monthly updates. Register at 《
www.reedsnauticalalmanac.co.uk

145

MILFORD HAVEN TO MUMBLES HEAD

(AC 1179, 1076) Milford Haven is a long natural, all-weather harbour with marinas beyond the oil terminals. Beware Turbot Bank (WCM lt buoy) 3M S of the entrance. Crow Rk (dries 5·5m) is 5ca SSE of Linney Hd, and The Toes are dangerous submerged rocks close W and SE of Crow Rock. There is a passage inshore of these dangers. There are overfalls on St Gowan Shoals which extend 4M SW of St Govan's Hd, and the sea breaks on the shallow patches in bad weather. There are firing areas from Linney Hd to Carmarthen Bay.

Caldey Is (lit) lies S of Tenby. Off its NW pt is St Margaret's Is connected by a rocky reef. Caldey Sound, between St Margaret's Is and Giltar Pt (AC 1482), is buoyed, but beware Eel Spit near W end of Caldey Is where there can be a nasty sea with wind against tide, and Woolhouse Rocks (dry 3·6m) 1ca NE of Caldey Is. Saundersfoot harbour (dries) is 2M N of Tenby, with an ⚓ well sheltered from N and W but subject to swell. Streams are weak here. Carmarthen Bay has no offshore dangers for yachts, other than the extensive drying sands at head of the bay and on its E side off Burry Inlet.

S of Worms Head, Helwick Sands (buoyed at each end) extend 7M W from Port Eynon Pt; least depth of 1·3m is near their W end. Stream sets NE/SW across the sands. There is a narrow channel inshore, close to Port Eynon Pt.

▶ *Between here and Mumbles Hd the stream runs roughly along coast, sp rates 3kn off headlands, but there are eddies in Port Eynon Bay and Oxwich Bay (both yacht anchorages), and overfalls SSE of Oxwich Pt.* ◀

FIRING RANGES – LINNEY HEAD TO BURRY INLET

For daily info on all range firing times call *Milford Haven CG* Ch 16/67 or ☎01646 690909.

Castlemartin Range Danger Area extends 12M WNW from Linney Hd, thence in an anti-clockwise arc to a point 12M S of St Govan's Hd. The exact Danger Area operative on any one day depends on the ranges/ammunition used; it is primarily a tank range. When firing is in progress R flags are flown (Fl R lts at night) along the coast from Freshwater West to Linney Head to St Govan's Head. Yachts are requested to keep clear of ranges when active.

Firing takes place on weekdays 0900–1630, exceptionally to 1700. Night firing takes place on Mon to Thurs, up to 2359, depending on the hours of darkness. In Jan only small arms are usually fired and the danger area is reduced.

Days/times of firing are published locally and can be obtained by VHF from *Castlemartin Range* Ch 16 or ☎01646 662367 (H24 answering service); Range safety launches Ch 16 or 12; and Milford Haven CG Ch 16. Also from the Range Office ☎(01646) 662287 or Warren Tower 01646 662336.

Manorbier Range (further E) covers a sector arc radius 12M centred on Old Castle Head; E/W extent is approximately between St Govan's Hd and Caldey Is (see AC Q6402). It is usually active Mon-Fri 0900-1700LT, occasionally Sat and Sun, and is primarily a surface to air missile range, but active areas depend on the weapons in use on any given day. On firing days warnings are broadcast on Ch 16, 73 at 0830, 1430 and on completion; red flags are flown either side of Old Castle Hd. Yachts on passage should either keep 12M offshore or transit close inshore via Stackpole Hd, Trewent Pt, Priest's Nose and Old Castle Hd. Firing days/times are available from local HMs and YCs. For further info call: *Manorbier Range Control* Ch 16, 73 (also manned by Range safety launches); *Milford Haven CG* Ch 16; or Range Control ☎(01834) 871282 ext 209, 🖷 871283.

Penally Range (further E at Giltar Pt) is for small arms only and seldom interferes with passage through Caldey Sound. Info ☎(01834) 843522.

Pendine Range (between Tenby and Burry Inlet) is a MOD range for testing explosive devices. It is usually possible to steer the rhumb line course from Tenby to Worms Hd without interference. Info ☎(01994) 453243. Broadcasts on VHF Ch 16, 73 at 0900 and 1400LT. Range active 0800-1615.

Pembrey Range (approx 5M NW of Burry Inlet) is used for bombing practice by the RAF. Info ☎(01554) 891224.

MUMBLES HEAD TO CARDIFF

(AC 1165, 1182) Off Mumbles Hd (Lt, fog sig) beware Mixon Shoal (dries 0·3m), marked by PHM buoy. In good conditions pass N of shoal, 1ca off Mumbles Hd. ⚓ N of Mumbles Hd, good holding but exposed to swell. At W side of Swansea Bay, Green Grounds, rky shoals, lie in appr's to Swansea.

Scarweather Sands, much of which dry (up to 3·3m) with seas breaking heavily, extend 7M W from Porthcawl (4.15) and are well buoyed (AC 1161). There is a chan between the sands and coast to E, but beware Hugo Bank (dries 2·6m) and Kenfig Patches (0·5m) with o'falls up to 7ca offshore between Sker Pt and Porthcawl.

Nash Sands extend 7·5M WNW from Nash Pt. Depths vary and are least at inshore end (dries 3m), but Nash Passage, 1ca wide, runs close inshore between E Nash ECM buoy and ledge off Nash Pt. ▶ *On E-going stream there are heavy overfalls off Nash Pt and at W end of Nash Sands. Between Nash Pt and Breaksea Pt the E-going stream begins at HW Avonmouth +0535, and the W-going at HW Avonmouth –0035, sp rates 3kn. Off Breaksea Pt there may be overfalls.* ◀

From Rhoose Pt to Lavernock Pt the coast is fringed with foul ground. Lavernock Spit extends 1·75M S of Lavernock Pt, and E of the spit is main chan to Cardiff; the other side of the chan being Cardiff Grounds, a bank drying 5·4m which lies parallel with the shore and about 1·5M from it.

SEVERN ESTUARY

(AC 1176, 1166) Near the centre of the Bristol Channel, either side of the buoyed fairway, are the islands of Flat Holm (Lt, fog sig) and Steep Holm. 7M SW of Flat Holm lies Culver Sand (0·9m), 3M in length, buoyed with W and ECM. Monkstone Rk (Lt, dries) is 2M NW of the buoyed channel to Avonmouth and Bristol. Extensive drying banks cover the North shore of the estuary, beyond Newport and the Severn bridges (AC 1176). Call Bristol VTS VHF Ch 12 when passing reporting points inwards/outwards.

▶ *The tidal range in the Bristol Channel is exceptional, 12·2m at sp and 6·0m np. Care must be taken to understand the changes in chart datum in the upper reaches of the estuary. Tidal streams are very powerful, particularly above Avonmouth. Between Flat and Steep Holm the E-going stream begins at HW Avonmouth –0610, sp 3kn, and the W-going at HW Avonmouth +0015, sp 4kn.* ◀

The entrance to the R Avon is just to the S of Avonmouth S Pier Hd. Bristol City Docks lie some 6M up-river. Approach the entrance via King Road and the Newcombe and Cockburn lt buoys and thence via the Swash channel into the Avon. The entrance dries at LW but the river is navigable at about half tide.

▶ *Tidal streams are strong in the approaches to Avonmouth, up to 5kn at sp. The tide is also strong in the R. Avon which is best entered no earlier than HW Avonmouth – 0200.* ◀

From Avonmouth it is 16M to Sharpness, which you should aim to reach at about HW Avonmouth. The passage between Avonmouth and Sharpness requires considerable attention to timing and tidal conditions if it is to be undertaken safely. Plan your passage to arrive off Sharpness no earlier than HW Sharpness –1 and no later than HW Sharpness. Information to assist in passage planning is available from Gloucester Harbour Trustees (see entry for Sharpness). Pilots are available (see entry for Sharpness). To ensure the safety of navigation of all vessels, the fairway between Avonmouth approaches and Sharpness old Dock entrance must be recognised as a 'narrow channel' and attention is drawn to the provisions of rule 9 of the 'collision regulations'.

▶ *Spring streams can run 8kn at the Shoots, and 6kn at the Severn bridges. At the Shoots the flood begins at HW Avonmouth –0430 and the ebb at HW Avonmouth +0045. The Severn Bore can usually be seen if Avonmouth range is 13·5m or more. For tidal streams 'Arrowsmiths' is recommended, from Arrowsmiths, Winterstoke Rd, Bristol, BS3 2NT.* ◀

4.13 TENBY

Pembrokeshire **51°40'·42N 04°41'·93W** ❀❀♦♦♠♠♠

CHARTS AC 5620, 1179, 1076, 1482; Imray C60, 2600

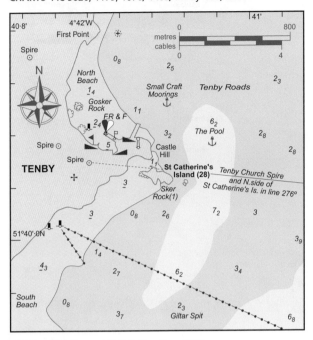

TIDES –0510 Dover; ML 4·5; Duration 0610

Standard Port MILFORD HAVEN (←)

Times				Height (metres)			
High Water		Low Water		MHWS	MHWN	MLWN	MLWS
0100	0800	0100	0700	7·0	5·2	2·5	0·7
1300	2000	1300	1900				
Differences TENBY							
–0015	–0010	–0015	–0020	+1·4	+1·1	+0·5	+0·2
STACKPOLE QUAY (7M W of Caldey Island)							
–0005	+0025	–0010	–0010	+0·9	+0·7	+0·2	+0·3

SHELTER Good, but hbr dries up to 5m. ⚓ in deep water off North Beach. Sheltered ⚓s, depending on wind direction, to NE in Tenby Roads, in Lydstep Haven (2·5M SW), and around Caldey Is as follows: Priory Bay to the N but shallow, Jones Bay (NE), Drinkim Bay (E) or Sandtop Bay (W).

NAVIGATION WPT 51°40'·02N 04°38'·08W, 279°/2·2M to monument on Castle Hill. The ⊕ WPT (off chartlet) is 2ca W of DZ2 SPM lit buoy. Beware Woolhouse Rks (3·6m) 1·5M SExE of the Hbr, marked by lit SCM buoy; and Sker Rk (1m high) closer in off St Catherine's Island (28m). From the W, Caldey Sound is navigable with care between Eel Pt SHM and Giltar Spit PHM lit buoys. Approaching Tenby Roads, keep outside the line of mooring buoys. For adjacent Firing ranges, see overleaf. Caldey Island is private and no landing without permission from the Abbot.

LIGHTS AND MARKS See 4.3 and chartlet. Church spire transit N side of St Catherine's Is 276°. FR 7m 7M on pier hd. Inside hbr, FW 6m 1M marks landing steps PHM beacon (unlit) marks outcrop from Gosker Rk on beach close N of hbr ent. Hbr is floodlit.

COMMUNICATIONS (Code 01834) CGOC (01646) 690909; Police 101; Dr 844161; 🏥 842040. HM 842717 (end May-end Sept), Mobile 07977 609947.

Ch 16, 80 (listening during HO).

FACILITIES Hbr ⚓ (<4·2m) ⚲. **Town** 🛠🗑🛒⛽✉Ⓑ🏦🛢🚿✕🗑 ⇌ ✈ (Swansea; and a small airfield at Haverfordwest).

OTHER ADJACENT HARBOURS (See AC 5620)

SAUNDERSFOOT, Pembrokeshire, **51°42'·60N 04°41'·76W**. AC 1179, 1076, 1482. HW –0510 on Dover; ML 4·4m; Duration 0605. See 4.13. A half-tide hbr with good shelter, but there may be a surge in prolonged E winds. On appr, beware buoys marking restricted area (power boats, etc) between Coppett Hall Pt and Perry's Pt. ⚲ may be available (see HM), or moorings in the middle. Pier hd lt Fl R 5s 6m 7M on stone cupola. VHF: HM 11 16. HM ☎(01834) 812094/(Home 831389). Facilities: ⚓ 6⚲⚓ (on SW wall) 🛠🗑🛠 🛢🏦. **Town** ✉Ⓑ🚿✕🗑⇌ (Tenby/Saundersfoot).

CARMARTHEN, Carmarthenshire, **51°46'·27N 04°22'·53W**. AC 1179, 1076. HW –0455 on Dover. See 4.14. R Towy & Taf dry. Beware Carmarthen Bar in S winds F4 and over with strong sp streams. Nav info is available from Carmarthen Bar Navigation Committee ☎ (01267) 231250 or YC's. Appr on N'ly hdg toward Wharley Pt, leaving DZ8 & 9 buoys 5ca to stbd. Chan shifts frequently and is unmarked so local knowledge reqd unless conditions ideal. ⚓ in mid-stream or ⚓s at R Towy YC off Ferryside (7M below Carmarthen) or R Towey Boat Club 1M N on W bank. 4 power lines cross in last 2·5M before Carmarthen, clearance 7·4m. **R Towy YC** ☎(01267) 238356, ⚓⚓🏦. **R Towy BC** ☎(01267) 238316. **Town** ⚓✉Ⓑ🗑 🛒⇌✈ (Cardiff).

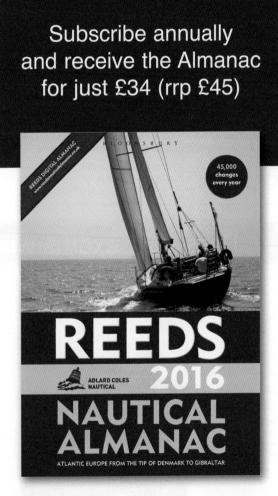

S Wales

4.14 BURRY PORT

Carmarthenshire 51°40'·52N 04°14'·93W (Burry Port) ✿✿♨♨✿

CHARTS AC 5620, 5608 1179, 1076; Imray C59, C60, 2600

TIDES −0500 Dover; ML 4·7; Duration 0555

Standard Port MILFORD HAVEN (←—)

Times				Height (metres)			
High Water		Low Water		MHWS	MHWN	MLWN	MLWS
0100	0800	0100	0700	7·0	5·2	2·5	0·7
1300	2000	1300	1900				
Differences BURRY PORT							
+0003	+0003	+0007	+0007	+1·6	+1·4	+0·5	+0·4
LLANELLI							
−0003	−0003	+0150	+0020	+0·8	+0·6	ND	ND
FERRYSIDE							
0000	−0010	+0220	0000	−0·3	−0·7	−1·7	−0·6
CARMARTHEN							
+0010	0000	DR	DR	−4·4	−4·8	DR	DR

SHELTER Good in Burry Port Marina via lock with flapgate controlled by R/G lts. Access HW±2 (max) over sill depth 2·5m. Sp tides run hard. Note: If bad weather precludes access, especially in W'lies, see 4.13 for ⚓s around Caldey Island.

NAVIGATION WPT 51°36'·50N 04°23'·00W, 090°/2·5M to Burry Holms, then about 5M to Burry Port over Lynch Sands which dry approx 1·5m. Carmarthen Bar and the approaches to Burry Port should not be attempted in W winds >F5, nor at night. Depths are changeable. Pendine Range may be active (look for red flags) but clear range procedures are in force and there are no restrictions on navigation.

From close NW of Burry Holms, with sufficient rise of tide, track 015° for 2·5M with the W edge of Burry Holms in transit astern with Worms Head. When Whiteford lighthouse (disused) bears 086° alter to approx 065° until Barrel Post bears 015°.

Near approaches to the harbour are marked by a buoyed channel, dries 3·2m. Barrel Post should not be rounded too close.

LIGHTS AND MARKS Whiteford lt ho is conspic, but no longer lit. On head of W bkwtr is Barrel post; 1½ca N is conspic old lt ho (W tr, R top) Fl 5s 7m 6½M, and flagstaff.

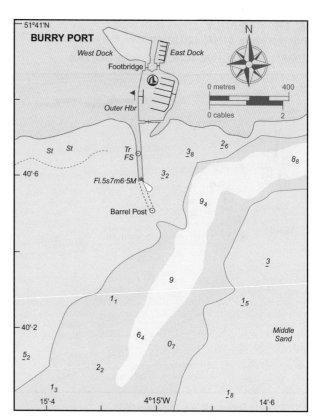

COMMUNICATIONS (Code 01554); CGOC (01646) 690909; Pendine Range (01994) 453243 Ext 240; Police 101; Dr 832240. HM 835691, mob (emergencies only) 07817 395710. Marina Ch M (HO).

FACILITIES Burry Port Marina 450 inc Ⓥ, £1.65, max LOA 11m, max draught 1·5m; Burry Port YC ☐; Services ⛴♂⚓✕🔧⊞⛽. Town ⛽🏧 (approx 1M), 🏦✉Ⓑ🛒✕☐⇌✈ (Cardiff).

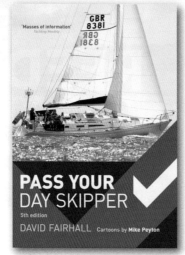
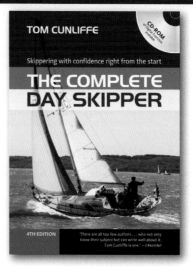

4.15   SWANSEA

Swansea 51°36'·43N 03°55'·67W ✸✸✸✥✥✥✿✿✿

CHARTS AC 5608, 1179, 1165, 1161; Imray C59, 2600

TIDES –0500 Dover; ML 5·2; Duration 0620

Standard Port MILFORD HAVEN (←)

Times				Height (metres)			
High Water		Low Water		MHWS	MHWN	MLWN	MLWS
0100	0800	0100	0700	7·0	5·2	2·5	0·7
1300	2000	1300	1900				
Differences SWANSEA							
+0004	+0006	–0006	–0003	+2·6	+2·1	+0·7	+0·3
MUMBLES							
+0001	+0003	–0012	–0005	+2·5	+2·0	+0·8	+0·4
PORT TALBOT							
0000	+0005	–0010	–0005	+2·7	+2·1	+1·0	+0·4
PORTHCAWL							
+0005	+0010	–0010	–0005	+2·9	+2·3	+0·8	+0·3

SHELTER Very good in marina.

NAVIGATION WPT 51°35'·53N 03°56'·08W (SHM buoy) 020°/0·92M to E bkwtr lt. Keep seaward of Mixon Shoal. When N of SW Inner Green Grounds (SWIGG) SCM lt buoy keep to W of dredged chan and clear of commercial ships. *Yachts must motor in approaches and in harbour,* max speed 4kn. In Swansea Bay tidal streams flow anti-clockwise for 9½ hrs (Swansea HW –3½ to +6), with at times a race off Mumbles Hd. From HW–6 to –3 the stream reverses, setting N past Mumbles Hd towards Swansea.

LOCKS Enter via R Tawe barrage locks, which operate on request HW±4½ (co-ordinated with the marina lock), 0700-2200BST; out of season, 0700-1900UT, but to 2200 at w/ends. There are pontoons in both locks.

Vessels usually exit Tawe barrage locks at H+00, and enter at H+30. Locks are closed when ht of tide falls to 1·5m above CD, usually at MLWS. At sp, do not enter river until LW+1½. Two large Or holding buoys below barrage in mid-stream; also, at W side of barrage lock, a landing pontoon (dries, foul ground).

LIGHTS AND MARKS See 4.3 and chartlet. Mumbles Hd, Fl (4) 20s35m16M, is 3M SSW of hbr ent. A conspic TV mast (R lts) NNE of hbr is almost aligned with the fairway. Ldg lts 020° mark E side of chan dredged 3m. When N of Swansea Middle West (QR) and Swansea Middle East (QG) chan buoys stay inside dredged chan. Barrage lock lit by 2FR/FG (vert) to seaward.

Port Traffic sigs are conspic at W side of ent to King's Dock; there are 9 lts, ● or ●, arranged in a 3 x 3 frame. Yachts arriving must obey the middle lt in left column:

   ● = Do not enter the river; hold SW of W Pier.
   ● = Yachts may enter the river, keeping to mid-chan, then to W of holding buoys.

Lock Master will advise on tfc movements Ch 18.
Lock sigs for barrage and marina locks alike are:

   ●] = Lock closed. Do not proceed

   ● = Wait

   ● = Enter with caution

   ●] = Free flow operating; proceed with caution

COMMUNICATIONS (Code 01792) CGOC 366534; Police 101; Ⓗ 205666; Dr 653452; DVLA (for SSR) 783355. HM 653787; Barrage 456014.

Barrage, *Tawe Lock* Ch 18. *Swansea Marina* Ch 80. For commercial docks call *Swansea Docks Radio* VHF Ch14 (H24).

FACILITIES Swansea Marina (340+50Ⓥ) ☎470310, £1·85, lock 9m wide ⚓ 🅿 🔥 🛢 ⛽ 🔧 ⚒ 🖉 Ⓔ ⚠ ⬛(25t) ◻(1t) 🔩 ACA, ice, ✕ ⬛ wi-fi.

Swansea Yacht & Sub Aqua Club (SY & SAC) ☎654863, No visitors, ⚓🛢⚓➴(5t static) ✕ ⬛.

City ✉ Ⓑ 🛒 ✕ ⬛ ⇌ ✈.

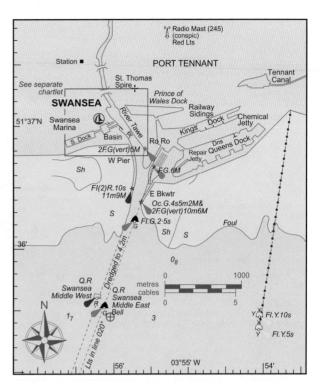

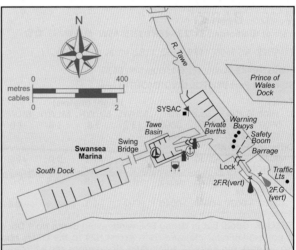

ADJACENT HARBOURS AND ANCHORAGES

Mumbles, 51°34'·2N 03°58'·2W. Good ⚓ in W'lies 5ca N of Mumbles **Bristol Chan YC** ☎(01792) 366000, ⚓ ➴; **Mumbles YC** ☎369321, ⚓ ➴ ➴ ◻ (hire).

R Neath, 51°37'·88N 03°49'·97W. Ent over bar HW±2½ via 1·5M chan, marked/lit training wall to stbd. Tfc info from *Neath Pilot* VHF Ch 77, if on stn. **Monkstone Marina**, W bank just S of bridge, dries 4m: ⚓, 2 Y ⚓s, ➴ 🔥 ▯(15t) ✕ ⬛. Visitors welcome. **Monkstone C & SC**, ☎(01792) 812229; VHF Ch **M** (occas).

PORTHCAWL, Bridgend, 51°28'·48N 03°42'·02W. AC 1165, 1169. HW –0500 on Dover; ML 5·3m. See 4.15. Hbr protected by bkwtr running SE from Porthcawl Pt. Beware rk ledges and appr drying 5m above CD. Porthcawl lt ho, F WRG (see 4.3). Tidal streams off bkwtr can reach 6kn at Sp. 3 ⚓s or ⚓ approx 3ca SSE of lt ho. Look out for swimmers. Marina access gate opens HW±3, R/G tfc lts, sill 3.5m above CD; Ⓥ by arrangement, HM ☎(01656) 815715 VHF Ch 80. Facilities: ➴ 70⚓➴ ◻. **Porthcawl Hbr B C** ☎782342. **Town** 🏨 🏨 🔩 ✉ Ⓑ 🛒 ✕ ⬛ ⇌(Bridgend) ✈(Cardiff).

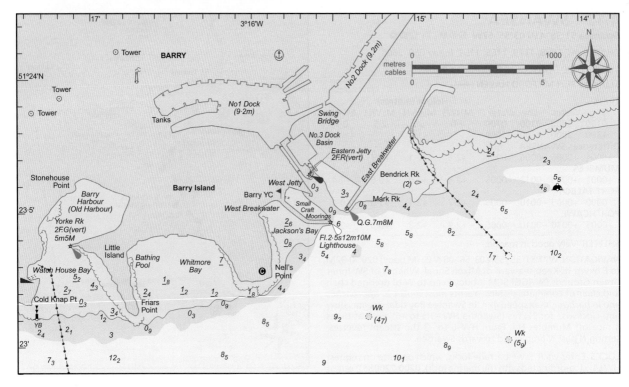

4.16 BARRY

Vale of Glamorgan **51°23´·48N 03°15´·45W** ❀❀❀♻♻♻❀❀

CHARTS AC 5608, 1179, 1152, 1182; Imray C59, 2600

TIDES –0423 Dover; ML 6·1; Duration 0630

Standard Port BRISTOL (AVONMOUTH) (→)

Times				Height (metres)			
High Water		Low Water		MHWS	MHWN	MLWN	MLWS
0600	1100	0300	0800	13·2	9·8	3·8	1·0
1800	2300	1500	2000				
Differences BARRY							
–0025	–0025	–0130	–0045	–1·5	–1·1	0·0	+0·2
FLAT HOLM							
–0015	–0015	–0035	–0035	–1·4	–1·0	–0·5	0·0
STEEP HOLM							
–0020	–0020	–0040	–0040	–1·7	–1·1	–0·5	–0·4

SHELTER Good, but in strong E/SE winds avoid Barry; No 1 Dock is not available for pleasure craft. Access H24 to the Outer hbr. No � or ⚓, but Barry YC administers all moorings and welcomes visitors. Temporary mooring may be available from Bristol Pilots on request.

NAVIGATION WPT 51°23´·03N 03°15´·08W, 332°/0·53M to entrance. Beware heavy commercial traffic. Approaching from E keep well out from the shore. Strong tidal stream across entrance.

LIGHTS AND MARKS Welsh Water Barry West PHM buoy, Fl R 5s, and Merkur PHM buoy, Fl R 2·5s, lie respectively 217°/1·5M and 191°/1·65M from harbour entrance. W bkwtr Fl 2·5s 10M. E bkwtr QG 8M.

COMMUNICATIONS (Code 01446) CGOC (01646) 690909; Police 101; Dr 733355. HM 0870 609 6699. BY 678186.
Barry Radio VHF Ch **11** 10 16 (HW–4 to HW+3); tidal info on request. *Bristol Pilot* via Ch 16 may advise on vacant moorings.

FACILITIES Barry YC (130) ☎735511, approaches dry approx 2m; ⚓⛝⚓✕✎ 🏪⌂🚻🅿(50t) 🗓. **Town** 🗓 🗓(2M) ⛽(2M) 🅿🚋✉ Ⓑ ✕ 🗓 ⇌ ✈ (Cardiff).

4.17 CARDIFF/PENARTH

Vale of Glamorgan **51°26´·74N 03°09´·92W** (marina)
❀❀❀♻♻♻❀❀❀

CHARTS AC 5608, 1179, 1176, 1182; Imray C59, 2600

TIDES –0425 Dover; ML 6·4; Duration 0610

Standard Port BRISTOL (AVONMOUTH) (→)

Times				Height (metres)			
High Water		Low Water		MHWS	MHWN	MLWN	MLWS
0600	1100	0300	0800	13·2	9·8	3·8	1·0
1800	2300	1500	2000				
Differences CARDIFF							
–0015	–0015	–0035	–0030	–0·9	–0·7	+0·2	+0·2
NEWPORT							
–0005	–0010	–0015	–0015	–0·9	–0·9	–0·2	–0·2
CHEPSTOW (River Wye)							
+0020	+0020	ND	ND	ND	ND	ND	ND

NOTE: At Newport the ht of LW does not normally fall below MLWS. Tidal hts are based on a minimum river flow; max flow may raise ht of LW by as much as 0·3m.

SHELTER Very good in marinas. See above for barrage locks. Waiting trot berths in outer hbr; or ⚓ off Penarth seafront in W'lies; in E'lies cramped ⚓ off Alexandra Dock ent in 2m.

NAVIGATION WPT 51°24´·03N 03°08´·81W (2½ca SW of S Cardiff SCM lt buoy), 349°/2·9M to barrage locks.

The outer approaches from W or SW are via Breaksea lt float and N of One Fathom Bk. Keep S of Lavernock Spit SCM lt buoy and NW of Flat Holm and Wolves NCM lt buoy drying rk. From NE, drying ledges and shoals extend >1M offshore. From E, appr via Monkstone Lt ho and S Cardiff SCM buoy. Ranny Spit (dries 0·4m) is 3½ca to the W, and Cardiff Grounds (dries 5·4m) 3½ca to the E.

The Wrach Chan is buoyed/lit and dredged 1·2m; it passes 1½ca E of Penarth Hd. The locks appr chan, buoyed, is dredged 0·7m below CD.

Do not impede merchant ships, especially those entering/leaving Alexandra Dock.

Cardiff Bay Barrage and Marina lock

- Call *Barrage Control* VHF Ch 18 or ☎02920 700234 to request lock-in or lock-out. Waiting berth on a barge in outer hbr.
- If entering near LW ask Barrage Control for up-to-date depths.
- Subject to VHF instructions, enter the outer hbr (Wpt 51°26'·71N 03°09'·84W) and lock in.
- IPTS (sigs 1, 2, 3, 5) are shown at lock ent.
- Departures on H and H +30. Arrivals at H +15 and H +45.
- Lock into marina operates H24 on free-flow from the bay.

LIGHTS AND MARKS Directional light, Oc WRG 10s 5m3M, on a W metal post marks Wrach Channel. SPM Fl Y 3s mark the 5kt limit.

COMMUNICATIONS (Code 02920) CGOC (01646) 690909; ⚓ 397020; Police101; Dr 415258; HM 400500; Barrage control 700234; Cardiff Bay Authority 877900.

Port VHF Ch **14** 16 (HW–4 to HW+3). *Barrage Control* Ch 18 H24. Penarth Quays Marina Ch 80 H24. Cardiff Marina Ch M.

FACILITIES Penarth Quays Marina ⚓ www.quaymarinas.com ☎705021, H24, 350⚓+Ⓥ welcome, £1.80 (short stay £11), max draught 3m, lock width 7·3m; ⊡ ♣ ♀(0930-1630, E pontoon) ♠ ✕ ♦ Ⓔ ⌂ ☐(20t) ⌂(20t) ⌂ ACA ✕.

Penarth YC ☎ 708196, ⚓ ⚓ ☐.

Mermaid Quay Ⓥ on pontons (£1/craft/hr) near city centre; many Rs and Bars.

Cardiff Marina www.themarinegroup.co.uk ☎396078, 320⚓ inc 50Ⓥ £2·20, ⊡ ♣ ♂ ⌂(4½t) ⌂(short walk).

Cardiff YC ☎463697, ⚓ (floating pontoon) ⚓ ⚓ ☐.

Cardiff Bay YC ☎226575, ⚓ ⚓ ⚓ ⚓ ⌂ ☐.

City ⊠ Ⓑ ⌂ ✕ ☐ ⇌ ✈ (15 mins).

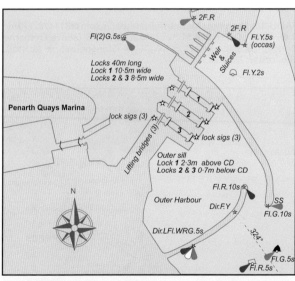

Penarth Quays Marina

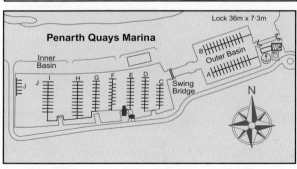

Penarth Quays Marina

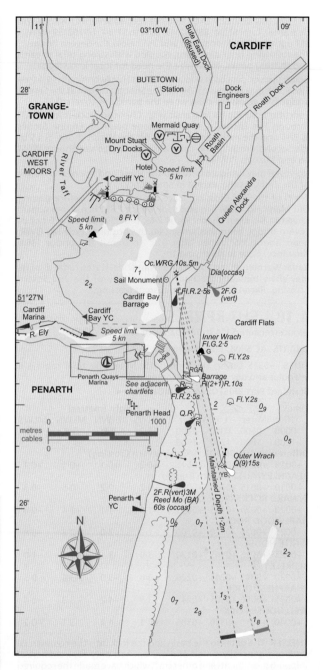

ADJACENT HARBOUR

NEWPORT, Newport, **51°32'·95N 02°59'·13W**. AC 5608, 1179, 1152, 1176. HW –0425 on Dover; ML 6·0m; Duration 0620. See 4.17. A commercial port controlled by ABP, but a safe shelter for yachts. Enter R Usk over bar (approx 0·5m) E of West Usk buoy, QR, and follow buoyed and lit chan to S Lock ent; turn NE (ldg lts 062°) for yacht moorings on S side between power stn pier and YC. Beware overhead cables in Julian's Pill, clearance 3·8m.

Lights, see 4.3. East Usk lt ho Fl (2) WRG 10s. Ldg lts 062°, both FG. Alexandra Dock, S lock W pier head 2 FR (vert) 9/7m 6M. E pier head 2 FG (vert) 9/7m 6M.

Port VHF, *Newport Radio,* and VTS: Ch 09, **71**, 74 (HW ±4). HM (ABP) ☎0870 609 6699. Facilities: ⌂ ⌂ ✕ ✕ Ⓔ. **Newport and Uskmouth SC** ☐ M. **Town** All facilities.

THE SEVERN BRIDGES (AC 1166) The Second Severn Crossing (37m clearance), from 51°34'·88N 02°43'·80W to 51°34'·14N 02°39'·82W, is 4M upriver from Avonmouth and 3M below the Severn Bridge. The following brief directions, coupled with strong tidal streams and shifting banks, emphasize the need for local knowledge.

Going upriver, pass both bridges at about HW Avonmouth –1¼ (see also 4.18); max sp stream is 8kn at The Shoots and 6kn at the Severn Bridge (set across the chan when the banks are covered).

Redcliffe F Bu ldg lts in transit with Charston Rock lt lead 013° through The Shoots, a narrow passage between English Stones (6·2m) and the rocky ledges (5·1m) off the Welsh shore. 5ca S of the Second Crossing, the chan is marked by Lower Shoots WCM bn and Mixoms PHM bn.

No vessel may navigate between the shore and the nearer Tower of the 2nd Crossing, except in emergency.

4ca N of the 2nd Crossing, leave the 013° transit before passing Old Man's Hd WCM bcn and Lady Bench PHM bcn. From abeam Charston Rk, keep Chapel Rk, Fl 2·6s, brg 050° until the E twr of Severn Bridge bears 068°; maintain this brg until Lyde Rk, QWR, bears about 355°, when alter 010° to transit the bridge (36m clearance) close to rks drying 1m.

Radar Warning. In certain conditions and tidal states, radar displays may show misleading echoes in the vicinity of the 2nd Severn Crossing. *Racon (O)* is at centre span of crossing.

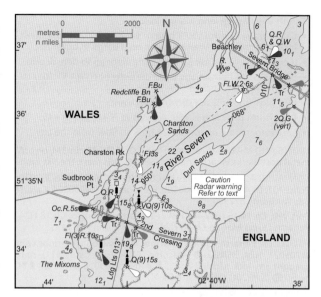

4.18 SHARPNESS

Gloucestershire 51°43'·03N 02°29'·08W ✳✳🌢🌢⚓🌸🌸

CHARTS AC 5608, 1166, Imray C59, 2600

TIDES –0315 Dover; Duration 0415. Note: The tidal regime is irregular and deviates from Avonmouth curve.

Standard Port BRISTOL (AVONMOUTH) (→)

Times				Height (metres)			
High Water		Low Water		MHWS	MHWN	MLWN	MLWS
0000	0600	0000	0700	13·2	9·8	3·8	1·0
1200	1800	1200	1900				
Differences SUDBROOK (Second Severn Crossing)							
+0010	+0010	+0025	+0015	+0·2	+0·1	–0·1	+0·1
BEACHLEY/AUST (Severn Bridge)							
+0010	+0015	+0040	+0025	–0·2	–0·2	–0·5	–0·3
INWARD ROCKS (River Severn)							
+0020	+0020	+0105	+0045	–1·0	–1·1	–1·4	–0·6
NARLWOOD ROCKS							
+0025	+0025	+0120	+0100	–1·9	–2·0	–2·3	–0·8
WHITE HOUSE							
+0025	+0025	+0145	+0120	–3·0	–3·1	–3·6	–1·0
BERKELEY							
+0030	+0045	+0245	+0220	–3·8	–3·9	–3·4	–0·5
SHARPNESS DOCK							
+0035	+0050	+0305	+0245	–3·9	–4·2	–3·3	–0·4
WELLHOUSE ROCK							
+0040	+0055	+0320	+0305	–4·1	–4·4	–3·1	–0·2

SHELTER The gates to the basin and the lock into the commercial dock are generally closed and are opened only for commercial shipping movements and other craft which have made the required booking and given appropriate notice (min. 24h). It is essential for arrangements to be made by contacting the Pierhead office which is generally manned during daylight tides, HW–4 to HW+1 (if unmanned leave a message). Plan your passage to arrive no sooner than HW–1 and no later than HW. Detailed information on lock fees and canal licences is available from the Pierhead office. Comprehensive information on the passage from Avonmouth is available from Gloucester Harbour Trustees. Fog signals are available from Sharpness Radio on VHF Ch 13 or Pierhead office.

NAVIGATION Use transits shown on AC 1166. Study guidance notes from Gloucester Harbour Trustees in good time.

- Leave King Road, Avonmouth (17M downriver) not before HW Sharpness –3, to be off Hbr ent about HW –½. Stem strong flood S of F Bu lt; beware tidal eddy.
- Do not proceed above the Severn Bridge except HW–1¼ /+2. There is a 5H flood and a 7H ebb.

LIGHTS AND MARKS Lights as chartlet, but night passage not advised without local knowledge/pilot (07774 226143).

COMMUNICATIONS (Code 01453) Police 101; ⊞ 810777. Pierhead 511968 (HW–4 to HW+1). Gloucester Harbour Trustees www.gloucesterharbourtrustees.org ☎811913 (HO).

Call Gloucester and Sharpness Canal Ch 74 for bridges (no locks). Call *Bristol VTS* VHF Ch 12 when passing reporting points inwards/outwards E/W Grounds PHM, Welsh Hook SCM and at Lower Shoots Bcn.

FACILITIES Sharpness Marina sharpness@f2s.com ☎811476. 170 inc 2 ♥, £8 all LOA. ♿ ⛽ 🛥 ✕ 🔧 🄱 🛒 🅰. **Town** 🅃 (above Fretherne Bridge), ✉ Ⓑ(Berkeley) 🍴 ✕ 🗐, ⇌ (Stonehouse), ✈ (Bristol). Gloucester: 🅃 🄻 ACA.

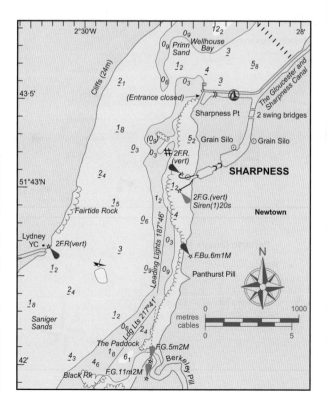

STANDARD TIME (UT) For Summer Time add ONE hour in **non-shaded** areas	**BRISTOL (AVONMOUTH)** LAT 51°30'N LONG 2°44'W TIMES AND HEIGHTS OF HIGH AND LOW WATERS	Dates in red are **SPRINGS** Dates in blue are NEAPS

YEAR **2016**

JANUARY

Time m	Time m
1 0513 2.6 / 1113 11.1 / F 1735 2.9 / 2335 10.6	**16** 0528 2.0 / 1129 12.3 / SA 1757 2.0 / ☽ 2352 11.8
2 0553 3.0 / 1156 10.5 / SA 1819 3.2 / ☽	**17** 0611 2.4 / 1222 11.6 / SU 1845 2.5
3 0022 10.1 / 0643 3.5 / SU 1253 10.1 / 1915 3.6	**18** 0049 11.1 / 0705 3.0 / M 1332 11.0 / 1949 3.1
4 0129 9.8 / 0749 3.8 / M 1408 9.9 / 2025 3.7	**19** 0207 10.7 / 0833 3.5 / TU 1456 10.8 / 2127 3.3
5 0248 9.9 / 0904 3.7 / TU 1522 10.2 / 2141 3.5	**20** 0330 10.8 / 1013 3.3 / W 1609 11.1 / 2246 2.8
6 0357 10.4 / 1017 3.2 / W 1624 10.8 / 2252 2.9	**21** 0439 11.3 / 1122 2.6 / TH 1712 11.7 / 2349 2.1
7 0454 11.2 / 1121 2.5 / TH 1718 11.5 / 2352 2.3	**22** 0537 12.1 / 1220 1.9 / F 1807 12.4
8 0544 12.0 / 1217 2.0 / F 1806 12.1	**23** 0044 1.5 / 0628 12.8 / SA 1314 1.4 / 1856 12.9
9 0045 1.8 / 0629 12.6 / SA 1310 1.6 / 1851 12.6	**24** 0136 1.1 / 0714 13.2 / SU 1404 1.1 / ○ 1941 13.2
10 0136 1.6 / 0712 13.0 / SU 1400 1.5 / ● 1935 12.9	**25** 0223 0.9 / 0757 13.4 / M 1450 1.1 / 2022 13.2
11 0223 1.5 / 0755 13.2 / M 1447 1.4 / 2019 13.1	**26** 0306 1.0 / 0836 13.3 / TU 1529 1.3 / 2100 13.0
12 0306 1.4 / 0837 13.4 / TU 1529 1.3 / 2101 13.2	**27** 0341 1.3 / 0911 13.0 / W 1600 1.6 / 2132 12.6
13 0344 1.5 / 0919 13.4 / W 1607 1.3 / 2142 13.1	**28** 0406 1.7 / 0942 12.6 / TH 1620 2.0 / 2200 12.2
14 0418 1.5 / 1001 13.2 / TH 1642 1.4 / 2223 12.9	**29** 0424 1.9 / 1011 12.2 / F 1637 2.2 / 2227 11.7
15 0452 1.7 / 1043 12.9 / F 1717 1.6 / 2305 12.5	**30** 0446 2.1 / 1040 11.7 / SA 1701 2.3 / 2257 11.2
	31 0516 2.4 / 1112 11.1 / SU 1734 2.6 / 2332 10.7

FEBRUARY

Time m	Time m
1 0554 2.9 / 1152 10.5 / M 1817 3.1 / ☽	**16** 0019 11.2 / 0633 2.9 / TU 1259 10.8 / 1908 3.2
2 0019 10.1 / 0645 3.4 / TU 1250 9.9 / 1917 3.7	**17** 0132 10.4 / 0740 3.7 / W 1430 10.2 / 2043 3.7
3 0128 9.7 / 0803 3.8 / W 1411 9.7 / 2043 3.9	**18** 0306 10.2 / 0948 3.7 / TH 1550 10.4 / 2223 3.3
4 0259 9.8 / 0929 3.6 / TH 1538 10.1 / 2207 3.4	**19** 0420 10.7 / 1103 3.0 / F 1656 11.1 / 2328 2.5
5 0417 10.6 / 1044 3.0 / F 1647 11.0 / 2319 2.7	**20** 0521 11.6 / 1201 2.1 / SA 1752 12.0
6 0516 11.5 / 1149 2.2 / SA 1743 11.9	**21** 0023 1.7 / 0611 12.4 / SU 1254 1.4 / 1839 12.7
7 0020 2.0 / 0607 12.4 / SU 1248 1.7 / 1832 12.6	**22** 0114 1.1 / 0657 13.0 / M 1343 1.0 / ○ 1922 13.1
8 0117 1.5 / 0654 13.1 / M 1343 1.3 / ● 1919 13.2	**23** 0202 0.8 / 0738 13.5 / TU 1428 0.9 / 2002 13.2
9 0209 1.2 / 0739 13.6 / TU 1434 1.0 / 2004 13.6	**24** 0245 0.8 / 0815 13.3 / W 1508 1.0 / 2036 13.0
10 0257 1.2 / 0823 13.9 / W 1520 0.8 / 2047 13.8	**25** 0321 1.0 / 0847 13.1 / TH 1540 1.4 / 2106 12.7
11 0338 0.8 / 0906 14.0 / TH 1600 0.7 / 2128 13.8	**26** 0348 1.4 / 0917 12.7 / F 1608 1.8 / 2133 12.4
12 0414 0.9 / 0947 13.9 / F 1634 0.8 / 2208 13.5	**27** 0404 1.7 / 0943 12.4 / SA 1611 1.9 / 2158 12.0
13 0445 1.1 / 1010 13.5 / SA 1704 1.2 / 2247 13.0	**28** 0419 1.8 / 1009 12.0 / SU 1629 2.0 / 2223 11.6
14 0515 1.5 / 1110 12.7 / SU 1736 1.7 / 2329 12.2	**29** 0444 2.0 / 1037 11.5 / M 1658 2.2 / 2254 11.1
15 0549 2.1 / 1157 11.8 / M 1815 2.4 / ◑	

MARCH

Time m	Time m
1 0517 2.4 / 1112 10.9 / TU 1734 2.7 / ☽ 2335 10.5	**16** 0608 2.8 / 1232 10.5 / W 1838 3.3
2 0559 3.0 / 1201 10.2 / W 1822 3.4	**17** 0102 10.1 / 0708 3.7 / TH 1407 9.8 / 1959 4.0
3 0032 9.9 / 0701 3.7 / TH 1310 9.7 / 1936 4.0	**18** 0243 9.9 / 0920 4.0 / F 1529 10.0 / 2158 3.7
4 0155 9.6 / 0839 3.9 / F 1446 9.8 / 2124 3.8	**19** 0357 10.4 / 1040 3.2 / SA 1634 10.8 / 2304 2.7
5 0336 10.1 / 1009 3.3 / SA 1616 10.6 / 2249 3.0	**20** 0458 11.3 / 1137 2.2 / SU 1729 11.7 / 2358 1.8
6 0448 11.2 / 1124 2.4 / SU 1719 11.7 / 2357 2.2	**21** 0549 12.1 / 1227 1.5 / M 1816 12.4
7 0544 12.3 / 1227 1.6 / M 1812 12.7	**22** 0047 1.1 / 0633 12.8 / TU 1315 1.0 / 1857 12.9
8 0056 1.5 / 0633 13.2 / TU 1324 1.0 / 1859 13.5	**23** 0134 0.8 / 0712 13.1 / W 1400 0.8 / ○ 1934 13.1
9 0151 0.9 / 0720 13.9 / W 1416 0.6 / ● 1944 14.0	**24** 0218 0.7 / 0748 13.1 / TH 1440 1.0 / 2008 13.0
10 0240 0.6 / 0805 14.3 / TH 1503 0.3 / 2028 14.2	**25** 0255 0.9 / 0821 12.9 / F 1514 1.3 / 2038 12.7
11 0323 0.4 / 0848 14.4 / F 1543 0.3 / 2109 14.2	**26** 0325 1.3 / 0850 12.6 / SA 1536 1.7 / 2105 12.4
12 0400 0.4 / 0930 14.3 / SA 1617 0.5 / 2149 13.9	**27** 0342 1.6 / 0917 12.3 / SU 1546 1.9 / 2130 12.1
13 0431 0.7 / 1010 13.7 / SU 1646 1.0 / 2227 13.3	**28** 0355 1.7 / 0941 12.0 / M 1602 1.9 / 2154 11.8
14 0458 1.3 / 1050 12.8 / M 1714 1.6 / 2307 12.3	**29** 0419 1.8 / 1009 11.7 / TU 1630 2.0 / 2225 11.4
15 0528 2.0 / 1134 11.7 / TU 1749 2.4 / ☽ 2353 11.2	**30** 0450 2.1 / 1045 11.2 / W 1704 2.4 / 2306 10.9
	31 0530 2.6 / 1132 10.6 / TH 1748 3.1 / ☽ 2359 10.2

APRIL

Time m	Time m
1 0624 3.3 / 1235 10.0 / F 1851 3.7	**16** 0216 9.8 / 0823 3.9 / SA 1500 9.9 / 2117 3.8
2 0113 9.8 / 0749 3.7 / SA 1401 9.8 / 2035 3.9	**17** 0327 10.3 / 1005 3.3 / SU 1603 10.5 / 2230 3.0
3 0252 10.1 / 0933 3.3 / SU 1541 10.5 / 2217 3.2	**18** 0426 11.0 / 1104 2.5 / M 1657 11.3 / 2325 2.1
4 0417 11.1 / 1056 2.4 / M 1652 11.6 / 2331 2.2	**19** 0517 11.8 / 1154 1.8 / TU 1744 12.1
5 0518 12.3 / 1202 1.6 / TU 1747 12.7	**20** 0014 1.4 / 0601 12.3 / W 1242 1.3 / 1825 12.6
6 0031 1.4 / 0609 13.3 / W 1300 0.9 / 1836 13.6	**21** 0101 1.0 / 0641 12.7 / TH 1326 1.1 / 1902 12.8
7 0126 0.8 / 0657 14.0 / TH 1352 0.4 / ● 1922 14.2	**22** 0145 1.0 / 0717 12.7 / F 1408 1.1 / ○ 1937 12.8
8 0216 0.4 / 0743 14.4 / F 1440 0.1 / 2006 14.4	**23** 0224 1.1 / 0752 12.6 / SA 1443 1.4 / 2009 12.6
9 0301 0.2 / 0828 14.5 / SA 1521 0.1 / 2048 14.4	**24** 0257 1.4 / 0823 12.5 / SU 1510 1.7 / 2038 12.4
10 0340 0.3 / 0910 14.3 / SU 1557 0.4 / 2129 14.0	**25** 0320 1.7 / 0852 12.2 / M 1525 1.9 / 2106 12.2
11 0414 0.7 / 0952 13.7 / M 1627 1.0 / 2208 13.3	**26** 0337 1.8 / 0920 12.0 / TU 1543 1.9 / 2133 11.9
12 0443 1.3 / 1033 12.7 / TU 1656 1.7 / 2248 12.3	**27** 0401 1.8 / 0951 11.8 / W 1611 2.0 / 2207 11.6
13 0512 2.0 / 1116 11.6 / W 1729 2.5 / 2333 11.2	**28** 0434 2.0 / 1029 11.4 / TH 1646 2.3 / 2248 11.2
14 0551 2.8 / 1211 10.5 / TH 1815 3.3 / ◑	**29** 0514 2.4 / 1115 10.9 / F 1730 2.8 / 2341 10.7
15 0039 10.2 / 0647 3.6 / F 1340 9.8 / 1926 4.0	**30** 0606 2.9 / 1215 10.4 / SA 1828 3.4 / ☽

Chart Datum: 6·50 metres below Ordnance Datum (Newlyn). HAT is 14·7 metres above Chart Datum.

Bristol Channel

STANDARD TIME (UT)
For Summer Time add ONE hour in **non-shaded areas**

BRISTOL (AVONMOUTH) LAT 51°30'N LONG 2°44'W
TIMES AND HEIGHTS OF HIGH AND LOW WATERS

Dates in red are **SPRINGS**
Dates in blue are NEAPS

YEAR 2016

MAY

Time	m		Time	m
1 SU	0049 10.3 / 0718 3.3 / 1331 10.2 / 1954 3.6		**16** M	0247 10.2 / 0853 3.5 / 1522 10.2 / 2133 3.3
2 M	0215 10.4 / 0855 3.1 / 1501 10.6 / 2141 3.2		**17** TU	0346 10.7 / 1013 3.0 / 1617 10.9 / 2240 2.6
3 TU	0341 11.2 / 1022 2.4 / 1619 11.5 / 2259 2.3		**18** W	0437 11.2 / 1111 2.3 / 1705 11.5 / 2334 2.0
4 W	0448 12.2 / 1131 1.7 / 1719 12.6		**19** TH	0524 11.8 / 1201 1.8 / 1749 12.1
5 TH	0002 1.5 / 0543 13.1 / 1231 1.0 / 1810 13.4		**20** F	0022 1.5 / 0605 12.2 / 1248 1.5 / 1828 12.4
6 F	0059 0.9 / 0633 13.8 / 1325 0.5 / ● 1858 14.0		**21** SA	0108 1.3 / 0645 12.4 / 1332 1.4 / ○ 1905 12.5
7 SA	0150 0.5 / 0721 14.2 / 1414 0.3 / 1943 14.3		**22** SU	0150 1.3 / 0722 12.4 / 1411 1.5 / 1941 12.5
8 SU	0238 0.3 / 0808 14.2 / 1458 0.3 / 2027 14.2		**23** M	0229 1.5 / 0758 12.3 / 1445 1.7 / 2015 12.4
9 M	0321 0.4 / 0852 14.0 / 1537 0.6 / 2110 13.8		**24** TU	0301 1.7 / 0833 12.2 / 1510 1.9 / 2048 12.3
10 TU	0358 0.8 / 0936 13.4 / 1611 1.1 / 2152 13.1		**25** W	0326 1.8 / 0906 12.1 / 1533 2.0 / 2120 12.1
11 W	0430 1.4 / 1018 12.6 / 1641 1.7 / 2232 12.3		**26** TH	0353 1.9 / 0941 12.0 / 1602 2.0 / 2157 11.9
12 TH	0501 2.0 / 1101 11.6 / 1714 2.4 / 2317 11.3		**27** F	0427 1.9 / 1020 11.7 / 1639 2.2 / 2239 11.6
13 F	0538 2.7 / 1150 10.7 / 1756 3.1 / ◗		**28** SA	0508 2.2 / 1106 11.4 / 1722 2.5 / 2330 11.2
14 SA	0013 10.4 / 0626 3.3 / 1300 10.4 / 1854 3.6		**29** SU	0557 2.5 / 1200 11.0 / 1816 2.9 / ◐
15 SU	0136 10.0 / 0732 3.6 / 1419 9.9 / 2009 3.7		**30** M	0031 10.9 / 0659 2.8 / 1306 10.8 / 1927 3.2
			31 TU	0146 10.9 / 0818 2.8 / 1425 10.9 / 2102 3.0

JUNE

Time	m		Time	m
1 W	0307 11.3 / 0946 2.5 / 1544 11.4 / 2227 2.5		**16** TH	0350 10.6 / 1006 2.9 / 1621 10.6 / 2241 2.6
2 TH	0417 11.9 / 1100 1.9 / 1650 12.2 / 2333 1.8		**17** F	0442 11.1 / 1112 2.4 / 1710 11.5 / 2339 2.1
3 F	0518 12.7 / 1202 1.3 / 1746 13.0		**18** SA	0530 11.6 / 1206 2.0 / 1755 12.0
4 SA	0032 1.2 / 0611 13.3 / 1259 0.9 / 1836 13.5		**19** SU	0030 1.7 / 0613 12.0 / 1256 1.7 / 1836 12.3
5 SU	0126 0.8 / 0701 13.6 / 1351 0.6 / ● 1923 13.8		**20** M	0118 1.4 / 0656 12.2 / 1341 1.6 / ○ 1917 12.5
6 M	0217 0.6 / 0750 13.7 / 1439 0.6 / 2009 13.8		**21** TU	0202 1.5 / 0737 12.3 / 1423 1.7 / 1956 12.6
7 TU	0304 0.7 / 0836 13.6 / 1522 0.8 / 2054 13.6		**22** W	0244 1.6 / 0816 12.4 / 1500 1.8 / 2034 12.5
8 W	0345 1.0 / 0921 13.2 / 1559 1.2 / 2136 13.1		**23** TH	0321 1.7 / 0855 12.3 / 1532 1.9 / 2112 12.5
9 TH	0421 1.5 / 1003 12.6 / 1630 1.7 / 2217 12.4		**24** F	0354 1.8 / 0934 12.3 / 1602 1.9 / 2150 12.4
10 F	0451 2.0 / 1044 11.8 / 1700 2.2 / 2257 11.6		**25** SA	0427 1.8 / 1014 12.2 / 1637 2.0 / 2232 12.2
11 SA	0522 2.4 / 1124 11.1 / 1736 2.7 / 2341 10.9		**26** SU	0505 1.9 / 1057 12.0 / 1717 2.1 / 2319 11.9
12 SU	0601 2.9 / 1212 10.4 / 1821 3.1 / ◐		**27** M	0549 2.1 / 1145 11.6 / 1804 2.5 / ◐
13 M	0037 10.3 / 0650 3.2 / 1314 10.0 / 1917 3.4		**28** TU	0013 11.5 / 0640 2.4 / 1243 11.2 / 1902 2.8
14 TU	0148 10.1 / 0749 3.4 / 1424 10.0 / 2023 3.5		**29** W	0119 11.2 / 0745 2.6 / 1353 11.0 / 2021 3.1
15 W	0253 10.2 / 0855 3.3 / 1526 10.3 / 2133 3.2		**30** TH	0236 11.2 / 0910 2.7 / 1513 11.1 / 2157 2.8

JULY

Time	m		Time	m
1 F	0351 11.5 / 1031 2.4 / 1624 11.7 / 2309 2.3		**16** SA	0359 10.5 / 1021 3.0 / 1632 10.9 / 2257 2.6
2 SA	0456 12.0 / 1138 1.9 / 1724 12.3		**17** SU	0456 11.1 / 1127 2.4 / 1724 11.6 / 2356 2.0
3 SU	0010 1.7 / 0553 12.6 / 1237 1.4 / 1818 13.0		**18** M	0546 11.7 / 1224 2.0 / 1811 12.2
4 M	0107 1.2 / 0645 13.1 / 1332 1.0 / ● 1907 13.4		**19** TU	0049 1.7 / 0632 12.2 / 1316 1.3 / ○ 1855 12.6
5 TU	0200 0.9 / 0735 13.3 / 1422 0.8 / 1954 13.5		**20** W	0141 1.5 / 0717 12.5 / 1405 1.6 / 1938 12.9
6 W	0249 0.9 / 0822 13.3 / 1508 0.9 / 2038 13.4		**21** TH	0230 1.4 / 0801 12.7 / 1451 1.6 / 2020 13.0
7 TH	0334 1.0 / 0906 13.1 / 1548 1.2 / 2120 13.1		**22** F	0314 1.4 / 0843 12.8 / 1531 1.6 / 2101 13.0
8 F	0411 1.4 / 0946 12.7 / 1619 1.6 / 2158 12.6		**23** SA	0353 1.4 / 0923 12.8 / 1605 1.6 / 2141 13.0
9 SA	0439 1.9 / 1021 12.1 / 1644 2.0 / 2232 12.0		**24** SU	0427 1.5 / 1003 12.8 / 1636 1.7 / 2221 12.8
10 SU	0502 2.2 / 1054 11.5 / 1711 2.3 / 2306 11.4		**25** M	0459 1.5 / 1043 12.5 / 1709 1.8 / 2304 12.4
11 M	0531 2.5 / 1129 10.9 / 1745 2.7 / 2345 10.8		**26** TU	0535 1.8 / 1127 12.1 / 1748 2.2 / ◐ 2352 11.9
12 TU	0609 2.8 / 1211 10.4 / 1830 3.1 / ◐		**27** W	0618 2.2 / 1218 11.5 / 1836 2.7
13 W	0036 10.2 / 0657 3.2 / 1308 10.0 / 1927 3.5		**28** TH	0052 11.2 / 0712 2.7 / 1324 10.9 / 1942 3.3
14 TH	0143 9.9 / 0759 3.4 / 1421 9.9 / 2036 3.5		**29** F	0211 10.8 / 0834 3.1 / 1447 10.7 / 2132 3.4
15 F	0255 10.0 / 0909 3.4 / 1531 10.2 / 2149 3.2		**30** SA	0331 10.9 / 1009 3.0 / 1604 11.1 / 2251 2.8
			31 SU	0440 11.4 / 1119 2.4 / 1708 11.8 / 2354 2.1

AUGUST

Time	m		Time	m
1 M	0540 12.1 / 1219 1.7 / 1804 12.5		**16** TU	0522 11.5 / 1158 2.2 / 1748 12.1
2 TU	0051 1.4 / 0632 12.7 / 1314 1.2 / ● 1853 13.1		**17** W	0027 1.8 / 0611 12.3 / 1255 1.8 / 1834 12.8
3 W	0144 1.0 / 0720 13.1 / 1405 0.9 / 1939 13.4		**18** TH	0122 1.4 / 0658 12.8 / 1348 1.5 / ○ 1919 13.3
4 TH	0233 0.8 / 0805 13.2 / 1452 0.8 / 2021 13.4		**19** F	0214 1.2 / 0742 13.2 / 1438 1.3 / 2003 13.6
5 F	0317 0.9 / 0847 13.1 / 1532 1.0 / 2100 13.2		**20** SA	0302 1.0 / 0826 13.4 / 1521 1.2 / 2044 13.7
6 SA	0354 1.3 / 0923 12.8 / 1604 1.4 / 2134 12.8		**21** SU	0343 1.0 / 0907 13.4 / 1558 1.2 / 2125 13.6
7 SU	0421 1.7 / 0954 12.3 / 1625 1.8 / 2203 12.3		**22** M	0418 1.1 / 0946 13.3 / 1629 1.3 / 2205 13.4
8 M	0438 2.1 / 1021 11.8 / 1644 2.1 / 2232 11.8		**23** TU	0448 1.3 / 1026 13.0 / 1657 1.6 / 2246 12.8
9 TU	0458 2.3 / 1050 11.3 / 1709 2.4 / 2302 11.1		**24** W	0517 1.7 / 1107 12.3 / 1729 2.1 / 2331 12.0
10 W	0526 2.6 / 1123 10.7 / 1743 2.8 / ◗ 2339 10.5		**25** TH	0554 2.3 / 1154 11.5 / 1810 2.8 / ◗
11 TH	0604 3.0 / 1206 10.1 / 1830 3.4		**26** F	0027 11.0 / 0641 3.0 / 1258 10.6 / 1909 3.6
12 F	0032 9.9 / 0658 3.6 / 1310 9.7 / 1941 3.9		**27** SA	0151 10.3 / 0801 3.7 / 1430 10.3 / 2116 3.9
13 SA	0151 9.6 / 0817 3.9 / 1440 9.7 / 2105 3.8		**28** SU	0318 10.4 / 0953 3.5 / 1550 10.7 / 2238 3.2
14 SU	0318 9.9 / 0940 3.6 / 1557 10.3 / 2222 3.2		**29** M	0428 11.0 / 1104 2.7 / 1655 11.5 / 2339 2.2
15 M	0426 10.7 / 1054 2.9 / 1657 11.2 / 2329 2.4		**30** TU	0526 11.8 / 1201 1.9 / 1749 12.4
			31 W	0033 1.4 / 0617 12.6 / 1254 1.2 / 1836 13.1

Chart Datum: 6·50 metres below Ordnance Datum (Newlyn). HAT is 14·7 metres above Chart Datum.

STANDARD TIME (UT)
For Summer Time add ONE hour in **non-shaded areas**

BRISTOL (AVONMOUTH)   LAT 51°30'N   LONG 2°44'W
TIMES AND HEIGHTS OF HIGH AND LOW WATERS

Dates in red are **SPRINGS**
Dates in blue are **NEAPS**

YEAR 2016

SEPTEMBER

Time	m		Time	m
1 0123	0.9	**16** 0101	1.3
0702	13.1	0636	13.1
TH 1344	0.8	F 1327	1.3
● 1920	13.4	○ 1857	13.7
2 0211	0.7	**17** 0154	0.9
0744	13.3	0721	13.6
F 1429	0.7	SA 1417	1.0
1959	13.5	1942	14.1
3 0254	0.8	**18** 0241	0.7
0822	13.2	0804	13.9
SA 1510	0.9	SU 1502	0.8
2035	13.3	2024	14.2
4 0331	1.2	**19** 0324	0.6
0855	12.9	0846	14.0
SU 1542	1.4	M 1541	0.9
2106	12.9	2106	14.1
5 0358	1.7	**20** 0400	0.8
0924	12.5	0926	13.7
M 1602	1.8	TU 1614	1.1
2133	12.4	2147	13.7
6 0411	2.1	**21** 0430	1.2
0949	12.0	1006	13.3
TU 1615	2.1	W 1642	1.5
2158	11.9	2227	13.0
7 0423	2.3	**22** 0458	1.7
1014	11.6	1047	12.5
W 1635	2.3	TH 1711	2.2
2224	11.4	2311	11.9
8 0446	2.5	**23** 0531	2.5
1042	11.0	1132	11.4
TH 1704	2.6	F 1749	3.0
2256	10.8	◑	
9 0518	2.9	**24** 0006	10.8
1118	10.4	0615	3.3
F 1742	3.2	SA 1237	10.4
◑ 2339	10.1	1845	3.9
10 0602	3.5	**25** 0136	10.0
1211	9.8	0733	4.1
SA 1838	3.9	SU 1417	10.0
		2101	4.1
11 0045	9.5	**26** 0303	10.1
0711	4.1	0936	3.8
SU 1336	9.4	M 1533	10.5
2018	4.2	2220	3.3
12 0230	9.5	**27** 0410	10.8
0858	4.1	1043	2.9
M 1522	9.9	TU 1635	11.4
2150	3.6	2318	2.3
13 0357	10.3	**28** 0506	11.7
1025	3.3	1138	2.0
TU 1630	11.0	W 1728	12.3
2304	2.7		
14 0458	11.4	**29** 0008	1.5
1134	2.5	0554	12.5
W 1724	12.1	TH 1229	1.2
		1813	13.0
15 0005	1.8	**30** 0057	1.0
0549	12.4	0638	13.0
TH 1233	1.8	F 1316	0.8
1812	13.0	1855	13.3

OCTOBER

Time	m		Time	m
1 0142	0.7	**16** 0127	0.8
0717	13.2	0657	13.9
SA 1401	0.8	SU 1351	0.9
● 1933	13.4	○ 1919	14.3
2 0225	0.8	**17** 0216	0.5
0753	13.2	0741	14.2
SU 1441	1.0	M 1438	0.7
2007	13.2	2003	14.5
3 0302	1.2	**18** 0259	0.5
0825	12.9	0825	14.3
M 1515	1.4	TU 1519	0.7
2037	12.8	2046	14.3
4 0329	1.7	**19** 0338	0.7
0853	12.5	0906	14.0
TU 1537	1.9	W 1556	1.0
2104	12.4	2129	13.8
5 0343	2.1	**20** 0411	1.2
0918	12.1	0947	13.4
W 1548	2.1	TH 1627	1.5
2129	12.0	2211	13.0
6 0352	2.3	**21** 0441	1.8
0942	11.7	1019	12.6
TH 1607	2.3	F 1658	2.2
2154	11.6	2255	11.9
7 0415	2.4	**22** 0514	2.6
1010	11.3	1115	11.5
F 1635	2.5	SA 1735	3.0
2226	11.1	◑ 2349	10.8
8 0446	2.7	**23** 0557	3.4
1046	10.7	1218	10.5
SA 1710	3.0	SU 1830	3.8
2308	10.4		
9 0526	3.3	**24** 0114	10.0
1135	10.1	0705	4.1
SU 1758	3.7	M 1340	10.1
◐		2019	4.2
10 0007	9.8	**25** 0238	10.0
0622	4.0	0903	4.0
M 1247	9.6	TU 1507	10.5
1919	4.2	2150	3.6
11 0134	9.5	**26** 0342	10.6
0802	4.3	1013	3.2
TU 1434	9.8	W 1606	11.2
2111	3.9	2247	2.7
12 0320	10.2	**27** 0437	11.4
0950	3.7	1107	2.3
W 1557	10.9	TH 1658	12.0
2233	2.9	2337	1.9
13 0429	11.3	**28** 0525	12.2
1105	2.7	1157	1.6
TH 1656	12.0	F 1744	12.6
2338	2.0		
14 0523	12.4	**29** 0024	1.3
1206	1.9	0608	12.8
F 1747	13.1	SA 1244	1.2
		1825	13.0
15 0035	1.3	**30** 0109	1.0
0611	13.3	0646	13.0
SA 1301	1.3	SU 1328	1.0
1833	13.8	● 1903	13.1
		31 0152	1.1
		0722	13.0
		M 1409	1.2
		1938	13.0

NOVEMBER

Time	m		Time	m
1 0229	1.3	**16** 0235	0.5
0755	12.8	0804	14.3
TU 1444	1.5	W 1459	0.7
2010	12.7	2029	14.2
2 0300	1.7	**17** 0318	0.7
0825	12.6	0848	14.1
W 1511	1.9	TH 1539	1.0
2040	12.4	2114	13.8
3 0319	2.1	**18** 0355	1.1
0853	12.2	0931	13.5
TH 1528	2.2	F 1616	1.5
2107	12.1	2158	13.0
4 0331	2.3	**19** 0429	1.7
0920	11.9	1015	12.7
F 1548	2.3	SA 1650	2.1
2134	11.7	2242	12.1
5 0355	2.4	**20** 0502	2.4
0949	11.6	1100	11.8
SA 1617	2.4	SU 1725	2.8
2208	11.4	2331	11.1
6 0427	2.6	**21** 0542	3.1
1027	11.1	1155	10.9
SU 1653	2.8	M 1811	3.4
2250	10.9	◐	
7 0507	3.0	**22** 0037	10.3
1115	10.6	0634	3.7
M 1739	3.3	TU 1314	10.3
◐ 2344	10.3	1914	3.9
8 0558	3.6	**23** 0158	10.0
1218	10.2	0748	4.0
TU 1844	3.8	W 1429	10.4
		2044	3.8
9 0056	10.0	**24** 0304	10.3
0713	4.0	0919	3.7
W 1342	10.2	TH 1529	10.8
2020	3.8	2201	3.3
10 0228	10.2	**25** 0400	10.9
0902	3.8	1025	3.0
TH 1514	10.8	F 1622	11.4
2153	3.1	2257	2.6
11 0351	11.1	**26** 0450	11.6
1028	3.0	1119	2.3
F 1622	11.8	SA 1710	11.9
2305	2.2	2347	2.0
12 0452	12.2	**27** 0535	12.1
1134	2.1	1207	1.8
SA 1718	12.8	SU 1753	12.4
13 0004	1.5	**28** 0033	1.6
0544	13.1	0615	12.6
SU 1231	1.4	M 1252	1.5
1809	13.6	1833	12.6
14 0059	0.9	**29** 0117	1.4
0632	13.9	0652	12.8
M 1324	1.0	TU 1335	1.4
○ 1856	14.2	● 1910	12.7
15 0149	0.6	**30** 0157	1.5
0719	14.2	0728	12.7
TU 1413	0.7	W 1414	1.6
1943	14.3	1946	12.6

DECEMBER

Time	m		Time	m
1 0232	1.7	**16** 0302	0.7
0802	12.6	0833	14.0
TH 1448	1.8	F 1527	0.9
2020	12.4	2101	13.7
2 0300	2.0	**17** 0343	1.0
0835	12.4	0918	13.6
F 1515	2.1	SA 1607	1.3
2052	12.2	2145	13.2
3 0321	2.2	**18** 0419	1.5
0906	12.1	0958	13.0
SA 1539	2.2	SU 1641	1.8
2123	12.0	2227	12.4
4 0345	2.3	**19** 0451	2.1
0939	11.9	1042	12.3
SU 1608	2.3	M 1712	2.4
2159	11.7	2308	11.7
5 0418	2.4	**20** 0523	2.6
1017	11.6	1126	11.5
M 1645	2.5	TU 1747	2.9
2240	11.4	2353	10.8
6 0457	2.7	**21** 0603	3.1
1102	11.3	1217	10.8
TU 1729	2.8	W 1830	3.3
2329	11.0	◐	
7 0545	3.1	**22** 0051	10.2
1157	10.9	0653	3.5
W 1823	3.1	TH 1326	10.3
◐		1925	3.6
8 0028	10.7	**23** 0205	10.0
0645	3.4	0755	3.7
TH 1305	10.7	F 1436	10.2
1933	3.3	2031	3.7
9 0142	10.6	**24** 0310	10.2
0805	3.6	0907	3.6
F 1427	10.9	SA 1537	10.5
2104	3.2	2148	3.4
10 0307	11.0	**25** 0407	10.7
0945	3.2	1023	3.1
SA 1545	11.5	SU 1631	11.0
2228	2.6	2258	2.8
11 0419	11.8	**26** 0458	11.3
1102	2.5	1124	2.5
SU 1650	12.3	M 1719	11.6
2334	1.9	2353	2.2
12 0519	12.6	**27** 0543	11.9
1204	1.8	1215	2.0
M 1746	13.1	TU 1804	12.0
13 0032	1.3	**28** 0041	1.8
0611	13.4	0625	12.4
TU 1300	1.2	W 1302	1.7
1837	13.7	1845	12.3
14 0126	0.8	**29** 0127	1.6
0700	13.9	0705	12.6
W 1353	0.9	TH 1347	1.6
○ 1927	14.0	● 1925	12.5
15 0216	0.7	**30** 0209	1.7
0747	14.1	0743	12.7
TH 1442	0.8	F 1429	1.7
2014	14.0	2003	12.5
		31 0247	1.8
		0820	12.6
		SA 1506	1.9
		2040	12.4

Chart Datum: 6·50 metres below Ordnance Datum (Newlyn). HAT is 14·7 metres above Chart Datum.

〉〉 FREE monthly updates. Register at 〈
www.reedsnauticalalmanac.co.uk 〈

Bristol Channel

155

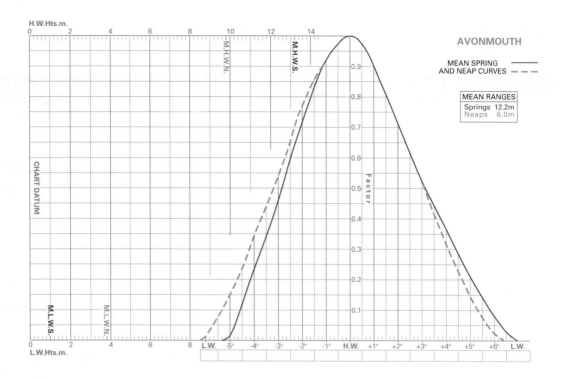

4.19 BRISTOL (CITY DOCKS)

Ent to R Avon **51°30'·44N 02°43'·31W** ✳✳◐◊◊◊✿✿✿

CHARTS AC 5608, 1179, 1176, 1859; Imray C59, 2600

TIDES –0410 on Dover; ML 7·0; Duration 0620. NB very large range

Standard Port BRISTOL (AVONMOUTH) (←)

Times				Height (metres)			
High Water		Low Water		MHWS	MHWN	MLWN	MLWS
0200	0800	0300	0800	13·2	9·8	3·8	1·0
1400	2000	1500	2000				
Differences SHIREHAMPTON (R Avon, 51°29'N 02°41'W)							
0000	0000	+0035	+0010	–0·7	–0·7	–0·8	0·0
SEA MILLS (R Avon, 51°29'N 02°39'W)							
+0005	+0005	+0105	+0030	–1·4	–1·5	–1·7	–0·1
CUMBERLAND BASIN (Ent)							
+0010	+0010	DR	DR	–2·9	–3·0	DR	DR

SHELTER Excellent in Bristol Floating Harbour. Avonmouth and Royal Portbury Docks are prohib to yachts, except in emergency. If early/late on the tide, ⚓ as close inshore as depth allows in Portishead Pool between Portishead Dock and Royal Portbury Dock, but avoid in onshore winds.

NAVIGATION From the south and west: from Avon SHM buoy (51°27'·92N 02°51'·73W) either follow the Bristol Deep shipping channel taking care not to impede the safe passage of commercial traffic or stay well clear to the S passing close to Portishead Pt. If to the north, cross the shipping channel by the most direct route keeping clear of inbound/outbound traffic.

From the north: Conform to the channel taking care not to impede the safe passage of commercial traffic.

- Beware large ships transiting/turning in the main channel.
- Beware ships and tugs leaving the docks at any time.
- When on passage up/down the Severn estuary without stopping at Bristol or Portishead, use the *Offshore Route*.

Entering R Avon keep N of shallows (Swash Bank) between Royal Portbury Dock and Avonmouth Docks. Speed limit in river: 6kn if draught > 2m; 9kn if draught < 2m.

LIGHTS AND MARKS Ldg lts 127°, both Iso R 2s, to R Avon ent abeam S pier lt, Oc RG 30s. St George ldg lts 173°, both Oc G 5s, front/rear W/Or posts, clear Swash Bank (dries). Upriver, G or R ✫s mark the outside of bends.

Entry signals to Bristol Hbr may be shown from E bank, 1½ and 2½ca S of Clifton Suspension Bridge: ● = continue with caution; ● = stop and await orders.

LOCKS Floating Harbour (approx 7M upriver) is accessed via Entrance Lock into Cumberland Basin and Junction Lock into Floating Hbr. Aim to reach the Ent lock no later than HW –0015. Ent lock opens approx HW –2½, –1½ and –¼hr for arrivals; departures approx 15 mins after these times. Plimsoll swing bridge opens in unison with lock, except weekday rush hours 0800–0900 and 1700–1800.

Junction lock is always open, unless ht of HW is >9·6m ('stopgate' tide) when it closes; read special instructions. If you miss the last lock-in, call Ch 12 for advice.

BRIDGES Prince St Bridge opens (by arrangement only) summer 0915–2130, winter 0915–1830. Call Duty Office ☎9031484 or VHF Ch 73. Same for Redcliffe Bridge, but only opened in exceptional circumstances. Clearances above HAT: St Augustine's Reach 1·8m & 0·7m; Prince St 0·7m; Redcliffe 2·1m; Bristol 2·6m. The R Avon leads to Netham lock ☎9776590, Keynsham, Bath and the Kennett & Avon canal.

COMMUNICATIONS (Code 0117) CGOC (01646) 690909; Police 101; Cumberland Basin Dock Master 9273633 Ⓗ 923 0000.

Bristol VTS, Ch 12, ☎0117 980 2638.

- All vessels are to maintain a listening watch on Ch 12 in Bristol VTS area and monitor commercial ship movements.
- At Black Rks (1M to run) call City Docks Radio Ch 14, 11 low power, (HW–3 to HW+1) for locking instructions.
- For berth: Bristol Floating Hbr Ch 73; Bristol Marina Ch 80.

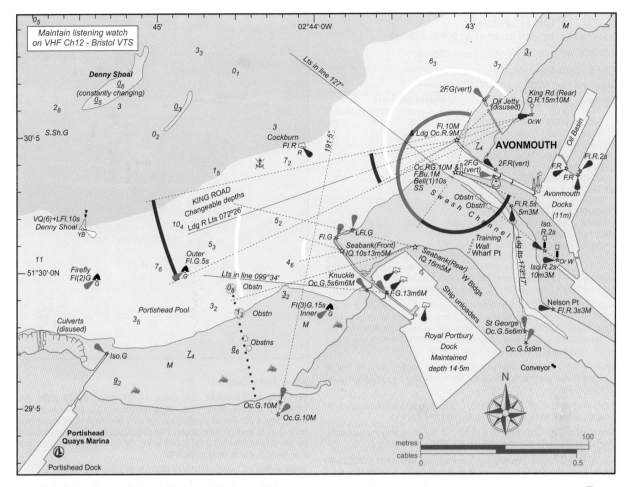

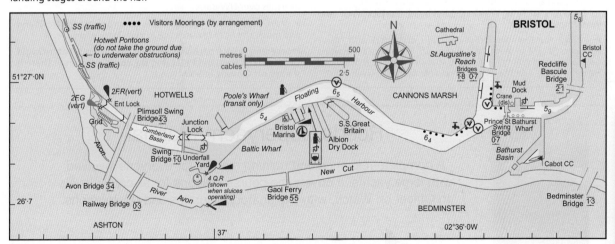

FACILITIES (from seaward) **Portishead Cruising Club** at Crockerne Pill, S bank, 5ca above M5 bridge; www.portisheadcruisingclub.org.uk ☎01275 373988, Drying 🅀 (soft mud) ⚓ grid (£5/day).

Bristol Hbr HM, Underfall Yard, Cumberland Rd, Bristol BS1 6XG. www.bristol-city.gov.uk ☎9031484; approx 40 🆅 consult website and HM in advance for detailed info on lock and bridge opening times ⚓ near ent to St Augustine's Reach, £2.67 inc licence fee. ⚓🕭🅑 ⚓⚓ (launching £9.22) 🅿🛢⚓×🗑; ferries ply between various landing stages around the hbr.

Baltic Wharf Leisure Centre contact HM ☎9031484, ⚓⚓ 🗑.

Bristol Marina Access–3 HW+1. www.bristolmarina.co.uk ☎9213198, 170⚓, inc about 5🆅 (21m max LOA) £2.00. 🅑⚓ (£2.25/m) 🅿🛢⚓ ⚓🍴🅑🅔 ✕ ⚓⚓🅑(6/12t) 🕭(50t) 🅿.

Bathurst Basin ⚓. **Cabot CC** ☎9268318, ⚓⚓⚓🗑.

City All domestic facilities, ACA, ⚒ ✈.

4.20 PORTISHEAD

Somerset **51°29′·56N 02°45′·41W** ※※◊◊◊◊❀❀❀

CHARTS AC 5608, 1176, 1859; Imray C59, 2600

TIDES –0405 Dover; ML 6·8

Standard Port BRISTOL (AVONMOUTH) (←)

Times				Height (metres)			
High Water		Low Water		MHWS	MHWN	MLWN	MLWS
0200	0800	0300	0800	13·2	9·8	3·8	1·0
1400	2000	1500	2000				
Differences PORTISHEAD							
–0002	0000	ND	ND	–0·1	–0·1	ND	ND
CLEVEDON							
–0010	–0020	–0025	–0015	–0·4	–0·2	+0·2	0·0
ST THOMAS HEAD							
0000	0000	–0030	–0030	–0·4	–0·2	+0·1	+0·1
ENGLISH AND WELSH GROUNDS							
–0008	–0008	–0030	–0030	–0·5	–0·8	–0·3	0·0
WESTON-SUPER-MARE							
–0020	–0030	–0130	–0030	–1·2	–1·0	–0·8	–0·2

SHELTER Good in marina. Access by lock 9m x 40m x 5m min depth over cill HW ±3½ (minimum). **Ⓥ**s available in marina. ‡ 1ca NE of pier hd (sheltered from SE - W) to await tide for marina or Sharpness.

NAVIGATION WPT 51°29′·96N 02°45′·35W, Firefly SHM lt buoy, 168°/500m to pier hd. Firefly Rks (0·9m) are close W of the 168° appr track. Appr's dry to mud and are exposed to N/NE winds. Close inshore a W-going eddy begins at HW –3 whilst the flood is still making E.

LIGHTS AND MARKS Portishead Pt, Q (3) 10s9m 16M, is 7ca W of Portishead pierhd, Iso G 2s 5m 3M. Lock ent has 2FG(vert) and 2FR(vert) lts.

COMMUNICATIONS (Code 01275) CGOC (01646) 690909; Police 101; Health centre 841630; Ⓗ (Clevedon) 01275 872212.

See Bristol. Monitor *Bristol VTS* Ch **12** for shipping movements. Portishead Quays Marina VHF Ch 80 24H.

FACILITIES Marina ⊕ www.quaymarinas.com ☎841941 (200◡+Ⓥ) £2·60 (min charge £21); ⅅ ► ♠ ♠ ♠ ♂ 🛢 ⚒ 📠 ⚠ ⛽ ⛴(35t) ⚓ 🏬 wi-fi.

Portishead Cruising Club ☎373988, 🏠.

Town ✉ Ⓑ ⇌ ✈ (Bristol). 3M to Junction 19 of M5.

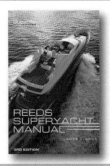

AVONMOUTH TO HARTLAND POINT

(AC 1152, 1165) From Avonmouth to Sand Pt, the part-drying English Grounds extend 3M off the S shore. Portishead Quays Marina offers good shelter. Extensive mud flats fill the bays S to Burnham-on-Sea. Westward, the S shore of Bristol Chan is cleaner than N shore. But there is less shelter since the approaches to harbours such as Watchet, Minehead, Porlock Weir and Watermouth dry out.

▶ In bad weather dangerous overfalls occur NW and NE of Foreland Pt. 5M to W there is a race off Highveer Pt. Between Ilfracombe and Bull Pt the E-going stream begins at HW Milford Haven +0540, and the W-going at HW Milford Haven –0025,

sp rates 3kn. Overfalls occur up to 1·5M N of Bull Pt and over Horseshoe Rks, which lie 3M N. There is a dangerous race off Morte Pt, 1·5M to W of Bull Pt. ◀

Shelter is available under the lee of Lundy Island; but avoid bad races to NE (White Horses), NW (Hen and Chickens), and SE; also overfalls over NW Bank.

▶ W of Lundy streams are moderate, but strong around the island and much stronger towards the Bristol Channel proper. ◀

Proceeding WSW from Rivers Taw/Torridge, keep 3M off to avoid the race N of Hartland Pt (Lt, fog sig, conspic radome). There is shelter off Clovelly in S/SW winds.

ADJACENT HARBOUR

WESTON-SUPER-MARE, Somerset, **51°21′·03N 02°59′·28W**. AC 5608, 1179, 1176,1152. HW –0435 on Dover; Duration 0655; ML 6·1m. See 4.20. Good shelter, except in S'lies, in Knightstone Hbr (dries) at N end of bay; access HW±1½. Causeway at ent marked by bn. Grand Pier hd 2 FG (vert) 6/5m. Or ‡ in good weather in R Axe (dries), enter only near HW.

Weston Bay YC (sited on beach) ☎01934 413366, VHF Ch 80, ⚓ 🏠.

Uphill Boat Centre ☎01934 418617. ⚓(lower R Axe-drying) ► ◡ ⚓♠♠✕⚒ 🏬 📠 ⛴(10t).

Town ⚓ 🏨 ✉ Ⓑ 🍴✕ ⇌ ✈ .

4.21 BURNHAM-ON-SEA

Somerset **51°14′·23N 03°00′·33W** ❀⚓❀❀

CHARTS AC 5608, 1179, 1152; Imray C59, 2600

TIDES –0435 Dover; ML 5·4; Duration 0620

Standard Port BRISTOL (AVONMOUTH) (←—)

Times				Height (metres)			
High Water		Low Water		MHWS	MHWN	MLWN	MLWS
0200	0800	0300	0800	13·2	9·8	3·8	1·0
1400	2000	1500	2000				
Differences BURNHAM-ON-SEA							
–0020	–0025	–0030	0000	–2·3	–1·9	–1·4	–1·1
BRIDGWATER							
–0015	–0030	+0305	+0455	–8·6	–8·1	DR	DR

SHELTER Ent is very choppy in strong winds, especially from SW to W and from N to NE. ⚓ S of town jetty or, for best shelter, ❷/⚓ in R Brue (dries). Contact HM by ☎ in advance.

NAVIGATION WPT 51°13′·46N 03°09′·80W, 0·5M S of Gore SWM buoy. Enter HW–2 to HW; not advised at night. From WPT track 090°/1·5M until abeam LH edge of Hinkley Pt C Power Station; then 070°/2M until close abeam No1 PHM buoy; 076°/2M in W sector of Low Lt; 112° on ldg lts; then 180° into river channel.

Banks and depths change frequently. Beware unmarked fishing stakes outside approach channels.

LIGHTS AND MARKS Lower lt ho Dir 076° as chartlet. Ldg lts/marks 112° (moved as chan shifts): front FR 6m 3M, R stripe on □W background on sea wall; rear FR 12m 3M, RH edge of church tr.

COMMUNICATIONS (Code 01278) Police 101; Ⓗ 773100. HM 01934 822666 H24; harbour.master@sedgemoor.gov.uk.

FACILITIES Burnham-on-Sea MB&SC ☎792911 (Wed eve and Sun am) ⚓ two drying pontoon berths in River Brue (free) ⬅⚓⚓ 🖉 ⬜. **Services** ✕ ✎ ⊞ ACA (Bristol).

Town ⬛ ✉ Ⓑ ⇌ (Highbridge), ✈(Bristol).

ADJACENT FACILITY

Combwich A cargo wharf has been constructed to facilitate the inload of large indivisible loads to Hinkley Pt C Power Station. The approaches can be busy on appropriate tides. Note: There is no access to Bridgwater Marina from sea or the R Parrett.

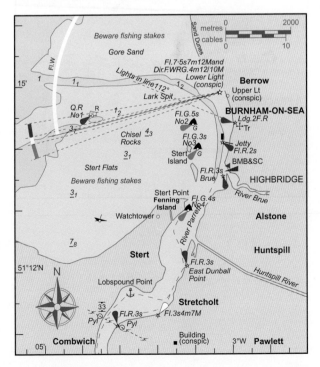

4.22 WATCHET

Somerset **51°11′·03N 03°19′·72W** ❀⚓⚓❀❀

CHARTS AC 5608, 1179, 1152, 1160; Imray C59, 2600

TIDES –0450 Dover; ML 5·9; Duration 0655

Standard Port BRISTOL (AVONMOUTH) (←—)

Times				Height (metres)			
High Water		Low Water		MHWS	MHWN	MLWN	MLWS
0200	0800	0300	0800	13·2	9·8	3·8	1·0
1400	2000	1500	2000				
Differences HINKLEY POINT							
–0032	–0028	–0055	–0049	–1·4	–1·1	–0·1	0·0
WATCHET							
–0035	–0050	–0145	–0040	–1·9	–1·5	+0·1	+0·1
MINEHEAD							
–0037	–0052	–0155	–0045	–2·6	–1·9	–0·2	0·0
PORLOCK BAY							
–0045	–0055	–0205	–0050	–3·0	–2·2	–0·1	–0·1
LYNMOUTH							
–0055	–0115	ND	ND	–3·6	–2·7	ND	ND

SHELTER Good, but open to N and E winds. Outer hbr (controlled by HM on VHF) dries 6·5m, but has about 6m depth at MHWS. Marina entered through a dropping sill gate (width 7m) which is open when the tide level is at or above CD +6.92m (retained water level). Min clearance over the gate is 2.5m. Approx gate opening times HW ±2½H sp, HW ±1½H np. **Outer harbour** 6 drying � on W wall (free), also used by commercial shipping.

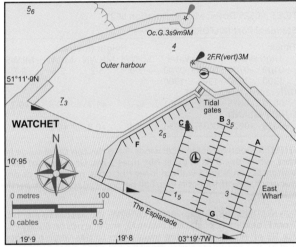

NAVIGATION WPT 51°12′·03N 03°18′·88W, 208°/1·1M to hbr ent. Rks/mud dry 5ca to seaward. Beware tidal streams 4-5kn at sp offshore and around W pier hd. The marina entrance is controlled by automatic stop/go R/G lts. Entrance max width 7m. Min retained water depths vary 1.5–3.0m. Marina subject to constant silting and some berths have limited accessibility. 3kn speed limit in marina.

LIGHTS AND MARKS Two unlit radio masts (206m) bearing 208° Station is conspic 7·5M to the E. W pier hd Oc G 3s 9m 9M on Red (R) tr. E pier hd 2 FR (vert) 3M.

COMMUNICATIONS (Code 01984) CGOC (01646) 690909; Police 101. HM 01643 703704 and ask for HM (WSDC at Minehead) see **Marina** ☎ below; Watchet Boat Owners Association (01643) 702569. Outer Harbour Ch 16 (only when vessel expected); Marina Ch 80.

FACILITIES Watchet Harbour Marina www.watchetharbour.co.uk ☎631264, mob 07969 138938, 250� inc ❷ £2·25 inc ⚡, 🖥 ⬛ ⬛ ⬜ (20t) ⛽ ACA. **Town** ✉ 🛒 ✕ ⬜. At Williton (2M): 🏧 🏧 ⬛; Ⓗ (Minehead 8M), ⇌ (Taunton 18M), ✈ (Bristol).

ADJACENT JETTY

Hinkley Pt C Power Station. The power station redevelopment includes the construction of a jetty and dolphins on Hinkley Pt. Craft are not allowed within 100m except in emergency.

HARBOURS ON THE SOUTH SHORE OF THE BRISTOL CHANNEL

MINEHEAD, Somerset, **51°12′·79N 03°28′·37W**. AC 1179, 1165, 1160. HW –0450 on Dover. ML 5·7m. See 4.22. Small hbr, dries 7·5m. Good shelter within pier curving E and then SE, over which seas may break in gales at MHWS; exposed to E'lies. Best appr from N or NW; beware The Gables, shingle bank (dries 3·7m) about 5ca ENE of pier. Keep E of a sewer outfall which passes ½ca E of pier hd and extends 1¾ca NNE of it; outfall is protected by rk covering, drying 2·8m and N end marked by SHM Bn QG 6m 7M. There are 2 R ⚓s at hbr ent just seaward of 3 posts or Med moor on quay, £1·80/m/day, at inner end of pier. Hbr gets very crowded. Holiday camp is conspic 6ca SE. Pierhd lt Fl (2) G 5s 4M, vis 127°-262°. VHF Ch 16 12 14 (occas). HM ☎(01643) 708101; Facilities: **Hbr** ⚓ ✠ (launching £7.00). **Town** 🏪🏨🛒⚔✎🖆⊠Ⓑ⛽✕⬭⇌ (Taunton).

PORLOCK WEIR, Somerset, **51°13′·17N 03°37′·64W**. AC 1179, 1165, 1160. HW –0500 on Dover; ML 5·6m. See 4.22. Access only near HW. Ent chan (250°), about 15m wide marked by withies (3 PHM and 1 SHM), between shingle bank/wood pilings to stbd and sunken wooden wall to port is difficult in any seas. A small pool (1m) just inside ent is for shoal draught boats; others dry out on pebble banks.

Or turn 90° stbd, via gates (but opening bridge usually closed), into inner drying dock with good shelter. No lts. HM ☎01643 863187 (not local). **Porlock Weir SC**. Facilities: ⚓ and limited 🛒.

LYNMOUTH, Devon, **51°14′·16N 03°49′·79W**. AC 1160,1165. HW–0515 on Dover. See 4.22. Tiny hbr, dries approx 5m, only suitable in settled offshore weather. Appr from Sand Ridge SHM lt buoy, 1·6M W of Foreland Pt and 9ca N of hbr ent. The narrow appr channel between drying boulder ledges is marked by 7 unlit posts. After first 2 posts keep 10m away from next SH post then next 2PH posts keep to middle of ent. Hbr ent is between piers, 2FR/FG lts, on W side of river course. Berth on E pier, which covers (beware) at MHWS. Resort facilities. Admin by Council ☎01598 752384.

WATERMOUTH, Devon, **51°13′·03N 04°04′·6W**. AC 1179, 1165. HW –0525 on Dover; ML 4·9m; Duration 0625. Use 4.23. Good shelter in drying hbr, but heavy surge runs in strong NW winds. Dir lt 153° Oc WRG 5s 1m, W sector 151·5°-154·5°, W △ on structure, 1½ca inside ent on S shore. Bkwtr, covered at high tide, has Y poles along its length and a G pole with conical topmark at the end. 9 Y ⚓s with B handles £6.50. HM ☎(01271) 865422. Facilities: **Hbr** ⚓ ✠ (cans) 🏨🛒(12t) 🛢; **YC**, 🍴. **Combe Martin** 1½M all facilities.

4.23 ILFRACOMBE

Devon **51°12′·65N 04°06′·65W** ❀❀◊◊✿✿

CHARTS AC 5608, *1179, 1165,* 1160; Imray C59, 2600

TIDES –0525 Dover; ML 5·0; Duration 0625

Standard Port MILFORD HAVEN (←)

Times				Height (metres)			
High Water		Low Water		MHWS	MHWN	MLWN	MLWS
0100	0700	0100	0700	7·0	5·2	2·5	0·7
1300	1900	1300	1900				
Differences ILFRACOMBE							
–0016	–0016	–0041	–0031	+2·2	+1·7	+0·6	+0·3
LUNDY ISLAND							
–0025	–0025	–0035	–0030	+1·0	+0·8	+0·2	+0·1

SHELTER Good except in NE/E winds. SW gales can cause surge in hbrs, which dry. 8 ⚓s in outer hbr, dries 2·7m. Or ⚓ clear of pier. Visitors ⚓ on N snd S walls of Inner Hbr, dries approx 4m, or dry out on chains off foot of N Pier. Call beforehand to confirm berth availability.

NAVIGATION WPT 51°13′·23N 04°06′·67W, 180°/0·55M to pier hd. From E, beware Copperas Rks (4M to E), and tide rips on Buggy Pit, 7ca NE of ent. On entry keep toward Pier to clear drying ledges and lobster keep-pots obstructing Hbr ent on SE side.

LIGHTS AND MARKS See 4.3 and chartlet.

COMMUNICATIONS (Code 01271) CGOC (01646) 690909; Police 101; Dr 863119. HM 862108 mob 07775 532606.

Ilfracombe Hbr VHF Ch 12 16 (not H24).

FACILITIES **Hbr** ⚓ (launching £5.84/day, £1·45/week) ⚓ and ⚓s £1·32 (inc use of ✎) ✠ 🔌(S Quay) 🔦⚔✎🖆🛢. **Ilfracombe YC** ☎863969, ⚓🔲🛠(35t as arranged) 🍴 **Town** ⊠Ⓑ⛽✕🍴 bus to Barnstaple (⇌), ✈ (Exeter).

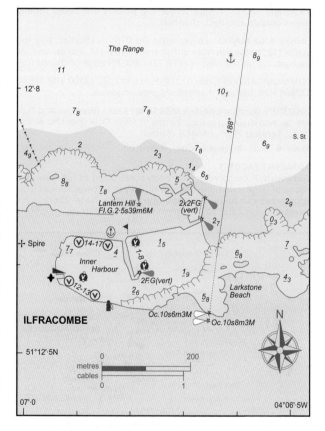

HARTLAND POINT TO LAND'S END

(AC 1156, 1149) The N coast of Cornwall and SW approaches to Bristol Chan are very exposed. Yachts need to be sturdy and well equipped since, if bad weather develops, no shelter may be at hand.

Bude dries, and is not approachable in W winds; only accessible in calm weather or offshore winds. Boscastle is a tiny hbr (dries) 3M NE of Tintagel Hd. Only approach in good weather or offshore winds; ⚓ off or dry out alongside.

Padstow can be a refuge, but in strong NW winds the sea breaks on bar and prevents entry. Off Trevose Hd beware Quies Rks which extend 1M to W. From here S the coast is relatively clear to Godrevy Is, apart from Bawden Rks 1M N of St Agnes Hd. Newquay Bay is good ⚓ in offshore winds, and the hbr (dries) is sheltered but uncomfortable in N winds. Off Godrevy Is are The Stones, drying rky shoals extending 1·5M offshore, marked by NCM lt buoy.

In St Ives Bay (AC 1168), Hayle is a commercial port (dries); seas break heavily on bar at times, especially with a ground swell. ▶ Stream is strong, so enter just before HW. ◀ The bottom is mostly sand. St Ives (dries) gives shelter from winds E to SW, but is very exposed to N; there is sometimes a heavy breaking sea if there is ground swell. Keep clear of the renewable energy development area centred approx 325°/10M from St Ives Bay (see AC 2565).

From St Ives to Land's End coast is rugged and exposed. There are o'falls SW of Pendeen Pt. Vyneck Rks lie awash about 3ca NW of C Cornwall. The Brisons are two high rky islets 5ca SW of C Cornwall, with rky ledges inshore and to the S. The Longships group of rks is about 1M W of Land's End. The inshore passage (001° on Brisons) is about 4ca wide with unmarked drying rks on the W side; only to be considered in calm weather and beware of fishing gear marker buoys..

 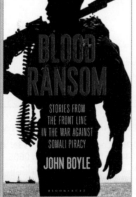

4.24 RIVERS TAW AND TORRIDGE

Devon 51°04'·37N 04°12'·88W ✿✿⚓⚓✿✿✿

CHARTS AC 5608, 1179, 1164, 1160; Imray C58, 2600

TIDES –0525 (Appledore) Dover; ML 3·6; Duration 0600
Standard Port MILFORD HAVEN (◀—)

Times				Height (metres)			
High Water		Low Water		MHWS	MHWN	MLWN	MLWS
0100	0700	0100	0700	7·0	5·2	2·5	0·7
1300	1900	1300	1900				
Differences APPLEDORE							
–0020	–0025	+0015	–0045	+0·5	0·0	–0·9	–0·5
YELLAND MARSH (R Taw)							
–0010	–0015	+0100	–0015	+0·1	–0·4	–1·2	–0·6
FREMINGTON (R Taw)							
–0010	–0015	+0030	–0030	–1·1	–1·8	–2·2	–0·5
BARNSTAPLE (R Taw)							
0000	–0015	–0155	–0245	–2·9	–3·8	–2·2	–0·4
BIDEFORD (R Torridge)							
–0020	–0025	0000	0000	–1·1	–1·6	–2·5	–0·7
CLOVELLY							
–0030	–0030	–0020	–0040	+1·3	+1·1	+0·2	+0·2

SHELTER Very well protected, but ent is dangerous in strong on-shore winds and/or swell. Yachts can ⚓ or pick up RNLI buoy (please donate to RNLI, Boathouse ☎473969) in Appledore Pool N of Skern Pt where spring stream can reach 5kn. Bideford quay dries to hard sand; used by commercial shipping.

NAVIGATION WPT 51°05'·43N 04°16'·11W, 118°/0·9M to Bar.

Bar and sands constantly shift; buoys are moved occasionally to comply. For advice on bar contact Bideford HM. Least depths over bar vary from 0·1m and 0·4m. Following 2014 storms a bank has formed which just dries at LW on the leading line. Estuary dries and access is only feasible from HW–2 to HW. Night entry not advised for strangers. Once tide is ebbing, breakers quickly form between Bideford Bar SHM lt buoy and Middle Ridge SHM lt buoy. Hold the ldg line 118° only up to Outer Pulley where chan deviates stbd toward Pulley buoy and Grey Sand Hill, thence to Appledore Pool. 2M passage to Bideford is not difficult. Barnstaple (7M): seek local advice or take pilot.

LIGHTS AND MARKS See 4.3 and chartlet. Ldg marks are W trs, lit H24. R Torridge: Lt QY at E end of Bideford bridge, 2FR vert & 2FG vert indicate preferred chan; then SHM bn, QG, on W bank.

COMMUNICATIONS (Appledore/Bideford: Code 01237) CGOC (01646) 690909; Police 101; Dr 474994. (Instow/Barnstaple: Code 01271) Dr 372672. Appledore HM 428700; Bideford HM/Pilot 475834, mob 07967 333725.
2 Rivers Port/Pilots VHF Ch 12 16 (From HW–2 occasional).

FACILITIES
APPLEDORE: no ⚲; slips at town quay. Services ⚓ 🔧 ✕ ⚒ ⚓ Ⓔ ⚓ ⚓(70t) ⚓.
BIDEFORD: some ⚲(contact HM) ⚓ ⚓ ⚒ ✕ ⚓. Ferry to Lundy Is.
INSTOW: North Devon YC, ☎861390, ⚓ ⚓ ✕ ⚓; Services ⚓ ⚲ via Instow Marine ☎861081, ⚓ ⚓ ⚓ Ⓔ ⚓(4t) ⚓. Town ⚓ ✕ ⚓.
BARNSTAPLE: ⚲ (free for short stay): limited facilities; ⚓ ⚓ ⚓ ⚓ ⚓ ⚓.
Towns ✉ (all four); Ⓑ (Barnstaple, Bideford) ⚐ (Barnstaple) ✈ (Exeter).
CLOVELLY, Devon, 51°00'·18N 04°23'·77W ✿⚓⚓✿✿✿✿. AC 1164. Tides see above. HW –0524 on Dover. Tiny drying hbr, 5M E of Hartland Pt, is sheltered from S/SW winds; useful to await the tide into Bideford or around Hartland Pt. Some ⚲ (max LOA 12m) £7 on pier, access only near HW; or ⚓ off in 5m. Lt Fl G 5s 5m 5M on hbr wall. HM mob: 07975 501830. Facilities: ⚓ ⚓ ✉ limited ⚒ ⚓ ⚓.

RIVERS TAW & TORRIDGE *continued*

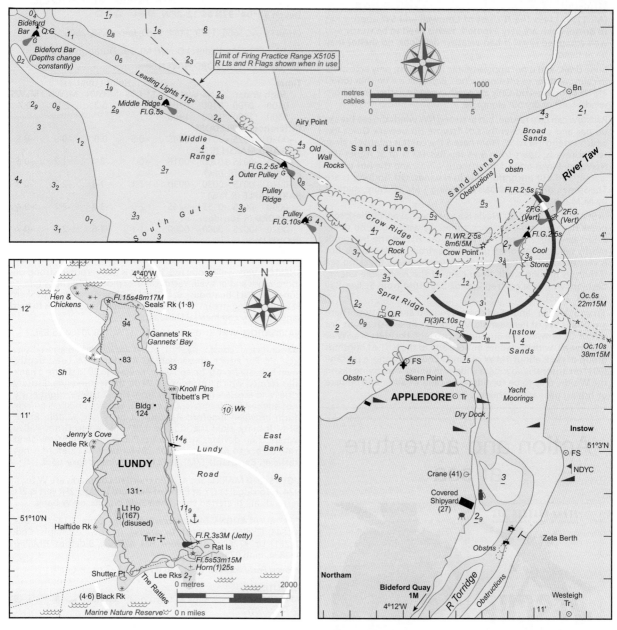

ISLAND IN BRISTOL CHANNEL, 10M NNW of Hartland Pt

LUNDY ISLAND, Devon, **51°09′·83N 04°39′·27W**. AC 5608, *1179, 1164*. HW −0530 on Dover; ML 4·3m; Duration 0605. See 4.23. Shore Office ☎01237 470074, Island ☎01237 431831. Beware bad tide races, esp on E-going flood, off the N and SE tips of the island; and to the SW on the W-going ebb. A violent race forms over Stanley Bank 3M NE of the N tip. Shelter good in lee of island's high ground (145m). In SSW to NW winds, usual ⚓ is close inshore to NW of SE Pt and Rat Island. In N'lies ⚓ in The Rattles, small bay on S side. In E'lies Jenny's Cove is safe if no W'ly swell. Lts: NW Pt, Fl 15s 48m 17M, vis 009°-285°, W ○ tr. On SE Pt, Fl 5s 53m 15M, vis 170°-073°, W ○ tr. Two Historic Wrecks (see 0.29) lie on the E side of island, at 51°11′N 04°39′·4W, and 4ca further E. Facilities: Landing by the ⚓ off SE end of island or using N side of jetty to disembark passengers only, boats may not remain alongside; £5.00/person landing fee. The waters around Lundy are a Marine Nature Reserve. **Lundy Co**: 🛢 ✉ 🏠 limited stores.

MINOR HARBOURS ON THE NW COAST OF CORNWALL

BUDE, Cornwall, **50°49′·93N 04°33′·37W**. AC 5608, 1156. HW −0540 on Dover. Duration 0605. See 4.25. Limited shelter in drying hbr, access near HW in daylight, quiet weather, no swell conditions but sea-lock gives access to canal basin with 2m. Conspic W radar dish aerials 3·3M N of hbr. Outer ldg marks 075°, front W spar with Y ◇ topmark, rear W flagstaff; hold this line until inner ldg marks in line at 131°, front W pile, rear W spar, both with Y △ topmarks. There are no lts. VHF Ch 16 12 (when vessel expected). Advise HM of ETA with 24H notice ☎(01288) 353111; ⚓ on quay; **Town** (½M); 🛢 ✉ Ⓑ 🛒 ✕ 🏠.

BOSCASTLE, Cornwall, **50°41′·48N 04°42·17W**. AC 5608, 1156. HW −0543 on Dover; see 4.25. A tiny, picturesque hbr, almost a land-locked cleft in the cliffs. Access near HW, but not in onshore winds when swell causes surge inside. An E'ly appr, S of Meachard Rk (37m high, 2ca NW of hbr), is best. 2 short bkwtrs at ent; moor as directed on drying S quay. HM ☎01840 250200.

4.25 PADSTOW

Cornwall **50°32'·51N 04°56'·17W** ✳❄⏃⏃✿✿✿✿✿

CHARTS AC 5608, 1156, 1168; Imray C58, 2400

TIDES –0550 Dover; ML 4·0; Duration 0600

Standard Port MILFORD HAVEN (←)

Times				Height (metres)			
High Water		Low Water		MHWS	MHWN	MLWN	MLWS
0100	0700	0100	0700	7·0	5·2	2·5	0·7
1300	1900	1300	1900				
Differences BUDE							
–0040	–0040	–0035	–0045	+0·7	+0·6	ND	ND
BOSCASTLE							
–0045	–0010	–0110	–0100	+0·3	+0·4	+0·2	+0·2
PADSTOW							
–0055	–0050	–0040	–0050	+0·3	+0·4	+0·1	+0·1
WADEBRIDGE (R Camel)							
–0052	–0052	+0235	+0245	–3·8	–3·8	–2·5	–0·4
NEWQUAY							
–0100	–0110	–0105	–0050	0·0	+0·1	0·0	–0·1
PERRANPORTH							
–0100	–0110	–0110	–0050	–0·1	0·0	0·0	+0·1
ST IVES							
–0050	–0115	–0105	–0040	–0·4	–0·3	–0·1	+0·1
CAPE CORNWALL							
–0130	–0145	–0120	–0120	–1·0	–0·9	–0·5	–0·1

NOTE: At Wadebridge LW time differences give the start of the rise, following a LW stand of about 5 hours.

SHELTER Good in inner hbr 3m+, access approx HW±2 sp, ±1½ nps via tidal gate. If too late for gate, moor in the Pool or ⚓ close N in 1·5m LWS. Drying moorings available for smaller craft. Good ⚓ at Wadebridge 4.5M up R Camel.

NAVIGATION WPT 50°34'·56N 04°56'·07W, 044° Stepper Pt 6ca. From SW, beware Quies Rks, Gulland Rk, The Hen, Gurley Rk, Chimney

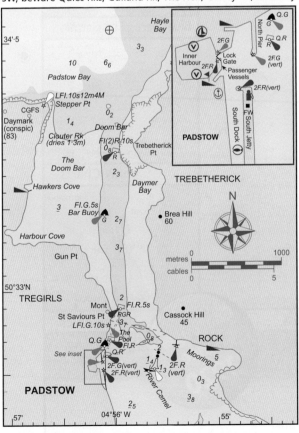

Rks and a wreck 5ca W of Stepper Pt (all off the chartlet). From N, keep well off Newland Island and its offlying reef.

- Best appr HW–2½, do not try LW±1½; least depth on the bar is 0·5m at MLWS. Waiting ⚓s in Port Quin Bay in lee of Rumps Pt and Mother Ivey's Bay 3M WSW Stepper Pt.
- Shifting banks in estuary require care and a rising tide (ditto the drying R Camel to Wadebridge, 4M). In doubt, consult HM.
- Identify the first 2 chan buoys before entry. In strong onshore winds or heavy ground swell, seas can break on Doom Bar and in the adjacent chan.
- S of St Saviour's Pt the chan lies very close to W shore.

LIGHTS AND MARKS See 4.3 and chartlet.

COMMUNICATIONS (Codes 01841) CGOC (01326) 317575; Police 101; Dr 532346. HM padstowharbour@btconnect.com , ☎532239; Ferry to Rock, (01326) 317575 it also acts as water taxi.

HM VHF Ch 12 16 (Mon-Fri 0800–1700 and HW±2). Ferry Ch 12.

FACILITIES Hbr ⚓ £2·00, M £1·01, ⚓ (£4·00 <10 hp engine<£6·00) ⚓⚓⚓⚓⚓ (extra) ⚓⚓. **Services** ⚓⚓⚓⚓⚓(60t) ⚓. **Town** ⚓⚓⚓⚓⚓✕⚓ Bus (to Bodmin ⚡/➔ Newquay). **Rock SC** ☎(01208) 862431, ⚓. **Wadebridge** HM as Padstow; ⚓ only; **Town** ⚓⚓⚓✕⚓.

MINOR HBRS BETWEEN BOSCASTLE AND LAND'S END

PORT ISAAC, Cornwall, **50°35'·75N 04°49'·57W**. AC 1156, 1168. HW –0548 on Dover; ML 4·0m. Small drying hbr. Conspic ✚ tr bears 171°/1·3M. Rks close E of 50m wide ent between short bkwtrs. HM ☎01208 880321, mob 07855 429422; ⚓⚓✕⚓ LB.

NEWQUAY, Cornwall, **50°25'·06N 05°05'·19W**. AC 1149, 1168. HW –0604 on Dover; ML 3·7m; see 4.25. Ent to drying hbr ('The Gap') between two walls, is 23m wide. Beware Old Dane Rk and Listrey Rk outside hbr towards Towan Hd. Swell causes a surge in the hbr. Enter HW±2 but not in strong onshore winds. Lts: N pier 2 FG (vert) 2M; S pier 2 FR (vert) 2M. VHF Ch 08 16 14. Facilities: ⚓⚓. **Town:** ⚓⚓⚓⚓✕⚓. Note: Shoal draught boats can dry out in Gannel Creek, close S of Newquay, but only in settled weather. Beware causeway bridge halfway up creek.

PORTREATH, Cornwall, **50°15'·88N 05°17'·57W**. AC 1149. HW –0600 on Dover. Conspic W daymark (38m) at E side of ent to small drying hbr. Gull Rk (23m) is 3ca W of ent and Horse Rk is close N. Keep close to pier on W side of chan. ⚓ in either of 2 basins, both dry. ⚓⚓✕⚓.

HAYLE, Cornwall, **50°12'·14N 05°26'·13W** (NCM) ✳❄✿. AC 1149, 1168. HW –0605 on Dover; ML 3·6m; Duration 0555. See 4.25. Drying hbr gives very good shelter, but is not advised for yachts. In ground swell dangerous seas break on the bar, drying 2·7m; approx 4m at ent @ MHWS. Cross in good weather HW±1. Marks do not necessarily indicate best water. Ldg marks/lts 180°: both W ☐ R horiz band, ✩ FW 17/23m 4M. NCM buoy, Q is about 7ca N of the front ldg lt. Training wall on W side of ent chan is marked by 5 lit perches, all Oc G 4s. The hbr is divided by long central island (about 700m long, with lt bn QG at NW end) which should be left to stbd. Follow the SE arm of hbr to Hayle; the S arm leads to Lelant Quay. Visitors must contact HM ☎(01736) 754043, Mob 07500993867, VHF Ch 16 prior to arrival. ⚓£5. Facilities: ⚓ (can) ⚓⚓⚓⚓⚓✕⚓⚡.

ST IVES, Cornwall, **50°12'·79N 05°28'·67W** ✳❄⏃⏃✿✿✿. AC 1149, 1168. HW –0610 on Dover; ML 3·6m; Duration 0555. See 4.25. Drying hbr with about 4·5m @ MHWS. Good shelter except in onshore winds when heavy swell works in. ⚓ in 3m between the hbr and Porthminster Pt to S and drying Or ⚓s in hbr. From the NW beware Hoe Rk off St Ives Hd, and obstn drying 0·9m at collapsed b'water E of Smeaton pier inshore of unlit SHM. From SE off Porthminster Pt avoid The Carracks and obstn drying 1·0m in Carbis Bay. Keep E of SHM buoy about 1½ ca ENE of E pier. Lts: E pier hd 2 FG (vert) 8m 5M. W pier hd 2 FR (vert) 5m 3M. VHF Ch 12 16 (occas). HM ☎ (01736) 795018. Facilities: ⚓s £12.13; **E Pier** ⚓. **Town** ⚓⚓⚓⚓⚓✕⚓⚡.

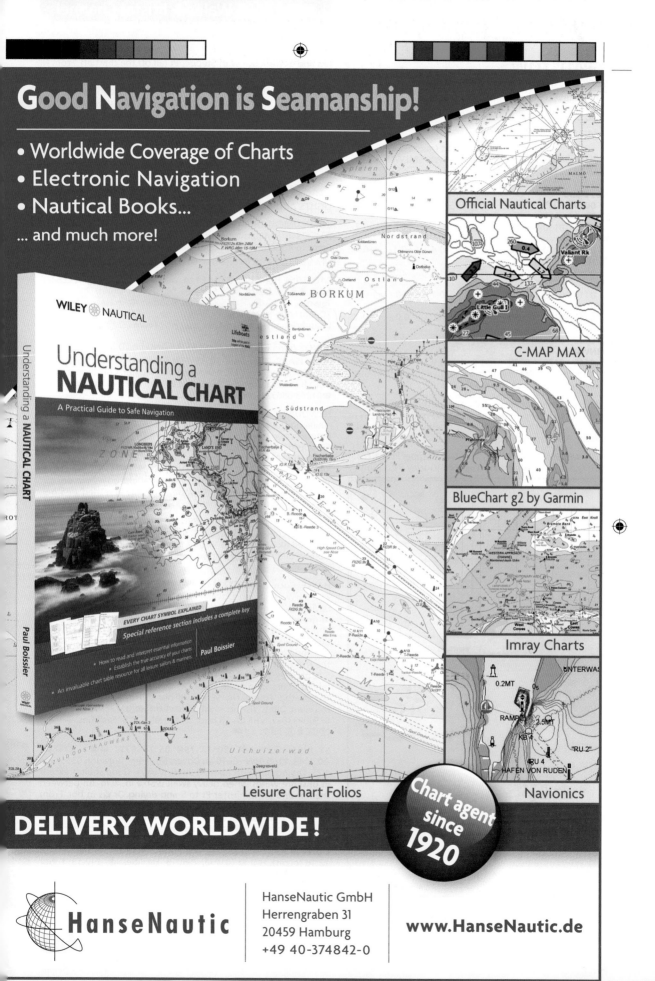

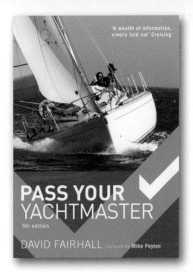
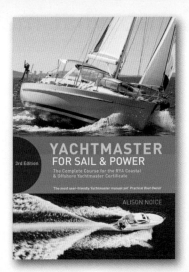
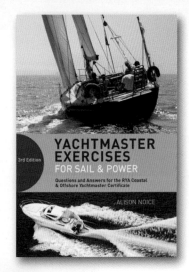
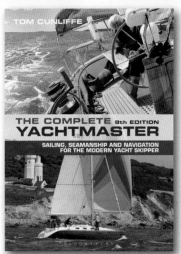
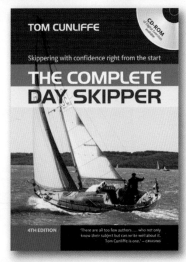
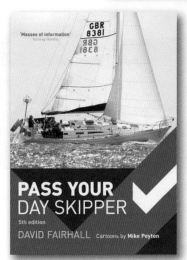
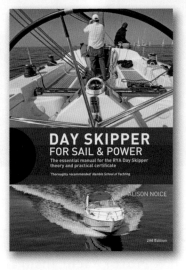
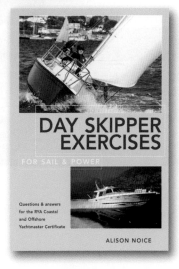

Come what may!

PANTAENIUS
Sail & Motor Yacht Insurance

Ireland

All Ireland

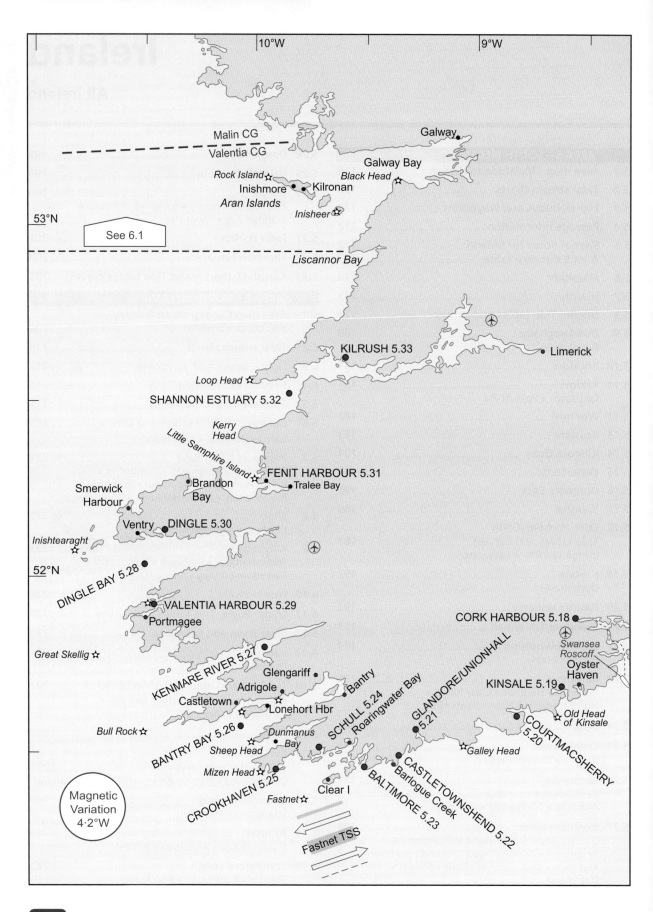

See 6.1

Magnetic
Variation
4·2°W

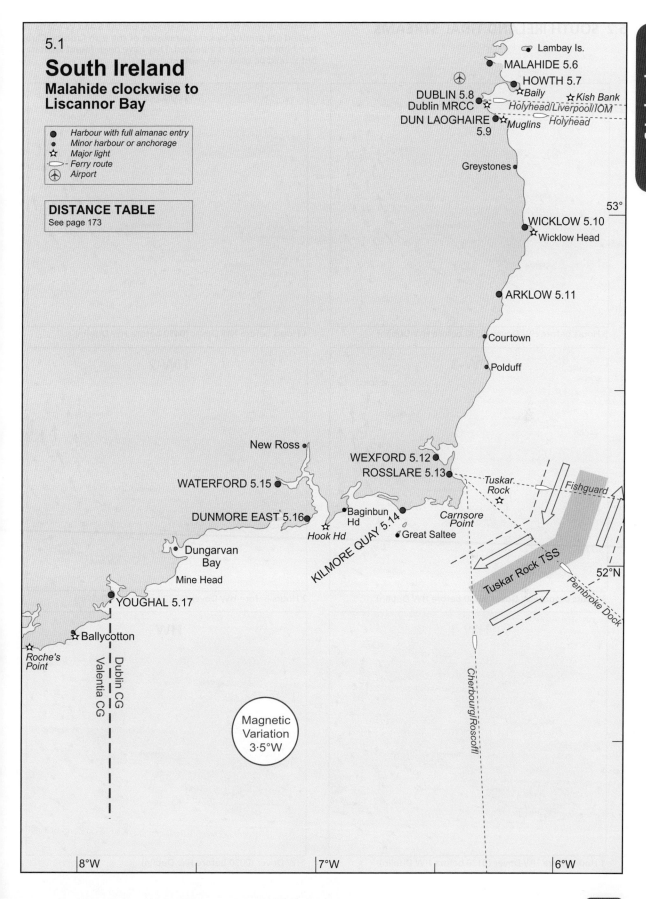

5.1

South Ireland
Malahide clockwise to Liscannor Bay

- ● Harbour with full almanac entry
- • Minor harbour or anchorage
- ☆ Major light
- ⬭ Ferry route
- ✈ Airport

DISTANCE TABLE
See page 173

Lambay Is.
MALAHIDE 5.6
HOWTH 5.7
Baily
DUBLIN 5.8 ☆ Kish Bank
Dublin MRCC ☆ Holyhead/Liverpool/IOM
DUN LAOGHAIRE ☆ Muglins Holyhead
5.9

Greystones

53°

WICKLOW 5.10
☆ Wicklow Head

ARKLOW 5.11

Courtown

Polduff

New Ross
WEXFORD 5.12
ROSSLARE 5.13
Tuskar Rock
Fishguard

WATERFORD 5.15
☆ Tuskar Rock

DUNMORE EAST 5.16
Baginbun Hd
Carnsore Point

Hook Hd
KILMORE QUAY 5.14
Great Saltee
Tuskar Rock TSS
52°N

Dungarvan Bay
Mine Head
Pembroke Dock

YOUGHAL 5.17

☆ Ballycotton

☆ Roche's Point
Dublin CG
Valentia CG

Cherbourg/Roscoff

Magnetic
Variation
3·5°W

8°W 7°W 6°W

5.2 SOUTH IRELAND TIDAL STREAMS

The tidal arrows (with no rates shown) off the S and W coasts of Ireland are printed by kind permission of the Irish Cruising Club, to whom the Editor is indebted. They have been found accurate, but should be used with caution.

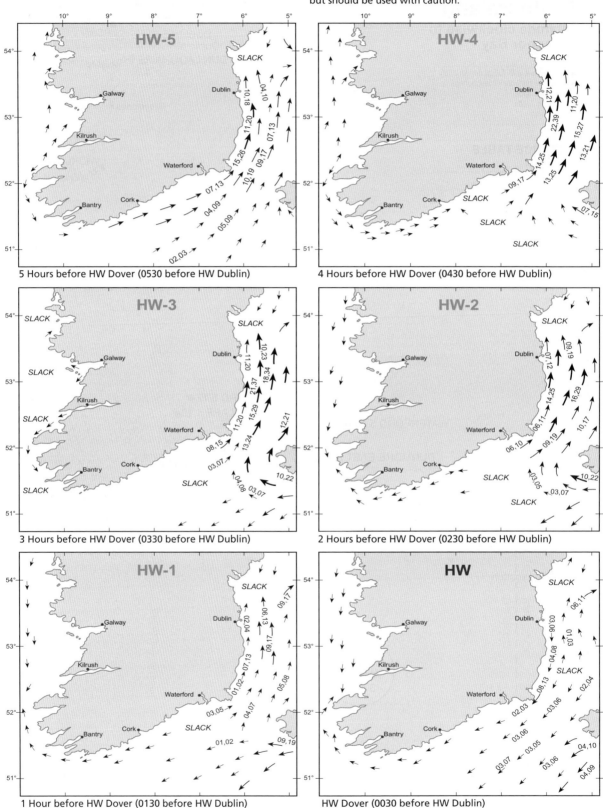

5 Hours before HW Dover (0530 before HW Dublin)

4 Hours before HW Dover (0430 before HW Dublin)

3 Hours before HW Dover (0330 before HW Dublin)

2 Hours before HW Dover (0230 before HW Dublin)

1 Hour before HW Dover (0130 before HW Dublin)

HW Dover (0030 before HW Dublin)

Northward 6.2   South Irish Sea 4.2

The tidal arrows (with no rates shown) off the S and W coasts of Ireland are printed by kind permission of the Irish Cruising Club, to whom the Editor is indebted. They have been found accurate, but should be used with caution.

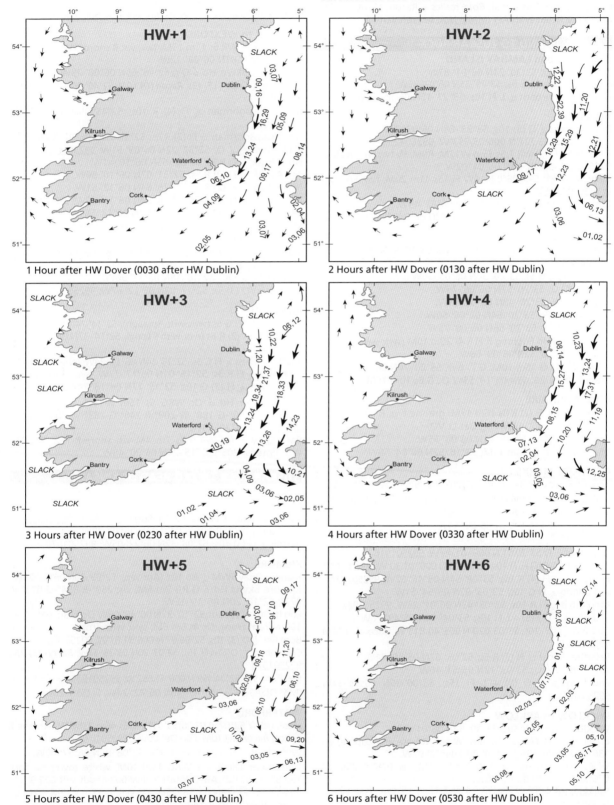

1 Hour after HW Dover (0030 after HW Dublin)

2 Hours after HW Dover (0130 after HW Dublin)

3 Hours after HW Dover (0230 after HW Dublin)

4 Hours after HW Dover (0330 after HW Dublin)

5 Hours after HW Dover (0430 after HW Dublin)

6 Hours after HW Dover (0530 after HW Dublin)

5.3 LIGHTS, BUOYS AND WAYPOINTS

Bold print = light with a nominal range of 15M or more. CAPITALS = place or feature. *CAPITAL ITALICS* = light-vessel, light float or Lanby. *Italics* = Fog signal. ***Bold italics*** = Racon. Many marks/buoys are fitted with AIS (<u>MMSI No</u>); see relevant charts.

LAMBAY ISLAND TO TUSKAR ROCK

MALAHIDE and LAMBAY ISLAND
Taylor Rks ⚓ Q; 53°30'·21N 06°01'·87W.
Burren Rocks ⚓ Fl G 5s; 53°29'·35N 06°02'·35W.
Malahide approach ⚓ L Fl 10s; 53°27'·12N 06°06'·87W.

HOWTH
Rowan Rocks ⚓ Q (3) 10s; 53°23'·88N 06°03'·27W.
Howth ⚓ 53°23.727'N 006°03.593'W; <u>992501250</u>.
E Pier Hd ⚓ Fl WR 7·5s 13m W12M, R9M; W twr; vis: W256°-R295°-256°; 53°23'·64N 06°04'·02W.
Baily ☆ 53°21'·69N 06°03'·16W Fl 15s 41m **20M**; twr. Fog Det Lt VQ; <u>992501010</u>.
Rosbeg E ⚓ Q (3) 10s; 53°21'·02N 06°03'·45W.
Rosbeg S ⚓ Q (6) + L Fl 15s; 53°20'·22N 06°04'·17W.

PORT OF DUBLIN
Dublin Bay ⚓ Mo (A) 10s; ***Racon (M)***; 53°19'·92N 06°04'·65W; <u>992351301</u>.
No. 1 ⚓ Fl (3) G 5s; 53°20'·30N 06°05'·56W.
No. 3 ⚓ IQ G; 53°20'·57N 06°06'·76W.
No. 4 ⚓ IQ R; 53°20'·48N 06°06'·93W.
No. 5 ⚓ Fl G 2s; 53°20'·64N 06°08'·60W.
No. 6 ⚓ Fl R 2s; 53°20'·56N 06°08'·75W.
Great S Wall Hd Poolbeg ⚓ Fl R 4s 20m 10M (*sync with N.Bull*); R ○ twr; 53°20'·52N 06°09'·08W.
N Bull ⚓ Fl G 4s 15m 10M; G ○ twr; 53°20'·70N 06°08'·98W.
N Bank ☆ 53°20'·69N 06°10'·59W Oc G 8s 10m **16M**; G □ twr.

DUN LAOGHAIRE
E Bkwtr Hd ⚓ Fl (2) R 8s 16m **17M**; granite twr, R lantern 7M; 53°18'·14N 06°07'·62W. Fog Det Lt VQ.
Outfall ⚓ Fl Y 5s; 53°18'·41N 06°08'·35W.
Muglins ⚓ Fl R 5s 14m 11M; 53°16'·52N 06°04'·58W.

OFFSHORE MARKS
Bennett Bank ⚓ Q(6)+ L Fl 15s; 53°20'·17N 05°55'·11W; <u>992501012</u>.
Kish Bank ☆ 53°18'·65N 05°55'·54W Fl (2) 20s 29m **21M** (H24); W twr, R band; ***Racon (T) 15M***; <u>992501017</u>.
N Kish ⚓ VQ; 53°18'·56N 05°56'·44W.
E Kish ⚓ Fl (2) R 10s; 53°14'·35N 05°53'·56W; <u>992501020</u>.
N Burford ⚓ Q 53°20.51'N 006° 01.49'W; <u>992501016</u>.
S Burford ⚓ VQ(6)+Fl 10s; 53°18.06'N 006° 01.30'W; <u>992501018</u>.
E Codling ⚓ Fl (4) R 10s; 53°08'·54N 05°46'·07W; <u>992501024</u>.
W Codling ⚓ Fl G 10s; 53°06'·97N 05°54'·51W.
Moulditch ⚓ Fl R 10s; 53°08'·43N 06°01'·23W; <u>992501022</u>.
S Codling ⚓ VQ (6) + L Fl 10s; 53°04'·74N 05°49'·76W.
Codling ⚓ Q(3) 10s; 53°03.020'N 005°40.815'W, ***Racon (G) 10M***, <u>992501028</u>.
Breaches Shoal ⚓ Fl (2) R 6s; 53°05'·67N 05°59'·81W.
North India ⚓ Q; 53°03'·12N 05°53'·46W.
South India ⚓ Q (6) + L Fl 15s; 53°00'·36N 05°53'·31W; <u>992501030</u>.

WICKLOW to ARKLOW
Wicklow ⚓ Fl (4) Y 10s; 52°59'·54N 06°01'·29W.
E Pier Hd ⚓ Fl WR 5s 11m 6M; W twr, R base and cupola; vis: 136°-R-293°-W-136°; 52°58'·99N 06°02'·07W.
W Packet Quay Hd ⚓ Fl WG 10s 5m 6M; vis: 076°-G-256°-W-076°; 52°58'·88N 06°02'·08W.
Wicklow Hd ☆ 52°57'·95N 05°59'·89W Fl (3) 15s 37m **23M**; W twr; <u>992501031</u>.

Horseshoe ⚓ Fl R 3s; 52°56'·84N 05°58'·47W; <u>992501032</u>.
N Arklow ⚓ Q; 52°53'·86N 05°55'·21W; <u>992501034</u>.
Arklow Bank Wind Farm from 52°48'·47N 05°56'·57W to 52°46'·47N 05°57'·11W, N and S Turbines Fl Y 5s14m 10M. No 7 Turbine <u>992501302</u>. Other turbines Fl Y 5s. See 5.4.

ARKLOW to WEXFORD
S Pier Hd ⚓ Fl WR 6s 11m 13M; twr; vis: R shore- W223°- R350°-shore; 52°47'·61N 06°08'·22W.
Roadstone Bkwtr Hd ⚓ QY; 52°46'·65N 06°08'·23W.
S Arklow ⚓ Q (6) + LFl 15s; ***Racon (O) 10M***; 52°40'·20N 05°58'·89W; <u>992501040</u>.
No. 2 Glassgorman ⚓ Fl (4) R 10s; 52°45'·35N 06°05'·34W; <u>992501038</u>.
No. 1 Glassgorman ⚓ Fl (2) R 6s; 52°37'·69N 06°07'·34W.
N Blackwater ⚓ Q; 52°32'·22N 06°09'·51W; <u>992501046</u>.
No. 6 Rusk ⚓ Fl R 3s; 52°32'·65N 06°10'·41W.
No. 4 Rusk ⚓ Fl (2) R 5s; 52°31'·07N 06°10'·86W.
No. 2 Rusk ⚓ Fl (2) R 5s; 52°28'·64N 06°12'·61W.
No. 1 Rusk ⚓ Fl (2) G 5s; 52°28'·54N 06°11'·80W; <u>992501048</u>.
W Blackwater ⚓ Fl G 6s; 52°25'·87N 06°13'·56W.
SE Blackwater ⚓ Q (3) 10s, 52°25'·62N 06°08'·42W; ***Racon (M) 10M***; <u>992501050</u>.
S Blackwater ⚓ Q (6) + L Fl 15s; 52°22'·76N 06°12'·87W.
North Long ⚓ Q; 52°21'·44N 06°17'·04W.
West Long ⚓ QG; 52°18'·18N 06°17'·96W.
Lucifer ⚓ VQ (3) 5s; 52°17'·02N 06°12'·67W; <u>992501054</u>.

ROSSLARE
S Long ⚓ Fl (2) G 6s (sync with Splaugh); 52°14'·74N 06°15'·80W.
Splaugh ⚓ Fl (2) R 6s (sync with S Long); 52°14'·37N 06°16'·76W; <u>992501062</u>.
South Holdens ⚓ Fl G 3s; 52°15'·14N 06°17'·24W. (sync Calmines).
Calmines ⚓ Fl R 3s; 52°15'·01N 06°17'·77W. (sync S Holdens).
W Holdens ⚓ Fl (3) G 10s; 52°15'·77N 06°18'·74W.
Rosslare Pier Hd ⚓ Oc WRG 5s 15m W13M, R10M, G10M; R twr; vis:098°-G-188°-W-208°-R-246°-W-286°-R-320°; 52°15'·43N 06°20'·29W.
Ballygeary ⚓ Oc WR 1·7s 7m 4M vis: shore-R-152°-W-200°-W(unintens)-205°; 52°15'·25N 06°20'·48W.

TUSKAR ROCK TO OLD HEAD OF KINSALE
Tuskar ☆ 52°12'·17N 06°12'·44W Q (2) 7·5s 33m **24M**; W twr; ***Racon (T) 18M***; <u>992501065</u>.
S Rock ⚓ Q (6)+L Fl 15s; 52°10'·80N 06°12'·84W; <u>992501068</u>.
Fundale ⚓ Fl (2) R 10s; 52°11'·04N 06°19'·78W.
Barrels ⚓ Q (3) 10s; 52°08'·32N 06°22'·05W; <u>992501070</u>.

KILMORE
Kilmore Quay SWM ⚓ Iso 10s; (Apr-Sep); 52°09'·20N 06°35'·30W.
Kilmore Bkwtr Hd ⚓ Q RG 7m 5M; vis: 269°-R-354°-G-003°-R-077°; 52°10'·20N 06°35'·15W.
Ldg lts 007·9°, Front 52°10'·37N 06°35'·08W Oc 4s 3m 6M. Rear, 100m from front, Oc 4s 6m 6M; sync with front.
Bore Rks ⚓ Q (3) 10s; 52°06.07'N 006°31.87'W; <u>992501072</u>.
Coningbeg ⚓ Q(6)+LFl 15s; 52°03'·20N 06°38'·57W; ***Racon (T) 7M***; <u>992501074</u>.
Red Bank W ; 52°04.499'N 006°41.652'W; <u>992501076</u>.
'M5' ODAS 35 ⚓ 51°41'·40N 06°42'·24W; Fl (5) Y 20s.

WATERFORD
Hook Hd ☆ 52°07'·42N 06°55'·77W Fl 3s 46m **23M**; W twr, two B bands; ***Racon (K) 10M***. Fog Det Lt VQ. <u>992501079</u>.
Waterford ⚓ Fl R 3s. Fl (3) R 10s; 52°08'·95N 06°57'·00W.
Duncannon Dir lt ⚓ F WRG 13m 10M, white tower on fort, 359·5°-FG-001·2°-Alt GW-001·7°-FW-002·4°-Alt WR-002·9°-FR-004·5°; 52°13'·23N 06°56'·25W; Oc WR 4s 13m W 9M R 7M on same tower, 119°-R-149°-W-172°.

Passage Pt ⌁ Fl WR 5s 7m W6M, R5M; R pile structure; vis: W shore- R127°-302°; 52°14'·26N 06°57'·77W.

Cheek Pt ⌁ Q WR 6m 5M; W mast; vis: W007°-R289°-007°; 52°16'·12N 06°59'·38W.

Sheagh ⌁ Fl R 3s 29m 3M; Gy twr; vis: 090°-318°; 52°16'·29N 06°59'·34W.

Snowhill Point Ldg lts 255°. Front, Fl WR 2·5s 5m 3M; vis: W222°- R020°- W057°-107°; 52°16'·39N 07°00'·91W. Rear, Flour Mill, 750m from front, Q 12m 5M.

Queen's Chan Ldg lts 098°. Front, QR 8m 5M; B twr, W band; vis: 030°-210°;52°15'·32N 07°02'·38W. Rear, 550m from front, Q 15m 5M; W mast.

Beacon Quay ⌁ Fl G 3s 9m; vis: 255°-086°; 52°15'·50N 07°04'·21W.

Cove ⌁ Fl WRG 6s 6m 2M; W twr; vis: R111°- G161°- W234°-111°; 52°15'·05N 07°05'·16W.

Smelting Ho Pt ⌁ Q 8m 3M; W mast; 52°15'·15N 07°05'·27W.

Ballycar ⌁ Fl RG 3s 5m; vis: G127°- R212°-284°; 52°15'·06N 07°05'·51W.

DUNMORE EAST

East Pier Head ☆ 52°08'·93N 06°59'·34W Fl WR 8s 13m **W17M,** R13M; Gy twr, vis: W225°- R310°-004°.

Dunmore East 1 ▲ Q G; 52°09'·06N 06°59'·38W.

Dunmore East 2 ▲ Fl G 2s; 52°09'·00N 06°59'·47W.

W Wharf ⌁ Fl G 2s 6m 4M; vis: 165°-246°; 52°08'·97N 06°59'·45W.

DUNGARVAN

Ballinacourty Pt ⌁ Fl (2) WRG 10s 16m W10M, R8M, G8M; W twr; vis: G245°- W274°- R302°- W325°-117°; 52°04'·69N 07°33'·18W.

Helvick ⌁ Q (3) 10s; 52°03'·61N 07°32'·25W.

Mine Head ⌁ 51°59'·56N 07°35'·23W Fl (4) 30s 87m 12M; W twr, B band; vis: 228°-052°; 992501085.

YOUGHAL

Bar Rocks ⌁ Q (6) + L Fl 15s; 51°54'·85N 07°50'·05W.

Blackball Ledge ⌁ 51°55'·34N 07°48'·53W Q (3) 10s.

W side of ent ☆ 51°56'·57N 07°50'·53W Fl WR 2·5s 24m **W17M,** R13M; W twr; vis: W183°- W273°- W295°- W307°- W351°-003°.

BALLYCOTTON

Ballycotton ☆ 51°49'·50N 07° 59'·13W Fl WR 10s 59m **W18M, R14M;** B twr, within W walls, B lantern; vis: 238°-W-048°-R-238°; 992501093.

The Smiths ≈ Fl (3) R 10s; 51°48'·62N 08°00'·71W.

Power ⌁ Q (6) + L Fl 15s; 51°45'·59N 08°06'·67W; 992501098.

CORK

Cork ⌁ L Fl 10s; 51°42'·92N 08°15'·60W; *Racon (T) 7M*; 992501100.

Daunt Rock ≈ Fl (2) R 6s; 51°43'·52N 08°17'·66W; 992501102.

Fort Davis Ldg lts 354·1°. Front, 51°48'·82N 08°15'·80W Dir WRG 29m **17M;** vis: FG351·5°-AlWG352·25°-FW353°-AlWR355°-FR355·75°-356·5°. Rear, Dognose Quay, 203m from front, Oc 5s 37m 10M; Or 3, synch with front.

Roche's Pt ☆ 51°47'·59N 08°15'·29W Fl WR 3s 30m **W20M, R16M;** vis: shore-R-292°-W-016°-R-033°, 033°- W (unintens)-159°-R-shore; 992501099.

Outer Hbr Rk E2 ≈ Fl R 2·5s; 51°47'·52N 08°15'·67W.

Chicago Knoll E1 ▲ Fl G 5s; 51°47'·66N 08°15'·54W.

W1 ▲ Fl G 10s; 51°47'·69N 08°16'·05W.

W2 ≈ Fl R 10s; 51°47'·69N 08°16'·34W.

White Bay Ldg lts 034·6°. Front, Oc R 5s 11m 5M; W hut; 51°48'·53N 08°15'·22W. Rear, 113m from front, Oc R 5s 21m 5M; W hut; synch with front.

Spit Bank Pile ⌁ Iso WR 4s 10m W10M, R7M; W house on R piles; vis: R087°- W196°- R221°- 358°; 51°50'·72N 08°16'·45W.

KINSALE and OYSTER HAVEN

Bulman ⌁ Q (6) + L Fl 15s; 51°40'·14N 08°29'·74W; 992501104.

Charlesfort ⌁ Fl WRG 5s 18m W9M, R6M, G7M; vis: G348°-W358°- R004°-168°; H24; 51°41'·75N 08°29'·84W.

Old Head of Kinsale ☆, S point 51°36'·29N 08°32'·02W Fl (2) 10s 72m **20M**; B twr, two W bands; 992501107.

COURTMACSHERRY

Barrel Rock ⌁ 51°37'·01N 08°37'·30W.

Black Tom ▲ Fl G 5s; 51°36'·41N 08°37'·95W; 992501110.

Wood Pt (Land Pt) ⌁ Fl (2) WR 5s 15m 5M; vis: W315°- R332°-315°; 51°38'·16N 08°41'·00W.

Galley Head ☆ summit 51°31'·80N 08°57'·21W Fl (5) 20s 53m **23M**; W twr; vis: 256°-065°.

GLANDORE and CASTLETOWNSHEND

Reen Point ⌁ Fl WRG 10s 9m W5M, R3M, G3M; W twr; vis: shore-G-338°-W-001°-R-shore; 51°30'·98N 09°10'·50W.

Kowloon Bridge ⌁ Q (6) + L Fl 15s; 51°27'·58N 09°13'·75W; 992501118.

BALTIMORE and FASTNET

Barrack Pt ⌁ Fl (2) WR 6s 40m W6M, R3M; vis: R168°- W294°-038°; 51°28'·33N 09°23'·65W.

Loo Rock ▲ Fl G 3s; 51°28'·44N 09°23'·46W; 992501119.

Lousy Rks ⌁; 51°28'·93N 09°23'·39W.

Wallis Rk ≈ Fl (3) R 10s; 51°28'·93N 09°22'·99W.

Lettuce Pt ⌁ VQ (3) 5s; 51°29'·32N 09°23'·81W.

Mealbeg ⌁ Q (6) + L Fl 15s; 51°29'·68N 09°24'·69W.

Inane Pt ⌁ Q (6) + L Fl 15s; 51°30'·02N 09°23'·66W.

Hare Is ⌁ Q; 51°30'·17N 09°25'·38W.

Fastnet ☆, W end 51°23'·35N 09°36'·19W Fl 5s 49m **27M**; Gy twr, *Racon (G) 18M*. Fog Det Lt VQ; 992501123.

SCHULL and LONG ISLAND CHANNEL

Amelia ▲; 51°29.979'N 009°31.461'W; 992501120.

Copper Point ⌁ 51°30'·25N 09°32'·06W Q (3) 10s 16m 8M.

Ldg lts 346° Front, Oc 5s 5m 11M, W mast; 51°31'·68N 09°32'·43W. Rear, 91m from front, Oc 5s 8m11M; W mast.

CROOKHAVEN

Rock Is Pt ⌁ L Fl WR 8s 20m W13M, R11M; W twr; vis: W over Long Is B to 281°-R-340°; inside harbour 281°-R-348°- towards N shore; 51°28'·59N 09°42'·27W; 992501124.

Mizen Head ⌁ Iso 4s 55m 12M; vis: 313°-133°; 51°26'·99N 09°49'·23W; 992501127.

Sheep's Hd ☆ 51°32'·59N 09°50'·92W Fl (3) WR 15s 83m **W15M** R9M; W bldg; vis: 011·3°-R-016·6°-W-212·5°-(partially obs) 233° (shore); 992501129.

BANTRY BAY, CASTLETOWN BEARHAVEN,
WHIDDY ISLE, BANTRY and GLENGARIFF

Roancarrigmore ⌁ Fl WR 5s 13m W11M, R9M, R(unintens)5M; s/steel twr; vis: 312°-W-050°-R-122°-R(unintens)-207°-obsc-246°-R-312°; 51°39'·18N 09°44'·82W. Old Lt ho W twr, B band; 992501130.

Ardnakinna Pt ⌁ 51°37'·10N 09°55'·09W Fl (2) WR 10s 62m W14M, R9M; W ○ twr; vis: 319°-R- 348°-W- 066°-R-shore; 992501131.

Walter Scott Rk ⌁ Q (6) + L Fl 15s; 51°38'·52N 09°54'·20W; 992501128.

Castletown (Dinish Is) Dir lt 023·25° ⌁ Oc WRG 5s 7m W15M, R12M, G12M; W hut, R stripe; vis: 019·5°-G-023°-W-023·5°-R-027°; 51°38'·78N 09°54'·32W; 992501125.

Castletown Ldg lts 008°. Front, Oc Bu 6s 4m 6M; W col, R stripe; vis: 005°-013°; 51°39'·16N 09°54'·40W. Rear, 80m from front, Oc Bu 6s 7m 6M; W with R stripe; vis: 005°-013°.

Bull Rock ☆ 51°35'·52N 10°18'·07W Fl 15s 91m **18M**; W twr; 992501131.

KENMARE RIVER, DARRYNANE and BALLYCROVANE
Illaunnameanla (Ballycrovane) ⚡ Fl R 3s; 51°42'·60N 09°57'·50W.
Book Rks ⚲ Fl(2) R 10s; 51°46'·54N 09°49'·74W.
Cuskeal ⚲ Fl R 5s; 51°46'·45N 09°48'·85W.
Bunaw Ldg Lts 041°. Front, Oc R 3s 9m 2M; B col, Y bands;
51°46'·80N 09°48'·40W. Rear, 200m from front Iso R 2s 11m 2M.
Maiden Rk ⚑ Fl G 5s; 51°48'·98N 09°47'·98W; 992501134.
Bat Rk ⚑ Fl G 5s; 51°50'·89N 09°40'·89W.
Carrignaronebeg ⚲ Fl R 5s; 51°50'·99N 09°41'·39W.
No1 ⚑ Fl G 5s; 51°52'·09N 09°36'·35W.
Carrignarone (Seal Rk) Fl 5s 2m 2M; 51°48'·58N 09°52'·65W.
Castlecove Ldg Lts 045°. Front, Oc 2s 5m 6M; concrete post W front;
51°46'·29N 10°02'·04W. Rear, 400m from front Oc 2s 18m 6M.
West Cove Hbr ⚡ Fl R 3s; post W front; 51°46'·00N 10°02'·93W.
West Cove Hbr Ldg Lts 312°. Front, Fl 2s 2m 6M; concrete post;
51°46'·11N 10°03'·08W. Rear, 200m from front Fl 2s 4m 6M.
Darrynane Ldg Lts 034°. Front, Oc 3s 10m 4M; 51°45'·90N
10°09'·20W. Rear, Oc 3s 16m 4M.

SKELLIG ISLANDS
Skelligs Rock ⚡ Fl (3) 15s 53m 12M; W twr; vis: 262°-115°; part obsc
within 6M 110°-115°; 51°46'·11N 10°32'·52W; 992501137.

VALENTIA and PORTMAGEE
Fort (Cromwell) Point ☆ 51°56'·02N 10°19'·28W Fl WR 2s 16m
W17M, R15M; W twr; vis: 304°-R-351°,102°-W-304°; obsc from
seaward by Doulus Head when brg more than 180°; 992501141.
Dir lt 141° ⚡ Oc WRG 4s 25m W11M, R8M, G8M (by day: W3M,
R2M, G2M); W twr, R stripe; vis:136°-G-140°-W-142°-R-146°;
51°55'·51N 10°18'·42W.
The Foot ↕ VQ (3) 5s; 51°55'·72N 10°17'·07W; 992501140.

DINGLE BAY TO LOOP HEAD
DINGLE BAY, VENTRY and DINGLE
Ldg lts 182° Oc 3s. Front 52°07'·41N 10°16'·59W, rear 100m behind.
Inishtearaght ☆, W end Blasket Islands 52°04'·54N 10°39'·67W Fl
(2) 20s 84m **19M**; W twr; vis: 318°-221°; *Racon (O)*; 992501143.

BRANDON BAY, TRALEE BAY and FENIT HARBOUR
Little Samphire Is ☆ 52°16'·26N 09°52'·91W Fl WRG 5s 17m
W16M, R13M; G13M; Bu ◯ twr; vis: 262°-R-275°, 280-R-090°-
G-140°-W-152°-R-172°.
Great Samphire I ⚡ QR 15m 3M; vis: 242°-097°; 52°16'·15N
09°51'·81W.
Fenit Hbr Pier Hd ⚡ 2 FR (vert) 12m 3M; vis: 148°-058°;
52°16'·24N 09°51'·55W.

SHANNON ESTUARY
Ballybunnion ↕ VQ; *Racon (M) 6M*; 52°32'·52N 09°46'·93W;
992501146.
Kilstiffin ⚲ Fl R 3s; 52°33'·80N 09°43'·83W; 992501148.

Kilcredaun ⚲ Q R (sync); 52°34'·42N 09°41'·16W.
Tail of Beal ⚑ Q G (sync); 52°34'·37N 09°40'·71W; 992501150.
Kilcredaun Head ⌂, W twr; 52°34'·78N 09°42'·58W.
Carrigaholt ⚲ Fl (2) R 6s (sync); 52°34'·90N 09°40'·47W.
Beal Spit ⚑ Fl (2) G 6s (sync); 52°34'·80N 09°39'·94W.
Beal Bar ⚑ Fl G 3s (sync); 52°35'·18N 09°39'·05W.
Doonaha ⚲ Fl R 3s (sync); 52°35'·54N 09°39'·01W; 992501154.
Letter Point ⚲ Fl R 7s; 52°35'·44N 09°35'·89W.
Asdee ⚲ Fl R 5s; 52°35'·09N 09°34'·55W.
Rineanna ⚲ QR; 52°35'·59N 09°31'·24W.
North Carraig ↕ Q; 52°35'·60N 09°29'·76W.
Scattery Is, Rineanna Pt ⚡ Fl (2) 8s 15m 10M; W twr; vis: 208°-
092°; 52°36'·35N 09°31'·07W.

KILRUSH
Marina Ent Chan Ldg lts 355°. Front, Oc 3s; 52°37'·99N 09°30'·27W.
Rear, 75m from front, Oc 3s.
Tarbert Is N Point ⚡ Q WR 4s 18m W14M, R10M; W ◯ twr; vis:
W069°- R277°- W287°-339°; 52°35'·52N 09°21'·83W.
Tarbert (Ballyhoolahan Pt) Ldg lts 128·2° ↕. Front, Iso 3s 13m
3M; △ on W twr; vis: 123·2°-133·2°; 52°34'·35N 09°18'·80W.
Rear, 400m from front, Iso 5s 18m 3M; G stripe on W Bn.
Garraunbaun Pt ⚡ Fl (3) WR 10s 16m W8M, R5M; W ☐ col, vis:
R shore - W072°- R242°- shore; 52°35'·62N 09°13'·94W.
Rinealon Pt ⚡ Fl 2·5s 4m 7M; B col, W bands; vis: 234°-088°;
52°37'·12N 09°09'·82W.

FOYNES
W Chan Ldg lts 107·9° (may be moved for changes in chan). Front,
Oc 4s 34m 12M; 52°36'·91N 09°06'·59W . Rear, Oc 4s 39m 12M.

RIVER SHANNON
Beeves Rock ⚡ Fl WR 5s 12m W12M, R9M; vis: 064·5°-W-091°-
238°-W-265°-W(unintens)-064·5°; 52°39'·01N 09°01'·35W .
North Channel Ldg lts 093°. Front, Tradree Rock Fl R 2s 6m 5M;
W Trs; vis: 246°-110°; 52°41'·00N 08°49'·87W. Rear 0·65M from
front, Iso 6s 14m 5M; W twr, R bands; vis: 327°-190°.

N side, Ldg lts 061°. Front, 52°40'·72N 08°45'·27W, Crawford
Rock 490m from rear, Fl R 3s 6m 5M. Crawford No. 2, Common
Rear, Iso 6s 10m 5M; 52°40'·85N 08°44'·88W.
Ldg lts 302·1°, Flagstaff Rock, 670m from rear, Fl R 7s 7m 5M;
52°40'·66N 08°44'·40W.
Ldg lts 106·5°. Meelick Rk, Front Iso R 4s 6m 5M; 52°40'·24N
08°42'·32W. Meelick No. 2, rear 275m from front Iso R 4s 9m
5M; both W beacons.

LOOP HEAD
Loop Head ☆ 52°33'·67N 09°55'·94W Fl (4) 20s 84m **23M**; vis:
280°-218°; 992501161.
Mal Bay ↕ Fl(5) Y 20s 52°46.42'N 009°35.15'W; *AIS*.

5.4 PASSAGE INFORMATION
More passage information is threaded between the harbours
in this area.The latest editions of the Irish Cruising Club Sailing
Directions are strongly recommended for all Irish waters (www.
irishcruisingclub.com). Particularly useful on the N and W coast
where other information is scarce they are published in two
volumes, *E and N coasts of Ireland* and *S and W coasts of Ireland*.
(Both available from Imray in UK or Todd Chart Services, Bangor,
Co Down, ☎028 9146 6640 (www.toddchart.com). See also *Cruising
Cork and Kerry* (Imray/Swanson).

For notes on crossing the Irish Sea, see 6.4; and for Distances
across it see 0.31. More Passage Information is threaded between
the harbours of this Area.

5.5 SPECIAL NOTES FOR IRELAND
Céad Míle Fáilte! One hundred thousand Welcomes!

**Lifejackets: It is compulsory to wear lifejackets in Irish waters
on all craft of <7m LOA. Children under 16 years must wear
a lifejacket or personal flotation device at all times on deck
when underway. Every vessel, irrespective of size, must carry a
lifejacket or personal flotation device for each person on board.
These regulations are mandatory.**

Irish Customs: First port of call should preferably be at Customs
posts in one of the following hbrs: Dublin, Dun Laoghaire,
Waterford, New Ross, Cork, Ringaskiddy, Bantry, Foynes, Limerick,
Galway, Sligo and Killybegs. Yachts may, in fact, make their first

call anywhere and if no Customs officer arrives within a reasonable time, the skipper should inform the nearest Garda (Police) station of the yacht's arrival. Only yachts from non-EU member states should fly flag Q or show ● over ○ lts on arrival. Passports are not required by UK citizens. All current Northern Ireland 5 and 6 digit telephone numbers have become 8 digits **028 90**12 3456.

Telephone: To call the **Republic of Ireland (RoI)** from the UK, dial **00 - 353**, then the area code minus the initial 0, followed by the number. To call UK from the RoI: dial 00-44, followed by the area code minus the initial 0, then the number.

Salmon drift nets are now illegal and should not be encountered. Draft netting (across a river or estuary) is still permitted, but is rare.

Liquefied petroleum gas: In RoI LPG is supplied by Kosan, a sister company of Calorgas Ltd, but the smallest bottle is taller than the Calor equivalent fitted in most yachts with different connections. Calor bottles can be filled in larger towns. Camping Gaz is widely available.

Useful Irish websites:

Commissioners of Irish Lights	www.cil.ie
Irish Sailing Association	www.sailing.ie
Irish Tourist Board	www.discoverireland.com
Sea Area Forecast	www.met.ie/forecasts/sea-area.asp

Currency is the Euro (€), readily available from ATMs. VAT is 23%.

Access by air: Intl airports in RoI are at Dublin, Cork & Shannon. Regional airports in Waterford, Farranfore (Kerry), Knock (Mayo) and Carrickfinn (Donegal) provide some scheduled flights between Ireland and Britain. For details, see http://www.irishairports.com/.

Northern Ireland: Belfast CG (MRCC) is at Bangor, Co Down, ☎(028 91) 463933. HM Customs (⊜) should be contacted H24 on ☎ (028 90) 358250 at the following ports, if a local Customs Officer is not available: Belfast, Warrenpoint, Kilkeel, Ardglass, Portavogie, Larne, Londonderry, Coleraine. Northern Ireland's main airport is Belfast (Aldergrove).

AIS stations: 73 AIS stations have been established on navigational marks around the coast of Ireland under the control of the Commissioners of Irish Lights. These are located at lighthouses, and in more remote areas fitted to dedicated lit Y buoys offshore.

GAELIC: It helps to understand some of the more common words for navigational features (courtesy of the Irish Cruising Club):

Ail, alt	cliff, height	Cladach	shore	Inish, illaun	island	Mara	of the sea
Aird, ard	height, high	Cuan, coon	harbour	Inver	river mouth	More, mor	big
Anna, annagh	marsh	Derg, dearg	red	Keal, keel	narrow place,	Rannagh	point
Ath	ford	Drum	hill, ridge		sound	Ron, roan	seal
Bal, Bally	town	Duff, dubh	black	Kill	church, cell	Roe, ruadh	red
Barra	sandbank	Dun, doon	fort	Kin, ken	promontory,	Scolt	split, rky gut
Bel, beal	mouth, strait	Ennis	island		head	Scrow	boggy,
Beg	little	Fad, fadda	long	Knock	hill		grassy sward
Ben, binna	hill	Fan	slope	Lag	hollow	Slieve	mountain
Bo	sunken rock	Fin	white	Lahan	broad	Slig	shells
Boy, bwee	yellow	Freagh, free	heather	Lea	grey	Stag, stac	high rock
Bullig	shoal, round	Gall	stranger	Lenan	weed-	Tawney	low hill
	rock, breaker	Glas, glass	green		covered rock	Tigh, ti	house
Bun	end, river mouth	Glinsk	clear water	Lis	ancient fort	Togher	causeway
Caher	fort	Gorm	blue	Long, luing	ship	Tra, traw	strand
Camus	bay, river bend	Gub	point of land	Maan	middle	Turlin	boulder, beach
Carrick	rock	Hassans	swift current	Maol, mwee	bare	Vad, bad	boat

---

1	*Carlingford Lough*	**1**																											
2	Malahide	36	**2**																										
3	Howth	39	4	**3**																									
4	**Dublin/Dun Laoghaire**	48	12	8	**4**																								
5	Wicklow	63	29	25	21	**5**																							
6	**Arklow**	75	43	37	36	15	**6**																						
7	Wexford (Bar Buoy)	104	71	66	62	43	30	**7**																					
8	**Rosslare**	108	75	70	66	47	34	4	**8**																				
9	Kilmore Quay	128	95	90	86	67	54	25	21	**9**																			
10	Waterford	154	127	116	117	99	84	51	47	32	**10**																		
11	**Dunmore East**	139	112	101	102	84	69	36	32	17	15	**11**																	
12	Youghal	172	143	134	133	115	100	69	65	51	52	37	**12**																
13	**Crosshaven**	192	165	154	155	137	122	89	85	69	74	59	25	**13**															
14	Kinsale	202	178	164	168	150	135	99	95	79	84	69	35	17	**14**														
15	Courtmacsherry	201	177	163	167	149	136	109	105	85	90	75	44	26	13	**15**													
16	Glandore	213	189	175	179	161	148	121	117	97	102	87	56	38	25	23	**16**												
17	Castletownshend	224	200	186	190	172	159	132	128	108	113	98	67	49	36	26	6	**17**											
18	**Baltimore**	239	205	201	196	177	164	136	132	112	117	102	70	54	42	34	16	12	**18**										
19	**Fastnet Rock**	250	216	212	207	189	174	148	144	122	127	112	78	60	49	42	24	20	10	**19**									
20	Schull	256	222	218	213	195	180	154	150	128	133	118	84	66	55	48	30	26	14	9	**20**								
21	Crookhaven	256	222	218	213	195	180	154	150	128	133	118	84	66	55	47	29	25	16	8	10	**21**							
22	Bantry	286	252	237	243	225	210	184	180	158	163	148	114	96	85	78	60	56	45	36	41	35	**22**						
23	Kenmare R (Scariff Is)	285	251	236	242	224	209	183	179	157	162	147	113	95	84	77	59	55	44	35	40	34	42	**23**					
24	Valentia Hbr	295	261	257	252	242	227	192	188	175	180	165	131	113	102	96	78	74	56	54	60	53	55	20	**24**				
25	Dingle	308	274	270	265	246	233	205	201	181	186	171	139	123	111	104	86	82	69	62	67	61	63	28	13	**25**			
26	Fenit Hbr	344	310	306	301	283	268	242	238	216	221	206	172	154	143	136	118	114	105	95	99	93	100	60	47	45	**26**		
27	Kilrush	361	333	323	318	299	286	258	254	234	239	224	192	176	164	155	137	133	122	114	116	109	116	78	66	64	32	**27**	
28	*Slyne Head*	317	355	351	346	328	313	287	283	261	266	251	217	199	188	180	162	158	153	139	141	133	144	103	97	95	70	75	**28**

DISTANCE TABLE
Approximate distances in nautical miles are by the most direct route, whilst avoiding dangers and allowing for Traffic Separation Schemes. Places in *italics* are in adjoining areas; places in **bold** are in 0.31, Distances across the Irish Sea.

5.6 MALAHIDE

Dublin **53°27′·20N 06°08′·90W** ❀❀⊗◊◊◊❀❀❀

CHARTS AC 1468, 633, 5621; Imray C61, C62

TIDES +0030 Dover; ML 2·4; Duration 0615

Standard Port DUBLIN (NORTH WALL) (→)

Times				Height (metres)			
High Water		Low Water		MHWS	MHWN	MLWN	MLWS
0000	0700	0000	0500	4·1	3·4	1·5	0·7
1200	1900	1200	1700				
Differences MALAHIDE							
+0002	+0003	+0009	+0009	+0·1	–0·2	–0·4	–0·2

SHELTER Excellent in marina, dredged approx 2·3m. Visitors berth on pontoon **A**. Moorings preclude ⚓ in the inlet.

NAVIGATION WPT: SWM LFl 10s 53°27′·12N 06°06′·87W. The approach channel, which is well marked by 12 lit PHM and SHM, lies between drying sandbanks. The entrance is straightforward, but there is less than 1m of water below CD at some points of the chan, so adequate height of tide is required for safe entry. The flood reaches 3kn sp, the ebb 3½kn and a strong flow may be experienced through the marina at some states of the tide. Steep seas are formed in strong onshore winds against the full ebb, during which extreme caution needs to be exercised. The speed limit is 5kn in the fairway and 4kn in the marina.

LIGHTS AND MARKS The marina and apartment blocks close S of it are visible from the WPT. The marina enrance is marked by occulting red and green lights to each side.

COMMUNICATIONS (Code 01) MRCC 6620922/3; ⊜8746571; Police 666 4600; Dr 845 5994; Ⓗ 837 7755.

Malahide Marina, Ch **M** 80 (H24). MYC, call *Yacht Base* Ch **M** (occas).

FACILITIES **Marina** ④ (349) ☎8454129, 20♥ €3·90, ⊕(charge varies) ◻ ⌦/ⓌⒸ 🚿 ⛟(H24) ⚓ Kos ⚒ Ⓔ ⌂ ◳(30t) ✕ ⌷ ice.

Malahide YC ☎8453372, ⛴ (for craft <5.5m, launching HW ±2).

Town ◻ ✉ Ⓑ ⇌ ✈ (Dublin).

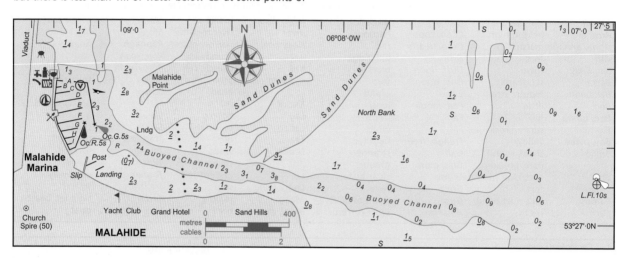

MALAHIDE TO TUSKAR ROCK

(AC 1468, 1787) Malahide, 4M from both Lambay Is and Howth, can be entered in most weather via a channel between drying sandbanks marked by R & G fixed perches. Ireland's Eye, a rky island which rises steeply to a height of 99m, lies about 7½ca N of Howth with reefs running SE and SW from Thulla Rk at its SE end. Ben of Howth, on N side of Dublin Bay, is steep-to, with no dangers more than 1ca offshore.

Rosbeg Bank lies on the N side of Dublin Bay. Burford Bank, on which the sea breaks in E gales, and Kish Bank lie offshore in the approaches. ▶ *The N-going stream begins at HW Dublin –0600, and the S-going at HW Dublin, sp rates 3kn.* ◀

From Dublin to Carnsore Pt as a cruising area, hbr facilities are being improved. The shallow offshore banks cause dangerous overfalls and dictate the route which is sheltered from the W winds. ▶ *Tidal streams run mainly N and S, but the N-going flood sets across the banks on the inside, and the S-going ebb sets across them on the outside.* ◀

Leaving Dublin Bay, yachts normally use Dalkey Sound, but with a foul tide or light wind it is better to use Muglins Sound. Muglins (lt) is steep-to except for a rk about 1ca WSW of the lt. Beware Leac Buidhe (dries) 1ca E of Clare Rk. The inshore passage is best as far as Wicklow. Thereafter yachts may either route offshore, passing east of Arklow Bank and its Lanby to fetch Tuskar Rock or Greenore Pt, or keep inshore of Arklow Bank, avoiding Glassgorman Banks. Stay E of the Blackwater Bank to Lucifer ECM buoy then pass W of Tuskar Rock to round Carnsore Pt to the SW. Avoid the Rusk Channel except in settled weather. Arklow is safe in offshore winds; Wexford has a difficult entrance. Rosslare lacks yacht facilities, but provides good shelter to wait out a SW'ly blow.

Arklow Bank Wind Farm, 7 miles east of Arklow, has 7 wind turbines, each 72.8m high with 104m diameter blades. They are lit, No 7 is fitted with an AIS transmitter.

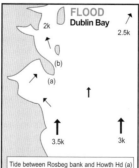

Tide between Rosbeg bank and Howth Hd (a) runs NE from HW Dublin +0300 for 9h30. In Howth Sd (b) the stream is NW going from +0430 to –0130.

New flood and ebb tides begin close to the S shore and N of Baily up to 1h before HW Dublin.

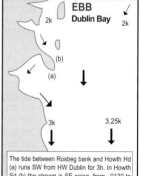

The tide between Rosbeg bank and Howth Hd (a) runs SW from HW Dublin for 3h. In Howth Sd (b) the stream is SE going from –0130 to +0430.

Strengths of streams increase S of Dublin Bay, and decrease N of it.

5.7 HOWHH

Dublin **53°23'·60N 06°04'·00W** ✿✿✿✿♦♦♦✿✿✿

CHARTS AC 1468, 1415, 5621; Imray C61, C62

TIDES +0025 Dover; ML 2·4; Duration 0625

Standard Port DUBLIN (NORTH WALL) (→)

Times				Height (metres)			
High Water		Low Water		MHWS	MHWN	MLWN	MLWS
0000	0700	0000	0500	4·1	3·4	1·5	0·7
1200	1900	1200	1700				
Differences HOWTH							
−0007	−0005	+0001	+0005	0·0	−0·1	−0·2	−0·2

SHELTER Excellent in marina, at all states of tide. After a severe ENE'ly storm, expect a dangerous scend in the app chan which has 11⚓, 6G & 5R. Caution: many moorings in E part of outer hbr. No ent to FV basin for yachts. Inside the inner hbr keep strictly to chan to avoid drying shoals either side and a substantial wavebreak (gabion). Marina depth 1·8m. R posts mark the outer limit of dredging around the marina. 4kn speed limit. There is a fair weather ⚓ in 2-3m at Carrigeen Bay, SW side of Ireland's Eye.

NAVIGATION WPT Howth SHM buoy, Fl G 5s, 53°23'·72N 06°03'·53W, 251°/0·27M to E pier lt. From the S beware Casana Rk 4ca S of the Nose of Howth and Puck's Rks extending about 50m off the Nose. Ireland's Eye is 0·6M N of hbr, with the Rowan Rks SE and SW from Thulla, marked by Rowan Rks ECM, and S Rowan SHM lt buoys. The usual approach passes S of Ireland's Eye, but beware many lobster pots between the Nose of Howth and the hbr, and rocks off both pier hds. Howth Sound has 2·4m min depth; give way to FVs (constrained by draught) in the Sound and hbr entrance. 2·5m in marina approach channel.

LIGHTS AND MARKS Baily Lt Ho, Fl 15s 41m 26M, is 1·5M S of Nose of Howth. Disused lt ho on E pier is conspic. E pier lt, Fl (2) WR 7·5s 13m 12/9M; 256°-W-295°, R elsewhere. W sector leads safely to NE pierhead which should be rounded 50m off. Trawler Dock moles are lit QR and Fl G 3s. Marina channel has 8 lateral marks (some lit) and perches with W reflective tape (2 bands = port, 1 = stbd).

COMMUNICATIONS (Code 01) MRCC 6620922/3; ⊖ 8746571; Police 666 4900; Dr 832 3191; ⊞ 837 7755. HM 8322252.

Marina Ch **M** 80. *Howth Harbour* VHF Ch 16 (Mon-Fri 0700–2300).

FACILITIES **Howth Marina** ☎8392777 (HO 0800-2130 Apr-Oct) 350 inc Ⓥ €3·65 (inc ⚡) ⛽ ♠ ⬳ (H24) 🅿 ♦(H24) 🅿 ⬚ 🛒(15t).

Howth YC www.hyc.ie ☎8322141 ⚙ 🅿 Scrubbing posts <20m LOA, ✕(☎8392100) ⬚(☎8320606).

Howth Boat Club (no facilities). **Services** LB, ⬛ Kos, ⚒ ⬘ ⬚ Ⓔ ⬚. **Town** ✉ Ⓑ 🅿 ⇌ ✈ (Dublin).

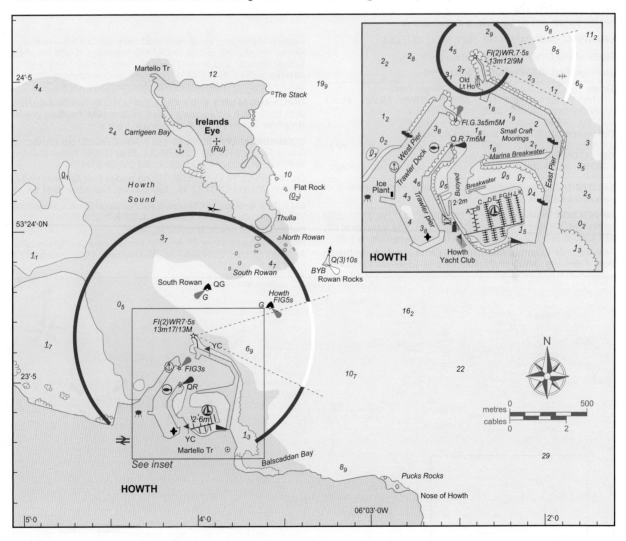

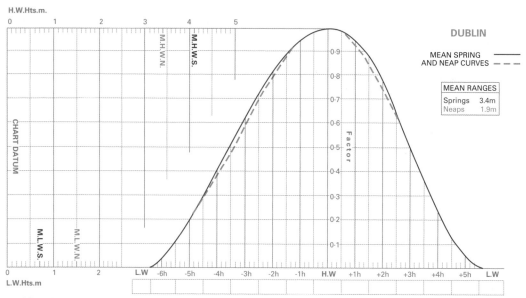

DUBLIN

MEAN SPRING ─────
AND NEAP CURVES ─ ─ ─

MEAN RANGES
Springs 3.4m
Neaps 1.9m

5.8 DUBLIN

Dublin **53°20'·85N 06°14'·80W** ✿✿✿✿◊◊✿✿✿

CHARTS AC 1468, 1415, 1447, 5621; Imray C61, C62

TIDES +0042 Dover; ML 2·4; Duration 0640

Standard Port DUBLIN (NORTH WALL) (⟶)

Times				Height (metres)			
High Water		Low Water		MHWS	MHWN	MLWN	MLWS
0000	0700	0000	0500	4·1	3·4	1·5	0·7
1200	1900	1200	1700				
Differences DUBLIN BAR and DUN LAOGHAIRE							
–0006	–0001	–0002	–0003	0·0	0·0	0·0	+0·1
GREYSTONES (53°09'N 06°04'W)							
–0008	–0008	–0008	–0008	–0·5	–0·4	ND	ND

SHELTER Dublin Port, excellent on Poolbeg YBC Marina, S of Alexandra Basin W.

NAVIGATION Dublin Port WPT 53°20'·50N 06°06'·71W, 275°/1·35M to hbr ent. Accessible H24, but the ent to R Liffey is rough in E'ly >F5 against ebb tide. Note Bull Wall covers 0.6 to 2.7m at HW.

For clearance to enter call *Dublin VTS* Ch 12. Conform to Dublin Port Company Small Craft Regulations (www.dublinport.ie).

Beware of shipping; small craft must keep outside fairway buoys. Yachtsmen wishing to visit Dublin City Moorings, N side between Samuel Beckett and Sean O'Casey Bridges, should check well in advance (+353 1 8183300), as restrictive bridge openings for East Link and especially Samuel Beckett Brs, may preclude this.

LIGHTS AND MARKS Entrance, N. Bull Lt Fl G 4s 15m 10M synchro with Gt. S. Wall Hd Poolbeg Lt Fl R 4s 20m 10M. Poolbeg power stn 2 R/W chimneys (VQ R) are conspic from afar.

COMMUNICATIONS (Code 00 353 1) MRCC 6620922/3; Coast/Cliff Rescue Service 2803900; ⊜2803992; ♨1550 123855; Police (Dublin) 6668000; Dr 2859244; ℍ2806901. HM Dublin 8748771.
Dublin VTS Ch **12** 13 16 (H24). Lifting bridge (call *Eastlink*) Ch 12. *Poolbeg Marina* Ch **37** 12 16. Dublin Coast Radio Stn 16 67 83.

FACILITIES Poolbeg YBC Marina www.poolbegmarina.ie ☎6689983 35♥ (<20m LOA in 2.4m),€3·80, ▬ ⚓ ⍭ 🛢 ⛽ 🛒 ⊠ ✕ 🛏.
Dublin City, all needs, @ at library, ⇌ ✈.
Ferries Holyhead; 4/day; 3¼ hrs; Irish Ferries (www.irishferries.com) & Stena Line (www.stenaline.co.uk). Liverpool; 18/wk (seasonal); 7 hrs; P&O (www.poferries.com).

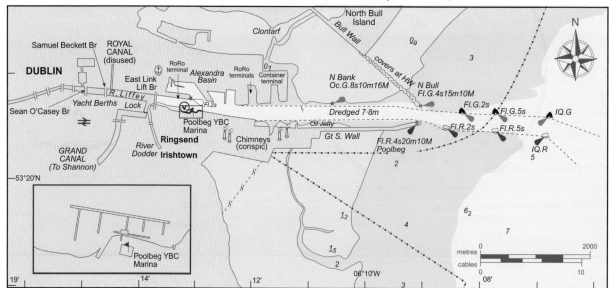

STANDARD TIME (UT)
For Summer Time add ONE hour in **non-shaded areas**

DUBLIN (NORTH WALL)   LAT 53°21'N   LONG 6°13'W
TIMES AND HEIGHTS OF HIGH AND LOW WATERS

Dates in red are **SPRINGS**
Dates in blue are **NEAPS**

YEAR **2016**

S Ireland

JANUARY

Time	m	Time	m
1 0408	3.5	**16** 0357	3.8
0945	1.4	0933	1.0
F 1627	3.7	SA 1613	4.0
2223	1.2	◗ 2209	0.8
2 0508	3.4	**17** 0458	3.7
1044	1.6	1037	1.2
SA 1727	3.5	SU 1715	3.9
◗ 2319	1.3	2315	1.0
3 0612	3.3	**18** 0608	3.7
1146	1.6	1148	1.3
SU 1832	3.4	M 1826	3.8
4 0018	1.4	**19** 0028	1.1
0713	3.4	0721	3.7
M 1251	1.7	TU 1303	1.3
1935	3.4	1941	3.7
5 0121	1.4	**20** 0142	1.2
0810	3.5	0829	3.8
TU 1353	1.6	W 1414	1.2
2032	3.5	2053	3.7
6 0218	1.4	**21** 0249	1.1
0900	3.6	0932	3.9
W 1447	1.4	TH 1517	1.0
2122	3.6	2157	3.8
7 0305	1.2	**22** 0345	1.0
0944	3.8	1026	4.0
TH 1530	1.3	F 1609	0.8
2206	3.7	2251	3.9
8 0344	1.1	**23** 0431	0.9
1022	3.9	1113	4.1
F 1606	1.1	SA 1655	0.7
2245	3.8	2335	3.9
9 0419	0.9	**24** 0511	0.8
1057	4.0	1153	4.1
SA 1641	0.9	SU 1736	0.6
2322	3.9	○	
10 0454	0.8	**25** 0012	3.9
1132	4.1	0547	0.8
SU 1717	0.7	M 1227	4.1
● 2359	4.0	1814	0.6
11 0531	0.7	**26** 0044	3.8
1210	4.2	0621	0.8
M 1756	0.6	TU 1259	4.1
		1851	0.6
12 0039	4.0	**27** 0117	3.8
0610	0.7	0656	0.8
TU 1253	4.3	W 1335	4.0
1838	0.5	1929	0.7
13 0123	4.0	**28** 0154	3.7
0654	0.7	0733	0.9
W 1338	4.3	TH 1413	4.0
1925	0.5	2008	0.8
14 0211	4.0	**29** 0233	3.7
0742	0.8	0813	1.0
TH 1426	4.2	F 1454	3.8
2015	0.6	2049	0.9
15 0302	3.9	**30** 0315	3.6
0835	0.9	0856	1.2
F 1518	4.2	SA 1537	3.7
2110	0.7	2133	1.1
		31 0402	3.4
		0946	1.3
		SU 1625	3.5
		2222	1.3

FEBRUARY

Time	m	Time	m
1 0457	3.3	**16** 0540	3.6
1046	1.5	1123	1.2
M 1723	3.3	TU 1809	3.6
◗ 2320	1.4		
2 0607	3.2	**17** 0000	1.3
1153	1.6	0657	3.5
TU 1839	3.2	W 1242	1.3
		1929	3.5
3 0025	1.5	**18** 0123	1.3
0719	3.3	0811	3.6
W 1301	1.6	TH 1401	1.2
1950	3.3	2044	3.6
4 0131	1.5	**19** 0238	1.2
0820	3.4	0918	3.7
TH 1405	1.5	F 1507	1.0
2050	3.4	2150	3.6
5 0230	1.3	**20** 0334	1.1
0911	3.6	1015	3.9
F 1458	1.2	SA 1558	0.8
2140	3.5	2244	3.7
6 0317	1.1	**21** 0418	0.9
0955	3.8	1102	4.0
SA 1541	1.0	SU 1641	0.7
2222	3.7	2326	3.8
7 0357	0.9	**22** 0457	0.8
1034	4.0	1141	4.0
SU 1619	0.7	M 1719	0.6
2301	3.9	○ 2358	3.8
8 0435	0.7	**23** 0531	0.7
1112	4.2	1210	4.0
M 1657	0.5	TU 1754	0.6
● 2339	4.0		
9 0513	0.5	**24** 0021	3.8
1150	4.3	0602	0.7
TU 1737	0.3	W 1237	4.0
		1827	0.6
10 0018	4.1	**25** 0049	3.8
0552	0.4	0633	0.7
W 1232	4.4	TH 1308	4.0
1819	0.2	1859	0.6
11 0101	4.1	**26** 0121	3.7
0634	0.4	0704	0.7
TH 1317	4.4	F 1342	3.9
1904	0.2	1932	0.7
12 0146	4.1	**27** 0155	3.7
0721	0.5	0736	0.8
F 1404	4.3	SA 1419	3.8
1953	0.4	2005	0.8
13 0235	4.0	**28** 0233	3.6
0812	0.6	0812	0.9
SA 1455	4.2	SU 1459	3.7
2046	0.5	2042	1.0
14 0328	3.9	**29** 0315	3.5
0909	0.8	0853	1.1
SU 1550	4.0	M 1544	3.5
2143	0.8	2124	1.2
15 0428	3.7		
1012	1.0		
M 1653	3.8		
◗ 2246	1.0		

MARCH

Time	m	Time	m
1 0403	3.4	**16** 0514	3.6
0941	1.3	1102	1.1
TU 1635	3.3	W 1756	3.5
◗ 2217	1.4	2333	1.3
2 0500	3.2	**17** 0634	3.5
1047	1.5	1220	1.2
W 1739	3.2	TH 1916	3.4
2329	1.5		
3 0614	3.2	**18** 0059	1.4
1210	1.5	0749	3.5
TH 1904	3.1	F 1343	1.1
		2031	3.5
4 0046	1.5	**19** 0219	1.3
0734	3.2	0858	3.6
F 1323	1.4	SA 1449	1.0
2016	3.3	2136	3.6
5 0154	1.3	**20** 0315	1.2
0835	3.4	0956	3.8
SA 1425	1.1	SU 1539	0.8
2112	3.5	2227	3.6
6 0249	1.1	**21** 0359	1.0
0925	3.7	1043	3.9
SU 1514	0.8	M 1620	0.7
2158	3.7	2307	3.7
7 0334	0.8	**22** 0436	0.8
1008	3.9	1120	3.9
M 1556	0.5	TU 1656	0.6
2238	3.9	2336	3.7
8 0414	0.5	**23** 0510	0.7
1049	4.2	1149	3.9
TU 1636	0.2	W 1729	0.6
2317	4.1	○ 2357	3.7
9 0453	0.3	**24** 0541	0.7
1129	4.3	1214	3.9
W 1717	0.1	TH 1800	0.6
● 2356	4.2		
10 0533	0.2	**25** 0021	3.7
1211	4.4	0609	0.7
TH 1759	0.0	F 1243	3.9
		1829	0.6
11 0037	4.2	**26** 0050	3.8
0615	0.2	0636	0.7
F 1256	4.4	SA 1315	3.8
1843	0.1	1857	0.7
12 0122	4.1	**27** 0123	3.8
0701	0.2	0706	0.7
SA 1344	4.3	SU 1351	3.7
1930	0.3	1928	0.8
13 0210	4.0	**28** 0201	3.7
0752	0.4	0740	0.8
SU 1436	4.1	M 1431	3.6
2022	0.5	2005	0.9
14 0302	3.9	**29** 0243	3.6
0850	0.6	0821	0.9
M 1532	3.9	TU 1515	3.5
2119	0.8	2048	1.1
15 0401	3.7	**30** 0329	3.5
0953	0.8	0908	1.1
TU 1638	3.7	W 1604	3.3
◗ 2221	1.1	2138	1.3
		31 0422	3.3
		1007	1.2
		TH 1704	3.2
		◗ 2243	1.4

APRIL

Time	m	Time	m
1 0526	3.2	**16** 0025	1.5
1125	1.3	0720	3.5
F 1820	3.1	SA 1314	1.1
		2006	3.4
2 0004	1.5	**17** 0146	1.4
0643	3.2	0829	3.6
SA 1245	1.2	SU 1420	1.0
1938	3.3	2110	3.5
3 0118	1.3	**18** 0246	1.3
0755	3.4	0927	3.7
SU 1351	1.0	M 1511	0.9
2039	3.5	2159	3.6
4 0218	1.1	**19** 0332	1.1
0852	3.7	1014	3.8
M 1445	0.7	TU 1553	0.8
2129	3.7	2237	3.6
5 0307	0.8	**20** 0411	0.9
0940	3.9	1052	3.8
TU 1532	0.4	W 1629	0.7
2213	3.9	2306	3.7
6 0350	0.5	**21** 0445	0.8
1025	4.1	1122	3.8
W 1614	0.1	TH 1702	0.7
2254	4.1	2331	3.7
7 0432	0.2	**22** 0517	0.8
1108	4.3	1151	3.8
TH 1656	0.0	F 1732	0.7
● 2334	4.2	○ 2355	3.8
8 0514	0.1	**23** 0545	0.7
1152	4.4	1219	3.8
F 1739	0.0	SA 1759	0.7
9 0016	4.2	**24** 0023	3.8
0558	0.1	0611	0.7
SA 1239	4.3	SU 1251	3.8
1823	0.1	1826	0.8
10 0101	4.2	**25** 0057	3.8
0645	0.2	0640	0.8
SU 1328	4.2	M 1327	3.7
1910	0.3	1859	0.8
11 0149	4.1	**26** 0135	3.8
0737	0.3	0716	0.8
M 1421	4.1	TU 1408	3.6
2002	0.6	1937	0.9
12 0241	3.9	**27** 0218	3.7
0834	0.5	0759	0.9
TU 1519	3.9	W 1453	3.6
2058	0.9	2022	1.0
13 0341	3.8	**28** 0305	3.6
0936	0.7	0848	1.0
W 1625	3.6	TH 1542	3.4
2158	1.1	2114	1.2
14 0451	3.6	**29** 0356	3.5
1042	0.9	0946	1.1
TH 1739	3.5	F 1639	3.3
◗ 2306	1.4	2216	1.3
15 0607	3.5	**30** 0456	3.4
1155	1.1	1056	1.1
F 1854	3.4	SA 1747	3.3
		◗ 2328	1.4

Chart Datum: 0·20 metres above Ordnance Datum (Dublin). HAT is 4·5 metres above Chart Datum.

>> **FREE** monthly updates. Register at <<
www.reedsnauticalalmanac.co.uk

DUBLIN (NORTH WALL) LAT 53°21'N LONG 6°13'W
TIMES AND HEIGHTS OF HIGH AND LOW WATERS

STANDARD TIME (UT)
For Summer Time add ONE hour in **non-shaded areas**

Dates in red are **SPRINGS**
Dates in blue are NEAPS

YEAR 2016

MAY

	Time	m		Time	m
1 SU	0605 1210 1900	3.4 1.1 3.4	**16** M	0058 0749 1340 2028	1.5 3.6 1.1 3.4
2 M	0040 0715 1318 2004	1.3 3.5 0.9 3.5	**17** TU	0205 0847 1435 2118	1.4 3.6 1.0 3.5
3 TU	0144 0817 1416 2059	1.1 3.7 0.6 3.7	**18** W	0258 0936 1520 2158	1.2 3.7 0.9 3.6
4 W	0238 0912 1507 2147	0.8 3.9 0.7 3.9	**19** TH	0340 1017 1558 2232	1.1 3.7 0.8 3.7
5 TH	0327 1002 1553 2232	0.5 4.1 0.2 4.1	**20** F	0417 1053 1632 2303	1.0 3.7 0.8 3.8
6 F ●	0412 1050 1638 2315	0.3 4.3 0.1 4.2	**21** SA ○	0450 1125 1703 2330	0.9 3.7 0.8 3.8
7 SA	0457 1137 1722 2359	0.2 4.3 0.1 4.2	**22** SU	0520 1156 1731 2359	0.9 3.7 0.8 3.8
8 SU	0544 1225 1806	0.2 4.3 0.2	**23** M	0547 1229 1800	0.8 3.7 0.8
9 M	0044 0632 1315 1853	4.2 0.2 4.2 0.4	**24** TU	0033 0618 1306 1835	3.9 0.8 3.7 0.9
10 TU	0132 0724 1408 1943	4.1 0.3 4.0 0.7	**25** W	0114 0656 1348 1915	3.9 0.8 3.7 0.9
11 W	0224 0819 1505 2037	4.0 0.5 3.8 0.9	**26** TH	0157 0741 1433 2001	3.9 0.8 3.7 1.0
12 TH	0322 0918 1607 2134	3.8 0.7 3.6 1.2	**27** F	0245 0832 1523 2054	3.8 0.9 3.6 1.1
13 F ◐	0427 1019 1713 2236	3.7 0.9 3.5 1.4	**28** SA	0336 0929 1618 2152	3.7 0.9 3.5 1.2
14 SA	0536 1124 1821 2343	3.6 1.1 3.4 1.5	**29** SU ◑	0432 1032 1719 2257	3.7 1.0 3.5 1.2
15 SU	0645 1233 1928	3.5 1.1 3.4	**30** M	0534 1139 1825	3.6 0.9 3.5
			31 TU	0005 0640 1246 1930	1.2 3.7 0.8 3.6

JUNE

	Time	m		Time	m
1 W	0110 0745 1348 2030	1.1 3.8 0.7 3.8	**16** TH	0214 0854 1441 2117	1.4 3.6 1.1 3.6
2 TH	0210 0846 1444 2124	0.9 3.9 0.6 3.9	**17** F	0305 0941 1524 2158	1.3 3.6 1.1 3.7
3 F	0305 0942 1535 2214	0.7 4.1 0.4 4.0	**18** SA	0346 1022 1601 2234	1.2 3.7 1.0 3.8
4 SA	0356 1035 1623 2301	0.5 4.2 0.4 4.1	**19** SU	0422 1100 1634 2306	1.1 3.7 0.9 3.8
5 SU ●	0445 1125 1708 2345	0.4 4.2 0.4 4.2	**20** M ○	0453 1134 1705 2337	1.0 3.7 0.9 3.9
6 M	0533 1214 1753	0.3 4.2 0.5	**21** TU	0524 1208 1738	0.9 3.8 0.8
7 TU	0030 0620 1303 1837	4.2 0.4 4.1 0.6	**22** W	0012 0558 1246 1814	4.0 0.8 3.8 0.8
8 W	0117 0710 1352 1924	4.1 0.4 3.9 0.8	**23** TH	0053 0638 1328 1855	4.0 0.8 3.8 0.8
9 TH	0206 0802 1444 2013	4.0 0.5 3.8 0.9	**24** F	0137 0723 1413 1941	4.0 0.7 3.8 0.9
10 F	0258 0856 1538 2106	3.9 0.7 3.6 1.1	**25** SA	0224 0813 1502 2032	4.0 0.7 3.8 1.0
11 SA	0355 0951 1636 2202	3.8 0.9 3.5 1.3	**26** SU	0314 0908 1554 2127	4.0 0.8 3.7 1.0
12 SU ◑	0457 1048 1738 2302	3.7 1.0 3.4 1.4	**27** M	0408 1007 1651 2228	3.9 0.8 3.6 1.1
13 M	0601 1147 1839	3.6 1.1 3.3	**28** TU	0507 1111 1754 2333	3.8 0.9 3.6 1.2
14 TU	0005 0703 1250 1937	1.5 3.5 1.2 3.4	**29** W	0612 1217 1901	3.8 0.9 3.6
15 W	0112 0801 1349 2030	1.5 3.5 1.2 3.5	**30** TH	0041 0720 1323 2006	1.1 3.8 0.9 3.7

JULY

	Time	m		Time	m
1 F	0147 0827 1425 2106	1.1 3.9 0.8 3.9	**16** SA	0225 0907 1448 2125	1.4 3.5 1.3 3.6
2 SA	0250 0930 1522 2201	0.9 3.9 0.7 4.0	**17** SU	0315 0954 1531 2206	1.3 3.6 1.1 3.8
3 SU	0346 1027 1613 2250	0.7 4.0 0.7 4.1	**18** M	0354 1035 1608 2242	1.1 3.7 1.0 3.9
4 M ●	0437 1118 1658 2335	0.6 4.1 0.6 4.2	**19** TU ○	0429 1112 1642 2316	1.0 3.8 0.9 4.0
5 TU	0524 1204 1740	0.5 4.0 0.6	**20** W	0502 1147 1716 2351	1.0 3.8 0.8 4.1
6 W	0017 0609 1248 1821	4.2 0.5 4.0 0.7	**21** TH	0538 1224 1753	0.7 3.9 0.7
7 TH	0059 0654 1331 1902	4.1 0.5 3.9 0.8	**22** F	0030 0618 1306 1833	4.2 0.6 3.9 0.7
8 F	0142 0740 1415 1946	4.1 0.6 3.8 0.9	**23** SA	0114 0702 1350 1918	4.2 0.5 3.9 0.7
9 SA	0227 0828 1501 2033	4.0 0.7 3.6 1.0	**24** SU	0200 0750 1437 2007	4.2 0.6 3.9 0.8
10 SU	0315 0917 1550 2124	3.8 0.9 3.5 1.2	**25** M	0250 0844 1528 2101	4.1 0.6 3.8 0.9
11 M	0408 1008 1644 2219	3.7 1.0 3.4 1.4	**26** TU	0343 0941 1623 2201	4.0 0.8 3.8 1.0
12 TU ◑	0507 1101 1745 2317	3.5 1.2 3.3 1.5	**27** W	0441 1043 1726 2306	3.9 0.9 3.7 1.1
13 W	0612 1158 1847	3.4 1.3 3.3	**28** TH	0548 1151 1837	3.8 1.0 3.6
14 TH	0020 0716 1257 1945	1.6 3.4 1.4 3.4	**29** F	0018 0703 1302 1948	1.2 3.7 1.1 3.7
15 F	0124 0814 1356 2038	1.5 3.4 1.3 3.5	**30** SA	0132 0818 1412 2054	1.2 3.7 1.1 3.8
			31 SU	0241 0925 1513 2153	1.0 3.8 1.0 3.9

AUGUST

	Time	m		Time	m
1 M	0340 1023 1604 2243	0.9 3.9 0.9 4.1	**16** TU	0328 1012 1543 2217	1.1 3.7 1.0 3.9
2 TU ●	0430 1113 1648 2326	0.7 3.9 0.8 4.1	**17** W	0404 1049 1619 2253	0.9 3.8 0.8 4.1
3 W	0515 1155 1727	0.6 3.9 0.7	**18** TH ○	0440 1125 1654 2329	0.6 3.9 0.7 4.2
4 TH	0003 0555 1231 1803	4.1 0.5 3.9 0.7	**19** F	0516 1202 1732	0.4 4.0 0.5
5 F	0037 0634 1305 1839	4.1 0.5 3.8 0.8	**20** SA	0007 0555 1242 1811	4.3 0.3 4.1 0.5
6 SA	0113 0714 1341 1917	4.1 0.6 3.8 0.9	**21** SU	0049 0638 1324 1855	4.4 0.3 4.1 0.5
7 SU	0153 0754 1421 1957	4.0 0.7 3.7 1.0	**22** M	0135 0726 1411 1943	4.3 0.3 4.0 0.6
8 M	0234 0838 1503 2042	3.9 0.8 3.6 1.1	**23** TU	0224 0817 1501 2037	4.2 0.5 3.9 0.8
9 TU	0319 0924 1548 2132	3.7 1.0 3.5 1.3	**24** W	0318 0915 1556 2138	4.1 0.8 3.8 1.0
10 W ◑	0409 1014 1641 2228	3.5 1.2 3.4 1.4	**25** TH ◑	0418 1018 1700 2245	3.9 0.9 3.7 1.1
11 TH	0511 1109 1746 2332	3.4 1.4 3.3 1.6	**26** F	0531 1128 1817	3.7 1.2 3.6
12 F	0627 1210 1858	3.3 1.5 3.3	**27** SA	0001 0655 1245 1933	1.3 3.6 1.3 3.6
13 SA	0039 0737 1313 2001	1.6 3.3 1.5 3.4	**28** SU	0122 0813 1400 2043	1.2 3.6 1.3 3.8
14 SU	0146 0837 1413 2054	1.5 3.4 1.4 3.6	**29** M	0235 0921 1503 2144	1.1 3.7 1.1 3.9
15 M	0244 0928 1503 2139	1.3 3.5 1.2 3.7	**30** TU	0332 1019 1552 2234	0.9 3.8 1.0 4.0
			31 W	0419 1105 1634 2315	0.7 3.9 0.9 4.1

Chart Datum: 0·20 metres above Ordnance Datum (Dublin). HAT is 4·5 metres above Chart Datum.

STANDARD TIME (UT)
For Summer Time add ONE hour in **non-shaded areas**

DUBLIN (NORTH WALL)   LAT 53°21'N   LONG 6°13'W

TIMES AND HEIGHTS OF HIGH AND LOW WATERS

Dates in red are **SPRINGS**
Dates in blue are NEAPS

YEAR 2016

S Ireland

SEPTEMBER

Time	m		Time	m
1 0459	0.6	**16** 0416	0.4
1143	3.9	1101	4.1
TH 1710	1.0	F 1632	0.5
● 2347	4.1	○ 2305	4.3
2 0536	0.5	**17** 0454	0.2
1211	3.8	1138	4.2
F 1744	0.7	SA 1710	0.4
		2344	4.4
3 0014	4.1	**18** 0534	0.1
0610	0.6	1217	4.2
SA 1238	3.8	SU 1751	0.3
1815	0.7		
4 0046	4.0	**19** 0026	4.5
0644	0.6	0615	0.2
SU 1309	3.8	M 1259	4.2
1848	0.8	1834	0.3
5 0121	4.0	**20** 0112	4.4
0719	0.7	0701	0.3
M 1344	3.8	TU 1346	4.1
1923	0.9	1922	0.5
6 0159	3.9	**21** 0202	4.2
0755	0.9	0753	0.6
TU 1423	3.7	W 1436	4.0
2001	1.0	2017	0.7
7 0240	3.7	**22** 0258	4.2
0835	1.0	0850	0.8
W 1504	3.6	TH 1533	3.9
2043	1.2	2119	0.9
8 0326	3.6	**23** 0402	3.8
0921	1.2	0955	1.1
TH 1550	3.5	F 1639	3.7
2133	1.4	◑ 2229	1.1
9 0419	3.4	**24** 0522	3.6
1017	1.4	1106	1.3
F 1645	3.3	SA 1758	3.6
◑ 2240	1.5	2346	1.2
10 0530	3.2	**25** 0646	3.5
1124	1.6	1226	1.5
SA 1759	3.3	SU 1916	3.7
2357	1.6		
11 0658	3.2	**26** 0109	1.2
1234	1.6	0803	3.6
SU 1919	3.3	M 1345	1.4
		2026	3.8
12 0108	1.5	**27** 0221	1.1
0807	3.3	0911	3.7
M 1340	1.5	TU 1446	1.3
2020	3.5	2127	3.9
13 0212	1.3	**28** 0316	0.9
0902	3.5	1005	3.8
TU 1434	1.3	W 1534	1.1
2109	3.7	2217	4.0
14 0300	1.0	**29** 0400	0.7
0947	3.7	1049	3.9
W 1517	1.0	TH 1614	0.9
2150	3.9	2258	4.1
15 0339	0.7	**30** 0439	0.6
1025	3.9	1124	3.9
TH 1555	0.7	F 1650	0.8
2228	4.2	2328	4.1

OCTOBER

Time	m		Time	m
1 0513	0.6	**16** 0432	0.2
1149	3.9	1115	4.3
SA 1723	0.8	SU 1650	0.3
● 2354	4.0	○ 2324	4.5
2 0545	0.6	**17** 0513	0.1
1212	3.8	1155	4.3
SU 1754	0.8	M 1732	0.2
3 0022	4.0	**18** 0007	4.5
0615	0.7	0555	0.2
M 1241	3.9	TU 1238	4.3
1823	0.8	1817	0.3
4 0055	3.9	**19** 0055	4.4
0645	0.8	0641	0.4
TU 1314	3.8	W 1325	4.2
1854	0.9	1907	0.4
5 0131	3.9	**20** 0147	4.2
0716	0.9	0732	0.6
W 1350	3.8	TH 1417	4.1
1928	1.0	2002	0.6
6 0211	3.7	**21** 0245	4.0
0753	1.1	0829	0.9
TH 1431	3.7	F 1515	4.0
2008	1.1	2104	0.9
7 0255	3.6	**22** 0352	3.8
0835	1.2	0932	1.2
F 1516	3.6	SA 1621	3.8
2054	1.3	◑ 2211	1.1
8 0346	3.4	**23** 0509	3.6
0928	1.4	1042	1.4
SA 1607	3.5	SU 1736	3.7
2153	1.4	2325	1.2
9 0448	3.2	**24** 0627	3.5
1037	1.6	1159	1.5
SU 1709	3.3	M 1850	3.7
◑ 2311	1.5		
10 0611	3.2	**25** 0045	1.2
1154	1.7	0742	3.6
M 1826	3.3	TU 1318	1.5
		2000	3.8
11 0029	1.5	**26** 0156	1.1
0729	3.3	0848	3.7
TU 1303	1.5	W 1421	1.4
1936	3.5	2101	3.9
12 0135	1.2	**27** 0251	1.0
0829	3.5	0941	3.8
W 1401	1.3	TH 1510	1.2
2032	3.7	2152	4.0
13 0228	0.9	**28** 0336	0.8
0917	3.7	1024	3.9
TH 1448	1.0	F 1552	1.1
2119	4.0	2233	4.0
14 0312	0.6	**29** 0414	0.8
0958	4.0	1058	3.9
F 1530	0.7	SA 1629	1.0
2201	4.2	2305	4.0
15 0353	0.3	**30** 0448	0.7
1036	4.1	1124	3.9
SA 1610	0.5	SU 1702	0.9
2242	4.4	● 2334	4.0
		31 0520	0.8
		1149	3.9
		M 1734	0.9

NOVEMBER

Time	m		Time	m
1 0002	3.9	**16** 0540	0.3
0548	0.8	1222	4.4
TU 1217	3.9	W 1805	0.3
1803	0.9		
2 0034	3.9	**17** 0043	4.3
0616	0.9	0625	0.5
W 1249	3.9	TH 1310	4.3
1832	0.9	1855	0.4
3 0109	3.8	**18** 0136	4.2
0646	1.0	0715	0.7
TH 1325	3.9	F 1402	4.2
1904	1.0	1949	0.6
4 0148	3.7	**19** 0234	4.0
0722	1.1	0809	1.0
F 1405	3.8	SA 1458	4.1
1943	1.1	2048	0.8
5 0232	3.6	**20** 0337	3.8
0804	1.2	0909	1.2
SA 1450	3.7	SU 1600	3.9
2029	1.2	2150	1.0
6 0322	3.5	**21** 0446	3.6
0855	1.4	1012	1.4
SU 1539	3.6	M 1708	3.8
2123	1.3	◑ 2255	1.1
7 0419	3.4	**22** 0557	3.5
0956	1.5	1122	1.6
M 1635	3.5	TU 1816	3.7
◑ 2230	1.4		
8 0528	3.3	**23** 0007	1.2
1110	1.6	0706	3.5
TU 1739	3.5	W 1237	1.6
2345	1.3	1922	3.7
9 0643	3.4	**24** 0118	1.2
1222	1.5	0810	3.6
W 1848	3.6	TH 1345	1.5
		2024	3.8
10 0054	1.2	**25** 0218	1.1
0748	3.6	0905	3.7
TH 1324	1.4	F 1441	1.4
1950	3.7	2117	3.8
11 0154	0.9	**26** 0307	1.0
0841	3.8	0949	3.8
F 1417	1.1	SA 1527	1.2
2045	4.0	2202	3.9
12 0244	0.7	**27** 0348	1.0
0928	3.9	1025	3.9
SA 1504	0.9	SU 1606	1.1
2135	4.2	2239	3.9
13 0330	0.4	**28** 0423	0.9
1012	4.2	1057	3.9
SU 1549	0.6	M 1642	1.0
2222	4.3	2313	3.9
14 0413	0.3	**29** 0455	0.9
1055	4.3	1127	4.0
M 1633	0.4	TU 1714	1.0
○ 2308	4.4	● 2344	3.9
15 0456	0.2	**30** 0525	0.9
1138	4.4	1156	4.0
TU 1718	0.3	W 1744	1.0
2354	4.4		

DECEMBER

Time	m		Time	m
1 0015	3.8	**16** 0035	4.2
0552	1.0	0612	0.6
TH 1227	4.0	F 1257	4.4
1812	1.0	1844	0.4
2 0050	3.8	**17** 0125	4.1
0622	1.0	0659	0.7
F 1302	4.0	SA 1346	4.3
1845	1.0	1935	0.5
3 0128	3.8	**18** 0218	4.0
0658	1.1	0748	0.9
SA 1343	4.0	SU 1438	4.2
1924	1.0	2027	0.7
4 0212	3.7	**19** 0313	3.8
0740	1.2	0842	1.1
SU 1427	3.9	M 1532	4.0
2008	1.0	2122	0.8
5 0259	3.6	**20** 0412	3.6
0828	1.3	0939	1.3
M 1515	3.8	TU 1631	3.9
2059	1.1	2219	1.0
6 0352	3.6	**21** 0515	3.5
0924	1.4	1040	1.5
TU 1607	3.8	W 1734	3.7
2157	1.1	◑ 2320	1.2
7 0451	3.5	**22** 0619	3.5
1027	1.5	1145	1.6
W 1704	3.7	TH 1837	3.6
◑ 2302	1.2		
8 0557	3.5	**23** 0026	1.3
1136	1.5	0720	3.5
TH 1806	3.7	F 1257	1.6
		1938	3.6
9 0012	1.1	**24** 0134	1.3
0704	3.6	0817	3.6
F 1244	1.4	SA 1404	1.5
1911	3.8	2036	3.6
10 0118	1.0	**25** 0232	1.3
0805	3.8	0907	3.6
SA 1345	1.2	SU 1459	1.4
2013	3.9	2127	3.7
11 0217	0.8	**26** 0319	1.2
0900	3.9	0951	3.8
SU 1441	1.0	M 1543	1.3
2112	4.1	2211	3.7
12 0310	0.6	**27** 0358	1.1
0951	4.1	1029	3.9
M 1532	0.7	TU 1621	1.2
2206	4.2	2250	3.7
13 0358	0.5	**28** 0431	1.1
1039	4.3	1104	3.9
TU 1621	0.5	W 1654	1.1
2257	4.3	2325	3.8
14 0444	0.5	**29** 0502	1.0
1125	4.4	1136	4.0
W 1709	0.4	TH 1724	1.0
○ 2346	4.3	● 2357	3.8
15 0528	0.5	**30** 0531	1.0
1210	4.4	1206	4.0
TH 1756	0.4	F 1753	0.9
		31 0030	3.8
		0601	0.9
		SA 1241	4.1
		1825	0.9

Chart Datum: 0·20 metres above Ordnance Datum (Dublin). HAT is 4·5 metres above Chart Datum.

》》 **FREE** monthly updates. Register at 《
www.reedsnauticalalmanac.co.uk 《

179

5.9 DUN LAOGHAIRE

Dublin (Port ent) 53°18'·16N 06°07'·68W ❀❀❀♟♟♟❁❁

CHARTS AC 1468, 1415, 1447, 5621; Imray C61, C62

TIDES +0042 Dover; ML 2·4; Duration 0640
Standard Port DUBLIN (NORTH WALL) (←)

Times				Height (metres)			
High Water		Low Water		MHWS	MHWN	MLWN	MLWS
0000	0700	0000	0500	4·1	3·4	1·5	0·7
1200	1900	1200	1700				
Differences DUBLIN BAR and DUN LAOGHAIRE							
0000	0000	+0002	+0003	0·0	+0·1	0·0	0·0
GREYSTONES (53°09'N 06°04'W)							
–0008	–0008	–0008	–0008	–0·5	–0·4	ND	ND

SHELTER Excellent. Breakwaters within main hbr protect 800+ berth marina from ferry wash. ❶ berths on end of pontoons or as directed. Additional berths inside Western Marina Breakwater. All YCs advertise ❶s and/or pontoon berths.

NAVIGATION Dun Laoghaire WPT 53°18'·40N 06°07'·00W, 240°/ 0·47M to ent. Accessible H24 Keep clear of commercial traffic turning off St Michael's Pier. Beware drying rks around E Pier Hd. **TSS:** Two TSS ½M long, one at either end of the Burford Bank lead to/from an anti-clockwise circular TSS radius 2·3ca centred on Dublin Bay SWM lt buoy (53°19'·90N 06°04'·58W, 2·5M NE of Dun Laoghaire/ 2·75M ESE of Dublin Port). Do not impede large vessels and keep clear of the TSS and fairway.

LIGHTS AND MARKS Ro Ro Berth 2 x Fl.W = 'Large vessel under way; small craft keep clear of No 1 Fairway (out to 600m seaward of ent). Traffic signals (Fl W) repeated at head of E Marina Breakwater. Marina Breakwater Hds marked by sync lts Fl G 2s and Fl R 2s.

COMMUNICATIONS (Code 00 353 1) MRCC 6620922/3; Coast/ Cliff Rescue Service 2803900; ⊖ 2803992; ♨ 1550 123855; Police 6665000; Dr 2859244; ⊞ 2806901. HM Dun Laoghaire 2801130.
Dun Laoghaire Hbr VHF Ch **14** 16 (H24); Marina Ch **M**; YCs Ch **M**. Dublin Coast Radio Stn 16 67 83.

FACILITIES Dun Laoghaire Harbour Marina, www.dlmarina.com
☎2020040; 800 � inc 20❶ €3.75, €5.00<6hrs, ♿◎♠▥☐.
Town ♠♨✖Ⓔ◫◪ ACA.

YACHT CLUBS (E→W):
Irish National SC ☎28444195.
National YC ☎2805725, ⊷ ♠◣⊤♠ ⌂(12t) ✖☐.
Royal St George YC ☎2801811, Boatman ☎2801208; ⌂ by prior agreement, €3.60, ⊷ ♠◣⊤♟ ⌂(5t) ✖☐.
Royal Irish YC ☎2809452, ♠◣⊷⊤♠ ⌂(5t) ✖☐.
Dun Laoghaire Motor YC ☎2801371, ⊷ ⌂⊷⊤ ✖☐.

ADJACENT HARBOUR

GREYSTONES 53°09'·05N 06°03'·80W midway between Dun Laoghaire and Wicklow. Harbour ent open to large seas in NE winds, with scend in outer basin. The redeveloped harbour encloses **Greystones Marina,** info@greystonesharbourmarina.ie ☎353 (086) 2718161; 100 ⌂, ❶ facilities tbc in N Basin.

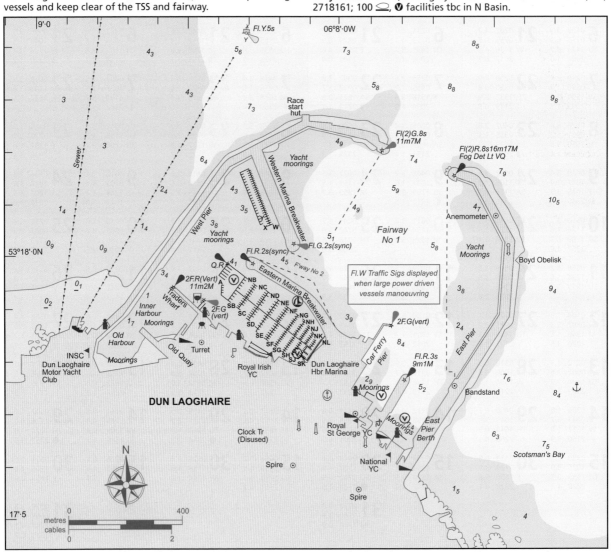

5.10 WICKLOW

Wicklow **52°58'·98N 06°02'·70W** ❀❀⊙♎♒♧♧

CHARTS AC 1468, 633, 5621; Imray C61

TIDES −0010 Dover; ML 1·7; Duration 0640

Standard Port DUBLIN (NORTH WALL) (←)

Times				Height (metres)			
High Water		Low Water		MHWS	MHWN	MLWN	MLWS
0000	0700	0000	0500	4·1	3·4	1·5	0·7
1200	1900	1200	1700				
Differences WICKLOW							
−0019	−0019	−0024	−0026	−1·4	−1·1	−0·4	0·0

SHELTER Very safe, access H24. Outer hbr is open to NE winds which cause a swell. Moorings in NW of hbr belong to SC and may not be used without permission. 4 berths on E Pier (2·5m) are convenient except in strong winds NW to NE, with fender boards/ladders provided. W pier is not recommended. ⚓ in hbr is restricted by ships' turning circle. Inner hbr (river) gives excellent shelter in 2·5m on N and S Quays, which are used by FVs. Packet Quay is for ships (2·5m), but may be used if none due; fender board needed. Yachts should berth on N or S quays as directed and/or space available.

NAVIGATION WPT 52°59'·20N 06°01'·80W, 220°/0·27M to ent. Appr presents no difficulty; keep in the R sector of the E pier lt to avoid Planet Rk and Pogeen Rk.

LIGHTS AND MARKS W pier head lt, Iso G 4s, is shown H24. ☆ Fl WG 10s on Packet Quay hd is vis 076°-G-256°-W-076°.

COMMUNICATIONS (Code 0404) MRCC (01) 6620922; Cliff Rescue

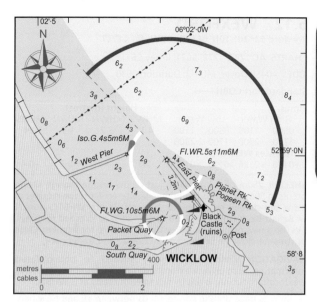

Service 086 8686009; ⊖ 67222; Police 60140; Dr 67381. HM 67455. Ch 12, **14**, 16. Wicklow SC Ch M 16 (occas).

FACILITIES East Pier, S and N Quays,⚓⚓⊆ €14.00/craft⚓🔧🛒 (bulk: see HM). **Wicklow SC** ☎67526, ⚓ (except LWS) ⚓⚓⚓🛒.

Service ⛽ Kos ⚒ 🖼 🛥. **Town** ✉ Ⓑ 🏦 🛒 ✕ 🖂 ≈ ✈(Dublin).

5.11 ARKLOW

Wicklow **52°47'·60N 06°08'·20W** ❀❀⊙♎♒♧♧

CHARTS AC 1468, 633, 5621; Imray C61

TIDES −0150 Dover; ML 1·0; Duration 0640

Standard Port DUBLIN (NORTH WALL) (←)

Times				Height (metres)			
High Water		Low Water		MHWS	MHWN	MLWN	MLWS
0000	0700	0000	0500	4·1	3·4	1·5	0·7
1200	1900	1200	1700				
Differences ARKLOW (Note small Range)							
−0315	−0201	−0140	−0134	−2·7	−2·2	−0·6	−0·1
COURTOWN							
−0328	−0242	−0158	−0138	−2·8	−2·4	−0·5	0·0

SHELTER Good, access H24. **Arklow Roadstone Hbr,** 1M S of Arklow, is not for yachts.

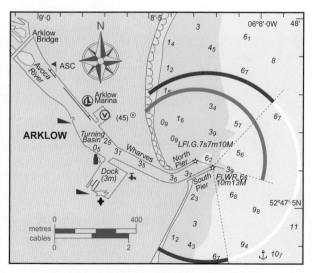

- Strong E'ly winds make the entrance unsafe and cause significant turbulence in the river.

A 60 berth marina lies on NE side of river. Good ⚓ in bay; avoid whelk pots. One ⊆ in 1.2m at ASC quay. ⊆ on SE wall of Dock (ent is 13·5m wide; 3m depth) in perfect shelter, but amidst FVs.

NAVIGATION WPT 52°47'·60N 06°07'·50W, 270°/0·40M to ent. No navigational dangers, but beware ebb setting SE across hbr ent; give S pierhd a wide berth. Ent is difficult without power, due to blanking by piers. 3kn speed limit. Night entry, see below. Caution: Upriver of Dock ent keep to NE side of river.

LIGHTS AND MARKS No ldg lts/marks, see 5.3 and chartlet Conspic factory chy 2·5ca NW of piers.

- Beware the Pier Hd lts are very difficult to see due to powerful orange flood lts near the root of both piers shining E/ENE onto them (to assist pilotage of departing shipping).
- Best advice to visitors is to approach from the NE with R sector just showing, or enter by day.

COMMUNICATIONS (Code 0402) MRCC (01) 6620922/3; ⊖ 67222; Cliff Rescue Service 32430; RNLI 32901; Police 32304; Dr 32421. HM 32466.

Marina Ch 16 12 (HJ); Arklow SC Ch 10.

FACILITIES Dock €15.00/craft (2nd day free), use 🚾/🚿 in LB Hse, ⛽ (Dock ent, HO); **Arklow SC** (NE bank, 500m upriver) 🛥; **Marina** ☎087 258 8078, 60⊆ inc Ⓥ €3·35. **Services** ⚓ ✕ ⚒ 🖼 🛥(20t) Kos. **Town** 🖼 🖼 limited 🏦 ✉ Ⓑ 🛒 ✕ 🖂 @ ≈ ✈(Dublin).

MINOR HARBOURS S OF ARKLOW
COURTOWN, Wexford, **52°38'·55N 06°13'·50W.** AC 1787. 9.6M S of Arklow is feasible in settled weather and offshore winds. Caution: 10m wide ent; only 1m (maintained by local YC) at MLWS due to silting. ⊆ on E wall or pick up vacant mooring.

POLDUFF PIER, Wexford, **52°34'·15N 06°11'·97W.** AC 1787. 14M S of Arklow. Pier, extends 100m NE from shore. NW side of pier has slipway from shore and 1m depth alongside. Local moorings W of pier. Good shelter for small boats in S to W winds. Swell in winds E of S. Appr in daylight only. Appr is clear from NE to E. Rks extend from shore E'ward 200m N of pier but steering along line of pier will clear them. Pub near pier. Village (Ballygarrett) 1·25M W.

5.12 WEXFORD

Wexford 52°20'·10N 06°27'·00W ✿◊◊✿✿

CHARTS AC 1787, 1772, 5621; Imray C61

TIDES –0450 Dover; ML 1·3; Duration 0630

Standard Port COBH (→)

Times				Height (metres)			
High Water		Low Water		MHWS	MHWN	MLWN	MLWS
0500	1100	0500	1100	4·1	3·2	1·3	0·4
1700	2300	1700	2300				
Differences WEXFORD							
+0126	+0126	+0118	+0108	–2·1	–1·7	–0·3	+0·1

SHELTER 250m of ⌓ available just below bridge though silting occurs in 50m closest to the bridge. Sheltered ⚓ off town quays in 2·3m, but streams are strong. ✪s are provided by WHBTC, close N of Ballast Bank (☎053 9122039 or Ch 16/69) or proceed to quays. FVs use a new quay on E bank with ⚓ and space for ■tanker. Close upstream below the bridge is an all-tide ⤙ and trailer park.

NAVIGATION Visitors are strongly advised to obtain latest information from www.wexfordharbour.com another site www. wexfordharbour.info is run by sailing enthusiasts as is WHBTC.

- Entry is hazardous in strong winds between SE and NE when the sea breaks on the bar.
- For strangers best entry is HW±2. It is difficult at any time for vessels with a draught >1.3m.

- Maintain a course on the rhumb line between marks as channel is narrow in places. Beware the S training wall (covers) and pass well S of Black Man SHM Bn at end of N training wall.
- To Wexford Bar SWM (52°19'·14N 06°19·39W): make good 214°/2·7M from North Long Buoy; from S make good 353°/3·4M from West Holdens Buoy. SWM is on 10m contour and marks the start of the buoyed channel to Wexford.

LIGHTS AND MARKS The narrow channel frequently shifts and marks are moved accordingly; positions on the chartlet are not reliable. They are sequentially numbered from 2–30. Outer channel buoys Nos 2–9 in position from Apr–Oct are removed seasonally; see www.wexfordharbour.com The 2 church spires / Opera Ho (conspic) at Wexford give useful general orientation. There are no ldg lts.

COMMUNICATIONS (Code 053) MRCC (01) 6620922/3; ⊜ 9133116; Police 9122333; Dr 9122524; ⊞ 9142233. Wexford Hbr BC 9122039. HM 9122300, email: harbourmaster@wexfordcoco.ie.

Wexford Hbr listening watch VHF 16, 09 (HO).

FACILITIES HM Capt Paul Murphy, based in Ballast Office on Crescent Quay, is the Marine Officer responsible for all Co. Wexford harbours except Rosslare Europort.

Wexford Quays ⤙ ⌓(free) ⚓ ⬛ delivery by road tanker ⚒ ⬚ 🛢.

Wexford Harbour Boat & Tennis Club, www.whbtc.ie ☎086 8131783, ⤙ ⍟(5t) ⬚.

Town ✉ Ⓑ 🛒 ⇌ ✈ (Waterford).

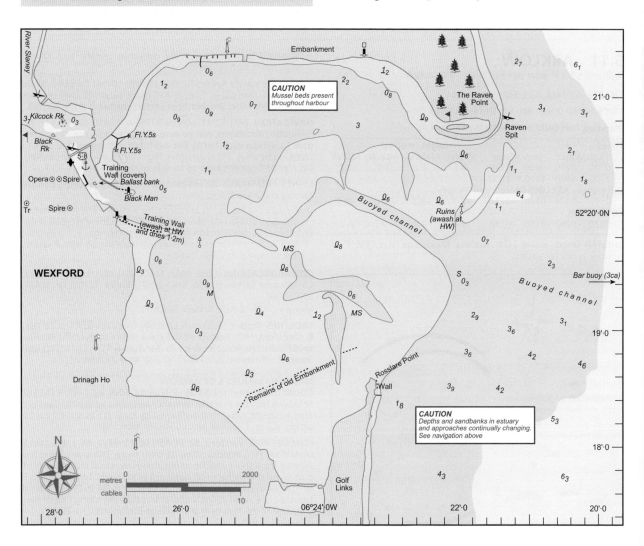

5.13 ROSSLARE ✿✿✿🌊✿✿

Dublin **52°15'·30N 06°20'·90W**

CHARTS AC 1787, 1772, 5621; Imray C61, C57

TIDES –0510 Dover; ML 1·1; Duration 0640

Standard Port COBH (→)

Times				Height (metres)			
High Water		Low Water		MHWS	MHWN	MLWN	MLWS
0500	1100	0500	1100	4·1	3·2	1·3	0·4
1700	2300	1700	2300				
Differences ROSSLARE EUROPORT							
+0045	+0035	+0015	–0005	–2·2	–1·8	–0·5	–0·1

SHELTER Useful passage shelter from SW'lies, but few facilities for yachts which may berth on E wall of marshalling area (⚓ on the chartlet, 3·7m), or ⚓ clear of harbour to the west. *Small craft harbour (5ca W) is not recommended in onshore winds and can become dangerous if winds freshen.* Rosslare Europort has 80 ferry movements per week.

NAVIGATION WPT 52°14'·70N 06°15'·80W (abeam S Long SHM buoy, Fl(2) G 6s), 287°/2·9M to 1ca N of breakwater light. Main approach from E, S and W is via S Shear, buoyed/lit chan to S of Holden's Bed, a shoal of varying depth; the tide sets across the chan. From S, beware rks off Greenore Pt, and overfalls here and over The Baillies. From the N, appr via N Shear. Tuskar TSS is approx 8M ESE of hbr. Yachts, bound N/S, will usually pass to the W of Tuskar Rk where the 3·5M wide chan lies to seaward of The Bailies. A passage inshore of The Bailies requires local knowledge and is not recommended at night. In heavy weather or poor vis, passage E of Tuskar Rk is advised.

LIGHTS AND MARKS Tuskar Rk, Q (2) 7·5s 33m 28M, is 5·8M SE of hbr. Water tr (R lt, 35m) is conspic 0·8M SSE of hbr ent. Bkwtr lt, Oc WRG 5s 15m 13/10M, see 5.3. Its two W sectors (188°-208° and 283°-286°) cover N and S Shear respectively. Note: Powerful floodlights in the hbr make identification of navigational lights difficult.

ROSSLARE EUROPORT

COMMUNICATIONS (Code 053) MRCC (01) 6620922/3; LB Lookout Stn 9133205; ⊖ 9133116; Police 053 9165200; Dr 9131154; Ⓗ 9142233. HM 9157921, mobile 087 2320251. Call on VHF Ch 12 (H24) before entering hbr.

FACILITIES Hbr Ops ☎9157929, No dues, ⚓⚓ (by hose on berths 2 and 3) 🏧🏧 Kos ⚒ 🅿️ 🛠 Divers. **Village** 🍴 ✕ 🏪 ✉ Ⓑ ⇌ ✈ (Dublin). **Ferries** Irish Ferries (www.irish ferries.com): Pembroke Dock, 2/day, 4 hrs; Cherbourg, 2 or 3/week, 18½ hrs; Roscoff, 1 or 2/week, 17½ hrs (seasonal). Stena (www.stenaline.co.uk): Fishguard, 2/day, 1¾ hrs.

TUSKAR ROCK TO COBH

(AC 2049) Dangerous rks lie up to 2ca NW and 6½ca SSW of Tuskar Rk and there can be a dangerous race off Carnsore Pt. In bad weather or poor visibility, use the Inshore Traffic Zone of the Tuskar Rock TSS, passing to seaward of Tuskar Rk (lt), the Barrels ECM lt buoy and Coningbeg buoy.

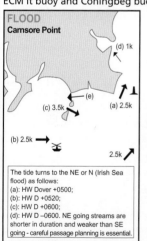

FLOOD
Carnsore Point

(d) 1k
(c) 3.5k (e) (a) 2.5k
(b) 2.5k
2.5k

The tide turns to the NE or N (Irish Sea flood) as follows:
(a): HW Dover +0500;
(b): HW D +0520;
(c): HW D +0600;
(d): HW D –0600. NE going streams are shorter in duration and weaker than SE going - careful passage planning is essential.

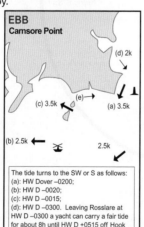

EBB
Carnsore Point

(d) 2k
(c) 3.5k (e) (a) 3.5k
(b) 2.5k 2.5k

The tide turns to the SW or S as follows:
(a): HW Dover –0200;
(b): HW D –0020;
(c): HW D –0015;
(d): HW D –0300. Leaving Rosslare at HW D –0300 a yacht can carry a fair tide for about 8h until HW D +0515 off Hook Head.

NOTE: The tide turns on St Patrick's Bridge (e) up to 2 hours earlier than in Saltee Sound

If taking the inshore passage from Greenore Pt, stay inside The Bailies to pass 2ca off Carnsore Pt. Beware of lobster pots. Steer WSW to pass N of Black Rk and the Bohurs, S of which are extensive overfalls. The small hbr of Kilmore Quay has been rebuilt with a marina, but beware rks and shoals in the approaches.

Saltee Sound (AC 2740) is a safe passage, least width 3ca, between Great and Little Saltee, conspic islands to S and N. ▶ *Sebber Bridge extends 7½ca N from the NE point of Great Saltee and Jackeen Rk is 1M NW of the S end of Little Saltee, so care is needed through the sound, where the stream runs 3·5kn at sp.* ◀

There are several rks S of the Saltees, but clear passage between many of them. There are no obstructions on a direct course for a point 1M S of Hook Head, clear of Tower Race which forms when the ebb (from Waterford Hbr) is stronger than the W going stream. In strong W winds Tower Race can be violent. Overfalls occur off Waterford Hbr entrance (AC2046) when the W'ly stream begins off Hook Hd and meets the strong outgoing stream from Waterford Hbr.

Dunmore East (AC 2046) is a useful passage port at the mouth of Waterford Hbr. To the W, beware Falskirt, a dangerous rk off Swines Pt. There are few offlying rocks from Tramore Bay to Ballinacourty Pt on the N side of Dungarvan Bay (AC 2017). Helvick is a small sheltered hbr approached along the S shore of the bay, keeping S of Helvick Rk (ECM lt buoy) and other dangers to the N.

Mine Hd (lt) has two dangerous rks, The Rogue about 2½ca E and The Longship 1M SW. To the W is a subm'gd rk 100m SE of Ram Hd. ▶ *Here the W-going stream starts at HW Cobh +0230, and the E-going at HW Cobh –0215, sp rates 1·5kn.* ◀ Pass 2ca off Capel Island; the sound between it and Knockadoon Hd is not recommended.

The N side of Ballycotton B is foul up to 5ca offshore. Ballycotton Hbr is small and crowded, but usually there is sheltered ⚓ outside. Sound Rk and Small Is lie between the mainland and Ballycotton Is (lit). From Ballycotton to Cork keep at least 5ca off for dangers including The Smiths (PHM lt buoy) 1·5M WSW of Ballycotton Island. Pass between Hawk Rk, close off Power Hd, and Pollock Rk (PHM lt buoy) 1.25M SE.

5.14 KILMORE QUAY

Wexford **52°10'·25N 06°35'·15W** ❀❀❀◊◊☆☆☆

CHARTS AC 2049, 2740, 5621; Imray C61, C57

TIDES –0535 Dover; ML No data; Duration 0605

Standard Port COBH (→)

Times				Height (metres)			
High Water		Low Water		MHWS	MHWN	MLWN	MLWS
0500	1100	0500	1100	4·1	3·2	1·3	0·4
1700	2300	1700	2300				
Differences BAGINBUN HEAD (5M NE of Hook Hd)							
+0003	+0003	–0008	–0008	–0·2	–0·1	+0·2	+0·2
GREAT SALTEE							
+0019	+0009	–0004	+0006	–0·3	–0·4	ND	ND
CARNSORE POINT							
+0029	+0019	–0002	+0008	–1·1	–1·0	ND	ND

SHELTER Excellent in marina (3m depth) with 0.8m below CD at LAT in ent. Hbr exposed to SE'lies. FVs berth on E and W piers close S of marina.

NAVIGATION WPT 52°09'·22N 06°35'·32W, SWM buoy (Apr-Sep), 007°/1·0M to pier hd lt, on ldg line. Great (57m) and Little (35m) Saltee Islands lie 3M and 1·7M to SSW and S, respectively, of hbr, separated by Saltee Sound. From the E, safest appr initially is via Saltee Sound, then N to WPT. Caution: In bad weather seas break on the Bohurs and The Bore, rks 2M E of Saltee Islands. Beware,

particularly on E-going stream, Goose Rk (2·6m) close W of Little Saltee and Murroch's Rk (2·1m) 6ca NW of Little Saltee. St Patrick's Bridge, 650m E of the WPT, is a 300m wide E/W chan used by FVs and yachts, but carrying < 2m; care needed in strong SW winds when a standing wave can form. It is marked by a PHM buoy, Fl R 6s, and a SHM buoy, Fl G 6s, (laid Apr to mid-Sep); general direction of buoyage is E. From the W, appr is clear but keep at least 5ca off Forlorn Pt to avoid Forlorn Rk (1·5m).

LIGHTS AND MARKS See 5.3 and chartlet. Ldg lts/marks lead 008° to the hbr.

- From W, ldg lts are obsc'd by piers until S of hbr ent. Turn 90° port into hbr ent, just past ☆ QRG at W Quay Hd; do not overshoot into shoal water ahead. The R sectors of this ☆ QRG warn of Forlorn Rock and The Lings to W of the ldg line and shingle banks drying 0·6m close E of the ldg line.

A white-gabled church is conspic from afar, as are two 20m high flood lt pylons on the E quay.

COMMUNICATIONS (Code 053) MRCC (01) 6620922/3; Emergency/ Dr/Police 999; ⊕ 9133741. HM 9129955, mob 087 9001037, assistant. marineofficer@wexfordcoco.ie.
VHF Ch 16, 09 (occas).

FACILITIES www.kilmorequaymarina.com or HM ☎(0800-2000); ♦ ⎯ 20Ⓥ €2.50 (€25 min) ▣ ♨ ⛟(24/7) ⚓ ⚒ Ⓑ cycle hire.
Village ⚓ ⚒ Ⓑ ⓘ ᴘ ⓕ ⓣ 3M away, ⊠ ⛟ ✕ ▢ Ⓗ(Wexford 15M).

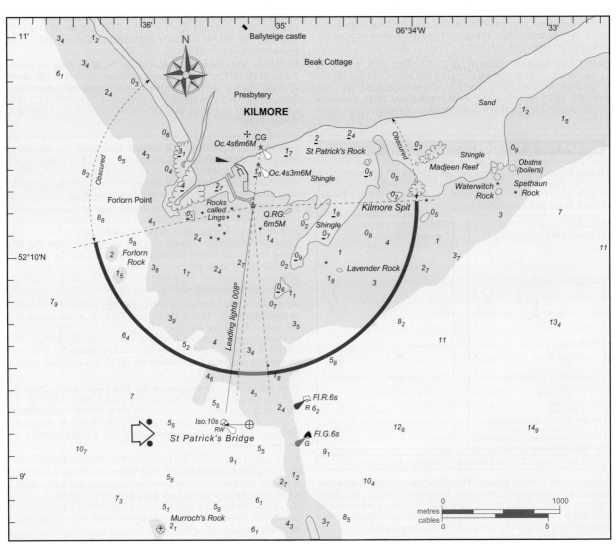

5.15 WATERFORD

Waterford 52°15′·50N 07°06′·00W ✦✦✦✦⚓⚓✿✿

CHARTS AC 2049, 2046, 5621, 5622; Imray C61, C57

TIDES −0520 Dover; ML 2·4; Duration 0605

Standard Port COBH (→)

Times				Height (metres)			
High Water		Low Water		MHWS	MHWN	MLWN	MLWS
0500	1100	0500	1100	4·1	3·2	1·3	0·4
1700	2300	1700	2300				
Differences WATERFORD							
+0053	+0032	+0015	+0100	+0·6	+0·6	+0·4	+0·2
CHEEKPOINT							
+0026	+0021	+0019	+0022	+0·5	+0·4	+0·3	+0·2
KILMOKEA POINT							
+0026	+0022	+0020	+0020	+0·2	+0·1	+0·1	+0·1
NEW ROSS							
+0100	+0030	+0055	+0130	+0·3	+0·4	+0·3	+0·4

SHELTER Very good on 4 long marina pontoons after Nanny pontoon (first one/private) on S bank, abeam cathedral spire. Beware strong tidal stream. Up the estuary are many excellent ⚓s: off S side of R Suir in King's Chan (only to be entered W of Little Is); and up the R Barrow near Marsh Pt (about 2M S of New Ross) and 0·5M S of New Ross fixed bridge.

NAVIGATION WPT 52°06′·50N 06°58′·50W, 002°/6·7M to Dir lt at Duncannon. From the E, keep clear of Brecaun reef (2M NE of Hook Hd). Keep about 1·5M S of Hook Hd to clear Tower Race and overfalls, especially HW Dover ±2. From the W beware Falskirt Rk (3m), 2ca off Swine Head and 2M WSW of Dunmore East (5.16). Marine Farms off Creadan Hd and Broomhill Pt; large ships go up to Waterford; beware ferry between Passage East and Ballyhack.

LIGHTS AND MARKS The estuary and R Suir are very well buoyed/lit all the way to Waterford. The estuary ent is between Dunmore East and Hook Hd. Duncannon dir lt, F WRG, leads 002° into the river. R Barrow is also well lit/marked up to New Ross. The railway swing bridge (now disused) at the river ent still opens at its W end. Call Bridge-keeper ☎086 816 7826 (no VHF).

COMMUNICATIONS (Code 051) MRCC (01) 6620922; ⊖ 832090; Police 305300; Dr 855411; Ⓗ848000.; HMs Waterford 301400, Mob 08725 98297 or 08722 24961; New Ross 421303.
Waterford and New Ross VHF Ch **14** 16. No VHF for marina.

FACILITIES Marina ☎309900 all tide access for 1·5m draught. Access/berth, call mob 087 2384944; 100◯ €16 (€80/wk)<7.6m>€20 (€95/wk)<10.7m>€30 (€130/wk)<13.7m. ⚓ ⊕ €2·50/10Kw, ⊫ ◻ at HM's office, ⬛(from Dunmore East by Coast2Coast ☎382797, mob 0872512170) ✕ ⚒ ⊡ ⬚ ⌂(Ballyhack ☎389164).

New Ross Marina newrossmarina@wexfordcoco.ie mob 086 388 9652; ⚓ ⊕ ⚓ 66◯ €10 (€50/wk)<9.5m>€20 (€100/wk) < 10.5m>€30 (€120/wk)<13.5m; ⬛ (as above) ⬛⊟.

Waterford Boatyard (R Suir), ☎857755 or 086 1727502 for bridge lift on approach. Waterford CC ☎076 1102020 for Rice Bridge lift.

City all facilities, bus to Rosslare for UK ferries, ✈ (Waterford) for UK/Continent.

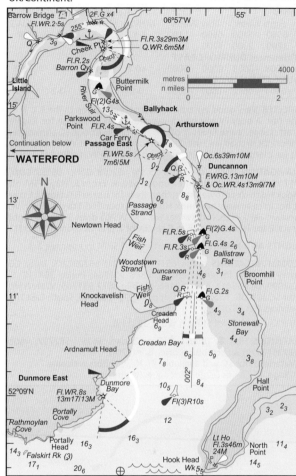

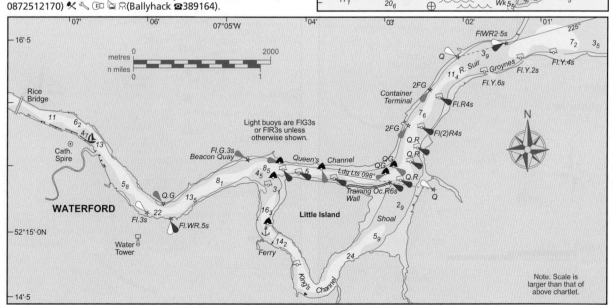

5.16 DUNMORE EAST

Waterford 52°08'·95N 06°59'·37W ✿✿✿✿◊◊✿✿

CHARTS AC 2049, 2046, 5621, 5622; Imray C61, C57

TIDES –0535 Dover; ML 2·4; Duration 0605

Standard Port COBH (→)

Times				Height (metres)			
High Water		Low Water		MHWS	MHWN	MLWN	MLWS
0500	1100	0500	1100	4·1	3·2	1·3	0·4
1700	2300	1700	2300				
Differences DUNMORE EAST							
+0008	+0003	0000	0000	+0·1	0·0	+0·1	+0·2
DUNGARVAN HARBOUR							
+0004	+0012	+0007	–0001	0·0	+0·1	–0·2	0·0

SHELTER Very good in harbour, but moorings open to the E. ⚓ N of the hbr. A busy FV hbr which may be a port of refuge for leisure craft. Large cruise liners ⚓ off. Waterford Harbour SC administer moorings. In bad weather berth alongside FVs at W Wharf, clear of ice plant, in at least 2m or go up R Suir to Waterford (5.15).

NAVIGATION WPT (see also 5.15) 52°08'·00N, 06°58'·00W, 317°/1·2M to bkwtr lt. Enter under power. From E, stay 1·5M off Hook Hd to clear Tower Race; then steer for hbr in R sector of E pier lt ho. In calm weather Hook Hd can be rounded 1ca off. From W, beware Falskirt Rk (off Swines Hd, 2M WSW) dries 3·0m. By night track E for Hook Hd until in R sector of E pier lt, then alter to N.

LIGHTS AND MARKS Lts as chartlet 2 lit SHM in appr see 5.3.

COMMUNICATIONS (Code 051) MRCC (01) 6620922/3; Duty CG (may be used for emergencies) 0868 501764; Police 383112; ⊖ 832090; Dr 855411. HM 383166, mobile 0877 931705; Waterford Hbr SC 383230. Tugs: Fastnet shipping 051 832946, South East Tug Services 051 852819.

VHF Ch 14 16 (Pilot Station ☎051 383119).

FACILITIES Hbr ⚓ (piers) ⚓(Coast2Coast ☎051 382797, mob 0872512170) ⬥ scrubbing grid, ⛽🅿(220t).
Waterford Hbr SC ⚓ if available, 🛒✕🚿; visitors welcome.
Village 🏨🏨 Kos ✉ Ⓑ 🍺 ✕ 🛒 ✈ (Waterford).

5.17 YOUGHAL

Cork 51°56'·54N 07°50'·20W ✿✿◊◊✿✿

CHARTS AC 2049, 2071, 5622; Imray C57

TIDES –0556 Dover; ML 2·1; Duration 0555

Standard Port COBH (→)

Times				Height (metres)			
High Water		Low Water		MHWS	MHWN	MLWN	MLWS
0500	1100	0500	1100	4·1	3·2	1·3	0·4
1700	2300	1700	2300				
Differences YOUGHAL							
0000	+0010	+0010	0000	–0·2	–0·1	–0·1	–0·1

SHELTER Good, but strong S'lies cause swell inside the hbr. Possible ⚓ in 1.3m (drying patches just off quay); seasonal short-stay pontoon, with ⚓ off landing jetty; 2 🅐s (see chartlet), €20/night, owned by Aquatrek (call on Ch 69 or ☎086 8593482). ⚓ as chartlet. Strong tidal streams run throughout ⚓orages.

NAVIGATION WPT, East Bar, 51°55'·62N 07°48'·00W, 302°/1·8M to Fl WR 2·5s lt. Beware Blackball Ledge (ECM lt buoy) and Bar Rks (SCM lt buoy), both outside hbr ent in R sector of lt ho. From W, appr via West Bar (1·7m) is shorter route and E Bar has 2·0m.

- Both Bars in E to SSW'lies >F6 are likely to have dangerous seas.
- Beware salmon nets set during June-July, Mon-Thurs 0400-2100.
- Red Bank is continually changing, obtain local knowledge.

LIGHTS AND MARKS See 5.3 and chartlet. Water tr is conspic from seaward; clock tr and ✠ tr within hbr. Upriver, 175° transit of convent belfry tr/town hall clears W of Red Bank.

COMMUNICATIONS (Code 024) MRCC (066) 9476109; Coast Guard 93252 or mob 0868 501769; ⊖ (021) 4325000; Police 92200; Dr 92702. HM Mobile 0872511143; Youghal Shipping 92577 (for poss ⚓).

VHF Ch 14 16 0900-1700 and when ships expected.

FACILITIES Services ⚓⚓⬥⚓ (☎Youghal Shipping).
Town 🏨🏨✉ Ⓑ 🍺 ✕ 🛒 Bus (Cork/W'ford) ✈(Cork). Wkly ferry to Roscoff www.brittanyferries.ie.

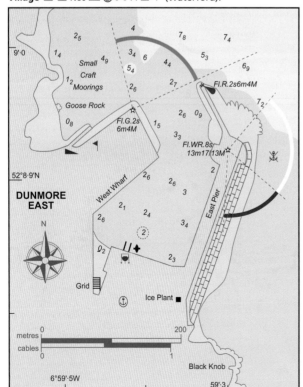

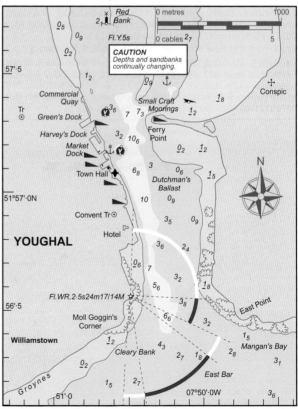

STANDARD TIME (UT)
For Summer Time add ONE hour in **non-shaded areas**

COBH LAT 51°51'N LONG 8°18'W
TIMES AND HEIGHTS OF HIGH AND LOW WATERS

Dates in red are **SPRINGS**
Dates in blue are NEAPS

YEAR 2016

S Ireland

JANUARY

Day	Time m	Time m	Time m	Time m
1 F	0357 1.1	0948 3.6	1625 1.2	2203 3.5
2 SA	0447 1.2	1036 3.5	1717 1.4	2255 3.4
3 SU	0543 1.3	1132 3.4	1817 1.4	2358 3.4
4 M	0646 1.4	1238 3.4	1920 1.4	
5 TU	0108 3.4	0747 1.3	1346 3.5	2019 1.3
6 W	0215 3.5	0846 1.2	1446 3.6	2115 1.1
7 TH	0312 3.7	0940 1.1	1539 3.7	2206 1.0
8 F	0403 3.9	1029 0.9	1625 3.9	2251 0.8
9 SA	0448 4.0	1113 0.7	1707 4.0	2332 0.6
10 SU ●	0530 4.2	1154 0.6	1746 4.1	
11 M	0012 0.5	0610 4.2	1234 0.6	1825 4.1
12 TU	0052 0.5	0650 4.2	1314 0.5	1905 4.1
13 W	0134 0.5	0732 4.2	1357 0.6	1948 4.1
14 TH	0218 0.5	0817 4.2	1441 0.6	2033 4.0
15 F	0305 0.6	0904 4.1	1528 0.7	2121 3.9
16 SA	0355 0.8	0954 3.9	1619 0.9	◗ 2213 3.8
17 SU	0450 0.9	1049 3.8	1717 1.0	2312 3.6
18 M	0554 1.0	1152 3.6	1825 1.1	
19 TU	0020 3.5	0707 1.1	1304 3.6	1941 1.1
20 W	0137 3.5	0824 1.0	1417 3.6	2056 1.0
21 TH	0252 3.7	0936 0.9	1524 3.7	2201 0.8
22 F	0356 3.9	1035 0.7	1621 3.9	2255 0.6
23 SA	0448 4.0	1124 0.5	1709 4.0	2340 0.5
24 SU ○	0533 4.2	1207 0.5	1751 4.1	
25 M	0020 0.4	0613 4.2	1245 0.5	1828 4.1
26 TU	0056 0.5	0649 4.2	1320 0.6	1903 4.1
27 W	0130 0.5	0724 4.1	1353 0.7	1935 4.0
28 TH	0204 0.7	0808 4.1	1426 0.8	2009 3.9
29 F	0238 0.8	0832 3.9	1501 0.9	2044 3.8
30 SA	0314 0.9	0909 3.8	1538 1.1	2123 3.7
31 SU	0355 1.1	0949 3.6	1621 1.2	2207 3.5

FEBRUARY

Day	Time m	Time m	Time m	Time m
1 M	0444 1.3	1035 3.5	1715 1.4	◗ 2300 3.4
2 TU	0545 1.4	1131 3.4	1821 1.4	
3 W	0005 3.3	0654 1.4	1242 3.3	1932 1.4
4 TH	0121 3.3	0803 1.3	1359 3.4	2038 1.3
5 F	0234 3.5	0907 1.1	1506 3.5	2137 1.0
6 SA	0334 3.7	1004 0.9	1601 3.8	2228 0.8
7 SU	0425 3.9	1053 0.7	1647 3.9	2313 0.5
8 M ●	0510 4.1	1137 0.5	1730 4.1	2355 0.4
9 TU	0552 4.3	1218 0.3	1810 4.2	
10 W	0035 0.3	0634 4.3	1259 0.3	1850 4.2
11 TH	0117 0.2	0716 4.3	1340 0.3	1932 4.2
12 F	0200 0.3	0759 4.2	1423 0.4	2015 4.1
13 SA	0246 0.4	0844 4.1	1508 0.5	2100 4.0
14 SU	0333 0.5	0931 3.9	1555 0.7	2149 3.8
15 M ◗	0425 0.7	1022 3.7	1649 0.9	2243 3.6
16 TU	0525 0.9	1123 3.5	1754 1.1	2351 3.4
17 W	0638 1.1	1237 3.3	1913 1.2	
18 TH	0114 3.3	0804 1.1	1359 3.4	2039 1.1
19 F	0237 3.5	0924 0.9	1510 3.5	2151 0.9
20 SA	0342 3.7	1024 0.7	1607 3.7	2245 0.6
21 SU	0434 3.9	1112 0.5	1654 3.9	2328 0.5
22 M ○	0516 4.1	1152 0.4	1735 4.0	
23 TU	0004 0.4	0554 4.1	1226 0.4	1809 4.1
24 W	0036 0.4	0627 4.1	1257 0.5	1841 4.0
25 TH	0105 0.5	0659 4.1	1325 0.6	1910 4.0
26 F	0133 0.6	0729 4.0	1354 0.7	1940 3.9
27 SA	0203 0.7	0759 3.9	1424 0.8	2013 3.9
28 SU	0236 0.8	0832 3.8	1458 0.9	2048 3.8
29 M	0313 1.0	0908 3.7	1536 1.1	2128 3.6

MARCH

Day	Time m	Time m	Time m	Time m
1 TU ◗	0357 1.1	0951 3.5	1623 1.3	2216 3.5
2 W	0453 1.3	1043 3.4	1726 1.4	2316 3.3
3 TH	0605 1.4	1149 3.2	1844 1.4	
4 F	0031 3.3	0721 1.3	1310 3.2	1959 1.3
5 SA	0153 3.4	0832 1.1	1429 3.4	2104 1.0
6 SU	0302 3.6	0934 0.9	1532 3.6	2201 0.7
7 M	0357 3.9	1028 0.6	1623 3.9	2249 0.4
8 TU	0445 4.1	1114 0.3	1708 4.1	2334 0.2
9 W ●	0530 4.3	1158 0.1	1750 4.2	
10 TH	0016 0.1	0612 4.3	1240 0.1	1831 4.3
11 F	0059 0.0	0655 4.3	1322 0.1	1913 4.3
12 SA	0142 0.1	0738 4.3	1404 0.1	1956 4.2
13 SU	0227 0.2	0823 4.1	1449 0.3	2040 4.0
14 M	0314 0.4	0909 3.9	1536 0.5	2127 3.8
15 TU ◗	0405 0.6	0959 3.6	1628 0.8	2220 3.6
16 W	0503 0.9	1058 3.4	1730 1.0	2327 3.3
17 TH	0615 1.1	1214 3.2	1850 1.1	
18 F	0055 3.2	0743 1.1	1339 3.2	2021 1.1
19 SA	0219 3.3	0905 0.9	1451 3.4	2134 0.8
20 SU	0322 3.6	1005 0.7	1547 3.6	2227 0.6
21 M	0412 3.8	1051 0.5	1633 3.8	2309 0.5
22 TU	0453 4.0	1130 0.4	1713 4.0	2343 0.4
23 W ○	0530 4.0	1202 0.4	1747 4.0	
24 TH	0012 0.4	0603 4.0	1231 0.5	1817 4.0
25 F	0038 0.5	0632 4.0	1256 0.5	1845 4.0
26 SA	0103 0.6	0700 3.9	1323 0.6	1913 3.9
27 SU	0132 0.6	0728 3.9	1353 0.7	1944 3.9
28 M	0205 0.8	0800 3.8	1426 0.8	2018 3.8
29 TU	0242 0.9	0835 3.7	1503 1.0	2057 3.7
30 W	0325 1.0	0917 3.6	1548 1.2	2143 3.5
31 TH ◗	0417 1.2	1008 3.4	1647 1.3	2240 3.4

APRIL

Day	Time m	Time m	Time m	Time m
1 F	0525 1.3	1113 3.2	1803 1.4	2352 3.3
2 SA	0643 1.3	1230 3.2	1921 1.2	
3 SU	0113 3.4	0756 1.2	1350 3.3	2029 1.0
4 M	0226 3.6	0901 0.8	1457 3.6	2129 0.7
5 TU	0325 3.8	0958 0.5	1553 3.9	2222 0.4
6 W	0417 4.1	1048 0.2	1642 4.1	2310 0.1
7 TH ●	0504 4.2	1135 0.1	1727 4.2	2355 0.0
8 F	0550 4.3	1219 0.0	1811 4.3	
9 SA	0040 -0.1	0634 4.3	1303 0.0	1854 4.3
10 SU	0125 0.1	0719 4.2	1348 0.1	1938 4.2
11 M	0211 0.1	0804 4.1	1433 0.2	2023 4.0
12 TU	0259 0.3	0850 3.9	1521 0.4	2110 3.8
13 W	0349 0.5	0940 3.6	1613 0.7	2203 3.5
14 TH	0446 0.8	1038 3.3	1713 1.0	2308 3.3
15 F	0555 1.0	1150 3.1	1828 1.1	
16 SA	0031 3.2	0716 1.0	1312 3.1	1951 1.0
17 SU	0150 3.3	0833 0.9	1422 3.3	2102 0.9
18 M	0251 3.5	0932 0.8	1517 3.5	2156 0.7
19 TU	0341 3.7	1020 0.6	1604 3.7	2239 0.6
20 W	0424 3.8	1100 0.5	1644 3.8	2314 0.5
21 TH	0502 3.9	1133 0.5	1719 3.9	2343 0.5
22 F ○	0535 3.9	1201 0.5	1751 3.9	
23 SA	0009 0.5	0605 3.9	1228 0.6	1819 3.9
24 SU	0036 0.6	0633 3.9	1256 0.6	1849 3.9
25 M	0106 0.7	0702 3.9	1328 0.7	1920 3.9
26 TU	0141 0.7	0734 3.8	1403 0.8	1955 3.8
27 W	0220 0.8	0812 3.7	1442 0.9	2035 3.7
28 TH	0304 1.0	0855 3.6	1528 1.0	2121 3.6
29 F ◗	0355 1.1	0946 3.5	1624 1.2	2217 3.5
30 SA ◗	0457 1.2	1047 3.4	1732 1.2	2324 3.4

Chart Datum: 0·13 metres above Ordnance Datum (Dublin). HAT is 4·5 metres above Chart Datum.

STANDARD TIME (UT)
For Summer Time add ONE hour in **non-shaded areas**

COBH LAT 51°51'N LONG 8°18'W
TIMES AND HEIGHTS OF HIGH AND LOW WATERS

Dates in red are SPRINGS
Dates in blue are NEAPS

YEAR 2016

MAY

Time	m		Time	m
1 0609	1.2	**16** 0108	3.3
1159	3.3	0747	1.0
SU 1846	1.1	M 1340	3.3
		2015	1.0
2 0039	3.5	**17** 0210	3.4
0721	1.0	0846	0.9
M 1314	3.4	TU 1437	3.4
1955	0.9	2111	0.9
3 0151	3.6	**18** 0302	3.5
0827	0.8	0937	0.8
TU 1422	3.6	W 1526	3.6
2057	0.7	2158	0.8
4 0253	3.8	**19** 0347	3.7
0927	0.5	1021	0.7
W 1521	3.9	TH 1609	3.7
2154	0.4	2237	0.7
5 0348	4.0	**20** 0429	3.8
1022	0.3	1058	0.7
TH 1615	4.1	F 1648	3.8
2247	0.2	2310	0.6
6 0440	4.2	**21** 0506	3.8
1112	0.1	1131	0.6
F 1704	4.2	SA 1723	3.9
● 2336	0.0	○ 2341	0.6
7 0529	4.3	**22** 0539	3.9
1200	0.0	1202	0.6
SA 1752	4.3	SU 1756	3.9
8 0023	0.0	**23** 0012	0.6
0615	4.3	0609	3.9
SU 1247	0.0	M 1234	0.6
1837	4.3	1828	3.9
9 0110	0.0	**24** 0046	0.7
0701	4.2	0641	3.9
M 1333	0.1	TU 1309	0.7
1922	4.2	1902	3.9
10 0157	0.1	**25** 0123	0.7
0747	4.0	0716	3.8
TU 1419	0.2	W 1347	0.7
2007	4.0	1939	3.9
11 0245	0.3	**26** 0204	0.8
0834	3.8	0756	3.8
W 1507	0.4	TH 1428	0.8
2055	3.8	2020	3.8
12 0335	0.5	**27** 0249	0.9
0922	3.6	0840	3.7
TH 1558	0.7	F 1515	0.9
2146	3.6	2107	3.8
13 0429	0.8	**28** 0339	0.9
1016	3.4	0931	1.0
F 1655	0.9	SA 1607	1.0
◗ 2245	3.4	2200	3.7
14 0530	1.0	**29** 0435	1.0
1119	3.2	1028	3.5
SA 1759	1.0	SU 1708	1.0
2355	3.3	◗ 2302	3.6
15 0639	1.0	**30** 0540	1.0
1231	3.2	1132	3.5
SU 1910	1.0	M 1815	1.0
		31 0009	3.6
		0648	1.0
		TU 1241	3.5
		1923	0.9

JUNE

Time	m		Time	m
1 0119	3.7	**16** 0216	3.4
0755	0.8	0846	1.0
W 1349	3.7	TH 1441	3.5
2028	0.7	2109	0.9
2 0223	3.8	**17** 0307	3.5
0858	0.6	0936	0.9
TH 1451	3.8	F 1530	3.6
2129	0.5	2155	0.9
3 0322	4.0	**18** 0354	3.7
0958	0.4	1021	0.8
F 1550	4.0	SA 1615	3.7
2226	0.3	2237	0.8
4 0419	4.1	**19** 0436	3.8
1053	0.3	1102	0.7
SA 1645	4.1	SU 1656	3.8
2319	0.2	2315	0.7
5 0511	4.2	**20** 0515	3.8
1144	0.2	1139	0.7
SU 1735	4.2	M 1734	3.9
●		○ 2352	0.6
6 0009	0.1	**21** 0550	3.9
0559	4.2	1215	0.6
M 1232	0.1	TU 1811	4.0
1822	4.2		
7 0056	0.1	**22** 0029	0.6
0646	4.1	0625	3.9
TU 1319	0.2	W 1253	0.6
1907	4.1	1847	4.0
8 0143	0.2	**23** 0108	0.6
0731	4.0	0703	3.9
W 1404	0.3	TH 1332	0.6
1952	4.0	1926	4.0
9 0229	0.4	**24** 0150	0.7
0816	3.9	0743	3.9
TH 1451	0.5	F 1415	0.7
2037	3.9	2008	3.9
10 0316	0.6	**25** 0234	0.7
0901	3.7	0828	3.8
F 1538	0.6	SA 1500	0.7
2123	3.7	2054	3.9
11 0405	0.8	**26** 0322	0.8
0948	3.5	0916	3.8
SA 1628	0.8	SU 1549	0.8
2213	3.5	2144	3.8
12 0457	0.9	**27** 0413	0.8
1039	3.4	1009	3.7
SU 1722	1.0	M 1643	0.8
◗ 2310	3.4	◗ 2239	3.7
13 0554	1.1	**28** 0511	0.9
1138	3.3	1107	3.6
M 1821	1.1	TU 1745	0.9
		2341	3.7
14 0014	3.3	**29** 0616	0.9
0654	1.1	1211	3.6
TU 1244	3.3	W 1852	0.9
1921	1.1		
15 0118	3.3	**30** 0048	3.7
0752	1.1	0725	0.9
W 1346	3.3	TH 1319	3.6
2017	1.0	2001	0.8

JULY

Time	m		Time	m
1 0156	3.7	**16** 0224	3.4
0833	0.8	0854	1.1
F 1427	3.7	SA 1452	3.5
2108	0.7	2116	1.0
2 0301	3.8	**17** 0319	3.5
0938	0.6	0947	0.9
SA 1531	3.9	SU 1544	3.7
2210	0.5	2207	0.9
3 0402	3.9	**18** 0408	3.7
1037	0.5	1035	0.8
SU 1630	4.0	M 1631	3.8
2306	0.4	2252	0.7
4 0456	4.0	**19** 0452	3.8
1130	0.3	1117	0.7
M 1722	4.1	TU 1713	3.8
● 2356	0.3	○ 2333	0.6
5 0546	4.1	**20** 0532	3.9
1218	0.3	1156	0.5
TU 1809	4.2	W 1752	4.0
6 0042	0.3	**21** 0012	0.5
0630	4.1	0609	4.0
W 1303	0.3	TH 1235	0.5
1851	4.1	1831	4.1
7 0125	0.3	**22** 0052	0.5
0713	4.0	0648	4.0
TH 1345	0.3	F 1315	0.5
1933	4.0	1910	4.1
8 0208	0.5	**23** 0133	0.5
0753	3.9	0728	4.0
F 1427	0.5	SA 1357	0.5
2013	3.9	1952	4.1
9 0250	0.6	**24** 0216	0.5
0833	3.8	0812	3.9
SA 1509	0.6	SU 1441	0.5
2054	3.8	2036	4.0
10 0332	0.8	**25** 0302	0.6
0914	3.6	0858	3.9
SU 1551	0.8	M 1528	0.6
2136	3.6	2124	3.9
11 0416	0.9	**26** 0350	0.7
0956	3.5	0947	3.8
M 1636	1.0	TU 1618	0.7
2221	3.5	◗ 2216	3.8
12 0504	1.1	**27** 0444	0.8
1044	3.4	1041	3.7
TU 1726	1.1	W 1716	0.8
◗ 2312	3.4	2314	3.7
13 0558	1.2	**28** 0545	0.9
1140	3.3	1143	3.6
W 1823	1.2	TH 1823	0.9
14 0013	3.3	**29** 0021	3.5
0657	1.2	0657	1.0
TH 1246	3.3	F 1255	3.5
1922	1.2	1937	0.9
15 0121	3.3	**30** 0135	3.5
0757	1.2	0813	0.9
F 1352	3.4	SA 1410	3.6
2021	1.1	2052	0.8
		31 0246	3.6
		0925	0.8
		SU 1520	3.7
		2200	0.7

AUGUST

Time	m		Time	m
1 0349	3.8	**16** 0341	3.6
1027	0.6	1007	0.8
M 1620	3.9	TU 1605	3.8
2256	0.5	2228	0.7
2 0444	3.9	**17** 0428	3.8
1119	0.4	1053	0.6
TU 1710	4.1	W 1650	4.0
● 2343	0.4	2311	0.5
3 0531	4.0	**18** 0510	4.0
1203	0.3	1134	0.4
W 1753	4.1	TH 1731	4.1
		○ 2352	0.4
4 0025	0.3	**19** 0549	4.0
0612	4.1	1213	0.3
TH 1244	0.3	F 1811	4.2
1832	4.1		
5 0104	0.4	**20** 0032	0.3
0651	4.0	0628	4.1
F 1321	0.4	SA 1254	0.3
1909	4.1	1850	4.2
6 0141	0.5	**21** 0113	0.3
0727	3.9	0709	4.1
SA 1357	0.5	SU 1336	0.3
1944	4.0	1932	4.2
7 0216	0.6	**22** 0155	0.4
0802	3.8	0752	4.0
SU 1432	0.6	M 1419	0.3
2020	3.8	2015	4.1
8 0252	0.8	**23** 0240	0.4
0837	3.7	0836	4.0
M 1508	0.8	TU 1505	0.5
2056	3.7	2102	4.0
9 0329	0.9	**24** 0327	0.6
0915	3.6	0924	3.8
TU 1546	1.0	W 1555	0.6
2135	3.6	2152	3.8
10 0410	1.1	**25** 0419	0.6
0957	3.5	1017	3.7
W 1629	1.1	TH 1651	0.8
◗ 2218	3.5	◗ 2249	3.6
11 0459	1.2	**26** 0520	1.0
1046	3.4	1119	3.5
TH 1723	1.3	F 1758	1.0
2310	3.3	2358	3.4
12 0601	1.3	**27** 0635	1.1
1146	3.3	1237	3.4
F 1829	1.3	SA 1919	1.1
13 0017	3.2	**28** 0119	3.4
0709	1.3	0759	1.0
SA 1300	3.2	SU 1401	3.4
1937	1.3	2044	1.0
14 0135	3.3	**29** 0236	3.5
0815	1.2	0917	0.8
SU 1414	3.4	M 1512	3.6
2041	1.1	2152	0.7
15 0245	3.4	**30** 0338	3.7
0915	1.0	1018	0.6
M 1515	3.6	TU 1608	3.9
2138	0.9	2245	0.5
		31 0430	3.9
		1106	0.4
		W 1655	4.0
		2329	0.4

Chart Datum: 0·13 metres above Ordnance Datum (Dublin). HAT is 4·5 metres above Chart Datum.

STANDARD TIME (UT)
For Summer Time add ONE hour in **non-shaded areas**

COBH LAT 51°51'N LONG 8°18'W
TIMES AND HEIGHTS OF HIGH AND LOW WATERS

Dates in red are SPRINGS
Dates in blue are NEAPS

YEAR **2016**

S Ireland

SEPTEMBER

Time m	Time m
1 0514 4.0 / 1147 0.4 / TH 1735 4.1 / ●	**16** 0443 4.0 / 1109 0.3 / F 1705 4.2 / ○ 2329 0.3
2 0006 0.4 / 0552 4.1 / F 1222 0.4 / 1810 4.1	**17** 0525 4.2 / 1151 0.2 / SA 1747 4.3
3 0040 0.4 / 0627 4.0 / SA 1254 0.4 / 1843 4.1	**18** 0010 0.2 / 0606 4.2 / SU 1232 0.1 / 1828 4.3
4 0110 0.5 / 0658 4.0 / SU 1323 0.5 / 1914 4.0	**19** 0052 0.2 / 0648 4.2 / M 1315 0.2 / 1910 4.3
5 0140 0.7 / 0729 3.9 / M 1353 0.7 / 1945 3.9	**20** 0135 0.2 / 0731 4.2 / TU 1359 0.2 / 1954 4.2
6 0210 0.8 / 0801 3.8 / TU 1424 0.8 / 2017 3.8	**21** 0220 0.4 / 0816 4.0 / W 1446 0.4 / 2040 4.0
7 0244 0.9 / 0837 3.7 / W 1459 1.0 / 2052 3.7	**22** 0308 0.5 / 0904 3.9 / TH 1536 0.6 / 2130 3.8
8 0321 1.1 / 0916 3.6 / TH 1540 1.1 / 2133 3.5	**23** 0401 0.8 / 0957 3.6 / F 1632 0.9 / ◗ 2228 3.5
9 0407 1.2 / 1002 3.4 / F 1631 1.3 / ◗ 2222 3.4	**24** 0502 1.0 / 1102 3.4 / SA 1740 1.1 / 2340 3.3
10 0507 1.4 / 1059 3.3 / SA 1739 1.4 / 2324 3.2	**25** 0619 1.1 / 1225 3.3 / SU 1906 1.1
11 0623 1.4 / 1211 3.2 / SU 1855 1.4	**26** 0105 3.3 / 0749 1.1 / M 1351 3.4 / 2033 1.0
12 0043 3.2 / 0737 1.3 / M 1334 3.3 / 2006 1.2	**27** 0222 3.4 / 0906 0.9 / TU 1458 3.6 / 2138 0.8
13 0206 3.4 / 0842 1.1 / TU 1443 3.5 / 2107 1.0	**28** 0322 3.7 / 1003 0.7 / W 1550 3.8 / 2227 0.6
14 0309 3.6 / 0937 0.8 / W 1536 3.8 / 2200 0.8	**29** 0410 3.9 / 1048 0.5 / TH 1634 4.0 / 2308 0.5
15 0359 3.8 / 1026 0.6 / TH 1623 4.0 / 2246 0.5	**30** 0452 4.0 / 1126 0.4 / F 1712 4.1 / 2343 0.5

OCTOBER

Time m	Time m
1 0529 4.1 / 1158 0.5 / SA 1746 4.1 / ●	**16** 0500 4.3 / 1129 0.2 / SU 1723 4.4 / ○ 2349 0.2
2 0012 0.5 / 0601 4.1 / SU 1225 0.5 / 1816 4.1	**17** 0544 4.3 / 1213 0.1 / M 1807 4.4
3 0039 0.6 / 0630 4.0 / M 1251 0.6 / 1844 4.0	**18** 0033 0.1 / 0628 4.3 / TU 1258 0.1 / 1851 4.3
4 0105 0.7 / 0659 3.9 / TU 1318 0.7 / 1912 3.9	**19** 0118 0.2 / 0713 4.3 / W 1344 0.2 / 1936 4.2
5 0134 0.8 / 0730 3.9 / W 1348 0.9 / 1942 3.9	**20** 0204 0.3 / 0759 4.1 / TH 1432 0.4 / 2023 4.0
6 0206 0.9 / 0804 3.8 / TH 1423 1.0 / 2017 3.8	**21** 0253 0.5 / 0848 3.9 / F 1522 0.7 / 2113 3.8
7 0244 1.1 / 0842 3.7 / F 1504 1.2 / 2057 3.6	**22** 0347 0.8 / 0942 3.7 / SA 1619 0.9 / ◗ 2210 3.5
8 0329 1.2 / 0927 3.5 / SA 1554 1.3 / 2145 3.5	**23** 0448 1.0 / 1046 3.5 / SU 1726 1.1 / 2320 3.3
9 0426 1.4 / 1022 3.4 / SU 1658 1.4 / ◗ 2246 3.3	**24** 0602 1.1 / 1206 3.3 / M 1848 1.2
10 0540 1.5 / 1131 3.3 / M 1815 1.5	**25** 0042 3.3 / 0728 1.1 / TU 1327 3.4 / 2009 1.1
11 0001 3.3 / 0657 1.4 / TU 1251 3.4 / 1930 1.3	**26** 0158 3.4 / 0841 1.0 / W 1432 3.6 / 2111 0.9
12 0123 3.4 / 0806 1.2 / W 1405 3.6 / 2034 1.0	**27** 0256 3.6 / 0936 0.8 / TH 1523 3.8 / 2200 0.8
13 0232 3.6 / 0905 0.9 / TH 1503 3.9 / 2130 0.7	**28** 0344 3.8 / 1021 0.7 / F 1606 3.9 / 2241 0.7
14 0327 3.9 / 0957 0.6 / F 1553 4.1 / 2220 0.6	**29** 0426 4.0 / 1059 0.6 / SA 1645 4.0 / 2315 0.6
15 0415 4.1 / 1044 0.3 / SA 1639 4.3 / 2305 0.3	**30** 0503 4.0 / 1131 0.6 / SU 1719 4.1 / ● 2344 0.6
	31 0536 4.1 / 1157 0.7 / M 1750 4.1

NOVEMBER

Time m	Time m
1 0010 0.7 / 0605 4.0 / TU 1223 0.7 / 1817 4.0	**16** 0018 0.2 / 0612 4.4 / W 1245 0.2 / 1835 4.3
2 0037 0.8 / 0634 4.0 / W 1251 0.8 / 1845 4.0	**17** 0104 0.3 / 0659 4.3 / TH 1332 0.3 / 1921 4.2
3 0107 0.8 / 0705 4.0 / TH 1323 0.9 / 1915 3.9	**18** 0152 0.4 / 0746 4.2 / F 1420 0.5 / 2008 4.0
4 0141 0.9 / 0739 3.9 / F 1400 1.0 / 1950 3.9	**19** 0241 0.5 / 0835 4.0 / SA 1511 0.7 / 2057 3.8
5 0219 1.1 / 0818 3.8 / SA 1441 1.2 / 2031 3.7	**20** 0333 0.8 / 0927 3.8 / SU 1604 0.9 / 2150 3.6
6 0305 1.2 / 0903 3.7 / SU 1530 1.3 / 2119 3.6	**21** 0430 1.0 / 1026 3.6 / M 1705 1.1 / ◗ 2252 3.4
7 0359 1.3 / 0956 3.6 / M 1629 1.4 / ◗ 2218 3.5	**22** 0536 1.1 / 1133 3.4 / TU 1815 1.2
8 0506 1.4 / 1100 3.5 / TU 1739 1.4 / 2327 3.4	**23** 0004 3.3 / 0649 1.2 / W 1247 3.4 / 1927 1.2
9 0619 1.4 / 1212 3.5 / W 1853 1.3	**24** 0117 3.4 / 0759 1.1 / TH 1352 3.5 / 2030 1.1
10 0042 3.5 / 0729 1.2 / TH 1325 3.7 / 2000 1.1	**25** 0218 3.5 / 0857 1.0 / F 1446 3.7 / 2122 1.0
11 0153 3.7 / 0832 0.9 / F 1427 3.9 / 2059 0.8	**26** 0309 3.7 / 0945 0.9 / SA 1532 3.8 / 2206 0.9
12 0253 3.9 / 0928 0.7 / SA 1522 4.1 / 2154 0.6	**27** 0354 3.9 / 1026 0.8 / SU 1614 3.9 / 2244 0.8
13 0347 4.1 / 1021 0.4 / SU 1613 4.3 / 2244 0.4	**28** 0434 4.0 / 1101 0.8 / M 1652 4.0 / 2317 0.8
14 0437 4.3 / 1111 0.3 / M 1702 4.4 / ○ 2332 0.2	**29** 0510 4.0 / 1132 0.8 / TU 1726 4.0 / ● 2346 0.8
15 0526 4.4 / 1158 0.2 / TU 1749 4.4	**30** 0544 4.1 / 1201 0.8 / W 1756 4.0

DECEMBER

Time m	Time m
1 0016 0.8 / 0615 4.1 / TH 1232 0.8 / 1825 4.0	**16** 0053 0.3 / 0647 4.4 / F 1321 0.3 / 1908 4.2
2 0048 0.8 / 0648 4.0 / F 1307 0.9 / 1857 4.0	**17** 0139 0.4 / 0733 4.2 / SA 1408 0.5 / 1953 4.1
3 0124 0.9 / 0723 4.0 / SA 1345 1.0 / 1933 3.9	**18** 0226 0.5 / 0819 4.1 / SU 1455 0.6 / 2038 3.9
4 0204 1.0 / 0802 3.9 / SU 1426 1.1 / 2014 3.8	**19** 0314 0.7 / 0906 3.9 / M 1543 0.8 / 2124 3.7
5 0248 1.1 / 0846 3.9 / M 1513 1.2 / 2101 3.7	**20** 0404 0.9 / 0956 3.7 / TU 1634 1.0 / 2214 3.5
6 0339 1.2 / 0936 3.8 / TU 1606 1.3 / 2155 3.6	**21** 0458 1.1 / 1050 3.5 / W 1731 1.2 / 2311 3.4
7 0437 1.3 / 1034 3.7 / W 1707 1.3 / ◗ 2257 3.6	**22** 0558 1.2 / 1151 3.4 / TH 1833 1.3
8 0543 1.3 / 1138 3.7 / TH 1815 1.3	**23** 0017 3.3 / 0702 1.2 / F 1258 3.4 / 1935 1.3
9 0005 3.6 / 0652 1.2 / F 1247 3.7 / 1924 1.1	**24** 0126 3.4 / 0803 1.2 / SA 1359 3.5 / 2033 1.2
10 0115 3.7 / 0759 1.0 / SA 1353 3.9 / 2029 0.9	**25** 0226 3.5 / 0859 1.1 / SU 1453 3.6 / 2125 1.1
11 0220 3.9 / 0902 0.8 / SU 1454 4.0 / 2130 0.7	**26** 0318 3.7 / 0949 1.0 / M 1542 3.8 / 2211 1.0
12 0321 4.1 / 1001 0.6 / M 1551 4.2 / 2225 0.5	**27** 0405 3.8 / 1032 0.9 / TU 1626 3.9 / 2251 0.9
13 0418 4.2 / 1056 0.4 / TU 1645 4.3 / 2317 0.4	**28** 0447 4.0 / 1110 0.9 / W 1705 4.0 / 2327 0.8
14 0511 4.3 / 1146 0.3 / W 1735 4.3 / ○	**29** 0525 4.1 / 1144 0.8 / TH 1740 4.0 / ●
15 0006 0.3 / 0600 4.4 / TH 1235 0.3 / 1822 4.3	**30** 0000 0.7 / 0600 4.1 / F 1219 0.8 / 1812 4.0
	31 0034 0.7 / 0634 4.1 / SA 1254 0.8 / 1845 4.0

Chart Datum: 0·13 metres above Ordnance Datum (Dublin). HAT is 4·5 metres above Chart Datum.

》》 **FREE** monthly updates. Register at 《
www.reedsnauticalalmanac.co.uk 《

189

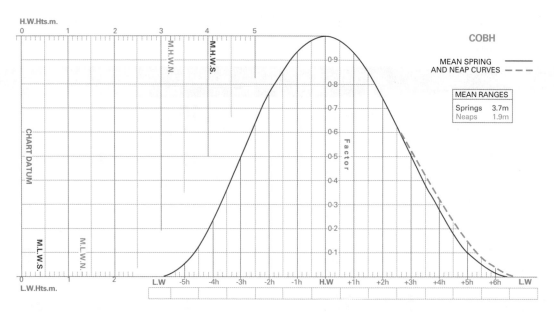

COBH

MEAN SPRING —
AND NEAP CURVES - - -

MEAN RANGES	
Springs	3.7m
Neaps	1.9m

5.18 CORK HARBOUR

Cork 51°47'·50N 08°15'·54W ✿✿✿✿♢♢♢♢✿✿✿

CHARTS AC 1765, 1777, 1773, 5622; Imray C57, C56

TIDES −0523 Dover; ML 2·3; Duration 0555

Standard Port COBH (←)

Times				Height (metres)			
High Water		Low Water		MHWS	MHWN	MLWN	MLWS
0500	1100	0500	1100	4·1	3·2	1·3	0·4
1700	2300	1700	2300				
Differences BALLYCOTTON (15M ENE of Roche's Point)							
−0011	+0001	+0003	−0009	0·0	0·0	−0·1	0·0
RINGASKIDDY							
+0005	+0020	+0007	+0013	+0·1	+0·1	+0·1	+0·1
MARINO POINT							
0000	+0010	0000	+0010	+0·1	+0·1	0·0	0·0
CORK CITY							
+0005	+0010	+0020	+0010	+0·4	+0·4	+0·3	+0·2
ROBERTS COVE (approx 4M SW of Roche's Point)							
−0005	−0005	−0005	−0005	−0·1	0·0	0·0	+0·1

SHELTER Very good in all conditions, esp in Crosshaven and East Passage. There are 3 marinas at Crosshaven, plus a small marina and several ⚓s up the Owenboy River, notably at Drake's Pool. There are marinas at East Ferry on Great Island and at Monkstown. Cobh, Ringaskiddy and Cork City are commercial and ferry ports; contact HM/Port berthing Master for advice on berths. 100m yacht pontoon in 4·5m at Custom House Quay, Cork City.

NAVIGATION WPT 51°46'·57N, 08°15'·39W, 005°/1M to Roche's Pt lt; also on 354°ldg line. Safe hbr with no dangers for yachts; ent is deep and well marked. Sp rate is about 1½kn in ent. Main chan up to Cork and the chan to E Ferry are marked, but shoal outside navigable chan. Ent to Crosshaven/Owenboy River carries at least 3m at LWS, and the chan is buoyed.

LIGHTS AND MARKS See 5.3. The 24·5m high hammerhead water tr S of Crosshaven and the R/W power stn chy NE of Corkbeg Is are conspic from seaward. Two set Ldg lts/marks lead through The Sound, either side of Hbr Rk (5·2m), not a hazard for yachts; but do not impede merchant ships. The chan to Crosshaven is marked by C1 SHM lt buoy, C1A SHM lt buoy; C2A PHM lt buoy, C2 PHM lt buoy; and C4 PHM lt buoy.

COMMUNICATIONS (Code 021) MRCC (066) 9476109; IMES 4831448; ⊖ 4311020; Police 4831222; Dr 4831716; ⊞ 4546400. HM/Port Berthing Master 4273125, info@portofcork.ie; Port Ops 4811380. Cork Hbr Radio (Port Ops) VHF Ch 12 14 16 (H24); Crosshaven BY Ch M (Mon–Fri: 0830–1730LT). Royal Cork YC Marina Ch M (0900–2359LT) and RCYC water taxi, Salve Marine Ch M 0830-1730.

FACILITIES Crosshaven BY Marina www.crosshavenboatyard.com ☎4831161, ⚓ 100⚓+20♥ €2.50, ⚓ ♨ ♙ ♪ ⚒ ⚓ Ⓑ Ⓔ ⚓ ☗(40t) ⚓(1½t).

Salve Marine ☎4831145, ⚓ ⚓ 45⚓+12♥ €2.50, ♙ ⚓ Koz ⚓ ⚒ ⚓ Ⓑ ⚓ ⚓ ⚓. Village: ⚓ ⚓ ⚓ ⚓ ✗.

Royal Cork YC Marina www.royalcork.com ☎4831023, ⚓ ⚓ ⚓ 170⚓+30♥ €3.00, ♙ ⚓ ⚒ Ⓑ ⚓ ✗ ⚓ wi-fi.

Crosshaven Pier/Pontoon ⚓€21.00 any size.

East Ferry Marina ☎(086) 7357785, access all tides, max draught 5·5m ⚓ 85⚓+15♥ €2.50, ♙.

Crosshaven Village FV pier in 3·5m at Town quay, HW±4(for RIBs small power craft) Dr ⚒ ⚓ grid ⚓ ⚓ Ⓒ ⚓ ✗ ⚓.

Cork Harbour Marina, www.monkstownmarina.com ☎(087) 3669009, access all tides, max length 17m, 80⚓ inc♥ facilities under development.

Cork City Marina, 150m ♥ pontoon ≤12m €20.

Cork City All facilities. ⚓ ✈, Ferries: Roscoff; weekly; 13 hrs; Brittany (www.brittany-ferries.ie).

Aghada Pontoon with 0.4m at LAT. ⚓ (enquire at petrol stn). Appr by 2 SHM 'A1' FL G 5s and 'A2' FL(2)G 10s which should be passed close to remining on a steady straight track; Facilities: ⚓ ✗ ⚓.

MINOR HARBOUR 16M ENE of YOUGHAL

DUNGARVAN BAY, Waterford, 52°05'·15N 07°36'·70W.✿✿✿♢♢✿✿✿ AC 2017, 5622. HW −0542 on Dover; Duration 0600. See 5.16. A large bay, drying to the W, entered between Helvick Hd to the S and Ballynacourty Pt to the N. Approach in W sector (274°-302°) of this lt to clear Carricknamoan islet to the N, and Carrickapane Rk and Helvick Rk (ECM buoy Q (3) 10s) to the S. 5ca W of this buoy are The Gainers, a large unmarked rocky patch (dries 0·8m). Beware salmon nets. Off Helvick harbour are 8 Y ⚓s or ⚓ in approx 4m. Dungarvan town harbour is accessible via buoyed chan which almost dries and shifts, the buoys being moved to suit. Approach is difficult in SE'lies >F6. ⚓ in the pool below the town or ⚓ on pontoon (dries to soft mud), S bank below bridge; craft can stay overnight beyond double Y lines. Facilities: ⚓ ⚓ Kos ⚓ Ⓑ ⚓ ⚓ ✗ ⚓.

MINOR HARBOUR 15M ENE of ROCHE'S POINT

BALLYCOTTON, Cork, 51°49'·70N 08°00·19W. AC 2424, 5622. HW −0555 on Dover; Duration 0550. See above. Small, NE-facing harbour at W end of bay suffers from scend in strong SE winds; 3m in entrance and about 1·5m against piers. Many FVs alongside piers, on which yachts should berth, rather than ⚓ in hbr, which is foul with old ground tackle. 6 Y⚓s are outside harbour, or good ⚓ in offshore winds in 6m NE of pier, protected by Ballycotton Is. Lt ho Fl WR 10s 59m 21/17M, B tr in W walls; 238°-W-048°-R-238°. Facilities: ⚓ on pier. Village LB, Kos ⚓ ⚓ Hotel ✗.

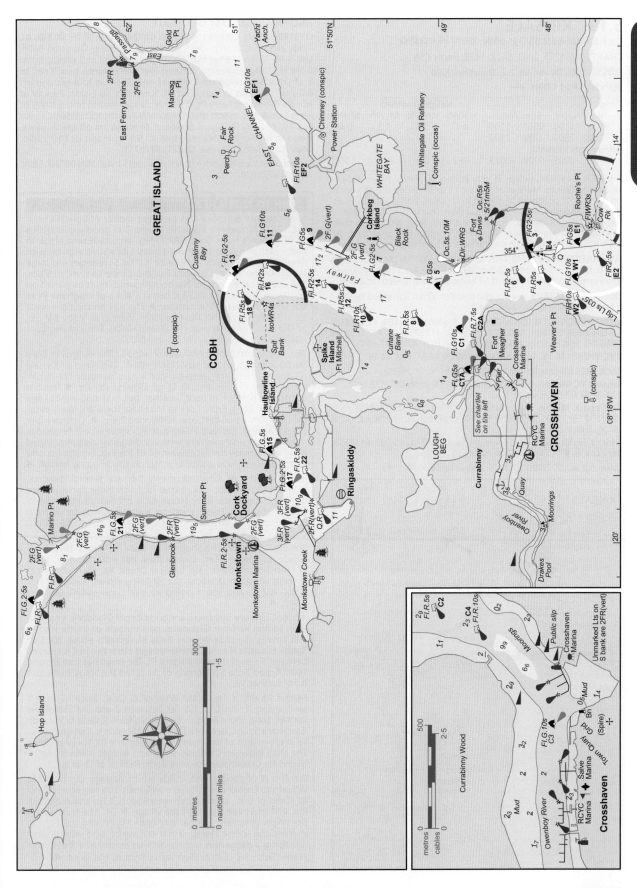

5.19 KINSALE

Cork **51°40′·80N 08°30′·00W** ❀❀❀◊◊◊✿✿✿

CHARTS AC 1765, 2053, 5622, 5623; Imray C56

TIDES –0600 Dover; ML 2·2; Duration 0600

Standard Port COBH (⟵)

Times				Height (metres)			
High Water		Low Water		MHWS	MHWN	MLWN	MLWS
0500	1100	0500	1100	4·1	3·2	1·3	0·4
1700	2300	1700	2300				
Differences KINSALE							
–0019	–0005	–0009	–0023	–0·2	0·0	+0·1	+0·2

SHELTER Excellent, except in very strong SE winds. Access H24 in all weathers/tides. Marinas at Kinsale YC and Castlepark; Ⓥ's berth on outside of pontoons in 10m in both cases; NNW of latter is FV pontoon and no ⚓ area. Possible ⊆ (Sun-Thurs) at Trident Hotel. 2 large Ⓥs NE of Kinsale Bridge (contact HM). No ⚓ allowed in main channel or within 700m of Town Pier. Contact HM prior to ⚓. All craft have to pay harbour dues as well as berthing/launching fees.

NAVIGATION WPT 51°40′·00N 08°30′·00W, 001°/1·7M to Charles's Fort lt. Beware: Bulman Rk (0·9m; SCM lt buoy) 4ca S of Preghane Pt and Farmer Rk (0·6m) ¾ca off W bank. Harbour speed limit 6kn.

LIGHTS AND MARKS See 5.3 and chartlet. Chan is marked by PHM lt buoys. Marina lts are 2 FG or FR.

COMMUNICATIONS (Code 021) MRCC (066) 9476109; Coast/Cliff Rescue 0868 501804; ⊖ 6027700; Police 4779250; Dr 4772253; Ⓗ 4546400. HM kharbour@iol.ie, 4772503 (HO), 4773047 (OT).

KYC VHF Ch M 16. Castlepark Marina 06 16 M. HM **14** 16.

FACILITIES Kinsale BY ☎4774774, Ⓥ ⛽ ✕ ⚒ Ⓔ ⛏(30t).

Kinsale YC Marina www.kyc.ie ☎4772196, mob 087 6787377 170+50Ⓥ €3·20, Ⓓ ⛴ ⛽ ✕ ⊡.

Castlepark Marina www.castleparkmarina.com ☎4774959, mob 0877502737, 130⊆ inc 20Ⓥ €3·50, deals for longer stays, ⛴ ⊡ Ⓔ ✕ ⊡ @.

Trident Hotel ⊆ ⛽ ⛽ Sovereign Sailing 4774145/087 6172555.

Services ⛽ ⛽ ⚒ Ⓔ Ⓔ ⚠ Divers ⛏(30t).

Town LB ⛴ ✉ Ⓑ ✕ ⊡ (bus to Cork, ⇶, ✈).

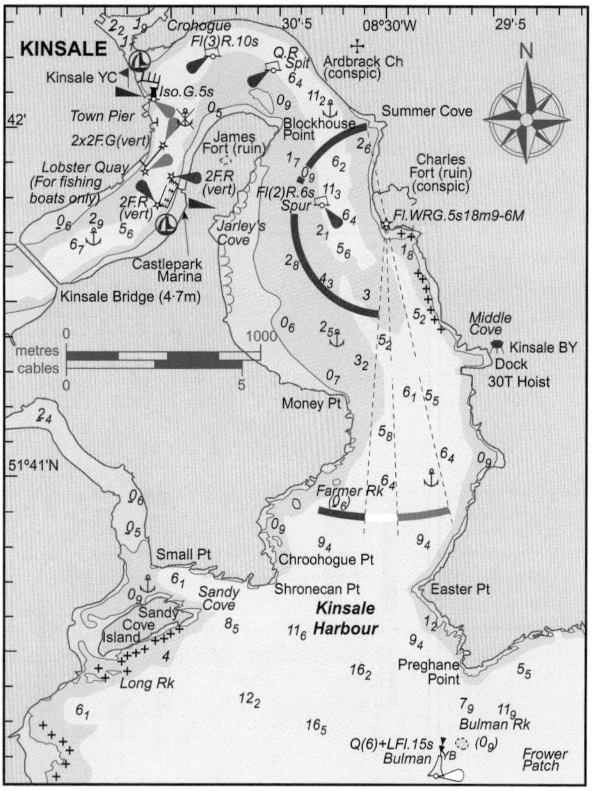

ANCHORAGE 2M EAST OF KINSALE

OYSTERHAVEN, Cork, **51°41′·20N 08°26′·90W**. ❀❀◊✿✿✿. AC 1765, 2053, 5622. HW –0600 on Dover; ML 2·2m; Duration 0600. Use 5.18. Good shelter but ⚓'s subject to swell in S winds. Enter 0·5M N of Big Sovereign, a steep islet divided into two. Keep to S of Little Sovereign on E side of ent. There is foul ground off Ballymacus Pt on W side, and off Kinure Pt on E side. Pass W of Hbr Rk (0·9m) off Ferry Pt, the only danger within hbr. ⚓ NNW of Ferry Pt in 4–6m on soft mud/weed. NW arm shoals suddenly about 5ca NW of Ferry Pt. Also ⚓ up N arm of hbr in 3m off the W shore. Weed in higher reaches may foul ⚓. No lts, marks or VHF radio. Coast/Cliff Rescue Service ☎(021) 4770711.

Oysterhaven Yacht Harbour (strictly private) 51°42′·10N 08°26′·58W, ☎(021) 4770878.

COBH TO MIZEN HEAD

Near the easy entrance and excellent shelter of Cork Harbour (AC 1777), Ringabella Bay offers temp ⚓ in good weather. 7ca SE of Robert's Hd is Daunt Rk (3·5m) on which seas break in bad weather; marked by PHM lt buoy. Little Sovereign on with Reanies Hd 241° leads inshore of it. The Sovereigns are large rks off Oyster Haven, a good hbr but prone to swell in S'lies. The ent is clear except for Harbour Rk which must be passed on its W side. Bulman Rk (SCM lt buoy) is 4ca S of Preghane Pt at the ent to Kinsale's fine harbour. ► *The tide on the Cork coast turns to the NE at HW Dover +0045. There is an eddy 5M ESE of Old Head of Kinsale at HW Dover +0400. The ingoing Cork Harbour tide begins at HW Dover +0055.*

The tide turns SW at HW Dover +0500. The outgoing Cork Harbour tide begins at HW Dover –0540. Old Head of Kinsale (lt, fog sig) is quite steep-to, but a race extends 1M to SW on W-going stream, and to SE on E-going stream. ◄ There is an inshore passage in light weather, but in strong winds keep 2M off. (AC 2424) From Cork to Mizen Hd there are many natural hbrs. Only the best are mentioned here. ► *Offshore the stream seldom exceeds 1·5kn, but it is stronger off headlands causing races and overfalls with wind against tide. Prolonged W winds increase the rate/duration of the E-going stream, and strong E winds have a similar effect on the W-going stream.* ◄

In the middle of Courtmacsherry Bay are several dangers, from E to W: Blueboy Rk, Barrel Rk (with Inner Barrels closer inshore), and Black Tom; Horse Rk is off Barry's Pt at the W side of the bay. These must be avoided going to or from Courtmacsherry, where the bar breaks in strong S/SE winds, but the river carries 2·3m.

Beware Cotton Rk and Shoonta Rk close E of Seven Heads, off which rks extend 50m. Clonakilty B has little to offer. Keep at least 5ca off Galley Hd to clear Dhulic Rk, and further off in fresh winds. ► *Offshore the W-going stream makes at HW Cobh +0200, and the E-going at HW Cobh –0420, sp rates 1·5kn.* ◄

Across Glandore Bay there are good ⚓s off Glandore, or Union Hall. Sailing W from Glandore, pass outside or inside High Is and Low Is; if inside beware Belly Rk (awash) about 3ca S of Rabbit Is. Castle Haven, a sheltered and attractive hbr, is entered between Reen Pt (lt) and Battery Pt. Toe Head has foul ground 100m S, and 7½ca S is a group of rks called the Stags. Baltimore is 7M further W.

Fastnet Rk (lit) is nearly 4M WSW of C Clear; 2½ca NE of it is an outlying rk. An E/W TSS lies between 2 and 8M SSE of the Fastnet. Long Island Bay can be entered from C Clear or through Gascanane Sound, between Clear Is and Sherkin Is. Carrigmore Rks lie in the middle of this chan, with Gascanane Rk 1ca W of them. The chan between Carrigmore Rks and Badger Island is best. If bound for Crookhaven, beware Bullig Reef, N of Clear Is.

Schull is N of Long Island, inside which passage can be made W'ward to Crookhaven. This is a well sheltered hbr, accessible at all states of tide, entered between Rock Is lt Ho and Alderman Rks, ENE of Streek Hd. ⚓ off the village. ► *Off Mizen Hd (lt ho) the W-going stream starts at HW Cobh +0120, and the E-going at HW Cobh –0500. The sp rate is 4kn, which with wind against tide forms a dangerous race, sometimes reaching to Brow Hd or Three Castle Hd, with broken water right to the shore.* ◄

5.20 COURTMACSHERRY

Cork **51°38'·22N 08°40'·90W** ❀❀⚓⚓☆☆

CHARTS AC 2092, 2081, 5622, 5623; Imray C56

TIDES HW –0610 on Dover; Duration 0545

Standard Port COBH (←—)

Times				Height (metres)			
High Water		Low Water		MHWS	MHWN	MLWN	MLWS
0500	1100	0500	1100	4·1	3·2	1·3	0·4
1700	2300	1700	2300				
Differences COURTMACSHERRY							
–0025	–0008	–0008	–0015	–0·1	–0·1	0·0	+0·1

SHELTER Good shelter upriver, but in strong S/SE winds seas break on the bar (<2m), when ent must not be attempted. Dry out in small inner hbr or � afloat on jetty (FVs) or on yacht pontoon (37m). ⚓ NE of Ferry Pt in about 2·5m or N of pontoon. Weed may foul ⚓; best to moor using two ⚓s.

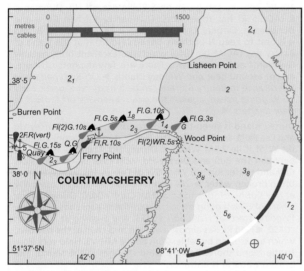

NAVIGATION WPT, 51°37'·50N 08°40'·17W, 324°/0·8M to Wood Pt. Appr in the W sector of Wood Pt lt, between Black Tom and Horse Rk (dries 3·6m); the latter is 3-4½ca E of Barry Pt on the W shore. Black Tom (2·3m), with SHM buoy Fl.G.5s 5ca SSE, is close NE of the appr. Further to NE, in centre of bay, Barrel Rk (dries 2·6m), has unlit perch (ruin). To NNW and E of it are Inner Barrels (0·5m) and Blueboy Rk. Hbr ent is between Wood Pt and SHM buoy 2ca NE, Fl G 3s. Chan (2m but 1·4m close inside ent) is marked by 5 SHM buoys and 1 PHM buoy (off Ferry Point). Upstream of Ferry Point there are moorings on both sides of the channel. The pier head is marked by 2 FR (vert) lights.

LIGHTS AND MARKS Wood Pt, Fl (2) WR 5s 15m 5M.

COMMUNICATIONS (023) Coast Rescue Service (Mob) 08685 01806; Dr 8846186 (HN 1850 335999); Police 8846122. HM (Mob) 0867394299; RNLI boathouse 8846600. No VHF.

FACILITIES Quay 🔌 LB ⚓ ⌂ (min €15/craft) ⚓ ⚡ 🚾 ⛽ (Pier 0930-1800 on request). **Village** ✕ 🛒 🛒 ≷ ✈ (bus to Cork).

5.21 GLANDORE/UNIONHALL

Cork, **51°33'·70N 09°07'·20W** ❀❀❀⚓⚓☆☆☆

CHARTS AC 2092, 5622, 5623; Imray C56

TIDES Approx as for 5.22 Castletownshend

SHELTER Excellent. 12 Y⚓s or ⚓ 1½ca SW of Glandore Pier in 2m or 1ca NE of the New pier at Unionhall in 3m.

NAVIGATION WPT 51°32'·35N 09°05'·10W, 309°/1·2M to Outer Dangers. Approach between Adam Is and Goat's Hd, thence keep

E of Eve Is and W of the chain of rocks: Outer, Middle and Inner Dangers and Sunk Rk. Before altering W for Unionhall, stand on to clear mudbank 1ca off S shore. Speed limit 3kn.

LIGHTS AND MARKS See 5.3. Galley Hd, Fl (5) 20s, is 5M E of ent. Middle and Inner Dangers are marked by 2 SHM bns; and Sunk Rk by a SHM lt buoy, Fl G 5s.

COMMUNICATIONS (Code 028) Coast Rescue 33115; Police (023) 23088; Dr 23456; HM Glandore/Unionhall 34737, mob 0866081944.

HM Ch 06.

FACILITIES **Glandore** GHYC, ⚓s €14.00/craft (contact Glandore Inn ☎33468/33518), ⚓ ✉ ✕ ⛽ Kos. **Unionhall** ⌂ (outside of FVs/ drying ⌂ Old Quay) €15.00/craft, ⚓ D(occ on quayside) or 📷 📷 (Leap 2M) ⚒ ⛽ ⚓ 🚾 ✉ ✕ 🛒.

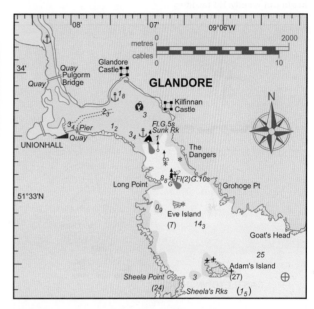

5.22 CASTLETOWNSHEND

Cork **51°30'·90N 09°10'·70W** ❀❀❀⚓⚓☆☆☆

CHARTS AC 2092, 2129, 5623; Imray C56

TIDES +0605 Dover; ML 2·2; Duration 0605

Standard Port COBH (←—)

Times				Height (metres)			
High Water		Low Water		MHWS	MHWN	MLWN	MLWS
0500	1100	0500	1100	4·1	3·2	1·3	0·4
1700	2300	1700	2300				
Differences CASTLETOWNSHEND							
–0020	–0030	–0020	–0050	–0·4	–0·2	+0·1	+0·3
CLONAKILTY BAY (5M NE of Galley Head)							
–0033	–0011	–0019	–0041	–0·3	–0·2	ND	ND

SHELTER Excellent ⚓ in midstream SE of Castletownshend slip, protected from all weathers and available at all tides; but the outer part of hbr is subject to swell in S winds. Or ⚓ N of Cat Island, or upstream as depth permits. Caution: An underwater cable runs E/W across the hbr from the slip close N of Reen Pier to the slip at Castletownshend.

NAVIGATION WPT 51°30'·28N, 09°10'·26W, 349°/7ca to Reen Pt lt. Enter between Horse Is (35m) and Skiddy Is (9m) both of which have foul ground all round. Black Rk lies off the SE side of Horse Is and is steep-to along its S side. Flea Sound is a narrow boat chan, obstructed by rks. Colonel's Rk (0·5m) lies close to the E shore, 2ca N of Reen Pt. Beware salmon nets.

Continued overleaf

CASTLETOWNSHEND *continued*

LIGHTS AND MARKS Reen Pt, Fl WRG 10s; a small slender W bn; vis shore-G-338°-W-001°-R-shore. A ruined tr is on Horse Is.

COMMUNICATIONS (Code 028) MRCC (066) 9746109; Coast/Cliff Rescue Service 21039; ⊖ Bantry (027) 50061; Police 36144; Dr 23456; Ⓗ 21677.

No VHF

FACILITIES Reen Pier ↘ ⚓; **Sailing Club** ☎36100; **Castletownshend Village** ↘ ⚓ ⌧ Ⓑ(Skibbereen) 🛒 ⤬ ▭ ⇌ ✈ (Cork).

BARLOGE CREEK, Cork, **51°29'·57N 09°17'·58W**. AC 2129. Tides approx as Castletownshend. A narrow creek, well sheltered except from S/SE winds. Appr with Gokane Pt brg 120°. Enter W of Bullock Is, keeping to the W side to clear rks S of the island. ⚓ W of the Is in 3m but weedy. No facilities.

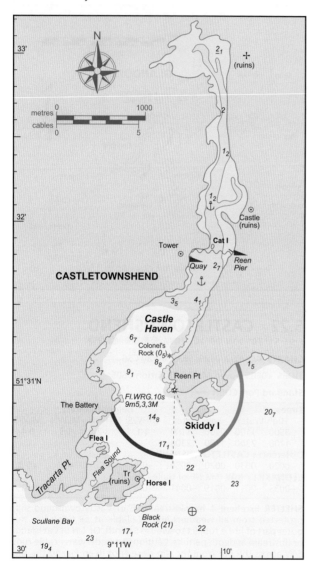

THE WEST COAST

This coast offers wonderful cruising, although exposed to the Atlantic and any swell offshore; but this diminishes mid-summer. In bad weather however the sea breaks dangerously on shoals with quite substantial depths. There is usually a refuge close by, but if caught out in deteriorating weather and poor vis, a stranger may need to make an offing until conditions improve, so a sound yacht and good crew are required. Even in mid-summer at least one gale may be met in a two-week cruise. Fog is less frequent than in the Irish Sea.

▶ *Tidal streams are weak, except round headlands.* ◀ There are few lights, so inshore navigation is unwise after dark, however coastal navigation is feasible at night in good visibility. Keep a good watch for lobster pots in inshore waters. Stores, fuel and water are not readily available.

MIZEN HEAD TO DINGLE BAY

(AC 2423) At S end of Dunmanus Bay Three Castle Hd has rks 1ca W, and sea can break on S Bullig 4ca off Hd. Dunmanus B (AC 2552) has three hbrs: Dunmanus, Kitchen Cove and Dunbeacon. Carbery, Cold and Furze Is lie in middle of B, and it is best to keep N of them. Sheep's Hd (lt) is at the S end of Bantry Bay (AC 1838, 1840) which has excellent hbrs, notably Glengariff and Castletown. There are few dangers offshore, except around Bear and Whiddy Islands. ▶ *Off Blackball Hd at W entrance to Bantry B there can be a nasty race, particularly on W-going stream against the wind. Keep 3ca off Crow Is to clear dangers.* ◀

Dursey Island is steep-to except for rk 7½ca NE of Dursey Hd and Lea Rk (1·4m) 1½ca SW. The Bull (lt, fog sig, Racon) and two rks W of it lie 2·5M WNW of Dursey Hd. The Cow is midway between The Bull and Dursey Hd, with clear water each side. Calf and Heifer Rks are 7½ca SW of Dursey Hd, where there is often broken water. ▶ *2M W of The Bull the stream turns NW at HW Cobh +0150, and SE at HW Cobh –0420. Dursey Sound (chart 2495) is a good short cut, but the stream runs 4kn at sp; W-going starts at HW Cobh +0135, and E-going at HW Cobh –0450.* ◀ Flag Rk lies almost awash in mid-chan at the narrows, which are crossed by cables 25m above MHWS. Hold very close to the Island shore. Beware wind changes in the sound, and broken water at N entrance.

Kenmare R. (AC 2495) has attractive hbrs and ⚓s, but its shores are rky, with no lights. The best places are Sneem, Kilmakilloge and Ardgroom. Off Lamb's Head, Two Headed Island is steep-to; further W is Moylaun Is with a rk 300m SW of it. Little Hog (or Deenish) Island is rky 1·5M to W, followed by Great Hog (or Scariff) Is which has a rk close N, and a reef extending 2ca W.

Darrynane is an attractive, sheltered hbr NNW of Lamb Hd. The entrance has ldg lts and marks, but is narrow and dangerous in bad weather. Ballinskelligs Bay has an ⚓ N of Horse Is, which has two rks close off E end. Centre of bay is a prohib ⚓ (cables reported).

Rough water is met between Bolus Hd and Bray Hd with fresh onshore winds or swell. The SW end of Puffin Island is steep-to, but the sound to the E is rky and not advised. Great Skellig (lit) is 6M, and Little Skellig 5M WSW of Puffin Is. Lemon Rk lies between Puffin Is and Little Skellig. ▶ *Here the stream turns N at HW Cobh +0500, and S at HW Cobh –0110.* ◀ There is a rk 3ca SW of Great Skellig. When very calm it is possible to go alongside at Blind Man's Cove on NE side of Great Skellig, where there are interesting ruins.

5.23 BALTIMORE

Cork 51°28'·30N 09°23'·40W ✳✳✳⚓✦✦⚓✿✿✿

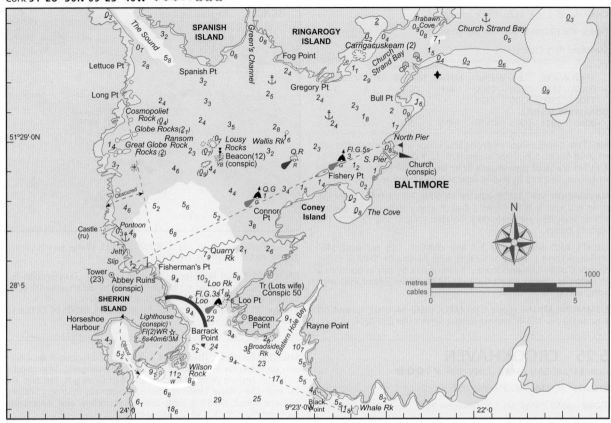

CHARTS AC 2129, 3725, 5623; Imray C56

TIDES −0605 Dover; ML 2·1; Duration 0610

Standard Port COBH (←—)

Times				Height (metres)			
High Water		Low Water		MHWS	MHWN	MLWN	MLWS
0500	1100	0500	1100	4·1	3·2	1·3	0·4
1700	2300	1700	2300				
Differences BALTIMORE							
−0025	−0005	−0010	−0050	−0·6	−0·3	+0·1	+0·2

SHELTER Excellent. Access H24 from the S. At Baltimore, pontoon (Apr-Sep) on S Pier, ⌒ for up to 20 yachts in 2·4m. Inner Hbr, partly dries between N and S piers, mostly used by ferries, local boats and FVs; the latter also berth on N pier (addition to pier in progress). Ro Ro berth SE of Bull Pt. ⚓ about 200m W of S pier, or about 200m N of N Pier. Beware extensive moorings. In strong NW'lies ⚓ in Church Strand Bay. Its are required. Do not ⚓ in dredged chan between Wallis Rk buoy and N Pier, or in chan to Church Strand Bay. In strong W winds ⚓ in lee of Sherkin Is off Castle ruins or berth on pontoon (see Adjacent Anchorages, Sherkin Island).

NAVIGATION WPT 51°27'·93N 09°23'·46W, 000°/5ca to Loo Rk SHM lt buoy. No passage between buoy and mainland. Beware Lousy Rks (SCM bn) and Wallis Rk (PHM lt buoy) in middle of the bay. Cardinal buoys mark rocks in The Sound, which demands care in pilotage; AC 3725 and ICC SDs essential. SCM marks isolated rk off Inane Pt in the R Ilen, which is navigable on the flood for at least 4M above The Sound. Speed limit 6kn in R Ilen and N/NE of Wallace Rock.

LIGHTS AND MARKS See 5.3 and chartlet. Ent easily identified by Barrack Pt lt ho and conspic W tr (Lot's Wife) on Beacon Pt.

COMMUNICATIONS (Code 028) MRCC and Coast/Cliff Rescue Service (066) 9476109; ✆ (027) 53210; Police 20102; Dr 23456/after hrs 1850 335999, Ⓗ 21677. HM 087 2351485.

VHF (HM) Ch 09, 16.

FACILITIES Berthing: May-Sept from €20/craft, ☎22145, 0872 351485 or www.atlanticboat.ie; ⌒ ⌒ ⚓(☎20106) ⚓ on pontoon; **Baltimore SC** ☎20426, visitors welcome ⚑ ⌑; **Glenans Irish Sailing School** ☎(01) 6611481, 028 20154; **Sherkin** Pontoon ⚓ access to shore in season. **Services** ⚓ ⚓ Kos ⚒ ⚓ 🖵 (on R Ilen at Old Court), 🛢 ACA ⚒. **Village** ⊠ 🖵 bus to Cork for ⇌ ✈.

ADJACENT ANCHORAGES

SHERKIN ISLAND on W side of harbour entrance. ⚓s: Horseshoe Harbour (keep well to the W in narrow entrance; unlit); and off Castle ruins, 5ca N, where there are also some ⌒ on pontoons (⚓ and electricity) belonging to nearby Islander's Rest Hotel.

CLEAR ISLAND, N HARBOUR, 51°26'·60N 09°30'·20W. AC 2129, 5623. Tides approx as Schull, 5.24. A tiny, partly drying inlet on N coast of Clear Is, exposed to N'ly swell. Rks either side of outer appr 196°. Inside the narrow (30m), rky ent keep to the E. Lie to 2 ⚓s on E side in about 1·5m or drying berth in Inner Hbr clear of ferry bad weather berth. Outer (N) bkwtr rebuilt with tidal gate (2015) which will permit vessels to remain afloat. Facilities ⚓ ⚓ 🖵 🖵 ⊠ 🛒 ✕ 🖵.

ROARINGWATER BAY, Long Island Bay AC 2129, 5623. Enter between Cape Clear and Mizen Hd, extends NE into Roaring-water Bay. *Beware extensive, low-lying unlit fish farms.* Safest appr, S of Schull, is via Carthy's Sound (51°30'N 09°30'W). From the SE appr via Gascanane Sound, but beware Toorane Rks, Anima Rk and outlying rks off many of the islands. Shelter in various winds at ⚓s clockwise from Horse Island: 3ca E and 7ca NE of E tip of Horse Is; in Ballydehob B 2m (Ballydehob has a good quay for tenders and most facilities); Poulgorm B 2m; 3ca SSW of Carrigvalish Rks in 6m. Rincolisky Cas (ru) is conspic on S side of bay. The narrow chan E of Hare Is and N of Sherkin Is has two ⚓s; also leads via The Sound into Baltimore hbr. Local advice useful. Temp'y fair weather ⚓s in Carthy's Islands. Rossbrin Cove safe ⚓ 2·5M E of Schull, but many local moorings; no access from E of Horse Is due to drying Horse Ridge.

5.24 SCHULL

Cork **51°30'·80N 09°32'·00W** ❀❀❀⚓⚓♨♨♨

CHARTS AC 2184, 2129, 5623; Imray C56

TIDES +0610 Dover; ML 1·8; Duration 0610

Standard Port COBH (←—)

Times				Height (metres)			
High Water		Low Water		MHWS	MHWN	MLWN	MLWS
0500	1100	0500	1100	4·1	3·2	1·3	0·4
1700	2300	1700	2300				
Differences SCHULL							
−0040	−0015	−0015	−0110	−0·9	−0·6	−0·2	0·0

SHELTER Good, except in strong S/SE winds when best shelter is N of Long Island. Schull Hbr access H24. 12 Y ⚓s in NE part of hbr or ⚓ in 3m 1ca SE of pier, usually lit by street lts all night; keep clear of fairway marked by 8 unlit lateral buoys (summer time only).

NAVIGATION WPT 51°29'·60N 09°31'·60W, 346°/2·1M to front ldg lt. In hbr ent, Bull Rk (dries 1·8m), R iron perch, can be passed either side. Beware unmarked isolated rock, 0·5m, close to the visitors' buoys.

LIGHTS AND MARKS See 5.3 and chartlet. Ldg lts, lead 346° between Long Is Pt, W conical tr, and Amelia Rk SHM lt buoy; thence E of Bull Rk and toward head of bay. By day in good vis 2 W radomes conspic on Mt Gabriel (2M N of Schull) lead 355° with Long Is Pt lt ho in transit.

COMMUNICATIONS (Code 028) MRCC (066) 9476109; Coast/Cliff Rescue Service 35318; Inshore Rescue Service 086 236 0206; ⊖ (027)

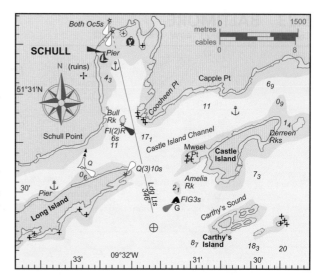

51562; Police 28111; Dr 28311; ⊞ (027) 50133. Water Sports Centre 28554; HM 086 039105. No VHF.

FACILITIES Schull Pier/Hbr ⚓ (not at LWS) FV pier/pontoon for tenders, ⛴ tempy, ⚓s €10/night, ⚒ ▯ (by arrangement) ⚓ ⚠.
Sailing Club ☎37352; **Services** Kos ☂ ⚒ ⚓ ⚒ ⚓.
Village ☎ ☎ (Ballydehob 5M), ☒ @, Charts, ✉ ⑧ ✕ ⚓ bus to Cork for ⇌ ✈ Ferries.

5.25 CROOKHAVEN

Cork **51°28'·50N 09°42'·00W** ❀❀ ♨♨♨♨

CHARTS AC 2184, 5623; Imray C56

TIDES +0550 Dover; ML 1·8; Duration 0610

Standard Port COBH (←—)

Times				Height (metres)			
High Water		Low Water		MHWS	MHWN	MLWN	MLWS
0500	1100	0500	1100	4·1	3·2	1·3	0·4
1700	2300	1700	2300				
Differences CROOKHAVEN							
−0057	−0033	−0048	−0112	−0·8	−0·6	−0·4	−0·1
DUNMANUS HARBOUR							
−0107	−0031	−0044	−0120	−0·7	−0·6	−0·2	0·0
DUNBEACON HARBOUR							
−0057	−0025	−0032	−0104	−0·8	−0·7	−0·3	−0·1

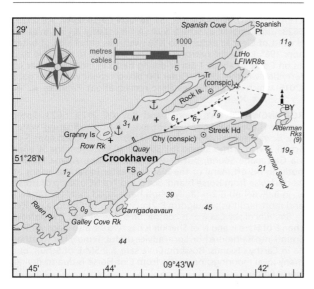

SHELTER Excellent. There are 8 Y ⚓s and 10 dayglow R ⚓s. Short stay pontoon for up to 4 boats (⚓/stores/passengers). ⚓s in middle of bay in 3m; off W tip of Rock Is; and E of Granny Is; last two are far from the village. Holding is patchy, especially in strong SW'lies; beware weed, shellfish beds around shoreline and submarine pipeline from Rock Is to Crookhaven.

NAVIGATION WPT 51°28'·50N 09°40'·50W, 274°/1M to Rock Is lt ho. Ent between this lt and NCM bn on Black Horse Rks (3½ca ESE). From S, keep 1ca E of Alderman Rks and ½ca off Black Horse Rks bn. Passage between Streek Hd and Alderman Rks is not advised for strangers. Inside the bay the shores are steep to. 1ca WSW of West end of Rock Is beware isolated rock, which is awash at LAT.

LIGHTS AND MARKS Lt ho on Rock Is (conspic W tr) L Fl WR 8s 20m 13/11M; vis outside hbr: W over Long Is Bay-281°-R-340°; inside hbr: 281°-R-348°-W-shore(N).

COMMUNICATIONS (Code 028) MRCC (066) 9476109; Coast/Cliff Rescue at Goleen 35318; ⊖ (027) 50061; Dr 35148; ✉ 35200. HM (O'Sullivan's Bar) 35319. No VHF.

FACILITIES Village ⚓s (☎086 356 7771) €8.00, pontoon for small craft ⚓ ☎ ⚒ ✉ ⑧(Schull) ⚒ ✕ ⚓, taxi to Goleen then bus to Cork, ✈ ⇌.

ADJACENT HARBOURS
GOLEEN (Kireal-coegea), Cork, **51°29'·65N 09°42'·21W**. AC 2184, 5623. Tides as Crookhaven. A narrow inlet 6ca N of Spanish Pt; good shelter in fair weather, except from SE. 2 churches are easily seen, but ent not visible until close. Keep to S side of ent and ⚓ fore-and-aft just below quay, where ⛴ also possible. Facilities: ☎ ⚒ ⚓.

DUNMANUS BAY, Cork. AC 2552, 5623. Tides see 5.25. Appr between Three Castle Hd and Sheep's Hd, Fl (3) WR 15s 83m 18/15M; no other lts. Ent to **Dunmanus Hbr**, 51°32'·70N 09°39'·86W, is 1ca wide; breakers both sides. ⚓ in 4m centre of B. **Kitchen Cove**, 51°35'·50N 09°38'·05W, best of the 3 hbrs; enter W of Owens Is and ⚓ 1ca NNW of it or 2ca further N in 3m. Exposed to S, but good holding. Quay at Ahakista village: ⛴(drying)⚓ ⚒ ⚒ ✕ ⚓. **Dunbeacon Hbr**, 51°36'·35N 09°33'·60W, is shallow and rock-girt. Quay possible ⛴ in 2m (used by FVs), ⚓; ⚓ E or SE of Mannion Is. Durrus (¾M): ☎ ☎ ✕ ⚓.

5.26 BANTRY BAY

Cork 51°34'N 09°57'W ✦✦✦♠♠♠♠✿✿✿

CHARTS AC 2552, 1840, 1838, 5623; Imray C56

TIDES +0600 Dover; ML 1·8; Duration 0610

Standard Port COBH (←)

Times				Height (metres)			
High Water		Low Water		MHWS	MHWN	MLWN	MLWS
0500	1100	0500	1100	4·1	3·2	1·3	0·4
1700	2300	1700	2300				
Differences BANTRY							
–0045	–0025	–0040	–0105	–0·7	–0·6	–0·2	+0·1
CASTLETOWN (Bearhaven)							
–0048	–0012	–0025	–0101	–0·8	–0·6	–0·2	0·0
BLACK BALL HARBOUR (51°36N 10°02W)							
–0115	–0035	–0047	–0127	–0·7	–0·6	–0·1	+0·1

SHELTER/NAVIGATION Bantry Bay extends 20M ENE from Sheep's Hd, Fl (3) WR 15s 83m 18/15M. Access is easy, but the Bay is exposed to W'lies. The shore is clear everywhere except off Bear Is and Whiddy Is. Some of the many well sheltered ‡s on the N shore are detailed on this page. The S shore has few ‡s.

CASTLETOWN BEARHAVEN 51°38'·80N 09°54'·45W. AC 1840, 5623. Castletownbere Fishery Harbour lies between Dinish Is and the mainland; also ‡ at **Dunboy Bay**, W of Piper Snd (open to E). 4 Y ✿s are laid Apr-Sep 3ca E of Dinish Is. Lts: At W ent, Ardnakinna Pt, Fl (2) WR 10s 62m 17/14M, H24. At E ent to Bearhaven: Roancarrigmore, Fl WR 5s 13m 11/9M. Appr W of Bear Is on 023·25° Dir lt, Oc WRG 5s 7m 15/12M (023°-W-023·5°); then inner ldg lts 008°, both Oc Bu 6s 4/7m 6M, vis 005°-013°, via ent chan which narrows to 50m where it is marked by lit bcns. Beware Walter Scott Rk (2·7m), SCM lt buoy, and Carrigaglos (0·6m high) S of Dinish Is. VHF Ch 14 16. HM e(027) 70220. Facilities: ⚓ 🛢 on quay; 🚗 on Dinish Is. **Town** 🅿 🅿 Kos ✕ ⚒ ⟟✉ ⓑ 🛒 ✕ 🍴 @.

LAWRENCE COVE MARINA 51°38'·28N 09°49'·28W; AC 1840, 5623. *See inset on chartlet below.* Good shelter on N side of Bear Island.

Marina on S side of cove has NE/SW pontoon 90m long (40⌇ in 3-3·5m). From E keep clear of Palmer Rock and a shoal patch, both 1·8m. ☎027 75044; VHF Ch 16 **M**. ⌇(€1.52), ⚓ 🗓 🄍 🛢 🔧. Friendly welcome at the only marina between Kinsale and Cahersiveen/Dingle. There are 4 yellow ✿s in 3m close S of Ardagh Point, or ‡ in 4m to W of Turk Is. At Rerrin ⚓ 🛢 🄍(storage) ✉ 🛒 ✕ 🍴 bus to Cork.

LONEHORT HARBOUR 51°38'·12N 09°47'·80W. AC 1840, 5623. At E tip of Bear Is, good shelter but keep S at ent to clear unmarked rks; then turn ENE to ‡ in 2·7m at E end of cove. Be aware of Firing Practice Area to east of harbour entrance (full clear range procedure in force).

ADRIGOLE 51°40'·51N 09°43'·22W. AC 1840, 5623. Good shelter, but squally in W/N gales. Beware Doucallia Rk, dries 1·2m, 1M SSW of ent. Beyond the 2ca wide ent, keep E of Orthons Is (rks on W side). 7 Y ✿s NE of Orthons Is. ‡s to suit wind direction: off pier on E shore 4m; N or NW of Orthons Is. Drumlave (½M E): ⚓ ⚓ 🗓 (sailing school) 🅿 🛢 ✉ 🛒.

Trafrask Bay, 2M east, has Y✿ at 51°40'·8N 09°40'·1W; 🛒 ✕ 🍴.

GLENGARRIFF 51°44'·20N 09°31'·90W. AC 1838, 5623. Tides as Bantry. Beautiful ‡ S of Bark Is in 7-10m; or to NE in 3m, where there are 6 Y ✿s. Better for yachts than Bantry hbr. Ent between Big Pt and Gun Pt. Keep 1ca E of rks off Garinish Island (Illnacullen) and Ship Is; chan marked to either side by lateral marks LFl R/G 4s. Beware marine farms. HT cables removed allowing access N of Garinish with local knowledge; but rocky chan W of should not be attempted. Facilities: Eccles hotel, 🗓. **Village** ⚓ (ferry berth 1800-1900) 🅿 🅿 Kos ✉ 🛒 ✕ 🍴 @.

BANTRY 51°40'·85N 09°27'·85W. AC 1838, 5623. Beware Gerane Rks ½M W of Whiddy Is. Appr via the buoyed/lit N chan to E of Horse and Chapel Is; keep 2ca off all islands to clear unlit marine farms. The S chan, fair weather only. Appr Relane Pt hdg 063° with HW mark S. Beach (seaward edge of airfield) ≠ Reenbeg Cliff (distant rounded hill) to clear Cracker Rk, then leave Blue Hill and S Beach to stbd. ✿s call Bantry Hbr Ch 14 or ☎027 51253; VHF 14 11 16 (H24). HM (027) 53277; ⊖ 50061; Police 50045; Dr 50405; 🄷 50133. MRCC (066) 9476109. Facilities: ⚓ **Pier** ⌇(drying) ⚓ 🛢; **Bantry Bay SC** ☎51724, Kos ✕ ✉ ⓑ 🛒 ✕ 🍴 bus to Cork.

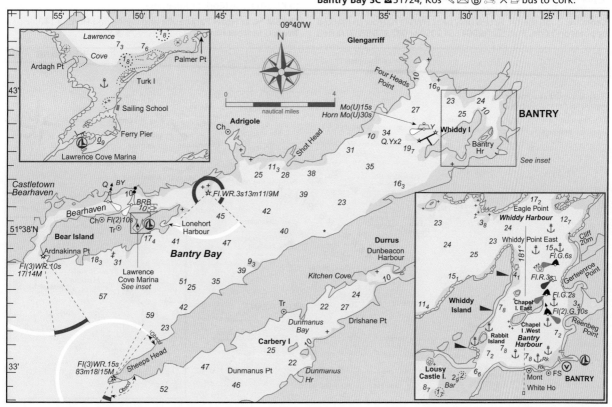

5.27 KENMARE RIVER

Kerry 51°45'·00N 10°00'·00W ✿✿✿✧✧ ✿✿✿

CHARTS AC 2495; Imray C56

TIDES +0515 Dover; Duration Dunkerron 0620

Standard Port COBH (←)

Times				Height (metres)			
High Water		Low Water		MHWS	MHWN	MLWN	MLWS
0500	1100	0500	1100	4·1	3·2	1·3	0·4
1700	2300	1700	2300				
Differences BALLYCROVANE HARBOUR (Coulagh Bay)							
−0116	−0036	−0053	−0133	−0·6	−0·5	−0·1	0·0
DUNKERRON HARBOUR							
−0117	−0027	−0050	−0140	−0·2	−0·3	+0·1	0·0
WEST COVE (51°46'N 10°03'W)							
−0113	−0033	−0049	−0129	−0·6	−0·5	−0·1	0·0
BALLINSKELLIGS BAY							
−0119	−0039	−0054	−0134	−0·5	−0·5	−0·1	0·0

SHELTER Garnish Bay (S of Long I): is only good in settled weather and W'ly winds. ⚓ either W or 1ca S of the Carrigduff concrete bn.

Ballycrovane: in NE of Coulagh B is a good ⚓, but open to W'ly swell which breaks on submerged rks in SE. N and E shores are foul 5ca NE of Bird Is.

Cleanderry: ent NE of Illaunbweeheen (Yellow Is) is only 7m wide and rky. ⚓ ENE of inner hbr. Beware marine farms.

Ardgroom: excellent shelter, but intricate ent over rky bar. Appr with B bn brg 135°; then 2 W bns (front on Black Rk, rear ashore) lead 099° over bar. Alter 206° as two bns astern come in transit. When clear, steer WNW to ⚓ 0·5 ca E of Reenavade pier. Beware marine farms off Ardgroom & Kilmakilloge.

Kilmakilloge: is a safe ⚓ in all winds. Beware mussel beds and rky shoals. On appr keep S side of ent, heading W of Spanish Is until past PHM buoy, Fl(2) R 10s, then steer approx 105°. Bunaw Hbr ldg lts 041°, front Oc R 3s, rear Iso R 2s (access only near HW; ⚓ for shoal draught). Keep S side of ent; ⚓ 2ca W of Carrigwee bn; S of Eskadawer Pt; or Collorus Hbr W side only.

Ormond's Harbour: good shelter except in SW or W winds, but beware rk 2½ca ENE of Hog Is. ⚓ in S half of bay.

Kenmare: good shelter. Access only near HW via narrow ch marked by poles on S side. Poss ⚓ (☎064 664 2059 or 087 250 8803) rafted

at end of pier (⚓ available) at N side of river, just below town. Beware very strong ebbs at springs and after heavy rains.

Dunkerron Harbour: ent between Cod Rks and The Boar to ⚓ 1ca NW of Fox Is in 3·2m; land at Templenoe pier. 4ca E of Reen Pt behind pier ⚓ available.

Sneem: enter between Sherky Is and Rossdohan Is. Hotel conspic NE of hbr. 3 Y ⚓s and ⚓ NE of Garinish Is, but uncomfortable if swell enters either side of Sherky Is. Beware of marine farms.

Darrynane: 1½M NW of Lamb's Hd, is appr'd from the S between Deenish and Moylaun Islands, but not with high SW swell. Enter with care on the ldg marks/lts 034°, 2 W bns, both Oc 3s 10/16m 4M. Safe ⚓ (3m) NE of Lamb's Is. Also ⚓s in Lehid Hbr (S shore), R Blackwater, Coongar Hbr & W Cove.

NAVIGATION WPT 51°40'·00N 10°17'·20W, 065°/15·6M to 0.5M S of Sherky Island. From SW, keep NW of The Bull and Dursey Is. From SE, Dursey Sound is possible in fair weather but narrow (beware Flag Rk 0·3m) and with cable car, 21m clearance. To clear dangerous rks off Coulagh Bay, keep twr on Dursey Is well open of Cod's Head 220°. From NW, there are 3 deep chans off Lamb's Head: between Scarriff Is and Deenish Is which is clear; between Deenish and Moylaun Is which has rky shoals; and between Moylaun and Two Headed Is which is clear and 4½ca wide. A night appr into the river is possible, but close appr to hbrs or ⚓s is not advised. Up-river from Sneem Hbr, keep clear of Maiden Rk(dries 0·5m); Church Rks and Lackeen Rks are unmarked; a buoyed chan lies between Carrignaronabeg and Bat Rock. Beware marine farms.

LIGHTS AND MARKS On Dursey Is: Old Watch Twr (conspic) 250m. Eagle Hill (Cod's Hd) 216m. Lights are as on chartlet.

COMMUNICATIONS (Code 064) MRCC (066) 9476109; ⊖ Bantry (027) 50061; Ⓗ 4108; Police 41177. No VHF.

FACILITIES

ARDGROOM Pallas Hbr 🕙 🕙 🍴 ✗ 🏠 Kos @ ✉ at Ardgroom village (2M SSW of Reenavade pier).

KILMAKILLOGE Bunaw Pier ⚓ 🍴 🏠; 2M to 🕙 Kos, ✉.

KENMARE ⚓. **Town** 🕙 🕙 Kos ⚓ ✗ 🍴 🏠 Ⓗ ✉ inc @ Ⓑ ⇌ (bus to Killarney) ✈ (Cork or Killarney).

SNEEM ⚓ at Hotel Parknasilla and Oysterbed Ho pier (⚓).
Town (2M from hbr), 🕙 🕙 ✗ 🏠 ✉ 🍴 ⚓ Kos.

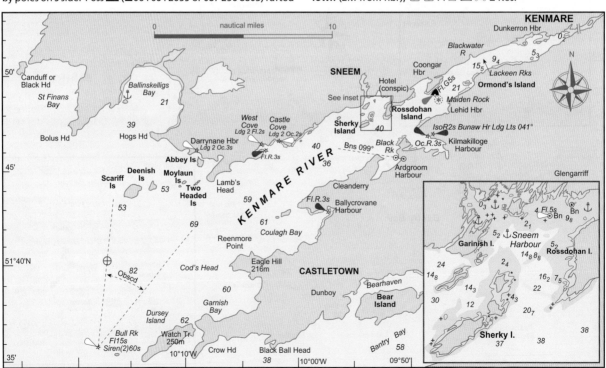

5.28 DINGLE BAY

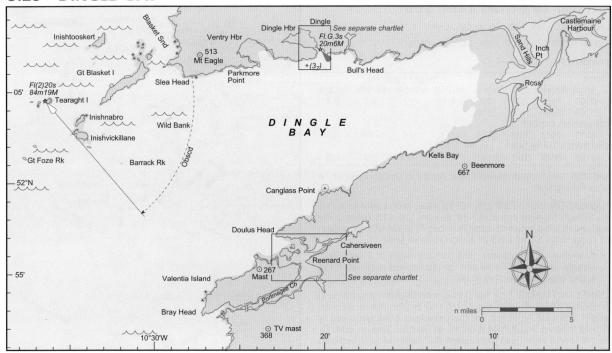

5.29 VALENTIA HARBOUR

Kerry 51°55'·7N 10°17'·1W ✿✿▲▲✿✿✿

CHARTS AC 2125; Imray C56

TIDES +0515 Dover

Standard Port COBH (←—)

Times				Height (metres)			
High Water		Low Water		MHWS	MHWN	MLWN	MLWS
0500	1100	0500	1100	4·1	3·2	1·3	0·4
1700	2300	1700	2300				
Differences VALENTIA HARBOUR (Knight's Town)							
–0118	–0038	–0056	–0136	–0·6	–0·4	–0·1	0·0

SHELTER Good ⌂s at: Glanleam B, 6ca S of Fort Pt in 4m; 1ca NW of LB slip in 2·5m (beware The Foot, spit drying 1·2m, marked by ECM lt buoy) SE of Ferry Pier at Knight's Town (E end of the island) in 4m; in bay on the S side of Beginish Is in 3m.

NAVIGATION WPT 51°56'·84N 10°20'·15W 147°/1M to Fort Pt lt. Appr the NE end of Valentia Is, either via:

- Beware rock outcrop 2.6m 1 Ca ENE Reenadrolaun Pt and other shoal patches within 10m contour.
- Doulus Bay, N of Beginish Is (avoid if swell is running). Clear Black Rks by ½ca then head for E end of Beginish Is as soon as Reenard Pt opens to port. When Lamb Is and the N point of Beginish are about to open astern, steer to keep them so till Reenard Point opens to the E of Church Is. Then steer to pass between Church Is and the WCM buoy marking Passage Rk.
- Better ent, between Fort Pt and Beginish Is (easy access except in strong NW'lies). Beware Hbr Rk, 2·6m, 3ca SE of Fort Pt marked by ECM lt Bn.

For **Cahersiveen Marina** from Valentia Is start as early on the tide possible to cross the Caher Bar, min depth 1·4m (buoyed), using the ldg lts/lines 019-199°, then keep to the middle of the river.

For appr S of Island via Portmagee chan see **Portmagee** overleaf for info on availability of the swing bridge across the chan.

LIGHTS AND MARKS See 5.3 and chartlet.

COMMUNICATIONS CG 9476109; ⊖ 7128540; Dr 9472121; Police 9472111; ⊞ 9472100; Knightstown HM (066) 9476124;

Cahersiveen Marina ☎947 2777, VHF Ch **M** www.cahersiveenmarina.ie.

FACILITIES Knight's Town Kos ▣ ✕ ⚒ 🍴 **Marina** ⌂ are readily available in expanding facility, some with ⬦. Ferry/bus to Cahersiveen (2½M) for usual shops; Bus to ⇌ (Tralee and Killarney) ✈ (Kerry, Shannon, Cork). **Cahersiveen Marina** 2M upriver, min depth 2.5m in basin, 93 inc Ⓥ €2.50, ▣ ▲ ✕ ⚒ 🛢 Ⓔ 🏳(14t) ⊠ Ⓑ 🛒 ✕ 🗺.

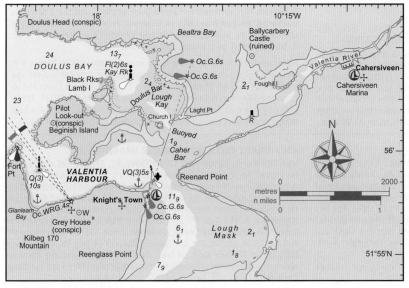

5.30 DINGLE

Kerry **52°07'·14N 10°15'·48W** ✳✳✳✳🌙🌙☆☆☆

CHARTS AC 2789, 2790; Imray C55, C56

TIDES +0540 Dover; ML 2·1m; Duration 0605

Standard Port COBH (←)

Times				Height (metres)			
High Water		Low Water		MHWS	MHWN	MLWN	MLWS
0500	1100	0500	1100	4·1	3·2	1·3	0·4
1700	2300	1700	2300				
Differences DINGLE							
–0111	–0041	–0049	–0119	–0·1	0·0	+0·3	+0·4
SMERWICK HARBOUR							
–0107	–0027	–0041	–0121	–0·3	–0·4	ND	ND

SHELTER Excellent at marina (3·3m depth) in landlocked hbr. A busy fishing port.

NAVIGATION WPT 52°06'·20N 10° 15'·48W, 360°/1·06M to lt Fl G 3s. Straightforward entrance H24. Beware Crow Rk (dries 3·7m) and shoals lying between it and Reenbeg Pt (0·8M NE). Keep clear of rocky ledge SW of Black Pt indicated by lit SHM.

- **Castlemaine Hbr,** approx 15M E at the head of Dingle Bay, largely dries and should not be attempted without local knowledge or inspection at LW.

LIGHTS AND MARKS Eask Twr (195m, with fingerpost pointing E) is conspic 0·85M WSW of ent. Lt trs, Fl G 3s 20m 6M on NE side, and Fl 5s 5m 3M SW of ent. Ent chan, dredged 2·6m, is marked by 5 SHM lt buoys and 3 PHM lt buoys, as chartlet. Ldg lts, both Oc 3s, (W ◊s on B poles) lead from astern 182° to hbr bkwtrs. Sectored Dir lt 002° Oc RWG 4s on W side of Main Pier.

COMMUNICATIONS (Code 066) Coastguard (066) 9476109; ⊖ 7121480; Dr 9152225; ⊞9151455; Police 9151522. All emergencies: 999 or 112.

Ch **14** 16 ⚓ but no calls required. Valentia Radio (Ch 24 28) will relay urgent messages to Dingle HM.

FACILITIES **Marina** dinglemarina.ie ☎087 9254115 ⚓ (launch €2) 60⚓+20🄥 €2·50, ⚒ 🔧 ⛽ ⛴(70t).

Town 🏨 🏨 🍴 Kos ⚒ 🅑🄷 🄔 △🅰 🖂 🅑 🛒 ✕ ◻ ⇌ Tralee (by bus) ✈ (Kerry 30M).

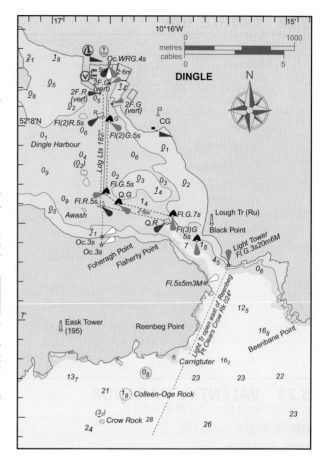

DINGLE BAY TO LISCANNOR BAY

(AC 2254) Dingle Bay (AC 2789, 2790) is wide and deep, with few dangers around its shores. Cahersiveen and Dingle have small marinas. The best ⚓s are at Portmagee and Ventry. At the NW ent to the bay, 2·5M SSW of Slea Hd, is Wild Bank (or Three Fathom Pinnacle), a shallow patch with overfalls. 3M SW of Wild Bank is Barrack Rk, which breaks in strong winds.

The Blasket Islands are very exposed, ▶ *with strong tides and overfalls* ◀ but worth a visit in settled weather (AC 2790).

Great Blasket and Inishvickillane each have ⚓ and landing on their NE side. Between lies Inishabro with a beach and impressive rock formations. Inishtearaght is the most W'ly Is (lt), but further W lie Tearaght Rks, and 3M S are Little Foze and Gt Foze Rks. Inishtooskert is the most N'ly. Blasket Sound is the most convenient N-S route, 1M wide, and easy in daylight and reasonable weather with fair wind or tide; extensive rks and shoals form its W side.

▶ *The N-going stream starts at HW Galway +0430, and the S-going at HW Galway –0155, with sp rate 3kn.* ◀

Between Blasket Sound and Sybil Pt there is a race in W or NW winds with N-going tide, and often a nasty sea. Sybil Pt has steep cliffs, and offlying rks extend 3½ca.

Smerwick hbr, entered between Duncapple Is and the E Sister, is sheltered, except from NW or N winds. From here the scenery is spectacular to Brandon Bay on the W side of which there is an ⚓, but exposed to N winds and to swell.

From Inishtearaght to Loop Hd, Little Samphire Is in Tralee B is the sole light, where Fenit hbr provides the only secure refuge until entering the Shannon Estuary. The coast from Loop Hd to Liscannor Bay has no safe ⚓, no lts, save an AIS buoy Fl(5)Y 20s in Mal Bay. Take care not to be set inshore, although there are few offlying dangers except near Mutton Is and in Liscannor Bay.

ANCHORAGE SW VALENTIA ISLAND

PORTMAGEE, Kerry, **51°53'·20N 10°22'·29W**. AC 2125. HW +0550 on Dover; ML 2·0m; Duration 0610; See 5.30. A safe ⚓ 2·5M E of Bray Head in Portmagee Sound between the mainland and Valentia Is. The ent to the Sound often has bad seas, but dangers are visible. Care required E of Reencaheragh Pt (S side) due rks either side. Deepest water is N of mid-chan. ⚓ off the pier (S side) in 5m, opposite Skelling Heritage Centre (well worth a visit). 🍴 on pier is not recommended due to strong tides. Facilities: ⚓ 🛒 🏨 (at hotel), ✕ ◻ Kos.

The swing bridge 1ca E of pier is currently closed; for further information check with Valentia RNLI or Valentia CG.

ANCHORAGE CLOSE W OF DINGLE HARBOUR

VENTRY Kerry, **52°06·70N 10°20'·30W**. AC 2789, 2790. HW +0540 on Dover; ML 2·1m; Duration 0605; Use 5.31. A pleasant harbour with entrance 1M wide 2M W of Eask Tr (conspic). Good holding on hard sand, open to swell from the SE; Sheltered from SW to N winds but in fresh w'lies prone to sharp squalls. Beware Reenvare Rocks 1ca SE of Parkmore Point; also a rocky ridge 2·9m, on which seas break, extends 2·5ca SSE of Ballymore Pt. No lts. ⚓s are in about 4m off Ventry Strand (✦ brg W, the village NE); or in 3m SW side of bay, 1ca N of pier keeping clear of marine and seaweed farms. Both piers access HW±3 for landing. Facilities: 🏨 ⚓ 🍴 Kos ✕ ◻ 🖂.

ANCHORAGES BETWEEN THE BLASKETS AND KERRY HD
SMERWICK HARBOUR, Kerry, **52°13'·00N 10°24'·00W**. AC 2789. Tides 5.31. Adequate shelter in 1M wide bay, except from NW'ly when considerable swell runs in. Ent between The Three Sisters (150m hill) and Dunacapple Is to the NE. Beacon Fl.R.3s at pier end at Ballynagall Pt. ⚓s at: the W side close N or S of the Boat Hr in 3-10m; to the S, off Carrigveen Pt in 2·5m; or in N'lies at the bay in NE corner inside 10m line. Facilities at Ballynagall village on SE side: pier (0·5m), limited 🛒, 🚌 bus.

BRANDON BAY, Kerry, **52°16'·10N 10°09'·92**W. AC 2739. Tides as Fenit 5.31. A 4M wide bay, very exposed to the N, but in moderate SW-W winds there is safe ⚓ in 6m close E of drying Brandon Pier, 2FG (vert). Cloghane Inlet in SW of Bay is not advised. Facilities at Brandon: limited ☎(1M) ⊠ 🛒 ✕ 🚌 bus.

TRALEE BAY, Kerry, **52°18'·00N 09°56'·00W**. AC 2739. HW −0612 on Dover; ML 2·6m; Duration 0605. See 5.31. Enter the bay passing 3M N of Magharee Islands. Pick up the W sector (W140°−152°) of Little Samphire Is lt, Fl WRG 5s 17m 16/13M; see 5.3 for sectors. Approach between Magharee Is and Mucklaghmore (30m high).

5.31 FENIT HARBOUR
Kerry **52°16'·20N 09°51'·61W** ✶✶✶⚓♨✿✿✿

CHARTS AC 2254, 2739; Imray C55

TIDES −0612 Dover; ML 2·6m; Duration 0605

Standard Port COBH (←—)

Times				Height (metres)			
High Water		Low Water		MHWS	MHWN	MLWN	MLWS
0500	1100	0500	1100	4·1	3·2	1·3	0·4
1700	2300	1700	2300				
Differences FENIT PIER (Tralee Bay)							
−0057	−0017	−0029	−0109	+0·5	+0·2	+0·3	+0·1

SHELTER Good shelter in marina (2.7m depth).

NAVIGATION Appr on 146° to WPT 52°16'·00N 09° 53'·00W, Little Samphire Is, conspic lt ho, Fl WRG 5s 17m 16/13M, thence 7ca E to Samphire Is; lt QR 15m 3M vis 242°−097°, leaving S breakwater bn FlR 6m 3M to N. Fenit Pier Hd 2 FR (vert) 12m 3M, vis 148°−058°. Easy ent H24.

LIGHTS AND MARKS See 5.3 and chartlet.

COMMUNICATIONS (Code 066) ⊖7121480. Port Manager ☎7136231; VHF Ch 16 **14 M** (0900-2100UT). Tralee SC ☎7136119. *Neptune* (Tralee SC) VHF Ch 14 16.

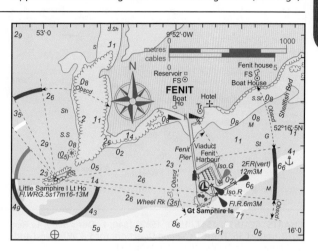

FACILITIES Marina www.fenitharbour.com, ⚓ 130 inc 15Ⓥ; max LOA 25m, €1.60 (min €16.00/craft) ♿ 🚿 ⛽ ⛵(at LB stn) ▲ ⚒ 📮 🏠 🚻 🛒.

Village ☎ ▮ Ⓑ 🛒 ✕ 📮.

Tralee (by bus, Fridays only) ✕ ♨ 🏧 ✕ 📮 ⇌ ✈ (Kerry 30M).

THE SHANNON ESTUARY
(AC 1819, 1547, 1548, 1549) The lower reaches of the Shannon are tidal for 50M, from its mouth between Loop Hd and Kerry Hd up to Limerick Dock, some 15M beyond the junction with R Fergus.
▶ *The tides and streams have roughly equal duration and similar flood and ebb streams. In the entrance the flood stream begins at HW Tarbert Is −0555, and the ebb at HW Tarbert Is +0015.* ◀

There are several ⚓s available for yachts on passage up or down the coast. Kilbaha Bay (AC 1819) is about 3M E of Loop Hd, and is convenient in good weather or N winds, but is open to SE and any swell. Carrigaholt B (AC 1547), entered about 1M N of Kilcredaun Pt, is well sheltered from W winds and has little tidal stream.

▶ *Off Kilcredaun Pt the ebb reaches 4kn at Sp, and in strong winds between S and NW a race forms. This can be skirted by keeping near the N shore, which is free from offlying dangers,*

cheating the worst of the tide. When leaving the Shannon in strong W winds, pass Kilcredaun Pt at slack water, and again keep near the N shore. Loop Hd (lt) marks the N side of Shannon Est, and should be passed 3ca off. Here the stream runs SW from HW Tarbert Is +0300, and NE from HW Tarbert Is −0300. ◀

In N winds ⚓ SE of Querrin Pt (AC 1547), 4½M above Kilcredaun on N shore. At Kilrush there is a marina and ⚓s E of Scattery Is and N of Hog Is. Note that there are overfalls 0·75M S of Scattery Is with W winds and ebb tide.

▶ *Above the junction with R Fergus (AC 1540) the characteristics become more riverine, ie the flood stream is stronger than the ebb, but it runs for a shorter time. In the Shannon the stream is much affected by the wind. S and W winds increase the rate and duration of the flood stream, and reduce the ebb. Strong N or E winds have the opposite effect.* ◀

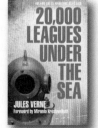

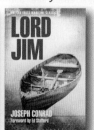

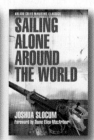

5.32 SHANNON ESTUARY

Clare (N); Kerry and Limerick (S) 52°35'·00N 09°40'·00W ✿✿✿⚓✿✿✿

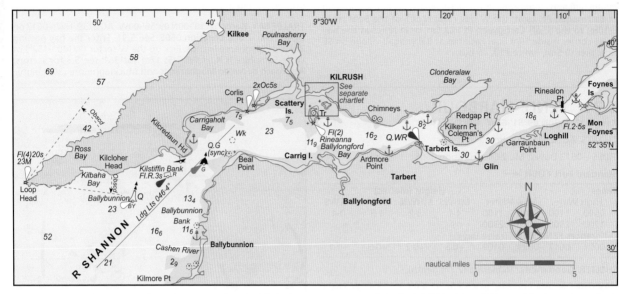

CHARTS AC 1819, 1547, 1548, 1549, 1540; L. Derg 5080; L. Ree 5078; Imray C55. The ICC's *Sailing Directions for S & W Ireland* and/or Admiralty *Irish Coast Pilot* are essential.

TIDES

HW at	HW Tarbert Is	HW Dover
Kilbaha & Carrigaholt	–0030	+0605
Coney Island	+0045	–0500
Foynes	+0030	–0515
Limerick	+0110	–0435

At Limerick strong S-W winds increase the height and delay the times of HW; strong N-E winds do the opposite.

SHELTER The Shannon Estuary is 50M long (Loop Hd to Limerick). For boats on passage N/S the nearest ⚓ is Kilbaha Bay, 3M inside Loop Hd; it has ⚓s sheltered in winds from W to NE, but is exposed to swell and holding is poor. 6M further E, Carrigaholt Bay has ⚓s and good shelter from W'lies; ⚓ just N of the new quay, out of the tide. Kilrush Marina (5.24) with all facilities is 7M further E. From Kilcredaun Head in the W to the R Fergus ent (about 25M) there are ⚓s or ⚓s, protected from all but E winds, at Tarbert Is, Glin, Labasheeda, Killadysert (pontoon) and among the islands in the Fergus mouth. There is a pontoon off the YC S of Foynes Is and drying quays at Ballylongford Creek (Saleen), Knock and Clarecastle (S of Ennis, off chartlet). Yachts may enter Limerick Dock, but this is a primarily a commercial port.

NAVIGATION WPT 52°32'·52N 09°46'·93W, Ballybunnion NCM Q 062°/4·0M to intercept Ldg lts, Oc. 5s, 046·4° on Corlis Pt, passing between Kilcredaun PHM Q.R(sync) and Tail of Beal buoy SHM, Q.G(sync). For notes on entrance and tidal streams see 5.4. The ebb can reach 4kn. The lower estuary between Kerry and Loop Heads is 9M wide, narrowing to 2M off Kilcredaun Pt.

Here the chan is well buoyed in mid-stream and then follows the Kerry shore, S of Scattery Is. From Tarbert Is to Foynes Is the river

narrows to less than 1M in places, before widening where the R Fergus joins from the N, abeam Shannon airport. Above this point the buoyed chan narrows and becomes shallower although there is a minimum of 2m at LWS. AC 1540 is essential for the final 15M stretch to Limerick.

RIVER SHANNON The Shannon, the longest navigable river in the UK or Ireland, is managed by Shannon Foynes Port Company up to Limerick. Upstream it effectively becomes an inland waterway; progress is restricted by locks and bridges. Info on navigation and facilities can be obtained from the Waterways Service, Dept of Art, Culture & the Gaeltacht, 51 St Stephen's Green, Dublin 2, ☎01-6613111; or from the Inland Waterways Association of Ireland, Kingston House, Ballinteer, Dublin 4, ☎01-983392; also from Tourist Offices and inland marinas.

LIGHTS AND MARKS See 5.3. There are QW (vert) aero hazard lts on tall chimneys at Money Pt power station 3M ESE of Kilrush. 2 chys at Tarbert Is are conspic (R lts).

COMMUNICATIONS Foynes Ch 12 13 16 (occas). *Shannon Estuary Radio* Ch 12 13 16 (HO).

FACILITIES Marine facilities are available at several communities on the Shannon; ⚓ ✠ 🏪 🏪 🛒 can be found at many villages. ⚓s are at Foynes and Glin Pier (pontoon). E of Aughanish Is on S shore, R Deal is navigable 3M to Askeaton. Deal BC may offer berths (tidal constraints). Ent, marked by RW bn, is 8ca SE of Beeves Rk with 1m in buoyed chan. ☆ at Massey's Pier ☎069 73100, ⚓s ⟍ 🏪 ✠ 🛒 🛒 🛒.

Facilities at Foynes and Limerick inc:

Foynes ⟍ ⟍ ⟍ ✠ 🏪 🏪 ✉ ⑧ 🛒 ✕ 🛒.

Foynes YC ☎(069) 65261, ⟍(pontoon) ✕ 🛒.

Limerick: Hbr Commission ☎(069) 73100; ⊖ ☎415366. **City** all usual city amenities, ⇌ ✈ (Shannon).

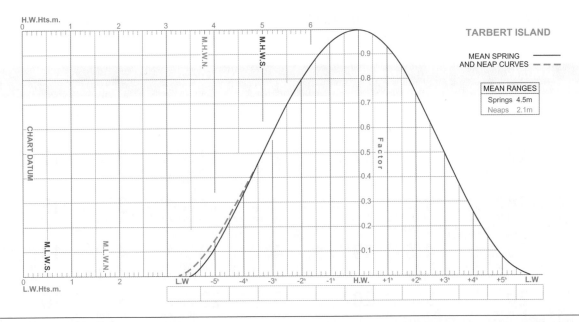

TARBERT ISLAND

MEAN SPRING
AND NEAP CURVES

MEAN RANGES
Springs 4·5m
Neaps 2·1m

5.33 KILRUSH

Clare **52°37'·90N 09°29'·70W** ✿✿△△✿✿

CHARTS AC 1819, 1547; Imray C55

TIDES –0555 Dover; ML 2·6; Duration 0610

Standard Port TARBERT ISLAND (→)

Times				Height (metres)			
High Water		Low Water		MHWS	MHWN	MLWN	MLWS
0500	1000	0000	0600	5·0	3·8	1·7	0·5
1700	2200	1200	1800				
Differences KILRUSH							
–0010	–0010	–0005	–0005	0·0	–0·1	0·0	0·0

SHELTER Excellent in Kilrush Marina (2·7m), access via lock (width 9m) H24. Day ⚓ in lee of Scattery Is.

NAVIGATION WPT 52°37'·18N 09°31'·64W, 063°/1M to SWM buoy. From seaward usual appr is N of Scattery Is (prominent Round Twr, 26m); beware Baurnahard Spit and Carrigillaun to the N. Follow ldg lts (355°) exactly in buoyed channel where the depth is reported to be 0·5m below CD. Coming downriver between Hog Is and mainland, beware unmarked Wolf Rk.

LIGHTS AND MARKS SWM buoy, L Fl 10s, at ent to buoyed chan, with ldg lts 355°, both Oc 3s, to lock. Fl G 3s on S side of lock.

COMMUNICATIONS (Code 06590) MRCC (066) 9476109; Coast/Cliff Rescue Service 51004; ⊜ (061) 415366; ⚕ (061) 62677; Police 51017; Dr (065) 51581 also 51470. Marina 52072 Mobile 086 2313870; Lock 52155. Marina Ch 80. Kilrush Ch 16, 12.

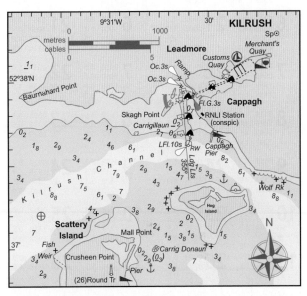

FACILITIES Marina ④ kilrushmarina.ie ☎ 52072, lock 52155; ⬛ 120⬛ inc ❶ €1·90 (min €16·00/craft) ⬛ ▲ ▲ Kos ☂ ▶(45t) ⬛(26t) **Town** ⬛ ✕ ⬛ ⬛ ⬛ ⬛ ⊠ ⬛ ⬛ ✕ ⬛ @ ⇌ (bus to Limerick) ✈ (Shannon).

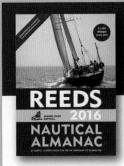

TARBERT ISLAND LAT 52°35'N LONG 9°21'W
TIMES AND HEIGHTS OF HIGH AND LOW WATERS

STANDARD TIME (UT)
For Summer Time add ONE hour in **non-shaded areas**

Dates in red are **SPRINGS**
Dates in blue are NEAPS

YEAR **2016**

JANUARY

Date	Time	m	Time	m	Time	m	Time	m
1 F	0331	1.5	1004	4.2	1611	1.5	2241	4.0
2 SA	0423	1.7	1059	4.0	1710	1.6	2340	3.9
3 SU	0527	1.9	1206	3.9	1818	1.7		
4 M	0045	3.9	0642	1.9	1317	3.9	1924	1.7
5 TU	0147	4.1	0751	1.8	1420	4.0	2022	1.6
6 W	0242	4.2	0849	1.5	1512	4.2	2113	1.4
7 TH	0330	4.4	0940	1.3	1559	4.4	2159	1.2
8 F	0414	4.6	1026	1.0	1642	4.6	2242	1.0
9 SA	0455	4.8	1110	0.8	1723	4.7	2324	0.8
10 SU	0536	5.0	1151	0.6	1804	4.8		
11 M	0004	0.7	0616	5.1	1231	0.5	1844	4.9
12 TU	0044	0.6	0656	5.1	1311	0.4	1926	4.9
13 W	0124	0.6	0738	5.1	1351	0.4	2009	4.8
14 TH	0205	0.7	0822	5.0	1434	0.5	2055	4.7
15 F	0250	0.8	0909	4.8	1521	0.7	2144	4.5
16 SA	0340	1.1	1002	4.6	1615	1.0	2241	4.4
17 SU	0440	1.3	1105	4.3	1719	1.2	2349	4.2
18 M	0553	1.4	1223	4.2	1833	1.3		
19 TU	0106	4.2	0713	1.4	1345	4.2	1947	1.3
20 W	0219	4.3	0829	1.3	1456	4.4	2054	1.2
21 TH	0322	4.5	0933	1.0	1555	4.6	2152	1.0
22 F	0416	4.7	1026	0.8	1646	4.7	2242	0.9
23 SA	0503	4.9	1113	0.6	1731	4.9	2326	0.7
24 SU	0546	5.0	1156	0.5	1813	4.9		
25 M	0006	0.7	0624	5.1	1235	0.5	1851	4.9
26 TU	0043	0.7	0701	5.1	1311	0.5	1927	4.9
27 W	0115	0.8	0736	5.0	1344	0.7	2001	4.8
28 TH	0147	0.9	0811	4.9	1416	0.9	2036	4.6
29 F	0220	1.1	0847	4.7	1449	1.2	2113	4.5
30 SA	0256	1.4	0925	4.4	1526	1.4	2155	4.3
31 SU	0337	1.6	1009	4.2	1612	1.7	2244	4.1

FEBRUARY

Date	Time	m	Time	m	Time	m	Time	m
1 M	0427	1.8	1106	4.0	1709	1.9	2344	4.0
2 TU	0533	2.0	1216	3.9	1821	2.0		
3 W	0052	4.0	0653	2.0	1332	3.9	1936	1.9
4 TH	0159	4.1	0810	1.8	1438	4.0	2040	1.7
5 F	0257	4.3	0912	1.5	1533	4.3	2134	1.4
6 SA	0348	4.6	1004	1.1	1621	4.5	2221	1.1
7 SU	0434	4.8	1050	0.8	1705	4.8	2305	0.8
8 M	0517	5.0	1132	0.5	1747	4.8	2347	0.5
9 TU	0559	5.2	1213	0.3	1828	5.1		
10 W	0028	0.4	0640	5.3	1254	0.2	1909	5.2
11 TH	0108	0.3	0721	5.3	1334	0.2	1951	5.1
12 F	0149	0.3	0804	5.2	1415	0.3	2034	5.0
13 SA	0231	0.6	0849	5.0	1459	0.6	2119	4.8
14 SU	0317	0.9	0939	4.7	1549	1.0	2212	4.5
15 M	0412	1.2	1039	4.4	1649	1.3	2315	4.2
16 TU	0521	1.5	1156	4.1	1804	1.6		
17 W	0035	4.1	0647	1.6	1327	4.1	1928	1.6
18 TH	0159	4.2	0813	1.4	1445	4.2	2042	1.4
19 F	0309	4.4	0921	1.2	1546	4.4	2141	1.2
20 SA	0405	4.6	1014	0.9	1636	4.7	2229	0.9
21 SU	0451	4.8	1058	0.7	1718	4.8	2311	0.8
22 M	0530	5.0	1138	0.5	1755	4.9	2348	0.7
23 TU	0605	5.1	1215	0.5	1829	5.0		
24 W	0022	0.7	0638	5.1	1248	0.6	1901	5.0
25 TH	0052	0.6	0710	5.1	1318	0.7	1932	4.9
26 F	0121	0.9	0743	4.9	1346	0.9	2004	4.8
27 SA	0151	1.0	0815	4.8	1416	1.1	2038	4.6
28 SU	0223	1.2	0848	4.6	1449	1.4	2114	4.4
29 M	0259	1.5	0926	4.3	1528	1.6	2157	4.2

MARCH

Date	Time	m	Time	m	Time	m	Time	m
1 TU	0342	1.7	1014	4.1	1617	1.9	2251	4.0
2 W	0439	1.9	1120	3.8	1724	2.1	2359	3.9
3 TH	0555	2.0	1242	3.8	1847	2.0		
4 F	0114	4.0	0724	1.9	1404	3.9	2007	1.8
5 SA	0223	4.2	0841	1.5	1507	4.2	2109	1.4
6 SU	0321	4.5	0938	1.1	1558	4.5	2159	1.1
7 M	0410	4.8	1026	0.7	1644	4.8	2245	0.7
8 TU	0456	5.1	1110	0.3	1727	5.1	2328	0.3
9 W	0539	5.3	1152	0.1	1809	5.3		
10 TH	0009	0.2	0621	5.5	1233	0.0	1849	5.4
11 F	0050	0.1	0703	5.5	1314	0.0	1930	5.3
12 SA	0130	0.2	0746	5.4	1355	0.2	2012	5.2
13 SU	0212	0.4	0831	5.1	1437	0.6	2056	4.9
14 M	0257	0.7	0920	4.7	1525	1.0	2146	4.5
15 TU	0348	1.1	1018	4.3	1623	1.4	2246	4.2
16 W	0455	1.4	1135	4.0	1739	1.7		
17 TH	0006	4.0	0622	1.6	1310	3.9	1909	1.7
18 F	0137	4.0	0754	1.5	1432	4.1	2028	1.5
19 SA	0252	4.2	0903	1.2	1531	4.3	2125	1.3
20 SU	0347	4.5	0953	0.9	1618	4.6	2210	1.0
21 M	0431	4.7	1036	0.7	1657	4.7	2250	0.8
22 TU	0508	4.8	1114	0.6	1732	4.9	2325	0.7
23 W	0542	4.9	1149	0.6	1803	4.9	2357	0.7
24 TH	0613	5.0	1220	0.6	1833	5.0		
25 F	0027	0.7	0643	5.0	1249	0.7	1903	4.9
26 SA	0056	0.8	0714	4.9	1317	0.9	1934	4.9
27 SU	0125	0.9	0745	4.8	1346	1.1	2006	4.7
28 M	0155	1.1	0816	4.6	1417	1.3	2040	4.5
29 TU	0229	1.3	0852	4.4	1453	1.5	2118	4.3
30 W	0309	1.5	0935	4.1	1537	1.8	2207	4.1
31 TH	0400	1.7	1036	3.9	1639	2.0	2311	3.9

APRIL

Date	Time	m	Time	m	Time	m	Time	m
1 F	0510	1.8	1157	3.8	1803	2.0		
2 SA	0028	3.9	0638	1.7	1328	3.9	1930	1.8
3 SU	0145	4.1	0801	1.4	1438	4.2	2040	1.4
4 M	0250	4.4	0905	1.0	1532	4.5	2134	0.9
5 TU	0344	4.8	0957	0.5	1620	4.9	2221	0.5
6 W	0432	5.1	1044	0.2	1704	5.2	2306	0.2
7 TH	0517	5.3	1128	0.0	1747	5.4	2349	0.0
8 F	0601	5.4	1210	-0.1	1829	5.4		
9 SA	0030	-0.1	0645	5.4	1253	0.0	1911	5.4
10 SU	0112	0.0	0729	5.3	1334	0.2	1953	5.2
11 M	0154	0.3	0815	5.0	1417	0.5	2037	4.9
12 TU	0239	0.6	0904	4.7	1504	1.0	2125	4.5
13 W	0329	1.0	1001	4.3	1600	1.4	2222	4.2
14 TH	0432	1.3	1114	4.0	1714	1.7	2336	3.9
15 F	0553	1.5	1244	3.8	1841	1.7		
16 SA	0103	3.9	0719	1.4	1404	4.0	1959	1.6
17 SU	0220	4.0	0829	1.3	1503	4.3	2056	1.3
18 M	0316	4.2	0921	1.0	1549	4.5	2142	1.1
19 TU	0401	4.4	1004	0.8	1629	4.6	2221	0.9
20 W	0439	4.6	1042	0.7	1703	4.7	2257	0.8
21 TH	0512	4.7	1117	0.7	1734	4.8	2330	0.7
22 F	0544	4.8	1150	0.7	1804	4.9		
23 SA	0001	0.7	0614	4.8	1220	0.8	1834	4.9
24 SU	0032	0.8	0646	4.8	1250	0.9	1906	4.8
25 M	0102	0.8	0718	4.7	1320	1.0	1939	4.7
26 TU	0133	0.9	0751	4.6	1312	1.2	2014	4.6
27 W	0207	1.0	0828	4.4	1428	1.3	2052	4.4
28 TH	0247	1.2	0912	4.2	1511	1.5	2138	4.2
29 F	0336	1.3	1008	4.0	1610	1.7	2236	4.0
30 SA	0440	1.5	1122	3.8	1727	1.8	2348	4.0

Chart Datum: 0·30 metres below Ordnance Datum (Dublin). HAT is 5·5 metres above Chart Datum.

STANDARD TIME (UT)
For Summer Time add ONE hour in **non-shaded areas**

TARBERT ISLAND   LAT 52°35'N   LONG 9°21'W
TIMES AND HEIGHTS OF HIGH AND LOW WATERS

Dates in red are **SPRINGS**
Dates in blue are NEAPS

YEAR 2016

MAY

Day	Time	m	Time	m
1 SU	0600 / 1249 / 1852	1.4 / 3.9 / 1.6		
2 M	0105 / 0720 / 1405 / 2006	4.1 / 1.2 / 4.2 / 1.3		
3 TU	0216 / 0828 / 1503 / 2105	4.3 / 0.8 / 4.5 / 0.9		
4 W	0314 / 0925 / 1554 / 2156	4.7 / 0.5 / 4.8 / 0.5		
5 TH	0406 / 1016 / 1641 / 2243	5.0 / 0.2 / 5.1 / 0.2		
6 F ●	0455 / 1103 / 1726 / 2329	5.2 / 0.0 / 5.3		
7 SA	0543 / 1148 / 1810	5.3 / 0.0 / 5.3		
8 SU	0013 / 0629 / 1233 / 1853	0.0 / 5.2 / 0.1 / 5.3		
9 M	0057 / 0715 / 1316 / 1937	0.0 / 5.1 / 0.3 / 5.1		
10 TU	0140 / 0802 / 1400 / 2021	0.2 / 4.9 / 0.6 / 4.8		
11 W	0224 / 0851 / 1446 / 2108	0.5 / 4.6 / 0.9 / 4.5		
12 TH	0312 / 0944 / 1538 / 2159	0.8 / 4.3 / 1.3 / 4.2		
13 F ☽	0408 / 1048 / 1643 / 2302	1.1 / 4.0 / 1.5 / 4.0		
14 SA	0516 / 1205 / 1759	1.3 / 3.8 / 1.7		
15 SU	0017 / 0630 / 1320 / 1912	3.8 / 1.4 / 3.9 / 1.6		
16 M	0132 / 0738 / 1422 / 2013	3.9 / 1.3 / 4.0 / 1.4		
17 TU	0232 / 0835 / 1511 / 2103	4.0 / 1.2 / 4.2 / 1.3		
18 W	0321 / 0922 / 1553 / 2146	4.2 / 1.0 / 4.4 / 1.1		
19 TH	0403 / 1004 / 1630 / 2225	4.3 / 0.9 / 4.5 / 0.9		
20 F	0439 / 1043 / 1703 / 2301	4.5 / 0.8 / 4.7 / 0.8		
21 SA ○	0513 / 1118 / 1735 / 2337	4.6 / 0.8 / 4.7 / 0.8		
22 SU	0547 / 1152 / 1808	4.6 / 0.8 / 4.8		
23 M	0010 / 0620 / 1226 / 1842	0.7 / 4.6 / 0.9 / 4.8		
24 TU	0043 / 0655 / 1259 / 1917	0.7 / 4.6 / 0.9 / 4.7		
25 W	0117 / 0733 / 1333 / 1954	0.8 / 4.5 / 1.0 / 4.6		
26 TH	0152 / 0813 / 1411 / 2034	0.8 / 4.4 / 1.1 / 4.5		
27 F	0233 / 0857 / 1456 / 2119	0.9 / 4.3 / 1.3 / 4.4		
28 SA	0321 / 0950 / 1550 / 2213	1.0 / 4.1 / 1.4 / 4.2		
29 SU ☽	0419 / 1055 / 1658 / 2317	1.1 / 4.0 / 1.5 / 4.1		
30 M	0528 / 1212 / 1817	1.1 / 4.0 / 1.4		
31 TU	0030 / 0642 / 1330 / 1931	4.1 / 1.0 / 4.2 / 1.2		

JUNE

Day	Time	m
1 W	0142 / 0752 / 1433 / 2035	4.3 / 0.8 / 4.5 / 0.9
2 TH	0246 / 0854 / 1528 / 2132	4.5 / 0.6 / 4.7 / 0.6
3 F	0343 / 0950 / 1619 / 2224	4.8 / 0.4 / 5.0 / 0.3
4 SA	0436 / 1041 / 1707 / 2313	4.9 / 0.3 / 5.1 / 0.1
5 SU ●	0527 / 1130 / 1754 / 2359	5.0 / 0.2 / 5.2 / 0.1
6 M	0615 / 1216 / 1839	5.0 / 0.3 / 5.1
7 TU	0043 / 0702 / 1301 / 1923	0.1 / 4.9 / 0.4 / 5.0
8 W	0127 / 0749 / 1344 / 2006	0.2 / 4.8 / 0.6 / 4.9
9 TH	0210 / 0835 / 1428 / 2050	0.4 / 4.6 / 0.9 / 4.6
10 F	0254 / 0923 / 1514 / 2136	0.7 / 4.3 / 1.1 / 4.4
11 SA	0341 / 1015 / 1606 / 2226	1.0 / 4.1 / 1.4 / 4.1
12 SU ☽	0435 / 1116 / 1709 / 2325	1.2 / 3.9 / 1.6 / 3.9
13 M	0538 / 1224 / 1818	1.4 / 3.8 / 1.7
14 TU	0032 / 0643 / 1329 / 1922	3.8 / 1.4 / 3.9 / 1.6
15 W	0138 / 0743 / 1425 / 2018	3.9 / 1.4 / 4.0 / 1.5
16 TH	0234 / 0837 / 1513 / 2108	4.0 / 1.3 / 4.2 / 1.3
17 F	0323 / 0925 / 1555 / 2153	4.1 / 1.2 / 4.4 / 1.1
18 SA	0405 / 1008 / 1633 / 2235	4.2 / 1.1 / 4.5 / 1.0
19 SU	0444 / 1049 / 1709 / 2314	4.4 / 1.0 / 4.6 / 0.8
20 M ○	0521 / 1128 / 1745 / 2351	4.5 / 0.9 / 4.7 / 0.7
21 TU	0559 / 1205 / 1822	4.5 / 0.8 / 4.8
22 W	0027 / 0637 / 1242 / 1859	0.7 / 4.6 / 0.8 / 4.8
23 TH	0104 / 0717 / 1319 / 1938	0.6 / 4.6 / 0.8 / 4.8
24 F	0141 / 0759 / 1359 / 2019	0.6 / 4.6 / 0.9 / 4.7
25 SA	0221 / 0843 / 1442 / 2103	0.7 / 4.5 / 1.0 / 4.6
26 SU	0307 / 0933 / 1533 / 2153	0.7 / 4.4 / 1.1 / 4.5
27 M	0359 / 1031 / 1633 / 2252	0.8 / 4.2 / 1.2 / 4.3
28 TU	0500 / 1140 / 1744	1.0 / 4.2 / 1.3
29 W	0000 / 0609 / 1256 / 1900	4.2 / 1.0 / 4.2 / 1.2
30 TH	0113 / 0721 / 1406 / 2011	4.2 / 1.0 / 4.4 / 1.0

JULY

Day	Time	m
1 F	0223 / 0828 / 1507 / 2114	4.4 / 0.8 / 4.6 / 0.8
2 SA	0325 / 0931 / 1602 / 2210	4.5 / 0.7 / 4.8 / 0.5
3 SU	0422 / 1027 / 1653 / 2301	4.7 / 0.6 / 5.0 / 0.3
4 M ●	0515 / 1118 / 1741 / 2348	4.8 / 0.5 / 5.1 / 0.2
5 TU	0604 / 1204 / 1826	4.9 / 0.4 / 5.1
6 W	0032 / 0649 / 1248 / 1908	0.2 / 4.9 / 0.5 / 5.0
7 TH	0114 / 0733 / 1328 / 1949	0.3 / 4.8 / 0.6 / 4.9
8 F	0153 / 0815 / 1407 / 2029	0.4 / 4.6 / 0.8 / 4.7
9 SA	0231 / 0856 / 1445 / 2109	0.7 / 4.5 / 1.0 / 4.5
10 SU	0310 / 0938 / 1526 / 2151	0.9 / 4.3 / 1.3 / 4.3
11 M	0351 / 1025 / 1614 / 2239	1.2 / 4.1 / 1.5 / 4.1
12 TU ☽	0441 / 1120 / 1714 / 2335	1.4 / 3.9 / 1.7 / 3.9
13 W	0541 / 1225 / 1826	1.6 / 3.9 / 1.8
14 TH	0040 / 0647 / 1332 / 1933	3.8 / 1.7 / 3.9 / 1.7
15 F	0145 / 0751 / 1430 / 2032	3.8 / 1.6 / 4.1 / 1.6
16 SA	0243 / 0847 / 1520 / 2124	3.9 / 1.5 / 4.2 / 1.4
17 SU	0333 / 0938 / 1604 / 2210	4.1 / 1.3 / 4.4 / 1.1
18 M	0418 / 1024 / 1645 / 2253	4.3 / 1.1 / 4.6 / 0.9
19 TU ○	0500 / 1106 / 1725 / 2333	4.4 / 0.9 / 4.8 / 0.7
20 W	0541 / 1147 / 1804	4.6 / 0.7 / 4.9
21 TH	0012 / 0621 / 1227 / 1842	0.5 / 4.7 / 0.7 / 5.0
22 F	0050 / 0702 / 1305 / 1922	0.4 / 4.8 / 0.6 / 5.0
23 SA	0128 / 0743 / 1345 / 2003	0.3 / 4.8 / 0.6 / 5.0
24 SU	0208 / 0827 / 1427 / 2046	0.4 / 4.7 / 0.7 / 4.8
25 M	0251 / 0914 / 1514 / 2135	0.5 / 4.6 / 0.9 / 4.7
26 TU ☾	0339 / 1007 / 1609 / 2230	0.7 / 4.4 / 1.1 / 4.4
27 W	0435 / 1111 / 1716 / 2336	0.9 / 4.3 / 1.3 / 4.2
28 TH	0542 / 1226 / 1836	1.1 / 4.2 / 1.3
29 F	0052 / 0658 / 1344 / 1954	4.1 / 1.2 / 4.2 / 1.2
30 SA	0209 / 0814 / 1453 / 2103	4.2 / 1.2 / 4.4 / 1.0
31 SU	0317 / 0921 / 1552 / 2201	4.4 / 1.0 / 4.6 / 0.7

AUGUST

Day	Time	m
1 M	0415 / 1019 / 1644 / 2252	4.5 / 0.8 / 4.8 / 0.5
2 TU ●	0507 / 1108 / 1730 / 2337	4.7 / 0.6 / 5.0 / 0.3
3 W	0552 / 1152 / 1812	4.8 / 0.6 / 5.1
4 TH	0018 / 0633 / 1233 / 1851	0.3 / 4.8 / 0.6 / 5.1
5 F	0057 / 0712 / 1309 / 1928	0.3 / 4.8 / 0.6 / 5.0
6 SA	0132 / 0748 / 1342 / 2003	0.5 / 4.7 / 0.6 / 4.8
7 SU	0204 / 0824 / 1414 / 2039	0.7 / 4.6 / 1.0 / 4.7
8 M	0236 / 0900 / 1449 / 2116	0.9 / 4.4 / 1.2 / 4.4
9 TU	0310 / 0939 / 1528 / 2157	1.2 / 4.2 / 1.5 / 4.2
10 W ☾	0351 / 1025 / 1616 / 2246	1.5 / 4.0 / 1.7 / 3.9
11 TH	0441 / 1124 / 1718 / 2347	1.7 / 3.9 / 1.9 / 3.8
12 F	0545 / 1234 / 1839	1.9 / 3.8 / 1.9
13 SA	0057 / 0701 / 1346 / 1956	3.7 / 1.9 / 3.9 / 1.8
14 SU	0207 / 0812 / 1447 / 2057	3.8 / 1.7 / 4.1 / 1.5
15 M	0306 / 0911 / 1538 / 2147	4.0 / 1.5 / 4.4 / 1.2
16 TU	0356 / 1001 / 1623 / 2232	4.3 / 1.2 / 4.6 / 0.9
17 W	0441 / 1046 / 1705 / 2313	4.5 / 0.9 / 4.8 / 0.6
18 TH ○	0523 / 1128 / 1745 / 2353	4.7 / 0.6 / 4.9 / 0.3
19 F	0604 / 1209 / 1824	4.9 / 0.4 / 5.2
20 SA	0032 / 0644 / 1249 / 1904	0.2 / 5.0 / 0.3 / 5.2
21 SU	0111 / 0725 / 1329 / 1945	0.1 / 5.0 / 0.3 / 5.2
22 M	0151 / 0808 / 1410 / 2029	0.2 / 5.0 / 0.5 / 5.0
23 TU	0232 / 0853 / 1456 / 2116	0.4 / 4.8 / 0.7 / 4.8
24 W	0318 / 0943 / 1548 / 2211	0.7 / 4.5 / 1.0 / 4.5
25 TH ☾	0412 / 1044 / 1653 / 2317	1.1 / 4.3 / 1.3 / 4.2
26 F	0519 / 1202 / 1818	1.4 / 4.1 / 1.4
27 SA	0039 / 0643 / 1330 / 1945	4.0 / 1.5 / 4.1 / 1.3
28 SU	0204 / 0808 / 1446 / 2056	4.1 / 1.4 / 4.3 / 1.1
29 M	0314 / 0917 / 1545 / 2152	4.3 / 1.2 / 4.5 / 0.8
30 TU	0410 / 1010 / 1635 / 2239	4.5 / 0.9 / 4.8 / 0.5
31 W	0457 / 1055 / 1718 / 2321	4.7 / 0.7 / 4.9 / 0.4

Chart Datum: 0·30 metres below Ordnance Datum (Dublin). HAT is 5·5 metres above Chart Datum.

》 **FREE** monthly updates. Register at 《
www.reedsnauticalalmanac.co.uk

205

STANDARD TIME (UT)
For Summer Time add ONE hour in **non-shaded areas**

TARBERT ISLAND   LAT 52°35'N   LONG 9°21'W
TIMES AND HEIGHTS OF HIGH AND LOW WATERS

Dates in red are **SPRINGS**
Dates in blue are NEAPS

YEAR 2016

SEPTEMBER

Time	m		Time	m
1 0537	4.8	**16** 0502	4.9	
1136	0.6	1108	0.4	
TH 1755	5.0	F 1724	5.2	
● 2359	0.4	○ 2331	0.1	
2 0613	4.9	**17** 0544	5.1	
1212	0.6	1149	0.2	
F 1830	5.0	SA 1805	5.3	
3 0034	0.4	**18** 0011	0.0	
0646	4.9	0624	5.2	
SA 1245	0.7	SU 1231	0.1	
1903	5.0	1846	5.4	
4 0105	0.6	**19** 0051	0.0	
0718	4.8	0706	5.2	
SU 1314	1.0	M 1311	0.2	
1935	4.9	1928	5.3	
5 0134	0.8	**20** 0132	0.1	
0750	4.7	0748	5.1	
M 1343	1.0	TU 1353	0.3	
2008	4.7	2012	5.1	
6 0203	1.0	**21** 0213	0.4	
0822	4.6	0832	4.9	
TU 1415	1.2	W 1438	0.6	
2042	4.5	2100	4.8	
7 0234	1.2	**22** 0258	0.8	
0858	4.4	0922	4.6	
W 1450	1.4	TH 1529	0.9	
2118	4.3	2155	4.4	
8 0310	1.5	**23** 0351	1.2	
0938	4.2	1021	4.2	
TH 1532	1.7	F 1635	1.3	
2202	4.0	◑ 2303	4.1	
9 0354	1.7	**24** 0501	1.5	
1030	4.0	1141	4.0	
F 1626	1.9	SA 1802	1.5	
◑ 2300	3.8			
10 0454	1.9	**25** 0030	3.9	
1139	3.8	0631	1.7	
SA 1741	2.0	SU 1316	4.0	
		1934	1.4	
11 0013	3.7	**26** 0158	4.0	
0611	2.0	0800	1.5	
SU 1301	3.8	M 1434	4.2	
1912	1.9	2043	1.1	
12 0134	3.8	**27** 0304	4.2	
0736	1.8	0904	1.3	
M 1413	4.0	TU 1531	4.4	
2027	1.6	2134	0.8	
13 0240	4.0	**28** 0356	4.4	
0845	1.5	0953	1.0	
TU 1510	4.3	W 1617	4.7	
2121	1.2	2218	0.6	
14 0333	4.3	**29** 0438	4.6	
0938	1.1	1035	0.8	
W 1558	4.6	TH 1658	4.8	
2207	0.7	2257	0.5	
15 0419	4.6	**30** 0515	4.8	
1024	0.8	1113	0.7	
TH 1642	4.9	F 1733	4.9	
2250	0.4	2333	0.5	

OCTOBER

Time	m		Time	m
1 0548	4.8	**16** 0522	5.2	
1147	0.6	1128	0.1	
SA 1805	4.9	SU 1744	5.3	
●		○ 2348	-0.1	
2 0006	0.5	**17** 0605	5.3	
0617	4.8	1211	0.0	
SU 1218	0.7	M 1828	5.4	
1835	4.9			
3 0036	0.6	**18** 0030	0.0	
0647	4.8	0646	5.3	
M 1247	0.8	TU 1254	0.1	
1906	4.8	1911	5.3	
4 0104	0.8	**19** 0112	0.1	
0717	4.6	0729	5.2	
TU 1316	0.9	W 1337	0.2	
1938	4.7	1957	4.9	
5 0132	1.0	**20** 0155	0.4	
0749	4.7	0814	4.9	
W 1346	1.1	TH 1422	0.5	
2010	4.5	2046	4.7	
6 0203	1.2	**21** 0240	0.8	
0823	4.5	0903	4.6	
TH 1420	1.3	F 1514	0.9	
2046	4.3	2141	4.3	
7 0237	1.4	**22** 0333	1.2	
0901	4.3	1000	4.2	
F 1459	1.5	SA 1617	1.2	
2128	4.1	◑ 2247	4.0	
8 0318	1.7	**23** 0440	1.5	
0948	4.1	1116	4.0	
SA 1549	1.7	SU 1737	1.4	
2222	3.8			
9 0414	1.9	**24** 0011	3.8	
1051	3.9	0606	1.7	
SU 1657	1.8	M 1249	3.9	
◑ 2333	3.7	1905	1.4	
10 0530	2.0	**25** 0135	3.9	
1211	3.8	0733	1.6	
M 1824	1.8	TU 1407	4.1	
		2014	1.2	
11 0057	3.8	**26** 0239	4.1	
0657	1.8	0837	1.4	
TU 1335	4.0	W 1504	4.3	
1948	1.5	2105	1.0	
12 0211	4.0	**27** 0329	4.3	
0814	1.5	0926	1.1	
W 1439	4.3	TH 1550	4.5	
2048	1.1	2148	0.8	
13 0307	4.4	**28** 0411	4.5	
0911	1.1	1007	0.9	
TH 1530	4.6	F 1630	4.6	
2138	0.7	2227	0.7	
14 0355	4.7	**29** 0447	4.7	
1000	0.7	1044	0.8	
F 1617	4.9	SA 1706	4.7	
2223	0.3	2303	0.6	
15 0439	5.0	**30** 0519	4.8	
1045	0.3	1119	0.7	
SA 1701	5.2	SU 1738	4.8	
2306	0.1	● 2336	0.7	
		31 0548	4.8	
		1151	0.7	
		M 1809	4.8	

NOVEMBER

Time	m		Time	m
1 0006	0.7	**16** 0011	0.1	
0617	4.8	0629	5.3	
TU 1222	0.8	W 1238	0.1	
1839	4.7	1857	5.2	
2 0036	0.9	**17** 0055	0.2	
0649	4.8	0714	5.1	
W 1253	0.9	TH 1323	0.2	
1911	4.7	1944	5.0	
3 0106	1.0	**18** 0138	0.5	
0722	4.7	0759	4.9	
TH 1324	1.0	F 1409	0.4	
1945	4.5	2033	4.7	
4 0138	1.2	**19** 0224	0.8	
0757	4.6	0846	4.6	
F 1358	1.1	SA 1458	0.7	
2022	4.3	2125	4.4	
5 0213	1.3	**20** 0313	1.1	
0834	4.4	0939	4.3	
SA 1437	1.3	SU 1555	1.0	
2104	4.1	2224	4.1	
6 0254	1.5	**21** 0413	1.5	
0919	4.2	1042	4.1	
SU 1524	1.5	M 1703	1.3	
2155	3.9	◑ 2336	3.9	
7 0345	1.7	**22** 0526	1.6	
1015	4.0	1202	3.9	
M 1625	1.6	TU 1817	1.4	
● 2300	3.8			
8 0454	1.8	**23** 0052	3.9	
1127	3.9	0643	1.7	
TU 1742	1.6	W 1322	3.9	
		1926	1.3	
9 0018	3.8	**24** 0158	4.0	
0616	1.7	0751	1.5	
W 1250	4.0	TH 1425	4.1	
1903	1.4	2022	1.2	
10 0136	4.1	**25** 0251	4.2	
0735	1.5	0846	1.3	
TH 1402	4.2	F 1515	4.3	
2010	1.0	2110	1.1	
11 0236	4.4	**26** 0336	4.4	
0839	1.1	0931	1.1	
F 1500	4.6	SA 1558	4.4	
2105	0.7	2152	0.9	
12 0327	4.7	**27** 0414	4.5	
0932	0.7	1012	1.0	
SA 1550	4.9	SU 1636	4.6	
2154	0.4	2230	0.9	
13 0415	5.0	**28** 0449	4.7	
1021	0.4	1050	0.9	
SU 1638	5.1	M 1711	4.6	
2241	0.2	2306	0.8	
14 0500	5.2	**29** 0520	4.8	
1108	0.1	1126	0.8	
M 1725	5.2	TU 1744	4.7	
○ 2326	0.1	● 2340	0.9	
15 0545	5.3	**30** 0553	4.8	
1153	0.0	1201	0.8	
TU 1811	5.3	W 1817	4.7	

DECEMBER

Time	m		Time	m
1 0013	0.9	**16** 0040	0.4	
0626	4.8	0700	5.1	
TH 1235	0.8	F 1311	0.2	
1850	4.6	1931	5.0	
2 0046	1.0	**17** 0123	0.5	
0701	4.8	0744	5.0	
F 1308	0.9	SA 1355	0.4	
1926	4.6	2017	4.8	
3 0120	1.1	**18** 0206	0.8	
0737	4.7	0829	4.8	
SA 1343	1.0	SU 1440	0.6	
2004	4.4	2104	4.5	
4 0156	1.2	**19** 0251	1.0	
0815	4.6	0915	4.5	
SU 1421	1.1	M 1528	0.9	
2046	4.3	2153	4.3	
5 0236	1.3	**20** 0339	1.3	
0858	4.4	1006	4.3	
M 1506	1.2	TU 1622	1.2	
2134	4.2	2249	4.1	
6 0324	1.4	**21** 0436	1.5	
0948	4.3	1106	4.1	
TU 1559	1.4	W 1724	1.4	
2231	4.0	◑ 2353	3.9	
7 0423	1.6	**22** 0544	1.7	
1051	4.1	1219	3.9	
W 1705	1.4	TH 1830	1.5	
◑ 2339	4.0			
8 0535	1.6	**23** 0101	3.9	
1205	4.1	0654	1.7	
TH 1819	1.3	F 1332	4.0	
		1932	1.5	
9 0054	4.1	**24** 0203	4.1	
0653	1.4	0757	1.6	
F 1322	4.2	SA 1433	4.1	
1929	1.1	2027	1.4	
10 0202	4.4	**25** 0255	4.2	
0804	1.2	0853	1.4	
SA 1428	4.5	SU 1523	4.2	
2032	0.8	2116	1.3	
11 0259	4.6	**26** 0340	4.4	
0906	0.9	0941	1.3	
SU 1525	4.7	M 1607	4.4	
2128	0.6	2200	1.2	
12 0351	4.9	**27** 0420	4.6	
1000	0.6	1025	1.1	
M 1618	4.9	TU 1646	4.5	
2219	0.4	2240	1.1	
13 0440	5.1	**28** 0456	4.7	
1051	0.3	1105	1.0	
TU 1708	5.1	W 1723	4.6	
2308	0.3	2318	1.0	
14 0528	5.2	**29** 0532	4.8	
1139	0.2	1143	0.9	
W 1757	5.1	TH 1758	4.6	
○ 2355	0.3	● 2354	0.9	
15 0615	5.2	**30** 0607	4.9	
1226	0.2	1219	0.8	
TH 1845	5.1	F 1833	4.7	
		31 0029	0.9	
		0643	4.9	
		SA 1254	0.7	
		1909	4.7	

Chart Datum: 0·30 metres below Ordnance Datum (Dublin). HAT is 5·5 metres above Chart Datum.

1	*Kilrush*	318	361	364	335	332	323	309	291	276	274	270	251	220	203	191	183	142	119	75	76	**1**
2	Galway	348	366	338	309	307	297	284	266	253	251	245	227	192	178	166	163	104	94	49	**2**	
3	Slyne Head	352	317	289	260	257	248	234	217	201	199	195	178	143	128	117	114	55	44	**3**		
4	Westport	337	323	295	266	249	240	226	207	193	191	187	168	137	120	108	100	57	**4**			
5	Eagle Island	297	262	234	205	198	193	175	162	147	145	136	123	88	72	62	59	**5**				
6	Sligo	281	246	218	189	179	177	156	146	123	121	117	107	72	51	30	**6**					
7	Killybegs	267	232	204	175	171	163	148	132	115	113	109	93	58	43	**7**						
8	Burtonport	218	182	153	130	130	116	108	90	74	72	68	49	18	**8**							
9	**Tory Island**	209	174	146	117	113	105	90	74	57	55	51	35	**9**								
10	**L Swilly (Fahan)**	200	166	138	109	104	96	81	65	48	46	42	**10**									
11	**Lough Foyle**	157	121	92	72	73	55	47	30	11	9	**11**										
12	River Bann	155	120	92	63	65	53	40	24	5	**12**											
13	**Portrush**	150	115	87	58	60	48	35	19	**13**												
14	Altacarry Head	135	102	74	45	45	31	21	**14**													
15	**Carnlough**	118	78	50	25	26	11	**15**														
16	**Larne**	108	73	45	16	16	**16**															
17	**Carrickfergus**	101	66	39	6	**17**																
18	**Bangor**	96	61	34	**18**																	
19	**Strangford L**	71	36	**19**																		
20	**Carlingford L**	50	**20**																			
21	*Dun Laoghaire*	**21**																				

DISTANCE TABLE
Approximate distances in nautical miles are by the most direct route, whilst avoiding dangers and allowing for Traffic Separation Schemes. Places in *italics* are in adjoining areas; places in **bold** are in 0.31, Distances across the Irish Sea.

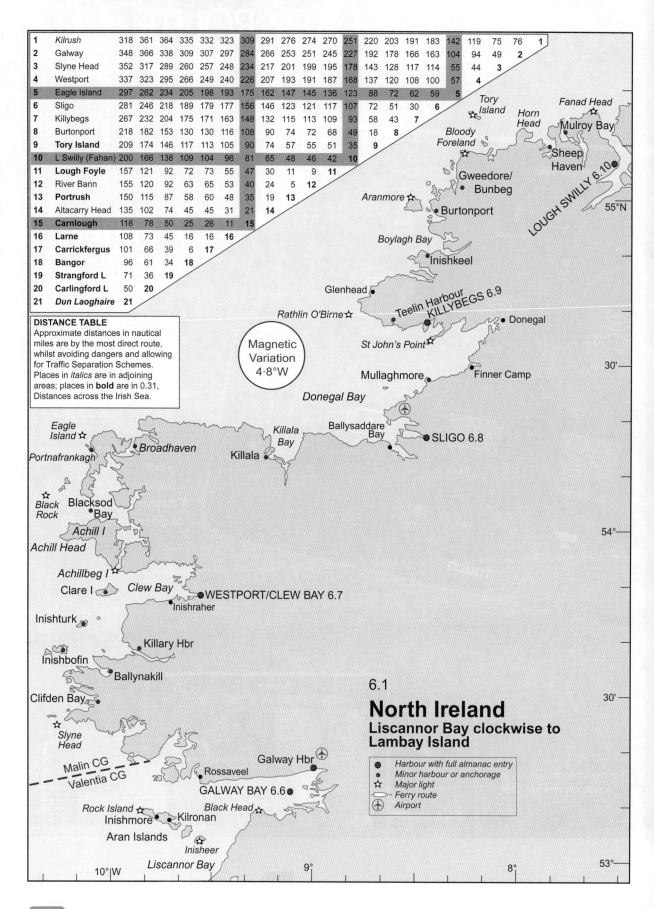

Magnetic Variation 4·8°W

6.1

North Ireland
Liscannor Bay clockwise to Lambay Island

- ● Harbour with full almanac entry
- • Minor harbour or anchorage
- ☆ Major light
- ⊂ Ferry route
- ✈ Airport

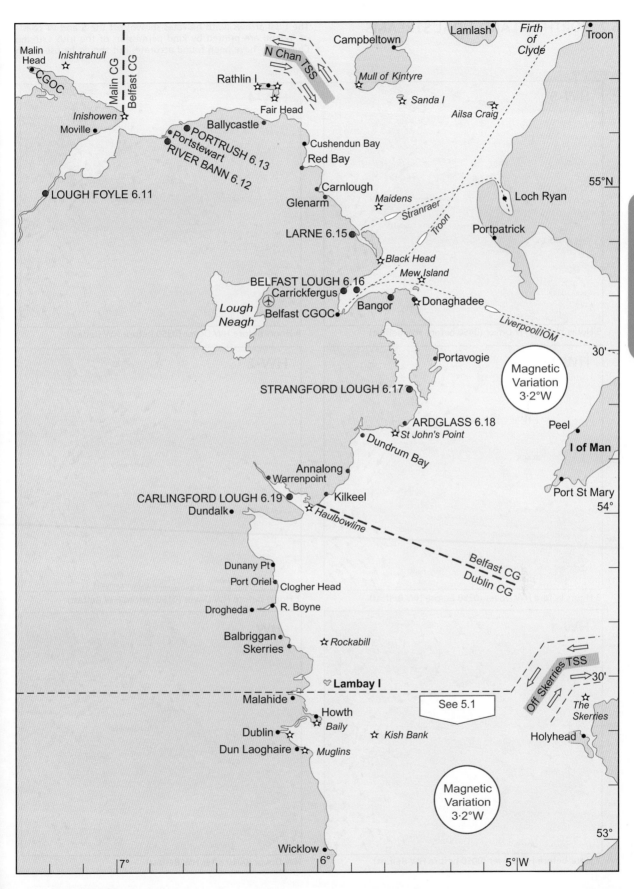

6.2 NORTH IRELAND TIDAL STREAMS

The tidal arrows (with no rates shown) off the S and W coasts of Ireland are printed by kind permission of the Irish Cruising Club. They have been found accurate, but should be used with caution.

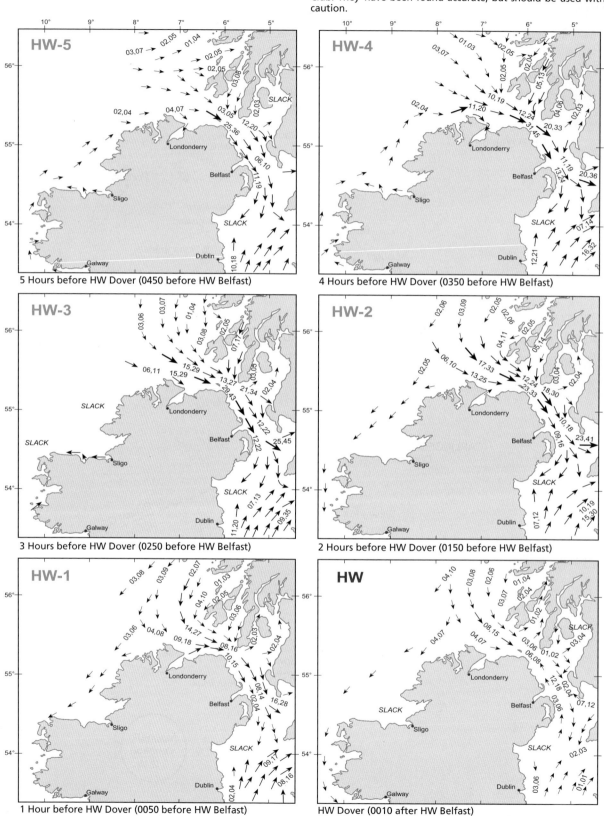

HW-5 — 5 Hours before HW Dover (0450 before HW Belfast)

HW-4 — 4 Hours before HW Dover (0350 before HW Belfast)

HW-3 — 3 Hours before HW Dover (0250 before HW Belfast)

HW-2 — 2 Hours before HW Dover (0150 before HW Belfast)

HW-1 — 1 Hour before HW Dover (0050 before HW Belfast)

HW — HW Dover (0010 after HW Belfast)

Rathlin Island 6.14
Mull of Kintyre 2.10
North Irish Sea 3.2

SW Scotland 2.2
South Ireland 5.2

The tidal arrows (with no rates shown) off the S and W coasts of Ireland are printed by kind permission of the Irish Cruising Club. They have been found accurate, but should be used with caution.

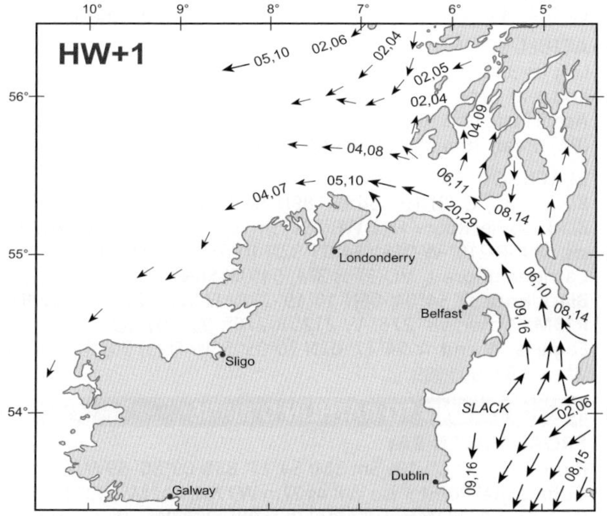

HW+1

1 Hour after HW Dover (0110 after HW Belfast)

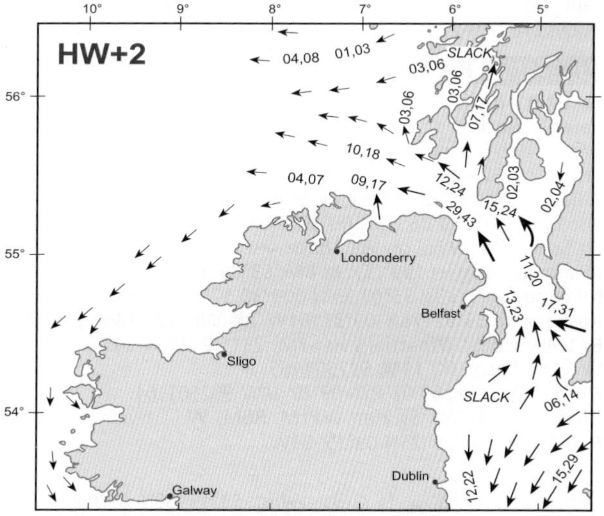

HW+2

2 Hours after HW Dover (0210 after HW Belfast)

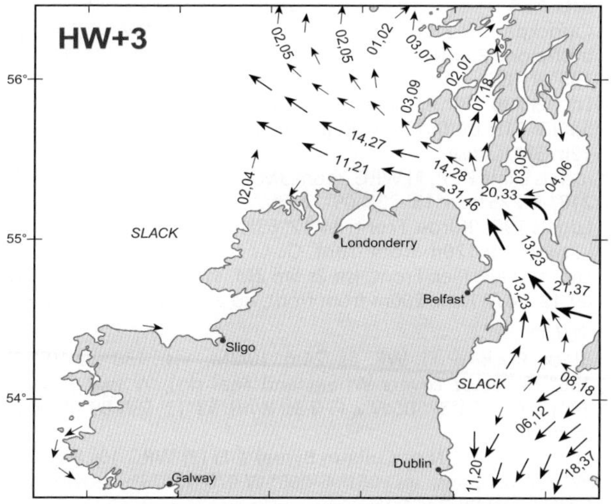

HW+3

3 Hours after HW Dover (0310 after HW Belfast)

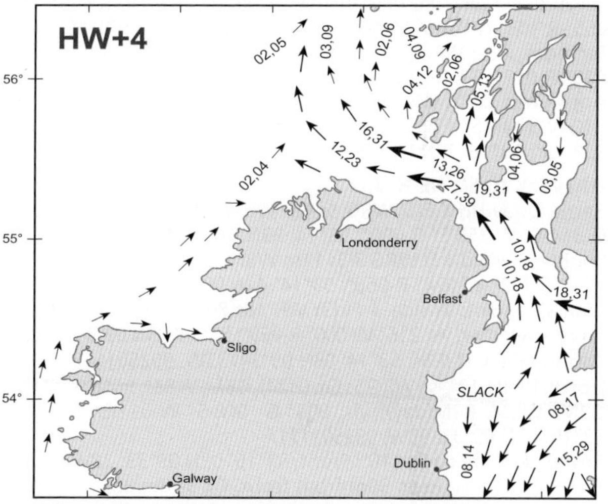

HW+4

4 Hours after HW Dover (0410 after HW Belfast)

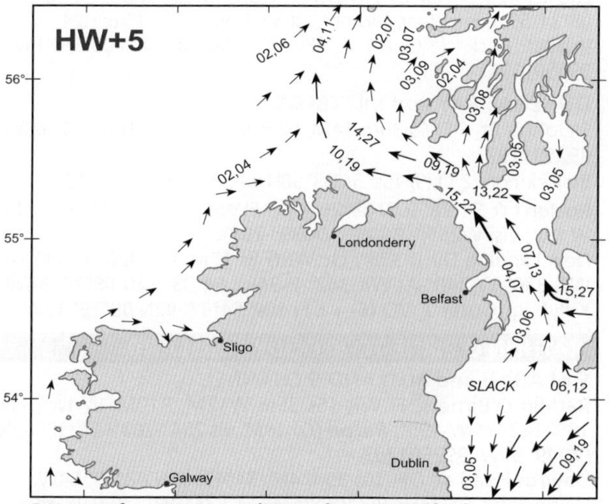

HW+5

5 Hours after HW Dover (0510 after HW Belfast)

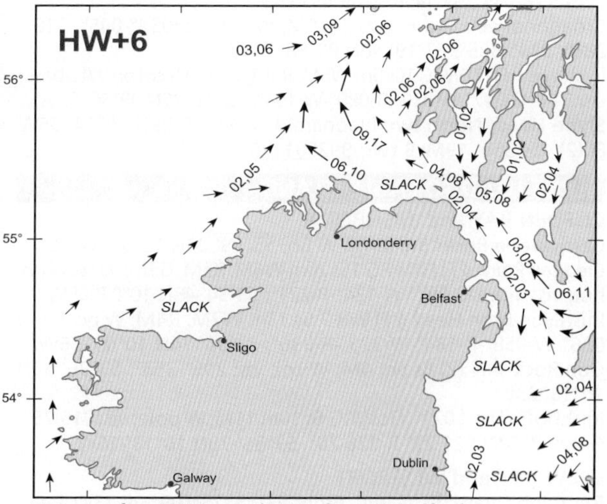

HW+6

6 Hours after HW Dover (0610 after HW Belfast)

N Ireland

6.3 LIGHTS, BUOYS AND WAYPOINTS

Bold print = light with a nominal range of 15M or more. CAPITALS = place or feature. *CAPITAL ITALICS* = light-vessel, light float or Lanby. *Italics* = Fog signal. ***Bold italics*** = Racon. Many marks/buoys are fitted with AIS, <u>MMSI No</u>; see relevant charts.

LISCANNOR BAY TO SLYNE HEAD

GALWAY BAY and INISHMORE

Eeragh, Rock Is ☆ 53°08'·91N 09°51'·40W Fl 15s 35m **18M**; W twr, two B bands; vis: 297°-262°; <u>992501172</u>.
Straw Is ⚓ Fl (2) 5s 11m 12M; W twr; 53°07'·08N 09°37'·82W.
Killeany Ldg lts 192°. Front, Oc 5s 6m 3M; W col on W □ base; vis: 142°-197°, 53°06'·25N 09°39'·74W. Rear, 43m from front, Oc 5s 8m 2M; W col on W □ base; vis: 142°-197°.
Inishmaan, Ldg lts 199°, Oc 6s 8M; 53°06'·08N 09°34'·77W.
Killeaney ⚓ Fl G 3s; 53°07.33N 009°38.37'W; <u>992501166</u>.
Inisheer ☆ 53°02'·76N 09°31'·61W Iso WR 12s 34m **W18M**, R11M; vis: 225°-W(partially vis >7M)-231°, 231°-W-245°-R-269°-W-115°; ***Racon (K) 13M***; <u>992501165</u>.
Finnis ⚓ Q (3) 10s; 53°02'·82N 09°29'·14W, <u>992501164</u>.
Black Hd ⚓ Fl WR 5s 20m W11M, R8M, W □ twr; vis: 045°-R268°-276°; 53°09'·25N 09°15'·83W.

GALWAY

Margaretta Shoal ⚓ Fl G 3s; *Whis;* 53°13'·68N 09°05'·99W, <u>992501170</u>.
Leverets ⚓ Q WRG 9m 10M; B□twr, W bands; vis: 015°-G-058°-W-065°-R-103°-G-143.5°-W-146.5°-R-015°; 53°15'·33N 09°01'·90W.
Rinmore ⚓ Iso WRG 4s 7m 5M; W □ twr; vis: 359°-G-008°-W-018°-R-027°; 53°16'·12N 09°01'·97W.
Appr Chan Dir lt 325°, WRG 7m 3M; vis: 322·25°-FG-323·75°-AlGW-324·75°-FW-325·25°-AlRW-326·25°-FR-331·25°-FlR-332·25°; 53°16'·12N 09°02'·83W.

GALWAY to SLYNE HEAD

Barna Quay Hd ⚓ Fl 2 WRG 5s 6m W8M, R5M, G5M; vis:250°-G-344·5°-W-355·5°-R-090°; 53°14'·93N 09°08'·90W.
Spiddle Pier Hd ⚓ Fl WRG 3·5s 11m W8M, R8M, G8M; Y col; vis: 265°-G-308°-W-024°-R-066°; 53°14'·42N 09°18'·54W.
Cashla Bay Ent, W side ⚓ Fl (3) WR 10s 8m W6M, R3M; W col on concrete twr; vis: 216°-W-000°-R-069°; 53°14'·23N 09°35'·20W.
Cannon Rk ⚓ Fl G 5s; 53°14'·08N 09°34'·35W, <u>992501173</u>.
Lion Pt Dir lt 010°, IsoWRG 5s 6m (H24), G6M, W8M, R6M, (night), G2M, W3M, R2M(day); vis: 005°-G- 008·5°-W-011·5°-R-015°; 53°15'·83N 09°33'·98W; <u>992501171</u>.
Rossaveel Pier Ldg lts 116°. Front, 53°16'·02N 09°33'·38W Oc 3s 7m 3M; W mast. Rear, 90m from front, Oc 3s 8m 3M.
Kiggaul Bay ⚓ Fl WRG 3s 5m W5M, R3M, G3M; vis: 310°-G-329°-W-339°-R-059°; 53°14'·03N 09°43'·02W.
Croaghnakeela Is ⚓ Fl 3·7s 7m 5M; W col; vis: 034°-045°, 218°-286°, 311°-325°; 53°19'·40N 09°58'·21W.
Inishnee ⚓ Fl (2) WRG 10s 9m W5M, R3M, G3M; W col on W□base; vis: 314°-G-017°-W-030°-R-080°-W-194°; 53°22'·75N 09°54'·53W.
Slyne Head, North twr, Illaunamid ☆ 53°23'·99N 10°14'·05W Fl (2) 15s 35m **19M**; B twr; <u>992501175</u>.

SLYNE HEAD TO EAGLE ISLAND

CLIFDEN BAY and INISHBOFIN

Carrickrana Rocks Bn, large W Bn; 53°29'·24N 10°09'·48W.
Cleggan Point ⚓ Fl (3) WRG 15s 20m W6M, R3M, G3M; W col on W hut; vis: shore-G-091°-W-124°-R-221°; 53°34'·48N 10°07'·69W.
Inishlyon Lyon Head ⚓ Fl WR 7·5s 13m W7M, R4M; W post; vis: 036°-W-058°-R-184°-W-325°-R-036°; 53°36'·74N 10°09'·56W.
Gun Rock ⚓ Fl (2) 6s 8m 4M; W col; vis: 296°-253°; 53°36'·59N 10°13'·23W.
Inishbofin Dir lt 021°, Oc WRG 6s 10m 11M; W pole; vis: 015·75°-G-020·75°-W-021·25°-R-026·25°; 53°36'·78N 10°13'·16W.

CLEW BAY and WESTPORT

Roonagh Quay Ldg lts 144°. Front 53°45'·75N 09°54'·23W. Rear, 54m from front, both Iso Bu 10s 9/15m.

Inishgort ⚓ L Fl 10s 10M; 53°49.59'N 009°40.25'W; <u>992501179</u>.
Cloughcormick ⚓ Q (9) 15s; 53°50'·56N 09°43'·20W.
Achillbeg I, S Point ☆ 53°51'·51N 09°56'·84W Fl WR 5s 56m **W16M, R18M**, R11M; W ○ twr on □ building; vis: 262°-R-281°-W-342°-R-060°-W-092°-R(intens)-099°-W-118°; <u>992501181</u>.

ACHILL SOUND

Ldg lts 330°, 53°52'·50N 09°56'·91W Whitestone Point. Front and rear both Oc 4s 5/6m; W ◊, B stripe.
Achill I Ldg lts 310°, Purteen, Oc 8s 5m; 53°57'·83N 10°05'·93W (PA). Rear, 46m from front Oc 8s 6m.

BLACKSOD BAY

Blacksod ⚓ Q (3) 10s; 54°05'·89N 10°03'·01W.
Blacksod Pier Root ⚓ Fl(2) WR 7·5s 13m W12M, R9M; W twr on bldg; vis: 189°-R-210°-W-018°; 54°05'·92N 10°03'·63W; <u>992501186</u>.
Carrigeenmore ⚓ VQ(3) 5s 3M; 54°06'·56N 10°03'·4W.
Black Rock ☆ 54°04'·06N 10°19'·23W Fl WR 12s 86m **W20M, R16M**; W twr; vis: 276°-W-212°-R-276°; <u>992501183</u>.
Eagle Is, W end ☆ 54°17'·02N 10°05'·56W Fl (3) 20s 67m **18M**; W twr; <u>992501189</u>.

EAGLE ISLAND TO RATHLIN O'BIRNE

BROAD HAVEN BAY

Rinroe Pt ⚓ Fl (2) 10s 5m 3M; 54°17'·83N 09°50'·59W.
Gubacashel Point ⚓ Iso WR 4s 27m **W17M**, R12M; 110°-R-133°-W-355°-R-021° W twr; 54°16'·06N 09°53'·33W.

KILLALA

Carrickpatrick ⚓ Q (3) 10s; 54°15'·56N 09°09'·14W; <u>992501192</u>.
Inishcrone Pier Root ⚓ Fl WRG 1·5s 8m 2M; vis: 098°-W-116°-G-136°-R-187°; 54°13'·21N 09°05'·79W.
Ldg lts 230°. Rinnaun Point. Front No. 1, Oc 10s 7m 5M; □ twr; 54°13'·21N 09°05'·79W. Rear, 150m from front, No. 2 Oc 10s 12m 5M; □ twr.
Inch Is Dir lt 215°, Fl WRG 2s 6m 3M; □ twr; vis: 205°-G-213°-W-217°-R-225°; 54°13'·29N 09°12'·30W.
Ldg lts 196°. Kilroe. Front, 54°12'·63N 09°12'·33W Oc 4s 5m 2M; □ twr. Rear,120m from front, Oc 4s 10m 2M; □ twr.
Ldg lts 236°. Pier. Front, Iso 2s 5m 2M; W ◊ on twr; 54°13'·02N 09°12'·84W. Rear, 200m from front, Iso 2s 7m 2M; W ◊ on pole.

SLIGO

Black Rock ⚓ Fl WR 5s 24m 10/8M; vis: 130°-W-107°-R-130° (R sector covers Wheat and Seal rks); W twr, B band; 54°18'·46N 08°37'·06W ⚓ Fl G 3s; *Whis;* 53°13'·68N 09°05'·99W, <u>992501195</u>.
Lower Rosses, (N of Cullaun Bwee) ⚓ Fl (2) WRG 10s 8m 10M; W hut on piles; vis: 061°-G-066°-W-070°-R-075°; shown H24; 54°19'·73N 08°34'·41W.
Ldg lts 125° Fl (3) 6s 7M (sync). Front, Metal Man; 54°18'·24N 08°34'·55W, 3m. Rear, Oyster Is, 365m from front, 13m; H24.
Wheat Rock ⚓ Q (6) + LFl 15s; 54°18'·84N 08°39'·10W; <u>992501196</u>.

DONEGAL BAY and KILLYBEGS

St John's Pt ⚓ Fl 6s 30m 14M; W twr; 54°34'·16N 08°27'·66W; <u>992501197</u>.
Bullockmore ⚓ Q (9) 15s; 54°33'·98N 08°30'·14W; <u>992501198</u>.
Rotten I ☆ 54°36'·97N 08°26'·41W Fl WR 4s 20m **W15M**, R11M; W twr; vis: W255°- R008°- W039°-208°.
New Landing Dir lt 338°, Oc WRG 8s 17m; vis: 328°-G-334°-Al WG-336°-W-340°-Al WR-342°-R-348°; 54°38'·14N 08°26'·38W.
Killybegs Outer ⚓ VQ (6) + L Fl 10s; 54°37'·92N 08°29'·15W.

RATHLIN O'BIRNE TO BLOODY FORELAND

S of ARAN and RUTLAND S CHANNEL

Rathlin O'Birne ⚓ Fl WR 15s 35m W12M, R10M; W twr; vis: 195°-R-307°-W-195°; ***Racon (O) 13M***, vis 284°-203°. 54°39'·82N 08°49'·95W; <u>992501203</u>.
Dawros Head ☆ L Fl 10s 39m 4M; 54°49'·63N 08°33'·64W.
Wyon Point ⚓ Fl (2) WRG 10s 8m W6M, R3M; W □ twr; vis: shore-G-021°-W-042°-R-121°-W-150°-R-shore; 54°56'·51N 08°27'·54W.

BURTONPORT
Ldg lts 068·1°. Front , FG 17m 1M; Gy Bn, W band; 54°58'·95N 08°26'·40W. Rear, 355m from front, FG 23m 1M; Gy Bn, Y band.

N SOUND OF ARAN and RUTLAND N CHANNEL
Rutland I Ldg lts 137·6°. Front, 54°58'·97N 08°27'·68W Oc 6s 8m 1M; W Bn, B band. Rear, 330m from front, Oc 6s 14m 1M.
Inishcoo Ldg lts 119·3°. Front, Iso 6s 6m 1M; W Bn, B band; 54°59'·43N 08°29'·63W. Rear, 248m from front, Iso 6s 11m 1M.
Ldg lts 186°. Front, Oc 8s 8m 3M; B Bn, W band; 54°58'·94N 08°29'·27W. Rear, 395m from front, Oc 8s 17m 3M; B Bn.
Aranmore, Rinrawros Pt ☆ 55°00'·90N 08°33'·67W Fl (2) 20s 71m **27M**; W twr; obsc by land about 234°-007° and about 013°. Auxiliary lt Fl R 3s 61m 13M, same twr; vis: 203°-234°; 992501205.

OWEY SOUND to INISHSIRRER
Cruit Is. Owey Sound Ldg lts 068·3°. Oc 10s. Front, 55°03'·06N 08°25'·85W. Rear, 107m from front.
Rinnalea Point ⚡ 55°02'·59N 08°23'·72W Fl 7·5s 19m 9M; ☐ twr; vis: 132°-167°.
Gola Is Ldg lts 171·2°. Oc 3s 2M (sync). Front, 9m; W Bn, B band; 55°05'·11N 08°21'·07W. Rear, 86m from front, 13m; B Bn, W band.
Glassagh. Ldg lts 137·4°. Front, Oc 8s 12m 3M; 55°06'·83N 08°18'·97W. Rear, 46m from front, Oc 8s 17m 3M; synch.
Inishsirrer, NW end ⚡ Fl 3·7s 20m 4M; W ☐ twr vis: 083°-263°; 55°07'·40N 08°20'·93W.

BLOODY FORELAND TO INISHTRAHULL
BLOODY FORELAND to SHEEPHAVEN
Bloody Foreland ⚡ Fl WG 7·5s 14m W6M, G4M; vis: 062°-W-232°-G-062°; 55°09'·51N 08°17'·03W.
Tory Island ☆ 55°16'·36N 08°14'·96W Fl (4) 30s 40m **18M**; B twr, W band; vis: 302°-277°; *Racon (M) 12-23M*; 992501211.
West Town Ldg lts 001° ⚡ Iso 2s 9m 7M △ on Y structure R stripe; 55°15'·79N 08°13'·50W. Rear Iso 2s 11m 7M ▽ ditto (sync).
Inishbofin Pier ⚡ Fl 8s 3m 3M; 55°10'·14N 08°10'·01W.
Ballyness Hbr. Ldg lts 119·5°. Front, Iso 4s 25m 1M; 55°09'·06N 08°06'·98W. Rear, 61m from front, Iso 4s 26m 1M.
Portnablahy Ldg lts 125·3°. Front Oc 6s 7m 2M; B col, W bands; 55°10'·79N 07°55'·65W. Rear, 81m from front, Oc 6s 12m 2M; B col, W bands.

MULROY BAY
Limeburner ⚡ Q Fl; 55°18'·54N 07°48'·40W; 992501214.
Ravedy Is ⚡ Fl 3s 9m 3M; vis 177°-357°; 55°15'·14N 07°46'·90W

LOUGH SWILLY, BUNCRANA and RATHMULLAN
Fanad Head ☆ 55°16'·57N 07°37'·92W Fl (5) WR 20s 39m **W18M**, R14M; W twr; vis 100°-R-110°-W-313°-R-345°-W-100°; 992501215.
Swillymore ⚡ Fl G 3s; 55°15'·12N 07°35'·79W; 992501216.
Dunree ⚡ Fl (2) WR 5s 49m W12M, R9M; vis: 320°-R-328°-W-183°-R-196°; 55°11'·89N 07°33'·25W.
Buncrana Pier near Hd ⚡ Iso WR 4s 11m W13M, R10M; R twr, W band; vis: R shore- over Inch spit, 052°-W-139°-R-shore over White Strand Rock; 55°07'·60N 07°27'·88W.
Rathmullan Pier Hd ⚡ Fl G 3s 5M; vis: 206°-345°; 55°05'·70N 07°31'·66W.
Inishtrahull ☆ 55°25'·89N 07°14'·63W Fl (3) 15s 59m **19M**; W twr; obscd 256°-261° within 3M; *Racon (T) 24M 060°-310°*. Fog Det Lt VQ; 992501229.

INISHTRAHULL TO RATHLIN ISLAND
LOUGH FOYLE
Foyle ⚡ L Fl 10s; 55°15'·32N 06°52'·62W; *Racon (M)*; 992501230.
Tuns ⚡ Fl R 3s; 55°14'·00N 06°53'·46W; 992501232.
Inishowen Dunagree ☆ 55°13'·60N 06°55'·70W Fl (2) WRG 10s 28m **W18M**, R14M, G14M; W twr, 2 B bands; vis: 197°-G-211°-W-249°-R-000°. Fog Det lt VQ 16m vis: 270°.

Greencastle S Bkwtr Dir lt 042·5°. Fl (2) WRG 3s 4m W11M, R9M, G9M; vis 307°-G- 040°-W-045°-R-055°; 55°12'·17N 06°59'·13W.
McKinney's ⚡ Fl R 5s; 55°10'·9N 07°00'·5W.
Moville ⚡ Fl WR 2·5s 11m 4M; W house on G piles vis: 240°-W-064°-R-240°; 55°10'·98N 07°02'·13W.

RIVER BANN, COLERAINE and PORTRUSH
River Bann Ldg lts 165°. Front, Oc 5s 6m 2M; W twr; 55°09'·96N 06°46'·23W. Rear, 245m from front, Oc 5s 14m 2M; W ☐ twr.
W Mole ⚡ Fl G 5s 4m 2M; vis: 170°-000°; 55°10'·25N 06°46'·45W.
Portstewart Point ⚡ Oc R 10s 21m 5M; R ☐ hut; vis: 040°-220°; 55°11'·33N 06°43'·26W.
N Pier Hd ⚡ Fl R 3s 6m 3M; vis: 220°-160°; 55°12'·34N 06°39'·58W.
Skerries ⚡ Fl R 5s; 53°13'·90N 06°36'·90W; 992351096.

RATHLIN ISLAND
Rathlin W 0·5M NE of Bull Pt ⚡ Fl R 5s 62m **22M**; W twr, lantern at base; vis: 015°-225°; H24. Fog Det Lt VQ; 992351000.
Drake Wreck ⚡ 55°17'·00N 06°12'·48W Q (6) + L Fl 15s.
Manor House ⚡ Oc WRG 4s 5M; vis: 020°-G-023°-W-026°-R-029°; 55°17'·52N 06°11'·73W.
Rue Pt ⚡ Fl(2) 5s 16m 14M; W twr B bands; 55°15'·53N 06°11'·47W; 992351131.
Altacarry Head ☆ 55°18'·11N 06°10'·31W Fl (4) 20s 74m **26M**; W twr, B band; vis: 110°-006° and 036°-058°; *Racon (G) 15-27M*; 992320707.

FAIR HEAD TO LAMBAY ISLAND
RED BAY, CARNLOUGH and LARNE
Red Bay Pier ⚡ Fl 3s 10m 5M; 55°03'·93N 06°03'·21W.
Carnlough Hbr N Pier ⚡ Fl G 3s 4m 5M; 54°59'·59N 05°59'·29W.
East Maiden ☆ Fl (3) 15s 29m **23M**; W twr, B band; *Racon (M) 11-21M*. Auxiliary lt Fl R 5s 15m 8M; 54°55'·75N 05°43'·71W; same twr; vis:142°-182° over Russel and Highland Rks; 992351110.
N Hunter Rock ⚡ Q; 54°53'·04N 05°45'·13W.
S Hunter Rock ⚡ VQ(6) + LFl 10s; 54°52'·69N 05°45'·22W; 992351007.
Larne No. 1 ⚡ QG; 54°51'·68N 05°47'·67W; *AIS*.
Chaine Twr ☆ Iso WR 5s 23m **W16M**, R12M; Gy twr; vis: 232°-W-240°-R-000° (shore); 54°51'·27N 05°47'·90W.
Larne Ldg lts 184°, No. 11 Front, 54°49'·60N 05°47'·81W Oc 4s 6m 12M; W 2 with R stripe on R pile structure; vis: 179°-189°. No. 12 Rear, 610m from front, Oc 4s 14m 12M; W 2 with R stripe on R ☐ twr; synch with front, vis: 5° either side of Ldg line.

CARRICKFERGUS
Black Hd ☆ 54°46'·02N 05°41'·34W Fl 3s 45m **27M**; W 8-sided twr; 992351002.
Cloghan Jetty ⚡ 54°44'·10N 05°41'·58W QG. Marina Ent Appr ⚡ Dir Oc WRG 3s 5m 3M; vis: G308°- W317·5°- R322·5°-332°; 54°42'·58N 05°48'·78W.

BELFAST LOUGH and BANGOR
Mew Is ☆ NE end 54°41'·92N 05°30'·82W Fl (4) 30s 35m **18M**; B twr, W band; *Racon (O) 14M*. Fog Det Lt VQ; 992351109.
Belfast Fairway ⚡ Iso 4s; 54°42'·32N 05°42'·30W; *Racon (G)*; *AIS*.
Kilroot ⚡ Fl QG (sync); 54°42'·85N 05°42'·85W.
Helen's Bay ⚡ QR (sync); 54°41'·86N 05°42'·85W.
No 1 ⚡ Fl G 2s (sync); 54°41'·67N 05°46'·51W.
No 2 ⚡ Fl R 2s (sync); 54°41'·55N 05°46'·43W.
Briggs ⚡ Fl (2)R 10s; 54°41'·52N 05°53'·70W; 992351133.

DONAGHADEE
Merandoragh ⚡ Fl (2) G 6s (sync); 54°39'·84N 05°32'·24W.
Foreland Spit ⚡ Fl (2) R 6s (sync); 54°39'·64N 05°32'·31W.
Governor's ⚡ Fl G 3s (sync); 54°39'·36N 05°31'·99W; 992351134.
Riggs Bank ⊙ V–AIS PHM; 54°38'·63N 05°27'·10W; 992356011.
Donaghadee ☆, S Pier Hd 54°38'·71N 05°31'·86W Iso WR 4s 17m **W18M**, R14M; twr; vis: shore-W-326°-R-shore; 002320792.

BALLYWATER and PORTAVOGIE

Ballywalter, Bkwtr Hd Fl WRG 3s 4m 9M; vis: 240°-G-267°-W-277°-R-314°; 54°32'·68N 05°28'·83W.

Skulmartin ⚓ L Fl 10s; 54°31'·82N 05°24'·80W; 992351022.
Portavogie Bkwtr Hd ⚡ Iso WRG 5s 9m W10M, R8M, G8M; ☐twr; vis: shore-G-258°-W-275°-R-348°; 54°27'·44N 05°26'·14W.
Plough Rock ⚓ 54°27'·40N 05°25'·12W Fl R 3s.
South Rock ⚓ Fl (3) R 30s 7M 54°24'·49N 05°22'·02W; 992351004.

STRANGFORD LOUGH

Strangford ⚓ L Fl 10s; 54°18'·63N 05°28'·69W; 992351028.
Bar Pladdy ⚓ Q (6) + L Fl 15s; 54°19'·34N 05°30'·51W; 992351135.
Dogtail Pt Ldg lts 341°. Front, Iso 4s 2m 5M; G Bn; 54°20'·79N 05°31'·84W. Rear, Gowlands Rk, 0·8M fm front, Iso 4s 6m 5M; W twr, G top, B base.

Swan Is ⚓ Q (3) 5m; BYB brick twr; 54°22'·38N 05°33'·16W.

Strangford East Ldg lts 256°. Front, Oc WRG 5s 6m W9M, R6M, G6M: vis: 190°-R-244°-G-252°-W-260°-R-294°; 54°22'·29N 05°33'·27W. Rear, 46m from front, Oc R 5s 10m 6M; vis: 250°-264°.

Portaferry Pier Hd ⚡ Oc WR 10s 9m W9M, R6M; Or mast; vis: W335°- R005°- W017°-128°; 54°22'·82N 05°33'·03W.

ARDGLASS

Inner Pier Hd ⚡ Iso WRG 4s 10m W8M, R7M, G5M; twr; vis: shore-G-308°-W-314°-R-shore; 54°15'·79N 05°36'·33W.

DUNDRUM BAY

St John's Point ☆ 54°13'·61N 05°39'·61W Q (2) 7·5s 37m **25M**; B twr, Y bands. **Auxiliary Light** ☆ Fl WR 3s 14m **W15M**, R11M; same twr; vis: 064°-W-078°-R-shore; Fog Det lt VQ 14m vis: 270°; 992351005.
DZ East ⚓ Fl (2) Y 10s; 54°12'·05N 05°45'·30W.
DZ West ⚓ Fl Y 5s; 54°11'·84N 05°50'·82W.

ANNALONG

E Bkwtr Hd ⚡ Oc WRG 5s 8m 9M; twr; vis: 204°-G-249°-W-309°-R-024°; 54°06'·51N 05°53'·73W.

KILKEEL

Pier Hd ⚡ Fl WR 2s 8m 8M; vis: R296°-W313°-017°; 54°03'·46N 05°59'·30W; 992356010 [emergency AIS 992356008].

CARLINGFORD LOUGH and NEWRY RIVER

Hellyhunter ⚓ Q(6) + LFl 15s; 54°00'·35N 06°02'·10W; 992351009.
Haulbowline ⚡ 54°01'·19N 06°04'·74W Fl (3) 10s 32m 10M; Grey twr; 992501235.
Ldg lts 310·4° Front, Oc 3s 7m 11M; R △ on twr; vis: 295°-325°; 54°01'·80N 06°05'·43W; 992501237. Rear, 457m from front, Oc 3s 12m 11M; R ▽ on twr; vis: 295°-325°; both H24.
Newry River Ldg lts 310·4°. Front, 54°06'·37N 06°16'·51W. Rear, 274m from front. Both Iso 4s 5/15m 2M; stone cols.

DUNDALK

Imogene ⚓ Fl (2) R 10s; 53°57'·41N 06°07'·02W; 992501238.
Pile Light ⚡ 53°58'·56N 06°17'·71W Fl WR 15s 10m 10M; W Ho.
Dunany ⚓ Fl R 3s; 53°53'·56N 06°09'·47W; 992501243.

SKERRIES BAY

Skerries Pier Hd ⚡ Oc R 6s 7m 7M; W col; vis: 103°-R-154°; 53°35'·09N 06°06'·49W

DROGHEDA to LAMBAY ISLAND

Port Approach Dir lt 53°43'·30N 06°14'·73W WRG 10m **W19M, R15M**, G15M; vis: 268°-FG-269°-Al WG-269·5°-FW-270·5°-Al WR-271°-FR-272°; H24.
Balbriggan ⚡ Fl (3) WRG 10s 12m W13M, R10M, G10M; W twr; vis: 159°-G-193°-W-288°-R-305°; 53°36'·76N 06°10'·80W.
Rockabill ☆ 53°35'·81N 06°00'·30W Fl WR 12s 45m **W17M, R13M**; W twr, B band; vis: 178°-W-329°-R-178°; 992501246.
Skerries Bay Pier Hd ⚡ Oc R 6s 7m 7M; W col; vis: 103°-154°; 53°35'·09N 06°06'·49W.

6.4 PASSAGE INFORMATION

More passage information is threaded between the harbours in this area. Admiralty Leisure Folio 5612 covers Carlingford Lough to Lough Foyle. The latest editions of the Irish Cruising Club Sailing Directions are strongly recommended for all Irish waters (www.irishcruisingclub.com). Particularly useful on the N and W coast where other information is scarce they are published in two volumes, *E and N coasts of Ireland* and *S and W coasts of Ireland*. (Both available from Imray in UK or Todd Chart Services, Bangor, Co Down, ☎028 9146 6640 (www.toddchart.com).

CROSSING THE IRISH SEA

(AC 1123, 1121, 1411) Passages across the Irish Sea range from the fairly long haul from Land's End to Cork (140M), to the relatively short hop from Mull of Kintyre to Torr Pt (11M). Such distances are deceptive, because the average cruising yacht needs to depart from and arrive at a reasonably secure hbr. See 0.31 for distances across the Irish Sea. Submarine exercise areas are at 2.17.

▶*Strong tidal streams in North Channel can cause heavy overfalls.*◀

Many yachts use the Land's End/Cork route on their way to and from the delightful cruising ground along the S coast of Ireland. Penzance Bay or one of the Scilly Islands' ⚓s are convenient places from which to leave, with good lights to assist departure. Although the Celtic Sea is exposed to the Atlantic, there are no dangers on passage and the tidal streams are weak.

A landfall between Ballycotton and Old Hd of Kinsale (both have good lights) presents no offlying dangers, and in poor vis decreasing soundings indicate approach to land. Outward bound under sail, it is likely that the boat will be on the wind – a possible benefit on the return passage. If however the wind serves, and if it is intended to cruise along the southern coast, a landfall at the Fastnet with arrival at (say) Baltimore will place the yacht more to windward, for a little extra distance (170M).

From Land's End another likely destination is Dun Laoghaire. A stop at Milford Haven enables the skipper to select the best time

for passing the Smalls or Bishops (see 4.4) and roughly divides the total passage into two equal parts of about 100M. From S Bishop onwards there are the options of making the short crossing to Tuskar Rk and going N inside the banks (theoretically a good idea in strong W winds) or of keeping to seaward.

▶*But in bad weather the area off Tuskar is best avoided; apart from the Traffic Separation Scheme, the tide is strong at Sp and the sea can be very rough.*◀

The ferry route Holyhead/Dun Laoghaire is another typical crossing (56M) and with relatively straightforward landfalls either end. Beware the TSS off The Skerries and Kish Bank wind farm.

▶*The tide runs hard round Anglesey at Sp, so departure just before slack water minimises the set N or S.*◀

Harbours on the Isle of Man provide convenient staging points for cruising in the Irish Sea, wherever bound.

CROSSING TO/FROM SCOTLAND

(AC 2198, 2199, 2724) Between Scotland and Ireland there are several possible routes, but much depends on weather and tide. Time of departure must take full advantage of the stream, and avoid tide races and overfalls (see 2.4). Conditions can change quickly, so a flexible plan is needed. The distance to Mull of Kintyre from Belfast Lough entrance is about 35M.

▶ *A departure at local HW (also HW Dover) provides at least 6hrs of N-going tides, and fair winds make it possible to get past the Mull or Sanda Is on one tide. To be more confident of reaching Gigha or Port Ellen, a departure from Glenarm Marina or Red Bay at HW makes a shorter passage with better stream advantage. The inshore side of the TSS coincides with the outer limit of the race S-SW off the Mull of Kintyre; this runs from HW Dover +0430 until +0610 when a local S-going stream opposes the main N-going stream.*◀

LISCANNOR BAY TO SLYNE HEAD

(AC 2173) The coast NE of Liscannor Bay is devoid of shelter. O'Brien's Tower is conspicuous just N of the 199m high Cliffs of

Moher. Eastward from Black Head there are many bays and inlets, often poorly marked, but providing shelter and exploration.

Galway is a commercial port, with a small marina. 3M SE, New Harbour (AC 1984) is a pleasant ⚓ with moorings off Galway Bay SC. The N side of Galway Bay is exposed, with no shelter. Normal approach to Galway Bay is through South Snd or North Snd. South Snd is 3M wide, with no dangers except Finnis Rock (0·4m) 5ca SE of Inisheer. North Snd is 4M wide from Eagle Rock and other dangers off Lettermullan shore, to banks on S side which break in strong winds. The other channels are Gregory Sound, 1M wide between Inishmore and Inishmaan, and Foul Sound between Inishmaan and Inisheer. The latter has one danger, Pipe Rock and the reef inshore of it, extending 3ca NW of Inisheer.

In good visibility the Connemara coast (AC 2709, 2096) and Aran Islands (AC 3339) give excellent cruising. But there are many rocks and few navigational marks. Between Slyne Hd and Roundstone Bay are many offlying dangers. If coasting, keep well seaward of Skerd Rocks. A conspicuous tower (24m) on Golan Head is a key feature. Going E the better harbours are Roundstone Bay, Cashel Bay, Killeany Bay, Greatman Bay and Cashla Bay. Kilronan (Killeany Bay) on Inishmore is the only reasonable harbour in the Aran Islands, but is exposed in E winds. Disused lighthouse on centre of island is conspicuous.

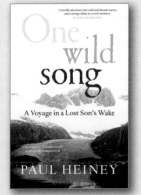

6.5 SPECIAL NOTES FOR IRELAND: See 5.5

6.6 GALWAY BAY

Galway 53°12'N 09°08'W ✳✳✳✳⚓⚓⚓🏳🏳🏳

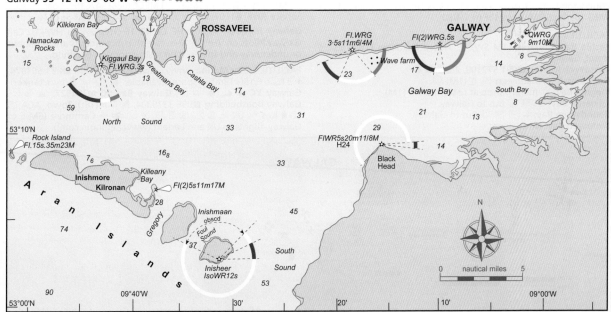

CHARTS AC 2173, 3339, 1984,1904; Imray C55, C54

TIDES −0555 Dover; ML 2·9; Duration 0620

Standard Port GALWAY (→)

Times				Height (metres)			
High Water		Low Water		MHWS	MHWN	MLWN	MLWS
0600	1100	0000	0700	5·1	3·9	2·0	0·8
1800	2300	1200	1900				
Differences KILKIERAN COVE							
+0005	+0005	+0016	+0016	−0·3	−0·2	−0·1	−0·2
ROUNDSTONE BAY							
+0003	+0003	+0008	+0008	−0·7	−0·5	−0·3	−0·3
KILLEANY BAY (Aran Islands)							
0000	0000	+0001	−0001	−0·1	+0·1	+0·1	+0·2
LISCANNOR							
−0003	−0007	+0006	+0002	−0·4	−0·3	ND	ND

SHELTER Galway Bay is sheltered from large swells by Aran Is, but seas get up in the 20M between the Aran Is and Galway. Beware salmon drift nets in the apps to many bays. On the S Shore:

Bays between Black Hd and Galway have rocks and shoals, but give excellent shelter. Kinvarra B, Aughinish B, South B and Ballyvaghan B are the main ones. Enter Kinvarra B with caution on the flood; beware rks. Berth in small drying hbr. Beware fish farm in South B. Ballvaghan B, entered either side of Illaunloo Rk, leads to two piers (both dry) or ⚓ close NE in pool (3m). Best access HW±2.

On the N coast there is no safe hbr from Galway to Cashla (20M).

Cashla Bay: Easiest all weather entry on this coast. To the East side: **Rossaveel** is a sheltered but busy fishing and ferry hbr, with small dedicated marina. To the West side: 8 Y ⚓s off Struthan Quay.

The better ⚓s in outer Galway Bay northward to Slyne Head are:

Greatman Bay: Beware English Rk (dries 1·2m), Keeraun Shoal (1.6m, seas break), Arkeena Rk, Trabaan Rk, Rin and Chapel Rks.

⚓ off Natawny Quay (E side), or on 4 Y ⚓s off Maumeen Quay (dries), ⌾ possible.

Kiggaul Bay: Easy ent, H24; ⚓ close W /NW of lt Fl WRG 3s 5/3M. Depth 3 to 4m; exposed to S/SE winds.

Kilkieran Bay: Easy ent abm Golam Tr (conspic). 12 Y ⚓s off Kilkieran. Many ⚓s in 14M long, sheltered bay.

Roundstone Bay: AC2709 (Off chartlet at 53°23'N 09°54'·5W). Safe shelter/access, except in SE'ly. 4 Y ⚓s are 5ca SSE of Roundstone, or ⚓ in 2m off N quay. Other ⚓s E in Bertraghboy and Cashel Bays.

Bunowen Bay: (53°24'·6N 10°06'·9W). Sheltered in W-NE winds; unsafe in S'ly. Easy appr with Bunowen House brg 000°, leaving Mullauncarrickscoltia Rk (1·1m) to port. ⚓ in 3-4m below conspic Doon Hill.

NAVIGATION Enter the Bay by one of four Sounds:
- North Sound between Inishmore and Golam Tr (conspic), 4½M wide, is easiest but beware Brocklinmore Bank in heavy weather.
- Gregory Sound between Inishmore and Inishmaan, is free of dangers, but give Straw Island a berth of 2-3ca.
- Foul Sound between Inishmaan and Inisheer; only danger is Pipe Rock (dries) at end of reef extending 3ca NW of Inisheer.
- South Sound between Inisheer and mainland. Finnis Rock (dries 0·4m) 4½ca SE of E point of Inisheer (marked by ECM buoy Q (3) 10s). From S, beware Kilstiffin Rocks off Liscanor Bay.

LIGHTS AND MARKS Cashla Bay: Killeen Pt Fl (3) WR 10s 6/3M; Lion Pt Dir lt 010°, Iso WRG 4s 8/6M, 008·5°-W-011·5°. Rossaveel ldg lts 116°, Oc 3s. Black Head lt Fl WR 5s 20m 11/8M H24, vis 045°-W-268°-R (covers Illanloo Rk)-276°.

Kiggaul Bay: Fl WR 3s 5m 5/3M, 329°-W-359°-R-059°.

Roundstone Bay: Croaghnakeela Is Fl 3·7s 7m 5M. Inishnee lt Fl (2) WRG 10s 9m 5/3M, W sector 017°-030°.

FACILITIES
Cashla Bay: Carraroe (1M SW) ⚓ Hotel. **Costelloe** (1½M E) ⌧ Hotel, Garage.
Rossaveel: Marina ☎091 572108, 28⌾ ⚓ ⌿.
Greatman Bay: Maumeen ⚓ ☏(1M) ⌾.
Kiggaul Bay: ⌾ (no ☎), shop at Lettermullen (1M).
Kilkieran Bay: ☏ ⚓ ⌾ Bus to Galway.
Roundstone Bay: ⚓ ⌧ ⚓ ⌾ Bus to Galway.
Bunowen Bay: No facilities.

ARAN ISLANDS Shelter at **Inishmore** in Killeany Bay with harbour at Kilronan, HM ☎099 20946. 8 Y ⚓s available or ⚓ S of Kilronan pier or ⚓ E of Killeany Pt, but exposed to E/NE wind. In good weather ⚓ at Portmurvy. Facilities: ⚓ ⚓ ⌧ ⚓; Ferry to Rossaveel, **Lights and marks**: Inishmore: Eeragh Island (Rk Is) Fl 15s 35m 23M, W tr, B bands. Killeany Bay: Straw Is, Fl (2) 5s 11m 17M. Ldg lts 192° Oc 5s for Killeany Bay. **Inishmaan** Ldg lts 199°, Oc 6s 8M, lead into small harbour with 3·5m and good shelter. Ferries have priority for ⌾, but do not stay overnight. Inisheer: Iso WR 12s 34m 20/16M, Racon, vis 225°-W-245° (partially obscd 225°-231° beyond 7M), R sector covers Finnis Rk.

GALWAY HARBOUR
53°16'·07N 09°02'·74W ❄❄❄⚓⚓⚓✿✿✿

SHELTER Very good in Galway hbr, protected from SW'lies by Mutton Island. Dock gates open HW–2 to HW. The approach channel is dredged to 3.4m. Enter Galway Dock and secure in SW corner of basin where there is a 31-berth marina, or ask HM for waiting berth on lead-in pier. Reclamation work at Rinmore Pt has improved shelter in the 'Layby' (a dredged cut NE of New pier) where an additional 8 berths are available on a 60m pontoon. New Harbour (2·5M ESE and home of Galway Bay SC) is nearest safe ⚓ to Galway. 5 Y ⚓s in lee of Mutton Island causeway in 2-4m, may be used while waiting for the dock gates to open.

NAVIGATION Galway WPT 53°14'·80N 09°03'·40W, 061°/1·1M to Leverets lt. Shipping information see www.aislive.com.

LIGHTS AND MARKS See 6.3 and chartlet. Leverets Q WRG 9m 10M; B tr, W bands; Rinmore Iso WRG 4s 7m 5M; W ☐ tr. Appr chan 325° is defined by a Dir lt WRG 7m 3M on New Pier.

COMMUNICATIONS (Code 091) MRCC (066) 9476109; Coast Rescue Service (099) 61107; Police 538000; Dr 562453. HM 561874.

Galway Harbour Radio VHF Ch **12** 16 (HW–2½ to HW+1). Call Galway Pilots on VHF Ch **12** in case ship movements are imminent or under way and follow their instructions on berthing.

FACILITIES City Marina: www.galwayharbour.com ☎091 561874, ⚓ 31⌾ €15(<13m) if space available, ⚓ ⚓ ⚓ ⚓(by r/tanker). **Galway YC** ⚓ ⚓ ⚓ ⌾; **Galway Bay SC** ☎794527, ⚓ ⚓ ⚓. **Galway Boatbuilding** ☎086 3379304, ⚓ ⚓ ☏(18t). **Town** ACA ☏ ☏ ⚓ Kos ⚓ ⚓ ⚓ ⚓ ⌧ Ⓑ ☏ ⚓ ⚓ ➔ Carnmore (6M E of Galway, flights to UK and Lorient (www.aerarann.com)).

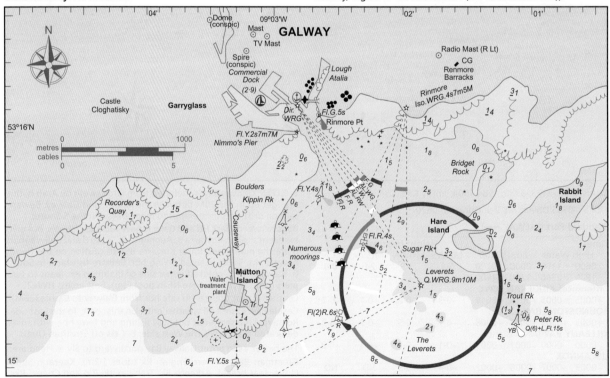

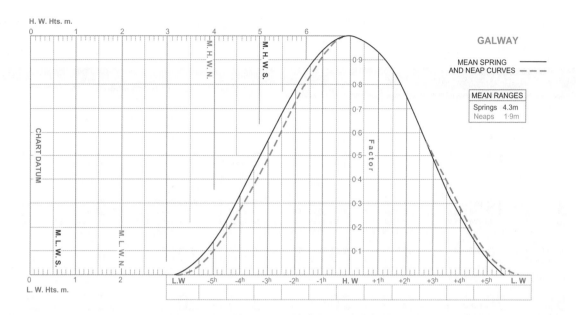

H. W. Hts. m.

GALWAY

MEAN SPRING AND NEAP CURVES

MEAN RANGES
Springs 4.3m
Neaps 1.9m

CHART DATUM

M. H. W. N.

M. H. W. S.

M. L. W. S.

M. L. W. N.

L.W -5h -4h -3h -2h -1h H. W +1h +2h +3h +4h +5h L. W

L. W. Hts. m.

SLYNE HEAD TO EAGLE ISLAND

(AC 2420) This coast has many inlets, some sheltered, but few lights.

▶ *Streams are weak offshore.* ◀

Slyne Hd Lt Ho marks SW end of the rocks and islets stretching 2M WSW from coast.

▶ *Here the stream turns N at HW Galway −0320, and S at HW Galway +0300. It runs 3kn at sp and in bad weather causes a dangerous race; keep 2M offshore.* ◀

Seas break on Barret Shoals, 3M NW of Slyne Hd. Cleggan B is moderate ⚓, open to NW but easy access. High Is Sound is usual coasting route, not Friar Is Sound or Aughrus Passage. Clifden Bay (AC 2708) has offlying dangers with breakers; enter 3ca S of Carrickrana Bn and ⚓ off Drinagh Pt, in Clifden Hbr or Ardbear Bay.

Ballynakill Hbr (AC 2706), easily entered either side of Freaghillaun South, has excellent shelter; Tully mountain is conspic to N. Beware Mullaghadrina and Ship Rk in N chan. ⚓ in Fahy, Derryinver or Barnaderg B. There is ⚓ on S side of Inishbofin (lt), but difficult access/exit in strong SW wind or swell. Rks and breakers exist E of Inishbofin and S of Inishshark; see AC 2707 for clearing lines. Lecky Rks lie 1M SSE of Davillaun. Carrickmahoy is a very dangerous rock (1·9m) between Inishbofin and Cleggan Pt.

Killary B (AC 2706) and Little Killary both have good ⚓s in magnificent scenery. Consult sailing directions, and only approach in reasonable weather and good vis.

Clare Is has Two Fathom Rk (3·4m) 5ca off NW coast, and Calliaghcrom Rk 5ca to the N; ⚓ on NE side. In Clew Bay Newport and Westport (AC 2667, 2057) need detailed pilotage directions. S of Clare Is beware Meemore Shoal 1·5M W of Roonagh Hd. 2M further W is the isolated rk Mweelaun. The islands of Caher, Ballybeg, Inishturk (with ⚓ on E side) and Inishdalla have few hidden dangers, but the coast to the E must be given a berth of 1·5M even in calm weather; in strong winds seas break much further offshore.

Achill Sound (ACs 2667/2704) is entered close N of Achillbeg Is and extends N for about 8M to Bull's Mouth. Passage is possible at HW for shallow draught craft (<2m) via a swing bridge, which is rarely opened. ⚓s at each end of Sound, but the stream runs strongly. Rough water is likely off Achill Hd (highest cliffs in the British Islands).

Blacksod B (AC 2704) has easy ent (possible at night) and good shelter. In the appr Black Rk (lt) has rks up to 1·25M SW. From N, in

good weather, there is chan between Duvillaun Beg and Gaghta Is, but in W gales beware breakers 1M SE of Duvillaun More.

Keep 5ca off Erris Hd, and further in bad weather. Unless calm, keep seaward of Eagle Is (lt) where there is race to N. Frenchport (AC 2703) is good temp ⚓ except in strong W winds. Inishkea Is (AC 2704) can be visited in good weather; ⚓ N or S of Rusheen Is. On passage keep 5ca W of Inishkea to avoid bad seas if wind over tide. The sound off Mullett Peninsula is clear, but for Pluddany Rk 6ca E of Inishkea N.

EAGLE ISLAND TO BLOODY FORELAND

Broad Haven (AC 2703) is good ⚓ and refuge, but in N/NW gales sea can break in ent. In approaches beware Slugga Rk on E side with offlier, and Monastery Rk (0·3m) on S side.

The coast E of Broad Haven is inhospitable. Only Portacloy and Belderg give a little shelter. The Stags, 1M N of Buddagh, are steep-to and high. Killala B has temp ⚓ 1M S of Kilcummin Hd, on W side. Proceeding to Killala beware St Patrick's Rks. Ent has ldg lts and marks, but bar is dangerous in strong NE winds.

In Donegal B (AC 2702) beware uncharted rks W of Teelin, a good natural hbr but exposed to S/SW swell. Killybegs has better shelter and is always accessible. Good shelter with fair access in Donegal Hbr (AC 2715). Good ⚓ or ⚓ via YC at Mullaghmore in fair weather; sea state is calm with winds from SE through S to NW. Inishmurray is worth a visit in good weather, ⚓ off S side. There are shoals close E and NE of the Is, and Bomore Rks 1·5M to N. Keep well clear of coast N from Sligo in onshore winds, and beware of lobster pots.

The coast and islands 15M NE from Aran Is give good cruising (AC 1883). An inshore passage avoids offlying dangers: Buniver and Brinlack shoals, which can break; Bullogconnell 1M NW of Gola Is; and Stag Rks 2M NNW of Owey Is. ⚓s include Bunbeg and Gweedore Hbr, and Cruit B which has easier access. Behind Aran Is are several good ⚓s. Use N ent, since S one is shallow (AC 2792). Rutland N Chan is main appr to Burtonport.

Boylagh B has shoals and rks N of Roaninish Is. Connell Rk (0·3m) is 1M N of Church Pool, a good ⚓, best approached from Dawros Hd 4·5M to W. On S side of Glen B a temp ⚓ (but not in W or NW winds) is just E of Rinmeasa Pt. Rathlin O'Birne Is has steps E side; ⚓ SE of them 100m offshore. Sound is 5ca wide; hold Is side to clear rks off Malin Beg Hd.

Off low-lying Bloody Foreland (lt) there is often heavy swell.

GALWAY LAT 53°16'N LONG 9°03'W
TIMES AND HEIGHTS OF HIGH AND LOW WATERS

STANDARD TIME (UT)
For Summer Time add ONE hour in **non-shaded areas**

Dates in red are **SPRINGS**
Dates in blue are NEAPS

YEAR 2016

JANUARY

Day	Time	m	Day	Time	m
1 F	0307 / 0936 / 1544 / 2209	1.9 / 4.4 / 1.8 / 4.2	**16** SA	0303 / 0935 / 1532 / ☾2210	1.3 / 4.8 / 1.3 / 4.5
2 SA	0412 / 1026 / 1653 / ☾2301	2.1 / 4.2 / 2.0 / 4.1	**17** SU	0402 / 1035 / 1633 / 2315	1.6 / 4.6 / 1.5 / 4.4
3 SU	0531 / 1121 / 1804	2.2 / 4.0 / 2.1	**18** M	0511 / 1147 / 1745	1.8 / 4.4 / 1.7
4 M	0000 / 0636 / 1226 / 1904	4.0 / 2.2 / 4.0 / 2.0	**19** TU	0034 / 0636 / 1310 / 1915	4.3 / 1.8 / 4.3 / 1.7
5 TU	0113 / 0733 / 1348 / 1958	4.1 / 2.1 / 4.1 / 1.9	**20** W	0150 / 0806 / 1421 / 2030	4.4 / 1.6 / 4.5 / 1.6
6 W	0219 / 0824 / 1447 / 2046	4.3 / 1.9 / 4.3 / 1.7	**21** TH	0251 / 0907 / 1518 / 2123	4.7 / 1.4 / 4.7 / 1.4
7 TH	0306 / 0910 / 1532 / 2129	4.5 / 1.6 / 4.5 / 1.5	**22** F	0342 / 0955 / 1608 / 2207	4.9 / 1.1 / 4.9 / 1.2
8 F	0348 / 0951 / 1613 / 2208	4.8 / 1.3 / 4.7 / 1.3	**23** SA	0428 / 1036 / 1653 / 2245	5.2 / 0.9 / 5.1 / 1.1
9 SA	0427 / 1029 / 1653 / 2244	5.0 / 1.1 / 4.9 / 1.1	**24** SU	0511 / 1111 / 1735 / ○2319	5.3 / 0.8 / 5.2 / 1.0
10 SU	0507 / 1106 / 1733 / ●2320	5.2 / 0.9 / 5.1 / 1.0	**25** M	0551 / 1143 / 1815 / 2353	5.3 / 0.8 / 5.2 / 1.0
11 M	0547 / 1143 / 1814 / 2358	5.3 / 0.7 / 5.1 / 0.9	**26** TU	0629 / 1216 / 1854	5.3 / 0.8 / 5.1
12 TU	0627 / 1223 / 1855	5.4 / 0.6 / 5.2	**27** W	0028 / 0706 / 1252 / 1930	1.1 / 5.2 / 0.9 / 5.0
13 W	0040 / 0709 / 1305 / 1938	0.9 / 5.4 / 0.7 / 5.1	**28** TH	0105 / 0742 / 1328 / 2007	1.2 / 5.0 / 1.1 / 4.8
14 TH	0124 / 0754 / 1350 / 2024	0.9 / 5.2 / 0.9 / 4.9	**29** F	0141 / 0821 / 1405 / 2047	1.4 / 4.8 / 1.4 / 4.6
15 F	0212 / 0842 / 1438 / 2114	1.1 / 5.1 / 1.0 / 4.7	**30** SA	0219 / 0902 / 1443 / 2130	1.6 / 4.6 / 1.6 / 4.4
			31 SU	0258 / 0948 / 1524 / 2217	1.9 / 4.3 / 1.9 / 4.2

FEBRUARY

Day	Time	m	Day	Time	m
1 M	0344 / 1038 / 1615 / ☾2308	2.1 / 4.1 / 2.1 / 4.1	**16** TU	0446 / 1124 / 1720	1.7 / 4.2 / 1.8
2 TU	0453 / 1133 / 1823	2.3 / 3.9 / 2.2	**17** W	0008 / 0615 / 1255 / 1856	4.2 / 1.8 / 4.1 / 1.9
3 W	0006 / 0700 / 1238 / 1929	4.0 / 2.2 / 3.9 / 2.1	**18** TH	0135 / 0756 / 1411 / 2020	4.2 / 1.7 / 4.2 / 1.8
4 TH	0114 / 0758 / 1356 / 2023	4.1 / 2.0 / 4.0 / 1.9	**19** F	0240 / 0902 / 1509 / 2116	4.4 / 1.4 / 4.5 / 1.5
5 F	0225 / 0849 / 1501 / 2110	4.3 / 1.7 / 4.3 / 1.6	**20** SA	0332 / 0949 / 1557 / 2158	4.7 / 1.2 / 4.8 / 1.3
6 SA	0319 / 0933 / 1548 / 2152	4.6 / 1.4 / 4.6 / 1.3	**21** SU	0416 / 1027 / 1639 / 2232	5.0 / 1.0 / 5.0 / 1.1
7 SU	0403 / 1014 / 1631 / 2230	4.9 / 1.0 / 4.9 / 1.0	**22** M	0457 / 1057 / 1718 / ○2301	5.1 / 0.8 / 5.1 / 1.0
8 M	0445 / 1051 / 1712 / ●2306	5.2 / 0.7 / 5.1 / 0.8	**23** TU	0534 / 1121 / 1755 / 2330	5.2 / 0.8 / 5.1 / 0.9
9 TU	0526 / 1128 / 1753 / 2344	5.5 / 0.5 / 5.3 / 0.6	**24** W	0610 / 1150 / 1830	5.2 / 0.7 / 5.1
10 W	0609 / 1206 / 1836	5.6 / 0.3 / 5.4	**25** TH	0003 / 0644 / 1223 / 1904	0.9 / 5.2 / 0.8 / 5.0
11 TH	0024 / 0652 / 1247 / 1918	0.5 / 5.6 / 0.1 / 5.3	**26** F	0037 / 0718 / 1256 / 1938	1.0 / 5.0 / 0.9 / 4.9
12 F	0106 / 0736 / 1330 / 2003	0.6 / 5.5 / 0.5 / 5.2	**27** SA	0110 / 0753 / 1330 / 2015	1.1 / 4.8 / 1.1 / 4.7
13 SA	0152 / 0823 / 1416 / 2051	0.8 / 5.2 / 0.8 / 4.9	**28** SU	0145 / 0831 / 1404 / 2054	1.3 / 4.6 / 1.4 / 4.5
14 SU	0241 / 0914 / 1507 / 2143	1.1 / 4.9 / 1.1 / 4.6	**29** M	0222 / 0913 / 1443 / 2138	1.6 / 4.3 / 1.7 / 4.3
15 M	0337 / 1012 / 1606 / ☾2245	1.4 / 4.5 / 1.5 / 4.3			

MARCH

Day	Time	m	Day	Time	m
1 TU	0304 / 1000 / 1527 / ☾2227	1.8 / 4.1 / 1.9 / 4.1	**16** W	0427 / 1104 / 1702 / 2343	1.6 / 4.1 / 1.9 / 4.0
2 W	0353 / 1054 / 1621 / 2324	2.1 / 3.9 / 2.2 / 3.9	**17** TH	0557 / 1241 / 1834	1.8 / 4.0 / 2.0
3 TH	0457 / 1156 / 1900	2.2 / 3.8 / 2.3	**18** F	0119 / 0734 / 1358 / 1958	4.1 / 1.7 / 4.1 / 1.9
4 F	0026 / 0732 / 1306 / 2000	3.9 / 2.1 / 3.9 / 2.1	**19** SA	0225 / 0845 / 1454 / 2057	4.3 / 1.5 / 4.3 / 1.6
5 SA	0138 / 0826 / 1426 / 2049	4.1 / 1.7 / 4.2 / 1.6	**20** SU	0316 / 0931 / 1540 / 2139	4.6 / 1.2 / 4.6 / 1.3
6 SU	0247 / 0912 / 1522 / 2132	4.5 / 1.3 / 4.6 / 1.2	**21** M	0359 / 1007 / 1620 / 2211	4.7 / 1.0 / 4.8 / 1.1
7 M	0337 / 0954 / 1606 / 2210	4.9 / 0.8 / 4.9 / 0.8	**22** TU	0437 / 1033 / 1657 / 2238	4.9 / 0.9 / 5.0 / 0.9
8 TU	0421 / 1031 / 1648 / 2247	5.3 / 0.5 / 5.3 / 0.5	**23** W	0513 / 1055 / 1731 / ○2306	5.0 / 0.8 / 5.0 / 0.8
9 W	0504 / 1108 / 1730 / ●2324	5.6 / 0.2 / 5.5 / 0.3	**24** TH	0547 / 1123 / 1804 / 2337	5.0 / 0.7 / 5.1 / 0.8
10 TH	0548 / 1145 / 1813	5.7 / 0.1 / 5.6	**25** F	0621 / 1154 / 1838	5.0 / 0.8 / 5.0
11 F	0004 / 0632 / 1226 / 1856	0.2 / 5.7 / 0.1 / 5.5	**26** SA	0010 / 0654 / 1227 / 1910	0.8 / 4.9 / 0.9 / 4.9
12 SA	0046 / 0717 / 1308 / 1941	0.3 / 5.6 / 0.3 / 5.3	**27** SU	0044 / 0728 / 1300 / 1944	0.9 / 4.8 / 1.0 / 4.7
13 SU	0131 / 0805 / 1353 / 2028	0.5 / 5.3 / 0.7 / 5.0	**28** M	0118 / 0803 / 1335 / 2020	1.1 / 4.6 / 1.2 / 4.5
14 M	0220 / 0855 / 1443 / 2119	0.9 / 4.9 / 1.1 / 4.7	**29** TU	0155 / 0841 / 1413 / 2101	1.3 / 4.3 / 1.5 / 4.3
15 TU	0316 / 0953 / 1544 / ☾2218	1.3 / 4.5 / 1.6 / 4.3	**30** W	0236 / 0927 / 1457 / 2150	1.6 / 4.1 / 1.8 / 4.1
			31 TH	0324 / 1021 / 1549 / ☾2247	1.8 / 3.9 / 2.1 / 3.9

APRIL

Day	Time	m	Day	Time	m
1 F	0422 / 1122 / 1656 / 2349	2.0 / 3.8 / 2.2 / 3.9	**16** SA	0054 / 0651 / 1335 / 1919	4.0 / 1.7 / 4.0 / 1.9
2 SA	0657 / 1230 / 1932	2.0 / 3.9 / 2.0	**17** SU	0201 / 0805 / 1430 / 2021	4.1 / 1.5 / 4.2 / 1.7
3 SU	0058 / 0758 / 1348 / 2024	4.1 / 1.6 / 4.1 / 1.6	**18** M	0252 / 0856 / 1516 / 2106	4.3 / 1.3 / 4.5 / 1.4
4 M	0211 / 0846 / 1452 / 2107	4.4 / 1.2 / 4.5 / 1.2	**19** TU	0335 / 0932 / 1555 / 2141	4.5 / 1.2 / 4.6 / 1.2
5 TU	0308 / 0928 / 1540 / 2146	4.8 / 0.7 / 5.0 / 0.7	**20** W	0413 / 0959 / 1630 / 2211	4.6 / 1.0 / 4.8 / 1.0
6 W	0356 / 1007 / 1623 / 2224	5.2 / 0.4 / 5.3 / 0.4	**21** TH	0447 / 1026 / 1703 / 2241	4.8 / 0.9 / 4.9 / 0.9
7 TH	0441 / 1044 / 1706 / ●2303	5.5 / 0.1 / 5.6 / 0.2	**22** F	0521 / 1056 / 1737 / ○2313	5.0 / 0.8 / 5.0 / 0.8
8 F	0527 / 1123 / 1750 / 2344	5.7 / 0.1 / 5.6 / 0.1	**23** SA	0556 / 1127 / 1811 / 2346	4.8 / 0.8 / 4.9 / 0.8
9 SA	0613 / 1203 / 1835	5.7 / 0.1 / 5.6	**24** SU	0631 / 1200 / 1844	4.8 / 0.9 / 4.9
10 SU	0026 / 0659 / 1246 / 1920	0.2 / 5.5 / 0.4 / 5.4	**25** M	0019 / 0704 / 1234 / 1917	0.9 / 4.7 / 1.0 / 4.7
11 M	0112 / 0747 / 1332 / 2007	0.4 / 5.2 / 0.8 / 5.1	**26** TU	0055 / 0738 / 1310 / 1950	1.0 / 4.5 / 1.2 / 4.6
12 TU	0202 / 0838 / 1424 / 2058	0.8 / 4.8 / 1.2 / 4.7	**27** W	0134 / 0815 / 1350 / 2029	1.2 / 4.4 / 1.4 / 4.4
13 W	0259 / 0935 / 1526 / 2155	1.2 / 4.4 / 1.6 / 4.3	**28** TH	0215 / 0859 / 1434 / 2118	1.4 / 4.2 / 1.7 / 4.2
14 TH	0411 / 1044 / 1645 / ☾2311	1.5 / 4.1 / 1.9 / 4.0	**29** F	0303 / 0953 / 1527 / 2215	1.6 / 4.0 / 1.9 / 4.1
15 F	0532 / 1220 / 1806	1.7 / 3.9 / 2.0	**30** SA	0401 / 1053 / 1633 / ☾2317	1.7 / 3.9 / 2.0 / 4.0

Chart Datum: 0·20 metres below Ordnance Datum (Dublin). HAT is 5·9 metres above Chart Datum.

STANDARD TIME (UT)
For Summer Time add ONE hour in **non-shaded areas**

GALWAY   LAT 53°16'N   LONG 9°03'W
TIMES AND HEIGHTS OF HIGH AND LOW WATERS

Dates in red are SPRINGS
Dates in blue are NEAPS

YEAR **2016**

N Ireland

MAY		JUNE		JULY		AUGUST	
Time m	Time m	Time m	Time m	Time m	Time m	Time m	Time m

1 0515 1.8 / 1159 4.0 / SU 1820 2.0
16 0125 4.0 / 0709 1.7 / M 1357 4.1 / 1935 1.8
1 0106 4.4 / 0726 1.2 / W 1350 4.6 / 2002 1.3
16 0227 4.1 / 0808 1.7 / TH 1447 4.3 / 2032 1.6
1 0155 4.5 / 0801 1.3 / F 1430 4.8 / 2037 1.2
16 0231 4.0 / 0825 1.7 / SA 1452 4.3 / 2051 1.6
1 0343 4.8 / 0944 1.1 / M 1604 5.1 / 2214 0.8
16 0336 4.4 / 0934 1.4 / TU 1549 4.7 / 2156 1.1

2 0024 4.1 / 0715 1.5 / M 1313 4.2 / 1949 1.6
17 0220 4.1 / 0803 1.5 / TU 1444 4.3 / 2025 1.6
2 0214 4.7 / 0827 1.0 / TH 1448 4.9 / 2054 0.9
17 0310 4.2 / 0853 1.5 / F 1527 4.5 / 2115 1.5
2 0257 4.8 / 0900 1.1 / SA 1524 5.0 / 2130 0.9
17 0319 4.2 / 0911 1.6 / SU 1535 4.5 / 2134 1.4
2 0431 5.0 / 1026 1.0 / TU 1650 5.3 / ● 2253 0.7
17 0416 4.7 / 1013 1.1 / W 1628 5.0 / 2234 0.8

3 0136 4.4 / 0813 1.2 / TU 1420 4.6 / 2037 1.2
18 0305 4.3 / 0847 1.4 / W 1524 4.5 / 2106 1.4
3 0311 5.0 / 0916 0.7 / F 1538 5.2 / 2141 0.6
18 0349 4.4 / 0933 1.4 / SA 1604 4.7 / 2155 1.3
3 0351 5.0 / 0949 0.9 / SU 1614 5.2 / 2217 0.7
18 0401 4.4 / 0953 1.4 / M 1615 4.8 / 2215 1.2
3 0516 5.1 / 1104 0.9 / W 1733 5.3 / 2329 0.6
18 0455 4.9 / 1048 0.8 / TH 1707 5.2 / ○ 2310 0.5

4 0240 4.8 / 0858 0.8 / W 1512 4.8 / 2120 0.7
19 0343 4.4 / 0924 1.2 / TH 1600 4.6 / 2142 1.2
4 0403 5.2 / 1001 0.6 / SA 1626 5.4 / 2227 0.5
19 0427 4.5 / 1011 1.3 / SU 1641 4.8 / 2232 1.1
4 0441 5.2 / 1034 0.8 / M 1701 5.4 / ● 2302 0.6
19 0441 4.6 / 1030 1.2 / TU 1653 4.9 / ○ 2252 0.9
4 0558 5.2 / 1139 0.9 / TH 1813 5.3
19 0534 5.1 / 1124 0.6 / F 1747 5.4 / 2346 0.4

5 0332 5.2 / 0940 0.5 / TH 1559 5.3 / 2201 0.4
20 0419 4.5 / 0958 1.1 / F 1634 4.8 / 2217 1.1
5 0452 5.4 / 1045 0.5 / SU 1712 5.5 / ● 2311 0.4
20 0506 4.6 / 1046 1.1 / M 1718 4.9 / ○ 2307 1.0
5 0529 5.2 / 1117 0.8 / TU 1746 5.4 / 2344 0.6
20 0520 4.8 / 1105 0.9 / W 1731 5.1 / 2328 0.8
5 0003 0.7 / 0638 5.1 / F 1214 0.9 / 1851 5.2
20 0614 5.2 / 1202 0.5 / SA 1828 5.5

6 0420 5.4 / 1020 0.3 / F 1644 5.5 / ● 2243 0.2
21 0455 4.7 / 1031 1.0 / SA 1709 4.9 / ○ 2251 1.0
6 0541 5.4 / 1129 0.6 / M 1759 5.5 / 2357 0.4
21 0544 4.7 / 1120 1.1 / TU 1755 5.0 / 2343 0.9
6 0614 5.2 / 1158 0.9 / W 1830 5.3
21 0559 4.9 / 1141 0.9 / TH 1810 5.2
6 0038 0.8 / 0716 5.0 / SA 1250 1.1 / 1929 5.0
21 0025 0.3 / 0654 5.2 / SU 1243 0.5 / 1911 5.4

7 0507 5.6 / 1101 0.2 / SA 1729 5.6 / 2325 0.2
22 0531 4.7 / 1104 1.0 / SU 1744 4.9 / 2324 0.9
7 0628 5.3 / 1213 0.8 / TU 1845 5.4
22 0621 4.8 / 1156 1.1 / W 1831 5.0
7 0026 0.7 / 0658 5.1 / TH 1239 1.0 / 1912 5.2
22 0005 0.6 / 0637 5.0 / F 1221 0.8 / 1848 5.2
7 0115 0.9 / 0753 4.8 / SU 1328 1.3 / 2007 4.8
22 0107 0.4 / 0737 5.1 / M 1327 0.7 / 1956 5.2

8 0555 5.6 / 1143 0.3 / SU 1815 5.5
23 0607 4.7 / 1137 1.0 / M 1819 4.9 / 2359 0.9
8 0042 0.6 / 0716 5.1 / W 1259 1.0 / 1931 5.1
23 0021 0.8 / 0658 4.7 / TH 1236 1.1 / 1907 4.9
8 0107 0.8 / 0742 4.9 / F 1321 1.2 / 1955 5.0
23 0046 0.6 / 0717 5.0 / SA 1302 0.9 / 1930 5.1
8 0153 1.2 / 0832 4.6 / M 1406 1.5 / 2048 4.5
23 0152 0.6 / 0823 4.9 / TU 1414 0.9 / 2045 4.9

9 0010 0.3 / 0642 5.4 / M 1228 0.6 / 1901 5.4
24 0643 4.7 / 1213 1.1 / TU 1852 4.8
9 0130 0.8 / 0804 4.9 / TH 1347 1.3 / 2018 4.9
24 0102 0.9 / 0736 4.7 / F 1318 1.2 / 1947 4.9
9 0150 1.0 / 0825 4.7 / SA 1405 1.4 / 2037 4.7
24 0128 0.6 / 0759 4.9 / SU 1347 1.0 / 2015 5.0
9 0232 1.5 / 0914 4.4 / TU 1447 1.8 / 2132 4.3
24 0240 0.9 / 0914 4.7 / W 1507 1.2 / 2141 4.6

10 0057 0.5 / 0731 5.1 / TU 1315 0.9 / 1948 5.1
25 0037 1.0 / 0717 4.6 / W 1251 1.2 / 1926 4.7
10 0221 1.1 / 0853 4.6 / F 1440 1.6 / 2106 4.6
25 0146 0.9 / 0819 4.6 / SA 1404 1.3 / 2033 4.7
10 0235 1.3 / 0908 4.5 / SU 1453 1.7 / 2122 4.5
25 0214 0.8 / 0846 4.7 / M 1436 1.1 / 2105 4.8
10 0315 1.7 / 1000 4.2 / W 1535 2.0 / ◑ 2220 4.0
25 0335 1.3 / 1012 4.4 / TH 1611 1.5 / ◑ 2247 4.3

11 0147 0.8 / 0822 4.8 / W 1407 1.3 / 2038 4.8
26 0117 1.0 / 0754 4.5 / TH 1333 1.3 / 2005 4.6
11 0317 1.4 / 0944 4.3 / SA 1542 1.8 / 2157 4.3
26 0233 1.0 / 0907 4.5 / SU 1455 1.4 / 2126 4.6
11 0326 1.6 / 0954 4.3 / M 1551 1.9 / 2209 4.2
26 0304 1.0 / 0938 4.5 / TU 1530 1.4 / ◑ 2201 4.6
11 0406 2.0 / 1050 4.0 / TH 1716 2.2 / 2314 3.9
26 0442 1.6 / 1126 4.2 / F 1730 1.7

12 0243 1.1 / 0916 4.5 / TH 1508 1.6 / 2132 4.4
27 0200 1.2 / 0838 4.3 / F 1419 1.5 / 2053 4.4
12 0419 1.6 / 1041 4.1 / SU 1650 2.0 / ◑ 2254 4.1
27 0325 1.2 / 1002 4.4 / M 1553 1.6 / ◑ 2224 4.5
12 0426 1.8 / 1043 4.1 / TU 1702 2.1 / ◑ 2301 4.0
27 0359 1.3 / 1037 4.4 / W 1633 1.6 / 2305 4.4
12 0556 2.1 / 1146 3.9 / F 1837 2.2
27 0012 4.1 / 0606 1.8 / SA 1257 4.2 / 1915 1.7

13 0350 1.4 / 1018 4.2 / F 1620 1.9 / ◑ 2234 4.1
28 0248 1.3 / 0929 4.2 / SA 1511 1.7 / 2148 4.3
13 0522 1.7 / 1150 4.0 / M 1754 2.0
28 0424 1.3 / 1103 4.3 / TU 1658 1.6 / 2328 4.4
13 0534 1.9 / 1138 4.0 / W 1810 2.1
28 0503 1.5 / 1147 4.3 / TH 1746 1.7
13 0014 3.8 / 0705 2.1 / SA 1251 4.0 / 1936 2.0
28 0137 4.1 / 0745 1.7 / SU 1410 4.4 / 2033 1.4

14 0500 1.6 / 1139 4.0 / SA 1732 2.0
29 0344 1.4 / 1027 4.1 / SU 1614 1.8 / ◑ 2249 4.2
14 0012 3.9 / 0622 1.8 / TU 1305 4.0 / 1852 2.0
29 0530 1.4 / 1212 4.3 / W 1812 1.6
14 0000 3.9 / 0637 2.0 / TH 1246 4.0 / 1909 2.0
29 0023 4.3 / 0619 1.6 / F 1309 4.3 / 1916 1.6
14 0133 3.9 / 0801 1.9 / SU 1409 4.2 / 2028 1.7
29 0242 4.4 / 0850 1.5 / M 1506 4.7 / 2125 1.1

15 0009 4.0 / 0607 1.7 / SU 1258 4.0 / 1836 1.9
30 0448 1.5 / 1131 4.1 / M 1727 1.8 / 2354 4.3
15 0133 3.9 / 0717 1.8 / W 1402 4.1 / 1945 1.8
30 0041 4.4 / 0645 1.4 / TH 1326 4.5 / 1932 1.4
15 0122 3.9 / 0734 1.9 / F 1359 4.1 / 2002 1.9
30 0144 4.3 / 0748 1.5 / SA 1418 4.6 / 2034 1.3
15 0249 4.1 / 0850 1.7 / M 1506 4.4 / 2114 1.4
30 0334 4.7 / 0937 1.2 / TU 1553 4.9 / 2206 0.9

31 0604 1.5 / 1241 4.3 / TU 1853 1.6
31 0248 4.5 / 0854 1.3 / SU 1515 4.8 / 2128 1.1
31 0418 4.9 / 1015 1.0 / W 1636 5.1 / 2240 0.7

Chart Datum: 0·20 metres below Ordnance Datum (Dublin). HAT is 5·9 metres above Chart Datum.

》》 FREE monthly updates. Register at 《
www.reedsnauticalalmanac.co.uk 《

219

STANDARD TIME (UT)	GALWAY	LAT 53°16'N	LONG 9°03'W	Dates in red are SPRINGS

For Summer Time add ONE hour in **non-shaded areas**

GALWAY LAT 53°16'N LONG 9°03'W
TIMES AND HEIGHTS OF HIGH AND LOW WATERS

Dates in red are SPRINGS
Dates in blue are NEAPS

YEAR **2016**

SEPTEMBER

Time m	Time m
1 0459 5.0 / 1047 0.9 / TH 1715 5.2 / ● 2308 0.6	**16** 0428 5.0 / 1027 0.7 / F 1642 5.4 / ○ 2247 0.3
2 0538 5.1 / 1116 0.8 / F 1752 5.2 / 2335 0.6	**17** 0508 5.3 / 1103 0.4 / SA 1723 5.6 / 2323 0.2
3 0614 5.1 / 1147 0.8 / SA 1828 5.1	**18** 0549 5.4 / 1141 0.3 / SU 1807 5.6
4 0007 0.7 / 0648 5.0 / SU 1220 0.9 / 1902 5.0	**19** 0002 0.1 / 0631 5.4 / M 1222 0.3 / 1851 5.5
5 0041 0.9 / 0722 4.9 / M 1255 1.1 / 1937 4.8	**20** 0044 0.3 / 0715 5.3 / TU 1306 0.5 / 1938 5.3
6 0115 1.1 / 0759 4.7 / TU 1330 1.3 / 2016 4.6	**21** 0128 0.6 / 0801 5.1 / W 1353 0.8 / 2028 4.9
7 0151 1.3 / 0838 4.5 / W 1407 1.6 / 2058 4.3	**22** 0217 1.0 / 0852 4.7 / TH 1448 1.2 / 2124 4.5
8 0228 1.6 / 0922 4.3 / TH 1447 1.8 / 2145 4.1	**23** 0314 1.4 / 0954 4.4 / F 1554 1.5 / ◐ 2232 4.2
9 0310 1.9 / 1011 4.1 / F 1536 2.1 / ◐ 2237 3.8	**24** 0426 1.8 / 1105 4.1 / SA 1721 1.7
10 0402 2.2 / 1105 3.9 / SA 1802 2.2 / 2336 3.7	**25** 0003 4.0 / 0557 1.9 / SU 1245 4.1 / 1903 1.7
11 0637 2.2 / 1206 3.9 / SU 1911 2.1	**26** 0129 4.1 / 0730 1.8 / M 1358 4.3 / 2020 1.4
12 0043 3.8 / 0738 2.0 / M 1316 4.0 / 2005 1.7	**27** 0231 4.3 / 0835 1.6 / TU 1452 4.6 / 2109 1.2
13 0213 4.0 / 0829 1.7 / TU 1431 4.3 / 2052 1.3	**28** 0319 4.6 / 0847 1.3 / W 1537 4.8 / 2148 1.0
14 0309 4.4 / 0913 1.3 / W 1520 4.7 / 2134 0.9	**29** 0401 4.8 / 0956 1.1 / TH 1617 5.0 / 2218 0.8
15 0350 4.7 / 0952 1.0 / TH 1601 5.1 / 2212 0.6	**30** 0438 5.0 / 1024 1.0 / F 1654 5.1 / 2241 0.7

OCTOBER

Time m	Time m
1 0513 5.0 / 1050 0.9 / SA 1729 5.1 / ● 2306 0.7	**16** 0442 5.4 / 1040 0.3 / SU 1701 5.6 / ○ 2259 0.1
2 0547 5.1 / 1120 0.8 / SU 1802 5.0 / 2337 0.8	**17** 0525 5.6 / 1119 0.2 / M 1746 5.7 / 2339 0.2
3 0620 5.0 / 1153 0.9 / M 1836 4.9	**18** 0609 5.6 / 1202 0.3 / TU 1833 5.6
4 0010 0.9 / 0653 4.9 / TU 1227 1.0 / 1911 4.6	**19** 0022 0.4 / 0654 5.4 / W 1247 0.5 / 1921 5.3
5 0044 1.1 / 0728 4.8 / W 1302 1.2 / 1947 4.6	**20** 0108 0.7 / 0742 5.2 / TH 1336 0.8 / 2012 4.9
6 0119 1.3 / 0805 4.6 / TH 1338 1.4 / 2027 4.3	**21** 0158 1.1 / 0833 4.8 / F 1432 1.2 / 2109 4.5
7 0156 1.6 / 0847 4.3 / F 1418 1.7 / 2112 4.1	**22** 0257 1.5 / 0930 4.5 / SA 1540 1.5 / ◐ 2216 4.2
8 0238 1.9 / 0934 4.1 / SA 1504 1.9 / 2204 3.9	**23** 0412 1.9 / 1041 4.2 / SU 1705 1.7 / 2346 4.0
9 0327 2.1 / 1028 4.0 / SU 1602 2.1 / ◐ 2302 3.8	**24** 0538 2.0 / 1221 4.1 / M 1829 1.7
10 0433 2.3 / 1128 3.9 / M 1840 2.1	**25** 0108 4.1 / 0656 1.9 / TU 1335 4.2 / 1945 1.5
11 0007 3.8 / 0711 2.1 / TU 1234 4.0 / 1937 1.7	**26** 0208 4.3 / 0803 1.7 / W 1430 4.4 / 2038 1.3
12 0123 4.0 / 0803 1.8 / W 1346 4.3 / 2026 1.3	**27** 0256 4.5 / 0852 1.5 / TH 1515 4.6 / 2117 1.2
13 0234 4.4 / 0847 1.4 / TH 1446 4.7 / 2108 0.9	**28** 0337 4.7 / 0929 1.3 / F 1554 4.8 / 2147 1.0
14 0319 4.8 / 0926 0.9 / F 1533 5.1 / 2146 0.6	**29** 0413 4.8 / 0958 1.1 / SA 1630 4.9 / 2212 1.0
15 0400 5.2 / 1003 0.6 / SA 1616 5.5 / 2222 0.3	**30** 0447 4.9 / 1026 1.0 / SU 1704 4.9 / ● 2240 0.9
	31 0520 5.0 / 1057 0.9 / M 1738 4.9 / 2312 0.9

NOVEMBER

Time m	Time m
1 0553 5.0 / 1130 0.9 / TU 1813 4.9 / 2344 1.0	**16** 0550 5.7 / 1146 0.4 / W 1817 5.5
2 0627 5.0 / 1204 1.0 / W 1848 4.8	**17** 0004 0.6 / 0636 5.5 / TH 1233 0.5 / 1906 5.3
3 0018 1.1 / 0701 4.8 / TH 1239 1.1 / 1924 4.6	**18** 0052 0.8 / 0724 5.3 / F 1322 0.8 / 1957 5.0
4 0054 1.3 / 0736 4.7 / F 1316 1.3 / 2001 4.4	**19** 0142 1.2 / 0815 5.0 / SA 1417 1.1 / 2052 4.7
5 0131 1.5 / 0814 4.5 / SA 1356 1.5 / 2043 4.2	**20** 0240 1.6 / 0909 4.7 / SU 1521 1.4 / 2153 4.4
6 0214 1.8 / 0859 4.3 / SU 1442 1.7 / 2133 4.0	**21** 0350 1.9 / 1010 4.4 / M 1635 1.6 / ◐ 2309 4.1
7 0303 2.0 / 0953 4.1 / M 1537 1.9 / ◐ 2231 3.9	**22** 0505 2.0 / 1136 4.2 / TU 1747 1.7
8 0405 2.2 / 1053 4.1 / TU 1650 2.0 / 2333 3.9	**23** 0030 4.1 / 0614 2.0 / W 1259 4.1 / 1852 1.7
9 0549 2.2 / 1157 4.1 / W 1857 1.8	**24** 0135 4.2 / 0717 1.9 / TH 1359 4.2 / 1950 1.6
10 0042 4.1 / 0728 1.9 / TH 1306 4.4 / 1952 1.4	**25** 0226 4.4 / 0811 1.8 / F 1447 4.4 / 2035 1.5
11 0153 4.4 / 0816 1.5 / F 1412 4.7 / 2037 1.0	**26** 0309 4.5 / 0854 1.6 / SA 1528 4.5 / 2112 1.4
12 0248 4.8 / 0859 1.0 / SA 1506 5.1 / 2118 0.7	**27** 0346 4.7 / 0930 1.4 / SU 1604 4.7 / 2145 1.2
13 0334 5.2 / 0939 0.7 / SU 1554 5.4 / 2157 0.4	**28** 0420 4.8 / 1004 1.2 / M 1639 4.8 / 2218 1.2
14 0419 5.5 / 1019 0.4 / M 1641 5.6 / ○ 2238 0.3	**29** 0454 5.0 / 1038 1.1 / TU 1715 4.8 / ● 2251 1.1
15 0504 5.6 / 1102 0.3 / TU 1729 5.6 / 2320 0.4	**30** 0529 5.2 / 1112 1.1 / W 1752 4.8 / 2325 1.1

DECEMBER

Time m	Time m
1 0605 5.0 / 1146 1.1 / TH 1828 4.8 / 2359 1.2	**16** 0623 5.6 / 1221 0.6 / F 1853 5.4
2 0639 4.9 / 1221 1.1 / F 1904 4.7	**17** 0038 0.9 / 0709 5.4 / SA 1308 0.8 / 1941 5.1
3 0035 1.3 / 0712 4.8 / SA 1259 1.2 / 1939 4.6	**18** 0125 1.2 / 0756 5.2 / SU 1357 1.0 / 2031 4.9
4 0114 1.5 / 0748 4.7 / SU 1340 1.3 / 2019 4.4	**19** 0216 1.5 / 0845 4.9 / M 1451 1.3 / 2122 4.6
5 0157 1.6 / 0831 4.6 / M 1425 1.5 / 2105 4.3	**20** 0314 1.8 / 0936 4.6 / TU 1552 1.6 / 2218 4.3
6 0245 1.8 / 0922 4.4 / TU 1516 1.6 / 2200 4.2	**21** 0421 2.0 / 1032 4.3 / W 1659 1.8 / ◑ 2324 4.1
7 0342 2.0 / 1020 4.3 / W 1617 1.7 / ◑ 2300 4.1	**22** 0529 2.1 / 1145 4.1 / TH 1802 1.9
8 0451 2.0 / 1122 4.3 / TH 1729 1.7	**23** 0041 4.1 / 0631 2.1 / F 1312 4.1 / 1900 1.9
9 0005 4.2 / 0613 1.9 / F 1231 4.4 / 1854 1.5	**24** 0145 4.2 / 0728 2.0 / SA 1412 4.1 / 1953 1.8
10 0116 4.5 / 0735 1.6 / SA 1341 4.7 / 2001 1.3	**25** 0235 4.3 / 0819 1.8 / SU 1459 4.3 / 2040 1.7
11 0219 4.8 / 0831 1.2 / SU 1443 5.0 / 2052 1.0	**26** 0317 4.5 / 0903 1.6 / M 1539 4.5 / 2121 1.5
12 0312 5.1 / 0919 0.9 / M 1536 5.3 / 2138 0.8	**27** 0354 4.7 / 0944 1.4 / TU 1617 4.6 / 2200 1.4
13 0401 5.4 / 1004 0.7 / TU 1627 5.5 / 2223 0.6	**28** 0431 4.9 / 1022 1.3 / W 1654 4.7 / 2236 1.3
14 0448 5.6 / 1050 0.5 / W 1716 5.5 / ○ 2307 0.6	**29** 0508 5.0 / 1058 1.1 / TH 1732 4.8 / 2311 1.2
15 0536 5.6 / 1135 0.5 / TH 1804 5.5 / 2352 0.7	**30** 0544 5.1 / 1132 1.1 / F 1809 4.9 / 2345 1.2
	31 0620 5.1 / 1207 1.0 / SA 1845 4.9

Chart Datum: 0·20 metres below Ordnance Datum (Dublin). HAT is 5·9 metres above Chart Datum.

》》FREE monthly updates. Register at 《
www.reedsnauticalalmanac.co.uk《

6.7 WESTPORT (CLEW BAY)

Mayo 53°47'·85N 09°35'·40W ✱✱✿✚✚✚✿✿✿

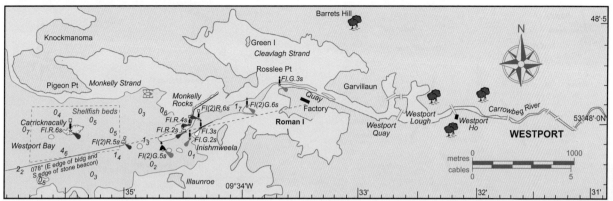

Standard Port GALWAY (←)

Times				Height (metres)			
High Water		Low Water		MHWS	MHWN	MLWN	MLWS
0600	1100	0000	0700	5·1	3·9	2·0	0·8
1800	2300	1200	1900				
Differences BROAD HAVEN							
+0035	+0035	+0040	+0040	−1·4	−1·0	−0·6	−0·2
BLACKSOD QUAY							
+0025	+0035	+0040	+0040	−1·2	−1·0	−0·6	−0·4
CLARE ISLAND							
+0015	+0021	+0039	+0027	−0·6	−0·4	−0·1	0·0
INISHGORT/CLEW BAY							
+0035	+0045	+0115	+0100	−0·7	−0·5	−0·2	0·0
KILLARY HARBOUR							
+0021	+0015	+0035	+0029	−1·0	−0·8	−0·4	−0·3
INISHBOFIN HARBOUR							
+0013	+0009	+0021	+0017	−1·0	−0·8	−0·4	−0·3
CLIFDEN BAY							
+0005	+0005	+0016	+0016	−0·7	−0·5	ND	ND

SHELTER Secure ⚓s amongst the islands at all times, as follows: E of Inishlyre in 2m; 2ca NE of Dorinish More, good holding in lee of Dorinish Bar (dries); 6 ⚓s in Rosmoney Hbr 53°49'·75N 09°37'·34W; Westport Quay HW±1½, to dry out on S side; Newport Hbr (dries) can be reached above mid-flood with careful pilotage (AC 2667); dry out against N quay or ⚓ at E end of Rabbit Is.

NAVIGATION WPT 53°49'·20N 09°42'·10W, 071°/1·2M to Inishgort lt ho. Approaches to Westport Channel between Monkellys Rks and Inishmweela are well marked by lit PHMs and SHMs. Beware fish farms E of Clare I and in Newport Bay. Do not ⚓ or ground in the Carricknacally Shellfish Bed Area.

LIGHTS AND MARKS Westport Bay ent via Inishgort lt, L Fl 10s 11m 10M (H24), and a series of ldg lines, but not advised at night. Final appr line 080° towards lt bn, Fl 3s. but beware of drying patches on this lead inwards from Pigeon PHM. Chan from Westport Bay to Westport Quay, 1½M approx, is marked by bns.

COMMUNICATIONS (Code 098) MRCC (01) 6620922/3; ⊖ (094) 9021131; Police 9025555; ℍ (094) 9021733. No VHF.

FACILITIES **Westport Quays** ⚓ ⚓ ⚲ Kos ⬛ Ⓔ ⬛ ✕ ⬛; **Town** ⬛ ⬛ ⊠ Ⓑ ⇄ ✈ (Galway/Knock). **Mayo SC Rosmoney** ☎9026160, ⚓ ⬛; **Glénans Irish SC** ☎9026046 (Collanmore Is).

OTHER ANCHORAGES FROM SLYNE HEAD TO EAGLE ISLAND

CLIFDEN BAY, Galway, 53°29'·40N 10°05'·90W. AC 1820, 2708. HW −0600 on Dover; duration 0610. Tides as 6.7.
Identify conspic W bn on Carrickrana Rks prior to entry; ldg marks: W bn at Fishing Pt on 080° with Clifden Castle (ruin). Avoid Coghan's and Doolick Rks to the E and beware bar 2·4m off Fishing Pt. 8 Y ⚓s are 3ca S of Castle ruins, or ⚓ NE of Drinagh Pt. Beware ruined training wall In the drying creek to Clifden; dry out against the quay or enter Ardbear Bay to ⚓ SE of Yellow Slate Rks in 3·4m. Keep clear of fish farms. Facilities: **Town** ⚓ ⬛ ⬛ Kos ⬛ ⊠ Ⓑ ⬛ ✕ ⬛ Dr ℍ bus to Galway.

BALLYNAKILL, Galway, 53°34'·95N 10°03'·00W. AC 2706. Tides as Inishbofin/Killary. Easy appr between Cleggan Pt, Fl (3) WRG 15s and Rinvyle Pt. Then pass N of Freaghillaun South Is, E of which is good passage ⚓ in 7m. Further E, Carrigeen and Ardagh Rks lie in mid-chan. Keep N for ⚓ in Derryinver B. S chan leads to ⚓s: off Ross Pt; S of Roeillaun; in Fahy Bay with 8 Y ⚓s sheltered by bar dries 0·2m. No facilities.

INISHBOFIN, Galway, 53°36'·60N 10°13'·20W. AC 1820, 2707. HW −0555 on Dover; ML 1·9m. Very safe inside narrow ent. Daymarks 2 conspic W trs lead 032° and Dir RWG lt leads 021° at night to increase separation from Gun Rock, Fl (2) 6s 8m 4M, vis 296°-253°. ⚓ between new pier and Port Is. Old pier to the E now refurbished and dredged may provide ⚲ ⚓ ⚓(on both piers) ⬛ ✕ ⬛ / B&B: ☎(095) 45829.

KILLARY HARBOUR, Mayo/Galway, 53°37'·83N 09°54'·00W, 4ca W of Doonee Is. AC 2706. Tides 6.7. A 7M long inlet, narrow and deep. Caution fish farms, some with Fl Y lts. Appr in good vis to identify Doonee Is and Inishbarna bns, both LFl G, ldg 099° to ent. ⚓s off Dernasliggaun, Bundorragha and, at head of inlet, Leenaun with 8 Y ⚓s. (Village: ⚓ ⬛ ⬛ hotel.) Enter **Little Killary Bay** 4ca S of Doonee Is; drying rks at ent. Good ⚓ in 3m at head of bay.

INISHTURK, Mayo, 53°42'·3N 10°05'·2W. 8 Y ⚓s Garranty Hbr. sheltered SW to NNW winds. ⚓ quay ⊠ ✕ ⬛ 6⚓s on E side.

CLARE ISLAND, Mayo, 53°48'·1N 09°56'·7W. 6⚓s on SE side untenable in E winds. Hotel ⬛ some shops.

BLACKSOD BAY, Mayo, 54°05'·00N 10°02'·00W. AC 2704. HW −0525 on Dover; ML 2·2m; Duration 0610. See 6.7. Easy appr, accessible by night. Safe ⚓s depending on wind: NW of Blacksod Pt 6 Y ⚓s in 3m; at Elly B in 1·8m; Elly Hbr 6 Y ⚓s; Saleen Bay (ldg lts 319°, both Oc 4s, lead to pier); N of Claggan Pt. Beware drying rk 3·5ca SSE of Ardmore Pt. Lts: Blacksod Pt, Fl (2) WR 7·5s 13m 9M, see 6.3. ECM buoy Q (3) 10s. Ldg lts 181°, Oc W 5s, lead to Blacksod pier hd. Few facilities; nearest town is Belmullet.

ACHILL SOUND ⚓s at each end sheltered by Achill Is. Mayo Co Council (+353 (0)97 81004) requires 2 days' notice to open bridge.

PORTNAFRANKAGH Mayo, 54°14'·95N 10°06'·00W. AC 2703. Tides approx as Broadhaven. A safe passage ⚓, close to the coastal route, but swell enters in all winds. Appr toward Port Pt, thence keep to the N side for better water; middle and S side break in onshore winds. ⚓ in 4–5m on S side, close inshore. ⚓ at new pier. Unlit, but Eagle Is lt, Fl (3) 15s 67m 26M H24, W tr, is 2M N. No facilities; Belmullet 4M, ⬛.

BROAD HAVEN, Mayo, 54°16'·00N 09°53'·20W. AC 2703. A safe refuge except in N'lies. Easy appr across Broadhaven Bay to the ent between Brandy Pt and Gubacashel Pt, Iso WR 4s27m 12/9M, W tr. 7ca S of this lt is Ballyglas Fl G 3s on W side. ⚓ close N or S of Ballyglas which has pier (2m) and 8 Y ⚓s. In E'lies ⚓ 3ca S of Inver Pt out of the tide. Further S off Barrett Pt, the inlet narrows and turns W to Belmullet. Facilities: ⊠ ⬛.

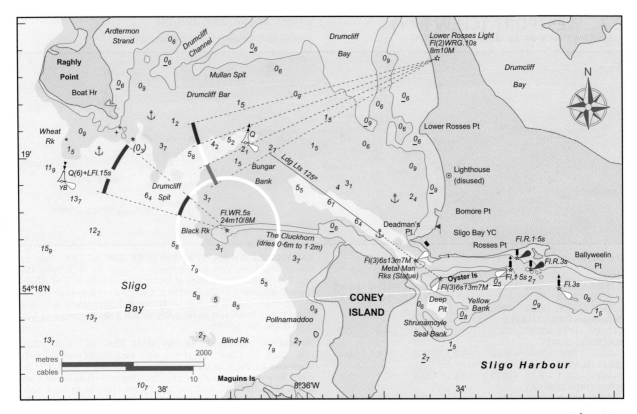

6.8 SLIGO

Sligo 54°18'·30N 08°34'·70W ✲✲✲◊◊✿✿

CHARTS AC 2767, 2852; Imray C54

TIDES –0511 Dover; ML 2·3; Duration 0620

Standard Port GALWAY (←)

Times				Height (metres)			
High Water		Low Water		MHWS	MHWN	MLWN	MLWS
0600	1100	0000	0700	5·1	3·9	2·0	0·8
1800	2300	1200	1900				
Differences SLIGO HARBOUR (Oyster Is)							
+0043	+0055	+0042	+0054	–1·0	–0·9	–0·5	–0·3
MULLAGHMORE							
+0036	+0048	+0047	+0059	–1·4	–1·0	–0·4	–0·4
BALLYSADARE BAY (Culleenamore)							
+0059	+0111	+0111	+0123	–1·2	–0·9	ND	ND
KILLALA BAY (Inishcrone)							
+0035	+0055	+0030	+0050	–1·3	–1·2	–0·7	–0·4

SHELTER The lower hbr is fairly exposed; ⌓ along N side of Oyster Island, or proceed 4M (not at night) up to the shelter of Sligo town; 2nd berth below bridge for yachts.

NAVIGATION WPT 54°19'·15N 08°36'·77W, 125°/1·6M to front ldg lt.

- The passage between Oyster Island and Coney Island is marked 'Dangerous'.
- Pass N of Oyster Is leaving Blennick Rks to port. Passage up to Sligo town between training walls. Appr quays at HW–3 or higher.
- Some perches are in bad repair. Pilots at Raghly Pt and Rosses Pt. *Tide Tables* (based on Inishraher/Inishgort, published by Westport Hbr Comm.) available locally.

LIGHTS AND MARKS See 6.3 and chartlet. Channel to Sligo Deepwater Quay is well marked by lit bcns.

COMMUNICATIONS (Code 071) MRCC (01) 6620922/3; ⊜9161064; Police 9157000; Dr 9142886; 🅷9171111. Hbr Office 9153819, mob 086 0870767.

Pilots VHF Ch 12 16. HM Ch 16.

FACILITIES 60m visitors pontoon, 20-30ft €19.00; ⌓ ⌂(15t) ⌂; **Sligo YC** ☎9177168, ⌂s ━ ⌓ ⌂. **Services** ⌂ ⌂ ⚒ ⚓ ⌂ ⌂. **Town** 🅿 🅣 ⌂ ⑧ ⌂ ☓ ⌂ ⇌ Irish Rail ☎9169888, Bus ☎9160066, ✈ Londonderry/Derry or Knock, Co Mayo (60-70M).

MINOR HARBOUR/ANCHORAGE TO THE WEST
KILLALA BAY, Sligo/Mayo, 54°13'·02N 09°12'·80W. AC 2715. Tides, see 6.18. The bay, open to the N-NE, is entered between Lenadoon Pt and Kilcummin Hd, 6M to the W. 1·1M W of Kilcummin Hd are 8 Y ⌂s off Kilcummin pier, well sheltered from W'lies. Carrickpatrick ECM lt buoy, in mid-bay marks St Patrick's Rks to the W. Thence, if bound for Killala hbr, make good Killala SHM lt buoy, 7½ca to the SSW. The Round Tr and cathedral spire at Killala are conspic. Four sets of ldg bns/lts lead via a narrow chan between sand dunes and over the bar (0·3m) as follows:

- 230°, Rinnaun Pt lts Oc 10s 7/12m 5M, ☐ concrete trs.
- 215°, Inch Is, ☐ concrete trs; the rear has Dir lt Fl WRG 2s.
- 196°, Kilroe lts Oc 4s 5/10m 2M, W ☐ trs, which lead to ⌓ in Bartragh Pool, 6ca NE of Killala hbr; thence
- 236°, Pier lts Iso 2s 5/7m 2M, W ◇ daymarks, lead via narrow, dredged chan to pier where ⌸ is possible in about 1·5m.

Facilities: ⌓ 🅿 🅣 ⌂ in town ½M.
Other hbrs in the bay: R Moy leading to Ballina should not be attempted without pilot/local knowledge. Inishcrone in the SE has a pier and lt; see 6.3.

MINOR HARBOUR ON S SIDE OF DONEGAL BAY
MULLAGHMORE 54°27'·90N 08°26'·80W. AC 2702. Tides see 6.8. Pierhead lit Fl G 3s 5m 3M. Fair weather ⌓ in 2-3m off hbr ent, sheltered by Mullaghmore Head, except from N/NE winds. For ⌂s near hbr ent, call Rodney Lomax, ☎071 9166124, mobile 0872 727538. Keep close to N pier to avoid shingle bank drying 1m, ⅔ of the way across the ent toward the S pier. Take the ground or dry out against the piers inside hbr berth on pontoon on bkwtr (min 1m at MLWS). Access approx HW±2 when least depth is 2m. VHF Ch 16, 8, 6. Facilities: ⌓ at S Pier and on bkwtr, 🅣 ⚒ ⌂ ⌂ ☓ ⌂.

6.9 KILLYBEGS

Donegal 54°36'·90N 08°26'·80W ✿✿✿✿♨♨♨✿✿✿

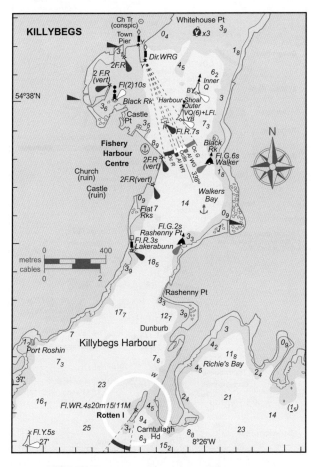

CHARTS AC 2702, 2792; Imray C53

TIDES –0520 Dover; ML 2·2; Duration 0620

Standard Port GALWAY (◄——)

Times				Height (metres)			
High Water		Low Water		MHWS	MHWN	MLWN	MLWS
0600	1100	0000	0700	5·1	3·9	2·0	0·8
1800	2300	1200	1900				
Differences KILLYBEGS							
+0040	+0050	+0055	+0035	–1·0	–0·9	–0·5	–0·2
GWEEDORE HARBOUR							
+0048	+0100	+0055	+0107	–1·3	–1·0	–0·5	–0·3
BURTONPORT							
+0042	+0055	+0115	+0055	–1·2	–1·0	–0·6	–0·3
DONEGAL HARBOUR (SALTHILL QUAY)							
+0038	+0050	+0052	+0104	–1·2	–0·9	ND	ND

SHELTER Secure natural hbr, but some swell in SSW winds. A busy major FV port, H24 access.60m pontoon orientated NNE/SSW is 100m N of Black Rk Pier, 3 ⚓ about 2½ca NE of Town Pier, or contact HM and berth at pier. **Bruckless Hbr**, about 2M E at the head of McSwyne's Bay, is a pleasant ⚓ in 1·8m but is severely restricted due to fish cages, sheltered from all except SW winds. Ent on 038° between rks; ICC SDs are essential.

NAVIGATION WPT 54°36'·00N 08°27'·00W, 022°/0·94M to Rotten Is lt. From W, beware Manister Rk (covers at HW; dries at LW) off Fintragh B. Keep mid chan until off new Killybegs Fishery Centre, then follow the Dir lt or Y ◊ ldg marks 338° into hbr.

LIGHTS AND MARKS Rotten Is lt, Fl WR 4s 20m 15/11M, W tr, vis W255°-008°, R008°-039°, W039°-208°. Dir lt 338°, Oc WRG 6s 17m; W sector 336°-340° (see 6.3). Harbour Shoal (2·3m) is marked by a SCM and NCM lt buoy.

COMMUNICATIONS (Code 07497) MRCC (01) 6620922/3; Bundoran Inshore Rescue ☎(071) 9841713; 📠31070; Police 31002; Dr 31148 (Surgery). HM 31032.

HM Ch **14**; essential to request a berth.

FACILITIES **Town Pier** ☎31032, ⚓ ━ ⚲(free) ⚓ ⚓ 📛 Kos ✕ ⚲ 🔌 Ⓔ ⚲(12t) ⚓ 🏪 ✕ ⬜.
Black Rock Pier ⚓ ━ ⚲⚓.
Town ✉ Ⓑ 🚂 (bus to Sligo).

OTHER HARBOURS AND ANCHORAGES IN DONEGAL

TEELIN HARBOUR, Donegal, **54°37'·50N 08°37'·87W**. AC 2792. Tides as 6.9. A possible passage ⚓, mid-way between Rathlin O'Birne and Killybegs. But Hbr is open to S'ly swell and prone to squalls in NW winds. Ent, 1ca wide, is close E of Teelin Pt lt, Fl R 10s, which is hard to see by day. 4 Y ⚓s and ⚓ on E side in 3m to N of pier, or ⚓ on E side near pier. Many moorings and, in the NE, mussel rafts. Facilities: ⚓ ⚓ 🏪 at Carrick, 3M inland.

INISHKEEL, Donegal, **54°50'·82N 08°26'·50W**. AC 2792. 6 Y ⚓s in Church Pool, 3ca E of Inishkeel. Open to N/NE'lies.

BURTONPORT, Donegal, **54°58'·93N 08°26'·60W**. AC 1879, 2792. HW –0525 on Dover; ML 2·0m; Duration 0605. See 6.9. Only appr via N Chan. Ent safe in all weathers except NW gales. Hbr very full, no space to ⚓; berth on local boat at pier or go to Rutland Hbr or Aran Roads: 6 Y ⚓s 250m NE of Black Rks, Fl R 3s. Ldg marks/lts: N Chan ldg lts on Inishcoo 119·3°, both Iso 6s 6/11m 1M; front W bn, B band; rear B bn, Y band. Rutland Is ldg lts 138°, both Oc 6s 8/14m 1M; front W bn, B band; rear B bn, Y band. Burtonport ldg lts 068°, both FG 17/23m 1M; front Gy bn, W band; rear Gy bn, Y band. HM ☎(075) 42155 (43170 home); VHF Ch 06, 12, **14**, 16. Facilities: ⚓ (just inside pier), ⚓ (root of pier), 📛 (½M inland). **Village** Kos ✉ 🏪 ✕ ⬜.

GWEEDORE HBR/BUNBEG, Donegal, **55°03'·75N 08°18'·87W**. AC 1883. Tides see 6.9. Gweedore hbr, the estuary of the R Gweedore, has sheltered ⚓s or temp ⚲ at Bunbeg Quay, usually full of FVs. Apprs via Gola N or S Sounds are not simple especially in poor visibility. N Sound is easier with ldg lts 171°, both Oc 3s 9/13m 2M, B/W bns, on the SE tip of Gola Is. (There are also ⚓s on the S and E sides of Gola Is.) E of Bo Is the bar 0·4m has a Fl

G 3s and the chan, lying E of Inishinny Is and W of Inishcoole, is marked by a QG and 3 QR. A QG marks ent to Bunbeg. Night ent not advised. Facilities: ⚓ ⚓ at quay; ✉ Ⓑ🏪 ⬜ at village ½M.

SHEEP HAVEN, Donegal, **55°11'·00N 07°51'·00W**. AC 2699. HW –0515 on Dover. See 6.10. Bay is 2M wide with many ⚓s, easily accessible in daylight, but exposed to N winds. Beware rks off Rinnafaghla Pt, and further S: Black Rk (6m) and Wherryman Rks, which dry, 1ca off E shore. ⚓ or 8 Y ⚓s in Downies Bay to SE of pier; in Pollcormick inlet close W in 3m; in Ards Bay for excellent shelter, but beware the bar in strong winds. Lts: Breaghy Hd LFl 10s 3m 6M, Portnablahy ldg lts 125°, both Oc 6s 7/12m 2M, B col, W bands; Downies pier hd, Fl R 3s 5m 2M, R post. Facilities: (Downies) EC Wed: ⚓ 📛 📛(300m) 🏪 ✕ ⬜; (Portnablahy Bay) 📛 📛 🏪 ✕ ⬜.

MULROY BAY, Donegal, **55°15'·30N 07°46'·30W**. AC 2699; HW (bar) –0455 on Dover. See 6.10. Beware Limeburner Rk, (NCM buoy, Q) 3M N of ent & the bar which is dangerous in swell or onshore winds. Obtain local advice as the depths on the bar change considerably. Ent at half flood (not HW); chan lies between Bar Rks (Low Bar Rk Fl G 2s) and Sessiagh Rks, it is rep'd to run along the alignment of the charted drying spit thence through First, Second (under bridge 19m) and Third Narrows to Broad Water. HW at the head of the lough is 2¼ hrs later than at the bar. ⚓s: Close SW of Ravedy Is (Fl 3s 9m 3M); Fanny's Bay (2m), excellent; Rosnakill Bay (3·5m) in SE side; Cranford Bay; Milford Port (3 to 4m). Beware power cable 6m, over Moross chan, barring North Water to masted boats. Facilities: **Milford Port**, pier derelict, ⚓ 🏪; **Fanny's Bay** ✉ Shop at Downings village (1M), hotel at Rosepenna (¾M).

6.10 LOUGH SWILLY

Donegal 55°17'N 07°34'W ❀❀❀❀❀🌢🌢✿✿✿

CHARTS AC 2697; Imray C53

TIDES –0500 Dover; ML 2·3; Duration 0605

Standard Port GALWAY (←—)

Times				Height (metres)			
High Water		Low Water		MHWS	MHWN	MLWN	MLWS
0200	0900	0200	0800	5·1	3·9	2·0	0·8
1400	2100	1400	2000				
Differences INISHTRAHULL							
+0100	+0100	+0115	+0200	–1·8	–1·4	–0·4	–0·4
TRAWBREAGA BAY							
+0115	+0059	+0109	+0125	–1·1	–0·8	ND	ND
FANAD HEAD							
+0115	+0040	+0125	+0120	–1·1	–0·9	–0·5	–0·3
RATHMULLAN							
+0125	+0050	+0126	+0118	–0·8	–0·7	–0·1	–0·3
MULROY BAY (BAR)							
+0108	+0052	+0102	+0118	–1·2	–1·0	ND	ND
SHEEP HAVEN (DOWNIES BAY)							
+0057	+0043	+0053	+0107	–1·1	–0·9	ND	ND

SHELTER Good, but beware downdrafts on E side. ⚓s N of 55°05'N may suffer from swell. ⚓s from seaward: Ballymastocker Bay, also 8 🅀s, but exposed to E'lies; inside Macamish Pt, sheltered from SE to N; Rathmullan Roads N of pier, where yacht pontoon lies N/S in 3·6m MLWS; Fahan Creek and marina ent at HW–1.

NAVIGATION WPT 55°17'·00N 07°34'·20W, 180°/5M to 5ca W of Dunree Hd lt. Entrance is easy and dangers are well marked. Off W shore: Swilly More Rocks, Kinnegar Spit and Strand; off E shore: Colpagh Rocks, White Strand Rocks and Inch Spit/Flats. Fahan Creek is buoyed; there is a shallow bar S of Inch Spit PHM and Inch Flats dry. Entry should not be attempted before LW+2. There are many marine farms and shellfish beds S from Scraggy Bay (☎074 50172/59071 for permission to use pier).

LIGHTS AND MARKS Fanad Hd lt, Fl (5) WR 20s 38m 18/14M, touching Dunree Hd lt, Fl (2) WR 5s 46m 12/9M, leads 151° into the Lough. Thence Ballygreen Point and Hawk's Nest in line 202°.

COMMUNICATIONS (Codes: both sides of lough 074) Malin Head MRSC 9370103; Police 9153114 (Milford) and 074 9320540 (Buncrana); Dr 9158416 (Rathmullan), 1850 400911 (out of hours), and 9363611 (Buncrana); Rathmullan Pontoon 9158131, 9158315 (eves). No VHF.

FACILITIES **Rathmullan** Pontoon (Easter–October) ☎087 2480132 €20/craft, 🛠 ⚓ Kos ⊠ 🚿 Hotel ✕ 🏪.

Ramelton 🛥(drying) 🍴 ☎9151082, 🛠 🏧 🏧 Kos 🛢 ⊠ ©️ ✕ 🏪.
Buncrana 🛥(congested) 🛢 🏧 🏧 Kos ⊠ Ⓑ 🛒 Hotel ✕ 🏪 @ (library).

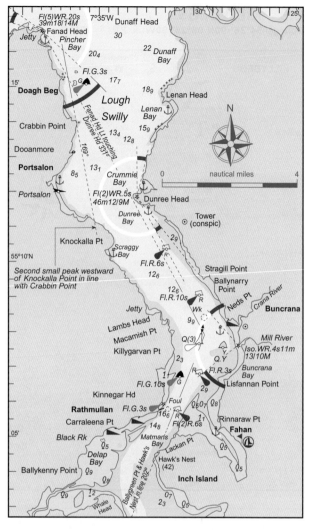

Lough Swilly Marina www.loughswillymarina.com ☎086 108211 200 🛥 some 🅥 €3/m, 🛠 🔌 (development ongoing).

Fahan 🛠 ✕ 🏪 **Lough Swilly YC** www.loughswillyyc.com.

Services (1M SE): 🏧 🏧 🛒 ⇌ ✈ (Londonderry 10M bus/taxi).

BLOODY FORELAND TO FAIR HEAD

(AC 2723, 5612) This is a good cruising area, under the lee of land in SW'lies, but very exposed to NW or N. Beware fishing boats and nets in many places and the North Channel TSS.

(AC 2752) Between Bloody Foreland and Horn Head are three low-lying islands: Inishbofin, Inishdooey and Inishbeg. The first is almost part of the mainland; it has a temporary ⚓ on S side and a more sheltered ⚓ on NE side in Toberglassan Bay. 6M offshore is Tory Is (Fl 4 30s) with rocks for 5ca off SW side. The harbour in Camusmore B provides the best shelter on this stretch of coast (details in ICC's SDs).

▶ *In Tory Sound the stream runs W from HW Galway +0230, and E from HW Galway –0530, sp rates 2kn.* ◀

Sheep Haven Bay is easy to enter between Horn Hd and Rinnafaghla Pt, and has good ⚓s except in strong NW or N winds. Beware Wherryman Rks, dry 1·5m, 1ca off E shore.

Between Sheep Haven and Mulroy Bay there is an inshore passage between Guill Rks & Carnabollion and S of Frenchman's Rock. Safe in good weather, otherwise keep 1M offshore. E to Lough Swilly the coast is very foul. Beware Limeburner Rk (2m),

6·8M WNW of Fanad Hd. Mulroy Bay has good ⚓s but needs accurate pilotage (see ICC SDs). Ent to L Swilly is clear except for Swilly Rks off the W shore, SSE of Fanad Hd. From Dunaff Hd at ent to Lough Swilly, keep 5ca offshore to Malin Hd. Trawbreaga Lough (AC 2697) gives shelter, but is shallow, and sea can break on bar; only approach when no swell, and at half flood. **At Malin Hd the direction of buoyage changes to W.**

Garvan Is, Tor Rks and Inishtrahull lie E and NE of Malin Hd. In bad weather it is best to pass at least 3M N of Tor Rks. Inishtrahull is lit and about 1M long; rocks extend N about 3ca into Tor Sound.

▶ *W of Malin Hd a W-going eddy starts at HW Galway +0400, and an E-going one at HW. Inishtrahull Sound, between Inishtrahull and Garvan Is, is exposed; tidal streams up to 4kn sp can raise a dangerous sea with no warning. Stream also sets hard through Garvan Isles, S of which Garvan Sound can be passed safely in daylight avoiding two sunken rks, one 1½ca NE of Rossnabarton, and the other 5ca NW. The main stream runs W for only 3 hrs, from HW Galway –0500 to –0200. W of Malin Hd a W-going eddy starts at HW Galway +0400, and an E-going one at HW Galway –0300.* ◀

Enter Lough Foyle by either the North Chan W of The Tuns, or S chan passing 2ca N of Magilligan Pt and allowing for set towards The Tuns on the ebb (up to 3·5kn).

Proceeding to Portrush, use Skerries Sound in good weather.

▶ *A fair tide is essential through Rathlin Sound, as sp rates reach 6kn, with dangerous overfalls. The main stream sets W from HW Dover +0030 for 5 hrs, and E from HW Dover –0530 for 5 hrs. The worst overfalls are S of Rue Pt (Slough-na-more) from HW Dover*

+0130 to +0230, and it is best to enter W-bound at the end of this period, on the last of fair tide. E-bound enter the Sound at HW Dover –0500. Close inshore between Fair Hd and Carrick-mannanon Rk a counter eddy runs W from HW Dover –0030, and an E-going eddy runs from HW Dover +0200 to +0300. ◀

Pass outside Carrickmannanon Rk (0·3m) and Sheep Is.
There are small hbrs in Church Bay (Rathlin Is) and at Ballycastle.

6.11 LOUGH FOYLE

Londonderry/Donegal **55°14'N 06°54'W** ✲✲✲✲⬤⬤✿✿

CHARTS AC 2723, 2798, 2511, 2510, 5612; Imray C53, C64

TIDES
Warren Point: –0430 Dover
Moville: –0350 Dover
Londonderry: –0255 Dover
ML 1·6; Duration 0615

Standard Port RIVER FOYLE (LISAHALLY) (⟶)

Times				Height (metres)			
High Water		Low Water		MHWS	MHWN	MLWN	MLWS
0100	0800	0200	0700	2·6	1·9	0·9	0·4
1300	2000	1400	1900				
Differences WARREN LIGHTHOUSE							
–0055	–0115	–0155	–0117	–0·3	0·0	ND	ND
MOVILLE							
–0042	–0057	–0127	–0058	–0·3	0·0	+0·1	0·0
QUIGLEY'S POINT							
–0020	–0027	–0040	–0027	–0·3	–0·1	0·0	–0·1
LONDONDERRY							
+0033	+0035	+0032	+0032	+0·1	+0·2	+0·3	+0·2

SHELTER The SE side of the Lough is low lying and shallow. The NW rises steeply and has several village hbrs between the ent and Londonderry (often referred to as Derry).

White Bay: close N of Dunagree Point is a good ⚓ in settled weather on passage.

Greencastle: a busy commercial fishing hbr, open to swell in winds SW to E. No formalised ⓥ. Only advised for yachts in emergency.

Moville: a quaint resort on the western shore. A wooden pier, with 1·5m at the end, is near the village (shops closed all day Wed), but is much used by FVs. ⚓ outside hbr is exposed; inside hbr for shoal draught only. 8 Y ⓐs are about 600m upstream.

Carrickarory: pier/quay is used entirely by FVs. ⚓ in bay is sheltered in winds from SW to NNW. Plans for possible new marina.

Culmore Bay: good shelter. ⚓ 1½ca W of Culmore Pt in pleasant cove, 4M from Londonderry.

NAVIGATION WPT Tuns PHM buoy, Fl R 3s, 55°14'·00N 06°53'·49W, 235°/2·5M to Warren Pt lt, 2·5M. The Tuns bank lies 3M NE of Magilligan Pt and may dry. The main or N Chan, ¾M wide, runs NW of The Tuns; a lesser chan, min depth 4m, runs 3ca off shore around NE side of Magilligan Pt. **Beware commercial traffic**. Transiting the Loch the main channel passes NW of McKinney's Bank and the commercial ⚓ off Moville. The maintained channel leads close to the NW shore to the N of North Middle Bank and into the West Channel towards the commercial port of Lisahally. The narrows at Culmore Pt, marked by a GW Twr and medieval castle on the N shore, experience strong currents as the Loch gives way to the river proper. Upstream at Gransha the Foyle Bridge has 31m clearance before the river winds round Madams Bank following the Rosses Bay Channel, which is well marked by leading beacons. The buoyed channel leads to the city itself where further passage is limited by the Peace Bridge (clearance 3·7m) and the Craigavon Bridge (clearance 1·2m). In June and July the channel is at times obstructed by salmon nets at night. In North Chan tidal streams reach 3½kn, and upriver the ebb runs up to 6kn.

LIGHTS AND MARKS Inishowen Fl (2) WRG 10s 28m 18/14M; W tr, 2 B bands; vis 197°–G–211°–W–249°–R–000°. Warren Pt Fl 1·5s 9m 10M; W tr, G abutment; vis 232°–061°. Magilligan Pt QR 7m 4M; ✕ structure. The main chan up to Londonderry is very well lit. Foyle Bridge centre FW each side; VQ G on W pier; VQ R on E.

COMMUNICATIONS (Code 028) CGOC 9146 3933; ⊖ 7126 1937 or 9035 8250; Police 101; Dr 7126 4868; Ⓗ 7034 5171. HM (at Lisahally) 7186 0555.
Yachts are to call *Harbour Radio* on CH 14 for berthing directions at Foyle Marina. When secure ☎7186 0313 for gate code and facilities.
VHF Ch **14** 12 16 (H24). Traffic and nav info Ch 14.

FACILITIES Culdaff Bay (10M W of Foyle SWM buoy) 6 Y ⓐs at 55°18'N 07°09'·1W, off Bunnagee Port.

Lisahally is the commercial port (55°02'·6N 07°15'·6W).

Londonderry Foyle Marina (pontoon) www.londonderryport.com billmccann@londonderryport.com, ☎71860555, mob 078 41580590 ⚭ in 5-7m, £15-£21/night, ⚓ ⬜£3, adjacent to city centre. All payments can be made at the coffee shop just outside the gate to the 'Northern' pontoon.

Prehen Boat Club (above Craigavon Bridge) ☎7034 3405.

City 🏠 🏠 🔧 🏪 ✉ Ⓑ 🛒 ✕ 🛏 ⇌ ✈.

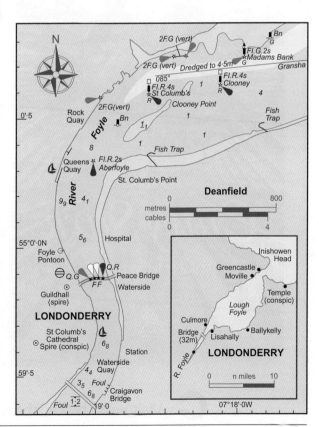

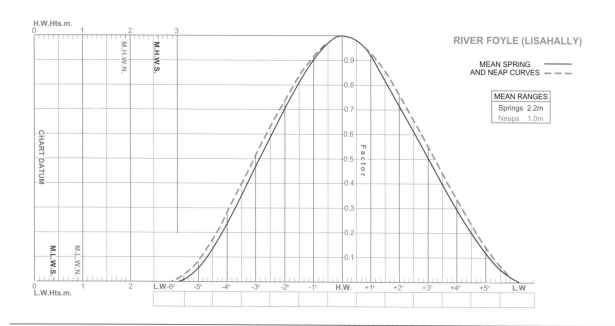

RIVER FOYLE (LISAHALLY)

MEAN SPRING
AND NEAP CURVES

MEAN RANGES
Springs 2.2m
Neaps 1.0m

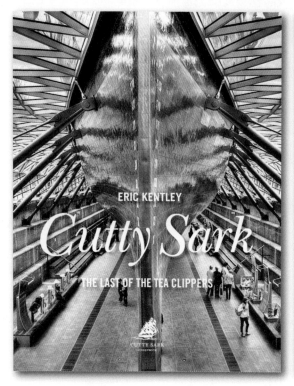
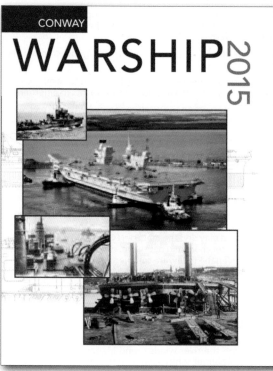

RIVER FOYLE   LAT 55°03'N   LONG 7°16'W

TIMES AND HEIGHTS OF HIGH AND LOW WATERS

STANDARD TIME (UT)
For Summer Time add ONE hour in **non-shaded areas**

Dates in red are **SPRINGS**
Dates in blue are NEAPS

YEAR 2016

N Ireland

JANUARY

Day	Time	m	Time	m		Day	Time	m	Time	m
1 F	0537	0.8	1216	2.1		16 SA	0600	0.7	1219	2.5
	1906	1.0					1845	0.8		◑
2 SA	0052	1.9	0630	0.9		17 SU	0041	2.1	0701	0.8
◑	1349	2.0	2011	1.0			1335	2.4	1949	0.8
3 SU	0209	1.9	0733	1.0		18 M	0208	2.0	0821	0.9
	1503	2.0	2118	1.0			1455	2.3	2102	0.9
4 M	0318	1.9	0842	1.0		19 TU	0335	2.0	0952	0.9
	1601	2.0	2217	0.9			1608	2.3	2219	0.8
5 TU	0418	2.0	0951	1.0		20 W	0451	2.2	1107	0.8
	1649	2.1	2309	0.8			1712	2.4	2324	0.7
6 W	0508	2.2	1055	0.9		21 TH	0547	2.4	1205	0.6
	1729	2.2	2354	0.7			1805	2.5		
7 TH	0550	2.4	1147	0.8		22 F	0015	0.6	0631	2.5
	1804	2.3					1255	0.6	1850	2.5
8 F	0035	0.6	0627	2.5		23 SA	0100	0.5	0710	2.6
	1235	0.7	1840	2.4			1340	0.5	1930	2.6
9 SA	0114	0.5	0704	2.7		24 SU	0140	0.5	0747	2.7
	1319	0.6	1918	2.5		○	1423	0.5	2007	2.6
10 SU	0153	0.5	0742	2.8		25 M	0217	0.4	0822	2.7
●	1404	0.6	1958	2.5			1502	0.5	2042	2.5
11 M	0231	0.4	0821	2.9		26 TU	0252	0.4	0856	2.7
	1448	0.5	2040	2.6			1538	0.6	2115	2.5
12 TU	0309	0.4	0902	2.9		27 W	0323	0.4	0930	2.6
	1533	0.5	2122	2.6			1612	0.6	2149	2.4
13 W	0348	0.4	0945	2.9		28 TH	0355	0.5	1003	2.5
	1617	0.5	2205	2.5			1645	0.7	2223	2.3
14 TH	0428	0.4	1030	2.8		29 F	0429	0.6	1037	2.3
	1702	0.6	2250	2.4			1721	0.8	2302	2.1
15 F	0511	0.5	1119	2.7		30 SA	0508	0.7	1115	2.1
	1750	0.6	2339	2.2			1805	0.9	2349	2.0
						31 SU	0554	0.8	1204	1.9
							1859	0.9		

FEBRUARY

Day	Time	m	Time	m		Day	Time	m	Time	m
1 M	0055	1.9	0652	0.9		16 TU	0129	1.9	0801	0.9
◑	1329	1.8	2003	1.0			1435	2.1	2026	0.9
2 TU	0220	1.8	0757	1.0		17 W	0316	1.9	0945	0.9
	1507	1.8	2116	0.9			1600	2.1	2155	0.9
3 W	0333	1.9	0905	1.0		18 TH	0444	2.1	1102	0.7
	1615	1.9	2228	0.8			1709	2.2	2306	0.8
4 TH	0434	2.1	1017	0.9		19 F	0541	2.3	1158	0.6
	1709	2.0	2325	0.7			1801	2.3	2358	0.7
5 F	0524	2.2	1125	0.8		20 SA	0623	2.4	1245	0.5
	1752	2.1					1844	2.4		
6 SA	0013	0.6	0607	2.4		21 SU	0043	0.5	0659	2.5
	1221	0.7	1831	2.3			1327	0.4	1919	2.4
7 SU	0057	0.5	0647	2.6		22 M	0123	0.4	0733	2.6
	1309	0.5	1909	2.4		○	1406	0.4	1952	2.4
8 M	0138	0.4	0726	2.8		23 TU	0159	0.4	0804	2.6
●	1355	0.4	1948	2.5			1442	0.4	2021	2.5
9 TU	0218	0.3	0805	2.9		24 W	0232	0.3	0834	2.6
	1438	0.3	2027	2.6			1514	0.4	2049	2.5
10 W	0257	0.2	0845	3.0		25 TH	0303	0.3	0903	2.5
	1520	0.3	2106	2.6			1543	0.5	2119	2.4
11 TH	0336	0.3	0927	3.0		26 F	0332	0.4	0932	2.4
	1600	0.4	2145	2.6			1610	0.5	2151	2.3
12 F	0415	0.3	1010	2.9		27 SA	0405	0.4	1004	2.3
	1641	0.4	2226	2.5			1640	0.6	2227	2.2
13 SA	0456	0.4	1057	2.7		28 SU	0442	0.5	1039	2.1
	1723	0.5	2310	2.3			1717	0.7	2308	2.1
14 SU	0543	0.5	1150	2.5		29 M	0525	0.7	1120	1.9
	1811	0.7					1804	0.8		
15 M	0003	2.1	0640	0.7						
	1304	2.2	1910	0.9 ◑						

MARCH

Day	Time	m	Time	m		Day	Time	m	Time	m
1 TU	0001	1.9	0619	0.8		16 W	0104	1.9	0753	0.8
◑	1217	1.7	1904	0.9			1416	1.9	1950	0.9
2 W	0121	1.8	0723	0.9		17 TH	0301	1.9	0934	0.8
	1357	1.7	2016	0.9			1543	1.9	2126	0.9
3 TH	0251	1.8	0832	0.9		18 F	0424	2.0	1046	0.7
	1540	1.7	2138	0.9			1653	2.0	2239	0.8
4 F	0400	2.0	0947	0.8		19 SA	0522	2.2	1140	0.5
	1648	1.8	2255	0.8			1745	2.1	2333	0.6
5 SA	0456	2.1	1106	0.7		20 SU	0605	2.4	1225	0.4
	1738	2.0	2348	0.6			1826	2.2		
6 SU	0543	2.3	1206	0.5		21 M	0018	0.5	0641	2.4
	1819	2.2					1305	0.4	1900	2.3
7 M	0034	0.5	0624	2.6		22 TU	0059	0.4	0713	2.4
	1255	0.4	1855	2.3			1342	0.3	1930	2.3
8 TU	0117	0.3	0705	2.8		23 W	0136	0.3	0741	2.4
	1339	0.2	1931	2.5		○	1417	0.3	1956	2.4
9 W	0158	0.2	0744	2.9		24 TH	0209	0.3	0808	2.4
●	1421	0.1	2008	2.6			1447	0.3	2022	2.4
10 TH	0238	0.1	0825	3.0		25 F	0239	0.3	0835	2.4
	1500	0.1	2045	2.6			1514	0.4	2051	2.4
11 F	0318	0.1	0907	3.0		26 SA	0308	0.3	0905	2.3
	1539	0.1	2123	2.6			1539	0.4	2123	2.4
12 SA	0358	0.1	0950	2.9		27 SU	0341	0.4	0937	2.2
	1616	0.2	2203	2.5			1606	0.5	2157	2.3
13 SU	0440	0.3	1035	2.7		28 M	0417	0.5	1012	2.1
	1655	0.4	2246	2.3			1638	0.6	2236	2.1
14 M	0527	0.5	1128	2.4		29 TU	0500	0.6	1052	1.9
	1739	0.6	2336	2.1			1718	0.7	2322	2.0
15 TU	0626	0.7	1239	2.1		30 W	0551	0.7	1141	1.7
◑	1834	0.8					1812	0.8		
						31 TH	0029	1.8	0653	0.8
						◑	1259	1.6	1923	0.9

APRIL

Day	Time	m	Time	m		Day	Time	m	Time	m
1 F	0206	1.8	0803	0.8		16 SA	0350	2.0	1014	0.6
	1454	1.6	2046	0.9			1619	1.8	2202	0.8
2 SA	0322	1.9	0918	0.7		17 SU	0449	2.1	1108	0.5
	1614	1.7	2212	0.8			1715	2.0	2259	0.6
3 SU	0421	2.1	1038	0.6		18 M	0536	2.2	1154	0.4
	1711	1.9	2315	0.6			1758	2.1	2347	0.5
4 M	0512	2.3	1141	0.4		19 TU	0615	2.3	1235	0.4
	1755	2.1					1834	2.2		
5 TU	0005	0.4	0557	2.5		20 W	0029	0.4	0647	2.3
	1232	0.3	1833	2.3			1313	0.3	1903	2.3
6 W	0050	0.2	0640	2.7		21 TH	0107	0.4	0715	2.3
	1316	0.1	1909	2.5			1347	0.3	1929	2.3
7 TH	0133	0.1	0722	2.9		22 F	0141	0.3	0740	2.3
●	1358	0.0	1946	2.6		○	1419	0.3	1956	2.4
8 F	0215	0.0	0803	3.0		23 SA	0212	0.3	0808	2.3
	1437	0.0	2023	2.7			1446	0.3	2025	2.5
9 SA	0257	0.0	0846	2.9		24 SU	0243	0.4	0840	2.3
	1519	0.1	2102	2.6			1512	0.3	2058	2.4
10 SU	0340	0.1	0931	2.8		25 M	0317	0.4	0915	2.2
	1552	0.2	2143	2.5			1539	0.4	2134	2.4
11 M	0425	0.2	1018	2.6		26 TU	0356	0.5	0953	2.1
	1631	0.4	2227	2.4			1611	0.5	2212	2.2
12 TU	0515	0.4	1111	2.3		27 W	0439	0.5	1035	2.0
	1713	0.5	2321	2.1			1648	0.6	2258	2.1
13 W	0617	0.6	1220	2.0		28 TH	0530	0.6	1124	1.8
	1804	0.7					1735	0.7	2357	2.0
14 TH	0053	2.0	0743	0.7		29 F	0630	0.7	1230	1.7
◑	1349	1.8	1915	0.9			1839	0.8		
15 F	0235	2.0	0908	0.7		30 SA	0122	1.9	0738	0.7
	1509	1.8	2046	0.9		◑	1403	1.6	2000	0.8

Chart Datum: 1·37 metres below Ordnance Datum (Belfast). HAT is 3·1 metres above Chart Datum.

STANDARD TIME (UT)
For Summer Time add ONE hour in **non-shaded areas**

RIVER FOYLE   LAT 55°03'N   LONG 7°16'W
TIMES AND HEIGHTS OF HIGH AND LOW WATERS

Dates in red are **SPRINGS**
Dates in blue are **NEAPS**

YEAR **2016**

MAY

Day	Time	m		Day	Time	m
1 SU	0242 / 0848 / 1527 / 2124	2.0 / 0.6 / 1.7 / 0.7		**16** M	0409 / 1027 / 1633 / 2219	2.0 / 0.6 / 1.8 / 0.7
2 M	0344 / 1001 / 1633 / 2235	2.1 / 0.5 / 1.9 / 0.6		**17** TU	0501 / 1116 / 1723 / 2311	2.1 / 0.5 / 1.9 / 0.6
3 TU	0439 / 1107 / 1725 / 2332	2.3 / 0.4 / 2.1 / 0.4		**18** W	0544 / 1200 / 1803 / 2356	2.1 / 0.4 / 2.1 / 0.5
4 W	0529 / 1202 / 1808	2.5 / 0.2 / 2.3		**19** TH	0619 / 1240 / 1835	2.1 / 0.4 / 2.2
5 TH	0021 / 0615 / 1250 / 1847	0.2 / 2.7 / 0.1 / 2.4		**20** F	0035 / 0647 / 1318 / 1903	0.5 / 2.2 / 0.3 / 2.3
6 F ●	0108 / 0700 / 1333 / 1925	0.1 / 2.8 / 0.1 / 2.6		**21** SA ○	0112 / 0714 / 1351 / 1933	0.4 / 2.2 / 0.3 / 2.4
7 SA	0153 / 0744 / 1414 / 2004	0.1 / 2.9 / 0.0 / 2.7		**22** SU	0146 / 0744 / 1422 / 2004	0.4 / 2.2 / 0.3 / 2.5
8 SU	0238 / 0829 / 1453 / 2045	0.1 / 2.8 / 0.1 / 2.6		**23** M	0220 / 0819 / 1450 / 2039	0.4 / 2.2 / 0.3 / 2.5
9 M	0325 / 0916 / 1532 / 2128	0.2 / 2.7 / 0.2 / 2.6		**24** TU	0258 / 0857 / 1520 / 2116	0.4 / 2.2 / 0.4 / 2.4
10 TU	0413 / 1004 / 1611 / 2215	0.3 / 2.5 / 0.3 / 2.4		**25** W	0339 / 0939 / 1554 / 2157	0.5 / 2.2 / 0.4 / 2.3
11 W	0506 / 1057 / 1652 / 2311	0.4 / 2.2 / 0.5 / 2.2		**26** TH	0425 / 1023 / 1631 / 2243	0.5 / 2.1 / 0.5 / 2.2
12 TH	0607 / 1158 / 1739	0.6 / 2.0 / 0.6		**27** F	0515 / 1112 / 1716 / 2338	0.5 / 1.9 / 0.6 / 2.1
13 F ◑	0033 / 0720 / 1312 / 1839	2.1 / 0.7 / 1.8 / 0.8		**28** SA	0612 / 1209 / 1811	0.6 / 1.8 / 0.7
14 SA	0200 / 0831 / 1424 / 1957	2.0 / 0.7 / 1.7 / 0.8		**29** SU ◑	0049 / 0714 / 1322 / 1924	2.1 / 0.6 / 1.7 / 0.7
15 SU	0309 / 0933 / 1532 / 2115	2.0 / 0.6 / 1.8 / 0.8		**30** M	0204 / 0819 / 1441 / 2043	2.1 / 0.5 / 1.8 / 0.7
				31 TU	0309 / 0925 / 1552 / 2158	2.2 / 0.5 / 1.9 / 0.6

JUNE

Day	Time	m		Day	Time	m
1 W	0408 / 1032 / 1654 / 2302	2.3 / 0.4 / 2.0 / 0.4		**16** TH	0510 / 1124 / 1730 / 2321	2.0 / 0.5 / 2.1 / 0.6
2 TH	0504 / 1132 / 1744 / 2358	2.5 / 0.3 / 2.2 / 0.3		**17** F	0549 / 1208 / 1808	2.0 / 0.5 / 2.1
3 F	0555 / 1224 / 1828	2.6 / 0.2 / 2.4		**18** SA	0005 / 0621 / 1249 / 1841	0.6 / 2.1 / 0.4 / 2.3
4 SA	0048 / 0643 / 1311 / 1909	0.2 / 2.7 / 0.2 / 2.5		**19** SU	0045 / 0652 / 1327 / 1914	0.5 / 2.1 / 0.4 / 2.4
5 SU ●	0137 / 0730 / 1355 / 1951	0.2 / 2.7 / 0.1 / 2.6		**20** M ○	0124 / 0726 / 1402 / 1948	0.5 / 2.2 / 0.3 / 2.5
6 M	0225 / 0816 / 1436 / 2033	0.2 / 2.7 / 0.2 / 2.6		**21** TU	0204 / 0803 / 1436 / 2024	0.5 / 2.2 / 0.3 / 2.5
7 TU	0314 / 0903 / 1515 / 2117	0.3 / 2.6 / 0.2 / 2.6		**22** W	0246 / 0844 / 1509 / 2103	0.5 / 2.2 / 0.3 / 2.5
8 W	0404 / 0951 / 1554 / 2203	0.3 / 2.4 / 0.3 / 2.5		**23** TH	0330 / 0927 / 1544 / 2145	0.4 / 2.2 / 0.3 / 2.5
9 TH	0454 / 1040 / 1633 / 2255	0.4 / 2.2 / 0.4 / 2.3		**24** F	0416 / 1011 / 1622 / 2230	0.4 / 2.2 / 0.4 / 2.4
10 F	0548 / 1131 / 1715 / 2358	0.6 / 2.0 / 0.5 / 2.1		**25** SA	0503 / 1057 / 1704 / 2320	0.4 / 2.1 / 0.5 / 2.3
11 SA	0647 / 1228 / 1803	0.6 / 1.9 / 0.6		**26** SU	0554 / 1147 / 1753	0.5 / 2.0 / 0.5
12 SU ◑	0115 / 0748 / 1332 / 1902	2.0 / 0.7 / 1.8 / 0.7		**27** M ◐	0021 / 0650 / 1247 / 1855	2.3 / 0.5 / 1.9 / 0.6
13 M	0225 / 0846 / 1438 / 2015	2.0 / 0.7 / 1.7 / 0.8		**28** TU	0131 / 0750 / 1400 / 2010	2.2 / 0.5 / 1.8 / 0.7
14 TU	0327 / 0942 / 1543 / 2128	2.0 / 0.6 / 1.8 / 0.8		**29** W	0240 / 0853 / 1517 / 2129	2.2 / 0.5 / 1.9 / 0.6
15 W	0422 / 1035 / 1642 / 2230	2.0 / 0.6 / 1.9 / 0.7		**30** TH	0344 / 1001 / 1628 / 2242	2.3 / 0.5 / 2.0 / 0.5

JULY

Day	Time	m		Day	Time	m
1 F	0445 / 1107 / 1728 / 2344	2.4 / 0.4 / 2.1 / 0.4		**16** SA	0522 / 1138 / 1743 / 2338	1.9 / 0.5 / 2.1 / 0.7
2 SA	0542 / 1205 / 1817	2.4 / 0.4 / 2.3		**17** SU	0601 / 1224 / 1822	2.0 / 0.5 / 2.2
3 SU	0037 / 0633 / 1255 / 1900	0.3 / 2.5 / 0.3 / 2.5		**18** M	0025 / 0636 / 1306 / 1857	0.6 / 2.1 / 0.4 / 2.4
4 M ●	0129 / 0721 / 1340 / 1942	0.2 / 2.5 / 0.2 / 2.6		**19** TU ○	0110 / 0713 / 1345 / 1933	0.5 / 2.1 / 0.3 / 2.5
5 TU	0218 / 0807 / 1422 / 2023	0.2 / 2.5 / 0.2 / 2.6		**20** W	0154 / 0751 / 1423 / 2010	0.5 / 2.2 / 0.3 / 2.6
6 W	0306 / 0851 / 1501 / 2104	0.3 / 2.5 / 0.2 / 2.6		**21** TH	0238 / 0831 / 1459 / 2049	0.4 / 2.3 / 0.3 / 2.7
7 TH	0352 / 0934 / 1537 / 2146	0.4 / 2.4 / 0.2 / 2.5		**22** F	0321 / 0912 / 1535 / 2129	0.4 / 2.3 / 0.2 / 2.7
8 F	0436 / 1016 / 1613 / 2230	0.4 / 2.3 / 0.3 / 2.4		**23** SA	0404 / 0953 / 1612 / 2212	0.3 / 2.3 / 0.3 / 2.6
9 SA	0520 / 1057 / 1649 / 2317	0.5 / 2.1 / 0.4 / 2.2		**24** SU	0447 / 1035 / 1651 / 2259	0.3 / 2.2 / 0.3 / 2.5
10 SU	0607 / 1142 / 1728	0.6 / 2.0 / 0.6		**25** M	0533 / 1120 / 1736 / 2353	0.4 / 2.1 / 0.4 / 2.4
11 M	0015 / 0657 / 1235 / 1817	2.0 / 0.7 / 1.8 / 0.7		**26** TU ◐	0623 / 1212 / 1831	0.6 / 2.0 / 0.6
12 TU ◑	0130 / 0753 / 1340 / 1918	1.9 / 0.7 / 1.7 / 0.8		**27** W	0100 / 0719 / 1322 / 1943	2.3 / 0.6 / 1.9 / 0.7
13 W	0240 / 0852 / 1451 / 2028	1.9 / 0.7 / 1.7 / 0.8		**28** TH	0216 / 0824 / 1449 / 2110	2.2 / 0.6 / 1.8 / 0.7
14 TH	0342 / 0951 / 1559 / 2140	1.8 / 0.7 / 1.8 / 0.7		**29** F	0329 / 0936 / 1614 / 2235	2.2 / 0.6 / 1.9 / 0.7
15 F	0436 / 1048 / 1657 / 2245	1.9 / 0.6 / 1.9 / 0.8		**30** SA	0437 / 1050 / 1724 / 2339	2.2 / 0.6 / 2.1 / 0.5
				31 SU	0538 / 1151 / 1814	2.3 / 0.5 / 2.3

AUGUST

Day	Time	m		Day	Time	m
1 M	0033 / 0629 / 1242 / 1855	0.4 / 2.4 / 0.4 / 2.5		**16** TU	0010 / 0623 / 1246 / 1838	0.6 / 2.2 / 0.4 / 2.4
2 TU ●	0122 / 0715 / 1326 / 1934	0.4 / 2.4 / 0.3 / 2.6		**17** W	0057 / 0659 / 1327 / 1914	0.5 / 2.2 / 0.3 / 2.6
3 W	0209 / 0756 / 1407 / 2011	0.3 / 2.4 / 0.2 / 2.6		**18** TH ○	0141 / 0736 / 1405 / 1951	0.4 / 2.3 / 0.2 / 2.7
4 TH	0253 / 0834 / 1444 / 2047	0.3 / 2.4 / 0.2 / 2.6		**19** F	0224 / 0813 / 1442 / 2029	0.3 / 2.4 / 0.2 / 2.8
5 F	0333 / 0910 / 1518 / 2123	0.4 / 2.4 / 0.2 / 2.6		**20** SA	0305 / 0851 / 1519 / 2109	0.3 / 2.5 / 0.1 / 2.9
6 SA	0411 / 0945 / 1549 / 2159	0.5 / 2.3 / 0.3 / 2.4		**21** SU	0345 / 0929 / 1556 / 2150	0.2 / 2.5 / 0.1 / 2.8
7 SU	0446 / 1021 / 1622 / 2236	0.5 / 2.2 / 0.4 / 2.3		**22** M	0425 / 1009 / 1635 / 2235	0.3 / 2.4 / 0.3 / 2.7
8 M	0523 / 1059 / 1657 / 2316	0.6 / 2.1 / 0.5 / 2.1		**23** TU	0506 / 1051 / 1718 / 2326	0.4 / 2.3 / 0.4 / 2.5
9 TU	0604 / 1144 / 1741	0.7 / 1.9 / 0.7		**24** W	0551 / 1140 / 1810	0.5 / 2.1 / 0.6
10 W ◐	0011 / 0654 / 1244 / 1835	1.9 / 0.8 / 1.8 / 0.8		**25** TH ◑	0031 / 0646 / 1249 / 1924	2.3 / 0.7 / 1.9 / 0.8
11 TH	0140 / 0755 / 1404 / 1942	1.8 / 0.8 / 1.7 / 0.9		**26** F	0158 / 0754 / 1433 / 2106	2.1 / 0.8 / 1.9 / 0.8
12 F	0301 / 0904 / 1521 / 2054	1.7 / 0.8 / 1.8 / 0.9		**27** SA	0321 / 0916 / 1610 / 2232	2.1 / 0.8 / 2.0 / 0.7
13 SA	0405 / 1013 / 1626 / 2211	1.8 / 0.7 / 1.9 / 0.9		**28** SU	0434 / 1035 / 1719 / 2333	2.1 / 0.7 / 2.2 / 0.6
14 SU	0500 / 1112 / 1719 / 2318	1.9 / 0.6 / 2.1 / 0.7		**29** M	0534 / 1135 / 1806	2.2 / 0.6 / 2.4
15 M	0545 / 1201 / 1801	1.9 / 0.5 / 2.2		**30** TU	0024 / 0621 / 1225 / 1844	0.4 / 2.3 / 0.4 / 2.5
				31 W	0110 / 0702 / 1308 / 1919	0.4 / 2.3 / 0.3 / 2.6

Chart Datum: 1·37 metres below Ordnance Datum (Belfast). HAT is 3·1 metres above Chart Datum.

STANDARD TIME (UT)
For Summer Time add ONE hour in **non-shaded areas**

RIVER FOYLE LAT 55°03'N LONG 7°16'W
TIMES AND HEIGHTS OF HIGH AND LOW WATERS

Dates in red are **SPRINGS**
Dates in blue are NEAPS

YEAR 2016

N Ireland

SEPTEMBER

Time	m		Time	m
1 0152	0.3	**16**	0121	0.3
0738	2.4		0714	2.4
TH 1347	0.3	F 1341	0.4
● 1952	2.6	○ 1926	2.9
2 0231	0.3	**17**	0202	0.3
0811	2.5		0749	2.5
F 1422	0.2	SA 1419	0.1
2024	2.6	2005	3.0
3 0307	0.4	**18**	0241	0.2
0842	2.4		0826	2.6
SA 1454	0.3	SU 1457	0.1
2055	2.6	2045	3.0
4 0339	0.4	**19**	0320	0.2
0912	2.4		0904	2.7
SU 1524	0.3	M 1536	0.1
2126	2.5	2127	3.0
5 0408	0.5	**20**	0358	0.3
0945	2.3		0943	2.6
M 1554	0.4	TU 1616	0.3
2157	2.3	2212	2.8
6 0439	0.6	**21**	0437	0.4
1020	2.2		1025	2.5
TU 1628	0.5	W 1701	0.4
2232	2.1	2302	2.5
7 0514	0.7	**22**	0520	0.6
1100	2.1		1114	2.3
W 1709	0.7	TH 1756	0.7
2313	1.9		
8 0559	0.8	**23**	0008	2.2
1152	1.9		0612	0.8
TH 1800	0.8	F 1225	2.1
		◐ 1915	0.8
9 0014	1.7	**24**	0143	2.1
0656	0.9		0721	0.9
F 1314	1.8	SA 1424	2.0
◐ 1904	0.9	2103	0.9
10 0214	1.7	**25**	0309	2.0
0806	0.9		0852	0.9
SA 1445	1.8	SU 1555	2.1
2017	1.0	2219	0.7
11 0334	1.7	**26**	0420	2.1
0930	0.8		1011	0.8
SU 1553	1.9	M 1700	2.3
2138	0.9	2317	0.6
12 0434	1.8	**27**	0517	2.2
1042	0.7		1111	0.7
M 1648	2.1	TU 1746	2.4
2256	0.8		
13 0523	2.0	**28**	0005	0.5
1135	0.6		0602	2.3
TU 1733	2.3	W 1201	0.5
2351	0.6	1824	2.5
14 0603	2.1	**29**	0047	0.4
1219	0.5		0641	2.4
W 1812	2.5	TH 1243	0.4
		1858	2.6
15 0037	0.5	**30**	0126	0.4
0639	2.3		0714	2.5
TH 1301	0.4	F 1322	0.4
1849	2.7	1928	2.6

OCTOBER

Time	m		Time	m
1 0203	0.4	**16**	0134	0.2
0744	2.5		0725	2.7
SA 1357	0.3	SU 1353	0.2
● 1957	2.6	○ 1940	3.1
2 0236	0.4	**17**	0214	0.2
0812	2.5		0802	2.8
SU 1427	0.3	M 1434	0.2
2024	2.5	2022	3.1
3 0305	0.5	**18**	0253	0.2
0840	2.5		0841	2.8
M 1456	0.4	TU 1516	0.2
2053	2.5	2106	3.0
4 0331	0.5	**19**	0332	0.3
0912	2.5		0922	2.8
TU 1526	0.5	W 1600	0.3
2123	2.4	2152	2.8
5 0358	0.6	**20**	0411	0.4
0946	2.4		1006	2.6
W 1601	0.6	TH 1648	0.5
2156	2.2	2244	2.5
6 0429	0.7	**21**	0453	0.6
1023	2.3		1056	2.4
TH 1641	0.7	F 1746	0.7
2234	2.0	2349	2.2
7 0508	0.8	**22**	0543	0.8
1107	2.1		1211	2.2
F 1729	0.9	SA 1908	0.9
2322	1.8	◑	
8 0558	0.9	**23**	0119	2.1
1211	1.9		0647	1.0
SA 1831	1.0	SU 1402	2.2
		2043	0.9
9 0048	1.7	**24**	0242	2.0
0704	1.0		0814	1.0
SU 1358	1.9	M 1523	2.2
◐ 1943	1.0	2153	0.8
10 0249	1.7	**25**	0351	2.1
0823	1.0		0936	0.9
M 1512	2.0	TU 1627	2.3
2101	0.9	2249	0.7
11 0357	1.8	**26**	0449	2.2
0952	0.9		1038	0.8
TU 1608	2.2	W 1717	2.5
2220	0.8	2336	0.6
12 0450	2.0	**27**	0536	2.3
1056	0.8		1129	0.7
W 1657	2.4	TH 1758	2.5
2320	0.6		
13 0534	2.2	**28**	0018	0.5
1145	0.6		0614	2.4
TH 1740	2.6	F 1214	0.6
		1832	2.5
14 0009	0.5	**29**	0056	0.5
0612	2.4		0647	2.5
F 1230	0.4	SA 1253	0.5
1820	2.8	1902	2.5
15 0053	0.3	**30**	0132	0.5
0648	2.5		0716	2.6
SA 1312	0.3	SU 1328	0.5
1900	3.0	● 1929	2.5
		31	0204	0.5
			0744	2.6
		M 1359	0.5
		1955	2.5

NOVEMBER

Time	m		Time	m
1 0233	0.5	**16**	0230	0.3
0813	2.7		0823	2.9
TU 1429	0.5	W 1459	0.3
2023	2.5	2049	3.0
2 0259	0.5	**17**	0310	0.3
0844	2.6		0906	2.9
W 1500	0.6	TH 1547	0.4
2054	2.4	2136	2.8
3 0325	0.6	**18**	0351	0.5
0918	2.4		0952	2.8
TH 1536	0.7	F 1637	0.6
2129	2.3	2228	2.5
4 0355	0.7	**19**	0432	0.6
0955	2.5		1043	2.6
F 1617	0.8	SA 1735	0.8
2208	2.1	2328	2.3
5 0432	0.8	**20**	0518	0.8
1037	2.3		1152	2.4
SA 1704	0.9	SU 1847	0.9
2254	2.0		
6 0516	0.9	**21**	0043	2.1
1129	2.2		0612	0.9
SU 1801	0.9	M 1326	2.3
2357	1.8	◑ 2008	0.9
7 0612	1.0	**22**	0200	2.0
1250	2.1		0722	1.0
M 1910	1.0	TU 1444	2.3
		2116	0.9
8 0140	1.8	**23**	0309	2.0
0724	1.0		0844	1.0
TU 1421	2.1	W 1549	2.3
2022	0.9	2213	0.8
9 0306	1.9	**24**	0410	2.1
0845	1.0		0956	1.0
W 1525	2.3	TH 1644	2.4
2134	0.8	2302	0.7
10 0408	2.0	**25**	0503	2.2
1003	0.9		1054	0.9
TH 1619	2.5	F 1729	2.4
2240	0.6	2345	0.7
11 0500	2.2	**26**	0546	2.3
0952	0.8		1141	0.8
F 1707	2.7	SA 1807	2.4
2335	0.5		
12 0544	2.4	**27**	0024	0.6
1157	0.5		0620	2.4
SA 1753	2.9	SU 1223	0.7
		1837	2.4
13 0023	0.4	**28**	0101	0.6
0624	2.6		0651	2.6
SU 1244	0.4	M 1259	0.7
1836	3.0	1903	2.5
14 0107	0.3	**29**	0135	0.5
0703	2.8		0720	2.6
M 1329	0.3	TU 1332	0.7
○ 1919	3.1	● 1929	2.5
15 0149	0.3	**30**	0206	0.5
0742	2.9		0750	2.7
TU 1414	0.3	W 1404	0.7
2003	3.1	1959	2.5

DECEMBER

Time	m		Time	m
1 0234	0.6	**16**	0254	0.4
0823	2.7		0854	2.9
TH 1438	0.7	F 1537	0.5
2033	2.4	2123	2.7
2 0303	0.6	**17**	0334	0.4
0859	2.7		0940	2.8
F 1516	0.7	SA 1626	0.6
2111	2.4	2211	2.5
3 0335	0.6	**18**	0414	0.5
0937	2.6		1028	2.7
SA 1558	0.7	SU 1717	0.8
2152	2.3	2301	2.3
4 0411	0.7	**19**	0455	0.7
1018	2.5		1123	2.5
SU 1645	0.8	M 1814	0.9
2237	2.2	2357	2.1
5 0452	0.8	**20**	0539	0.8
1106	2.4		1235	2.3
M 1738	0.8	TU 1918	1.0
2330	2.0		
6 0541	0.9	**21**	0104	2.0
1207	2.3		0632	0.9
TU 1839	0.9	W 1356	2.2
		◑ 2026	1.0
7 0040	1.9	**22**	0215	1.9
0643	0.9		0738	1.0
W 1327	2.3	TH 1506	2.2
◑ 1945	0.9	2127	0.9
8 0208	1.9	**23**	0322	1.9
0757	1.0		0855	1.0
TH 1441	2.4	F 1609	2.2
2052	0.8	2222	0.9
9 0322	2.0	**24**	0423	2.0
0915	0.9		1010	1.0
F 1543	2.5	SA 1701	2.2
2200	0.7	2310	0.8
10 0425	2.2	**25**	0514	2.2
1028	0.8		1107	0.9
SA 1639	2.6	SU 1744	2.3
2302	0.6	2353	0.7
11 0517	2.4	**26**	0554	2.3
1130	0.6		1153	0.8
SU 1731	2.8	M 1817	2.3
2357	0.5		
12 0604	2.6	**27**	0033	0.6
1223	0.5		0628	2.5
M 1819	2.9	TU 1234	0.8
		1844	2.3
13 0646	2.8	**28**	0111	0.6
0646	2.8		0700	2.6
TU 1313	0.4	W 1311	0.7
1905	3.0	1911	2.4
14 0130	0.3	**29**	0145	0.6
0728	2.9		0733	2.7
W 1401	0.4	TH 1347	0.7
○ 1950	3.0	1943	2.4
15 0213	0.3	**30**	0218	0.5
0811	2.9		0807	2.7
TH 1449	0.4	F 1425	0.7
2037	2.9	2019	2.4
		31	0250	0.5
			0844	2.8
		SA 1504	0.7
		2058	2.4

Chart Datum: 1·37 metres below Ordnance Datum (Belfast). HAT is 3·1 metres above Chart Datum.

»» FREE monthly updates. Register at ««
www.reedsnauticalalmanac.co.uk
229

6.12 RIVER BANN AND COLERAINE

Londonderry/Antrim 55°10'·32N 06°46'·35W ❀❀♨♨✿✿

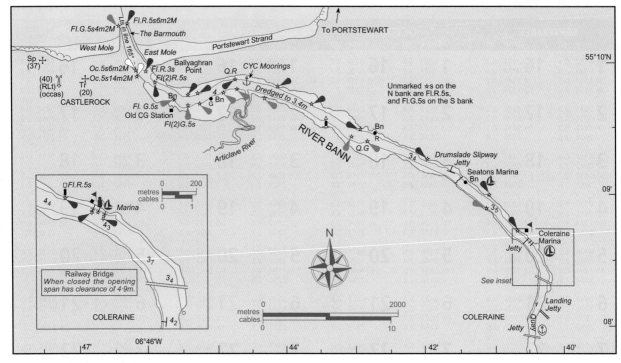

CHARTS AC 2723, 2798, 2494, 5612; Imray C53, C64

TIDES –0345 Dover (Coleraine); ML 1·1; Duration 0540

Standard Port RIVER FOYLE (←)

Times				Height (metres)			
High Water		Low Water		MHWS	MHWN	MLWN	MLWS
0100	0800	0200	0700	2·6	1·9	0·9	0·4
1300	2000	1400	1900				
Differences COLERAINE							
–0004	–0106	–0109	–0005	–0·4	–0·1	0·0	0·0

SHELTER Good, once inside the river ent (The Barmouth) between 2 training walls, extending 2ca N from the beaches. Do not try to enter in strong onshore winds or when swell breaks on the pierheads. If in doubt call Coleraine Hbr Radio or ring HM. ⚓ upstream of old CG stn, or berth at Seaton's or Coleraine marinas, 3½M & 4½M from ent, on NE bank.

NAVIGATION WPT 55°11'·00N, 06°46'·65W, 165°/0·72M to ent. Appr from E of N to bring ldg lts into line at bkwtr ends. The sand bar is constantly moving but ent is dredged to approx 3·5m. Beware commercial traffic.

LIGHTS AND MARKS Ldg lts 165°, both Oc 5s 6/14m 2M, front on W pyramidal metal tr; rear W ☐ tr. Portstewart Pt, Oc R 10s, is 2M ENE.

COMMUNICATIONS (Code 028) CGOC 91463933; Police 101; Ⓗ 70344177; Dr 70344831; HM 70342012; Rly Bridge 70325400. Coleraine Hbr Radio Ch 12 (Mon-Fri: HO and when vessel due). Coleraine Marina Ch M.

FACILITIES **Coleraine Hbr** ☎70342012, ⚓(35t).

Coleraine Marina ☎70344768, ⚓ 90+5Ⓥ £21, ⚓(H24) ♒ ⚒ ▣ ⚸ ⚓(12½t).

Seatons Marina ☎07718 883099, ⚓(£3) ⚓(12t).

Coleraine YC ☎70344503, ⚓ ☐.

Town ☎ ☎ ⚓ ⚒ Ⓔ ⚓ ⚓ ⚓ ✉ Ⓑ ⚓ ✗ ⚓ ✈ (Belfast).

MINOR HARBOUR TO THE EAST

Portstewart, Antrim, **55°11'·21N 06°43'·21W**. AC 2494, 5612. Tides as for Portrush. A tiny hbr 1·1ca S of Portstewart Pt lt, Oc R 10s 21m 5M, vis 040°–220°, obscd in final appr. A temp, fair weather berth (£10) at S end of inner basin in 0·8–1·7m; the very narrow ent is open to SW wind and swell. Visitors should obtain fuel at Portrush before proceeding to Portstewart. Beware rocks close to S bkwtr. Facilities: ⚓⚓⚓⚓ ✗ ☐ @ at library.

6.13 PORTRUSH

Antrim **55°12'·34N 06°39'·49W** ❀❀♦♦♧♧♧

CHARTS AC 2798, 2494, 5612; Imray C53, C64

TIDES –0400 Dover; ML 1·1; Duration 0610

Standard Port RIVER FOYLE (⟵)

Times				Height (metres)			
High Water		Low Water		MHWS	MHWN	MLWN	MLWS
0100	0800	0200	0700	2·6	1·9	0·9	0·4
1300	2000	1400	1900				

Differences PORTRUSH
| –0046 | –0052 | –0117 | –0057 | –0·5 | –0·3 | +0·1 | +0·1 |

SHELTER Good in hbr, except in strong NW/N winds. Berth on N pier or on pontoon at NE end of it and see HM. A ⚓ may be available, but very congested in season. ⚓ on E side of Ramore Hd in Skerries Roads 1ca S of Large Skerrie gives good shelter in most conditions, but open to NW sea/swell.

NAVIGATION WPT 55°13'·00N 06°41'·00W, 128° to N pier lt, 1·1M.

Ent with onshore winds >F 4 is difficult. Beware submerged bkwtr projecting 20m SW from N pier. Depth is 2·8m in hbr entrance.

LIGHTS AND MARKS Ldg lts 028° (occas, for LB use) both FR 6/8m 1M; R △ on metal bn and metal mast. N pier Fl R 3s 6m 3M; vis 220°-160°. S pier Fl G 3s 6m 3M; vis 220°-100°.

COMMUNICATIONS (Code 028) CGOC 9146 3933; Police 101; Dr 7082 3767; ⊞ 7034 4177. HM 7082 2307.

VHF Ch 12 16 (0900-1700LT, Mon-Fri; extended evening hrs June-Sept; Sat-Sun: 0900–1700, June-Sept only).

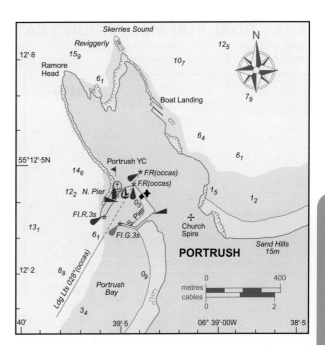

FACILITIES Hbr ⚓ ⛴(£3) ⬭ £14, ⚒ ⛽ ⚓(0900-1800) ⬛ ⬜ Ⓔ; Portrush YC ☎7082 3932, ⬜; **Town** ⬜⬜⬜⬜⬜⬜✕⬜@ Library ⇌ ✈ (Belfast). Giant's Causeway is 10M ENE.

FAIR HEAD TO LAMBAY ISLAND

(AC 2199/8, 2093, 44) Fair Hd is a bold 190m headland, steep-to all round, but with extensive overfalls in Rathlin Sound. The coast is fairly steep-to except in larger bays, particularly Dundalk.

▶Streams in North Channel can reach more than 4½kn. S of Belfast Lough they are weaker, but run up to 2·5kn S of Rockabill.◀

⚓ in offshore winds in Cushendun Bay, 5M NNW of Garron Pt, and in Red Bay 4M further S. They provide useful ⚓s on passage to/from the Clyde or Western Is. Glenarm Marina provides good shelter for small craft and is useful for on passage to the W coasts of Scotland or Ireland. (AC 2198) 4M N of Larne are the Maidens, two dangerous groups of rks extending 2·5M N/S; E Maiden is lit. Hunter Rk (0·8m), S of the Maidens, is marked by N & S cardinals.

N of Belfast Lough, Muck Island is steep-to on its E side, as is Black Hd. Three routes lead into Belfast Lough from the south:
a. E of Mew Is.

▶Beware Ram Race (N'thly on the ebb and S'thly on the flood.◀

b. Copeland Sound, between Mew Is and Copeland Is, is passable but not recommended.

▶Here the stream runs SSE from HW Belfast +0420 and NW from HW Belfast –0115.◀

c. Donaghadee Sound is buoyed and a good short cut for small craft (see AC 3709).

▶Here the stream runs SSE from HW Belfast +0530 and NW from HW Belfast –0030, 4·5kn max. An eddy extends S to Ballyferris Pt, and about 1M offshore.◀

From Belfast Lough to Strangford Lough, the coast has numerous rocky dangers close inshore, but is reasonably clear if keeping about 2M offshore. In fair weather and good vis, there is a passage between North Rocks and South Rock, otherwise pass to the E using South Rock superbuoy as a guide. Pass E of Butter Pladdy and 5ca off Ballyquintin Point.

▶The tidal cycle is approx 3 hours later than in the N Channel. Flood runs for 6 hours from HW Belfast –0330 (HW Dover –0345), with a maximum rate of 7.5kn at Rue Point. The strong flow flattens the sea in onshore winds and entrance can be made in strong winds. The ebb runs for 6 hours from HW Belfast +0230 (HW Dover +0215), max rate 7.5kn, E of Angus Rk. If entering against ebb use West Channel with care. Smoothest water near Bar Pladdy Buoy when leaving.◀

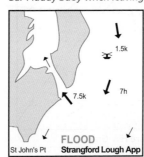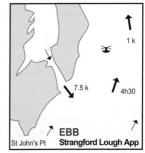

5M SSW of the entrance to Strangford Lough there is a marina at Ardglass.

There are no offshore dangers SW of Strangford to Carlingford Lough. Skerries Islands (Colt, Shenick's and St Patrick's) are 1M E and SE of Red Island, to E of Skerries hbr. Shenick's Island is connected to shore at LW. Pass between Colt and St Patrick's Islands, but the latter has offliers 3ca to S. Rockabill, two steep-to rks with lt ho, is 2·5M E of St Patrick's Island. Lambay Island is private, and steep-to except on W side, where there can be overfalls.

6.14 TIDAL STREAMS AROUND RATHLIN ISLAND

North Ireland 6.2   Off Mull of Kintyre 2.10   South Ireland 2.2
North Irish Sea 3.2   SW Scotland 2.2

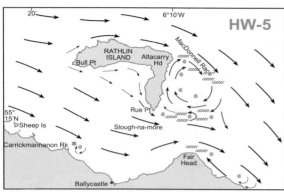

5 Hours before HW Dover (0605 after HW Greenock)

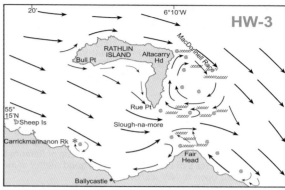

3 Hours before HW Dover (0420 before HW Greenock)

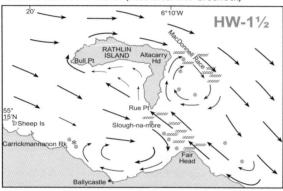

1½ Hours before HW Dover (0250 before HW Greenock)

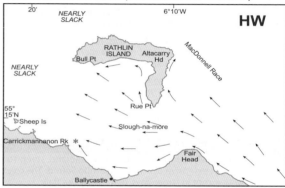

HW Dover (0120 before HW Greenock)

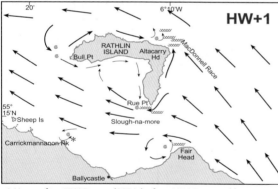

1 Hour after HW Dover (0020 before HW Greenock)

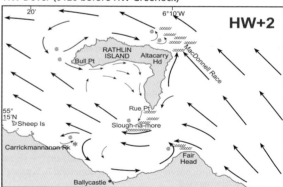

2 Hours after HW Dover (0040 after HW Greenock)

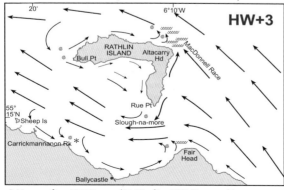

3 Hours after HW Dover (0140 after HW Greenock)

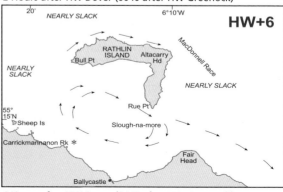

6 Hours after HW Dover (0440 after HW Greenock)

HARBOURS & ANCHORAGES BETWEEN PORTRUSH & LARNE

RATHLIN ISLAND, Antrim, **55°17'·47N 06°11'·78W**. AC 2798, 2494, 5612. HW sp –0445, nps –0200 on Dover. Small harbour in NE corner of Church Bay, sheltered from winds NW through E to SSE. Ferries run from the the Inner Harbour to Ballycastle. Beware sp streams up to 6kn in Rathlin Sound (6.14) and the North Channel TSS, just 2M NE of the island. Pass N or E of a wreck 6ca SW of hbr, marked on its SE side by a SCM lt buoy. When clear, appr on NNE to the W and S piers which form an outer hbr. The white sector of Manor House lt, Oc WRG 4s, leads 024·5° to Inner Harbour (2m) ent via channel dredged to 3·5m (2013). ⌷ on yacht pontoons just S of Inner Harbour. ⌘ in outer hbr on NW side in about 1.2m clear of ferry ramp. Outside hbr, close to W pier ⌘ possible in about 5m, but holding poor in rock/weed. Facilities: Church Bay ⊠ ⩙ ⌷ ✕ ferry to Ballycastle.

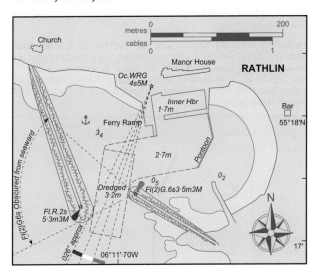

BALLYCASTLE, Antrim, **55°12'·47N 06°14'·27W**. AC 2798, 2494, 5612. Tides as for Rathlin Is; ML 0·8m; –0320 on Dover. Ferries to Rathlin Island berth inside the N breakwater; Ro-Ro disused. The marina is in the S part of the harbour with 2·3m. Outside the harbour is a fair weather ⌘ clear of strong tidal streams, but liable to sudden swell and exposed to onshore winds. Lights: see chartlet and 6.3. CG ☎20762226; Ⓗ 20762666. **Marina** ☎(028) 20768525, mob 07803 505084 74 ⌷£2·10, short stay £4/hr. ⌑ ⩙ ⊹Ⓓ ⚓ ⬚ ⚓ ⊙ ⊡. **Town** ⊠ Ⓑ ⩙ ✕ ⌷.

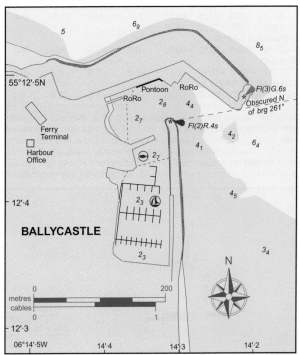

RED BAY, Antrim, **55°03'·91N 06°03'·13W**. AC 2199, 5612. HW +0010 on Dover; ML 1·1m; Duration 0625. See 6.15. Good holding, but open to E winds. Beware rocks, 2 ruined piers W of Garron Pt and on S side of bay, approx ½M from shore, fish farms, marked by lit buoys. Glenariff pier is lit Fl 3s 10m 5M. In S and E winds ⌘ 2ca off W stone arch near head of bay in approx 3·5m; in N or W winds ⌘ S of small pier in 2–5m, ½M NE of Glenariff (Waterfoot) village. **Waterfoot** ✕ ⌷ ⊠.

Cushendall (1M N of pier) ⌷ ⊡ ⊡ ⌑ ⚓ ⊹Ⓓ ⊠ ✕ ⩙ ⚓.

CARNLOUGH HARBOUR, Antrim, **54°59'·87N 05°59'·20W**. AC 2198, 5612. HW +0006 on Dover, +0005 on Belfast; HW –1·6m on Belfast; ML no data; Duration 0625. Good shelter, except in SE gales; do not enter in fresh/strong onshore winds. Entrance shoaling due to build up of kelp, minimum depth 1m (2004). Ldg marks 310°, Y ▽s on B/W posts. N pier lt, Fl G 3s 4m 5M; S pier Fl R 3s 6m 5M, both lts on B/W columns. Beware fish farms in the bay marked by lt buoys (unreliable); and rocks which cover at HW on either side of ent. Small harbour used by yachts and small FVs; visitors welcome. HM mob 07703 606763.

Quay ⌷ £1, ⊹Ⓓ (see HM) ⚓ (by arrangement) ⚓ ⌑. **Town** ⊡ ⊡ ⚓ ⊠ ✕ ⩙ ⌷ ⊡.

GLENARM, Antrim, **54°58'N 05°57'W**. AC 2198, 2199, 5612. HW +0006 on Dover, +0005 on Belfast; HW –1·6m on Belfast; ML no data; Duration 0625. Good shelter in marina, which reports 3m at LW. Hbr ent lts G.3s 3M and R.3s 3M. Beware fish farm about 0·5M NE of entrance. HM / Marina ☎028 2884 1285, Mob 07703 606763. **Marina** 40 ⌷ inc 10 Ⓥ in 4-6m, £2.20, ⚓ ⚓ ⊹Ⓓ ⊙. **Village** ⩙ ⊡ ⊡.

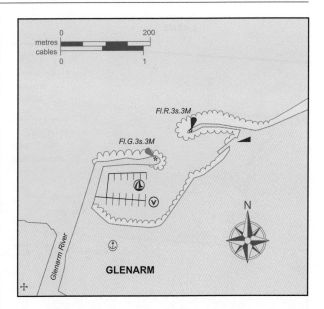

6.15 LARNE

Antrim 54°51'·20N 05°47'·50W ✳✳✳⚓⚓❀❀

CHARTS AC 2198, 1237, 5612; Imray C62, C64, C69

TIDES +0005 Dover; ML 1·6; Duration 0620

Standard Port BELFAST (→)

Times				Height (metres)			
High Water		Low Water		MHWS	MHWN	MLWN	MLWS
0100	0700	0000	0600	3·5	3·0	1·1	0·4
1300	1900	1200	1800				
Differences LARNE							
+0005	0000	+0010	−0005	−0·7	−0·5	−0·3	0·0
RED BAY							
+0022	−0010	+0007	−0017	−1·9	−1·5	−0·8	−0·2
CUSHENDUN BAY							
+0010	−0030	0000	−0025	−1·7	−1·5	−0·6	−0·2

SHELTER Secure shelter in Larne Lough or ⚓ overnight outside hbr in Brown's Bay (E of Barr Pt) in 2-4m. Hbr can be entered H24 in any conditions. Larne is a busy commercial and ferry port; W side is commercial until Curran Pt where there are two YCs with congested moorings. ⚓ S of Ballylumford Power Stn. No 🛟 available for visitors. Yachts should not berth on any commercial quays, inc Castle Quay, without HM's permission. Boat Hbr (0·6m) 2ca S of Ferris Pt only for shoal draft craft.

NAVIGATION WPT 54°51'·70N 05°47'·47W, 184°/2·1M to front ldg lt. Beware Hunter Rk 2M NE of hbr ent. Magnetic anomalies exist near Hunter Rk and between it and the mainland. Inside the narrow ent, chan is close to the E shore. Tide in the ent runs at up to 3½kn.

LIGHTS AND MARKS No1 SHM Q G 1½ca off chartlet N edge; Ldg lts 184°, Oc 2.5s 6m / 5s14m 12M, synch and vis 179°-189°; W ◇ with R stripes. Chaine Tr and fairway lts as chartlet. Note: Many shore lts on W side of ent may be mistaken for nav lts.

COMMUNICATIONS (Code 02828) CGOC 9146 3933; Pilot 273785; Dr 275331; Police 101. HM 872100.

VHF Ch **14** 11 16 *Larne Port Control*. Traffic, weather and tidal info available on Ch 14.

FACILITIES Pier ☎279221, ⚓🛢🛟 🗑(33t); **E Antrim Boat Club** ☎277204, Visitors should pre-contact Sec'y for advice on ⚓; ⚓🛢🛟🚿🍴🗑; **Services** 🛢⛽🔧🅿. **Town** 🛢(delivered, tidal) 🛒 🏦✉🅱🔌✕🍴 ⇌ **Ferries** Cairnryan; 8/day; 1¾ hrs; P&O (www. poferries.co.uk). Troon; 17/week; 1¾ hrs; P&O. ✈ (Belfast City and Belfast/Aldergrove).

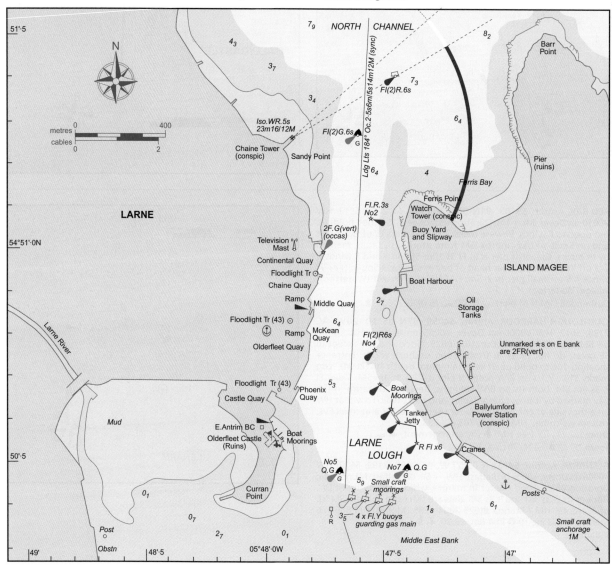

6.16 BELFAST LOUGH

County Down and County Antrim **54°42'N 05°45'W**

Bangor ✲✲✲⚓⚓⚓✿✿; Carrickfergus ✲✲✲⚓⚓⚓✿✿

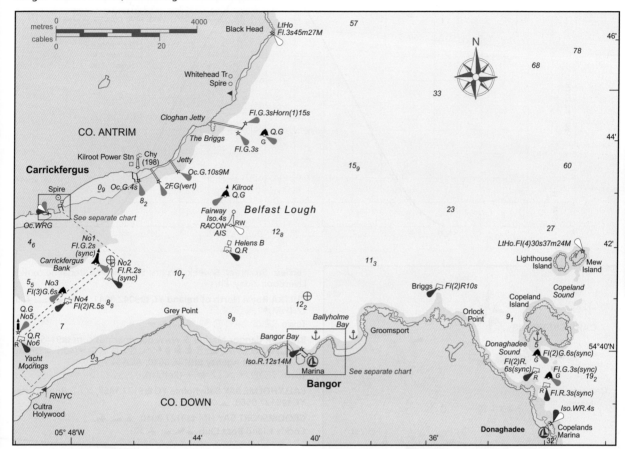

CHARTS AC 2198, 1753, 1752, 5612; Imray C62, C64, C69

TIDES +0007 Dover; ML Belfast 2·0, Carrickfergus 1·8; Duration 0620

Standard Port BELFAST (→)

Times				Height (metres)			
High Water		Low Water		MHWS	MHWN	MLWN	MLWS
0100	0700	0000	0600	3·5	3·0	1·1	0·4
1300	1900	1200	1800				
Differences CARRICKFERGUS							
+0005	+0005	+0005	+0005	–0·3	–0·3	–0·2	–0·1
DONAGHADEE							
+0020	+0020	+0023	+0023	+0·5	+0·4	0·0	+0·1

SHELTER Main sailing centres, clockwise around Belfast Lough, are at Bangor, Cultra and Carrickfergus.

Donaghadee: small marina at SE ent to the Lough.

Ballyholme Bay: good ⚓ in offshore winds.

Bangor: exposed to N winds, but well sheltered in marina (depths 2·9m to 2·2m). Speed limits: 4kn in marina, 8kn between Luke's Pt and Wilson's Pt.

Cultra: in offshore winds good ⚓ & moorings off RNoIYC.

Belfast Harbour is a major commercial port, but there are 40 ◡ in Abercorn Basin, just NE of Lagan Bridge, in the River Lagan.

Carrickfergus: very good in marina, depths 1·8m to 2·3m (2015). The former commercial hbr has 10 yacht berths on the W quay. A stub bkwtr, marked by 2 PHM bns, extends NNE into the hbr from the W pier. The ent and SW part of the hbr are dredged 2·9m (2015); the NE part of the hbr dries 0·7m. Good ⚓ SSE of Carrickfergus Pier, except in E winds.

NAVIGATION Belfast Fairway SWM buoy, 54°42'·32N 05°42'·30W, Traffic passes inbound to N between SWM and Kilroot SHM,

outbound between SWM and Helens Bay PHM. The Lough is well marked. WPT Carrickfergus 54°41'·71N 05°46'·16W, marks start of the buoyed chan to Belfast Hbr. It bears 121°/301° from/to Carrickfergus Marina, 1.7M. Carrickfergus Bk liable to shift. Deep draught yachts should not enter/leave before LW±2. Beware HSS ferry operation. WPT Bangor 54°41'·00N 05°40'·00W, 190°/1M to bkwtr lt. Rounding Orlock Pt beware Briggs Rks extending ¾M offshore.

LIGHTS AND MARKS Chan to Belfast Hbr is well marked/lit by buoys and bns. Beyond No 12 PHM bn it is dangerous to leave the chan. Carrickfergus is easily recognised by conspic castle to E of Marina. On Marina Bkwtr, 30m W of the ✲ QR 7m 3M, is a Dir lt 320°, Oc WRG 3s 5m 3M, (H24).

COMMUNICATIONS (Codes: Belfast 028) CGOC 91463933; ⚓ (08494) 22339; Police 101; Dr 91468521. HM Bangor 91453297; HM Belfast 90553012; Belfast VTS 9055 3504. 0845 600 8000 Bangor Marina Ch **80** M (H24); Bangor HM Ch 11 (H24). Royal N of Ireland YC (at Cultra) Ch **16**; 11 (H24) 80. *Belfast Port Control* (at Milewater Basin) Ch **12** 16 (H24); VTS provides info on request to vessels in port area. The greater part of Belfast Lough is under radar surveillance. Carrickfergus Marina Ch M, 80, M2.

FACILITIES Anti-clockwise around the Lough:

CARRICKFERGUS Marina www.carrickfergus.org/site/marina ☎93366666; entry HW±2; 300 inc ♥ £2.50 (2nd night free), short stay (max 6 hrs) £1.00 (min charge £7.35) ⚒ ⚓ ⬥ ⎙ Ⓔ. **Carrick SC** ☎351402, ⚓ ⚓⚓◡◟. **Hbr:** 10◡ ⚓ ⌷(45t).

Town ✉ Ⓑ ⚒ ✕ ⚡ ✈ (Belfast).

BELFAST Abercorn Basin www.belfast-harbour.co.uk 40◡ £15<10m>£25<12m LOA; short stay (5 hrs) £8; ⚓ ⬥ 🆆🅲.

City all facilities, ⚡ ✈.

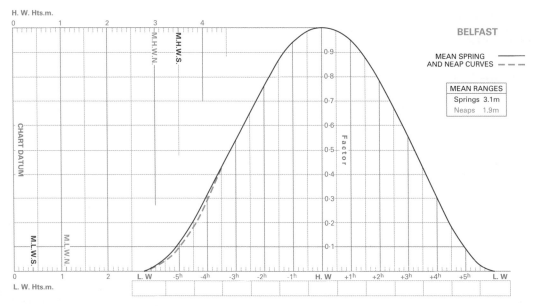

BELFAST

MEAN SPRING ———
AND NEAP CURVES – – –

MEAN RANGES	
Springs	3.1m
Neaps	1.9m

H. W. Hts.m.

L. W. Hts.m.

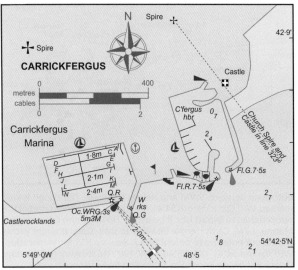

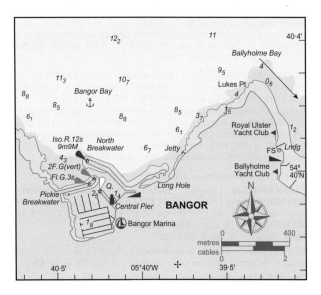

Ferries: Stranraer; 6/week; 2½ hrs; Stena (www.stenaline.co.uk). Liverpool; 2/day; 8hrs.

CULTRA Royal North of Ireland YC ☎9042 8041, ⚓⚓⚓⚓⚓⚓ ⚓(½M)⚓⚓⚓⚓⚓.

Town ⚓⚓⚓⚓⚓⚓⚓⚓⚓⚓.

BANGOR Bangor Marina ⚓ www.quaymarinas.com ☎9145 3297, 550⚓+40⚓ £2·55, ⚓⚓⚓⚓⚓⚓⚓⚓⚓⚓⚓⚓(40t) ⚓ Diving ⚓. **Todd Chart Agency** ☎9146 6640, ACA ⚓.

Town ⚓⚓⚓⚓⚓⚓⚓ (Belfast).

BALLYHOLME BAY Ballyholme YC ☎9127 1467, ⚓⚓; **Royal Ulster YC** ☎9127 0568, ⚓⚓⚓.

GROOMSPORT BAY HM ☎9127 8040, ⚓⚓⚓.

Cockle Island Boat Club ⚓⚓⚓⚓⚓.

HARBOURS BETWEEN BELFAST AND STRANGFORD LOUGHS

DONAGHADEE, Down, 54°38′·71N 05°31′·85W. ⚓⚓⚓⚓⚓⚓⚓. AC 1753, 5612. HW +0025 on Dover; see 6.16; ML no data; Duration 0615. Excellent shelter and basic facilities in tiny marina, access HW±4 over sill; covers approx 1·1m at half tide. Appr on about 275° on ldg marks, orange △s to tricky ent with sharp 90° port turn into marina (pilots available). Appr in strong winds or at night not advised. 3ca to the N, the Old Hbr is small and very full; scend often sets in. Beware rocky reef with less than 2m extends 1·5ca ENE from S pier hd. Max depth in hbr is approx 2·5m, dries at SW end; best berth alongside SE quay. S pier lt, Iso WR 4s 17m 18/14M, W shore–326°, R326°–shore. HM ☎9188 2377. Police 101. Facilities: **Copelands Marina** ☎9188 2184, mob 07802 363382; VHF Ch **16** 11 80; ⚓ for 6 ⚓⚓⚓ (20t). **Old Hbr** ⚓ £4. **Town** ⚓⚓⚓⚓⚓⚓⚓⚓ ⚓⚓ (Bangor), ✈ (Belfast).

PORTAVOGIE, Down, 54°27′·45N 05°26′·08W. ⚓⚓⚓⚓⚓. AC 2156, 5612. HW +0016 on Dover; ML 2·6m; Duration 0620. See 6.17. Good shelter, but hbr so full of FVs as to risk damage; best only for overnight or emergency. Entrance dangerous in strong onshore winds. Beware Plough Rks to SE marked by PHM buoy, Fl (2) R 10s, and McCammon Rks to NE of ent. Keep in W sector of outer bkwtr lt, Iso WRG 5s 9m 9M, shore-G-258°-W-275°-R-348°. Inner bkwtr 2 FG (vert) 6m 4M. Monitor VHF Ch **14** on entry/exit. (Mon-Fri: 0900-1700LT). HM ☎(028) 4277 1470. Facilities: ⚓⚓ (on central quay) ⚓⚓⚓. **Town** ⚓⚓⚓⚓⚓⚓⚓.

STANDARD TIME (UT)
For Summer Time add ONE hour in **non-shaded areas**

BELFAST LAT 54°36′N LONG 5°55′W
TIMES AND HEIGHTS OF HIGH AND LOW WATERS

Dates in red are **SPRINGS**
Dates in blue are NEAPS

YEAR 2016

N Ireland

JANUARY

Day	Time m	Time m	Time m	Time m		Day	Time m	Time m	Time m	Time m
1 F	0336 3.1	0925 1.1	1553 3.4	2150 0.9		16 SA	0320 3.3	0917 0.7	1536 3.6	2159 0.6
2 SA	0426 3.0	1019 1.2	1644 3.3	2248 1.0		17 SU	0420 3.2	1016 0.9	1637 3.4	2306 0.7
3 SU	0519 3.0	1126 1.3	1738 3.2	2356 1.1		18 M	0526 3.2	1125 0.9	1749 3.3	
4 M	0616 3.0	1238 1.3	1836 3.1			19 TU	0021 0.8	0640 3.1	1244 1.0	1913 3.2
5 TU	0101 1.1	0716 3.0	1340 1.2	1938 3.1		20 W	0130 0.8	0751 3.2	1356 0.9	2025 3.2
6 W	0158 1.0	0820 3.1	1434 1.1	2039 3.2		21 TH	0232 0.7	0853 3.3	1500 0.8	2125 3.3
7 TH	0247 0.9	0915 3.2	1521 0.9	2131 3.3		22 F	0327 0.7	0947 3.5	1554 0.6	2216 3.4
8 F	0330 0.8	0959 3.4	1603 0.8	2214 3.4		23 SA	0416 0.6	1035 3.6	1641 0.6	2303 3.4
9 SA	0411 0.7	1037 3.5	1643 0.7	2251 3.4		24 SU	0459 0.6	1119 3.7	1723 0.5	2346 3.3
10 SU	0451 0.7	1108 3.6	1722 0.6	2326 3.4		25 M	0540 0.6	1200 3.7	1802 0.5	
11 M	0530 0.6	1141 3.6	1802 0.5			26 TU	0026 3.3	0617 0.7	1239 3.7	1837 0.5
12 TU	0004 3.5	0610 0.6	1220 3.7	1842 0.4		27 W	0103 3.2	0652 0.7	1317 3.7	1911 0.6
13 W	0047 3.4	0652 0.6	1304 3.7	1925 0.4		28 TH	0139 3.2	0726 0.8	1355 3.6	1945 0.6
14 TH	0135 3.4	0737 0.6	1351 3.7	2011 0.4		29 F	0218 3.2	0802 0.8	1435 3.5	2021 0.7
15 F	0226 3.4	0825 0.7	1442 3.7	2102 0.5		30 SA	0259 3.1	0842 0.8	1518 3.4	2103 0.8
						31 SU	0345 3.1	0927 1.0	1604 3.3	2149 0.9

FEBRUARY

Day	Time m	Time m	Time m	Time m		Day	Time m	Time m	Time m	Time m
1 M	0434 3.0	1020 1.1	1655 3.1	2245 1.1		16 TU	0458 3.1	1102 0.8	1730 3.2	2359 0.9
2 TU	0529 2.9	1131 1.2	1752 3.0			17 W	0613 3.1	1226 0.9	1859 3.0	
3 W	0001 1.1	0627 2.9	1258 1.2	1854 2.9		18 TH	0113 0.9	0733 3.1	1343 0.8	2015 3.0
4 TH	0121 1.1	0731 2.9	1403 1.1	1958 3.0		19 F	0219 0.8	0839 3.2	1451 0.7	2115 3.1
5 F	0219 1.0	0835 3.1	1456 0.9	2100 3.1		20 SA	0318 0.7	0933 3.4	1547 0.6	2205 3.2
6 SA	0309 0.8	0928 3.2	1542 0.7	2148 3.2		21 SU	0406 0.7	1020 3.5	1631 0.5	2249 3.2
7 SU	0352 0.7	1008 3.4	1624 0.5	2228 3.3		22 M	0447 0.6	1103 3.6	1707 0.4	2330 3.2
8 M	0433 0.5	1044 3.5	1704 0.3	2306 3.4		23 TU	0522 0.6	1142 3.6	1740 0.4	
9 TU	0512 0.5	1121 3.6	1743 0.3	2346 3.4		24 W	0006 3.2	0555 0.6	1218 3.6	1811 0.5
10 W	0552 0.4	1203 3.7	1824 0.2			25 TH	0039 3.2	0626 0.6	1252 3.5	1841 0.5
11 TH	0030 3.4	0633 0.4	1249 3.7	1906 0.2		26 F	0110 3.2	0656 0.6	1326 3.5	1912 0.6
12 F	0118 3.4	0718 0.4	1337 3.7	1951 0.3		27 SA	0143 3.2	0729 0.6	1403 3.4	1946 0.6
13 SA	0208 3.4	0804 0.4	1427 3.7	2040 0.4		28 SU	0220 3.2	0806 0.7	1440 3.4	2024 0.6
14 SU	0300 3.3	0855 0.5	1520 3.5	2134 0.5		29 M	0258 3.1	0848 0.8	1521 3.2	2107 0.8
15 M	0356 3.2	0952 0.7	1619 3.4	2240 0.7						

MARCH

Day	Time m	Time m	Time m	Time m		Day	Time m	Time m	Time m	Time m
1 TU	0341 3.0	0935 0.9	1610 3.1	2157 0.9		16 W	0433 3.2	1043 0.7	1716 3.0	2338 0.9
2 W	0435 2.9	1034 1.1	1710 2.9	2259 1.1		17 TH	0545 3.0	1210 0.8	1846 2.9	
3 TH	0539 2.8	1213 1.2	1815 2.8			18 F	0053 1.0	0710 3.0	1327 0.8	2000 2.9
4 F	0039 1.1	0645 2.8	1333 1.0	1921 2.9		19 SA	0203 0.9	0818 3.1	1436 0.7	2058 3.0
5 SA	0152 1.0	0751 2.9	1430 0.8	2025 3.0		20 SU	0303 0.8	0913 3.3	1532 0.5	2147 3.1
6 SU	0245 0.8	0850 3.1	1518 0.5	2118 3.2		21 M	0352 0.7	0959 3.4	1613 0.5	2229 3.2
7 M	0331 0.6	0936 3.3	1601 0.3	2202 3.3		22 TU	0430 0.6	1041 3.5	1645 0.4	2307 3.2
8 TU	0412 0.5	1018 3.5	1642 0.2	2243 3.4		23 W	0501 0.6	1119 3.5	1714 0.5	2342 3.2
9 W	0451 0.3	1100 3.6	1721 0.1	2327 3.5		24 TH	0531 0.6	1153 3.4	1743 0.5	
10 TH	0531 0.3	1145 3.7	1801 0.1			25 F	0012 3.2	0600 0.6	1225 3.4	1811 0.5
11 F	0012 3.5	0612 0.2	1233 3.7	1843 0.1		26 SA	0039 3.2	0629 0.6	1256 3.4	1842 0.5
12 SA	0101 3.5	0657 0.2	1324 3.7	1929 0.2		27 SU	0108 3.2	0701 0.6	1329 3.4	1915 0.6
13 SU	0151 3.5	0744 0.3	1415 3.6	2018 0.3		28 M	0140 3.2	0737 0.6	1404 3.3	1952 0.6
14 M	0242 3.4	0835 0.4	1509 3.5	2112 0.5		29 TU	0214 3.2	0816 0.7	1443 3.2	2034 0.7
15 TU	0334 3.3	0932 0.5	1606 3.3	2217 0.8		30 W	0253 3.1	0901 0.8	1531 3.1	2121 0.9
						31 TH	0341 3.0	0955 0.9	1632 2.9	2219 1.1

APRIL

Day	Time m	Time m	Time m	Time m		Day	Time m	Time m	Time m	Time m
1 F	0447 2.9	1110 1.0	1741 2.8	2334 1.1		16 SA	0026 1.0	0638 3.0	1301 0.7	1937 2.9
2 SA	0602 2.8	1259 0.9	1848 2.9			17 SU	0134 1.0	0749 3.1	1407 0.7	2034 3.0
3 SU	0117 1.1	1126 2.9	1400 0.7	1952 3.0		18 M	0236 0.9	0845 3.2	1501 0.6	2121 3.1
4 M	0217 0.9	0813 3.1	1451 0.4	2048 3.2		19 TU	0326 0.8	0932 3.3	1542 0.5	2203 3.1
5 TU	0305 0.6	0906 3.3	1535 0.2	2135 3.4		20 W	0405 0.7	1014 3.4	1614 0.5	2240 3.2
6 W	0348 0.4	0953 3.5	1616 0.1	2221 3.5		21 TH	0437 0.6	1051 3.4	1644 0.5	2314 3.2
7 TH	0428 0.3	1039 3.7	1656 0.0	2306 3.6		22 F	0506 0.6	1125 3.4	1714 0.6	2344 3.2
8 F	0509 0.2	1127 3.7	1738 0.0	2354 3.6		23 SA	0536 0.6	1155 3.3	1744 0.6	
9 SA	0552 0.2	1217 3.7	1822 0.1			24 SU	0010 3.3	0606 0.6	1225 3.3	1815 0.6
10 SU	0043 3.6	0637 0.2	1309 3.7	1908 0.2		25 M	0038 3.3	0638 0.6	1257 3.3	1849 0.6
11 M	0134 3.6	0726 0.2	1402 3.6	1958 0.4		26 TU	0109 3.3	0713 0.6	1333 3.3	1927 0.7
12 TU	0224 3.5	0817 0.3	1455 3.4	2052 0.6		27 W	0145 3.3	0752 0.6	1415 3.2	2009 0.7
13 W	0315 3.4	0915 0.5	1552 3.2	2157 0.8		28 TH	0225 3.3	0837 0.7	1504 3.1	2056 0.9
14 TH	0410 3.3	1026 0.6	1700 3.0	2313 1.0		29 F	0312 3.2	0929 0.8	1603 3.0	2152 1.0
15 F	0515 3.1	1148 0.7	1826 2.9			30 SA	0410 3.0	1036 0.9	1710 2.9	2258 1.1

Chart Datum: 2·01 metres below Ordnance Datum (Belfast). HAT is 3·9 metres above Chart Datum.

FREE monthly updates. Register at www.reedsnauticalalmanac.co.uk

STANDARD TIME (UT)
For Summer Time add ONE hour in **non-shaded areas**

BELFAST LAT 54°36'N LONG 5°55'W
TIMES AND HEIGHTS OF HIGH AND LOW WATERS

Dates in red are **SPRINGS**
Dates in blue are NEAPS

YEAR 2016

MAY

Day	Time	m	Day	Time	m
1 SU	0521 / 1213 / 1818	3.0 / 0.8 / 2.9	**16** M	0054 / 0706 / 1325 / 2000	1.1 / 3.1 / 0.7 / 2.9
2 M	0022 / 0634 / 1324 / 1921	1.1 / 3.0 / 0.6 / 3.1	**17** TU	0154 / 0808 / 1419 / 2048	1.0 / 3.1 / 0.7 / 3.0
3 TU	0138 / 0740 / 1419 / 2019	0.9 / 3.2 / 0.4 / 3.2	**18** W	0248 / 0858 / 1503 / 2131	0.9 / 3.2 / 0.7 / 3.1
4 W	0233 / 0839 / 1506 / 2110	0.7 / 3.4 / 0.2 / 3.4	**19** TH	0332 / 0942 / 1540 / 2209	0.8 / 3.3 / 0.6 / 3.2
5 TH	0321 / 0931 / 1550 / 2159	0.5 / 3.5 / 0.1 / 3.5	**20** F	0409 / 1020 / 1613 / 2243	0.7 / 3.3 / 0.6 / 3.3
6 F ●	0406 / 1020 / 1633 / 2247	0.4 / 3.7 / 0.1 / 3.6	**21** SA ○	0441 / 1056 / 1646 / 2316	0.7 / 3.3 / 0.6 / 3.3
7 SA	0450 / 1110 / 1717 / 2336	0.3 / 3.7 / 0.1 / 3.7	**22** SU	0513 / 1128 / 1719 / 2345	0.7 / 3.3 / 0.6 / 3.4
8 SU	0535 / 1201 / 1803	0.2 / 3.7 / 0.2	**23** M	0547 / 1158 / 1754	0.6 / 3.3 / 0.7
9 M	0025 / 0622 / 1253 / 1851	3.7 / 0.2 / 3.6 / 0.4	**24** TU	0011 / 0621 / 1230 / 1829	3.4 / 0.6 / 3.3 / 0.7
10 TU	0116 / 0711 / 1346 / 1941	3.7 / 0.2 / 3.5 / 0.5	**25** W	0044 / 0657 / 1308 / 1908	3.4 / 0.6 / 3.3 / 0.7
11 W	0205 / 0803 / 1439 / 2036	3.6 / 0.3 / 3.5 / 0.7	**26** TH	0122 / 0736 / 1352 / 1950	3.4 / 0.6 / 3.2 / 0.8
12 TH	0254 / 0859 / 1534 / 2136	3.5 / 0.5 / 3.2 / 0.9	**27** F	0204 / 0819 / 1441 / 2038	3.4 / 0.6 / 3.2 / 0.8
13 F ◐	0345 / 1005 / 1635 / 2244	3.4 / 0.6 / 3.0 / 1.0	**28** SA	0252 / 0911 / 1538 / 2131	3.3 / 0.7 / 3.1 / 0.9
14 SA	0442 / 1117 / 1750 / 2351	3.2 / 0.7 / 2.9 / 1.1	**29** SU ◑	0346 / 1011 / 1641 / 2232	3.2 / 0.7 / 3.0 / 1.0
15 SU	0549 / 1224 / 1902	3.1 / 0.7 / 2.9	**30** M	0448 / 1125 / 1748 / 2340	3.2 / 0.7 / 3.0 / 1.0
			31 TU	0559 / 1243 / 1852	3.2 / 0.6 / 3.1

JUNE

Day	Time	m	Day	Time	m
1 W	0054 / 0710 / 1345 / 1952	0.9 / 3.3 / 0.5 / 3.2	**16** TH	0205 / 0811 / 1422 / 2051	1.0 / 3.1 / 0.8 / 3.1
2 TH	0201 / 0815 / 1438 / 2048	0.8 / 3.4 / 0.4 / 3.4	**17** F	0255 / 0904 / 1505 / 2134	0.9 / 3.1 / 0.8 / 3.2
3 F	0257 / 0912 / 1528 / 2140	0.6 / 3.5 / 0.3 / 3.5	**18** SA	0339 / 0948 / 1544 / 2213	0.8 / 3.2 / 0.7 / 3.3
4 SA	0349 / 1005 / 1615 / 2230	0.4 / 3.6 / 0.3 / 3.6	**19** SU	0416 / 1028 / 1620 / 2249	0.7 / 3.3 / 0.7 / 3.3
5 SU ●	0437 / 1056 / 1701 / 2319	0.3 / 3.6 / 0.3 / 3.7	**20** M ○	0452 / 1103 / 1657 / 2321	0.7 / 3.3 / 0.7 / 3.4
6 M	0524 / 1146 / 1749	0.3 / 3.6 / 0.4	**21** TU	0528 / 1134 / 1734 / 2347	0.6 / 3.3 / 0.7 / 3.4
7 TU	0008 / 0611 / 1237 / 1836	3.7 / 0.3 / 3.5 / 0.5	**22** W	0605 / 1206 / 1813	0.6 / 3.3 / 0.7
8 W	0057 / 0659 / 1328 / 1926	3.7 / 0.3 / 3.4 / 0.6	**23** TH	0020 / 0642 / 1245 / 1852	3.5 / 0.5 / 3.3 / 0.7
9 TH	0144 / 0747 / 1418 / 2017	3.7 / 0.4 / 3.3 / 0.7	**24** F	0101 / 0722 / 1330 / 1935	3.5 / 0.5 / 3.3 / 0.7
10 F	0231 / 0838 / 1508 / 2110	3.6 / 0.5 / 3.1 / 0.9	**25** SA	0145 / 0805 / 1419 / 2021	3.5 / 0.5 / 3.2 / 0.7
11 SA	0319 / 0933 / 1600 / 2207	3.5 / 0.6 / 3.0 / 1.0	**26** SU	0232 / 0853 / 1513 / 2111	3.5 / 0.5 / 3.2 / 0.8
12 SU ◐	0408 / 1036 / 1656 / 2308	3.4 / 0.7 / 2.9 / 1.1	**27** M ◑	0324 / 0948 / 1612 / 2207	3.4 / 0.6 / 3.1 / 0.8
13 M	0502 / 1139 / 1756	3.2 / 0.8 / 2.9	**28** TU	0421 / 1053 / 1716 / 2310	3.3 / 0.6 / 3.1 / 0.9
14 TU	0009 / 0600 / 1239 / 1902	1.1 / 3.1 / 0.8 / 2.9	**29** W	0527 / 1206 / 1822	3.3 / 0.6 / 3.1
15 W	0108 / 0706 / 1334 / 2001	1.1 / 3.1 / 0.8 / 3.0	**30** TH	0021 / 0641 / 1316 / 1927	0.9 / 3.3 / 0.6 / 3.2

JULY

Day	Time	m	Day	Time	m
1 F	0135 / 0755 / 1417 / 2029	0.8 / 3.3 / 0.5 / 3.3	**16** SA	0218 / 0819 / 1432 / 2054	1.0 / 3.0 / 0.9 / 3.1
2 SA	0240 / 0859 / 1511 / 2125	0.7 / 3.4 / 0.5 / 3.5	**17** SU	0308 / 0916 / 1516 / 2142	0.9 / 3.1 / 0.8 / 3.2
3 SU	0337 / 0955 / 1602 / 2217	0.5 / 3.4 / 0.4 / 3.6	**18** M	0351 / 1002 / 1557 / 2221	0.8 / 3.2 / 0.7 / 3.3
4 M ●	0428 / 1046 / 1650 / 2305	0.4 / 3.5 / 0.5 / 3.7	**19** TU ○	0431 / 1039 / 1636 / 2253	0.6 / 3.3 / 0.6 / 3.4
5 TU	0516 / 1134 / 1736 / 2352	0.3 / 3.4 / 0.5 / 3.7	**20** W	0509 / 1111 / 1715 / 2322	0.5 / 3.3 / 0.6 / 3.5
6 W	0601 / 1221 / 1822	0.3 / 3.4 / 0.6	**21** TH	0546 / 1144 / 1754 / 2357	0.5 / 3.3 / 0.6 / 3.5
7 TH	0038 / 0644 / 1308 / 1906	3.7 / 0.4 / 3.3 / 0.7	**22** F	0625 / 1223 / 1834	0.5 / 3.3 / 0.6
8 F	0122 / 0727 / 1353 / 1950	3.7 / 0.4 / 3.2 / 0.8	**23** SA	0038 / 0704 / 1308 / 1915	3.6 / 0.4 / 3.3 / 0.6
9 SA	0206 / 0808 / 1437 / 2034	3.6 / 0.5 / 3.1 / 0.8	**24** SU	0124 / 0746 / 1357 / 2000	3.6 / 0.4 / 3.3 / 0.6
10 SU	0250 / 0851 / 1523 / 2119	3.5 / 0.6 / 3.1 / 0.9	**25** M	0212 / 0832 / 1449 / 2049	3.6 / 0.4 / 3.3 / 0.6
11 M	0335 / 0937 / 1610 / 2209	3.4 / 0.7 / 3.0 / 1.0	**26** TU ◑	0303 / 0924 / 1546 / 2143	3.5 / 0.5 / 3.2 / 0.7
12 TU ◑	0423 / 1032 / 1700 / 2310	3.3 / 0.9 / 2.9 / 1.1	**27** W	0359 / 1024 / 1647 / 2244	3.4 / 0.6 / 3.2 / 0.8
13 W	0515 / 1138 / 1753	3.1 / 0.9 / 2.9	**28** TH	0502 / 1137 / 1754 / 2358	3.3 / 0.7 / 3.1 / 0.9
14 TH	0017 / 0611 / 1244 / 1851	1.1 / 3.0 / 1.0 / 2.9	**29** F	0620 / 1255 / 1907	3.2 / 0.7 / 3.2
15 F	0121 / 0713 / 1341 / 1953	1.1 / 3.0 / 1.0 / 3.0	**30** SA	0119 / 0744 / 1401 / 2016	0.9 / 3.1 / 0.7 / 3.3
			31 SU	0229 / 0853 / 1459 / 2115	0.7 / 3.2 / 0.7 / 3.4

AUGUST

Day	Time	m	Day	Time	m
1 M	0329 / 0949 / 1551 / 2206	0.6 / 3.3 / 0.6 / 3.5	**16** TU	0326 / 0934 / 1534 / 2149	0.7 / 3.2 / 0.7 / 3.3
2 TU ●	0420 / 1038 / 1638 / 2253	0.5 / 3.3 / 0.6 / 3.6	**17** W	0408 / 1013 / 1614 / 2223	0.5 / 3.3 / 0.6 / 3.5
3 W	0505 / 1123 / 1722 / 2336	0.4 / 3.3 / 0.6 / 3.7	**18** TH ○	0446 / 1047 / 1653 / 2256	0.4 / 3.4 / 0.6 / 3.6
4 TH	0546 / 1205 / 1803	0.4 / 3.3 / 0.6	**19** F	0524 / 1122 / 1731 / 2334	0.3 / 3.4 / 0.5 / 3.6
5 F	0018 / 0624 / 1246 / 1840	3.7 / 0.4 / 3.2 / 0.7	**20** SA	0602 / 1202 / 1810	0.3 / 3.4 / 0.5
6 SA	0058 / 0658 / 1324 / 1916	3.6 / 0.5 / 3.2 / 0.7	**21** SU	0017 / 0641 / 1248 / 1852	3.7 / 0.2 / 3.4 / 0.5
7 SU	0138 / 0732 / 1404 / 1952	3.6 / 0.5 / 3.1 / 0.8	**22** M	0104 / 0723 / 1336 / 1937	3.7 / 0.3 / 3.4 / 0.5
8 M	0218 / 0807 / 1445 / 2030	3.5 / 0.6 / 3.1 / 0.8	**23** TU	0153 / 0808 / 1428 / 2026	3.7 / 0.4 / 3.4 / 0.6
9 TU	0300 / 0846 / 1529 / 2113	3.4 / 0.7 / 3.1 / 0.9	**24** W	0245 / 0859 / 1523 / 2120	3.6 / 0.5 / 3.3 / 0.7
10 W ◐	0345 / 0930 / 1617 / 2203	3.3 / 0.8 / 3.0 / 1.1	**25** TH ◑	0341 / 0958 / 1623 / 2222	3.4 / 0.7 / 3.2 / 0.8
11 TH	0434 / 1023 / 1709 / 2309	3.1 / 1.0 / 3.0 / 1.2	**26** F	0446 / 1114 / 1731 / 2343	3.2 / 0.9 / 3.1 / 0.9
12 F	0529 / 1134 / 1805	3.0 / 1.1 / 2.9	**27** SA	0609 / 1239 / 1851	0.9 / 0.9 / 3.1
13 SA	0037 / 0630 / 1300 / 1905	1.2 / 2.9 / 1.1 / 2.9	**28** SU	0109 / 0738 / 1349 / 2004	0.9 / 3.0 / 0.8 / 3.2
14 SU	0144 / 0735 / 1401 / 2009	1.1 / 2.9 / 1.0 / 3.0	**29** M	0221 / 0846 / 1450 / 2103	0.8 / 3.1 / 0.8 / 3.4
15 M	0239 / 0842 / 1451 / 2106	0.9 / 3.0 / 0.9 / 3.2	**30** TU	0322 / 0940 / 1542 / 2153	0.6 / 3.2 / 0.7 / 3.5
			31 W	0411 / 1026 / 1626 / 2238	0.5 / 3.3 / 0.7 / 3.6

Chart Datum: 2·01 metres below Ordnance Datum (Belfast). HAT is 3·9 metres above Chart Datum.

》》 FREE monthly updates. Register at 《《
www.reedsnauticalalmanac.co.uk

BELFAST   LAT 54°36'N   LONG 5°55'W
TIMES AND HEIGHTS OF HIGH AND LOW WATERS

STANDARD TIME (UT)
For Summer Time add ONE hour in **non-shaded areas**

Dates in red are **SPRINGS**
Dates in blue are NEAPS

YEAR 2016

N Ireland

SEPTEMBER

Day	Time	m	Day	Time	m
1 TH	0451	0.4	16	0421	0.3
	1108	3.3		1022	3.5
	1705	0.7	F	1628	0.5
●	2318	3.6	○	2232	3.7
2 F	0526	0.4	17	0458	0.2
	1146	3.2	SA	1101	3.5
	1740	0.7		1706	0.5
	2356	3.6		2314	3.7
3 SA	0557	0.5	18	0536	0.2
	1221	3.2	SU	1143	3.6
	1812	0.7		1746	0.4
				2359	3.8
4 SU	0032	3.6	19	0616	0.2
	0626	0.6	M	1229	3.6
	1254	3.2		1829	0.4
	1842	0.7			
5 M	0108	3.5	20	0048	3.8
	0656	0.6	TU	0659	0.3
	1328	3.2		1319	3.6
	1914	0.8		1915	0.4
6 TU	0145	3.5	21	0140	3.7
	0728	0.6	W	0746	0.4
	1406	3.2		1410	3.5
	1950	0.8		2005	0.5
7 W	0224	3.4	22	0233	3.6
	0805	0.7	TH	0837	0.6
	1447	3.2		1504	3.4
	2031	0.9		2100	0.6
8 TH	0305	3.3	23	0331	3.4
	0847	0.8	F	0936	0.8
	1532	3.1	◑	1603	3.3
	2117	1.0		2205	0.8
9 F	0352	3.1	24	0437	3.2
	0934	1.0	SA	1055	1.0
◑	1623	3.0		1711	3.2
	2213	1.1		2331	0.9
10 SA	0449	3.0	25	0603	3.0
	1033	1.2	SU	1222	1.1
	1722	2.9		1832	3.2
	2342	1.2			
11 SU	0552	2.9	26	0056	0.9
	1205	1.3	M	0728	3.0
	1824	2.9		1335	1.1
				1946	3.3
12 M	0111	1.1	27	0209	0.8
	0658	2.9	TU	0832	3.1
	1330	1.2		1438	1.0
	1927	3.0		2045	3.4
13 TU	0210	0.9	28	0310	0.6
	0804	3.0	W	0923	3.2
	1424	1.0		1530	0.8
	2026	3.2		2134	3.5
14 W	0259	0.7	29	0356	0.6
	0900	3.2	TH	1007	3.3
	1510	0.8		1611	0.7
	2113	3.4		2217	3.6
15 TH	0342	0.5	30	0431	0.5
	0943	3.3	F	1047	3.3
	1550	0.6		1645	0.7
	2153	3.5		2257	3.6

OCTOBER

Day	Time	m	Day	Time	m
1 SA	0459	0.6	16	0431	0.2
	1123	3.3	SU	1040	3.7
	1715	0.7		1641	0.4
●	2333	3.6	○	2257	3.8
2 SU	0527	0.6	17	0510	0.2
	1155	3.3	M	1125	3.7
	1744	0.8		1723	0.4
				2345	3.8
3 M	0005	3.5	18	0552	0.3
	0554	0.7	TU	1213	3.7
	1224	3.3		1808	0.4
	1812	0.8			
4 TU	0037	3.5	19	0036	3.8
	0623	0.7	W	0637	0.4
	1254	3.4		1303	3.7
	1844	0.8		1856	0.4
5 W	0111	3.5	20	0130	3.7
	0656	0.6	TH	0726	0.5
	1328	3.4		1355	3.7
	1919	0.8		1947	0.5
6 TH	0148	3.4	21	0224	3.6
	0732	0.8	F	0819	0.7
	1404	3.4		1448	3.6
	1958	0.9		2044	0.6
7 F	0227	3.3	22	0322	3.4
	0813	0.9	SA	0919	1.0
	1443	3.3	◑	1544	3.5
	2043	1.0		2150	0.8
8 SA	0312	3.2	23	0427	3.2
	0859	1.0	SU	1035	1.1
	1530	3.2		1649	3.3
	2135	1.1		2314	0.9
9 SU	0410	3.0	24	0548	3.0
	0954	1.2	M	1158	1.2
	1633	3.0		1806	3.3
◑	2243	1.2			
10 M	0517	2.9	25	0033	0.9
	1104	1.3	TU	0707	3.0
	1742	3.0		1309	1.2
				1919	3.3
11 TU	0032	1.2	26	0143	0.8
	0624	2.9	W	0809	3.1
	1249	1.3		1413	1.1
	1847	3.0		2019	3.4
12 W	0136	1.0	27	0243	0.8
	0729	3.0	TH	0859	3.2
	1352	1.1		1507	1.0
	1948	3.2		2109	3.5
13 TH	0228	0.7	28	0328	0.7
	0826	3.2	F	0943	3.3
	1441	0.9		1548	0.9
	2041	3.4		2153	3.5
14 F	0312	0.5	29	0401	0.7
	0914	3.4	SA	1022	3.4
	1523	0.7		1622	0.8
	2127	3.6		2233	3.5
15 SA	0352	0.3	30	0429	0.7
	0957	3.6	SU	1058	3.4
	1602	0.5		1651	0.8
	2211	3.7	●	2308	3.5
			31	0458	0.7
			M	1129	3.4
				1720	0.8
				2340	3.5

NOVEMBER

Day	Time	m	Day	Time	m
1 TU	0527	0.8	16	0534	0.4
	1157	3.5	W	1158	3.9
	1750	0.8		1754	0.4
2 W	0010	3.5	17	0024	3.8
	0557	0.8	TH	0621	0.5
	1225	3.5		1249	3.9
	1821	0.8		1842	0.4
3 TH	0043	3.5	18	0118	3.7
	0630	0.8	F	0711	0.7
	1257	3.5		1339	3.8
	1856	0.8		1934	0.5
4 F	0118	3.4	19	0212	3.5
	0707	0.8	SA	0804	0.8
	1331	3.5		1431	3.7
	1934	0.8		2029	0.6
5 SA	0157	3.3	20	0308	3.4
	0747	0.9	SU	0902	1.0
	1409	3.4		1524	3.6
	2017	0.9		2132	0.7
6 SU	0242	3.2	21	0408	3.2
	0833	1.0	M	1010	1.2
	1453	3.3	◑	1621	3.5
	2107	1.0		2245	0.9
7 M	0337	3.1	22	0519	3.0
	0926	1.2	TU	1123	1.2
	1548	3.2		1727	3.3
●	2208	1.1		2357	0.9
8 TU	0443	3.0	23	0633	3.0
	1029	1.3	W	1230	1.2
	1656	3.1		1840	3.3
	2328	1.1			
9 W	0551	3.0	24	0101	0.9
	1145	1.3	TH	0735	3.1
	1807	3.2		1333	1.2
				1944	3.3
10 TH	0052	1.1	25	0159	0.9
	0655	3.1	F	0828	3.2
	1306	1.2		1429	1.1
	1912	3.3		2038	3.4
11 F	0151	0.7	26	0248	0.9
	0754	3.3	SA	0914	3.3
	1404	1.0		1517	1.0
	2011	3.5		2125	3.4
12 SA	0239	0.6	27	0326	0.8
	0846	3.5	SU	0955	3.4
	1453	0.8		1555	0.9
	2103	3.6		2206	3.5
13 SU	0323	0.4	28	0400	0.8
	0934	3.6	M	1032	3.4
	1538	0.6		1628	0.9
	2153	3.8		2244	3.5
14 M	0406	0.3	29	0432	0.8
	1021	3.8	TU	1106	3.5
	1622	0.5		1700	0.8
○	2242	3.8	●	2318	3.5
15 TU	0449	0.3	30	0504	0.8
	1109	3.8	W	1137	3.5
	1707	0.4		1732	0.8
	2332	3.8		2349	3.4

DECEMBER

Day	Time	m	Day	Time	m
1 TH	0538	0.8	16	0012	3.7
	1205	3.6	F	0609	0.6
	1806	0.8		1234	3.9
				1833	0.4
2 F	0019	3.4	17	0104	3.6
	0612	0.8	SA	0658	0.7
	1233	3.6		1323	3.9
	1841	0.8		1922	0.4
3 SA	0053	3.4	18	0155	3.5
	0649	0.9	SU	0748	0.8
	1307	3.6		1411	3.8
	1918	0.8		2013	0.5
4 SU	0132	3.4	19	0247	3.3
	0729	0.9	M	0840	0.9
	1346	3.5		1500	3.7
	2000	0.8		2107	0.7
5 M	0217	3.3	20	0340	3.2
	0813	1.0	TU	0937	1.1
	1430	3.5		1550	3.6
	2046	0.8		2207	0.8
6 TU	0308	3.2	21	0435	3.1
	0903	1.1	W	1040	1.2
	1519	3.4		1644	3.4
	2141	0.9	◑	2311	0.9
7 W	0407	3.1	22	0536	3.0
	1000	1.1	TH	1144	1.2
	1617	3.3		1742	3.3
◑	2245	0.9			
8 TH	0513	3.1	23	0014	1.0
	1104	1.2	F	0643	3.0
	1724	3.3		1246	1.2
	2359	0.9		1848	3.2
9 F	0620	3.2	24	0112	1.0
	1215	1.1	SA	0747	3.0
	1835	3.3		1345	1.2
				1956	3.2
10 SA	0109	0.8	25	0205	1.0
	0722	3.3	SU	0841	3.1
	1326	1.0		1440	1.1
	1942	3.4		2053	3.2
11 SU	0208	0.6	26	0252	0.9
	0821	3.4	M	0927	3.3
	1426	0.8		1526	1.0
	2043	3.6		2140	3.3
12 M	0300	0.5	27	0332	0.9
	0914	3.6	TU	1008	3.4
	1520	0.7		1606	0.9
	2138	3.7		2221	3.4
13 TU	0348	0.5	28	0409	0.8
	1005	3.7	W	1045	3.5
	1609	0.5		1641	0.8
	2230	3.7		2259	3.4
14 W	0435	0.5	29	0445	0.8
	1055	3.8	TH	1120	3.5
	1657	0.4		1716	0.8
○	2321	3.7	●	2333	3.4
15 TH	0522	0.5	30	0521	0.8
	1144	3.9	F	1149	3.6
	1745	0.4		1751	0.7
			31	0001	3.4
			SA	0557	0.8
				1213	3.6
				1827	0.7

Chart Datum: 2·01 metres below Ordnance Datum (Belfast). HAT is 3·9 metres above Chart Datum.

》》 FREE monthly updates. Register at 《
www.reedsnauticalalmanac.co.uk 《

239

STRANGFORD LOUGH

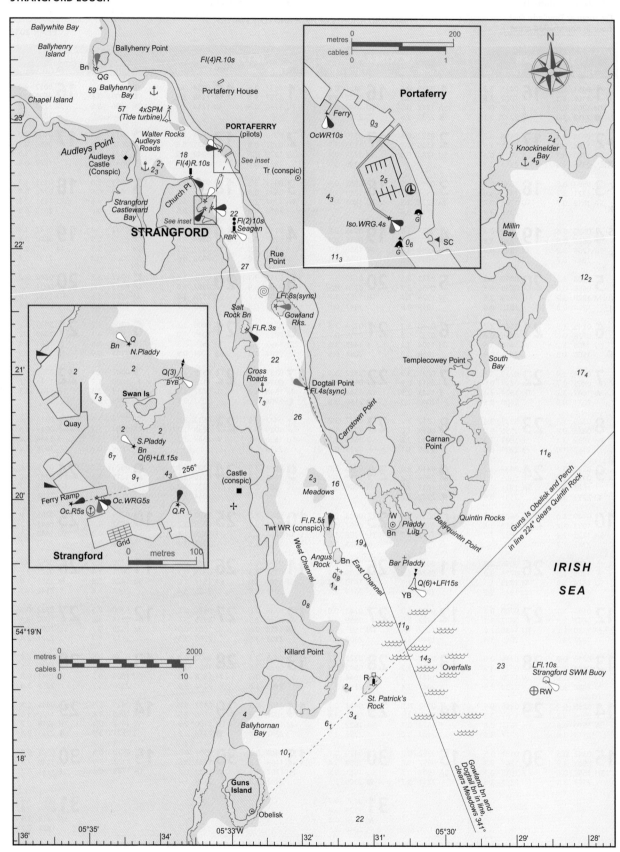

6.17 STRANGFORD LOUGH
Down 54°19'·33N 05°30'·85W (Narrows) ✿✿✿♧♧❀❀❀

CHARTS AC 2156, 2159, 5612; Imray C62, C69

TIDES Killard Pt 0000, Strangford Quay +0200 Dover; ML 2·0; Duration 0610

Standard Port BELFAST (←—)

Times				Height (metres)			
High Water		Low Water		MHWS	MHWN	MLWN	MLWS
0100	0700	0000	0600	3·5	3·0	1·1	0·4
1300	1900	1200	1800				
Differences STRANGFORD (The Narrows)							
+0147	+0157	+0148	+0208	+0·1	+0·1	−0·2	0·0
KILLARD POINT (Entr)							
+0011	+0021	+0005	+0025	+1·0	+0·8	+0·1	+0·1
QUOILE BARRIER							
+0150	+0200	+0150	+0300	+0·2	+0·2	−0·3	−0·1
KILLYLEAGH							
+0157	+0207	+0211	+0231	+0·3	+0·3	ND	ND
SOUTH ROCK							
+0023	+0023	+0025	+0025	+1·0	+0·8	+0·1	+0·1
PORTAVOGIE							
+0010	+0020	+0010	+0020	+1·2	+0·9	+0·3	+0·2

SHELTER Excellent; largest inlet on E coast. ⚓ in the Narrows at Cross Roads, off Strangford clear of moorings, in Audley Roads (in about 15m) and in Ballyhenry Bay. Limited ⚓ at Strangford; moorings may be available in Audley Roads (check with Sailing Club). Small marina at Portaferry, where stream runs fast; best to enter near slack water. Many good ⚓ (NB Marine Nature Reserve) and some ⚓s up the lough, by villages and YCs.

NAVIGATION WPT: SWM buoy, L Fl 10s, 54°18'·63N 05°28'·69W, 306°/2·04M to Angus Rk lt twr Fl R 5s 5M. Visitors should use E Chan. Disregard W Chan ≠ 320·5° shown on old editions of AC 2159. Beware St Patricks Rk, Bar Pladdy and Pladdy Lug; overfalls occur in the SE apprs and at the bar, which can be dangerous when ebb meets the NW set outside. Strong tidal streams (7kn at sp) in the Narrows. The bar is passable during the flood; best to enter on young flood or at slack water. The flood starts in the Narrows at HW Belfast −3½ and runs for about 6 hrs; the ebb starts at HW Belfast +2½. Beware car ferry between Strangford, S and E of Swan Is, and Portaferry. Swan Island, seen as a grassy mound at HW, is edged with rks and a reef extends 32m E ending at W bn, Q (3). Further up the lough, despite improved marks and lights, unmarked drying shoals (pladdies) abound; AC 2156 or equivalent is essential.

LIGHTS AND MARKS Off Strangford *Seagen* tide turbine consists of pile with cross beam 50m wide, 3.1m deep at LAT when submerged. Marked as IDM, Fl(2)10s it forms a 43m wide obstruction when raised for maintenance. Vessels should keep 50m clear – info at www.marineturbines.com. Further turbine 1¾Ca WNW of Walter Rks marked by 2 pair Y SPM; outer pr Fl(2) 10s, inner pr FlY 5s.

COMMUNICATIONS (Code 028) CGOC 91463933; Police 101; Medical Clinic 4488 1209. HM at Strangford Ferry Terminal 4488 1637. HM Ch 16 (Mon-Fri 0900-1700). Some YCs Ch 80 M.

FACILITIES Strangford, Portaferry and Killyleagh are easy to access and offer good shops, pubs and restaurants.
STRANGFORD ⚓ 25m Ⓥ pontoon, ⚓ ⚓; Cuan Inn ▮▸ Ⓓ.
Islander Marine ☎4488 1449, ◣ ▮▮ ⚓ ✕ ⓒ Ⓔ.
PORTAFERRY Marina portaferrymarina.co.uk, mob 7703 209780, ⚓(limited) £1·50, ⚓ ⤵ Ⓓ. Village ▮▮▮▮ ⊠ Ⓑ ▦ ✕ ⌂.
Cook St Pier (2ca S), limited ⚓, ⚓.
QUOILE RIVER: Quoile YC ☎4461 2266, ⚓ ◣ ⚓ ⚓.
KILLYLEAGH ⚓◣ ▮▮ Ⓓ▮ Kos ✕ Ⓖ⚓ (Irish Spars & Rigging ☎9751 2830) ▮ ▦ ⊠ Ⓑ ✕ ⌂.
Killyleagh YC ☎07801 291410, N of village.
East Down YC ☎4482 8375, ⚓ (about 1M NE of town).
RINGHADDY QUAY CC, ⚓ ⚓ drying, ⚓.
SKETRICK ISLAND In White Rk B,
Strangford Lough YC ☎9754 1883, ◣ ⚓ ⚓ ⚓ ⚓ ✕ ⌂.
Down CC, (Old Lightship to NW in Dorn) ⚓ ▮ ⌂.
KIRCUBBIN (tidal) ▮▮ Ⓓ▮ ⊠ Ⓑ ▦ ✕ ⌂.

6.18 ARDGLASS
Down 54°15'·63N 05°35'·96W ✿✿✿♧♧❀❀

CHARTS AC 2093, 633, 5612; Imray C62

TIDES HW +0025 Dover; ML 3·0; Duration 0620

Standard Port BELFAST (←—)

Times				Height (metres)			
High Water		Low Water		MHWS	MHWN	MLWN	MLWS
0100	0700	0000	0600	3·5	3·0	1·1	0·4
1300	1900	1200	1800				
Differences KILKEEL							
+0040	+0030	+0010	+0010	+1·2	+1·1	+0·4	+0·4
NEWCASTLE							
+0025	+0035	+0020	+0040	+1·6	+1·1	+0·4	+0·1
KILLOUGH HARBOUR							
0000	+0020	ND	ND	+1·8	+1·6	ND	ND
ARDGLASS							
+0010	+0015	+0005	+0010	+1·7	+1·2	+0·6	+0·3

SHELTER Good, except in strong winds from E to S. It is the only all-weather, all-tide shelter between Howth and Bangor. Phennick Cove/Ardglass marina is on W side of hbr, with depths 1·0m to 2·8m. Visitors should check depth of berth offered by marina against depth drawn. The busy fishing port is in South Hbr, with quays (2·1m) on inside of extended S pier. At NW end of hbr, old drying N Dock is also used by FVs.

NAVIGATION WPT 54°15'·30N 05°35'·32W, 131°/5ca to hbr ent. Appr 311° in W sector of WRG Dir lt. Depth in chan 2·4m. Off the tip of the inner breakwater the buoyed marina channel commences in a depth of 1.3m. It is marked by lit PHM and SHM (not shown on chartlet) and turns sharply to port to approach the marina on a heading of 230°. Do not cross the drying SW portion of inner bkwtr, marked by two unlit SCM perches.

LIGHTS AND MARKS Dir lt, 311°, conspic W tr at inner hbr, Iso WRG 4s 10m 8/7/5M, 308°-W-314°; reported hard to see against shore lts. S bkwtr Fl R 3s 10m 5M. W roof of shed on S bkwtr is conspic. If entering S Hbr, avoid Churn Rk, unlit SCM bn. Entrance to marina is buoyed. Castle, spire and water tr (off plan) are conspic to W.

COMMUNICATIONS (Code 028) CGOC 91463933; Police 101; Dr 9084 1242. HM 4484 1291, mob 07790 648274.

Monitor VHF Ch 12 on entry/exit. Marina Ch ⚓ 80.

FACILITIES
Ardglass Marina www.ardglassmarina.co.uk ☎4484 2332, ◣
(£8·00) 55 inc 22Ⓥ £2·40+⤵ £1/day, ⚓ Ⓓ ▮ Ⓓ.
Town ▮▮ ▮▮ ▮ ⊠ ▦ ✕ ⌂.

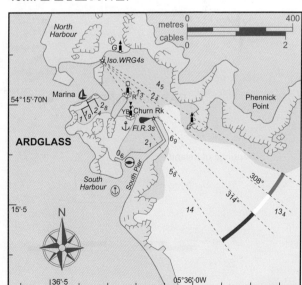

MINOR HARBOURS SOUTH OF ARDGLASS

DUNDRUM BAY, Down. AC 44, 5612. Tides see 6.18. This 8M wide bay to the W of St John's Pt is shoal to 5ca offshore and unsafe in onshore winds. The small drying hbr at **Newcastle** (54°11'·8N 05°53'·0W) is for occas use in fair weather. HM ☎(02843) 722804, mob 07803 832515. **Dundrum Hbr (54°14'·2N 05°49'·4W)** No longer used by commercial tfc and only to be used with caution, provides ⚓ in 2m for shoal draught; the bar carries about 0·3m. A steep sea can run at the bar in onshore winds. HW Dundrum is approx that of HW Liverpool; see also 6.18 Newcastle. *The Irish Cruising Club's Sailing Directions* are essential for the 1M long, buoyed approach channel. 2 lit DZ buoys offshore are part of the Ballykinler firing range, 2M E of hbr; R flag/lts indicate range active.

ANNALONG HBR, Down, 54°06'·50N 05°53'·65W. AC 44, 5621, 5612. Tides as Kilkeel, see 6.7. Slight silting rep't 2006. Entry HW ±2. Excellent shelter in small drying hbr, dredged to 1·5m 80m beyond pier with 30m pontoon (£12/craft), ⚓. Appr in W sector of S breakwater light, Oc WRG 5s 8m 9M, vis 204°-G-249°-W-309°-R-024°. Hug N side of the breakwater to avoid rocky shore to starboard. Surge gate at harbour entrance may be closed in SE winds (3R lts vert shown). IPTS shown at entrance. HM mob 07739 527036. Facilities: 🛒 🏠 ✉.

KILKEEL, Down, 54°03'·47N 05°59'·26W. AC 44, 2800, 5612. HW +0015 on Dover; ML 2·9m; Duration 0620. See 6.18. Do not appr in E-SW winds >F4. Inner basin is sheltered, but crowded by FVs; depth off quays approx 1m. Secure in inner basin and see HM. There are drying banks both sides of ent chan and SW gales form a sandbank across ent. This is dredged or slowly eroded in E winds. S bkwtr lt Fl WR 2s 8m 8M, 296°-R-313°-W-017°, storm sigs. Meeney's pier (N bkwtr) Fl G 3s 6m 2M. Monitor VHF Ch **12** on entry/exit. HM ☎(028 417) 62287. Facilities: ⚓ on quay, ℛ (between fish market and dock). ✕ ⚒ ⛽. **Town** (¾M) 🛢 ✉ 🛒 ⓞ ✕ 🏠.

6.19 CARLINGFORD LOUGH

Louth/Down **54°01'·25N 06°04'·30W** ❀❀◊◊❁❁❁

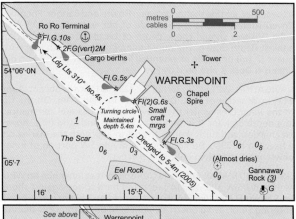
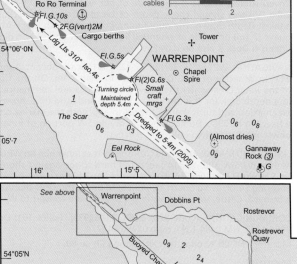

CHARTS AC 44, 2800, 5621, 5612; Imray C62

TIDES Cranfield Pt +0025 and Warrenpoint +0035 Dover; ML 2·9; Duration Cranfield Pt 0615, Warrenpoint 0540

Standard Port DUBLIN (NORTH WALL – AREA 12) (←)

Times				Height (metres)			
High Water		Low Water		MHWS	MHWN	MLWN	MLWS
0000	0700	0000	0500	4·1	3·4	1·5	0·7
1200	1900	1200	1700				
Differences CRANFIELD POINT							
–0027	–0011	+0005	–0010	+0·7	+0·9	+0·3	+0·2
WARRENPOINT							
–0020	–0010	+0025	+0035	+1·0	+0·7	+0·2	0·0
NEWRY (VICTORIA LOCK)							
+0005	+0015	+0045	Dries	+1·2	+0·9	+0·1	DR
DUNDALK (SOLDIERS POINT)							
–0010	0000	0000	+0045	+1·0	+0·8	+0·1	–0·1
DUNANY POINT							
–0028	–0018	–0008	–0006	+0·7	+0·9	ND	ND
RIVER BOYNE BAR							
–0005	0000	+0020	+0030	+0·4	+0·3	–0·1	–0·2
BALBRIGGAN							
–0021	–0015	+0010	+0002	+0·3	+0·2	ND	ND

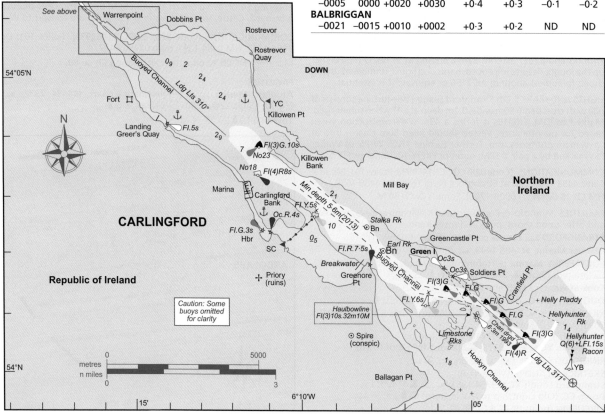

SHELTER

Carlingford Marina is protected on S side by sunken barge; depths 1·5m at LW (check with Marina). Appr from N with Nos 18 and 23 buoys in transit astern 012°, to clear the tail of Carlingford Bank (dries) and beware of marine farms in vicinity.

Carlingford Hbr (dries 2·2m), ⌇ at piers.

Warrenpoint has pontoons on NW side of breakwater (Fl G 3s); access dredged 1·1m. ⌄s clockwise from ent include: off Greenore Pt, between SW end of quay and bkwtr, in 3m clear of commercial traffic; off Greer's Quay in 2m; off Rostrevor Quay, Killowen Pt (YC) and off derelict pier at Greencastle Pt (beware rks). Limited space may be available for short-stay visiting craft in the mussel fishing complex (approx £15/night). Call at least 24 hours before arrival.

NAVIGATION WPT 54°00'·09N 06°02'·00W, (2½ ca S of Hellyhunter SCM lt buoy) 311°/1M to first chan buoys. The main chan is Carlingford Cut (6·3m), about 3ca SW of Cranfield Pt, and passing 2ca NE of Haulbowline lt ho. Drying rocks and shoals obstruct most of the entrance. Small craft should at all times keep clear of commercial shipping in the narrow dredged channel. The ent is impassable in strong on-shore winds. The NE bank is **Northern Ireland**, SW bank is **Republic of Ireland**.

The lough becomes choppy in S'ly winds and, due to the funnelling effect of the mountains, NW winds can cause a higher sea state within the lough than outside it.

Tides run up to 5kn off Greenore Pt through a channel with a minimum depth of 5.6m. Entry is impracticable against the ebb. Beware sudden squalls and waterspouts.

Extensive shellfish beds exist along the NE side of the lough; beware fishing vessels on both sides of the channel, and give them a wide berth.

LIGHTS AND MARKS Haulbowline Fl (3) 10s 32m 10M; granite tower. Ldg lts 310°26': both Oc 3s 7/12m 11M, vis 295°-325°; R △ front, ▽ rear, on framework trs. Greenore Pier Fl R 7·5s 10m 5M. Newry R: Ldg lts 310°, both Iso 4s 5/15m 2M, stone columns. Channel from Green Is to Warren Pt marked by lit lateral buoys.

COMMUNICATIONS (Code Greenore/Carlingford 042; Warrenpoint 028). MRCC (01) 6620922/3 or (02891) 463933; Irish ⊖: Dundalk (042) 34114; Dr (042) 73110; ℍ Newry (028) 3026 5511, Dundalk (042) 34701; Police Newry 101, Dundalk (042) 9373102.

Greenore (*Ferry Greenore*) Ch 12 16 (HJ). Carlingford Marina Ch M 16. Warrenpoint Ch 12 16 (H24); call Ch 12 at By No. 23 to enter dredged chan. Dundalk Ch 14 16 (HW±3).

FACILITIES **Carlingford Marina** www.carlingfordmarina.com ☎0429373072, mob 0872 321567, ⌇ 290 inc ♥ €4.00 (min€20), short stay <5hrs €12.50, ⌷ ▲(0900-2100) ☒(50t) ⌇ ✕ ✕ ⌷ @.

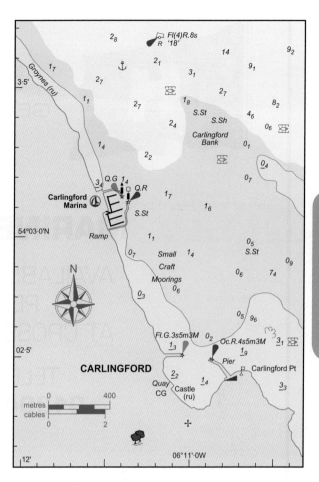

Services ⚓ ☎0872 301319, ⚑ ☎(048)44 828882, Divers,.

Carlingford YC ☎(041) 685 1951, ⚓ ⬥ ⚒ ⌷.

Carlingford Hbr ⌇ ⌇ ⬥ Kos ✕ ⚓ ⌷.

Village ⌷ ⌷ ✉ ⑧ ⌷ ✕ ⌷.

Warrenpoint HM ☎(02841) 752878; ⚓ (but no access at LW) ⌇ ⚒ ⬥ ⬥ ✉ also at Rostrevor, ⑧ also Dundalk, ⇆ (Dundalk, Newry), ✈ (Dublin).

MINOR HARBOURS AND ANCHORAGES BETWEEN CARLINGFORD LOUGH AND LAMBAY ISLAND

PORT ORIEL, Louth, **53°47'·94N 06°13'·37W**. AC 44. Tides see 6.19 (Dunany Pt). Good shelter in small new harbour except in strong ENE winds when a dangerous scend can enter the harbour. Entry reported to be difficult in strong NE winds. Approach from NE on leading marks 174·9°, front and rear Fl 3s (sync) avoiding Wk 1·6m 2.7ca from entrance; Pier Head Light Mo(A) R 9s. ⌇ on pier in 4m, €25.00/craft, or dry out in inner harbour. HM ☎087 2628777. No facilities; ⬥ by tanker, ⌷ in Clogher Head village (1·2M).

BALBRIGGAN, Dublin, **53°36'·76N 06°10'·84W**. AC 44, 1468. Tides see 6.19. Good shelter in small harbour which dries about 1m. Harbour often crowded with FVs and is not recommended for yachts. Approach from E to open the outer harbour; enter from NE but beware severe shoaling on W side of harbour mouth and on both sides of outer harbour. Thence to ⌇ on SE quay in inner harbour. Lt, Fl (3) WRG 10s 12m 13/10M, conspic W tr on East breakwater head, vis 159°-G193°-W-288°-R-305°. Facilities: ⚒ ⬥ (by tanker from Skerries) ⌇ ⬥ (HW±2) ⌷ ✕ ⌷.

SKERRIES, Dublin, **53°35'·09N 06°06'·49W**. AC 633. Tides as Balbriggan, 6.19. E & SE of Red Island (a peninsula) lie Colt, Shenick's and St Patrick's Islands, the latter foul to S and SW. Inshore passage between Colt and St Patrick's Is uses transit/brg as on chart to clear dangers. Good shelter and holding in 3m at Skerries Bay, W of Red Is. Approach from E or NE outside PHM buoy, Fl R 10s, off Red Is. ⌄ WNW of pier, Oc R 6s 7m 7M, vis 103°-154°; clear of moorings. Most facilities; Skerries SC ☎1-849 1233, ⌇ (HW±3). Rockabill Lt, Fl WR 12s 45m 17/13M, is conspic 2·4M ENE of St Patrick's Is.

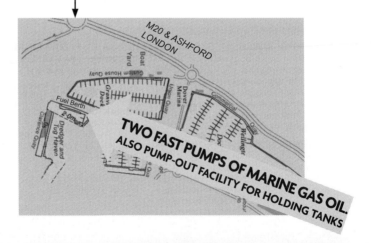

Index

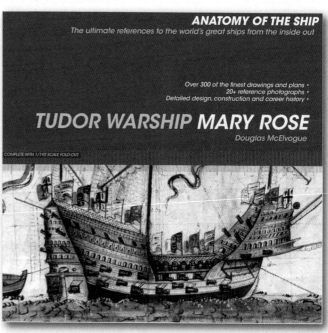
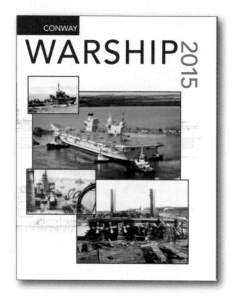
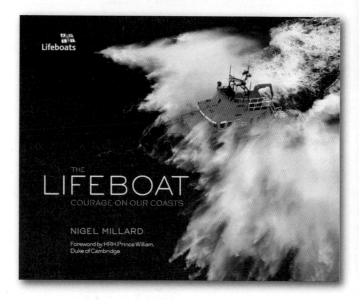